FEEDING FRENZY

*How Attack Journalism Has
Transformed American Politics*

Larry J. Sabato

With a New Afterword

THE FREE PRESS
A Division of Macmillan, Inc.
NEW YORK
Maxwell Macmillan Canada
TORONTO
Maxwell Macmillan International
NEW YORK OXFORD SINGAPORE SYDNEY

The Free Press
A Division of Macmillan, Inc.
866 Third Avenue, New York, N. Y. 10022

Maxwell Macmillan Canada, Inc.
1200 Eglinton Avenue East
Suite 200
Don Mills, Ontario M3C 3N1

Macmillan, Inc. is part of the Maxwell Communication Group of Companies.

First Free Press Paperback Edition 1993

Printed in the United States of America

printing number

1 2 3 4 5 6 7 8 9 10

Library of Congress Cataloging-in-Publication Data

Sabato, Larry.
    Feeding frenzy : how attack journalism has transformed American politics / Larry J. Sabato.
        p.   cm.
    Includes bibliographical references and index.
    ISBN 0-02-927636-5
    1. Press and politics—United States.   2. Journalism—Political aspects—United States.   3. Libel and slander—United States.
4. Press law—United States.   5. United States—Politics and government–1945—   I. Title.
PN4888.P6S23   1991
302.23′0973–dc20   91-10611
                                                                CIP

For my Piranhas,
who remind me why
I chose to teach.

Contents

Preface to the Paperback Edition   vii

Preface and Acknowledgments   ix

CHAPTER 1.
Inquisition, American Style   1
Attack Journalism and Feeding Frenzies

CHAPTER 2.
The Press of Yesteryear   25
From Canard to Cover-up to Exposé

CHAPTER 3.
The Boys in the Bush   52
The Attack Mentality Within the New Media

CHAPTER 4.
A Thousand Points of Gossip   94
How the Politicians, the Public, and the Pundits Feed the Frenzy

CHAPTER 5.
Rumor and Excess   136
Junkyard Dog Journalism on the Prowl

CHAPTER 6.
Frenzies That Weren't   187
The Other Side of the Story

CHAPTER 7.
Consequences   200

CHAPTER 8.
Remedies   213

AFTERWORD   247
The Frenzies of '92

APPENDIX
Interviews Conducted for This Study   301

Notes   307

Selected Bibliography   351

Name Index   357

Subject Index   367

Preface to the Paperback Edition

Your book saved me.
GEORGE STEPHANOPOULOS, Clinton campaign and (later) White House communications director, referring to his use of *Feeding Frenzy* during Clinton's Gennifer Flowers crisis[1]

Thanks for going after the sleaze-mongers.
MARVIN BUSH, son of George and Barbara, in a comment concerning the author's criticism of 1992 press reports about President Bush's supposed "mistress"[2]

Timing is everything in sex, politics, and publishing, and the first edition of this book was badly timed. As chance would have it, the book's release date was August 19, 1991, and its elaborate multimedia promotional launching collapsed under the weight of that day's attempted Russian coup aimed at ousting Mikhail Gorbachev from power. *Feeding Frenzy* might well have sunk without a trace, an innocent victim of a massive international frenzy—save for the American press.

The news media's behavior in the 1992 campaign revived the book and its central arguments, and made the phrase "feeding frenzy" a vital part of the political lexicon. From Bill Clinton's Gennifer Flowers to George Bush's "other Jennifer," and a dozen other episodes, too, the airwaves and the headlines hummed and bristled with press excesses from start to finish in 1992. And for all of it I am perversely grateful to my friends in the media, for they have made this updated paperback edition possible. Yet I still hope for the time when this book can be classified as history and not current events, perhaps after some of the modest press reforms proposed in these pages are finally adopted. More on this—and the frenzies of '92—in the newly added Afterword (see pp. 247).

The first edition had its intended effect of provoking discussion among journalists about declining standards in political coverage. I have benefited enormously from the reactions of dozens of newspersons and other citizens to my recommendations, and I appreciate the time many took to write or call with their thoughts. Of course, some in the press reacted favorably while others expressed disagreement or even anger. To the latter group, at least, I managed to prove that, just as journalists are the politician's burden, so also can academics be the journalist's burden.

Along the way to this second edition I was fortunate to have the services of yet another superb research assistant, Michael J. Ard, a graduate student in government and foreign affairs at the University of Virginia. He was ever resourceful, dependable, and industrious, and I hereby declare him to be an official Piranha. Mike joins me in thanking Mark Stencel for his continuing research help to this project. One of the original band of Piranhas, Mark has since gone on to greater things on the staff of the *Washington Post*, and it is a source of pride and relief to me that his association with a news critic did not make him a pariah as well as a Piranha in his newsroom.

The staff members of The Free Press have truly been a delight to work with over the past two years, and I sincerely thank them all—especially Suzanne Herz. I have been fortunate to have had two fine Free Press editors: first Peter Dougherty, and now Bruce Nichols, a friend whose prodigious talents have been applied to several of my earlier projects and, lately, to this one. May this edition be equal to the result of the remarkable effort that the Free Press's staff put into the original.

Charlottesville, Virginia
March 1993

Preface and Acknowledgments

In the course of my research for this volume, the feisty Texas journalist Sarah McClendon, a member of the White House press corps, made an observation to one of my student assistants that is worth citing at the outset:

You know, it's foolish the way all these professors write these books about something they've never experienced. You can tell him I said that. . . . What the hell is he [doing]? He knows nothing about the subject. Why doesn't he leave it to people who do know something about it? He has to come to us to get information to write his book.

In truth, any academic writing about the press is on the outside looking in, dependent on the journalistic guild for cooperation and insight. Fortunately for this professor, about 150 broadcast and print reporters plus several dozen candidates, political consultants, and campaign staffers, were willing to be helpful (including the redoubtable Ms. McClendon). Most were exceptionally frank, with relatively few exercising the closemouthed discretion of master Republican operative Stuart Spencer, who—when asked to reveal a few of his presidential campaign secrets—perhaps wisely replied, "If I had terminal cancer, I'd tell you." I am deeply indebted to all those who so generously shared their time and memories, and, following Ms. McClendon's advice, I have tried to let those who "know something" about the subject share that knowledge by means of this book.

A few notes about the 208 interviews conducted for this volume: All quotations in the text are taken from on-the-record interviews unless otherwise noted. Minor grammatical and structural errors were corrected, and when an interviewee specifically asked me to do so during the course of an interview, off-color language was sanitized. With the main exception of interviewees who requested that their sessions not be recorded, all interviews were taped and the tapes

ix

have been preserved. A handful of interviewees (fewer than two dozen) agreed to talk only on deep background: No tapes were made, their names appear nowhere in this volume, and no direct anonymous quotations have been drawn from their sessions.

Those selected—sometimes serendipitously—for interviews comprise a reasonably diverse group of print and broadcast journalists, but no claim is made either for the representativeness or comprehensiveness of the chosen scribes and broadcasters. The vast majority are either veterans in senior positions who have had the opportunity to view their profession from a number of perspectives during lengthy careers or more-junior reporters who had covered one or more of the specific case studies surveyed for this book. Only about a dozen interviews that were requested were denied. A complete listing of on-the-record interviews appears in the Appendix.

I have come away from these sessions with many of journalism's best, with genuine respect and admiration for what their life's work has produced, as well as a greater appreciation for the difficulties they face in undertaking it. From the outside it is easy to romanticize journalism and equally easy to be hypercritical of it. I hope I have avoided both extremes, though I have not been shy in making observations and in second-guessing my interviewees. As a member of the only two groups of professionals—academics and authors—thinner-skinned than journalists, I can appreciate the reactions of some reporters and editors to this volume. I can only ask their forbearance if not their forgiveness for any hurtful comments it contains.

Not incidentally, I have been faced with some of the same agonizing decisions reporters and editors confront every day: Which conflicting version of events is closer to the truth? Which memories are more accurate? Which interpretations are more fair and balanced? What should be included and what excluded about the foibles of those making (and reporting) the news? Concerning accuracy, I have done my best to separate wheat from chaff, but undoubtedly I have not always succeeded. The full truth about many past political controversies seems destined to remain elusive. In my decisions about what to publish, I have tried to err on the side of caution, deleting surnames where unnecessary embarrassment would accrue and being only specific enough to make my point. On the other hand, where sources permitted and details were required to prove a significant allegation or assertion, I have not hesitated to do so.

In two and a half years of research for this book, I have benefited from the efforts, support, and guidance of many. Generous financial backing was provided by the Faculty of Arts and Sciences of the University of Virginia and the Center for the Humanities of the Virginia Foundation for the Humanities and Public Policy. For this essential help I would like to thank my departmental chairman, Clifton McCleskey; University of Virginia Provost Hugh P. Kelly; Dean of the Faculty of Arts and Sciences Raymond J. Nelson; and Virginia Foundation Executive Director Robert C. Vaughan and his staff. I also wish to acknowledge a travel grant from the Gerald R. Ford Foundation for research at the Ford presidential library.

Few investigators have ever been blessed with such remarkable student assistants. My University of Virginia group called themselves the Piranhas and adopted the slogan, "We Feed on Frenzies." Their enthusiasm and hard work thrilled and delighted me. Three were especially dedicated: Leslie Greenwald, whose meticulous administrative abilities were a godsend; Katie Dunn, who expertly supervised the manuscript in its later stages; and Mark Stencel, a very talented budding journalist whose keen interviewing skills were superbly applied to this project. The other splendid Piranhas were Christopher Barbuto, Jonathan Blank, Aaron Book, Mark Brazeal, Lewis Brissman, Ned Lilly, Miguel Monteverde, Richard Strulson, and Richard Winston. I salute them all.

Many others deserve acknowledgment as well, including a number of my University of Virginia faculty colleagues, Henry J. Abraham, Michael Cornfield, Martha Derthick, Steven E. Finkel, J. J. Murray, and David O'Brien; Scott M. Matheson, Jr., for his wise legal counsel; colleagues at other institutions, Timothy E. Cook of Williams College, Robert M. Entman of Duke University, and Charles O. Jones of the University of Wisconsin at Madison; Alan Ehrenhalt, Marcus D. Rosenbaum, and Sandra Stencel, all of Congressional Quarterly, Inc.; Rossita Thomas of the Congressional Research Service; friends Jill Abramson, Wyatt G. Andrews, E. J. Dionne, Jerald terHorst, and Kent Jenkins; Glenn Simpson of *Roll Call*; Bruce Nichols of Macmillan, Inc.; Barry Jackson of the Center for Public Service, University of Virginia, who designed Figure 4.1; my patient, long-suffering secretary, Nancy Rae; champion transcriber Linda Miller and her associate Regina Rae; skilled typist Debbie LaMori; Steven Johnson and Steven Teles, who professionally scripted background papers on many of the case studies cited in this book; University of Virginia students Tao Bernstein, Greg Golladay, Charles Kromkowski, John Kirincich, and C. Gray Wheeler; Weldon and Mildred Cooper, for their usual sustenance; Jo McCleskey and Nancy Bowles for their friendship; and last but certainly not least,

Erwin Glikes, president and publisher, and Peter Dougherty, senior editor, The Free Press, whose suggestions, encouragement, and belief in the importance of this project have been instrumental in its completion, and Edith Lewis of The Free Press for her superb shepherding of the manuscript to publication.

My thanks to all for helping me find some news and commentary that is fit to print. The remaining errors unfit for publication but in cold print nonetheless are my responsibility alone.

Charlottesville, Virginia
January 1991

1

Inquisition, American Style

Attack Journalism and Feeding Frenzies

I would never have comprehended the anguish visited by the "death watch" of the media. To have people surrounding our home with a real carnival atmosphere, shouting questions at you with a boom microphone and long-lens cameras, it makes one feel like a hunted animal driven to his lair.

JIM WRIGHT, former Speaker of the House[1]

This is guilt by press. We might as well have hanging by the press. We [shouldn't] have Gestapo tactics by the media in this country.

ROGER AILES, media consultant to the 1988 Bush/Quayle campaign, commenting on the coverage of Dan Quayle[2]

It has become a spectacle without equal in modern American politics: the news media, print and broadcast, go after a wounded politician like sharks in a feeding frenzy. The wounds may have been self-inflicted, and the politician may richly deserve his or her fate, but the journalists now take center stage in the process, creating the news as much as reporting it, changing both the shape of election-year politics and the contours of government. Having replaced the political parties as the screening committee for candidates and office-holders, the media propel some politicians toward power and unceremoniously eliminate others. Unavoidably, this enormously influential role—and the news practices employed in exercising it—has provided rich fodder for a multitude of press critics.

These critics' charges against the press cascade down with the fury of rain in a summer squall. Public officials and many other observers see journalists as rude, arrogant, and cynical, given to exaggeration, harassment, sensationalism, and gross insensitivity. From the conservative perspective, their reporting is, more often than not, viewed as evidence of blatant liberal bias, with the facts being fitted to pre-conceived notions. At the same time, the left indicts the media for being too hesitant to find fault with the status quo and too close to the very establishment they are supposed to check. Moreover, critics of all stripes see journalists as hypercritical of others yet vengeful when criticized themselves, quick to accuse yet slow to correct error, willing to violate the constitutional values of due process and fair trial in the Fifth and Sixth Amendments by acting as judge and jury, yet insistent on wrapping themselves in the First Amendment when challenged on virtually anything. Especially in the post-Watergate era of institutionalized investigative reporting and "star journalism," the press is perceived as being far more interested in finding sleaze and achieving fame and fortune than in serving as an honest broker of information between citizens and government.

In the wake of recent elections and political scandals, feelings about the news media are running particularly strong. This intensity shows in the kind of modifiers that were added to the word *journalism* during the course of research and interviewing for this study:

blood-sport	peek-a-boo
character cop	peeping-Tom
cheap-shot	skinhead
food-fight	soap opera
gotcha	tabloid
hit-and-run	totalitarian
jugular	trash
keyhole	voyeur
paparazzi	

Some of these insulting adjectives came from a suspect class: politicians speared by the pens of scribes. All losing candidates naturally blame the press—politicians are never responsible for their own defeats—and surprisingly few winners have much good to say about the profession that they believe made victory more difficult. Such universal condemnation by politicians may ironically be taken as welcome proof that the press is doing its job.

Less reassuring, however, is another chorus of critics of modern journalism. A host of the most senior, respected, and experienced news professionals are themselves becoming equivocal about, embarrassed over, even repulsed by the conduct of some of their colleagues. While disagreeing with many of the criticisms leveled at reporters from outside the profession, they are nonetheless concerned about the media's growing distortion of the political process and deeply disturbed that legitimate press inquiry sometimes gets quickly and completely out of hand. And they fear a rising tide of antipress sentiment if the excesses are left unchecked. Already, several public opinion studies (discussed in chapter 7) have revealed a dramatic decline in citizens' confidence in, and respect for, the news media: Most Americans no longer believe that the press generally "gets the facts straight," and they rate journalism among the professions with the "lowest ethical standards." Fully 78 percent in one study agreed that "the media spend too much time focusing on [campaign] things that are irrelevant, like candidates' personal lives" rather than centering their coverage on "the most important issues."[3] The evidence also suggests that recent controversies have weakened public support for First Amendment press freedoms.

These thoughtful and credible practitioners, many of them interviewed for this book, are less worried about the press's obsession with scandal—a staple of news in virtually every free society and certainly for the whole of American history—than with the *kinds* of scandals now considered reportable and the *manner* in which they are investigated and reported. First of all, scandal coverage is no longer restricted to misuse of public office, incompetence in the exercise of public responsibilities, or some other inadequacy or malfeasance in a *public* role; it extends to purely *private* misbehavior, even offenses, some of them trivial, committed long before an individual's emergence into public life. No wise politician today dares utter St. Augustine's legendary prayer: "Give me chastity and continency, but not just yet." Even a college student contemplating a political career had best think twice about youthful indulgences, given degenerating press standards. When *New York Times* columnist William Safire wrote the following words in protest just after Gary Hart's 1987 presidential withdrawal, they seemed alarmist:

If we do not turn the tables on the titillaters, we will load future news conferences with such significant policy questions as: "Sir, there are widespread reports of your impotence; when was the last time you and your wife had sexual relations?" "Madam, how do you deal with the persistent rumors that your national security adviser is a herpes victim?" "Have you or any member of your family ever taken illegal drugs?" "Some say that you once saw a psychiatrist—exactly what was your problem?"[4]

Since Safire's predictions appeared, variations of the latter two questions have already been asked of candidates, and one wonders only half whimsically whether fellow *Times* columnist Russell Baker's vision of "adultery disclosure forms" to be filed before the New Hampshire primary will also come to pass someday.[5] Soon no public figure may be too unimportant for close scrutiny. Editors and reporters at several major publications are seriously considering expanding their circle of legitimate targets for private life investigations to include top aides to candidates and even people uninvolved in politics who are "in the news" prominently. Similarly, no offense may be too minor to ignore in this "bare-all" age. Journalist Timothy Noah, while at *Newsweek*, was called with a scandal tip about Republican presidential candidate Alexander Haig: He was observed parking in a spot reserved for the handicapped in a supermarket parking lot. At this rate it seems almost inevitable that a candidate will be exposed for using an express checkout lane when purchasing more than the ten-item limit.[6]

Press invasion of privacy is leading to the gradual erasure of the line protecting a public person's purely private life. This makes the price of public life enormously higher, serving as an even greater deterrent for those not absolutely obsessed with holding power—the kind of people we ought least to want in office. Rather than recognizing this unfortunate consequence, many in journalism prefer to relish their newly assumed role of "gatekeeper," which, as mentioned earlier, enables them to substitute for party leaders in deciding which characters are virtuous enough to merit consideration for high office. As ABC News correspondent Brit Hume self-critically suggests:

We don't see ourselves institutionally, collectively anymore as a bunch of journalists out there faithfully reporting what's happening day by day. . . . We have a much grander view of ourselves: we are the Horatio at the national bridge. We are the people who want to prevent the bad characters from crossing over into public office.

Hume's veteran ABC colleague Sander Vanocur agrees, detecting "among some young reporters a quality of the avenging angel: they are going to sanitize American politics.'"[7] More and more, the news media seem determined to show that would-be emperors have no clothes, and if necessary to prove the point, they personally will strip the candidates naked on the campaign trail. The sheer number of journalists participating in these public denudings guarantees riotous behavior, and the "full-court press" almost always presents itself as a snarling, unruly mob more bent on killing kings than making them. Not surprisingly potential candidates deeply fear the power of an inquisitorial press, and in deciding whether to seek office, they often consult journalists as much as party leaders, even sharing private vulnerabilities with newsmen to gauge reaction. The *Los Angeles Times*'s Washington bureau chief, Jack Nelson, had such an encounter before the 1988 campaign season, when a prospective presidential candidate "literally asked me how long I thought the statute of limitations was" for marital infidelity. "I told him I didn't know, but I didn't think [the limit] had been reached in his case!" For whatever reasons, the individual chose not to run.

As the reader will see later in this volume, able members of the news corps offer impressive defenses for all the practices mentioned thus far, not the least of which is that the press has become more aggressive to combat the legions of image makers, political consultants, spin doctors, and handlers who surround modern candidates like a nearly impenetrable shield. Yet upon reflection, most news veterans recognize that press excesses are not an acceptable antidote for consultant or candidate evils. In fact, not one of the interviewed journalists even attempted to justify an increasingly frequent occurrence in news organizations: the publication of gossip and rumor _without convincing proof_. Gossip has always been the drug of choice for journalists as well as the rest of the political community, but as the threshold for publication of information about private lives has been lowered, journalists sometimes cover politics as "Entertainment Tonight" reporters cover Hollywood. A bitter Gary Hart observed: "Rumor and gossip have become the coins of the political realm,"[8] and the *New York Times*'s Michael Oreskes seemed to agree: "1988 was a pretty sorry year when the *National Enquirer* was the most important publication in American journalism." With all the stories and innuendo about personal vice, campaigns appear to be little more than a stream of talegates (or in the case of sexual misadventures, tailgates).

The sorry standard set on the campaign trail is spilling over into coverage of governmental battles. Ever since Watergate, government scandals have paraded across the television set in a roll call so lengthy and numbing that they are inseparable in the public consciousness, all joined at the Achilles' heel. Some recent lynchings, such as John Tower's failure to be confirmed as secretary of defense, rival any spectacle produced by colonial Salem. At the same time more vital and revealing information is ignored or crowded off the agenda. *Real* scandals, such as the savings-and-loan heist or the influence peddling at the Department of Housing and Urban Development in the 1980s, go undetected for years. The sad conclusion is inescapable: The press has become obsessed with gossip rather than governance; it prefers to employ titillation rather than scrutiny; as a result, its political coverage produces trivialization rather than enlightenment. And the dynamic mechanism propelling and demonstrating this decline in news standards is the "feeding frenzy."

LIKE SHARKS IN A FEEDING FRENZY

I feel like bait rather than a senior member of Congress. [The press are] investigative sharks.

U.S. Congressman JACK BROOKS (D., Texas)[9]

The term *frenzy* suggests some kind of disorderly, compulsive, or agitated activity that is muscular and instinctive, not cerebral and thoughtful.[10] In the animal world, no activity is more classically frenzied than the feeding of sharks, piranhas, or bluefish when they encounter a wounded prey. These attack-fish with extraordinarily acute senses first search out weak, ill, or injured targets. On locating them, each hunter moves in quickly to gain a share of the kill, feeding not just off the victim but also off its fellow hunters' agitation. The excitement and drama of the violent encounter builds to a crescendo, sometimes overwhelming the creatures' usual inhibitions.[11] The frenzy can spread, with the delirious attackers wildly striking any object that moves in the water, even each other. Veteran reporters will recognize more press behavior in this passage than they might wish to acknowledge. This reverse anthropomorphism can be carried too far, but the similarity of piranha in the water and press on the campaign trail can be summed up in a shared goal: If it bleeds, try to kill it.

The kingdom of politics and not of nature is the subject of this volume, so for our purposes, a feeding frenzy is defined as the press coverage attending any political event or circumstance where a critical mass of journalists leap to cover the same embarrassing or scandalous subject and pursue it intensely, often excessively, and sometimes uncontrollably. No precise number of journalists can be attached to the term *critical mass,* but in the video age, we truly know it when we see it; the forest of cameras, lights, microphones, and adrenaline-choked reporters surrounding a Gary Hart, Dan Quayle, or Geraldine Ferraro is unmistakable. Table 1.1 contains a list of thirty-six events that surely qualify as frenzies. They are occasions of sin for the press as well as the politicians, and thus ideal research sites that will serve as case studies for this book. A majority (twenty-one) are drawn from presidential politics, while seven examples

TABLE 1.1
FEEDING FRENZIES: CASE STUDIES USED FOR THIS BOOK

From Presidential Politics

1952	Richard Nixon's "secret fund"
1968	George Romney's "brainwashing" about Vietnam
1968	Spiro Agnew's "fat Jap" flap
1969	Ted Kennedy's Chappaquiddick
1972	Edmund Muskie's New Hampshire cry
1972	Thomas Eagleton's mental health
1976	Jimmy Carter's "lust in the heart" *Playboy* interview
1976	Gerald Ford's "free Poland" gaffe
1979	Jimmy Carter's "killer rabbit"
1980	Billygate (Billy Carter and Libya)
1983	Debategate (Reagan's use of Carter's debate briefing books)
1984	Gary Hart's age, name, and signature changes
1984	Jesse Jackson's "Hymietown" remark
1984	Geraldine Ferraro's family finances
1985/86	Jack Kemp's purported homosexuality
1987	Gary Hart and Donna Rice
1987	Joseph Biden's plagiarism and Michael Dukakis's "attack video"
1987	Pat Robertson's exaggerated résumé and shotgun marriage
1988	Dukakis's mental health
1988	Dan Quayle (National Guard service, Paula Parkinson, academic record, rumors such as plagiarism and drugs)
1988	George Bush's alleged mistress

From the State and Local Levels

1987/88	Governor Evan Mecham on the impeachment trail (Arizona)
1987/88	Chuck Robb and the cocaine parties (Virginia)
1983/90	Mayor Marion Barry's escapades (District of Columbia)
1987	Governor Dick Celeste's womanizing (Ohio)
1988	Mayor Henry Cisneros's extramarital affair (San Antonio, Texas)
1989/90	Governor Gaston Caperton's "soap opera" divorce (West Virginia)
1990	Texas governor's election: drugs, rape, and "honey hunts"

Noncampaign Examples

1973/74	The Watergate scandals
1974	Congressman Wilbur Mills and stripper Fanne Foxe
1986/87	The Iran-Contra affair
1987	Supreme Court nominee Douglas Ginsburg's marijuana use (and campaign repercussions)
1989	John Tower's losing fight to become secretary of defense
1989	Speaker Jim Wright's fall from power
1989	Tom Foley's rocky rise to the Speakership
1989/90	Barney Frank and the male prostitute

come from the state and local levels, with the remaining eight focused on government scandals or personal peccadilloes of nationally
recognized political figures. What follows is a brief case-by-case historical account of each selected frenzy. (Longer sketches of the presidential campaign cases that receive most of the attention in this
volume are available from the author.)

FEEDING FRENZIES: CAPSULE SUMMARIES
OF SELECTED CASE STUDIES

From Presidential Politics

Richard Nixon's "Secret Fund" (1952): Nixon, then a U.S. senator
from California and the Republican vice presidential nominee, was
accused of maintaining a hidden political fund of about eighteen
thousand dollars collected from home-state supporters. The
Democratic-leaning New York Post carried the first reports of the
fund—somewhat sensationalized accounts that, in Nixon's words,
"let [him] have it with both barrels." An avalanche of coverage followed, and soon the "secret fund" was the central issue of the presidential campaign. Though legal, the previously undisclosed nest
egg caused such a stir that Nixon was nearly forced from Dwight
Eisenhower's ticket. Some of Eisenhower's staff and key party elders
wanted Nixon to step down; former GOP presidential nominee and
New York Governor Thomas E. Dewey personally urged Nixon to
resign. Nixon saved himself with a dramatic if maudlin television appeal that became known as the "Checkers speech," so named because of a black-and-white cocker spaniel a supporter had given to
Nixon's young daughters, which Nixon swore never to give up,
come what might in the political wars.

George Romney's "Brainwashing" (1968): Governor Romney of
Michigan was a leading contender for the Republican presidential
nomination until September 4, 1967, when he told Detroit television
newsman Lou Gordon that he had been "brainwashed" by American generals into supporting the Vietnam war effort while touring
Southeast Asia in 1965. Though Romney tried in earnest to explain
himself, he became the target of blistering press and partisan attacks.
Romney's candidacy never recovered from the furor he created with
his statement.

Spiro Agnew's "Fat Jap" Flap (1968): Shortly after characterizing
Polish-Americans as "Polacks," Agnew, the Greek-American Re-

publican candidate for vice president, referred to Gene Oishi, a Japanese-American campaign reporter from the *Baltimore Sun*, as "the fat Jap." Agnew had known the journalist for years and claimed the remark was in jest, but others saw the quip as more evidence of Agnew's ethnic insensitivity. After some initial hesitation due in part to Oishi's reluctance to go public, the *Washington Post* eventually broke the story, forcing a flustered Agnew to offer excuses and then apologies.

Ted Kennedy's Chappaquiddick (1969): On the evening of July 19, 1969, Senator Edward M. Kennedy of Massachusetts drove his Oldsmobile off a wooden bridge on Chappaquiddick Island, drowning his passenger, a young campaign worker named Mary Jo Kopechne. The senator left the scene of the accident, did not report it to the police for many hours, and according to some accounts, considered concocting an alibi for himself in the interim. At the time, Kennedy managed to escape severe legal and political consequences for his actions thanks to his family's connections (which helped to contain the inquest and grand jury) as well as a nationally televised "Checkers"-like speech a week after the accident. But virtually no journalist who has closely examined the evidence fully believes Kennedy's story, and more than twenty years later, the tragedy still trails the senator, with aggressive press investigations revived in five-year-anniversary intervals. Probably more than any other single factor, Chappaquiddick—a frenzy without end—has ensured that Ted Kennedy will not follow his brother John to the White House.

Edmund Muskie's New Hampshire "Cry" (1972): Angered by *Manchester Union-Leader* publisher William Loeb's attacks on his wife and himself, Muskie—the early favorite for the Democratic presidential nod—raged against Loeb in front of the newspaper's building during a late February snowstorm. The *Washington Post's* David Broder, among many others, reported that Muskie had "tears streaming down his face," though in retrospect Broder and his colleagues acknowledge that the "tears" could have been melting snow. Whatever the truth, these dispatches about Muskie's lack of composure damaged his stable, steady image and contributed to Muskie's poorer-than-expected showing in the New Hampshire primary. Muskie's "cry" was a signal event in his surprising decline and eventual collapse as a credible front-runner.

Thomas Eagleton's Mental Health (1972): Democratic nominee George McGovern's presidential hopes virtually evaporated when it was revealed shortly after the party convention that his newly chosen vice presidential running mate, Missouri Senator Eagleton, had been hospitalized on three occasions for depression and had undergone electroshock therapy. Eagleton had withheld the explosive information from McGovern at the convention, but too many Missouri politicians and others knew his secret for it to be kept under wraps. An anonymous tip to the *Detroit Free Press* about Eagleton's past began the chain of events that eventually brought the Democrat's sad episodes to public view. The least responsible coverage of the ensuing frenzy was provided by columnist Jack Anderson, who—based on a questionable and unverified tip—falsely reported a half dozen Eagleton "arrests" for drunk driving and other traffic offenses. Anderson's gross breach of journalistic ethics in printing unproved gossip generated some sympathy for Eagleton, but it could not save him. Under pressure from McGovern and many senior Democrats, Eagleton withdrew from the ticket, but not before McGovern had swallowed a suicide pill by declaring himself to be "1000 percent" behind his doomed partner.

Jimmy Carter's "Lust in the Heart" Playboy Interview (1976): Carter admitted in an unsolicited comment to two *Playboy* free-lance writers that he had "looked on a lot of women with lust" and had "committed adultery in my heart many times," strange revelations all the more damaging because they appeared in a soft-porn magazine. A separate *New York Times Magazine* interview with Norman Mailer, also published during the general election campaign, added fuel to the frenzy's fire thanks to Carter's impolitic remark, "I don't care if people say fuck." The press had a field day with Carter's oddball offerings, but some journalists correctly saw the controversy as a warning sign of the future direction of American politics. As the *New York Times* editorialized, the erosion of "the legitimate boundaries of [politicians'] private lives and intimate feelings" had begun.

Gerald Ford's "Free Poland" Gaffe (1976): During a critical debate with Jimmy Carter a month before the presidential election, Ford declared in response to a question from Max Frankel of the *New York Times*, "There is no Soviet dominance of Eastern Europe." While the statement was prophetic given events a decade later, it seemed absurd to reporters at the time—so much so that Ford's chances of being elected president in his own right were diminished considerably. The press pounced on this passage of the debate and talked of little else for days afterward, so much so that a public initially convinced that Ford had won the debate soon turned overwhelmingly against him.

Jimmy Carter's "Killer Rabbit" (1979): While home fishing in Georgia during a summer when his popularity was at low tide, Carter's small boat was "attacked" by a mysterious swimming rabbit, which the president warded off with a paddle. Once leaked into print by Brooks Jackson of the Associated Press, the bizarre story captured the press's and the public's imagination, becoming a metaphor for Carter's hapless, enfeebled presidency. The incident encouraged Senator Edward Kennedy's primary challenge to Carter's renomination, and it became a symbolic preamble to Carter's landslide loss in November 1980.

Billygate (1980): President Carter's colorful brother Billy created a major headache for his elder sibling when he became an agent of the government of radical Libya. After three trips to the land of dictator Muammar Qaddafi and the receipt of hundreds of thousands of dollars from the Libyans, Billy became the center of a swirling storm of allegations about influence-peddling, and the sea swell quickly engulfed President Carter, then in the middle of a difficult campaign for renomination and reelection. "Billygate" also generated a press war between Washington, D.C.'s two newspapers, the *Post* and the *Star;* each one overdid the story in a glut of one-upmanship journalism that subsided only after conservative columnist James J. Kilpatrick pointed out the excesses in coverage. The president eventually answered all the serious charges to the satisfaction of both newspapers and most fair-minded observers, but the damage to his reelection bid was substantial.

Debategate (1983): When candidate Ronald Reagan was studying for a presidential debate with Jimmy Carter in October 1980, he and his staff had the advantage of having the very briefing book being used by Carter to prepare for the same encounter. The book had apparently been delivered by a still-unidentified Reagan "mole" who had access to the Carter White House. The revelation of this two-and-a-half-year-old espionage came from a mere two-paragraph mention in a 511-page book on Reagan by *Time* correspondent Laurence I. Barrett. The rest of the press was even less interested than Barrett in the information until former Carter Press Secretary Jody Powell began urging closer scrutiny. A Democratic congressional investigation into the matter helped to arouse the press and generate a summer frenzy in 1983. The subsequent yearlong inquiry linked the 1980 campaign with its successor in 1984.

Gary Hart(pence) (1984): With an upset victory over Walter Mondale in the New Hampshire Democratic primary, Hart became the wonder boy of 1984 politics, causing reporters and voters to ask, "Who is Gary Hart?" Some of the answers were perplexing: Hart had shortened his name (from Hartpence), shaved a year off his age, and changed his signature several times. Hart compounded his problems by offering vague or misleading explanations for the alterations, leaving the truth to be discovered piecemeal by investigative reporters for a dozen newspapers and magazines. The disclosures gave many voters pause, taking some of the luster off his rising star.

Jesse Jackson's "Hymietown" Remark (1984): Jackson referred to Jews as "Hymies" and to New York City as "Hymietown" in January 1984 during a conversation with a black *Washington Post* reporter, Milton Coleman. Jackson had assumed the references would not be printed because of his racial bond with Coleman, but several weeks later Coleman permitted the slurs to be included far down in an article by another *Post* reporter on Jackson's rocky relations with American Jews. A storm of protest erupted, and Jackson at first denied the remarks, then accused Jews of conspiring to defeat him. The Nation of Islam's radical leader, Louis Farrakhan, an aggressive anti-Semite and old Jackson ally, made a difficult situation worse by threatening Coleman in a radio broadcast and issuing a public warning—in Jackson's presence—to Jews: "If you harm this brother [Jackson], it will be the last one you harm." Finally, Jackson doused the fires in late February with an emotional speech admitting guilt and seeking atonement before national Jewish leaders in a Manchester, New Hampshire, synagogue. Yet Jackson refused to denounce Farrakhan, and lingering, deep-rooted Jewish suspicions guaranteed an enduring split between Jackson and the Jews. The frenzy also heightened tensions between Jackson and the "white" establishment press.

Geraldine Ferraro's Family Finances (1984): The first woman nominated for vice president by a major party, Ferraro was Walter Mondale's last best hope for an upset victory against Ronald Reagan. That hope was extinguished when the finances of Ferraro and her husband, John Zaccaro, became the dominant issue of the pre–Labor Day campaign. Charges of suspect real estate deals and unethical campaign funding filled the airwaves and newsprint for two weeks.

Some publications, especially the *Wall Street Journal*, also pursued Zaccaro's purported, extremely tenuous Mafia connections—so intensely, in fact, that many observers perceived anti-Italian prejudice in the quest. Finally Ferraro held a cathartic late-August press conference before an audience of 150 journalists and three dozen television cameras to clear the air, and the campaign was then able to move on to other issues.

Jack Kemp's Purported Homosexuality (1985–86): Kemp has suffered harm from a sordid rumor that keeps turning up like the proverbial bad penny. As an aide to California Governor Ronald Reagan in 1967, Kemp was indirectly and unfairly linked to a "homosexual ring" that existed within the Reagan circle. Kemp's immediate boss was one of the group, and Kemp had had some financial dealings with him that included the purchase of a lodge where, completely unknown to Kemp, gay parties were held. (Kemp had never even visited the lodge.) These flimsy connections allowed the rumor to follow him, however, and he has been forced to fight the recurrent gossip over nearly a quarter-century. Repeatedly the rumors have arisen, been debunked, and come alive again after the passage of a few years. In 1985 and 1986, preparing to campaign for the 1988 Republican presidential nomination, Kemp ran the gauntlet of investigation first by one news outfit, then another, then another, with unanimous findings of innocence but no final vindication. Occasionally, as with NBC's "Today" show, a media organization would use the earlier inquiries not as a reason to abjure further investigation but as a pretext to pursue the same tired subject.

Gary Hart and Donna Rice (1987): In the public's mind, probably no event from the 1988 campaign proved more memorable than the undoing of Democratic candidate Hart. Long plagued by rumors of "womanizing," the front-running Hart watched his chances for the presidential nomination evaporate in May, when the *Miami Herald* reported that Hart had spent the night with an attractive young model named Donna Rice. Acting on an anonymous tip, the *Herald* had staked out Hart's Washington town house, and though the surveillance was flawed (it was not continuous, and both house entrances were not always covered), the circumstances were suspicious enough to generate a massive media frenzy. Hart fought back, but his damage-control operation collapsed in the face of other real or threatened disclosures, such as the revelation that Hart and Rice had earlier taken an overnight cruise to Bimini on the aptly christened yacht *Monkey Business.* The denouement came after a *Washington Post* reporter asked Hart, "Have you ever committed adultery?" Hart refused to answer the question at the time, but the meaning of the query soon became clear. The *Post* had identified another woman with whom Hart had had a long-standing relationship. Faced with that potential disclosure and caught up in an overwhelming media maelstrom, Hart went home to Colorado, withdrawing from the presidential race in a bitter farewell speech on May 8.

Joseph Biden's Plagiarism; Michael Dukakis's "Attack Video" (1988): Democratic presidential candidate Biden, a U.S. senator from Delaware, was driven from the nomination battle after delivering, without attribution, passages from a speech by British Labour party leader Neil Kinnock. A barrage of subsequent press revelations also contributed to Biden's withdrawal: a plagiarism incident during his law school years; the senator's boastful exaggerations of his academic record at a New Hampshire campaign event; and the discovery of other quotations in Biden's speeches, these pilfered from past Democratic politicians. The controversy became two frenzies in one when it was disclosed that the Dukakis campaign had earlier secretly distributed to several news media outlets an "attack video" juxtaposing the Biden and Kinnock speeches and revealing Biden's word theft. The Dukakis campaign at first stonewalled and denied any part in the tape's distribution, but when the truth emerged Dukakis was forced to fire his campaign manager, John Sasso, who had orchestrated the maneuver, as well as his political director, Paul Tully, a less involved but knowing participant. Dukakis himself insisted he had no prior knowledge of their actions, and though wounded by it, his candidacy survived the incident.

Pat Robertson's Checkered Past (1988): The political preacher of the Christian right was forced to come to public terms with past sins during his unsuccessful presidential bid. Robertson was challenged on three fronts: military service, marriage, and résumé. In a controversy first broached in a syndicated column by Rowland Evans and Robert Novak, critics charged he had pulled strings to avoid hard combat duty in Korea, an allegation that Robertson steadfastly denied in the face of considerable testimony to the contrary. The *Wall Street Journal* discovered the reverend's marriage (in the period before his religious rebirth) to have been of the "shotgun" variety, with the couple's first son born just ten weeks after the wedding. And Robertson's résumé was found to be padded with several exaggerations. These difficulties did not appear to affect his die-hard fundamentalist supporters, but they may have contributed to his inability to expand a limited base.

Dukakis's Mental Health (1988): Rantings by the Lyndon LaRouche cult about Michael Dukakis's supposed visits to a psychiatrist became an especially sordid chapter of the 1988 presidential campaign. Followers of the extremist LaRouche circulated leaflets containing unsubstantiated claims about Dukakis's mental health at the Democratic National Convention. Within weeks the allegations found their way into print, assisted by Dukakis's refusal to release his full medical records as well as rampant speculation on the subject in a few media outlets (especially the *Washington Times*). A "joking" reference to the matter by President Reagan triggered full-blown press disclosure of the rumor. The president quickly apologized for his crude remark ("I'm not going to pick on an invalid"), and the incident faded with no evidence at all emerging to confirm the baseless gossip.

Quayle Season (1988): George Bush's selection of little-known Indiana Senator Dan Quayle as his Republican running mate proved to be one of the most controversial vice presidential choices in history. In fact, most major news organizations devoted far more resources to investigating rumors about Quayle than they did to covering the two presidential candidates. Within hours of Bush's announcement, Quayle was embroiled in a melee with the media about his Vietnam War service in the National Guard. The intense inquiry into whether Quayle's wealthy family had pulled strings to help him avoid combat by gaining him admission to the guard nearly provoked a press riot at times. Other mini-"scandals," some related to the guard issue and some not, erupted as well, including Quayle's poor academic record, his admission to law school despite his college grades, and a golf trip to Florida whose other participants included the lobbyist-seductress Paula Parkinson. Rumors of purported Quayle wrongdoing—from youthful drug use to college plagiarism—also occasionally reached print without a shred of supporting evidence.

George Bush's Alleged Mistress (1988): A decade-old rumor about Bush's purported extramarital affairs received new circulation several times during the 1988 campaign. In June 1987 the vice president's eldest son attempted to spike the adultery allegation by denying it bluntly to *Newsweek*: "The answer to the Big A question is N.O." In mid-October 1988 a minor Los Angeles paper, the *L.A. Weekly*, resurrected the subject with an article detailing the gossip (without any proof) and accusing major news organizations of not pursuing the matter. A few days later inaccurate Wall Street speculation that the *Washington Post* was on the verge of revealing Bush's "secret life" caused the Dow Jones average to drop twenty-two points. Discreet news coverage of the market's slide became more explicit as Dukakis campaign aide Donna Brazile called on Bush to "fess up" and tell "the American people . . . [who] will share that bed with him in the White House." Brazile had to resign because of her remarks, and the undocumented rumor sank back into the political sewer.

From the State and Local Levels

Arizona's Evan Mecham on the Impeachment Trail (1987–88): In April 1988 Mecham became the seventh governor in American history to be removed from office through impeachment, after seventeen months of near-continuous controversy and turmoil that were covered in great detail by the national media as well as the state press corps. On his inauguration day in January 1987 Mecham began his divisive reign by rescinding the Martin Luther King, Jr., holiday, thus alienating blacks from the start. In succeeding months Mecham antagonized many other groups with insensitive statements, careless, occasionally bizarre, pronouncements, and unconventional appointments (such as a tax commissioner who had not paid his state taxes). Faced with a recall election after more than three hundred thousand citizens signed petitions, Mecham lost his governorship even before his near-certain defeat could be administered at the polls. The Arizona Senate ousted Mecham by convicting him of obstructing justice and committing malfeasance in office. Mecham's supporters blamed the hostility of the "liberal media" in large part for their hero's travails; more-neutral observers acknowledged the presence of a media circus but nonetheless saw Mecham willingly playing chief clown.

Chuck Robb and the Cocaine Parties (1987–88): Robb's lengthy association, while Virginia's governor, with a fast and loose Virginia Beach crowd—and his knowing or unknowing participation in parties at which cocaine was used—became a major focus in his successful, lightly contested campaign for U.S. Senate in 1988. First discussed in the *Richmond Times-Dispatch* in May 1987, Robb's questionable activities became the target of a year-long investigation by the Norfolk *Virginian-Pilot*, culminating in a major *Pilot* exposé in August 1988. Reports also mentioned Robb's socializing with women other than his wife, Lynda Bird Johnson Robb (former President Lyndon Johnson's daughter).

Mayor Marion Barry's Escapades (1983–90): Few public officials—with the possible exceptions of Louisiana Governor Huey Long and Boston Mayor James Curley—have ever survived politically so many flagrant run-ins with the law and polite society for so long as did Washington, D.C.'s Mayor Marion Barry. The nation's capital had been abuzz with reports of the mayor's possible use of illegal drugs and numerous extramarital affairs for years before a January 1990 FBI sting aimed at Barry finally revealed the truth for all to see. While the police operation seemed like entrapment to some, Barry was arrested at the Vista International Hotel after he indisputably bought and smoked crack cocaine with a longtime paramour-turned-informant. The FBI usefully filmed the incident to convince doubting Thomases, not to mention a federal grand jury, which indicted the mayor on a cluster of cocaine and perjury charges. Despite the admission by Barry's own lawyer that the mayor had used drugs, a deeply divided, racially mixed jury deadlocked on most of the counts in August 1990, convicting Barry of a single misdemeanor charge of cocaine possession. The judge and the voters of D.C. were less sympathetic: Barry was sentenced to a jail term, a relatively harsh penalty for a first drug conviction, and then the beleaguered mayor lost his bid for a city council seat in the fall. Barry retained the support of about a quarter of his city, however, and his case badly strained race relations. Many local African-Americans directed their ire not just at white prosecutors but also at white-owned media, especially the *Washington Post*, which had been strongly critical of Barry.

Governor Dick Celeste's Womanizing (1987): When the presidential bug bit Ohio's Celeste prior to the 1988 Democratic primaries, the Cleveland *Plain Dealer* newspaper provided the antidote: a front-page headline announcing that the governor's ''links to three women may imperil presidential ambitions.'' His wife of twenty-five years was publicly supportive and forgiving, but in the post–Gary Hart climate, Celeste decided not to run.

Mayor Henry Cisneros's Extramarital Affair (1988): San Antonio's Cisneros had been a rising star in national and state Democratic politics until he unexpectedly withdrew from public life in 1988. After he declined to seek another term as mayor, citing personal reasons, local newspapers trumpeted accounts of an ongoing extramarital relationship that appeared to be responsible in part for Cisneros's early retirement. In one case a newspaper (the *San Antonio Express*) published information about the affair Cisneros had given them on an off-the-record basis, in order to prevent a competing paper from scooping them.

Governor Gaston Caperton's "Soap Opera" Divorce (1989–90): Newly inaugurated as governor of West Virginia, the wealthy Caperton shocked the state in 1989 by announcing his impending divorce from his beauty-queen wife, Dee. Once the divorce was final, Dee Caperton filed her own lawsuit charging the governor and his campaign manager with defrauding her of millions in family insurance company stock, and she also announced her candidacy for state treasurer. (The suit was later dropped, and she lost the Democratic primary election to boot.) More spice was added when completely unsubstantiated rumors about the governor's possible homosexuality reached print in a March 1990 *Washington Post* profile of the Peyton Place–like saga.

The 1990 Texas Governor's Election: Of Drugs, Rape, and "Honey Hunts": Few recent state elections have provided as much entertainment for the entire country as Texas's did in 1990. In the Democratic primary contest for governor, the eventual winner, State Treasurer Ann Richards, was accused by an opponent, State Attorney General Jim Mattox, of having repeatedly used drugs (marijuana, cocaine, and possibly others) during the 1970s—charges the self-admitted recovering alcoholic refused to confirm or deny. Mattox himself was then accused of earlier marijuana use. Meanwhile Richards's GOP opponent, wealthy rancher Clayton Williams, was creating his own set of controversies. First, he compared bad weather to rape: "If it's inevitable, just relax and enjoy it." Then he admitted to a *Houston Post* reporter he had used prostitutes as a teenager and college student, explaining that whorehouses "were the only place you got serviced then." But Williams denied unproved rumors (which the press published anyway) that he had sponsored "honey hunts"—that is, hiring prostitutes to frolic around the ranch while chased on horseback by eager cowhands. These gaffes, and others, eventually sunk Williams and helped elect Richards governor.

Noncampaign Examples

Watergate (1973–74): The grandest scandal of modern times, Watergate led to the resignation of President Nixon and the convictions of many White House aides—even two U.S. attorneys general—on various charges. The scandal began with the bugging of Democratic National Committee headquarters in Washington's Watergate office-apartment complex by officials of the Committee to Reelect the President on June 17, 1972. A cover-up of White House links to the burglary ensued, orchestrated by Nixon's closest staffers with the president's participation. The nation then endured two years of damaging revelations by Congress and the press—especially the *Washington Post* team of Bob Woodward and Carl Bernstein. After forced resignations, indictments galore, and a tissue of presidential lies, Nixon's defenses collapsed with the Supreme Court–mandated release of the tapes of his White House meetings about Watergate. Ironically these tapes had been made secretly by Nixon himself, and they contained a "smoking gun"—clear proof of Nixon's involvement in the cover-up. Faced with near-certain impeachment in the House and conviction in the Senate, Nixon became the only president ever to resign, on August 9, 1974. In an unrelated but coordinate scandal, Vice President Spiro Agnew had resigned his office earlier (in October 1973) after a bribery and corruption probe. His resignation was part of a plea bargain that included no contest to a charge of income tax evasion. In many ways Watergate transformed journalism, not least by elevating the practitioners of investigative reporting to hero status.

Congressman Wilbur Mills and Stripper Fanne Foxe (1974): A chance encounter between police and a speeding car on October 7, 1974, eventually ended the career of one of America's most powerful congressmen. When police stopped the automobile of Arkansas Democratic Congressman Wilbur Mills, Mills's passenger, burlesque performer Fanne Foxe, dived into the Potomac River—and into Washington folklore. Before long the details of Mills's alcoholism, extramarital relationship with Ms. Foxe, and bizarre behavior were splashed onto the front pages. Even though he had (briefly) been a candidate for president in 1972, Mills lost first his chairmanship of the House Ways and Means Committee and then his seat in Congress, choosing retirement in 1976 rather than a difficult reelection campaign.

The Iran-Contra Affair (1986–87): One of the most complicated and intrigue-filled scandals in recent decades, the Iran-Contra affair dominated the news for many months. It consisted of three interconnected parts: The Reagan administration sold arms to Iran, a country desperate for military materiel during its lengthy war with Iraq; in exchange for the arms, Iran was to use its influence to help gain the release of Americans held hostage in Lebanon; additionally, the U.S. assistance was supposed to strengthen so-called "moderate" elements of the Iranian leadership less hostile to America; and the arms were purchased at high prices, with the excess profits diverted to fund the Reagan-favored "Contras" fighting the Sandinista government in Nicaragua. It was a grand scheme that violated American law and policy all around: Arms sales to Iran were prohibited, the U.S. government had long forbidden ransom of any sort for hostages, and it was illegal to fund the Contras above the limits set by Congress. The first press revelations occurred in November 1986 and were followed by three investigations conducted by a presidentially appointed commission (headed by former Texas Senator John Tower), Congress (in televised hearings in mid–1987), and finally a special federal prosecutor. Charges brought by the prosecutor eventually resulted in the convictions of a number of individuals, including Reagan's national security adviser, Admiral John Poindexter, and his deputy, Col. Oliver North. (North's multicount conviction was set aside on appeal.) Reagan himself was never charged with any offense, although opinions differed about his knowledge of, and culpability for, the affair.

Judge Douglas Ginsburg's Marijuana Use (1987): In November 1987 Ginsburg was forced to withdraw as President Reagan's nominee for the vacant U.S. Supreme Court seat that had earlier been denied to Robert Bork. The cause was Ginsburg's admission that he had used marijuana in the 1960s and 1970s both as a college student and a Harvard Law School professor. The disclosures about Ginsburg, made first by National Public Radio's Nina Totenberg and the *Washington Post's* Al Kamen, sparked a series of confessions to the press by other politicians about youthful drug experimentation, from Senator Claiborne Pell (D., Rhode Island) on the left to Congressman Newt Gingrich (R., Georgia) on the right. Included among the penitents were two Democratic presidential candidates, Senator Albert Gore of Tennessee and former Arizona Governor Bruce Babbitt. Neither contender appeared at all damaged by their admissions that they had used drugs while they were in their twenties.

John Tower's Nomination as Secretary of Defense (1989): U.S. Senate confirmation of a new president's cabinet choices is usually *pro forma*, all the more so when the nominee is a former U.S. senator. But the treatment of George Bush's pick for secretary of defense, ex-Texas senator John Tower, was anything but standard. After five grueling weeks of testimony, debate, and rumormongering, Tower's nomination was defeated by a mostly party-line Senate vote in March 1989. Accusations of extensive womanizing and heavy drinking filled the airwaves and newsprint, supplementing more traditional charges of conflict of interest in Tower's previous work for defense contractors. Many media organizations unquestionably let their standards slip, with unproven allegations receiving equal weight with legitimate commentary. By the time of the final Senate vote, Tower felt compelled to make a humiliating public pledge on national television to abstain from drinking if confirmed, on pain of resignation if he broke his promise.

Speaker Jim Wright's Downfall (1989): On May 31, 1989, Wright became the first Speaker of the House to resign from office because of scandal. The unraveling of Democrat Wright's thirty-four-year congressional career began with a yearlong House Ethics Committee investigation of his finances, which resulted in a finding that Wright might have violated House rules in sixty-nine instances. The charges centered around $145,000 in gifts Wright and his wife had received from a Fort Worth developer, and the profits from a collection of Wright's speeches that allegedly were sold in bulk in lieu of speaking fees, which were limited by House rules. Wright's personal scandal was supplemented by the May resignations of his chief aide (after a *Washington Post* interview with a woman brutally assaulted by the aide in 1973) and of House Democratic Whip Tony Coelho because of an unrelated financial controversy.

Speaker Tom Foley's Rocky Rise (1989): Wright's resignation was only the first of several acts in the 1989 House degradation play. His natural successor as Speaker, Democratic Majority Leader Foley, had hoped for a coronation anointment; instead he received a baptism of smear. For weeks unsubstantiated rumors of Foley's homosexuality had been circulating in the corridors of Capitol Hill, spread by a few Wright supporters—hoping to make the alternative to Wright less palatable—as well as some Republicans. Several news outlets, including *The New Republic* and CBS News, had stoked the fires by offering their own teases about Foley's potential problem in print or over the airwaves. The allegations finally broke into full public view with the release of a Republican National Committee memo comparing Foley's record to that of avowedly gay Congressman Barney Frank (D., Mass.) under the headline, Out of the Liberal Closet. The

author of the memo, Mark Goodin, was fired in the subsequent uproar, and every Republican from President Bush to Party Chairman
Lee Atwater apologized, but Foley was forced to declare on national
television his devotion to heterosexuality.

Barney Frank and the Male Prostitute (1989): The era of sour feelings
on Capitol Hill continued through a third blockbuster scandal, as
Frank admitted a lengthy relationship with a male hooker who ran a
bisexual prostitution service out of Frank's apartment. The story was
broken by the conservative *Washington Times*, which trumpeted
every juicy morsel with front-page hype. Though Frank was apparently ignorant of some of the prostitute's activities, his indiscretion
had been so great that his standing in the House was greatly damaged. His home district in Massachusetts was more forgiving, re-
electing him easily in 1990 despite a House reprimand of Frank
passed overwhelmingly in July of that year.

Cumulatively, these capsule summaries yield several insights
about feeding frenzies. First, there has been a far greater concentration of frenzies in recent years, the reasons for which will be examined in later chapters. Second, the classic American scandal
centering on financial impropriety (the "Teapot Dome" genus) has
been overtaken by new types appropriate to our culture in the media
age—gaffes, "character" issues, and personal life-style questions.
Third, all frenzies are not equal. Some are extended and monumen-
tally important megafrenzies (such as Watergate), others blessedly
brief and less damaging all around ("frenziettes," if you will). Some
are simple one-ring media circuses, others the complex, three-ring
variety. Some are triggered by a major, real event (such as Ted
Kennedy's deadly Chappaquiddick accident), while others are press-
sustained or -exaggerated "medialities," political scientist Michael J.
Robinson's term for "events, developments, or situations to which
the media have given importance by . . . featuring them in such a
way that their real significance has been modified, distorted, or obscured."[12] These differences acknowledged, all case-study events
nevertheless have in common the kind of press coverage contained
in the definition of feeding frenzy.

Several cautions are in order. By no means are the chosen cases
meant to be an exhaustive list of modern feeding frenzies. However,
while not comprehensive, the list is representative of the phenomenon, and the conclusions reached later in the volume are applicable
to many other examples. Nor is press treatment of special feeding

frenzy events necessarily indicative of day-to-day coverage of politics and government, though one suspects it is becoming more so. After all, the potential for coverage to spin out of control is always present, and the standards and excesses observed during frenzies inevitably affect everyday journalism. Finally, it should be emphasized that not all consequences of frenzies are bad. To the contrary, some questionable candidacies and some regrettable governmental practices have been ended as a result, and intense coverage has attracted the public's attention to certain abuses as nothing else could have. Yet the means chosen by the media certainly do not always justify even the most golden ends.

The means and ends of frenzies will be examined at length in the pages that follow. After a chapter on the history and modern development of the American news media and their relationships with elected officials, the internal and external dynamics of the frenzy process will be charted and explained in chapters 3 and 4. The parade of excesses visible during frenzies will march by in chapter 5, with particular emphasis on the publication and airing of rumors without adequate proof. After a brief chapter on "frenzies that weren't"— potential or eventual frenzies whose coverage was delayed or muted—chapter 7 will focus on the positive and negative consequences of the frenzy phenomenon for the press, candidates, voters, and the political system. Finally, a prescriptive concluding chapter will propose some remedies for the media excesses and abuses identified throughout this book. As argued later, the press must assume most of the housecleaning chores, but candidates and voters need to pitch in as well.

Throughout this book, the reader may wish to consider the weighty obligations that should accompany the press's exceptional privileges. No group in American life is as constitutionally protected as is the press; no profession is afforded such wide latitude for unfettered enterprise as is journalism; no individuals are so entrusted with enormous yet nearly unchecked influence as are newspersons. In exchange for this position of privilege, the press has a special and coordinate obligation to be extraordinarily painstaking and eminently fair in exercising its freedoms. The abuses painfully visible during feeding frenzies damage the political fabric of America by cheapening public discourse, trivializing the campaign agenda, breeding cynicism, and discouraging able people from seeking public office. Just as importantly for the press, journalism's excesses undermine the very credibility of the news profession. This serious threat to the press's

most valuable asset inevitably menaces press freedom and, therefore, the democratic system that relies greatly on the check provided
by the news media.

The stakes are high, then, not just for the press but for the rest of
us. The future quality of American democracy and its politics depends in good measure on reversing the deterioration in journalistic
standards—a decline that will be documented in this volume.

2

The Press of Yesteryear

From Canard to Cover-up to Exposé

The journalists of the United States [possess] a vulgar turn of mind. The character-
istics of the American journalist consist in an open and coarse appeal to the passions
of his readers; he abandons principles to assail the characters of individuals, to track
them into private life and disclose all their weaknesses and vices. Nothing can be
more deplorable than this abuse of the powers of thought.

It was not Gary Hart nor John Tower nor any modern political figure who uttered these words, though it is easy to imagine it so.
Rather, Alexis de Tocqueville penned these lines in 1835,[1] proving
beyond question that some of the press abuses of the present day
have a long and distinguished history. It is that history which will be
examined in this chapter, with particular emphasis on the latter half
of the twentieth century.

The press has played many roles and assumed many postures in
U.S. history. Moreover, like every other American institution, its
power, promise, and performance has varied greatly from era to era.
Just in the modern age—from World War II to the present—the
breadth, depth, and influence of the news media have expanded
enormously, as political journalism has passed through three successive phases in its recent development:

From about 1941 to 1966, journalists engaged in what I would call
"lapdog" journalism—reporting that served and reinforced the political establishment. In this period, mainstream journalists rarely challenged prevailing orthodoxy, accepted at face value much of what
those in power told them, and protected politicians by revealing little
about their nonofficial lives, even when private vices affected their

public performance. Wartime necessities encouraged the "lapdog" mentality that had already become well established in Franklin Roosevelt's earlier administrations. But lapdog journalism perhaps reached its zenith under another Democratic president, John F. Kennedy.

From about 1966 to 1974 was a period of "watchdog" journalism, when reporters scrutinized and checked the behavior of political elites by undertaking independent investigations into statements made by public officials. The Vietnam War and the Watergate scandals stimulated this kind of journalism. In the later years of this period, the first discussions of private lives appeared, though usually only in the context of public performance.

Since about 1974, political reporters have engaged in what I would term "junkyard-dog" journalism—political reporting that is often harsh, aggressive, and intrusive, where feeding frenzies flourish, and gossip reaches print. Every aspect of private life potentially becomes fair game for scrutiny as a new, almost "anything goes" philosophy takes hold. This form of attack journalism was briefly sketched in the previous chapter.

These descriptions only generally describe the prevailing mainstream attitude of journalism in each time period: There are many exceptions to each categorization, and the periods overlap in some respects. For instance, as we shall see, even as Lyndon Johnson and Richard Nixon were being pummelled on policy (Vietnam and Watergate, respectively) by the newly activated "watchdog" press, their private lives remained protected in most respects thanks to the waning effects of "lapdog" journalism. Nonetheless these three phases are useful overall barometers of the behavioral changes that have occurred in recent years.

The evolution of the modern press through these phases is the focus of chapter 2, which will discuss journalism's changing modes and rules of operation from the country's earliest days up to the modern age.

Press Past as Press Prologue   [History of]

Journalism—the process and profession[2] of collecting and disseminating new information about subjects of public interest (i.e., the news)—has been with us in some form since the dawn of civilization.[3] Yet its practice has often been remarkably uncivilized, and far more so at the beginning of the American Republic than today.

A hint of future directions appeared in the very first newspaper published in America in 1690, which carried a report that the king of

France "used to lie with" his son's wife.[4] George Washington escaped most press scrutiny of his private life, but he detested journalists nonetheless; his battle tactics in the Revolutionary War had been much criticized in print, and an early draft of his "Farewell Address to the Nation" at the end of his presidency contained a condemnation of the press described as "savage."[5] Thomas Jefferson was treated especially harshly by elements of the early American press. Jefferson's attempt, while young and single, to seduce a neighbor's wife became a "character issue" for a viciously partisan press, while one Richmond newspaper editor, angered by Jefferson's refusal to appoint him a postmaster, concocted a falsehood that survives to this day: that Jefferson kept a slave as his concubine and had several children by her.[6] One can understand why Jefferson, normally a defender of a free press, also commented "even the least informed of the people have learned that nothing in a newspaper is to be believed."

Jefferson probably did not intend that statement to be taken literally, since he himself was instrumental in establishing the *National Gazette*, the newspaper of his political faction and viewpoint. The *Gazette* was created to compete with a similar paper founded earlier by Alexander Hamilton and his anti-Jefferson Federalists. The era of party newspapers extended from Washington's tenure through Andrew Jackson's presidency. The editor of Jackson's party paper, the *Globe*, was included in the president's influential if informal Kitchen Cabinet, and all of Jackson's appointees with annual salaries greater than one thousand dollars were required to buy a subscription. Incidentally, from George Washington through James Buchanan, all government printing contracts were awarded to the newspaper associated with the incumbent administration.[7]

The partisan press eventually gave way to the "penny press." In 1833 Benjamin Day founded the *New York Sun*, costing a penny at the newsstand. Politically a more independent publication, not inextricably tied to one party, it was the forerunner of the modern press built on mass circulation and commercial advertising to produce profit. By 1861 the penny press had so supplanted its partisan predecessor that President Abraham Lincoln announced his administration would have no favored or sponsored newspaper.

The press thus became markedly less partisan but not necessarily more respectable. Mass-circulation dailies sought wide readership, and readers were clearly attracted by the sensational and the scandalous. The sordid side of politics became the entertainment of the times. One of the best-known examples occurred in the presidential campaign of 1884, when the *Buffalo Evening Telegraph* headlined "A Terrible Tale" about Democratic nominee Grover Cleveland.[8] In 1871, while sheriff of Buffalo, the bachelor Cleveland had allegedly fathered an illegitimate child. Even though the woman in question had been seeing other men too, Cleveland willingly accepted responsibility since all the other men were married, and he had dutifully paid child support for years. Fortunately for Cleveland, another newspaper, the *Democratic Sentinel*, broke a story that helped to counterbalance his own scandal: Republican presidential nominee James G. Blaine and his wife had had their first child just three months after marriage. (Shades of 1988, when a "miracle baby" would again come front and center in a presidential campaign—that of Rev. Pat Robertson.) There is a lesson for politicians in this double-edged morality tale: Cleveland admitted his vice forthrightly and took his lumps, while Blaine backed and filled and told a fabulously elaborate, completely unbelievable story about having had two marriage ceremonies six months apart. Cleveland won the election.

The era of the intrusive press was in full flower. First, "yellow journalism" and then "muckraking" were in fashion. Pioneered by such prominent publishers as William Randolph Hearst and Joseph Pulitzer, yellow journalism[9] featured pictures, comics, and color designed to capture a share of the burgeoning immigrant population. The front-page "editorial crusade" became common, the motto for which frequently seemed to be Damn the Truth, Full Speed Ahead. The muckrakers—so named by President Theodore Roosevelt after a special rake designed to collect manure[10]—took charge after the turn of the century. Such journalists as Upton Sinclair and David Graham Phillips searched out and exposed real and apparent misconduct by government, business, and politicians in order to stimulate reform.[11] There was no shortage of corruption to reveal, of course, and much good came from their efforts. But an unfortunate side effect of the emphasis on crusades and investigations was increasing violation of legitimate privacy rights. The current controversy about press intrusiveness is in some ways an echo of the one that raged a century ago, when Louis D. Brandeis—later to become a distinguished Supreme Court justice—and his law partner Samuel D. Warren published these all-too-familiar thoughts about journalistic excesses:

The press is overstepping in every direction the obvious bounds of propriety and of decency. Gossip is no longer the resource of the idle and of the vicious, but has become a trade, which is pursued with industry as well as effrontery. To satisfy a prurient taste the details of sexual relations are spread broadcast in the columns of the daily papers. To occupy the indolent, column upon column is filled with idle gossip, which can only be procured by intrusion upon the domestic circle.[12]

If the modern press corps shows little enlightened advancement in the area of privacy rights, it has achieved great progress on another front. Throughout the nineteenth century payoffs to the press were not uncommon. Andrew Jackson gave one in ten of his early appointments to loyal reporters,[13] for instance, while in the 1872 presidential campaign the Republicans slipped cash to about three hundred newsmen.[14] Wealthy industrialists also sometimes purchased editorial peace or investigative cease-fire for tens of thousands of dollars.[15] Examples of press corruption today are exceedingly rare, and not even the most extreme of the modern media's critics charge otherwise.[16]

News Rules for New Times

As the news business grew, its focus gradually shifted from passionate opinion to corporate profit. Newspapers hoping to maximize profit were more careful not to alienate the advertisers and readers who produced their revenues, and the result was less harsh, more "objective" reporting. Meanwhile, media barons became pillars of the establishment, no longer the antiestablishment insurgents of yore, and in some cases they were perhaps less willing to give offense to fellow elites who occupied public office. World War I also seemed to change the rules of engagement for many journalists, as patriotism made victory a common cause for newsmen and politicians alike. After the war, real scandal—the massive Teapot Dome uproar of Warren Harding's administration—occupied those still in the muckraking tradition, as did the 1927 revelations about Harding's White House mistress, Nan Britton, and their illegitimate child. The press was apparently unaware of Harding's torrid affair with Britton, which was sometimes consummated in a closet near the Oval Office. The truth came out only after the deaths of President and Mrs. Harding, when Britton published a best-selling account.[17]

As in so many other areas of American life, Franklin D. Roosevelt's presidency rewrote the rules of engagement for the relationship between the press and the politicians they covered. That relationship became more "correct," in diplomatic parlance, with the tone of press coverage increasingly sedate. Perhaps it was partially the crisis atmosphere and sobering effect of the Great Depression, whose dire consequences for most Americans even the end of Prohibition in 1933 could not lighten. Then, too, most working reporters were probably strong personal supporters of Roosevelt who rooted for him to succeed, and those who did not still recognized his overwhelming popularity. Later World War II had its effects; reporters practiced self-censorship and refused to publish any information about America's leader that might give aid and comfort to the Axis powers. Whatever the precise combination of causes, Roosevelt was protected by the press in ways that would have amazed some of his harassed predecessors. Roosevelt, a polio victim, was wheelchair-bound, but of thirty-five thousand press photographs of FDR, only two showed his wheelchair.[18] When the president occasionally fell in public, photographers would take no pictures and live radio broadcasters would make no mention of the fact.[19] In 1944, as a desperately ill Roosevelt sought a fourth term, publishers such as Henry Luce—a GOP supporter, incidentally—refused to print photos hinting at FDR's poor state of health. And many supporters knew of or strongly suspected the president's estrangement from his wife Eleanor, while others were clearly aware of Roosevelt's relationship with Lucy Mercer, who resided in the White House at times and was with FDR in Warm Springs at his death. Not a word of any of it reached print. At least the press extended the same courtesies to some of Roosevelt's opponents. For instance, journalists in 1940 never reported that Republican presidential nominee Wendell Willkie had for many years openly kept a mistress, with whom he was in almost daily communication while on the campaign trail.[20]

The Rooseveltian rule of thumb for press coverage of politicians was simple, and it endured for forty years: The private life of a public figure should stay private and undisclosed unless it seriously impinged on his or her public performance. (In many cases even *serious* infringement did not warrant publication, as we shall see.) The rule's variations and practical applications were many. Politicians could earn special absolution for sins committed on the road, for example, as the *Washington Post*'s David Broder recalls:

The first campaign I covered was 1960 and I remember being formally initiated on the press bus by Bill Lawrence of the *New York Times* into something he called the "West of the Potomac" rule, which was basically that anything that happened west of the Potomac, you didn't talk about east of the Potomac. And it was a protective rule both for what was then substantially an all-male press corps and also for the candidates. We gave them kind of a license to live whatever way they wanted to live on the road.

The *Wall Street Journal's* Albert Hunt remembers that hypocrisy alone was not reason enough to break "the rule." Early in his career he knew a congressman "who not only slept around, but was actually living with someone on his staff, while his wife and family were back home . . . [Nevertheless] he ran for re-election every two years with a picture of the wife and the four kids. I never wrote about it, though today . . . I surely would." Not only mortal sin was off limits; the press rarely mentioned the venial variety either. Journalists willingly projected the sunny image President Eisenhower and his managers preferred, for instance. Americans never knew the fact of which the White House press corps was fully aware: Beneath the dazzling, charitable smile lay a man who could display a terrible temper and swore like the trooper he had been.

The post-Roosevelt Washington press corps, according to veteran journalist Paul Duke, was "rather sleepy" and "content to report from handouts and routine news briefings. There wasn't a hell of a lot of penetrating coverage back then." The press and the pols were frequently pals, socializing together extensively and assisting one another in various ways. A few journalists, such as Walter Lippmann, gave private advice and contributed speeches to favored senators and presidents.[21] Others made introductions; Eisenhower first met a young senator named Richard Nixon by way of Bert Andrews, the Washington correspondent of the New York *Herald Tribune*.[22] Politicians returned the favors, most of them in the traditional way with story tips and preferred treatment, a few with unusual courtesies. Louisiana's Huey Long, for example, would sometimes have state troopers pull cars over—not to issue tickets for violations but instead to suggest that drivers subscribe to the *New Orleans Tribune*, a newspaper friendly to him.[23]

Occasionally reports would hint at private impropriety by the use of code words or euphemisms, although many were too obscure to be fully comprehended by the average reader. The *Baltimore Sun's* veteran political columnist Jack Germond remembers:

When I first got into politics, a politician who was a notorious drunk would be described as somebody with a reputation for excessive conviviality. A politician who chased women was known as someone who appreciated a well-turned ankle. And this was the way we went at this. Everybody knew except the reader.

More often, though, unpleasant personal vices would be ignored completely, even when an official's public performance was manifestly impaired. Alcohol abuse is the most obvious example; nary a senior reporter interviewed for this book could not recall outrageously drunken public conduct by major politicians that was kept completely off the record. Three reminiscences will suffice here.

Benjamin Bradlee of the *Washington Post:*

I remember as a kid reporter going up to the Senate to watch a filibuster and seeing [Senator] Thruston Morton [R., Ky.] almost fall down as he was talking, and I was just stunned [because] nobody ever reported it; it was all a big club.

George Herman of CBS News:

When I first came to Washington there were a lot of senators who were well known as terrible drunks, including one Senator Herman Welker of Idaho, who burst out of the Senate Republican Cloak Room just in time to hear a unanimous consent motion on something like declaring National Pickle Week, shouted "I object" and fell over in a dead faint on the floor, half drunk, and was carried away. No reporter, including the reporters covering for his state, ever mentioned to the voters that their elected official was drunk on the floor of the Senate.

Jack Germond (then of Gannett News):

In 1962 Senator Pete Williams [D., N.J.] was running for reelection and he had a drinking problem. We decided we were going to do the [alcoholic] story about this guy [even though] that was almost never done. Well, we got him pegged finally because he showed up drunk at an NAACP function and they passed a resolution chastising him for his behavior. This gave us a way to get at this story. But when we wrote the piece, [the news service's key] paper in New Jersey refused to use it. . . . Everybody in Washington knew Williams had a drinking problem, but they weren't going to tell their readers.

Reporters who did try to tell the truth often received an unsympathetic hearing from their editors. In the mid-1960s, when Eileen Shanahan of the *New York Times* attempted to report that Louisiana Democratic Senator Russell Long was drunk on the Senate floor and thereby impeding the passage of a major tax bill, her editors rejected the topic as unfit for print.[24] Long's excessive drinking was hardly a secret; his nickname among reporters was Jack Daniels,[25] and colleagues had once escorted him—shouting while greatly inebriated—forcibly from the floor of the Senate. Also widely known were the bottle exploits of a host of other powerful congressmen, from Majority Leader Hale Boggs (D., La.) and Rules Committee Chairman Richard Bolling (D., Mo.) to Armed Services Committee Chairman L. Mendel Rivers (D., S.C.) and House Administration Committee Chairman Frank Thompson, Jr. (D., N.J.). Yet nothing of their problems was published or broadcast in their heyday. The dispensation from disclosure extended even to enemies of the press, such as the heartily disliked Senator Joseph McCarthy (R., Wis.). A victim at age forty-eight of cirrhosis of the liver, McCarthy had carried liquor in his briefcase and swallowed half sticks of butter so that he could hold his spirits—all observed by reporters, all unreported.[26]

In certain relatively rare circumstances, the rule did not apply because public comment became almost unavoidable. For example, the tempestuous love affair of Louisiana Governor Earl Long with stripper Blaze Starr was so flagrant that publicity was inevitable.[27] Financial scandals also did not come under the rule's umbrella, and the press feasted on them throughout the post–World War II era. The questionable financial affairs of Eisenhower's powerful White House chief of staff, Sherman Adams, and Lyndon Johnson's wheeler-dealer aide, Bobby Baker, are but two of many prominent examples from the 1950s and 1960s.[28] It was, in fact, a money scandal of sorts that triggered the first modern campaign feeding frenzy—Richard Nixon's "secret fund" in 1952. In retrospect, the small amount Senator Nixon collected from California supporters for legitimate public expenses seems trivial, especially in light of more recent campaign finance schemes and speaking-fee abuses. But this impression may be a measure of how our society's views of political propriety have changed over the decades. Moreover, press coverage of the Nixon fund matter in particular, and financial corruption in general, may have been intense in part because so many other scandalous subjects of potentially greater interest to journalists and their audiences were considered off limits.

The most taboo topic of all in the 1950s and 1960s was sex, of course. The Roosevelt example notwithstanding, John F. Kennedy's presidency provided the most severe test ever of the rule. Kennedy's reputation, and the press's, would be shaped by the outcome.

The Media's Camelot: JFK and the Press

By many credible accounts, John F. Kennedy was not King Arthur but Sir Lancelot in the Camelot of his presidency. Even thirty years later, it is not the large number of his sexual dalliances so much as his sheer recklessness in pursuing them that stuns. Garry Wills, author of *The Kennedy Imprisonment*, has written of "the calculated regimen of John Kennedy, the daily dose of sex taken, as it were, for muscle tone."[29] And indeed, Kennedy put Warren Harding, Franklin Roosevelt, and his other adulterous predecessors to shame with a "regimen" that included, over the years, many dozens of liaisons.[30] Marilyn Monroe, Jayne Mansfield, Angie Dickinson, and stripper Blaze Starr are only a few of the better-known paramours with whom JFK has been linked, not to mention a healthy dose of anonymous airline stewardesses, secretaries, and aides. There was apparently no slackening of Kennedy's sexual pursuits after his election. To the contrary, the presidency facilitated his desires, with frequent travel, time away from his wife, guaranteed privacy courtesy of the ever-discreet Secret Service, and the alluring aphrodisiac of his supremely powerful office.

It is now well established that one of Kennedy's principal mistresses was Judith Campbell (née Immoor, later Exner), a striking brunette introduced to Kennedy by Frank Sinatra in Las Vegas in early 1960. Shortly thereafter Sinatra played matchmaker for Campbell again, this time to Sam Giancana, the notorious Chicago mob boss and successor to Al Capone as head of a billion-dollar crime syndicate. Campbell was close to both men over much of the same period, and the evidence is strong that each man was fully aware of the other. Campbell appears to have acted as a courier, and there was no lack of business to be conducted between these scions of politics and crime. Giancana assisted Kennedy's presidential campaign with a substantial financial contribution before the crucial West Virginia primary and later in Cook County, Illinois, where a squeaker election was won for Kennedy, possibly corruptly. More important, Giancana had been recruited by the CIA for a Mafia-U.S. government collaborative effort: the assassination of Cuban Premier Fidel Castro, to be attempted sometime during the early 1960s. The motives for cooperation were different but complementary. The United States wanted to rid itself of a Communist dictatorship just ninety miles from its shores, while the Mafia bosses intended to avenge Castro's shutdown of all their Cuban casinos as well as curry favor with American politicians who had the power to prosecute them.

These extraordinary revelations came to light not because of a persistent, inquisitive press but indirectly by means of a governmental inquiry. A dozen years after Kennedy's assassination, the U.S. Senate Select Intelligence Committee was investigating the CIA's plans to kill foreign leaders when Campbell's role was uncovered. The committee, headed by Idaho Democratic Senator, and Kennedy family friend, Frank Church, downplayed the JFK–Campbell relationship, and its report cited only an unnamed, genderless "friend" of the president when referring to Campbell.

Did an aggressive, post-Watergate press leap to uncover the whole truth? Hardly. The initial story was leaked exclusively to Watergate's lead attack dog, the *Washington Post*, whose editors chose to minimize and bury it deep inside the November 16, 1975 edition. The by-lined reporter, Lawrence Stern, and his *Post* colleague George Lardner both thought it was a front-page story because it was a scoop and Stern was able to provide many details about the incident, including Campbell's name.[31]

There the matter rested for a month, with no widespread interest expressed by the news media, until a report surfaced that Senate committee staffers were being ordered to swear they were not the source of the earlier leak to the *Post*. This sparked *New York Times* columnist William Safire to launch a virtual one-man crusade[32] against an attempted cover-up by Senator Church, who was at that time also a presidential aspirant. Among Safire's observations in his first column on the subject was this compelling justification for his examination of Kennedy's private life even under terms of the Rooseveltian rule of coverage: "The private life of any public figure is nobody's business but his own. . . . But when the nation's Chief Executive receives even a few calls from the *home telephone* of the leader of the Mafia in Chicago, that crosses the line into the public's business."[33]

Safire's agitation opened the sluice, and the JFK–Campbell relationship became fair game for extensive review in virtually all major publications. Some went further. *Time* magazine, for instance, used the opportunity to discuss Kennedy's long-protected wild side; back-door tales of JFK's White House trysts and the names of many of his flames first achieved respectable print there.[34] While controversial at first—the strong reaction to the *Time* piece demonstrated that many preferred not to hear of Kennedy's foibles[35]—the truth about the private JFK has gradually emerged since that time. Judith Campbell Exner herself, well paid to do so by publishers and magazines, told sordid tales of White House intrigue.[36] For those who care to see, the presidential knight's once-shining armor has been tarnished badly.

The most pressing question left to answer is why the press did not see anything worth reporting about the president's shocking behavior *at the time*. There surely can be no doubt of the seriousness of

Kennedy's offenses; these were indiscretions that mattered. Consider the elements:

- The possibilities for blackmail of the president were many and substantial. Kennedy was reportedly quite casual about his flings, once openly discussing his need for frequent sex with British Prime Minister Harold Macmillan and Macmillan's foreign secretary. Unfriendly as well as friendly intelligence services might well have known of the president's entangling alliances. Inside the U.S. government there is evidence that one official used his knowledge of JFK's compromised private life to his personal advantage. FBI Director J. Edgar Hoover learned of the Campbell love triangle, and at a private luncheon with the president in March 1962 laid out his findings. It would logically follow that Hoover's tacit or overt threat to expose Kennedy's philandering with a mob moll made Hoover virtually untouchable by the normal chain of command control. Indeed, the autocratic FBI chief seemed to have carte blanche authority to do as he wanted in many sensitive areas.
- Public funds, facilities, and personnel were involved in JFK's illicit affairs with Campbell and others. From the White House to *Air Force One* to hotels around the country, some aides and security men must have scheduled and facilitated Kennedy's meetings with women. Some have claimed that members of the Secret Service actually procured "appropriate" women for the president, especially at non-Washington sites in advance of his trips.[37]
- The president's recklessness had potentially grave consequences bearing directly on his public responsibilities. On occasion Kennedy reportedly shook his guards and the military aide carrying the nuclear code "football" to seek more privacy with a sexual partner. This was at the height of the Cold War era, when a president might have only a few minutes' response time before a Russian missile attack.[38]
- Exner and others have told of JFK's intermittent use of marijuana and amphetamines.[39] Mind-altering drugs affect anyone's judgment, and in the nuclear age such a presidential transgression would be exceptionally foolhardy.

White House reporters during the Kennedy administration were not aware of all this, of course. Some may have known nothing at all, but virtually every major journalist had heard and suspected plenty. As columnist Mary McGrory puts it, "The classic question has become, 'What did you know about John Kennedy's private life and when did you know it?' " For many newsmen of the time, the answer can only be a confessional. Granted, as Jack Germond cautions, "After the fact, reporters always claim they knew." But the abundance of proof available to reporters before and during Kennedy's presidency is indisputable.

The rumors about Kennedy circulated widely from the start of his presidential campaign. Hal Bruno of ABC News, who worked for *Newsweek* then, remembers the press corps' jokingly suggested slogan for JFK in the Wisconsin primary: "Let's sack with Jack." But more than rumor was available. Kennedy had long been conducting an affair with one of his young secretarial aides, whose devoutly Catholic landlords were outraged when they observed the Catholic senator's behavior. They booby-trapped the woman's apartment with tape recorders and personally photographed Kennedy leaving the woman's apartment late at night. The evidence was shared with newspapers, magazines, and television stations, to no avail.[40] Even when the landlord couple began appearing at Kennedy's rallies and picketing in other public places in an attempt to draw attention to the candidate's morals, they were ignored by the news media. CBS's White House correspondent Robert Pierpoint knew firsthand of Kennedy's activities as a senator. As he explains it:

Even before Kennedy was in the White House I happened to know a young woman who had a romance with him. It was one of those summer romances when his wife was away, and this young woman was a close friend who was quite upset. She'd had a brief love affair with the senator and she was kind of overwhelmed by the whole thing. She confided in me and I tried to be a sympathetic sounding board for her.

Once Kennedy was installed in the Oval Office, of course, reporters were normally in close proximity to his every move, and the signs of his adultery were obvious. Barbara Gamarekian of the *New York Times* remembers that on trips without Mrs. Kennedy, "There were lots of women in strange comings and goings." Robert Novak cited the "classic story" of JFK's visit to New York sans Jackie in early 1963:

He came back from a weekend at Hyannis Port [Mass.] early to go to New York, leaving his wife at Hyannis, so that he could meet on Sunday night with the U.N. ambassador, Adlai Stevenson. He stayed at the Carlyle Hotel and met Adlai there. Everybody in the press corps soon found out that Adlai, after talking to JFK for about 10 or 15 minutes, whipped out the back

door, leaving JFK with a woman—a famous actress. Everybody knew it, and
it was a wonderful story, but nobody wrote it.

One reporter from the *New York Times* did alert his editor to the
actress's suspicious movements with Kennedy, but the editor declared the matter to be insufficiently newsworthy.[41]

Robert Pierpoint also had several unforgettable intersections with
Kennedy's love life while attending to his White House press duties
for CBS. In March 1962, while covering Kennedy's visit to Palm
Springs, Pierpoint and Douglas Cornell of the Associated Press witnessed the president and a young woman in a lengthy warm embrace inside and outside the executive limousine.[42] (JFK was unaware
of the reporters, who were sitting in a parked car some yards away
late in the evening.) Neither reporter included the incident in his
subsequent account of the president's activities. However, knowledge of JFK's amorous escapades was not really impeded as a result;
even Mrs. Kennedy was well aware of them, as another of
Pierpoint's anecdotes reveals:

I was sitting in the White House press room one day shortly after noon. And
through the corridor came a French magazine correspondent who worked
for *Paris Match* and he said, "Bob, I've just had a very unusual experience. I
have to tell somebody about it." He was somewhat agitated and said that he
had been invited to have lunch with Jackie upstairs in the private area and
the President joined them, and then after lunch the President said, "Jackie,
why don't you show our friend around?" She did, and brought him over to
the west wing. Between the Cabinet room and the Oval Office there is a
small room where the secretaries sit. As she ushered him into that room she
said in French, "And there is the woman that my husband is supposed to be
sleeping with." He was quite upset and didn't know what to answer; it was
kind of embarrassing for him.

As if all this were not enough for one reporter, Pierpoint was able
to learn still more from another Kennedy bedmate, this one an airline
stewardess who served the presidential entourage, and especially
the president, on *Air Force One* voyages. Pierpoint became her confi-
dant through an odd connection: She was Scandinavian and he was
the only one around who spoke fluent Swedish.

Pierpoint's experiences were not typical of White House reporters,
but a number of his contemporaries have confided similar stories
over the years.[43] Given the widespread knowledge of at least the out-
lines of Kennedy's shenanigans, we return to the central question:
Why did none of the incidents ever reach print or air during

Kennedy's lifetime? According to Pierpoint, this was a subject of active debate among some journalists at the time:

There was quite a bit of discussion in the White House press corps about how we should handle this. It was an ethical problem of concern to us in part because he was fairly blatant about it. But overall the basic feeling was that we shouldn't touch it because it wasn't our business or the public's business.

This adherence to the Rooseveltian "rule," which benefited the press as well as politicians, was indisputably part of the explanation. David Broder suggests as much:

The reason we didn't follow up [on the womanizing rumors] is clearly because of that "gentleman's understanding" that boys will be boys—and it was all boys. Nobody wanted to spoil the fun for anybody else, and besides, the attitude back then was, what the hell difference does it make? . . . The hypocrisy was evident, was acknowledged, and indeed was institutionalized. But I would argue that it was as much self-protective of the press corps as it was protective of the candidate. What people said was, "Well, shit, if you're going to whistle on this guy . . . are we going to go back and start telling about each other? Is that the next step?"

This "institutionalized hypocrisy" would be less offensive in retrospect if the media had been a bit more reluctant (if not guilt-ridden) while participating. Yet in some cases adherence to the rule seemed downright enthusiastic. As the *Wall Street Journal*'s Brooks Jackson sums up the problem, here was a case where "reporters got too close to their source." Many journalists liked Kennedy, agreed with his politics, and revelled in their acceptance by, and association with, the glamorous, dashing, wealthy, jet-setting Kennedys. Kennedy also had a disarming ability to charm journalists by taking them into his confidence, soliciting their views, and making them "part of the action." Broder again:

One of Kennedy's techniques for dealing with the press was to say things that were so goddamn candid—to some about sexual things but even his political comments—so that you knew if you printed it, you would be ending your intimate relationship: that is, the president would say, "you couldn't have thought that I would say something like that on the record." It was a way of co-opting us.

Using this device and others, says Howell Raines of the *New York Times*, "Kennedy was alarmingly successful at turning journalists into cheerleaders."

It is also true that the press may have been doing what much of the public wanted. People cherish their myths and heroes; while they love gossip, many also shrink from a painful or shocking truth, and in retrospect they would prefer not to know. When JFK's secret life became public in the mid-1970s—long after emotions about Camelot had had a chance to cool—some publications were inundated with letters denouncing them for "destroying" Kennedy's reputation and "assassinating" him anew.[44] In the heyday of the Kennedy era, playing the role of skunk at the garden party was considerably less appealing. Longtime *Detroit News* White House correspondent Jerald F. terHorst, later President Ford's first press secretary, explains, "No paper wanted to look like it was going out of its way to find something nasty about this very popular president." TerHorst also pointed out that Kennedy served before the courts weakened the libel laws, and the threat of legal action served as a deterrent to publication of anything but an airtight case.

So private foibles were not exposed in Kennedy's era, and for the reasons already discussed, the press was unwilling to buck tradition and to investigate, despite whispers aplenty and bits of evidence that the potential for blackmail of a president existed. Though this was clearly not the press's finest hour, in fact it was more reprehensible still. Not only did the media not want to dig for the unpleasant truth, they willingly communicated a lie, becoming part and parcel of the Kennedy public relations team. In the press reports, Jack Kennedy, champion philanderer, became the perfect husband and family man. Jackie Kennedy, often negligent in her duties and of difficult temperament, became the nation's paragon of virtue, one of the most splendid first ladies ever. Veteran CBS News correspondent George Herman (now retired) remembers the reality as quite different from the projected image:

I saw some things both Jackie and JFK did that I thought were disgusting and would shock the American people, and nobody reported them even though they were done in public. The press gave JFK a very, very good break; it was a kind of love affair. . . . For instance, Jackie would skip out on a White House dinner and the word would be that she was ill or that she had other responsibilities. And the next day the New York newspapers would show pictures of her dancing at a ball in New York or water-skiing while the president was entertaining some head of state that she wasn't anxious to meet. And yet everybody was talking about what a wonderful first lady she was. Baloney, she was one of the worst first ladies. She didn't want to bother with many duties. She only came to a dinner or took part in a thing when it was something she liked.

During JFK's administration, Michael Deaver (President Reagan's image manager) was found not on the White House staff but in the press pool. The news media that correctly took Lyndon Johnson and Richard Nixon to task for lying to the public during the Vietnam War and the Watergate scandal were guilty in the first degree of the same offense during the Kennedy presidency.

Many newsmen of the Camelot era excused their lack of aggressiveness by noting, as one did, "We were political reporters, not gumshoes." Yet there was one exceptional circumstance that spurred a few reporters into investigative high gear. Ironically, the exception was made in order to do President Kennedy's bidding, to clear him of a charge widely circulated in private that he had been secretly wed to a twice-divorced socialite in 1947 before his marriage to Jacqueline Bouvier in 1953. While it had reached print mainly in the publications of various right-wing extremist groups, the White House feared it would eventually get some kind of legitimate airing, especially since it was based on a written record—a privately published book entitled *The Blauvelt Family Genealogy*[45] (copyrighted in 1957). The president's close friend *Newsweek* reporter Benjamin Bradlee (later executive editor of the *Washington Post*) came to the rescue.[46] Having gotten "the complete story from the president himself," Bradlee was fully convinced the tale was untrue; his theory today is that "probably Joe Kennedy, [Jack's] brother, used to screw this girl, and that's how the connection was made." Bradlee then arranged through JFK's press secretary, Pierre Salinger, for temporary use of "some solid FBI documentation about the character of the organizations and people involved in spreading the Blauvelt story." In return the president was given the extraordinary right of approval and clearance of the story before publication. As it happened, Kennedy could have had no problems with the piece, published in September of 1962.[47] Bradlee and his coauthor Charles Roberts flatly discounted the poisonous "sensation" and attributed its spread to "hate groups and gossip columnists," helpfully concluding:

The President and Mrs. Kennedy—who celebrated their ninth wedding anniversary last week—are philosophical about the "Blauvelt campaign." They recognize that it is motivated by extremist groups and circulated for political purpose.

In one way this is an admirable example the current press would do well to emulate: A publication took the time and trouble to expose a false rumor rather than promote one. On the other hand, presidential preclearance was an appalling breach of journalistic independence and integrity, and the sycophantic tone had a whitewash quality to it given the press's refusal to investigate the other side of the larger story—Kennedy's flagrant and dangerous violations of his marriage vows.

Incidentally, Bradlee claims to have been totally ignorant of the other side of the story, even though most reporters with far less White House access had developed strong suspicions by that time. Insists Bradlee: "I did not know, and one of the people he was having an affair with was [someone in my family]; I had no idea about it [and] neither did my wife." Some of Bradlee's friends are not convinced. "He's said that to me many times. I don't believe him—and I adore him," admitted CBS News producer Andrew Lack. In his 1975 book about Kennedy, Bradlee himself hinted he knew more than he now acknowledges. In a conversation with the president and first lady, he informed JFK and Jackie of the notes he was keeping for later publication: "[President Kennedy] insisted that he was glad that someone was keeping some kind of record of the more intimate details without which the real story of any administration cannot be told. I am not convinced he knows how intimate those details might get, but I suspect Jackie does, but that's for another decade."[48]

Whatever the truth about Bradlee's knowledge of Kennedy's private transgressions, his compromising intimacy with the powerful was symptomatic of journalism's "lapdog" inadequacies during the period. In what is an apt commentary on the entire era as much as about his *Post* colleague, David Broder notes, "Ben's precepts are better than his example when it comes to defining what ought to be the relationship between reporters and presidents."

Lyndon Johnson, Richard Nixon, and the Media

Kennedy's two successors as president, Lyndon B. Johnson and Richard M. Nixon, are often viewed today as having endured an unremittingly hostile and critical press, by contrast to the kid-gloves treatment accorded JFK. While that may have been true on some policy matters, especially Vietnam for Johnson and Watergate for Nixon, the reality was quite different in the area of private life. Both LBJ and Nixon benefited from the liberal expansion of the Rooseveltian rule under Kennedy; while suffering the bark and bite of the newly developed "watchdog" journalism—engendered in good part because of press opposition to the Vietnam War (and the governmental lying attending the war)—these presidents still enjoyed the full private-life protections more typical of journalism's "lapdog" era.

Naturally enough, it was Johnson, the vulgar Texan, far more than the uptight Nixon, who pushed the rule to its limits. Johnson's lack of couth was legendary and for the most part went unreported. When presented with a prize bull by Tennessee's governor one day, Johnson punched a male reporter in the ribs and in earshot of the entire press corps, including women, he is said to have asked, "Hey, how'd you like to be hung like that?" Even in more formal settings, Johnson could exhibit foul-mouthed coarseness that made Nixon sound like a piker when he cursed in the taped privacy of the Oval Office. When asked a tough question by a persistent reporter during an impromptu press conference in Texas, an irritated Johnson replied, "What are you trying to do, fuck me?"[49] The physically unappealing Johnson was almost certainly less successful with women than Kennedy, but it was not for want of trying—and again, the press knew about some of his attempts. A White House secretary and friend of Douglas Kiker (then of the *Atlanta Constitution*) told him how Johnson "used to chase her around and around his desk. She would have to crawl through it just to get away from him." Jerry ter-Horst, in his book on *Air Force One*, told an eye-opening tale about Vice President LBJ's pursuit of Nancy Dickerson (then Nancy Hanschman) of NBC News.[50] Conducted over a radio telephone line accessible to eavesdropping by any radio operator sweeping the airwaves, Johnson, flying over the Atlantic toward Europe, pleaded with Dickerson, then in Vienna, to meet him for dinner in Paris. As terHorst phrased it, Johnson's interest in Dickerson "was something other than fatherly," and his attempts to corral Dickerson and many other women were no secret in the White House press corps.

Of greater fascination for an observer in the 1990s is the press's lack of concern about Johnson's occasional drinking bouts. Long before he became president, LBJ was known as a hard drinker. Robert Novak recalls a National Press Club party when Johnson, then Senate majority leader, was "drunk as a skunk. He was just raving. A friend and I shepherded him into the elevator and then his limousine. The next day at his regular morning press conference, Johnson said, 'Oh, Novak—had a little too much to drink last night, did you?' " Everybody in the know laughed, and no one reported a word. Far more serious were LBJ's drinking episodes during his Cold War presidency. CBS News's George Herman remembers one incident—ironically, during the 1964 presidential campaign when Johnson's Republican opponent, Arizona U.S. Senator Barry Goldwater, was portrayed as too unstable for the presidency:

We had arrived in Evansville, Indiana to pick up Lady Bird and there was no scheduled appearance. And Lyndon came reeling out of the plane and climbed up on a truck bed and made a speech anyway. Unfortunately, since it wasn't on the schedule, none of us had taken our cameras or our tape recorders off the plane. And as Lyndon made a rambling, incoherent speech I said to one of the Secret Service, "Is that man drunk?" and the Secret Service guard said, "If aged scotch will make you drunk, he's drunk." Well, we all realized he was drunk and it's not so hilarious. Remember, the theme of that campaign against Goldwater was, in Lyndon's inestimable words, "Whose finger do you want to mash that button?" And here was the man whose finger *was* on the button as drunk as can be in a campaign that was centered around responsibility. But none of us reported it. . . .

   I got back to Washington and called my bosses in New York, and I said, "I want some guidance: what do I do under our First Amendment responsibilities when the president of the United States is drunk in public? Even though I have no filmed proof, I know as well as I know any story that I've ever used on the air that he was drunk." They said, "Oh Christ, let's think about it and we'll call you back," and that was twenty-five years ago and they haven't called me back yet.

   Not all of the press's omissions in coverage during the 1960s are disturbing. Some in fact are praiseworthy, especially compared to current practice, which may go to the other extreme of complete disclosure even if meaning is distorted and legitimate privacy compromised. George Herman again provides an excellent example in the aftermath of the arrest of Walter Jenkins, Johnson's White House chief of staff, who was caught engaging in homosexual activity in a Washington YMCA in October 1964. Shortly afterward, Johnson was on a campaign swing in California when, in response to a local reporter's question, the president said, "A lot of presidents have had similar troubles. I remember President Eisenhower had it with one of his appointments secretaries." Johnson was incorrect, however, and had misremembered an incident involving an Eisenhower campaign aide before the general was even nominated for president. This presented a dilemma for the press, as Herman saw it:

Neither of President Eisenhower's two appointments secretaries were guilty, and if we were to report Johnson's remarks accurately, we would in effect damage innocent people. So we all tried to think what to do about it and without really consulting, we all did the same thing: we diluted it. We all said, "Johnson said Eisenhower had the same problem with one of his aides." I remember one of the young reporters looking at me in astonishment and complaining, "But you lied, you deliberately misquoted the President of the United States." And I came back quick as a whip and said, "Oh, shut up."

Would that Herman could similarly admonish today's press corps, where such a presidential gaffe would be repeated endlessly—and hang the consequences for the innocent!

It will surprise many—probably none less than the press-loathing Richard Nixon[51]—to learn that Nixon also benefited from the news media's reluctance to discuss private matters. In both the 1960 and 1968 campaigns, journalists refrained from making public some information about the Republican presidential candidate's consultations with a New York psychotherapist in the 1950s and possibly later.[52] (Columnist Drew Pearson disclosed the matter in a 1968 National Press Club speech only *after* the November election.) Even during the height of the Watergate scandals, when damaging revelations about Nixon tumbled forth with great regularity and eager acceptance, the press considered certain matters to be off limits. Several high-ranking White House correspondents received anonymous but seemingly authoritative telephone calls claiming the beleaguered president was having a homosexual affair with his close friend Charles ("Bebe") Rebozo. (The calls were made during Nixon's weekend visits with Rebozo on Key Biscayne, Florida.) The charge appeared ridiculous on its face—and no evidence whatsoever has been unearthed to support it in the years since—yet many ludicrous allegations were thoroughly investigated and sometimes printed or aired in the highly charged atmosphere of Watergate. But this particular indictment was simply too personal for the times. Said one newsman on the receiving end of the calls: "I didn't think it was my role to look into it. If he was having an affair with Rebozo, fine. Maybe he needed it; he was under a lot of strain."

Nixon was one of the last presidential politicians not to be challenged on a major private matter, and in his case it may partly have been a reluctance to pile on since he was already sinking under the weight of Watergate. By the 1970s the standards were changing rapidly, and the Rooseveltian rule was being sharply revised. Some of the causes, such as relaxation of libel laws, predated Watergate (as the next chapter will discuss). But the seminal event, the apocalypse that spawned both a major feeding frenzy and the "character issue," was Ted Kennedy's accident at Chappaquiddick.

For years Senator Edward Kennedy, like his brother Jack, had enjoyed an adoring press. During his first campaign for the Senate in 1962, the *Boston Globe* broke the bombshell story of Ted's undergraduate expulsion from Harvard for cheating under the subdued and kindly headline TED KENNEDY TELLS ABOUT HARVARD EXAMINATION INCIDENT with the text presented as Kennedy's admirable, straightforward attempt "to set the record straight."[53] After JFK's assassination the press, perhaps partly out of grief and partly in hopes of one day recapturing the glory of Camelot, was even more protective of Ted and hid the truth of the excessive drinking, compulsive womanizing, and erratic behavior so obvious to newspeople who covered him.[54] Then came Chappaquiddick, and the press never looked the other way again. Kennedy had been too flagrant, his actions too costly for one young woman, and his excuses too flimsy and insulting to the many perceptive minds in the press corps.[55] Good reporters were ashamed of, and the press as a whole was severely criticized for, the process of concealing Kennedy's manifest vices that had preceded the senator's own cover-up of the facts surrounding the accident.

With Chappaquiddick, many journalists began to believe that private life and individual character traits had such profound effects on politics and public policy that politicians' personal lives could no longer be ignored. This attitude was reinforced and extended by two other political upheavals that occurred in rapid succession: the dumping of Senator Thomas Eagleton from the 1972 Democratic ticket on account of his previously hidden psychiatric problems, and the Watergate revelations—not just about corruption but about Nixon's personality, tendencies, and frame of mind. From this "unholy trinity" of Chappaquiddick, Eagleton, and Watergate was created a new godhead to replace the Rooseveltian one. The new rule of political coverage was as open as its predecessor had been closed: Since any aspect of private life is potentially relevant to an official's public performance, the reasoning went, everything is fair game— personal relationships, private behavior, and any matter exhibiting an official's "character" or "judgment." Furthermore, literally anything that affects the political players and outcome—including unproved rumor and innuendo—can be made public in the process.

This new "anything goes" rule has evolved along with the "junkyard dog" journalism it encourages. The new rule has also been gradually broadened over the two decades of its development, as new circumstances and fresh frenzies have pushed the frontiers of acceptable scrutiny ever forward. For instance, Nixon's possible psychotherapy was not an issue in 1968, but after the 1972 Eagleton frenzy, a mere hint—false as it turned out—that a stressed Gerald Ford had also been a patient of Nixon's presumed psychiatrist became one of the major issues investigated in his Senate confirmation as vice president in 1973.[56] And after Chappaquiddick, Congressman Wilbur Mills (D., Ark.) helped to make alcohol abuse and sexual misconduct a permanent part of the reportable political landscape. The downfall of the powerful chairman of the House Ways and Means Committee was long in the making, since many journalists were well aware of his drinking problem. The *Wall Street Journal's* Albert Hunt even spent "seven or eight" nights hovering outside Mills's northern Virginia apartment in 1974 "to see if he'd stumble or to observe any bizarre happenings." (Press stakeouts did not begin with Gary Hart.) Mills himself eventually provided the smoking gun (or firecracker) on October 7, 1974, when he was stopped for speeding and driving with his headlights off. His passenger, Washington stripper Fanne Foxe (known as the Argentine Firecracker), seized the moment to dash out of the car and into the Potomac River's Tidal Basin in what appeared to be a suicide attempt. While no arrests were made, the sensational story soon found its way into print, augmented by Mills's intoxicated December appearance onstage with Ms. Foxe at a strip joint. Stripped of his own committee chairmanship as a result, and in and out of alcohol treatment centers, Mills quietly retired from the House in 1976. He was joined, not so quietly, by sixty-five-year-old Congressman Wayne Hays (D., Ohio), who had put his thirty-three-year-old mistress, Elizabeth Ray, on his congressional office payroll as a secretary despite the fact that by her own admission she could not type. Upset about Hays's impending marriage, Ray went to the *Washington Post* in May 1976. Following the exposé Hays first attempted suicide, then resigned from the House. A third congressional sexual adventure in 1976 also ensured that the bedroom habits of candidates would continue in future years as a topic of the country's living-room conversations. During the initial Senate campaign by Congressman Donald Riegle (D., Mich.) in 1976, the *Detroit News* published a transcript of explicit, erotic telephone calls Riegle had made in 1969 to a volunteer in his House office who was one of his mistresses at the time.[57] Incredibly, the calls were taped by the woman with Riegle's permission, but Riegle won despite the scandal and his own stupidity.

Just as sex and alcohol (and later drugs) were firmly established as legitimate subjects for journalistic inquiry, other aspects of the campaign and the candidate have come to be dissected with a heretofore-unknown precision. For instance, every phrase, quip, and gaffe has become grist for the character mill. George Romney's "brainwashing" claim, Spiro Agnew's "fat Jap" remark, Jimmy Carter's "lust in the heart" admission, and Jesse Jackson's "Hymietown" slur were presented as mirrors into their souls, the contents of their characters. Edmund Muskie's alleged "cry" in the New Hampshire snow and Gary Hart's change of name, age, and signature led to press psychoanalysis of their supposedly derivative personalities and personal inadequacies. Ground once off limits has been converted into territory worth fighting for. Jerry terHorst characterizes the press corps of the 1950s and 1960s this way: "We stayed a hundred yards away from anything that had a sexual overtone." By contrast, an ambitious reporter today would do almost anything to get to a political sex scandal first. The standards of financial propriety for legislators have become much stricter; yesterday's accepted norm for private enrichment is today's career-threatening conflict of interest, as Jim Wright discovered in 1989. Forty years ago the campaign associates and government staffers surrounding public officials had little to fear unless their hands were in the till; one of JFK's major aides had a child out of wedlock, and this fact, well-known among the White House press, was of course never reported. In today's environment the private lives of these aides, even those not on the public payroll, are sometimes as closely scrutinized as those of the elected representatives they serve. "Anything goes" coverage extends to the state and local levels as well, with similar effects.[58]

There is even evidence of the spread of the feeding frenzy mentality to other countries. Great Britain has long been a trailblazer, with its unrivaled love of sordid sex scandals involving public officials, combined with salacious tabloids that exploit every prurient opportunity.[59] But extensive reports on the real and rumored private lives of leading politicians have recently taken center stage in countries as diverse as Australia, Argentina, Greece,[60] and Japan. In Japan, for example, a classic feeding frenzy comparable to the Gary Hart/Donna Rice affair brought down a new prime minister. Sosuke Uno was forced to resign after only a month in office in July 1989, following unprecedented press disclosures about his extramarital relationships with geisha girls and bar hostesses. For centuries, Japanese politicians had taken such mistresses, but journalistic comment on private lives had been considered taboo. A similar revelation brought down a key minister in the government of Uno's successor, Prime Minister Toshiki Kaifu, who was himself rocked by the publication of a completely erroneous report claiming he had fathered an illegitimate child. The rising tide of international press interest in such matters is also reflected in the intensity with which foreign journalists cover the frenzies attending American politics. Several reporters interviewed for this book told of being inundated with telephone calls from colleagues around the world as word spread they were working on various angles of 1988 campaign frenzies. "The American feeding frenzy is now a global feeding frenzy," said one.

This chapter has traced the path of American journalism from its partisan origins to the current day, with particular emphasis on the evolution from "lapdog" to "watchdog" to "junkyard dog" in the years since Franklin Roosevelt's presidency. As it has happened, the abandonment of "lapdog" journalism and the press's desire to check the policy excesses of government is praiseworthy. So, too, is the press's newfound determination to reveal the personal excesses of those running the government when the vices affect their public performance. But along the way, legitimate "watchdog" journalism has spun out of control and has developed the nasty demeanor and side effects of the "junkyard dog" variety. In the next two chapters, we will examine more thoroughly the reasons for this unfortunate turn in the press's evolution, and discuss in detail the development of the modern feeding frenzy. Before proceeding to these tasks, a few of the most vital current conditions affecting U.S. print and broadcast media will be briefly reviewed.

A Note on the Contemporary Media Scene

Paradoxically and simultaneously, the news media have expanded in some ways and contracted in others, dramatically changing the ways in which they cover politics. The growth of the political press corps is obvious to anyone familiar with government or campaigns. Just since 1983, for example, the number of print (newspaper and magazine) reporters accredited at the U.S. Capitol has jumped from 2,300 to more than 4,100; the gain for broadcast (television and radio) journalists was equally impressive and proportionately larger, from about 1,000 in 1983 to more than 2,400 by 1990.[61] On the campaign trail a similar phenomenon has been occurring. In the early primaries in the 1960s, a presidential candidate would attract a press entourage of at most a couple of dozen, while in the 1980s a hundred or more print and broadcast journalists could be seen tagging along with a frontrunner. A politician's every public utterance is thus made and intensively scrutinized in a media pressure-cooker.

At the same time, more journalists are not necessarily attracting a larger audience, at least on the print side. Daily newspaper circulation has been stagnant for twenty years, at 62 to 63 million papers per day, and on a per-household basis, circulation has actually fallen 44 percent.[62] Barely half of the adult population reads a newspaper every day; among young people aged eighteen to twenty-nine, only a third are daily readers—a decline of 50 percent in two decades. Along with the relative decline of readership has come a drop in the overall level of competition. In 1880 61 percent of U.S. cities had at least two competing dailies, but by 1990 a mere 2 percent of cities did. Not surprisingly, the number of dailies has declined significantly, from a peak of 2,600 in 1909 to 1,622 today.[63] And most of the remaining dailies are owned by large media conglomerates called "chains"; whereas in 1940 83 percent of all daily newspapers were independently owned, by 1990 just 24 percent remained out of the clutches of a chain (such as Gannett, Hearst, Knight-Ridder, or Newhouse).

Partly, of course, newspapers have been losing their audience to television. At the dawn of the 1960s a substantial majority of Americans reported that they got most of their news from newspapers, but by the latter half of the 1980s television was the people's choice by almost two to one.[64] Moreover, by a 55 to 21 percent margin, Americans now say they are inclined to believe television over newspapers when conflicting reports about the same story arise.[65] Of course, most individuals still rely on *both* print and broadcast sources,[66] but there can be little question that television news is increasingly important, that despite its many drawbacks (simplicity, brevity, entertainment orientation, and so on) it is "news that matters."[67] While not eclipsing newspapers, television frequently overshadows them, even as it often takes its agenda and lead stories from the headlines produced by print reporters (especially those working for the "print elite," such as the *New York Times*, the *Washington Post*, the *Wall Street Journal*, AP, UPI, *Time*, *Newsweek*, and *U.S. News & World Report*).

The television news industry differs from its print cousin in a variety of ways. For one, the number of outlets has been increasing, not declining as with newspapers. The three networks now receive broadcast competition from CNN, Headline News, C-Span, and PBS's "MacNeil/Lehrer NewsHour." While the audiences of all the alternate shows are relatively small compared to the networks, they are growing while the networks' market shares contract. The potential for cable expansion is still large, too; less than half of all American households are currently wired for cable. In addition, the national TV news corps is often outnumbered on the campaign trail by local television reporters. Satellite technology has offered any of the thirteen hundred local stations willing to invest in the hardware an opportunity to beam back reports from the field. Local TV news is watched by more people than is network news—67 percent of adults compared to 49 percent for the networks on a daily basis[68]—so increased local attention to politics has some real significance.

The decline of the networks' market shares and the local stations' decreasing reliance on the networks for news—coupled with stringent belt-tightening ordered by the networks' corporate managers—resulted in severe news staff cutbacks at NBC, CBS, and ABC during the 1980s.[69] These "economy measures" had an obvious impact on the morale of television journalists. CBS News correspondent Wyatt Andrews describes the effect in his organization:

CBS was almost like a Japanese company: it was presumed that when you joined CBS, that it was something of a fraternity that you were initiated into, as opposed to a company you were hired for—that this wasn't a job, this was a high moral calling. A lot of that has been lost, and now virtually every employee sees CBS as [just another] business, so if you see something better, you're going to jump for it. The highly cultivated cult or pact of corporate loyalty at CBS was broken in the round of firings that occurred in the middle 1980s, and the currency of being loyal to CBS has been greatly devalued.

More important, the cutbacks have affected the quality of broadcast journalism. Many senior correspondents bemoan the loss of many desk assistants and junior reporters who did much of the legwork necessary to get less superficial, more in-depth pieces on the air. "Even critical interviews sometimes just don't get done," one network newsman noted. As a consequence, campaign stories requiring extensive research are often discarded in favor of the simplistic, eye-catching, sexy items that frequently form the core of a feeding frenzy incident.

3

The Boys in the Bush

The Attack Mentality Within the News Media

As you look into press coverage of various things, you discover there's no rational explanation to it. There just isn't.

journalist PAUL DUKE

Anyone who has ever worked in the news media, or studied the subject dispassionately, knows full well that the conspiracy theorists are wrong. "The media" constitute no monolith, and news organizations are too disorganized and too competitive for much plotting to occur, much less succeed. Feeding frenzies are certainly not the result of intentionally coordinated action, and the chaos surrounding press coverage of most of them surely proves it. Rather, frenzies are a product of other conditions and forces both internal and external to the media, some that have fermented for many years, some of relatively recent vintage. Paul Duke is unquestionably correct in his assessment of the often nonsensical basis of much press coverage, yet academics by nature are inclined to search out the method in the madness. Such an attempt will be made in this chapter, where the frenzy's causes within the structure and development of journalism will be discerned, and in the next chapter as well, when factors outside the guild's immediate circle (but still in its orbit) will be examined.

Growing Intensity and Declining Civility in Coverage

Conditions are always ripe for the spawning of a frenzy in the brave new world of omnipresent journalism. Advances in media technology have revolutionized campaign coverage. Handheld miniature cameras (minicams) and satellite broadcasting have enabled television to go live anywhere, anytime with ease. Instantaneous transmission (by broadcast and fax) to all corners of the country has dramatically increased the velocity of campaign developments today, accelerating events to their conclusion at breakneck speed. Gary Hart, for example, went from front-runner to ex-candidate in less than a week in May 1987. Continuous public-affairs programming, such as C-SPAN and CNN, helps put more of a politician's utterances on the record, as Senator Joseph Biden discovered to his chagrin when C-SPAN unobtrusively taped Biden's exaggeration of his résumé at a New Hampshire kaffeeklatsch in 1987. (This became a contributing piece of the frenzy that brought Biden down.) C-SPAN, CNN, and satellite broadcasting capability also contribute to the phenomenon called "the news cycle without end," which creates a voracious news appetite demanding to be fed constantly, increasing the pressure to include marginal bits of information and gossip and producing novel if distorting "angles" on the same news to differentiate one report from another. The extraordinary number of local stations covering national politics today—up to several hundred at major political events—creates an echo chamber producing seemingly endless repetitions of essentially the same news stories. This local contingent also swells the corps traveling the campaign trail. In 1988 an estimated two thousand journalists of all stripes flooded the Iowa caucuses, for instance.[1] Reporters not infrequently outnumber participants at meetings and whistlestops.[2]

In such situations any development is almost inevitably magnified and overscrutinized; the crush of cameras, microphones, and people combined with the pressure of instant deadlines and live broadcasts hype events and make it difficult to keep them in perspective. When a frenzy begins to gather, the intensity grows exponentially. Major newspapers assign teams of crack reporters and researchers to the frenzy's victim. When Democratic vice presidential candidate Geraldine Ferraro was the focus of investigation in August 1984, for example, the *Philadelphia Inquirer* assigned a dozen employees to the story full-time, and the *Washington Post* and the *New York Times* five each. Television news time is virtually turned over to the subject of the frenzy. Republican vice presidential nominee Dan Quayle was the subject of ninety-three network evening news stories over the twelve days of his frenzy in August 1988— more coverage than twelve of the thirteen presidential candidates had received during all the primaries combined.[3] Much like the vice presidential candidates who had preceded him as frenzy victims (Eagleton and Ferraro), Quayle alone garnered three-quarters of all the evening network time devoted to the presidential campaign during his August dog-days tribulations. By comparison the Reagan-Gorbachev summit meeting in December 1987 registered considerably less network news interest.[4]

Oddly enough, just as the coverage of major political events is expanding with the increased number of media outlets on the campaign trail, the quality is simultaneously declining. Superficial "horserace" reporting—a focus on who's ahead, who's behind, and who's gaining—is now the norm. Of seven thousand print news stories surveyed between Labor Day and Election Day 1988, 57 percent were horserace items and only 10 percent concentrated on real policy issues.[5] On television network news shows during the 1988 primary campaign, two and a half times more horserace pieces aired than did policy-issue ones.[6] Reporters love the horserace and not policy for many different reasons. Most journalists are generalists, unfamiliar with the nuances and complexities of many issues and therefore unprepared to produce stories on them. Then, too, the horserace fits many reporters' rather cynical view of politics: Elections are but a game, not a contest of the power of competing ideas. And a focus on the horserace is partisanly unbiased, far more "objective" and disinterested than is the construction of an issue agenda for coverage. The length of modern campaigns also plays a part; reporters may be trying to stave off boredom. Tom Rosenstiel of the *Los Angeles Times* compares American elections not to a horserace but a football game where "we play about forty-seven quarters before any of the fans have come into the stadium. The players are on the field and the press is in the press box, and we have played for months before anybody cares or watches." The boredom is such that the press from time to time stops analyzing the game and concentrates attention on individual players—the source of more than one feeding frenzy over the years. Moreover, this gamesmanship coverage of politics aids in developing frenzies by discouraging sober discussion of policy choices while fostering personal conflict, controversy, and confrontation.

The emphasis on the sensational and the dramatic has always been the stuff of news, of course. Tammany Hall boss George Washington Plunkitt complained in 1905 that the New York newspapers favored the rival reformers because they provided more conflict to fill the headlines:

The newspapers like the reform administration. Why? Because these administrations, with their daily rows, furnish as racy news as prizefights or divorce cases. Tammany don't care to get in the papers. It goes right along attendin' to business quietly and only wants to be let alone. That's one reason why the papers are against us.[7]

But by comparison to Plunkitt's day, most modern print and broadcast journalists have insisted on upholding certain standards of proof and probity in their work. Unfortunately, those standards are eroding, as the more frequent use of gossip and rumor suggests. (Chapter 5 will address this problem.) Howell Raines of the *New York Times* regrets both "the decline in the standards of broadcast journalism" and "the shrinking number of quality newspapers that approach journalism as an intellectual activity of high seriousness." The concentration on the trivial and the titillating pervades not just the tabloid newspapers of publishers such as Rupert Murdoch and the "trash TV" talk shows of Geraldo Rivera and Phil Donahue. The cheapening of public discourse extends to respected newspapers and public affairs television programming. Gossipy pieces in newspaper "life-style" sections (and occasionally in the news pages, too) include rumors and innuendos once considered wholly unacceptable. On television, viewers have witnessed a decline in civility and a new acceptability of rudeness that is disturbing to many news veterans. Says the *Times*'s Raines: "My worry is when the public sees Sam Donaldson [of ABC News] shouting at a barricade, or when they see John McLaughlin [host of the 'McLaughlin Group'] sneering at some politician, they think that is the model of deportment for journalists." Such deportment surely raises the temperature of politics, and feeding frenzies thrive in the resulting hothouse.

Competitive Pressures

The first lady of Ohio had a succinct explanation for the Cleveland *Plain Dealer*'s front-page focus on her husband, Governor Richard Celeste, and his alleged extramarital affairs. "They're not in the business to promote Dick Celeste. They're in the business to sell papers. And this sells papers."[8] Scandal and sex do indeed sell well—a great deal better than dispassionate discussion of policy issues. Some of "Nightline"'s highest ratings ever were achieved for shows featuring scandal-ridden Christian broadcasters Jim and Tammy Faye Bakker. ABC News's Peter Jennings admitted that he and his cohorts "deliberately exploited them for the sheer prurient entertainment value." The same could be said of the media's handling of Donna Rice in Gary Hart's travails, Billy Carter during Billygate, or Barney Frank and his male prostitute. The *Miami Herald*'s Tom Fielder con-

ceded that the Hart/Rice story had embedded in it "a salaciousness
that attracted the tabloid press . . . and accounted for a great deal of
the feeding frenzy in that incident." The more tantalizing the offense, or the more it breaks new ground (as did the discussion of
mental illness in the Eagleton affair[9]), or the more volatile the mix of
vices (as in John Tower's combination of sex, alcohol, and political
intrigue), the more irresistible the subject is for the news media.[10]

While it has ever been so, today there are added inducements for
scandal coverage. First and foremost, contemporary corporate managers of broadcast and print media are closely attuned to the contribution each outlet makes to the overall profit or loss of the company.
Ratings and circulation increasingly matter, and executives are not
unaware of the experiences of newspapers such as the *Washington
Times*, where screaming front-page headlines about Barney Frank
and an unrelated homosexual "call boy" scandal boosted newsstand
sales by 25 percent in the summer of 1989. Nor are individual reporters oblivious to the reward system in the age of "star journalism."
Fame and fortune are the gold waiting at scandal's end for some in
journalism today, as columnist Robert Novak explains: "There are
very high rewards in both money and in fame, much more than
when I started. A lot of very bright young men and women want the
rewards, and they know damn well that carefully covering Fairfax
County [Virginia] is not going to do it for them."

The competitive philosophy governing this new generation of go-
getters can be summed up by their fevered adherence to journalism's
two ultimate imperatives: "Don't get beaten to a story by another
media outlet," and, "If we don't break this, someone else will."
Both axioms, and especially the second one, serve to encourage bad
judgment and premature decisions to publish or air stories. As the
Washington Post's managing editor Len Downie concedes, "A lot of
half-baked things get into newspapers including ours because people
begin writing too much before they have enough facts." Some of the
worst situations occur when competing media outlets become duel-
ing entrepreneurs, as the *Post* and the *Washington Star* did over
"Billygate" in 1980. With one newspaper and then the other raising
the stakes of coverage, the miniscandal was blown out of all fair proportion, and many of the reporters and editors involved admitted it
afterward.[11] Competitive pressures also encourage the conversion of
balanced reporting into sensationalized headlines. For example, the
Wall Street Journal broke the story of Pat Robertson's "miracle
baby"—born ten weeks after his marriage—but did so deep in a long
profile of Robertson, keeping that one fact in the perspective of the
preacher's admitted youthful roguishness, his later born-again con-

version, and his long, happy marriage.[12] The follow-up by other papers was all too typical of the second-wave one-upmanship that
helps to create frenzies. The *Washington Post*, for instance, found
room on its front page for the headline, PAINFULLY, ROBERTSON COR-
RECTS RECORD, which reported the shocking news that Robertson had
earlier fibbed about his wedding date to save his family embarrassment.[13]

Competitive pressures also propel each newspaper and network
to try to make a contribution, no matter how small and insignificant,
to the unfolding frenzy. Each new fact merits a new story, complete
with a recapitulation of the entire saga. This press pile-on by means
of minor, "wiggle" disclosures is an ordeal akin to water torture
(drip, drip, drip, day after day after day) and well known to many
frenzy victims. Every newly uncovered, unattributed quotation borrowed by a Biden speechwriter became a news item. "Every day
there is another story about another building," sighed an exasperated Geraldine Ferraro in her time of trial over family finances in
1984.[14] Wiggle disclosures extend and intensify a feeding frenzy,
while stretching the available news thin and reiterating it excessively.

Good judgment can be impaired and high standards lowered in
the heat of competitive battle. The *Washington Post* at first wisely ignored the grandstanding headlines of its minor rival, the *Washington
Times*, in the summer of 1989 when the *Times* claimed to have uncovered a massive homosexual "call boy" scandal entangling "key officials" of the Reagan and Bush administrations. But after much
goading from the *Times* (which sent newsboys to hawk their "exclusive" editions in front of the *Post*'s building) as well as internal criticism from the *Post* ombudsman, *Post* editors gave in to baser instincts
and devoted considerable resources to the sleazy enterprise. In the
end, the group of "key officials" caught in the web consisted merely
of the two very minor presidential appointees mentioned in the first
Times article.[15] This unfortunate episode in the annals of competition
pales beside others, however, where ethical judgment has occasionally been suspended entirely. In July 1972 columnist Jack Anderson
aired on his radio show a reprehensible story about Democratic vice
presidential nominee Thomas Eagleton's nonexistent drunk-driving
arrests. Anderson later ascribed his decision to broadcast the damaging information without securing proof to "the press of competition
. . . I knew there were a dozen reporters going after this [and] I used
it . . . to cover myself."[16] Another, more recent example comes from
San Antonio, Texas, where *Express-News* columnist Paul Thompson
broke a front-page story about Mayor Henry Cisneros's extramarital
affair in October 1988. Cisneros had told Thompson of the romance

on condition of confidentiality, but Thompson unilaterally violated the ground rule because he feared his rival newspaper was about to publish the story. "I wasn't going to be shut out on some ethical punctilio," noted Thompson.[17]

These travesties are exceptional. What is becoming more common, and more disturbing, is the domino effect of a kind of "lowest-common-denominator" journalism: If one newspaper prints or one broadcaster airs a story, however questionable or poorly documented it may be, other media outlets will then publish or broadcast the news without independently verifying it. This abdication of journalistic responsibility encourages the purveyors of campaign smut to search out the weak media link. Many newsmen cited experiences similar to those of ABC News's Hal Bruno, who received a series of telephone calls in the summer of 1987 about a major presidential campaign rumor:

I got calls from people saying, "The *New York Times* is gonna break the story on the weekend." And every week it would be a different news organization you were told had pictures and was gonna break the story. At one time a person called me and said he understood that ABC is gonna break this story. And I said to this person, "You're talking to ABC," and the person said, "Oh, I meant NBC," and hung up.

"All you need anymore is to get to the right reporter and the right paper, which is to say the wrong reporter and the wrong paper, to get a rumor published," notes the *Washington Post*'s Benjamin Weiser. Some journalists, such as the *New York Times*'s Michael Oreskes, bemoan the loss of vigilant gatekeeping by many in the media:

When we refuse to publish it, someone else publishes it. Then the fact that they published it becomes a story, so it still gets into our paper even though we originally decided it wasn't worth publishing. So you really lose control over your role as the gatekeeper. . . . On account of this some people begin to weaken their standards and say, "Well, it's going to get published anyway, so I'll go ahead and publish it first."

In good part then, a feeding frenzy is a manifestation of an adrenaline-charged news competition, with the initial contest won by the outlet breaking the story, the middle-round honors captured by the worst dramatic and sensational revelations, and the endgame trophy captured by the organization that checkmates the candidate and thereby takes him or her out of the race.

Pack Journalism

Oddly enough, the intense competitive pressures we have just discussed cause reporters (and editors and producers) to move forward together in essentially the same story direction, rather than on different story tracks. It is called "pack journalism," a condition former U.S. Senator Eugene McCarthy (D., Minn.) once likened to blackbirds on a telephone wire: When one moves to another wire, they all move. Timothy Crouse, in his delightful book *The Boys on the Bus*, described pack journalism by comparing the press to "a pack of hounds sicked on a fox."[18] A third animal metaphor, fish schooling, may be even more telling. Fish in schools keep close tabs on each other and copy every school movement reflexively. The reason for the behavior is obvious: Any fish out of school loses the safety of numbers and is vulnerable prey.[19]

For partly the same reason, the free market of journalism often leads to sameness instead of diversity. "Journalists want to do something their peers think is meaningful," notes Jim Gannon, formerly of the *Des Moines Register*. "Peer pressure matters in this big fraternity, and so you tend to turn to the sexy topic of the hour." "CBS Evening News" anchor Dan Rather puts it in practical terms for a newsman competing for an audience:

With journalists, as with almost everybody else, fear is the great motivator. Now, if you don't run the big scandal story of the day, Mabel is going to lean over the back of the fence and say to Ann, "what do you think about X's mistress?" and Ann's going to say "What are you talking about?"

"Where have you been, Ann, on planet Pluto?"

"Well, no, I just watched Dan Rather and he didn't say anything about it."

"Well, I watched Jimmy Jones and they did a lead piece and a follow-up piece on it."

That's the fear. That's what drives this. Once the herd moves, it's really hard to turn it and you find yourself just galloping along.

Most frequently, a major newspaper breaks the initial "big scandal story," and points the herd in a certain direction. But equally often today, a widely watched television broadcast—the evening news or a Sunday commentary show—will be the first indication of the conventional wisdom that will develop in reaction to the print story. David

Brinkley's Sunday morning panel on ABC ("This Week with David Brinkley") did the honors for Gary Hart after the *Miami Herald*'s same-day publication of the Donna Rice affair, with Sam Donaldson, among others, suggesting the effective end of Hart's candidacy was nigh.

It is remarkable to observe just how quickly even the heavy-weights fall into line with the pack when a frenzy begins. In retro-spect, when one weighs the real importance of Gerald Ford's "free Poland" remark in his October 1976 debate with Jimmy Carter com-pared to the other vital subjects covered that night, the *Washington Post*'s decision not to mention the "gaffe" until the thirty-third para-graph of its story was commendable and balanced. It was also clearly an independent one, since virtually every other major paper had placed the so-called slip of the tongue front and center. Yet within twenty-four hours the *Post* had capitulated and headlined the com-ment as well. Occasionally a reporter bucks the tide, as did the *Post*'s Michael Barone in writing an insightful and remarkably fair analysis of Dan Quayle's modestly successful Senate record in the midst of the pack's portrayal of Quayle as a hopelessly inadequate cipher.[20] Barone's temperance, however, seemed to have little effect on most of his peers, then or later.

Some have seen changes in Crouse's "bus" pack that offer hope for reduced groupthink.[21] For example, networks and newspapers for the most part no longer assign correspondents to travel for the duration of a campaign with a single candidate, potentially lessening the cocoonlike effect of a static entourage. Yet there is little evidence that pack journalism has abated, and in some ways it may be strengthening its grip on the press corps, especially television reporters. ABC's Ted Koppel remembers that nonconformist journalism was easier when production expectations were lower for a TV newsman:

When I was a foreign correspondent twenty years ago, I worked just for the evening news. Now a foreign correspondent for ABC has got to worry about the demands of "World News Tonight," "Good Morning America," "Nightline," "Prime Time Live," "David Brinkley," and "20/20." What does that mean? More and more pressure to get the pieces on the air quickly. Less and less time to go out and do the actual reporting. So you end up going with the flow. It takes much more time to dig into a story on your own than it does simply to match what you know your competition is doing.

Whether on the rise or not, the unfortunate effects of pack journal-ism are apparent to both news reporters and news consumers: conformity, homogeneity, and formulaic reporting. Innovation is discouraged, and the checks and balances supposedly provided by competition evaporate. Press energies are devoted to finding mere variations on a theme (new angles and wiggle disclosures), while a mob psychology catches hold that allows little mercy for the frenzy victim. CNN's Frank Sesno captures the pack mood perfectly:

I've been in that group psychology; I know what it's like. You think you're on to something, you've got somebody on the run. How dare they not come clean? How dare they not tell the full story? What are they trying to hide? Why are they hiding it? And you become a crusader for the truth. Goddammit, you're going to get the truth!

Watergate's Watermark on the Media

Sesno's crusader spirit can be traced directly to the lingering effects of the Watergate scandal, which had the most profound impact of any modern event on the manner and substance of the press's conduct. In many respects Watergate began the press's open season on politicians in a chain reaction that today allows for scrutiny of even the most private sanctums of public officials' lives. Moreover, coupled with Vietnam and the civil rights movement, Watergate shifted the orientation of journalism away from mere description—providing an accurate account of happenings—and toward prescription—helping to set the campaign's (and society's) agendas by focusing attention on the candidates' shortcomings as well as certain social problems.

A new breed and a new generation of reporters were attracted to journalism, and particularly its investigative arm. As a group they were idealistic, though aggressively mistrustful of all authority, and they shared a contempt for "politics as usual." Critics called them do-gooders and purists who wanted the world to stand at moral attention for them. Twenty years later the Vietnam and Watergate generation dominates journalism: They and their younger cohorts hold sway over most newsrooms, with two-thirds of all reporters now under the age of thirty-six and an ever-increasing share of editors and executives drawn from the Watergate-era class.[22]

Of course, many of those who found journalism newly attractive in the wake of Watergate were not completely altruistic. The ambitious saw the happy fate of the *Washington Post's* young Watergate sleuths Bob Woodward and Carl Bernstein, who gained fame and fortune, not to mention big-screen portrayals by Robert Redford and Dustin Hoffman in the movie *All the President's Men*. As *U.S. News & World Report's* Steven Roberts sees it:

A lot of reporters run around this town dreaming of the day that Dustin Hoffman and Robert Redford are going to play them in the movies. That movie had more effect on the self-image of young journalists than anything else. Christ! Robert Redford playing a journalist? It lends an air of glamour and excitement that acts as a magnet drawing young reporters to investigative reporting.

The young were attracted not just to journalism but to a particular *kind* of journalism. The role models were not respected, established reporters but two unknowns who refused to play by the rules their seniors had accepted. "Youngsters learned that deductive techniques, all guesswork, and lots of unattributed information [were] the royal road to fame, even if it wasn't being terribly responsible," says Robert Novak. After all, adds columnist Mark Shields, "Robert Redford didn't play Walter Lippmann and Dustin Hoffman didn't play Joseph Kraft." (Kraft, like Lippmann, had a long and distinguished career in journalism.)

In the post-Watergate press there is also a volatile mix of guilt and fear at work. The guilt stems from regret that experienced Washington reporters failed to detect the telltale signs of the Watergate scandal early on; that even after the story broke, most journalists underplayed the unfolding disaster until forced to take it more seriously by two wet-behind-the-ears *Post* cubs; that over the years journalism's leading lights had gotten too close to the politicians they were supposed to check and thus for too long failed to tell the public about JFK's and LBJ's dangerous excesses, the government's lies about Vietnam, and the corruption in the Nixon administration and in Congress. The press's ongoing fear is deep seated and complements the guilt. Every journalist is apprehensive about missing the next "big one," of being left on the platform when the next scandal train leaves Union Station. The guilt and the fear are reinforced every time an Iran-Contra episode occurs. Left-wing critics had already fired at the press for being too kind to, and cozy with, the Reaganites—and then, sure enough, a *Lebanese*, not an American, publication (Beirut's *al Shiraa*) broke the biggest scandal of the Reagan administration.

The guilt and fear combined to produce revisionism about old scandals and overreaction to new ones. In the 1970s and 1980s (long after it was most needed), John Kennedy and Lyndon Johnson received harsh criticism for their private offenses, and the assessments of Edward Kennedy's Chappaquiddick actions have grown increasingly scathing with each passing anniversary of the accident.[23] By contrast, the only revisionism necessary for most modern scandals is a downward scaling. The everlasting press search for another Watergate has produced one oversize "-gate" after another (Billygate, Debategate, and so on). Ironically, the Watergate analogy can actually help the targeted politician, as Ronald Reagan happily discovered during "Irangate." Despite his mismanagement and ignorance aplenty, in the end Reagan was judged "innocent by reason of analogy" because the investigations turned up no smoking-gun equivalent of the Watergate tapes directly implicating the president.[24]

Reagan's case was exceptional, and it was not for want of the press's trying that he escaped permanent damage. Ever since Watergate, most investigative journalists' goal has been not just sensational revelation but the downfall of their target, a trophy head for their wall that is the (im)moral equivalent of Richard Nixon. "We look for and hope for a really bad character to pursue because it can do wonders for our careers," observes ABC's Brit Hume. The sizable financial and personnel investments many major news organizations have made in investigative units almost guarantee that greater attention will be given to scandals and that probably more of them—pseudo and real—will be uncovered. The healthy adversarial relationship that naturally exists between the press and politicians has been sharpened to a razor's edge in the process. Many in the press are not merely skeptical of the pols, they are contemptuous of and corrosively cynical about them, and some reverse the usual presumption of innocence into "guilty unless proven otherwise." Partly this is an understandable reaction to their own earlier naïveté and betrayal. Robert Novak recalls, "When the Agnew story broke, the mood was, 'Come on, you've got to be kidding.' There was a disbelief among journalists that there was anything to it. But when you had a vice president accepting bags of money in the Executive Office Building, and Watergate—something out of a cheap Washington novel—on top of it, then anything seems possible." Yet the resulting cynicism, especially among their young colleagues, worries thoughtful veterans. "At times we're too adversarial," says Los Angeles Times Washington bureau chief Jack Nelson. "You shouldn't just assume politicians are lying." NBC News commentator John Chancellor somewhat wistfully recounts the days when he could "win an argument by citing U.S. government statistics" because they were considered the unquestionable "final word." Then came Vietnam, Watergate, and "hero worship for Woodward and Bernstein. Skepticism turned to cynicism, and in the White House press corps old-fashioned comity dissolved into a pack of attack dogs," notes Chancellor, regretfully. The Watergate-fed dogs are now used to red meat, and the pack is deeply addicted to the "-gate" scenario.[25]

The Character Issue Takes Hold

A clear consequence of Watergate and other recent historical events was the increasing emphasis placed by the press on the character of candidates. As journalists reviewed the three tragic but exceptionally capable figures who had held the presidency since 1960, they saw that the failures of Kennedy, Johnson, and Nixon were not those of intellect but of ethos. Chappaquiddick, Spiro Agnew, and the Eagleton affair reinforced that view. The party affiliations and ideology of these disappointing leaders varied, but in common they possessed defects of personality, constitution, and disposition. In the world of journalism (or academe), as few as two data points can constitute a trend; these six together constituted an irrefutable mother lode of proof. "We in the press learned from experience that character flaws could have very large costs," says David Broder, "and we couldn't afford to ignore them if we were going to meet our responsibility."

The issue of character has always been present in American politics—not for his policy positions was George Washington made our first president—but rarely if ever has character made such a mark for so many consecutive elections as it did from 1976 onward. The 1976 Carter campaign was characterized by much moral posturing; Edward Kennedy's 1980 candidacy was in part destroyed by lingering character questions; Walter Mondale finally overcame Gary Hart's 1984 challenge in the Democratic preliminaries by using character as a battering ram; and 1988 witnessed an explosion of character concerns so forceful that several candidates were eliminated and others badly scarred by it. The character issue now dominates many state and local elections and a sprinkling of Supreme Court nominations, cabinet appointments, and Speakership selections for good measure. Psychoanalysis of public figures has become so common that, in advising today's students interested in political journalism, one is tempted to recommend both *The Almanac of American Politics* and *The Collected Works of Sigmund Freud*.

The character issue may in part have been an outgrowth of the "new journalism" popularized by author Tom Wolfe in the 1970s.[26] Contending that conventional journalism was sterile and stripped of color, Wolfe and others argued for a reporting style that expanded the definition of news and, novel-like, highlighted all the personal details of the newsmaker. Then, too, reporters had witnessed the success of such books as Theodore H. White's series *The Making of the President* and Joe McGinniss's *The Selling of the President 1968*, which offered revealing behind-the-scenes vignettes of candidates with their hair down.[27] Why not give readers and viewers this information before the election, the press reasoned? And there was encouragement from academic quarters as well. "Look to character first" when evaluating and choosing among presidential candidates, wrote Duke University political science professor James David Barber in an acclaimed and widely circulated 1972 volume, *The Presidential Character.*[28]

Whatever the precise historical origins of the character trend in reporting, it is undergirded by certain assumptions—some valid and others dubious. First, the press correctly perceives that it has mainly replaced the political parties as the "screening committee" that winnows the field of candidates and filters out the weaker or more unlucky contenders. (This fact is yet another reason to support the strengthening of the political parties and the restoration of true "peer review" of candidates by their real professional colleagues.[29]) Second, many journalists, again correctly, recognize their mistakes under the old Rooseveltian rule and see the need to tell people about candidate foibles that affect public performance. *Time* magazine's Ted Gup frames this point by contrasting the press's crimes of commission with those of omission:

If a guy has got a psychological problem, if he can't keep his zipper up, if he can't keep away from a bottle or whatever, we are not serving the public by concealing that fact from them. The press gets a lot of heat for the crime of commission, what it writes about. But we're equally guilty of crimes of omission, because if we have an obligation to write about something and we don't, that's just as egregious as if we write about something that we're not supposed to.

The press's third realistic presupposition is that it is giving the public what it wants and expects, more or less. The social factors that have led Americans to prefer more information about the private lives of public officials will be discussed in the next chapter. For now, though, television itself is a sufficient answer, having served as handmaiden and perhaps mother to the age of personality politics. Television has not only personalized campaigns but has also conditioned its audience to thinking about the private "lives of the rich and famous." The rules of television prominence now apply to all celebrities equally, whether they reside in Hollywood or Washington.

Less convincing, however, are a number of other assumptions made by the press about elections and the character issue. Some journalists insist that they have an obligation to reveal everything of significance discovered about a candidate's private habits; to do otherwise, they say, is antidemocratic and elitist.[30] Such arguments ignore the press's unavoidable professional obligation to exercise reasonable judgment about what is fit to print and air as well as what is most important for a busy and inattentive public to absorb. Other reporters claim that character matters so much because policy issues matter so little. The issues change frequently, they say, and the pollsters and consultants determine the candidate's policy stands anyway. Brooks Jackson, now of CNN, voices typical sentiments:

The candidate stands for whatever his pollster tells him the public wants to hear at the moment. The question is not what his party stands for because party is irrelevant. We have candidates who have the ability to market themselves as anything they want. They're chameleons. And so the central issue in a campaign must be the character of the person running for office.

Bob Schieffer of CBS News adds, "We wind up with candidates who say about the same thing . . . but because it's a contest, people try to find a difference. The difference is character." Granted, journalists covering media-manipulating candidates who mouth tape-recorded, sound-bite answers to all questions can be forgiven a measure of cynicism. Nonetheless, even in contests between relative moderates, such as the 1976 presidential matchup, substantial policy differences exist—and the distinctions become a chasm in ideologically polarized years such as 1972, 1980, 1984, and 1988. The illusion of issueless races cannot justify an overemphasis on character.

Perhaps most troubling is the nearly universally accepted belief that private conduct is a road map to public action. Unquestionably, private behavior can have public consequences, as chapter 2's review of recent history suggested. However, it is a far-from-settled matter whether private vice inevitably leads to corrupt, immoral leadership or whether private virtue produces public good. An argument can be made that many lives run on two separate tracks (one public, one private) that ought to be judged independently. (This debate will be renewed in the concluding chapter.) Too often, the press defines character just as Gary Hart once complained: "in a totally negative sense as everything a candidate lacks or every mistake a candidate has made.''[31] A focus on character becomes not an attempt to construct the mosaic of attributes and features that make up an individual but a strained effort to find a sometimes real, sometimes manufactured ''pattern'' of errors or shortcomings that will automatically disqualify a candidate. It is a rare life that does not contain enough embarrassing incidents to give critics the opportunity to shred it. Similarly, there is not a human being who has not repeatedly exercised ''bad judgment''—the standard flaw used to raise the character issue.

On the other hand, some public figures have made it impossible, and unwise, for the press to ignore the evidence of character defects. Before and after Chappaquiddick, Senator Edward Kennedy has rarely been accused of exercising much discretion in his personal affairs. *Washington Monthly* editor Charles Peters believes the press was compelled to examine this presidential aspirant's vices: ''When you mix the womanizing with the excessive drinking and speeding, you get a combination of dangerous recklessness, a self-destructive pattern that very definitely needed to be reported.'' Despite his many protestations to the contrary, Senator Gary Hart can reasonably be classed with Ted Kennedy or brother John. Hart's bravado in asking the press to follow him around while he ran unacceptable risks with his reputation and future was reminiscent of President Kennedy's derring-do. Ken Bode, formerly of NBC News and one of the most experienced political correspondents in the nation, capsules the JFK-Hart comparison this way:

People who supported Hart said to me, ''Well, what about John Kennedy?'' And my answer . . . was that John Kennedy was also too reckless to have been president. . . . In fact, those people who say Kennedy proves one point, I think, got it backwards. Kennedy proves the point that adultery is something that must be looked into if it happens in the case of a presidential candidate.

The Hart character frenzy was nevertheless worrying to many journalists. Lines had been crossed, and methods used, that gave pause. Steven Roberts of *U.S. News & World Report* ''object[s]'' in many ways'' to the Hart story:

I just don't like the idea of reporters sitting in the bushes watching someone's bedroom, which is basically what the *Miami Herald* reporters did. But in hindsight I think it was very important that the material came out. I didn't like the means, but I liked the end, because the end clearly told us something critically important about Hart's ability to be president. It told us something profoundly important about his sense of judgment, something directly relevant to his capacity to be president. So in the end, the process worked, but I was always very uncomfortable with the way it worked.

Roberts's doubts were widely shared, but so was his conclusion. Bad means had yielded a good end; that is, Hart's demise as a serious presidential contender. In the process, however, those bad means may have been sanctified and, without doubt, the character issue had become even more firmly rooted in journalistic practice. The press would continue to play "character cop," its thin blue line society's first cordon of defense against vice-ridden candidates.

More Women in the Press Corps

Instrumental in the emergence of the character issue were women journalists, who have broken the "good ol' boy" mentality—and morality—prevalent in the press corps for decades.[32] Right on target in her analysis is Cokie Roberts of National Public Radio and ABC News:

Until a lot of women came into the press corps, the unwritten rule was that the guys worked together during the day and caroused together at night, and nobody reported on anybody. And on the bus, they pretended there were no marriages. We women all started arriving on the bus and we sort of pruded it up. There we were, friends of their wives, not that any of us were gonna run home and tell tales—but they couldn't be sure of it.

Fred Barnes of *The New Republic* confirms Roberts's observation from a somewhat different, male perspective: "You have all these women around now, and they're mostly humorless. It isn't as much fun and you don't have the same kind of camaraderie."

The numbers alone tell a good part of the story. In 1971 the newsroom work force was just 22 percent female; by 1989, women had a contingent comprising 35 percent of the total. Moreover, about half of all newly hired print and television reporters today are women, and current journalism school enrollments are 60 percent female.[33] Women journalists do not yet have anything approaching equal visibility, especially on network television, where progress has lagged well behind that of newspapers. But great strides have been made since 1972, when CBS's Bob Schieffer recalls only two women traveling regularly with the McGovern campaign. "Today half the seats in most campaign planes are usually filled by women," claims Schieffer. (Others agreed with the thrust of Schieffer's comment but placed the proportion at 30 to 40 percent.)

As the boys on the bus—or plane—have gone coed, and as the press fraternity has made room for a sorority, the journalistic consensus about character has been profoundly influenced by feminism. In 1979, when *Washington Monthly*'s Charles Peters published a watershed article on Ted Kennedy's personal problems,[34] he was much criticized for broaching the subject. The author of the piece, Suzannah Lessard, had difficulty getting on-the-record comments from committed feminists who were nonetheless deeply disturbed by Kennedy's behavior and found it abhorrent and disrespectful to women. The reluctant interviewees feared being seen as untrendy and unworldly. As Lessard later noted, those concerns had dissolved in time for Gary Hart to reap the whirlwind in 1987.[35] John Tower suffered a similar fate in 1989; "How could a womanizer be a real role model for women in the military?" asked former *Wall Street Journal* reporter Ellen Hume. The feminist perspective had triumphed: A man who cheated on his wife was now seen as possibly also given to deception, untrustworthiness, power lust, and recklessness in state as well as personal matters.[36] This new-wave thinking has "raised collective consciousness in the press corps," according to Schieffer. The most significant effect has been to reinforce the character issue and prepare the way for more feeding frenzies based on private vices.

Loosening of the Libel Law[37]

In the old days, a reporter would think twice about filing a story critical of a politician's character, and his editors probably would have killed it had he been foolish enough to do so. The reason is clear: fear of a libel suit. Veteran journalist Jerry terHorst recalls the first question his supervisors asked about even an ambiguous, suggestive phrase about a congressman: "If we're sued, can you prove beyond a doubt what you just wrote?" The chilling effect of libel laws tilted the press-politician relationship firmly in the direction of the pols, reinforcing the Rooseveltian rule that governed coverage of elected officials.

Such inhibitions were ostensibly lifted in 1964, when the Supreme Court ruled in *New York Times Co.* v. *Sullivan*[38] that simply publishing a defamatory falsehood was not enough to incur a libel judgment. Henceforth a public official would have to prove "actual malice," a requirement extended three years later to all public figures, such as Hollywood stars and prominent athletes.[39] The Supreme Court declared that the First Amendment requires elected officials and candidates to prove that the publisher either believed the challenged statement was false or at least entertained serious doubts about its truth and acted recklessly in publishing it in the face of those doubts.[40] The "actual malice" rule has made it very difficult for a politician to prevail in a libel case. The most comprehensive empirical study on the subject suggests that the *Sullivan* standard has reduced public plaintiffs' success rate in libel cases by as much as 60 percent,[41] with only about one in ten "public person" libel plaintiffs winning against the press.[42]

Nonetheless, the threat of libel litigation has not dissipated, and some deterrent effect on the press is still visible. At least two reasons account for this persistent libel chill. First, the *Sullivan* protections do little to reduce the expense of defending defamation claims.[43] The monetary costs have grown enormously,[44] as have the required commitments of reporters' and editors' time and psychic energy.[45] Small news organizations without the financial resources of a national network or the *New York Times* are sometimes reluctant to publish material that might invite a lawsuit because the litigation costs could threaten their existence.[46]

The second reason for the continuing libel threat is what defamation expert Rodney Smolla calls "the general thinning of the American skin,"[47] a cultural phenomenon of heightened sensitivity to the harm that words can do to an individual's emotional tranquillity. As a result, politicians are often more inclined to sue their press adversaries, even when success is unlikely. For example, despite the stringent *Sullivan* standards, elected officials and candidates brought 20 percent of all the defamation suits between 1974 and 1984.[48]

But high costs and the American propensity to sue cut both ways. The overall number of libel suits filed in recent years has dropped because plaintiffs also incur hefty legal bills, and—perhaps more important—they have despaired of winning.[49] Some news outlets have added another disincentive by filing countersuits charging their antagonists with bringing frivolous or nuisance actions against them.

In practice, then, the loosening of libel law has provided journalists with a safer harbor from liability in their reporting on elected officials and candidates. Whether it has truly diminished the chill of press self-censorship, especially for less financially endowed media outlets, is a more difficult question. However, at least for the wealthy newspapers and networks, the libel laws are no longer as severe a restraint on "character" or private-life reporting about public officials, and this once-formidable barrier to certain types of feeding frenzies has been lowered considerably.

The Search to Validate the Subtext

With the threat of a libel judgment greatly diminished, reporters are relatively free to make known their frank evaluations of a candidate's basic character. Frequently, a near consensus (accurate or not) forms around a politician's personality and faults, and each pol is typecast with shorthand labeling of various sorts. This set of preconceived images and stereotypes becomes the candidate's subtext—that is, the between-the-lines character sketch that guides and sets the tone for press coverage. Journalists are always on the lookout for circumstances that fit the common perceptions and preconceptions about a candidate, especially his or her shortcomings. A major incident that validates the subtext (and therefore the press's own judgment) has a good chance of being magnified and becoming a feeding frenzy. The subtext is the "fertile ground in which a story is planted," observes "Nightline" 's Ted Koppel, "and when it rains, the story grows explosively like Jack's beanstalk." In other words, a campaign development that corroborates the news media's conventional wisdom about a candidate resonates and intensifies because it rings true to the scribes and broadcasters. When a politician seems to confirm his or her own subtext, a collective gleeful shout from the press of "I knew it, I told you so" becomes a reinforcing part of many feeding frenzies. Table 3.1 reviews the subtexts that have helped to define selected presidential frenzies. Pack journalism and the development of the character issue are much in evidence throughout the table's listing. Some of the subtexts are accurate, if incomplete, readings of the candidates, others are off base, all are simplistic and usually unidimensional judgments on complex people.

It is important to understand just how pervasive the subtext interpretations frequently are. In several dozen discussions of Joseph Biden with this volume's interviewees, for example, not one journalist departed from the conventional wisdom. "We all thought he was a blowhard, didn't have much to say, wasn't very deep," said ABC's Brit Hume. E. J. Dionne, formerly of the *New York Times* (which played a key role in Biden's demise), characterized the widespread impression of Biden as that of "mostly talk." Columnist Jack Germond's epitaph of a reminiscence sums up the sentiment: "All he was known as was a guy who gave a good speech. As it turned

TABLE 3.1

PRESS SUBTEXT OF SELECTED PRESIDENTIAL FEEDING FRENZIES

FRENZY	SUBTEXT PREDATING FRENZY
George Romney's "brainwashing" (1968)	Reporters did not have a high regard for Romney's intelligence and acuity and considered him an inept lightweight.
Spiro Agnew's "fat Jap" flap (1968)	Agnew was viewed by many newsmen as insensitive and out of his depth.
Edward Kennedy's Chappaquiddick (1969)	Journalists knew of Kennedy's womanizing, drunkenness, tendency to speed, and general recklessness.
Edmund Muskie's New Hampshire "cry" (1972)	Muskie was seen as moody, temperamental, and given to emotional outbursts.
Jimmy Carter's "lust in his heart" *Playboy* interview (1976)	Some newspeople detected in Carter a false piety and sanctimony; others feared the religious zealotry of Carter's Southern Baptist religion; still others sensed a "weirdness" about Carter that worried them.
Gerald Ford's "free Poland" gaffe (1976)	Ford was seen as clumsy, ill-equipped mentally for the presidency and not up to the job, an amiable dunce given to malapropisms.
Jimmy Carter's "killer rabbit" (1979)	Carter's presidency had soured, and the press perceived him as managerially incompetent and politically impotent.
Billygate (1980)	Much like the "killer rabbit" incident, Billygate confirmed the impression of an out-of-control presidency with a chief executive so weak he could not even rein in his own brother.
Gary Hart's name, age, signature changes (1984)	Journalists believed Hart to be aloof, arrogant, rootless, strange, and a loner who refused to play by the rules.
Jesse Jackson's "Hymietown" remark (1984)	Jackson's (and many blacks') tensions with the Jewish community were well known; Jackson's embrace of the Palestine Liberation Organization and previous anti-Jewish statements were also remembered.
Geraldine Ferraro's family finances (1984)	Ferraro's Italian heritage may have sparked tacit suspicions; this was combined with a previous lack of scrutiny and an initial press so positive that some in the news media were concerned about bias and imbalance.

TABLE 3.1 *(Cont.)*

FRENZY	SUBTEXT PREDATING FRENZY
Gary Hart and Donna Rice (1987)	Hart's past factual and rumored womanizing, as well as the recklessness perceived in his character, served as backdrop.
Joseph Biden's plagiarism (1987)	The adjectives reporters privately (and sometimes publicly) used to describe Biden were *consultant programmed, glib,* and *shallow.*
Pat Robertson's résumé enhancement and shotgun marriage (1987)	Robertson's televangelism in an era of religious scams raised the press's antennae to search for signs of phoniness and misrepresentation.
Michael Dukakis's mental health (1988)	The press had typecast Dukakis as a cold technocrat, who had difficulty showing emotion, and this rumor seemed to confirm the stereotype in part.
Dan Quayle's past (1988)	Many in the news media knew little of Quayle, but first impressions suggested a "pretty boy" lightweight who was out of his league, a rich kid who had led a life of cushioned privilege.
George Bush's "mistress" (1988)	Rumors of Bush's supposed liaisons had circulated widely among the press for almost a decade.

NOTE: Subtext descriptions, and many of the specific adjectives used here, are drawn from newspaper and broadcast stories printed or aired *before* the onset of the corresponding frenzies. Journalists' recollections during the interviews conducted for this volume also served as source material.

out, they were good speeches other people had already given." The prefrenzy coverage reflected precisely these evaluations. Noting "Biden's verbal excesses" and "the perception that he is a gabby lightweight," *Time* quoted a prescient Iowa activist months before Biden's troubles began, saying, "He just might talk himself out of the nomination."[50] Even earlier, *Business Week* had headlined its feature article, "Is Joe Biden More Than 'Just a Speech'?"[51] *The Economist* declared at the outset that Biden's overriding task was to show that he was "not just a pretty face and articulate voice."[52]

This uniform perspective on Biden has undeniable elements of truth in it. Yet a fair evaluation of Biden's long legislative career shows it to be more substantive and accomplished than his typecasting would suggest.[53] What mattered in the frenzy that engulfed

Biden, however, was not a balanced view of his record but the nearly universally embraced substance of his subtext.

Biden is not the only candidate to have been victimized by an unleavened subtext. There are substantial elements of unfairness in the cases of George Romney, Geraldine Ferraro, and Dan Quayle, among others. Certainly, no year featured more misleading subtexts than did 1976. President Gerald Ford had long been haunted by his predecessor Lyndon Johnson's slashing remark that Ford "couldn't walk and chew gum at the same time," and he had been ridiculed by comics for his unfortunate habit of bumping into things, tripping, and falling on the ski slopes. Yet not only did Ford, a Yale Law School graduate, possess an able mind, he was (with the possible exception of Theodore Roosevelt) the most fit, athletic president of the twentieth century. Ironically, Ford's opponent in 1976 was doomed to a series of even more unjust subtexts during both his candidacy and his subsequent unhappy presidency. As a Southerner and a Baptist, Jimmy Carter suffered from a double prejudice in his presidential contest. Even before the "lust in the heart" *Playboy* interview that was granted to counteract fears about his religious beliefs, Carter had undergone a firestorm in the Democratic primary season about "ethnic purity." Carter had used the unfortunately worded term to describe his support for preservation of ethnic urban neighborhoods. It was interpreted by the press as a racist remark confirming their innate suspicions about any successful Southern politician. *Time*'s Walter Shapiro, an aide during the Carter administration, noted the "bizarre journalistic notion" that "these two words negated" Carter's impressive civil rights record in Georgia and his strong support among black leaders. Says Shapiro:

The press seized on that phrase because it fed the Northern "anti-Southern-Baptist" prejudice—if you get them alone late at night, the white sheets come on. The subtext was "he's a Baptist racist and this is George Wallace all over again; He's just trying to camouflage it."

There are many reasons why in hindsight Jimmy Carter was ill suited to be president of the United States. But no one in his right mind could say a lack of sympathy to civil rights was one of them. Yet three weeks when the country should have been getting to know the real Jimmy Carter were spent chasing down a totally irrelevant side issue.

Later, during his presidency, Jimmy Carter also demonstrated that even a grossly insignificant incident could become a debilitating frenzy, given the right press subtext and spin. In the summer of 1979 when Brooks Jackson, then an AP reporter, first sent out the story of the swamp rabbit's "attack" on President Carter's Plains rowboat, he missed its significance. It was only when editors across the country began to beseech the AP to permit early publication of the item that Jackson realized how the story fitted into the journalistic subtext about Carter.[54] The "killer rabbit" became a press parable of Carter's political impotence, a perfect metaphor for a president at the mercy of plagues big and small. That even a "banzai bunny," as Jackson called it, would be free to trouble this weakened leader exposed Carter to an avalanche of ridicule at a make-or-break point in his presidency. Jackson himself called "irresponsible" some of the exaggerated play given his footnote of a story, but the subtext—and the intensity of the personal dislike many in the working press felt for Carter—made the result almost inevitable.

Other cases provide more justifiable examples of the news media's seizing on one specific incident or phrase to trumpet their subtext. In the era before frank "character" profiles were common, many in the press simply waited for a suitable pretext to tell their audience what they had long known. In 1972, for instance, key journalists were well aware of Democratic presidential nominee Edmund Muskie's terrible temper and emotional outbursts.[55] Jack Germond remembers a number of occasions when a challenged Muskie privately began screaming obscenities, banging on the table, or erupting into furious anger. "Once when he was at our home my wife heard his yelling through several floors of the town house." The day Muskie choked up in the snow of New Hampshire, Germond caught the first plane from Washington to the Granite State "because I knew Muskie was through"; Germond understood reporters would focus on the incident in order to show the dark side of Muskie's personality. Similarly, in 1984 a number of journalists had been privately disturbed by what they had seen and heard of Jesse Jackson's attitudes toward Jews. Jackson had had a long history of making anti-Jewish statements.[56] So when Jackson's use of the slur "Hymietown" (a reference to New York City) crept into print—buried deep in a *Washington Post* story about Jackson–Jewish relations—the press jumped at the opportunity to vent legitimate concerns about Jackson's prejudice.

Sometimes the press is unable to publish or air much about the subtext because it is based on unproved rumor. Gossip about George Bush's "mistress" and Thomas Foley's "homosexuality" had circulated for years, oil in the media barrel, ready for the match to be applied as it eventually was in both cases. Occasionally, too, one feeding frenzy can create the subtext for a successor. The *Washington Post*'s Bob Woodward saw Debategate as "the preface to the Iran-contra scandal," since it demonstrated that some on the Reagan staff had "the level of knowledge and willingness to [engage in] subterfuge." In another sense, however, Iran-Contra reversed the previously prevailing subtext of the Reagan presidency: that Reagan, the ultimate delegator, had been a superb manager.[57] The media's wish to atone for their earlier misjudgment, and the anger they felt at having to do so, perhaps led to a special ferocity in the Iran-Contra coverage.

Finally, Gary Hart's evolving and expanding subtext over two presidential campaigns neatly encapsules many of the principles suggested here about subtexts. In 1984 Hart emerged so quickly from the Democratic pack that most reporters had not focused their energies on him, but many veterans remembered Hart in his role as George McGovern's 1972 campaign manager, and others had had contact with Hart on Capitol Hill during his years in the Senate. Bob Shogan of the *Los Angeles Times,* one of the most senior and respected reporters in the political corps, spoke for many if not a large majority of his peers in stating the common view of Hart as "one strange and quirky person." Fred Barnes of *The New Republic* gives a blunt evaluation: "Hart is a weird man, a very distant figure and the strangest guy I ever talked to." Adds the *Washington Post*'s George Lardner, who first discovered Hart's misrepresentation of his age, "There was always something strange and inexplicable about him, like he was trying to carve out a new identity and transform himself into somebody else." Individually, Hart's shortening of his name (from Hartpence) earlier in life, his changes in signature, his claim to be a year younger than he actually was, and his seemingly studied imitation of JFK's body language were not all that bothersome.[58] After all, millions of Americans have altered their names, tens of millions lie about their age, and every third politician tries to emulate John Kennedy. But as a package, and in combination with Hart's aloof manner, lack of close friends in the Senate, drifting marriage (at times), and estrangement from his strict upbringing and the fundamentalist religion of his early life, they constituted a convincing pattern to the press. "They seemed to symbolize to some reporters something that was inherently nongenuine in Gary Hart, and they were trying to figure out what it was. He seemed to be unable to come to terms with who he was and who he had been, and that seemed to bother a lot of reporters," says Hart's 1984 press secretary, Kathy Bushkin. Not just the changes but Hart's enigmatic lack of convincing explanation for some of them was puzzling to the press. *Washington Post* columnist

Richard Cohen remembers a conversation about the age question with Hart during the 1984 primaries:

I said to Gary, "I've got to ask you this one more time, why did you change your age?" And he said, "Well, lots of people sort of forget their age." And it's true, it happens to everyone. But you never forget your date of birth. And he had put down a different date of birth on records. So I said, "It doesn't add up, Gary." He said, "Well, why do you think I did it, to get out of the Army, the draft?" "No, that doesn't make sense." And we went through all the possibilities, and none of it made any sense. If he had done it for a reason, even if it was immoral or unethical or criminal, at least you'd understand the reason. I still don't know why he did it. And when you're talking about the guy who's sitting next to the [nuclear] button . . .

The other main feature of Hart's subtext right from the start of his first presidential effort was his image as a womanizer. Hart's own actions had fueled it, of course. In the 1972 McGovern campaign some reporters covering the campaign closely had been surprised to learn Hart was a married man, and he was quoted in the *Washington Post* then as saying, "Let's just say I believe in reform marriage."[59] Both Hart and his wife Lee had also dated openly during two separations in the late 1970s and early 1980s. Further, reporters who had known Hart well were all too familiar with his extracurricular activities. NBC's Ken Bode, who had both a friendship and a professional relationship with Hart dating back to 1969, claims he personally knows of "eleven women" Hart has dated at various times. Howard Fineman of *Newsweek* was in close touch during 1970 to 1972 with a college friend who was a ranking McGovern aide, and his chum described in some detail Hart's "kind of pathological sleeping around." A distressed woman correspondent for a prominent newspaper chain confided to a few of her colleagues that she had been propositioned by Hart in the spring of 1984 while interviewing him in his U.S. Senate office. Despite these assorted rumors and hints in published articles, the womanizing subtext never became a frenzy in 1984. No current incident that could have been used to highlight this aspect of Hart's character ever became public, and the campaign simply refused to talk about the subject. Recalls Bushkin: "When people asked me a general, vague question like, 'Gee, we hear there are rumors,' I'd say, 'Fine, if you can come back with something specific, then maybe there's something to talk about. If you don't have a specific allegation, don't raise it.' And that's about as far as it ever got in eighty-four."

All that smoke had convinced many in the media that Hart had started forest fires and never been caught. They were determined not to let him continue to break the post-Rooseveltian rules. The press was primed for 1988, particularly since Hart was the clear Democratic front-runner. This time around "Hart could get away with less than anyone else because he was perceived as getting away with more," Robert Novak surmises. "I love danger," Hart had once told journalists after shooting the rapids in 1984,[60] and everyone was on the watch now to see how risky Hart would be, whether he would try to evade the ordinary rules that applied to everyone else. At the *Washington Post*, according to political reporter Edward Walsh, "a conscious decision was made early on that we would basically declare a statute of limitations on whatever Hart may have done in the past, but if the behavior continued in the eighty-eight campaign cycle, if more rumors and allegations surfaced, then we would pursue them." *Newsweek*'s Fineman, in a piece published just before Hart's 1987 declaration of candidacy, quoted John McEvoy, a key Hart aide in 1984, warning that Hart would "always [be] in jeopardy of having the sex issue raised if he can't keep his pants on."[61] The day after Hart's April 13 announcement, the main story filed was about the womanizing issue. *Time*'s Larry Barrett asked Hart about the "rumors" allegedly being circulated by other campaigns concerning his private life, and Hart briefly suggested rumormongering would accomplish no good for any campaign guilty of it. This inconsequential exchange containing no hard news sent "virtually every single reporter on the campaign plane" diving for his computer keyboard, according to Hart's then press secretary Kevin Sweeney. By now the womanizing subtext was overpowering. Less than a month later, Donna Rice and the *Miami Herald* provided the subtext its full-blown outlet. Gary Hart's character quilt now had its centerpiece.

Interestingly, the centerpiece had very nearly been provided in 1984. In late spring of that year, NBC News producer Glen Rochkind noticed Gary Hart's Secret Service motorcade on Capitol Hill during an afternoon. A little after 6:30 P.M., having returned to his Washington Circle home, and while walking his dog, he came upon the very same motorcade in his residential area, with agents waiting inside the idling cars. It was clear to Rochkind that the cars had been there for some time "because there's no way they would have found three spaces together in this congested area where parking is at a premium, unless they put them there before 6:30 P.M., when parking is illegal." Becoming curious, Rochkind "walked the dog ninety-seven times around the block" (taking about twenty-five minutes) until he saw the agents jump out of their cars as Hart emerged, alone, from the front door of an apartment. "The cars were gone in seconds, and I quickly walked down to the apartment. Looking out the window, wearing a bathrobe, was an attractive woman." Rochkind generally recognized her because of the car she drove (a burnt orange Datsun 240-Z), since they (like all neighbors in the area) had jousted for the few available parking spaces. He got the car's license number and the next day gave it to his superior at NBC, producer John Holland, who within a short time was able to get the owner's name. Rochkind and others at NBC seriously discussed organizing a stakeout based on two premises, one substantive ("If an NBC producer could stumble on this, imagine what the KGB or a blackmailer could do, given Hart's recklessness") and one practical ("Even if we don't use it now, one day someone's going to go with this story, and we'd have our own pictures"). But NBC News executives vetoed the idea, apparently in the main because the contest was essentially over and Hart was not going to win the nomination. The fortuitous timing of the discovery had saved Hart from a likely 1984 disaster. There is little question the stakeout would have borne fruit. The woman Rochkind accidentally found with Hart was the same woman the *Washington Post* would link to Hart three years later, when the *Post* accelerated Hart's decision to withdraw from the presidential race by presenting "documented evidence of a recent liaison between Hart and a Washington woman with whom he has had a long-term relationship."[62]

Timing and Special Circumstances

As the Hart example demonstrates, timing matters in both sex and politics. It also matters in press coverage. Feeding frenzies are more likely to develop in slow news periods such as the doldrums of summer, for example. The absence of much hard news in those weeks allows relatively insignificant events such as Billygate, the "killer rabbit," and Debategate to be blown well out of proportion. Candidates should simply beware the Ides of August, says Steve Roberts: "If you are going to fuck up, don't fuck up in the middle of August when there is nothing else to write about."

Other time pressures affect the likelihood and coverage of frenzies. Because of the sheer concentration of media focusing on politics in election seasons, transgressions that might be unseen or ignored at other times are closely examined then. So many potential stories flow past the desks of editors in peak seasons that the element of fortune becomes part of the mix. As Roberts notes,

How much attention a story gets, where it gets played, what kind of attention it gets, is always a comparative judgment. The *New York Times* is going to have eight stories on its front page every day. Some days fifteen stories are going to be worth the front page. Some days three are going to be worth the front page. But there is always going to be eight and there is always going to be twenty-two minutes on the nightly news, whether they have ten minutes or forty-five minutes of good stuff. Luck and accident determine what the competition is for public attention on any given day.

A candidate's good or bad luck in timing is thus reflected in the press coverage. Republican vice presidential candidate Spiro Agnew had the misfortune to utter his "fat Jap" comment in 1968 just before a three-day campaign tour of the Hawaiian Islands, whose population includes many people of Japanese descent. As a consequence, the remark took on added significance for the press. By contrast, Gary Hart's dark 1987 cloud had at least one silver lining for him, owing to his timing. He dropped out just before the *Post* would certainly have published the full story of his affair with the Washington woman, according to *Post* reporters Ann Devroy and David Hoffman.[63] By the time Hart chose to reenter the race (in December 1987), he was no longer taken seriously. "His candidacy was a joke," says Hoffman, with Devroy adding, "At that point, [publishing the Hart affair] would have been like doing a sex-life story on Al Haig after New Hampshire." (Former Secretary of State Haig was a minor candidate for the Republican presidential nomination in 1988 and dropped out of the contest shortly before the New Hampshire primary.)

The fact that front-runners get rougher treatment and closer scrutiny than back-of-the-pack contenders is but one of the many special press circumstances that govern feeding frenzies. Other factors include the following examples:

- Nonpolarized races bereft of big events (war, major recession, and the like) tend to breed frenzies. The 1976 and 1988 presidential elections fall into this category. So do party nomination races in many years, when large fields of lookalike, soundalike Democrats or Republicans compete to be their party's standard bearer.
- Candidates who may reap a windfall of favorable news coverage one day will probably have to pay the press piper the next. Geraldine Ferraro well understands this "zero-sum" principle of journalism. Having benefited from enormously positive, even euphoric media attention as the first woman nominated by a major

party for national office, Ferraro came in for especially intense examination shortly thereafter by a press trying to restore balance to its coverage.[64]

- The context of an incident or offense—including its age and extenuating circumstances—greatly affects a frenzy's development. For example, a "statute of limitations" is in effect at some media outlets for examination of private, illicit relationships. As earlier mentioned, Gary Hart benefited (however briefly) from such an amnesty at the *Post* in 1987. Marijuana use provides another illustration of the importance of context. The youthful indiscretions of 1988 Democratic presidential candidates Albert Gore and Bruce Babbitt had little political impact on their campaigns, but Douglas Ginsburg lost his chance at a Supreme Court seat because he had smoked pot as a law professor in his thirties, and in the presence of students. Ginsburg's drug use was also given heightened relevance because of the vigorous antidrug policies of his sponsor, President Reagan.

- Certain frenzies gain greater relevance because they complement current fad or fashion in press coverage. Dan Quayle's membership in the National Guard became "one of those stories that reverberate because they tell other stories. . . . The United States had just gone through a period of rediscovering Vietnam again," notes E. J. Dionne. Moreover, Vietnam service and drug use are two story categories of ear-pricking interest for the baby-boom journalists now dominating American newsrooms.

- While the press sometimes triggers a frenzy by initiating its own investigation (as with the *Miami Herald* stakeout), it is frequently reactive in nature. Congressional action or partisan politics can jumpstart a reluctant press. For instance, the media viewed the case of Debategate as "politics as usual," and resisted taking it seriously until pressed by former Carter aides (such as press secretary Jody Powell) and a Michigan Democratic congressman, Donald J. Albosta, who began a formal congressional inquiry into the Reagan theft of the Carter debate briefing books.[65]

The most recurrent and important of all the special circumstances helping to explain frenzies is the exceptional nature of the presidency and vice presidency, and the distinctive forum in which nominees for those offices are chosen. Because of a president's life-or-death power, because he and his family become national role models, and because of the retrospective judgments rendered on past presidents' character flaws, most journalists are firmly convinced that there should be no limits to the scrutiny undergone by nominees for the office. "For the presidency there is virtually no reservoir of privacy left," says Jim Gannon of the *Detroit News*. ABC's Hal Bruno draws an admittedly crude comparison to his days on the crime beat:

When I started out as a police reporter, we used to say, with every crime, except murder, certain things don't have to be revealed, but when it's murder, everything comes out; there is nothing left in the closet. And it's true in politics. When you run for president, unlike lesser offices, there can be nothing left in the closet; everything has to come out.

Eric Engberg of CBS News offers a "Manchurian Candidate" defense of the proctoscopic examination endured by today's leading presidential contenders. Referring to the 1962 movie of that name starring Frank Sinatra, in which a soldier brainwashed by Red China assists the rise of a political candidate who is a tool of Communist foreign powers, Engberg asserts:

Anybody who would think that he could lead the free world ought to have every single thing about his past life [exposed] and every moment of it accountable. . . . It's very important that the man who gets elected president doesn't stand up some day and say "Oh, by the way, I happen to be a Soviet agent. During that year my official biography says I was a Rhodes Scholar at Oxford, I was actually a KGB trainee in Moscow."

These same rationales and standards are applied as rigidly today to vice presidential nominees, who were all but ignored just a few decades ago. The post–World War II era's experience with vice presidents easily explains why: Of the ten men serving in the post from Harry Truman to George Bush, fully half have become president (three by direct succession upon the president's death or resignation), and two more have been unsuccessful presidential nominees. The press feels more secure with some veep nominees than others, of course. Well-known national leaders who are picked for the position often get a mere once-over-lightly since it is presumed, perhaps incorrectly, that they have already been closely scrutinized. This axiom applies particularly to previous losing presidential candidates who wind up in the second slot, such as Walter Mondale in 1976, George Bush in 1980, and Lloyd Bentsen in 1988.[66] Nominees who are virtual unknowns, though, are guaranteed microscopic inspection, as Geraldine Ferraro and Dan Quayle learned to their chagrin.

Ferraro's time of trial came postconvention, once the glow of her "historic first" had dimmed. Quayle had no such chit to use. Not only was he almost completely anonymous—one matronly GOP national convention delegate mistook the middle-aged, dark-haired comedian Mark Russell for the youthful, blond Quayle a full day after Quayle was chosen[67]—Quayle was a *tabula rasa* (a blank slate) for most of the press corps. Jack Nelson of the *Los Angeles Times* recalls, "Here was a guy who was suddenly thrust on the stage by Bush, as a surprise to everybody, including most of Bush's closest associates, for God's sake. . . . We'd had no chance to check him out because there were no credible trial balloons." In the memorable words of GOP media consultant Roger Ailes, Bush "dropp[ed] a hot dog in a tank of 15,000 bluefish [journalists]. . . . That hot dog goes quick, you know what I mean?"[68]

The national political convention itself is a tailor-made accessory to a feeding frenzy crime. Filled to the gills by the print and electronic press and tens of thousands of political activists, with no escape or surcease even in the hotels and restaurants, the convention becomes an amplified echo chamber where every whisper of a rumor can quickly grow into a deafening roar. The late Republican National Committee Chairman Lee Atwater was an acknowledged master of the convention scene, and he analyzed the press's role in it by stressing the convention's built-in ingredients of disaster:

A convention is the most unique thing in American politics because a convention is a world of its own and has a life of its own. And recent conventions have all been coronations. So what you're faced with is a self-contained world where every political reporter in the United States does *not* have a story. A convention more than anything else is an automatic breeding ground for a frenzy. You've got them all down there. They got to go with *something* everyday. Add to that the regular intense competitiveness among reporters multiplied by ten.[69]

The synthesis of crowds, competition, and news famine is a stampede when a delicious morsel is produced. Robert Novak explains the mad mood when Quayle was served up as the chef's surprise:

Suddenly, you've got one of the great stories of all time. Here's a guy who is supposedly a multi-millionaire, draft dodger, sex fiend, Paula Parkinson's boyfriend, stupid. . . . Are they going to dump him? Is it over? . . . People call in with some tidbit that he dunked his donut somewhere sometime. . . . There's nothing else to write about—the platform has been put to bed, there are no floor fights. So everybody's a little guilty. I plead a little guilty: I think I hyped that story.

Quayle, Ferraro, and a host of others (from Spiro Agnew to Joseph Biden) are proof positive that the state and local news media do not generally provide the same kind of exhaustive scrutiny as the national press. Partly, this is because looser standards of probity are accepted for lower offices; then, too, many state and local media outlets are understaffed and plagued by high turnover with resources stretched very thin.[70] Some politicians have benefited from the state press's adherence to the old Rooseveltian rule, as in the case of Senator Thomas Eagleton. Some in the Missouri press corps had known or had strong suspicions about his lengthy hospitalizations in the 1960s. Yet the mental health question was never broached in print until the national press forced Eagleton's hand after his nomination for vice president. More recently a newspaper chose to publish damaging information about a public official's private life only when he indicated strong interest in the presidency. Richard Celeste had been governor of Ohio for six years (and a major political figure in the state for much longer) before the *Cleveland Plain Dealer* revealed the news of his extramarital affairs—relationships about which the newspaper had long known.[71]

Even if state and local media were more aggressive, however, most politicians would still be unprepared for the X-ray illumination and searing heat of the presidential spotlight. "Nothing can prime you for it. I've seen the best of them come unglued over it," observes Hal Bruno. "All of them think they know what it's going to be like and none of them do," says Steve Roberts. Few people care about the fine print of a legislator's finances until he or she is chosen for a national ticket. Congressmen need not weigh the nuance of every word, but presidential candidates must. No one examines every line of a senator's or a religious leader's résumé, but when they seek the presidency a minor misstatement can become a major story. Incidents already examined and consigned to history on the state level are reborn when a politician steps into the national circle. *U.S. News & World Report*'s Kenneth Walsh, as a reporter for the *Denver Post* in the 1970s, covered the "name change" issue when Hart first ran for the Senate, but it apparently had little impact on the Colorado electorate. The national press, by linking the name alteration to other transformations, raised serious questions about Hart in many voters' minds.

While contenders for most offices are unlikely ever to be held by the press to the same stringent standards as candidates for the presidency and vice presidency, there is clearly some movement in that direction. In some state and local cases, the distinction has diminished, as the frenzies discussed in this volume suggest. For some cabinet posts, such as secretary of defense or state, the distinction may already have disappeared entirely. Republican New Right leader Paul Weyrich, instrumental in the confirmation defeat of Defense Secretary-designate John Tower, suggests as much:

At Defense and State, just as with the president, you have to be concerned with life-style questions. These posts require people who are capable of making judgments at any time of the day or night. You can't have somebody with an alcohol problem, or a problem with women. Such a person could be subject to some kind of blackmail from foreign or big business interests.

So far the "blackmail" standard has not been applied to other cabinet posts, but in principle it could be.

Press Frustration

Not surprisingly, politicians react rather badly to the treatment they receive from the modern press. Convinced that the media have but one conspiratorial goal—to hurt or destroy them—the pols respond by restricting journalists' access, except under highly controlled conditions. Kept at arm's length and out of the candidate's way, the press feels enclosed behind trick mirrors: They can see and hear the candidate but he or she does not see and hear them. Journalists' natural, human frustrations grow throughout the grueling months on the road, augmented by many other elements, including a campaign's secrecy, deceptions, selective leaks to rival newsmen, and the well-developed egos of candidates and their staffs. Despite being denied access, they are expected to provide visibility for the candidate, to retail his bromides. Broadcast journalists especially seem trapped by their need for good video and punchy sound bites and with regret find themselves falling into the snares set by the campaign consultants—airing verbatim the manufactured message and photo clip of the day. The press's enforced isolation and the programmed nature of its assignment produces boredom as well as disgruntlement, yet the professionalism of the better journalists will not permit them to let their personal discontent show in the reports they file.

These conditions inevitably cause reporters to strike back at the first opportunity. Whether it is giving emphasis to a candidate gaffe or airing an unconfirmed rumor or publicizing a revelation about personal life, the press uses a frenzy to fight the stage managers, generate some excitement, and seize control of the campaign agenda. Press emotions have been so bottled and compressed that even the smallest deviation from the campaign's prepared script is trumpeted as a major development. A slip of the tongue or a scandal is especially welcome so that reporters can freely release their pent-up emotion on a nonideological subject, with less fear that they can credibly be charged with bias.

This scenario describes the 1988 presidential campaign, and especially the general election, quite well. George Bush and his experienced aides were exceptionally successful in keeping the press at bay. (The expertly media-managed Reagan presidency may have served as training ground and role model.) Reporters were forced to buy megaphones to shout questions at the distant candidate, and binoculars were standard equipment at some events.[72] Because he was so inaccessible and ran a relatively mistake-free post–Labor Day campaign, Bush's message was rarely "stepped on," as the terminology goes; that is, the press never really got control of the agenda again after the Quayle frenzy died out. Nonetheless, reporters' frustration showed in the intense coverage showered on Bush's main verbal gaffe—his innocuous misstating of the date of Pearl Harbor Day. (Bush moved up the day that lived in infamy three months, to September 7.) As in so many other ways, Michael Dukakis's organization proved slow to grasp and match Bush's strategy. After granting easy access for months and stepping all over his message as a consequence, Dukakis began to emulate Bush and become less available to the press in October. But it was far too little, too late.

Bias

Does press frustration, among other factors, ever result in uneven treatment of candidates, a tilt to one side or the other? In other words, are the news media biased? One of the enduring questions of journalism, its answer is simple and unavoidable: Of course they are. Journalists are fallible human beings who inevitably have values, preferences, and attitudes galore—some conscious and others subconscious, all reflected at one time or another in the subjects or slants selected for coverage. To paraphrase Iran-Contra defendant Oliver North's attorney Brendan Sullivan, reporters are not potted plants. The far-more-vital questions are: In what ways is the press biased? and When and how do the biases show?[73]

"There is a liberal tilt among the press that we refuse to recognize, and it is pointless not to acknowledge it because it is obvious," asserts *U.S. News & World Report*'s Michael Barone. In fact, a surprising number of our interviewees from the ideological right, left, and middle did acknowledge the bias. Liberal *Washington Monthly* editor Charles Peters concedes, "The conservatives have a point about liberal tilt"; the *Washington Post*'s relatively nonpartisan public editor, Richard Harwood, observes, "Most journalists are pigeonholed fairly as liberal Democrats"; conservative columnist James J. Kilpatrick perceives "a natural tilt in personal inclination toward the liberal side of the spectrum." Aside from the far right[74] and far left, no one believes the bias to be overwhelming. As Kilpatrick put it, "Walter Cronkite and I used to agree on eighteen of the twenty items that should be on the 'CBS Evening News' on an average night, but our clashing vantage points could spark quite an argument over the other two!"

Cumulatively, of course, those two stories per night—assuming they always veered to the left—could make quite a difference. And, truth be told, they would indeed most likely have a liberal bias. First of all, the relatively small group of professional journalists (not much over one hundred thousand, compared to over four million teachers in the United States)[75] are drawn heavily from the ranks of highly educated social and political liberals, as a number of studies, some conducted by the media themselves, have shown.[76] Journalists are substantially Democratic in party affiliation and voting habits, progressive and antiestablishment in political orientation, and well to the left of the general public on most economic, foreign policy, and especially social issues (such as abortion, affirmative action, gay rights, and gun control). Second, many dozens of the most influential reporters and executives entered (or reentered) journalism after stints of partisan involvement in campaigns or government, and a substantial majority worked for Democrats.[77] Third, this liberal press bias does indeed show up frequently on screen and in print. A study of reporting on the abortion issue, for example, revealed a clear slant to the pro-choice side on network television news, matching in many ways the reporters' own abortion rights views.[78] The *Washington Post* gave extensive coverage to a 1989 pro-choice rally in Washington that drew 125,000 (a dozen stories, leading the front page), while nearly ignoring a pro-life rally that attracted 200,000 (two stories in the Metro section).[79] *Post* reporters have also repeatedly been observed cheering speeches at pro-choice rallies.[80] Additionally, the press lists to the left on the agenda of topics they choose to cover.[81] In the latter half of the 1980s for instance, television gave enormous attention to the homelessness issue; in the process, some experts in the field believe the broadcasters both exaggerated the problem and grossly overstated the role of unemployment in creating the homeless.[82]

Not only does liberal tilt help to predict the stories chosen for coverage, it can determine which subjects are avoided by the press. "Where you look for a story depends on your view of the world," explains Michael Barone, "and you tend to find the stories you look for and *not* find the ones you *don't* look for." The alleged sexual preference of a public official is one such story. The cases of Speaker Tom Foley and Congressman Barney Frank might suggest otherwise, but many reporters insist that homosexuality, in and of itself, does not interest them even if it scandalizes their readers and viewers. "I don't care if someone's gay," declares CNN's Frank Sesno. "To me it's not a story and I wouldn't participate in covering it." Sesno also admits his decision is based on his own values; he recognizes that a substantial part of his audience believes homosexuality to be a major issue and might well object to being represented by a gay person. *Washington Post* managing editor Len Downie does not even concede that the public holds different values than he: "I believe we live at a time in which homosexual relationships between consenting adults, as far as society generally is concerned, are not thought to be illegal or immoral. I don't see that as something we need to inform people about."

The public, incidentally, senses that most members of the press have somewhat different beliefs than the citizenry at large. The Times Mirror Center for the People and the Press, which has commissioned an enlightening series of Gallup surveys on public attitudes toward journalism, found in 1989 that 76 percent of a random sample of the U.S. adult population saw "a great deal" or "a fair amount" of political bias in news coverage.[83] And 68 percent believed that news organizations tended to favor one side rather than dealing fairly with all sides on political and social issues. (Just four years earlier the proportion citing one-sidedness had been only 53 percent.) By decisive margins, respondents who chose to classify press bias saw it as liberal leaning rather than conservative or moderate.

Conservative politicians do not need a Gallup survey to convince them the press is biased against their ilk. For decades, right-of-center Republican leaders have railed against the "liberal media." When former President Dwight Eisenhower attacked the "sensation-seeking" press at the 1964 GOP convention that nominated Barry Goldwater for president, delegates raged against the media assemblage, cursing and shaking their fists at them.[84] No one has ever launched a more vigorous assault against the American media than did Vice President Spiro T. Agnew in November 1969, when he derided the "small band of network commentators and self-appointed analysts . . . who not only enjoy a right of instant rebuttal to every presidential address but more importantly wield a free hand in selecting, presenting, and interpreting the great issues in our nation."[85] And conservative journalists such as Republican activist Patrick J. Buchanan have built careers assailing their liberal brethren: Wrote Buchanan in a 1988 column, "America is bitter because the front pages of the prestige press and the major network 'news' shows are saturated with liberal bigotry, the practitioners of which are either too blind to see it or too dishonest to concede it."[86]

From their perspective, there has been no shortage of evidence in recent years to prove their point. To many conservatives the small things seem to be as memorable as the large. During Senator Gary Hart's separations from his wife, he lived for two lengthy periods with the *Washington Post*'s crack investigative reporter Bob Woodward—exactly the sort of cozy relationship between the newspaper's key personnel and liberal pols that confirms conservatives' worst suspicions. ("He was using the house as a mail drop" while dating women, says Woodward, who was generally aware of Hart's private activities. "In retrospect I think it's something I would never do again. . . . In this case I should have foreseen [the problems] a little better.") Another relatively minor matter that speaks volumes to some conservatives is the occasional financial contribution made by a journalist to a political party or candidate. In 1989, for example, Ed Bradley of CBS's "60 Minutes" and Charlayne Hunter Gault of the "MacNeil/Lehrer NewsHour" donated money (five hundred and seven hundred dollars, respectively) to the Virginia gubernatorial campaign of Democrat L. Douglas Wilder. Bradley defended his gift "as part of my life as a private citizen,"[87] but many colleagues are critical of the practice. "We should *never* make political contributions," declares Sam Donaldson. "Even if we don't cover the area, the perception counts. It's the Caesar's wife thing."

The events of many national election years underscore conservative complaints. Barry Goldwater's supporters can still recount alleged media horrors from 1964, and Richard Nixon's claims of a Democratic tilt during his 1968 presidential race were supported in a much circulated and greatly criticized book by *TV Guide*'s Edith Efron, *The News Twisters*.[88] More recently, the 1984 and 1988 campaigns have stoked conservative fires. Despite the frenzy surrounding Geraldine Ferraro's finances, the Mondale-Ferraro ticket received far kinder, more positive coverage than did the Reagan-Bush team, according to a study by political scientists Michael J. Robinson and Maura Clancey.[89] Four years later George Bush still received a highly negative press, though Michael Dukakis fared not much (if at all) better.[90] Most rankling to conservatives, though, was this pair of findings: The most liberal candidate for president in 1988, Jesse Jackson, garnered the best press,[91] and the most conservative of the four national party nominees, Dan Quayle, secured the worst. Quayle's treatment has become a right-wing cause célèbre, with attention given to alleged press excesses large and small. The intensely critical focus on Quayle's avoidance of Vietnam service, his contacts with Paula Parkinson, and the publication of rumors about his past enraged conservatives, as did unflattering characterizations of Quayle such as the insistence on calling the candidate by his full formal name (the elitist-sounding ''J. Danforth Quayle'') by some television broadcasters in the days following his nomination. No such moniker was forced on James Earl Carter—who was just ''Jimmy'' to the press, noted conservatives. And why, they asked, was Quayle derided as unqualified for the vice presidency after twelve years in the House and Senate when Geraldine Ferraro, with just three terms in the House and fewer legislative accomplishments to her name than Quayle, was hailed by the media (at least at first) in 1984? Incidentally, conservatives get some support within the press for their assertions about Quayle's coverage. ABC's Brit Hume, for instance, recalls hearing some newspeople make ''vitriolic comments'' about Quayle that made him ''ashamed to be a reporter'':

I was stunned by the extraordinary level of personal animus to this guy from major reporters. They knew enough about him to know they didn't like him. He was a conservative Republican, a young, attractive, apparently rich kid from Indiana who seemed to have coasted into the position in which he found himself. And that was good enough for a lot of reporters who decided they hated the guy.

The right wing is not alone in its disgruntlement with the news media. For very different reasons, the left wing joins in the condemnation. Liberals, while acknowledging the press's tough line on Quayle in August 1988, have taken the media to task for not keeping the pressure on him throughout the fall. The failure of the media to analyze and criticize the sometimes exaggerated claims made in Bush's anti-Dukakis advertisements is also cited, and many on the left are still furious that the media did not fully air the ''Bush mistress'' story. To the left, the perceived press kindness toward Bush was merely a continuation of its genuflection to Ronald Reagan during his presidency. ''Because of government manipulation and voluntary self-censorship the major American news organizations too often abdicated their responsibility . . . during the Reagan years," wrote left-wing media critic Mark Hertsgaard.[92] Like others of his persuasion over the years,[93] Hertsgaard points to the conservative status-quo interests of the corporate elites who run most media organizations to explain why a Reagan or a Bush would be pampered by the press. And there are many conservatives well placed in the television and print commentary areas to do the pampering, whether prompted by the media moguls or not. Right-of-center television hosts (John McLaughlin, William F. Buckley, Patrick J. Buchanan, and so on) dominate the public broadcasting agenda, and conservative columnists (especially James J. Kilpatrick, George Will, William Safire, and Rowland Evans and Robert Novak) have much larger circulations than most of their liberal counterparts. Conservative Paul Harvey is the premier radio commentator, too. Even the mainstream news shows rely disproportionately on white, male, moderate-to-conservative voices, as a recent study of guests on "Nightline" and the "MacNeil/Lehrer NewsHour" has shown.[94] This generous measure of conservative commentary is supplemented by the heavily Republican tilt of newspaper editorial pages. In the fifteen presidential elections from 1932 to 1988, a majority of the nation's dailies editorially supported the Republican nominee on fourteen of these occasions.[95] (The only exception was 1964.)

From left to right, all of these criticisms have some validity in different times and circumstances, in one media forum or another. But this cornucopia of critiques ignores some nonideological factors probably more essential to an understanding of press bias. Owing to competition and the reward structure of journalism, the deepest bias most political journalists have is the desire to get to the bottom of a good campaign story (which is usually negative news about a candidate). In search of this holy grail of journalism was conservative Dan Quayle laid low—as were a host of candidates near and dear to reporters' assumed partisan preferences (Eagleton, Ferraro, Biden, and Hart). Pack journalism more than bias leads all media outlets to the same developing "good story" and encourages them to adopt the same slant. One of the newspapers that broke important information about Quayle's National Guard service was none other than the Quayle family–owned paper, the *Indianapolis News*.[96] Commenting on the totality of his frenzy, Quayle himself remarked, "It just became so overwhelming [that] for anyone to step out and write something different about Dan Quayle, they would just [have] sort of said, 'Are you nuts?' "[97]

A related nonideological bias is the effort to create a horse race where none exists.[98] Newspeople whose lives revolve around the current political scene naturally want to add spice and drama, minimize their boredom, and increase their audience. Runaway elections such as 1984 almost inevitably find the press welcoming a new face (Hart)[99] or trying to poke holes in the campaign of the heavy favorite (Reagan).

Other human, not just partisan, biases are at work. Whether the press likes or dislikes a candidate personally is often vital. Former Governor Bruce Babbitt and U.S. Representative Morris K. Udall, both wisecracking, straight-talking Arizona Democrats, were press favorites in their presidential bids (in 1988 and 1976, respectively), and both enjoyed favorable coverage. Richard Nixon, Jimmy Carter, and Gary Hart were all roundly disliked by many reporters who covered them; from Watergate to Billygate to Donnagate the press used exposed Achilles' heels to spear politicians it rated as overall heels. In Carter's case his press secretary, Jody Powell, concluded that "by August 1979, if the President had been set upon by a pack of wild dogs, a good portion of the press would have sided with the dogs and declared that he had provoked the attack."[100] During the 1980 general election season, Carter's unfavorable press coverage was far greater than Ronald Reagan's[101]—even though a Republican as conservative as Reagan should have been the bête noire of journalists (at least according to the right wing's reckoning).

Finally, in their quest to avoid bias, reporters frequently seize on nonideological offenses such as gaffes, ethical violations, and campaign finance problems. These "objective" items are intrinsically free from partisan taint and can be pursued with the frenzied relish denied the press on "hot button," party-polarizing issues.

For all the emphasis here on bias, it is undeniably true that the modern news media are far fairer than their American ancestors ever were, as chapter 2 suggested. News blackouts of the editors' enemies, once shockingly common, are now exceedingly rare and universally condemned.[102] For all the excesses associated with feeding frenzies, few respectable newspapers are as blatantly one sided and partisan as the old left-wing *New York Post* (which shamelessly hyped Nixon's "secret fund")[103] or the right-wing *Manchester* (New Hampshire) *Union Leader* whose now-deceased ultraconservative publisher William Loeb used to rant, rave, and name-call with impunity.[104] (As his widow and more subdued successor as publisher, Nackey Loeb, put it, "Bill used to say that he ought to charge a medical fee for getting people's adrenaline going in the morning.") No longer do organized groups of reporters take out advertisements to support or oppose candidates, or send telegrams to the president and congressmen advocating certain public policies—events that occurred as late as the 1970s.[105] Very occasionally a high-profile journalist will be caught crossing the line to give Walter Lippmann–style aid and comfort to the enemy. ABC News's George Will did so in predebate coaching of candidate Ronald Reagan in 1980, after which Will declared on the air, postdebate, that Reagan had performed like a "thoroughbred."[106] Such instances are heartily denounced when they occur, and in the wake of the Will episode sensible journalists seek to avoid such occasions of sin.

In sum, then, press bias of all kinds—partisan, agenda-setting, and nonideological—can and does influence the development of feeding frenzies and the day-to-day coverage of politicians as well. But bias is not the absolutist be-all and end-all critics on both the right and left often insist it is. Press tilt has a marginal-to-moderate effect, no more and no less; it is but one facet of the mosaic that forms a frenzy.

As this chapter has shown, numerous factors inherent in the structure and operation of modern journalism contribute to the frenzy process. The next chapter will review other elements from the frenzy mix that are not in the immediate dominion of the news media but still shape their world.

4

A Thousand Points of Gossip

How the Politicians, the Public, and the Pundits Feed the Frenzy

Several powerful frenzy forces removed from the press's direct and full control are analyzed in the pages that follow. The sources adopted by journalists have a profound effect on the course and substance of any public controversy, yet they use the press as much as they are used by it. The politicians often bring the frenzy on themselves through stupidity, duplicity, and hypocrisy. Their mistakes, independent of the news media, provide the match that lights the frenzy's fire. Frenzies build on each other as well: The taboos broken and doors opened in one frenzy sometimes lead naturally to a new set of precedents and portals. Public opinion also influences the conduct of a frenzy. What the public wants, tolerates, is interested in, and judges to be right or wrong has clear impact on the press's pursuit of any offense. A fifth force, popular humor, is less powerful than the others but still of moment, especially when it is introduced and promoted by late-night television. Each of these components will be reviewed in turn, and a model of the feeding frenzy's dynamics—integrating both internal and external factors—will be proposed.

Sources—the Tips of the Trade

Tips and leaks from sources are the chief currency of investigative journalism, and most frenzies could not be sustained without them. All skilled journalists cultivate sources, and most recognize the dangers inherent in the undertaking, such as "sweetheart" arrangements whereby a frequent tipster (perhaps a political consultant) is immune from critical coverage or guaranteed an enviable quota of kudos in print.[1] Nonetheless it would be impossible for journalism to function well without these press "providers." They are the bits of string that, when pulled, frequently enable reporters to unravel the fabric of hidden scandal.

Sources for political stories come in three main varieties: intrapartisan (a Democrat or Republican providing a tip about a same-party rival); partisan (a Democrat feeding negative information about a Republican, or the reverse); and nonpartisan (generally a journalist's friend or a politician's associate with a nonpolitical motivation of some sort). Tips are "planted" by regular sources, especially the ubiquitous political consultants, but not uncommonly the unknown, even permanently anonymous source can be the bearer of a jackpot story.

INTRAPARTISAN SOURCES

Occasionally a former party opponent tries to even an old score by slipping a damaging dossier to a reporter. For instance, diplomat William True Davis, who lost the 1968 Democratic U.S. Senate nomination in Missouri to Thomas Eagleton, was the one who told Jack Anderson about Eagleton's supposed (and nonexistent) drunk driving arrests. Dan Quayle also suffered at the hands of Republican rivals, some disappointed that they had not gained the vice presidential nomination. "Most of the negative information about Quayle that I got came from Republicans who were infuriated for one reason or another," discloses Robert Novak. More usually, though, a campaign staffer or consultant will have a less personal but equally mischievous motive: to win a current contest by injuring a rival. "They try to get us to do their dirty work for them," explains the *Washington Post*'s Eleanor Randolph. The operatives rightly figure that charges will have greater credibility coming from a neutral press than from a competing campaign, so they often seek to break the findings of their "opposition research" via journalists instead of paid television advertisements.

There were plenty of examples of such shenanigans in 1988. Front-runner George Bush was the main target in the GOP. According to many press interviewees, some in the Robert Dole camp pushed the "Bush mistress" rumors particularly strenuously. Jack Kemp's operatives played a role, too, but with a secret-agent twist. As one of Bush's managers put it (on a not-for-attribution basis):

There were some Kemp people who were [calling reporters] masquerading as Dole people—a double whammy, that's a great technique. I'm Kemp, right? I want to get it out. I get a "two-for" if I get the rumor out to fuck Bush and I also get the Dole people fucked in the process because they're being blamed for the rumor.

Democrats understand the "double whammy," too. In the most infamous 1988 episode of intraparty skulduggery, Michael Dukakis's campaign surreptitiously sent out the "attack video" showing Joseph Biden's use of British Labour party leader Neil Kinnock's speech, and later tried to shift blame by suggesting Richard Gephardt's staff had been responsible. The reason many reporters were willing to believe Gephardt guilty was that one of his key consultants, Robert Shrum, was a former partner but now a blood enemy of Biden's consulting guru, Patrick Caddell. NBC's Ken Bode remembers calling up Shrum to hurl the j'accuse. When Shrum denied it and cited his recent trip to Paris at the time of the maneuverings, Bode replied, "Now I know you did it; you just went to Paris to give yourself cover!"[2]

Bode's instincts about Shrum were wrong in this specific but perhaps correct in another. A few weeks later Shrum apparently played an intermediary role in spreading the word of Biden's law school plagiarism that finally helped to sink Caddell's candidate. The somewhat circuitous route of the "sourcing" in this instance is instructive. The plagiarism story originated with a tip from a Miami legal academic to a reporter friend who worked for the *Miami Review,* a legal newspaper. While dining recently with a former dean of Biden's alma mater, Syracuse University College of Law, the academic had heard about the candidate's plagiarism.[3] The reporter passed along the tip (which had no apparent political motive) to the *Review*'s sister newspaper in Washington, the *Legal Times,* where a journalist began the process of checking it out. One of the calls went to Shrum under the assumption that Caddell's enemy might be willing to share his knowledge of a skeleton in the Caddell-sponsored candidate's closet. This was a miscalculation, however, because Shrum knew nothing of the incident beforehand but now possessed the disparaging information. In short order Gephardt staffers began spreading the story to reporters who worked for prestige news organizations (such as *Time* magazine), which, if they published it, could do more damage to Biden than could the *Legal Times.* Ironically, the *Legal Times* reporter was called by journalists at these newly informed publications, who insinuated that the *Legal Times* was spearheading a partisanly motivated attempt to "get Biden"—a perhaps reasonable conclusion, since they had been informed of Biden's problem by Gephardt's staff. (Shrum firmly denies playing this intermediary role, although he admits passing along the intelligence to some of his working associates.)

It is head-spinning source scenarios like the Biden plagiarism matter that convince many political players there are conspiracies afoot even when there are not. Such was the case with the female caller to the *Miami Herald* who revealed Gary Hart's ill-fated weekend plans with Donna Rice. At the time of the *Herald* exposé, little was said about the tipster because, as the *Herald*'s Jim Savage explained, "We were able to confirm independently nearly everything the woman told us, so her identity wasn't important for our purposes." Nonetheless, many journalists at the *Herald* and elsewhere immediately and understandably wondered whether Hart had been set up. As Wayne King of the *New York Times* (which had a team of reporters working on the conspiracy theories) characterized the scene:

It did seem very suspicious. Donna Rice . . . had a propensity to show up on yachts with men twice her age. She had, shall we say, a reputation. So one could easily see how she might be recruited to sink Hart. [Also there were the] coincidences. Hart meets her in Colorado [at a New Year's Eve party], then he runs into her on a yacht in Miami because she happens to be at an adjoining disco. Those things can happen, but it still looked a little funny.

While the public focus remained fixed on Hart's peccadillo, substantial resources were privately devoted to uncovering the purported conspiracy behind Hart's "seven days in May." Hart's Democratic rivals were immediately suspect. After all, as Hart's press secretary Kevin Sweeney explained, they "had been trying to push character to the forefront" as a way of attacking Hart. So when suggestions reached the *New York Times* that Joseph Biden's chief consultant, Patrick Caddell, knew Rice, Caddell became a suspect—not just because of the Biden connection but because Caddell, formerly a close adviser of Hart's, was now on very unfriendly terms with Hart. Even greater scrutiny was directed to George Bush's campaign manager, Lee Atwater, devotee of Machiavelli's *The Prince*. Donna Rice was from Lee Atwater's hometown (Columbia, South Carolina), and he acknowledged to this author having met Rice many years ago, though he said he did not remember it until she reminded him at a Washing-

ton dinner in 1988. In any event the Carolina connection was sufficient to generate a number of inquiries to Atwater by inquisitive reporters. "Nothing ever happens that I'm not blamed for," laughed
Atwater, but he had a convincing reply that satisfied most callers: "I
wasn't behind it, but if I had been, I would have waited until the son
of a bitch got the nomination and I'd have broken it then!"

Not all the conspiracy theories were political. For instance, investigators for ABC's "20/20," among others, pursued a possible connection with organized crime. Donna Rice's female companion during
her Washington and Bimini escapades with Hart, Lynn Armandt,
had close relatives connected with the seedier side of life, including a
Sicilian brother-in-law linked to the mob by Florida and federal law
enforcement agents.[4] Armandt's former husband and Rice's ex-boy-
friend had also reportedly been involved in drug dealing.[5] As the
"20/20" report suggested, "Attempts by organized crime to com-
promise politicians are not unheard of."

Yet in the end, "20/20," the *New York Times*, and the other organizations examining the conspiracy theories could prove none of them,
and most of these experienced journalists concluded that the
tipster's motives were probably not partisanly or criminally inspired.
The source's impulse might have been idealistic, in fact: She told the
Miami Herald's Tom Fiedler, the able political editor who spoke to her
over the phone, that she was a liberal Democrat upset at Hart's hypocrisy in denouncing "rumors" about him that were actually true.
It is also very possible that the caller saw an opportunity to gain eventual fame and money—or was put up to it by someone of similar desire. Lynn Armandt had taken the to-be-famous picture of Rice
sitting in Gary Hart's lap on the *Monkey Business*'s dock in Bimini,
and Rice had given her a copy of that photo and others. After Hart's
withdrawal, Armandt sold the pictures to the *National Enquirer* for a
reported $100,000, and she received another $190,000 from *People* for
the photos and her version of the story.

However, Armandt was *not* the *Herald*'s tipster, though many believe she was nonetheless behind the effort. Tom Fiedler has flatly
denied his source was Armandt,[6] stating that instead she was
"one of Donna's [other] good friends and associates." Both the
Atlanta Constitution[7] and "20/20" have identified the individual as
another Miami model and Rice/Armandt chum, Dana Weems;
"20/20" reported that Weems had unsuccessfully tried to sell the
story of her role to the Phil Donahue show for $250,000. Weems
has denied being the source and told the *Constitution* she had been
"set up."

PARTISAN SOURCES

As this tale of intrigue shows, the precise motivations of sources are not always apparent, but the easiest to analyze are those of clearly identified partisans. Their goal in the great game of politics has remained unchanged through the ages: to get the other party's rascals out and to get their party's rascals in.

Not a single major presidential campaign rumor in recent years has been spread without the assistance of partisan operatives. Most of the time the party apparatchiks' motivations are so transparent and the tips so flimsy that reporters offer a polite thank-you and place the material in File 13. Late in the autumn of 1988 one Democratic political consultant called around to Washington gossip columnists, while his party's presidential ticket was sinking into the sunset, offering "the name, address, and phone number of a woman who's servicing Dan Quayle," with no proof cited, according to Bill Thomas, formerly of *Roll Call*. (Thomas and apparently all the the other recipients of this desperate scurrilous rumor discarded it.) Journalists suggest that many partisans overdo it in another way: killing reporters with kindness by overwhelming them with damaging information about the opposition. Republicans in Virginia, for instance, helped to dampen the impact of Chuck Robb's attendance at parties where cocaine was used by "constantly ringing up every reporter in town with each little tidbit they had read on a men's-room wall," said Jeff Schapiro of the *Richmond Times-Dispatch*. The Virginia GOP even helped recruit a private detective to investigate Robb's activities. Party operatives, including the chairman and the executive director, later compounded the error by denying their role in hiring and paying the gumshoe.[8]

The more astute party activists recognize that they can best achieve their objectives when they provide newspeople with specific, provable information. By serving as research assistants gratis, they can earn goodwill and facilitate the further development of breaking frenzies. For example, a relatively low-level Reagan White House aide extended Joseph Biden's plagiarism miseries by informing the *New York Times* of Biden's unattributed use of certain Robert Kennedy phrases.[9] (Oddly, for a Republican, he was a fan of Bobby Kennedy's and knew his speeches by heart, thus enabling him to recognize Biden's borrowing.) More-senior Reagan White House and campaign staffers were involved in 1984 efforts to spread and emphasize the emerging character questions (age, name change, and so on) about Gary Hart. Concerned about Hart's youthful appeal and about their polls showing Hart to be Reagan's strongest potential Democratic opponent for the fall, the top Reagan people each called several journalists in the wake of Hart's New Hampshire victory to point out the problematic pattern in Hart's past—which at that juncture had not been made explicit in news media coverage. "These things were already on the public record," says Ken Bode, then of NBC, "but they had not been packaged together. The White House was one of the driving forces behind the age/signature business, and press interest was stirred up as a result."[10]

NONPARTISAN SOURCES

While dependent on their regular sources, reporters often find that the tips rounded up by their usual suspects are shopworn and well known, since most experienced partisans peddle their wares on a regular basis from media outlet to media outlet. The truly stunning revelations are frequently served up by nonpolitical sources who may be only indirectly or not at all connected to public life. Family, friends, and jilted lovers of public officials seem especially ripe for sourcing. In fact, the lesson learned by some pols is an ancient one: With family and friends like these, who needs partisan enemies?

One source of unflattering information about Jesse Jackson over the years has been Jackson's former allies in the civil rights movement of the 1960s. The *Atlanta Constitution*, for example, has been the beneficiary of stories supplied by some Atlanta residents connected to the late Dr. Martin Luther King, Jr. These individuals resented Jackson's claim to King's mantle, according to Bill Kovach, formerly of the *Constitution*. The associates who prove to be most damaging are not professional coworkers but spouses and "significant others." From Wayne Hays to Barney Frank, former lovers who choose to kiss and tell can be poisonous. John Tower's second ex-wife, Lilla, was an important source of derogatory background for Sarah McClendon and others. The former Mrs. Tower's divorce from the senator had been messy, and she remained angry. ("I hope to God I never get a woman as mad at me as she was at him," said one of our interviewees, who was familiar with the situation.)[11]

A bitter ex-lover also played a critical and hidden role in the unraveling of Douglas Ginsburg's nomination to the Supreme Court. While teaching at Harvard, Ginsburg had dated a liberal Boston public-interest lawyer who (unfortunately for Ginsburg) had maintained an extensive personal diary of their relationship, including notations of the nominee's attendance at parties where marijuana was used. Almost immediately after President Reagan announced Ginsburg's selection, the woman contacted a fellow well-known public-interest lawyer in Washington who was a member of a behind-the-scenes co-ordinating group opposing Ginsburg's confirmation. (The same informal group had helped to orchestrate the defeat of Ginsburg's predecessor as a Supreme Court nominee, Robert Bork.) In short order the unexploded dynamite was passed along to at least two reporters, and it was detonated after calls to Ginsburg's Harvard associates, who confirmed his participation in the pot-laced parties. Only Ginsburg's colleagues, and not his former girlfriend, were quoted as sources in the published and aired accounts.

Other nonpartisan sources with less-direct personal interest than some of the tipsters just cited can also provide a reporter with paydirt. Foremost among them are Secret Service agents who are aware of a presidential candidate's every movement. All the agents' observations are supposed to be confidential, but reporters frequently develop social friendships with them—they are together on the road a great deal—and over a drink or a game of tennis, gossip will inevitably be exchanged. About a dozen newsmen interviewed for this study cited Secret Service personnel as having been useful in developing stories (especially about Gary Hart and Jesse Jackson). This is true on the state level as well, where a governor's troopers or highway patrol guards will be privy to information that can be passed along to reporters. Some newsmen and others looking into the private activities of Governor Dick Celeste of Ohio and Chuck Robb of Virginia received assistance from this quarter. Virginia journalists' search for revelations about Robb's activities was aided by representatives of another part of the law enforcement community: members of the legal fraternity familiar with an ongoing federal grand jury investigation into cocaine trafficking. Several newspapers, including the *Richmond Times-Dispatch* and the *Virginian-Pilot*, were tipped partly in this fashion. For example, Michael Hardy of the *Richmond Times-Dispatch*, who (along with reporter Jeff Schapiro) first broke the story of Robb's attendance at Virginia Beach parties where drugs were used, was informed by a well-placed Hampton Roads, Virginia, lawyer who was both an old friend of his and an active Democrat with no personal or political animosity to Robb. The motivation for the lawyer's call to Hardy was exquisitely nonpartisan: Hardy's rivals from other newspapers had been making inquiries, and his friend wanted to make sure he had the story as well. Not just law enforcement officers but those on the other side of the jailhouse door occasionally serve as sources. As the next chapter will explore, prisoners stoked the fires of unsubstantiated rumors about both Dan Quayle and Tom Foley.

Reporters are fierce competitors but also comrades in arms, and under certain conditions they will share good intelligence with a colleague. Alfredo Corchado, a Dallas bureau reporter for the *Wall Street Journal*, attended a conference of Hispanic journalists in San Antonio in 1988 and expressed interest in the private-life rumors about San Antonio's Mayor Henry Cisneros. On his return to Dallas he had a "wild two weeks" with calls on the sly "every single day at work or at home" from San Antonio reporters frustrated because of their own editors' initial reluctance to publish the Cisneros story. Corchado's colleague-competitors were willing to give him their scoop, though eventually the San Antonio papers succumbed to temptation and told all. More often reporters from an unrelated beat will pass along a tip they cannot use to journalist friends covering the subject of the tip, or perhaps human nature intervenes, and one newsperson's gossiping or bragging may alert others to a potential story. Additionally, reporters feed off each other's published work. There is a food chain in journalism, and the larger publications (the big fish) not infrequently develop stories first discovered by less-visible publications, such as the hundreds of Washington policy and trade newsletters (the plankton) and elite-circulation papers like *Roll Call* and *Legal Times* (the small fish). As Washington journalist-writer Bill Thomas correctly saw it, "The young unknowns working for the less important publications often dig deeper and ask questions a big-time reporter might be embarrassed to ask." Those tough questions can lead to discoveries that become fodder for the frenzies that only larger papers can initiate and sustain.

For all the intentional cultivation of well-placed individuals, the accidental revelations from unwitting sources can prove just as golden. Gary Hart suffered from these happenstances in both 1984 and 1988. The careful background reporting of the *Washington Post*'s George Lardner, Jr., had taken him to Hart's birthplace, Ottawa, Kansas, in 1983 for an interview with his uncle, George Hartpence. During the course of the conversation, "Uncle George said, 'You know, I've always thought Gary was a year older than he says he is,' " remembers Lardner. Sure enough, his wife had recorded Hart's birth in the family "baby book," and the uncle clearly remembered visiting Hart's parents that same year when "there was a baby in the crib." After Lardner repeatedly confronted Hart with his relative's recollection, the candidate "just shrugged and weaseled around," eventually admitting, "It's whatever the records say." (Incidentally, Lardner and others are convinced that Hart's deception began sometime during the 1960s, when the in-vogue slogan was Don't Trust Anyone over Thirty—or in this case, twenty-nine.)[12] In the next presidential cycle, Hart's womanizing was the focus of partly coincidental exposure. The *Washington Post* first learned of Hart's longtime relationship with a local woman two days after the *Miami Herald* published the Hart-Rice exposé, when *Post* reporter Thomas B. Edsall received a copy of a Washington, D.C., private detective's report that included photographs of Hart entering the woman's house at night and leaving the next morning.[13] The detective had been hired to follow Hart by a former U.S. senator (a Democrat and ex-Hart supporter) who was a jealous husband convinced that Hart was having an affair with his wife. The stakeout uncovered no evidence of that purported liaison but apparently by chance documented the other relationship. "Uncomfortable with that kind of story" and also convinced that Hart was "dead meat already, so piling on was unnecessary," Edsall decided not to pursue the matter personally, but out of a sense of obligation to his newspaper, he passed it along to executive editor Benjamin C. Bradlee, who decided to carry it further and assigned it to other reporters. After their painstaking verification of details contained in the detective's report (such as Hart's schedule and itinerary on the day and night in question), as well as the gathering of other suggestive evidence, a Bradlee intimate contacted Hart's mistress, who confirmed her relationship with Hart in exchange for a guarantee that the *Post* would not publish her name in connection with the presidential candidate.[14]

By no means, however, are sources always critical to the breaking of a good story. The *Wall Street Journal's* Brooks Jackson, on a hunch, had collected Geraldine Ferraro's financial disclosure forms just before she was selected by Mondale in the summer of 1984. He simply followed the paper trail, and Ferraro's problems "just jumped out at me instantly," recalls Jackson, who did some groundbreaking spadework on the frenzy.

Other stories are delayed or never see the light of day because sources will not come forward. The *Washington Post's* Tom Sherwood, like other newspeople covering Mayor Barry, had had "very strong suspicions" about the mayor's drug use for years, and in fact had been given off-the-record but insufficiently documented confirmations by Barry's friends and associates. Sherwood did everything he could "to persuade the people who said they had used drugs with the mayor to come forward. I even went to several and told them, 'You're responsible because you know the mayor is drowning in public. I'm going to come back to you when the mayor dies of an overdose and ask why you protected the mayor instead of helping him.' " Sadly, even after Barry's drug arrest, the silence of many of these sources was deafening. It is a case like this that causes most journalists to agree with the *Post*'s Ann Devroy: "I want anybody on God's earth to call me up and tell me anything they want to about anybody in politics. Let us check it out."

The Politicians Themselves

Marion Barry's case is extraordinary but not unique in at least one vital respect: Virtually all frenzy victims are responsible to varying degrees for the unhappy fate that befalls them; the blood they shed that drives the press to frenzy seeps mainly from self-inflicted wounds. Yes, press excesses intensify the frenzy; bad luck can magnify the unfairness; and the punishment may not fit the crime. But the politicians' own substantive offenses (hypocrisy, lying, gaffes, greed, lawbreaking, or sexual misadventures) as well as procedural errors (lack of full disclosure, refusal to admit error quickly, or inadequate preparation for scrutiny) loom large, as table 4.1 suggests. In many cases, the candidate's mistake confirmed the preconceived press "subtext" about him or her—a subtext the candidate was well aware existed and ought to have been on guard not to reinforce.

Procedural errors can be every bit as politically damaging as the substantive ones. Dan Quayle's selection as a vice presidential nominee is a case study of blunder and mishap. (Again, see table 4.1.) The actual wisdom of Bush's choice aside, the much-vaunted Bush campaign team did a remarkably poor job of preparing the way for Quayle's acceptance by press and public alike. Even David Beckwith, then a *Time* correspondent and later Quayle's vice presidential press secretary, admitted: "Quayle was not prepared and the Bush campaign was not prepared [when Quayle was announced]. . . . It could have been handled better." Brooks Jackson of the *Wall Street Journal* adds: "The Quayle frenzy resulted because we and they didn't have all the facts. . . . If the whole story had been presented at the beginning, no feeding frenzy would probably have resulted." Even some senior aides had been left in the dark about Bush's choice and were in no mood to sell the party line. "We weren't getting any passionate defenses of Quayle from some of Bush's close associates," recalls NBC's John Chancellor. "To the contrary, we were getting winks and nods that Quayle was a strange choice and Bush hadn't thought

TABLE 4.1

How Politicians Bring Frenzies on Themselves: A Few Case Studies

Frenzy Category	Selected Frenzy	Substantive Error(s)	Procedural Error(s)
Financial	Nixon's "secret fund" (1952)	*Nixon chose to finance his political activities in an unconventional fashion that would invite extra scrutiny. *Eisenhower had chosen the corruption issue to use against the incumbent Democrats without carefully checking the background of his vice presidential nominee.	*Nixon had not previously publicized the existence of the fund. *The fund turned out to be 14 percent larger than first disclosed. *Eisenhower and his staff vacillated about Nixon's fate, sending out mixed signals and extending the length of the controversy. *Despite some advance warning that the story was about to break, Nixon did not take it seriously enough at first to prepare adequately.
	Ferraro's finances (1984)	*Ferraro first promised to release her husband's tax returns, then reneged, throwing down the gauntlet to the press and Republican party. *Some financial improprieties were in fact in the records, once they were fully disclosed—though her husband was apparently responsible for the lion's share.	*Mondale and his staff had conducted only a cursory examination of Ferraro's finances. *Mondale refused to insist privately that Ferraro disclose all. *Ferraro and Mondale let the controversy build for two long weeks, draining all their energies at a critical time.
Gaffe	Carter's "lust in the heart" *Playboy* interview (1976)	*Playboy* magazine was an inappropriate place for a major presidential candidate interview, especially in a year when personal values were being stressed. *The odd phrases and offensive language used by Carter in the interview were not accidental, but clearly intentional, designed to counteract his image of holier-than-thou religiosity.	*Carter and his staff failed to recognize the explosiveness of his remarks and did not organize an appropriate damage-control operation in anticipation of their release.

(cont.)

105

TABLE 4.1 (Cont.)

FRENZY CATEGORY	SELECTED FRENZY	SUBSTANTIVE ERROR(S)	PROCEDURAL ERROR(S)
Gaffe	Ford's "free Poland" remark (1976)	*Ford's defensible argument about Eastern Europe was inartfully phrased and confusing. Ford also passed up opportunities in the debate to clarify his comments, despite clear signals from Carter and the press panel that his statement was being misinterpreted.	*Ford's own stubbornness kept him for days from admitting that he misspoke. *His campaign staff did not end the "presidential bubble" isolation that prevented Ford from seeing the real damage that had been done to his campaign.
Character	Eagleton's mental health (1972)	*When asked directly whether he had any "skeletons in the closet," Eagleton said no, deciding not to divulge his mental hospitalizations to McGovern and his staff. *McGovern's actions proved both indecisive and devious after the crisis developed. First McGovern said he was "1,000 percent" behind Eagleton, then he undermined him behind the scenes to ease him off the ticket. This helped to destroy his clean "new politics" image.	*McGovern staff (led by Gary Hart) gave the most cursory examination to Eagleton's record and past; the senator had been well down on the list of possibilities. *McGovern wasted most of his time in the vice presidential search on a fruitless quest to woo Edward Kennedy onto the ticket. *The staff missed many signals at the convention, including warnings from prominent Democrats phoned directly to McGovern's headquarters, about Eagleton's problems.
	Gary Hart and Donna Rice (1987)	* After warnings galore that his alleged womanizing would be an issue, and that he might even be tailed, Hart maintained a relationship with Rice, using little discretion and putting himself in extraordinarily compromising situations.	*Hart actively invited close scrutiny, telling one reporter, "Follow me around . . . put a tail on me." *Hart refused to try to resolve lingering character questions from his 1984 campaign, thereby reinforcing the subtext for 1988.

106

FRENZY CATEGORY	SELECTED FRENZY	SUBSTANTIVE ERROR(S)	PROCEDURAL ERROR(S)
Character	Dan Quayle (1988)	*Bush picked a virtual unknown as his running mate, and someone not regarded as a person of great accomplishment who was prepared to be president. *The hypocrisy factor was present: Quayle was a hawk but chose not to go to Vietnam. *Quayle was ill-prepared for the national spotlight, and not well briefed for his first few public appearances after Bush announced his selection; he fanned the National Guard controversy by mishandling inquiries about his motives for serving and admission to the Guard.	*Republican party leaders, the press, and citizens were not prepared for the announcement through private consultations, tips, and trial balloons. *Bush made a momentous decision in virtual isolation, without properly gauging reactions in advance. *The surprised Bush staff was disorganized and unable to get ahead of the press curve at the convention. Some were not particularly supportive of Quayle in off-the-record conversations with newspeople. *The early convention announcement of Quayle gave the frenzy more time to build in the convention's news-starved echo chambers.

SOURCES: Interviews conducted for this volume.

it through." Compounding the difficulties was Quayle's own un-
steady performance now that the klieg lights were on him. Though
he defended his overall presentation, Lee Atwater acknowledged
that "a couple of times [convention] week Quayle appeared like a
doe with headlights shining in his face, and the media saw and
smelled weakness." Atwater and others also rue the decision to announce Quayle's selection on Tuesday, instead of the traditional
Thursday of the convention. As one top Bush adviser explained:

If we'd done it Thursday Quayle would have been out of there before a
frenzy would have had time to build in the special convention atmosphere.
But by going with it Tuesday, we took away the only story [the vice presidential pick] the press tribe had, and so they had to gin up another story.
And the ridiculous thing is we did it all because we didn't want to mess with
[Senator Robert] Dole's ego and wanted to end his misery [since he was not
selected], and in retrospect, Dole's gonna be mad about something everyday anyhow.

Of some consolation to the Bush veterans is the knowledge that they
were hardly the first presidential team to prepare inadequately for
the vice presidential selection. Richard Nixon in 1968, George Mc-
Govern in 1972, and Walter Mondale in 1984 each added his chapter
to the book of campaign blunders. In 1984, for example, only the Republicans seemed ready for the financial revelations that followed
Democrat Ferraro's nomination. ABC News's Ann Compton remembers a dinner party she hosted the night before Mondale chose
Ferraro: "A Democrat said to the chairman of the Republican National Committee as he left with his briefcase, 'What'cha got in there?
All the stuff on Mondale?' And he said, 'No, all the stuff on Geraldine Ferraro's husband.' "

Procedural mishandling heightens the effect of the substantive
mistakes candidates make, but it is those substantive errors that trigger a feeding frenzy. The misdeeds come in all varieties. Candidate
gaffes are responsible for much mischief-making on the campaign
trail. Texas's Republican gubernatorial nominee Clayton Williams
added to the mother lode in 1990 by first likening rape to bad weather
("If it's inevitable, just relax and enjoy it") and then offering that, as
a teenager and college student, he had been "serviced" by prostitutes. William's gaffes join a long and undistinguished line stretching from George Romney's "brainwashing" and Spiro Agnew's use
of "Polack" and "fat Jap" to Jimmy Carter's "lust in the heart" interview and Gerald Ford's "free Poland" remark. The latter was one

of the most costly misspeaks in U.S. history, since it may have drained Ford of just enough momentum at a critical time to deprive him of his unelected presidency. David Gergen, one of Ford's aides in 1976, attributes the president's stubborn refusal to admit the error and cut his losses to the "presidential bubble" insulating all chief executives from reality. "Ford didn't think he had erred, and nobody in the warm, cheering, enthusiastic crowds he saw after the debate told him he had erred either," says Gergen. In truth Ford's assertion was not the blooper it was portrayed as being, and the events of the late 1980s proved it.[15] Even in 1976 "we figured out what he was trying to say," recalled ABC's Sam Donaldson. "But at best Ford was ambiguous, and at worst his statement suggested he didn't understand what was happening in Eastern Europe." History may have vindicated Ford, but no doubt he would have preferred to win the election.

Unlike gaffes, which are generally interpreted as indicating pure stupidity, other substantive misdeeds are seen as evidence of poor judgment and impure character. Gary Hart is the prototype, of course, though his case also blends in a generous measure of obdurate obtuseness. Hart had been warned repeatedly by staff, friends, and even sympathetic reporters that he would have to be on his best behavior and might well find himself under surveillance.[16] The candidate repeatedly assured newspeople as well as aides that he was observing all the conventional rules. Just seven days before Hart's weekend with Donna Rice, Jack Germond had dinner with him, and the columnist was assured that "There's nothing to the womanizing charges" and that he was being careful to "observe community standards." Later that week Hart reiterated essentially the same message on videotape for NBC's Ken Bode. The crowning imbecility was Hart's declaration to *New York Times* reporter E. J. Dionne to "Follow me around. I don't care. I'm serious, if anybody wants to put a tail on me, go ahead. They'd be very bored."[17] Dionne himself was stunned by the statement, published in his *New York Times Magazine* profile of Hart the same morning the *Miami Herald* printed the Donna Rice exposé:

As soon as I heard the "follow me" quote ten percent of me thought maybe he really has changed and ninety percent of me thought, 'Why did you say this?' Because I immediately started imagining all the ways either the media or his opponents would use that quote as an excuse for something.

Interestingly, while the *Miami Herald* had already made the decision to conduct the Hart stakeout, *Herald* reporters Tom Fiedler and Jim

Savage had an advance copy of Dionne's story in hand when they flew to Washington for the surveillance and eventual confrontation with Hart. Dionne's story reinforced their rationale for the stakeout, though Hart had made similar "I have nothing to hide" comments earlier to Fiedler.

Most reporters found the Hart case an "easy call," as one put it, because he had been so blatant and had asked for intense scrutiny. A number of reporters such as *U.S. News*'s Steve Roberts drew a distinction between Hart's behavior with Donna Rice and George Bush's alleged and unsubstantiated dalliances:

Whatever was true about Bush's sex life, he clearly was not reckless about his private life. If in fact he has had a mistress or a series of mistresses over the years, he has been extremely discreet about it. Now this sounds odd in a way, but a lot of people saw that as a defining difference. It wasn't how many times he cheated on his wife, it was how he handled it.

Some of his own staff members came to believe that Hart had adopted not just JFK's gestures but his reckless persona—in an age no longer tolerant of such shenanigans. Calling Hart's demise "unfortunate but inevitable," his 1984 press secretary, Kathy Bushkin, surmised, "He tempted fate and got caught." While denying immorality, Hart himself conceded "a mistake by putting myself in circumstances that could be misconstrued."

The Hart model of bad judgment and flawed character has been replicated to various degrees many times in recent years. Wilbur Mills, John Tower, and scores of others forgot the sage advice of Tammany Hall boss George Washington Plunkitt: "No matter how well you learn to play the political game, you won't make a lastin' success of it if you're a drinkin' man."[18] Congressman Barney Frank (D., Mass.) hired as a personal aide a male prostitute possessing a criminal record after first buying sex from him; whatever good intentions may have prompted Frank to offer the job cannot erase the congressman's incredibly poor judgment in the matter. Senator Charles Robb (D., Va.) is as outwardly cautious as Frank is flamboyant, yet they share a penchant for choosing bad company. While serving as governor, Robb received warnings from business and political associates about the "comely" social set of his friends in Virginia Beach[19]—his wife also disapproved[20]—but he continued regularly attending late-night parties without his spouse, where drugs, prostitutes, and other suspect individuals were sometimes present.[21] As the *Richmond Times-Dispatch*'s Jeff Schapiro notes, "The issue was, and remains today, a matter of judgment. Chuck Robb had been warned about the company he was keeping, but he continued to move in some very questionable circles." Adds the *Los Angeles Times*'s Rose Ellen O'Connor, who did most of the *Virginian Pilot*'s investigative work on the Robb scandal as a reporter for the Norfolk-based paper:

A lot of the parties Robb attended were small—a half dozen people sometimes. The organizer of many of them was Robb's best friend at the Beach, and you can't say [the friend's] name in the area without [someone] bringing up cocaine. A number of people at these parties were also the focus of a federal Drug Enforcement Administration cocaine probe.

Robb's actions were all the more surprising, and disillusioning to some, because of the image he and his handlers had carefully nurtured and projected over the years—that of the clean-cut, straight-laced, milk-drinking ex-Marine. However oxymoronic that description might appear to other Marines, it was a facade that sold well in Virginia. With a successful term as governor to his credit, Robb's store of goodwill in the state was sufficient to overcome the impact of the revelations, and he easily won an open U.S. Senate seat in 1988 after Republicans nominated an exceptionally weak candidate.[22] Robb has also emphatically denied knowing that drugs were used at the parties.

None of the politicians discussed so far can compare to Republican Evan Mecham of Arizona and Democrat Marion Barry of Washington, D.C. The former governor and the former mayor were living, breathing, walking, talking feeding frenzies during their embarrassing terms of office. Mecham, the first state governor impeached and convicted in the United States since 1929, was ousted by his state's legislature in 1988 after serving just fifteen months of his four-year term. Those months were littered with some of the most appalling gaffes, slurs, and appointments in American history.[23] From defending the racist term *pickaninny*, to charging that his conversations were being bugged via laser beams, to the selection of a number of high state officials with convictions and court-martials in their backgrounds, Mecham kept the news media in hot copy from his inauguration to his demise. As for Marion Barry, his frenzy was "the world's longest strip-tease act," according to Tom Sherwood of Washington's WRC-TV. A review of the Barry mayoral years (1978–90) yields a scandal-studded calendar stretching from his relationship with a female cocaine dealer, to his attendance at a club favored by prostitutes and drug users, to harassment of a beautiful twenty-three-year-old model on the pretext of meeting her three-year-old son, to a sordid sex-and-crack sting arrest after other drug-related brushes with the authorities.[24] Press excesses such as sensationalism existed in the Barry and Mecham cases, but not even the most severe media critic would dispute that these two pols richly deserved their fate and brought it on themselves.

The frenzy offenses—whether major or minor—committed by politicians are amplified by any appearance of hypocrisy or attempt at lying and coverup. (See the examples in table 4.2, where in some cases reporters expressed strong emotions of disgust and outrage at candidates' perceived duplicity.) The hypocrisy angle has particularly influenced the coverage of the private lives of public officials. To the extent that candidates portray themselves as family oriented and use their spouses and children as video backdrop, they ask for scrutiny of their life's private sector, says CNN's Frank Sesno: "We hear so much from our candidates about family values. If they're going to preach this stuff then they better be practicing it, and the more pious the candidate becomes, the more he or she opens up personal life to inspection." Hal Bruno of ABC agrees, and adds: "If the candidate stands there with his wife and family all exchanging loving glances, he's conveying the image of the solid family man. If it turns out that this is fraud, [press exposure] is perfectly legitimate." Gary Hart is not the only recent public official to discover this aspect of media coverage. When San Antonio Mayor Henry Cisneros announced he would neither run for Texas governor nor a fifth term as mayor, he left the misleading impression with many in the media that his one-year-old son's heart problems were responsible. The revelations about his extramarital affair cast his political exit in a new light, especially because Cisneros had been so willing to picture himself as a devoted husband and father.[25] The Hart and Cisneros sagas suggest the downside of warm'n'fuzzy political family coverage: Candidates who willingly invite the media into their homes should not be surprised when the press follows them to motel rooms.

There are many other varieties of hypocrisy, and since it is the oil that greases politics, a rare campaign is without any trace. In the situational ethics of hypocrisy, any action that contradicts a candidate's central image or motif is ripe for targeting. Joseph Biden's claim of high idealism and inspirational oratory was tarnished by his past and present plagiarism; Michael Dukakis's "attack video" violated the "open honesty" theme in his projection of presidential character; Pat Robertson's exaggerations about his accomplishments and war record undermined his attempt to make moral values and integrity the backbone of a White House crusade. Oddly enough, the absence of hypocrisy at a critical moment can also prove damaging to a politician. Dan Quayle's most candid remark of the 1988 campaign, in response to a question about his Vietnam-era National Guard service shortly after he was chosen for the GOP ticket, was also one of his most injurious: "I did not know in 1969 that I would be in this room today." (Translation: He would have served in the military had he foreseen a big-league political career.)

Press hypocrisy does not deter full scrutiny of candidate hypocrisy, of course. Judge Ginsburg's drug history was examined with relish (and good cause) despite widespread reported cocaine and marijuana usage among younger journalists.[26] For example, Bob Woodward estimated in 1984 that forty *Washington Post* employees regularly used cocaine.[27] Ann Compton of ABC News recalled another instance of press hypocrisy when television reported Pat Robertson's "miracle baby":

I looked at two networks that evening. One correspondent and one anchor, both of whom have children born less than nine months after marriage, were doing the story. They handled it very straighforwardly, but I guess that knowing them, I recognized a bit of hypocrisy, a double standard there.

As Compton herself noted, the broadcasters were not seeking political office—an important distinction—yet the press has also been more willing of late to investigate the private lives of even nonpolitical public figures, a category into which celebrity journalists must surely fall. As for politicians, they can expect none of the dispensation granted famous reporters, and they must always be on their guard against deeds that communicate hypocrisy. It may have been a sign of the times that when Senators Edward Kennedy and Chuck Robb voted against John Tower's confirmation as secretary of defense, both announced that the conflict-of-interest charges and not the "party-boy" allegations against Tower had turned their thumbs down.

Lying is even more deadly than hypocrisy to the modern campaigner. George Washington established the yardstick as a boy with his cherry tree, though standards slipped somewhat during the heyday of the Rooseveltian rule. Lyndon Johnson, for example, used to brag in speeches that his great-great grandfather had died at the Battle of the Alamo, when actually he had died at home in bed; no one in the contemporary press apparently ever checked or corrected the

TABLE 4.2
REPORTERS' VIEWS OF HYPOCRISY AND LYING
IN SELECTED FEEDING FRENZIES

EXAMPLES OF HYPOCRISY

ON DOUGLAS GINSBURG'S SUPREME COURT NOMINATION
We were talking about the "law and order" candidate for the Supreme Court. . . .
He was not only a user but a frequent user and essentially the supplier—he would
bring it. At the time he was a professor and not a student. Also at this time the
Reagan administration had an official policy that it wouldn't hire anybody for any
position in the Justice Department who had admitted using drugs, including marijuana, after they had been admitted to the Bar. One of the follow-up stories I did
was about a guy who was almost identical to Ginsburg in every respect and had
been hired for an assistant U.S. attorney job. When he told the truth on a form that
asked had he ever used marijuana, and he said he had done so about eight years
earlier, the job offer was revoked.

Nina Totenberg, National Public Radio

ON VIRGINIA'S CHARLES ROBB
If the governor is espousing a policy of "tough on drugs," and yet he's associating
with people who are heavily into drugs, then he's presenting himself as something
that he's not, and it's fair for the press to look into that . . .

Rose Ellen O'Connor, formerly of the *Virginian-Pilot*

ON GARY HART
Gary Hart was trying to persuade the press that he was leading one kind of life,
that he and his wife had patched up whatever differences they had and that their
marriage had been repaired, and he challenged the press to go out and find otherwise. The press did find otherwise, so the issue to me was not so much that the
press was looking through peepholes at Gary Hart's private life but that the press
was exposing Gary Hart as a hypocrite.

Paul Duke, "Washington Week in Review"

Hart was making a real big show of traveling with his wife at gatherings, and he
was always bringing up his church background and the fact that he had gone to di-
vinity school. The image he was trying to project was basically that of a very religious family man.

Karen Tumulty, *Los Angeles Times*

The weekend before Hart spent the weekend in Washington with Donna Rice, he
was campaigning with his wife. She was with him in the car when I interviewed
him. He talked about his marriage, how it had been rocky, how they'd gone
through this tough period and now they were back together and their marriage
was more solid than ever. So the Donna Rice episode comes along, and it's obvious
Hart has been presenting a lie about his life to the public, to me. He was exposed
as a fraud.

Fred Barnes, *The New Republic*

ON DAN QUAYLE
Here's a man who is from the right wing of his party, a real hawk. It is not that I
faulted him for deciding that he didn't want to go toVietnam. Rather, it was the hypocrisy of it that was driving me. What did that mean for someone who might ultimately be sending people to war? Is this guy going to do one thing and say
another?

Ellen Hume, formerly of the *Wall Street Journal*

TABLE 4.2 (*Cont.*)

What made the Quayle National Guard story was the fact that he was such a hawk on Vietnam and in Congress. If he hadn't been such a hawk, it would have meant little.

Jack Germond, *Baltimore Sun*

EXAMPLES OF LYING

ON THOMAS EAGLETON

He had hidden his medical history from McGovern. When he was called and asked about his skeletons, he said there weren't any. Well, there was actually a hell of a skeleton in the closet. Either his judgment was so bad he didn't know a skeleton when he saw one, or he lied.

Brooks Jackson, formerly of the Associated Press

ON JESSE JACKSON AND "HYMIETOWN"

The controversy was heightened by the fact that Reverend Jackson largely ignored the lessons of Damage Control 101, and for about two weeks denied, ducked and dodged, gave these non-denial denials—"something like that would be out of character for me."

Milton Coleman, *Washington Post*

ON PAT ROBERTSON'S KOREAN WAR RECORD

I was in the same war he was, and my war record was even less heroic than his was. But the difference is that he bragged about [combat experience he did not have]; he misrepresented and lied about his record. That gets into the question of what kind of president he'd be if he can't tell the truth about his past.

Robert Novak, columnist and commentator

ON GARY HART

I wandered over to the courthouse in Hart's home town, and looked up the records on his name change. He had said that it was his family's wishes—that he was off in school when it happened. That was nonsense—he was there. He was the one who appeared in court, and he gave reasons of his own for the change.

George Lardner, Jr., *Washington Post*

Here Hart was, fresh from a television performance in which he said he had changed; he wasn't [womanizing]. But the fact of the matter was that a night or two before he had called on this [Washington] woman [with whom he had had a long-term affair]. And so we thought that the leading candidate for president of the United States was plainly lying and that was worth a story.

Benjamin Bradlee, *Washington Post*

ON DAN QUAYLE

Quayle had clearly opted out of active duty during Vietnam for which I have the utmost sympathy since I did the same thing. The guy had clearly used influence to get into the National Guard, too. . . . After having done that, he said he couldn't remember how he got into the National Guard. I want to tell you something, if you were facing the draft during the Vietnam War, and you didn't want to fight in this war, you remember how you got into the National Guard the same way you remember your first sexual experience. That was a lie and that was damning.

Richard Cohen, *Washington Post*

SOURCE: Interviews conducted for this volume.

record.[28] Truth telling became a sacrament again after Watergate, and a number of frenzies have been started or accelerated by lies, fibs, and half-truths. (See table 4.2 again for a sampling.) Sometimes the lie itself becomes the pretext for revealing a hidden private vice. The Cleveland *Plain Dealer* cited Governor Celeste's denial that he had a 'Gary Hart problem' as one key reason for its exposé of his extramarital affairs, for instance.[29] More often, a politician's refusal to admit the truth worsens the original offense, as suggested by aspects of the frenzies involving Ted Kennedy, Tom Eagleton, Gary Hart, Jesse Jackson, Pat Robertson, Michael Dukakis, and Dan Quayle. Documented lying in past instances usually toughens the scrutiny, whether the deceit was willful (Hart on his name, age, and so on, in 1984) or relatively innocent (Dukakis misleading the press about the purpose of his wife's 1982 hospitalization for drug dependency.[30]) The coverup—a politically perfected form of mendacity—always compounds the original error whenever the disguise is discovered, and Watergate is of course the modern original. Even the appearance of a coverup is enough to send a shiver down the spine of most campaign managers. Eagleton's refusal to release his full hospitalization records and Quayle's insistence that his college academic transcript remain private inevitably produced more ink and air time on the embarrassing subjects than they already merited. (The press speculation about a matter is frequently worse than the reality—though in Eagleton and Quayle's cases that may not be true.[31]) Finally subterfuge and dirty tricks, once common techniques out of style since Watergate, are forms of deception guaranteed to shake a campaign's foundations. Dukakis's managers learned this anew after the anti-Biden "attack video" chicanery was uncovered. The irony was that Biden's plagiarism was a perfectly legitimate subject for campaign debate, but the surreptitious manner of its introduction and the shameless buck-passing that followed produced damage to Dukakis that almost equalled Biden's penalty.[32]

Frenzies Build on One Another

Frenzies get their rocket thrust not only from the fuel provided by candidates but also from the booster generated by other frenzies past and present. In short, frenzies build on one another. They do so by incorporation; that is, topics from each frenzy are incorporated into the repertoire of legitimate journalistic inquiry. In this fashion every frenzy sets new precedents that can be cited to justify another.

Sometimes the attempt is made to spawn more frenzies in the wake of a major one. An Associated Press reporter in Louisiana surveyed each candidate for governor after Gary Hart's fall, asking point-blank, "Have you ever committed adultery?"[33] The Hart-Rice frenzy also encouraged the publication of Governor Celeste's affairs, and set the tone for consideration of the "Bush mistress" rumor, Henry Cisneros's extramarital relationship, and even John Tower's confirmation hearings. More importantly, candidates were given notice that the press would be scrutinizing this area of their lives in the future. And not just national politicians were affected; inevitably, frenzies have a trickle-down effect, and state and local campaigns adopt most of the same rules as federal ones.

The press's search for a trend line is obvious in all the "character frenzies" of recent years. A sensational revelation in one political camp leads reporters to search for similar discoveries and patterns elsewhere, as demonstrated by the roving confessional on drug use that followed the Ginsburg admission. Two Democratic presidential candidates, U.S. Senator Albert Gore of Tennessee and former Arizona Governor Bruce Babbitt, acknowledged youthful marijuana indulgence, as did a number of other Democratic liberals (such as U.S. Senators Claiborne Pell of Rhode Island and Lawton Chiles of Florida) and Republican conservatives (such as U.S. Representative Newt Gingrich of Georgia and Connie Mack of Florida). Perhaps because their drug use, unlike Ginsburg's, was basically restricted to casual experimentation, none suffered any noticeable political damage. Massachusetts politicians decided that on this issue there was safety in numbers. In 1990 about a dozen officeholders—including U.S. Senator John Kerry, U.S. Congressman Joseph Kennedy, and several statewide officials—rushed to confess mistakes of the past. The mass mea culpa was sparked by the state attorney general's admission of drug use, and it seemed to be a useful strategy. The developing frenzy was short-circuited and quickly converted into a revival meeting flooded by repentant sinners; all were guilty so no one stood out, and everyone's soul was cleansed in the process. Another lesson is apparent from the drug-use frenzies that have been building around the country: Only ye without sin had better cast that stone. In the 1990 Texas Democratic primary runoff for governor, state Attorney General Jim Mattox charged his opponent, State Treasurer Ann Richards, with use of marijuana and cocaine dating back about a decade. Richards admitted being a recovering alcoholic but refused all comment on the drug allegations, leading many to conclude they were true. In good part because of the issue, Mattox appeared to be making some headway in the campaign until just a few days before the election, when two newspapers printed statements from a Hous-

ton attorney and a former Dallas vice-squad officer swearing they
had witnessed Mattox smoke marijuana in the early 1970s.[34] Richards
then won the primary.

Most other candidates have not been as fortunate as Richards once
they found themselves in the vortex of a frenzy. Normally, once a
politician is wounded, open season is declared, and any damaging
item—related or unrelated to the pattern of the first offense—can be
introduced for public consumption. This pyramiding or pile-on can
finish off a pol who has survived the first onslaught, since "once a
guy is bloody, it is awfully easy to assume that seven other assertions
are true," explains ABC News's Jeff Greenfield. Several news organizations checked every shred of Joseph Biden's campaign position
papers and speeches to find a new "old" unattributed sentence or
phrase. After its original revelations about Donna Rice, the *Miami
Herald* was "besieged with hundreds of people calling and writing
with the 'ultimate' news story about Hart and his various girlfriends,
imaginary and otherwise," according to the *Herald*'s Jim Savage.
(Hart was out of the race before most of the credible-sounding items
could be checked out.) Interestingly, the Hart frenzy also generated
"allegations to the *Herald*—from homosexuality to drug use—about
nearly every other candidate in the contest," Savage recalls, and
many of our interviewees said this phenomenon was observed at
their news outlets as well. Reporters, it would seem, are not the only
ones driven into frenzy by the scent of blood; party activists, the
staffs of rival candidates, and even a few average citizens take part
when circumstances allow.

Another fascinating aspect of pyramidal frenzies is the resurrection of dead-and-buried charges when a frenzy develops. A good
example is the allegation against Dan Quayle by Paula Parkinson,
the former Washington lobbyist best known for her bedside manner.
In 1980 Quayle was one of three congressmen who shared a cottage
with Parkinson during a Florida golfing trip, but long ago he had
been cleared of any role in the sex-for-influence scandal by an FBI
investigation. Yet almost immediately after his nomination was
announced, the print and especially the broadcast media began linking Quayle's name to Parkinson again. This recycled canard was
given extended life when Parkinson's two former lawyers later said
their ex-client, possessing not the best of reputations coupled with an
affinity for publicity, had claimed in 1981 that Quayle made an unre-
quited pass at her.[35] Understandably, Quayle may have longed for
the era, not long past, when a Southern senator running for reelection is said to have silenced an opponent who was dredging up an-

cient sins with this retort: "You can't bring that up. They proved that on me in the last election!"

The Quayle frenzy, in fact, is the paradigm of pyramiding. The pile-on of charges that took place from the convention onwards was perhaps unprecedented in its scope. The National Guard issue and the Paula Parkinson matter were quickly joined by controversies about his academic record, possible favoritism in his admission to law school, and extensive rumors about womanizing and drug use. At the time the swirl of allegations around Quayle might have seemed a bit familiar in content and tone because his frenzy was the culmination and consolidation of a series of prior ones. Not only was the manner of the Quayle journalistic inquest shaped by the precedents set during the previous vice presidential frenzies surrounding Ferraro and Eagleton, but the variety of charges lodged against him included aspects of the four character antecedents in 1987 and 1988: Hart's womanizing, Biden's grades, Robertson's war record, and Ginsburg's drug use were all revisited in one grand campaign spectacular.

As suggested in an earlier section, partisanship plays a major role in stoking the frenzy fires in most cases. Not infrequently, frenzies build on one another as a direct result of partisan hijinks, oneupmanship, and revenge. These "tit-for-tat" frenzies include the ethics scandals that engulfed Washington in 1989. Republicans angered by John Tower's treatment pointed to questionable episodes in some Democrats' pasts, assisted by allies in the media. The *Wall Street Journal* reprinted a 1972 *Atlanta Journal* account of a quarter-century-old alcohol-related hit-and-run offense to which Georgia Democratic U.S. Senator Sam Nunn—one of Tower's main antagonists—pleaded guilty.[36] The *Washington Times* chimed in with a graphic, lurid account of sexual misconduct and alcohol abuse by some leading congressmen, including, of course, Senator Ted Kennedy.[37] The author of the piece, George Archibald, explained:

Some of our editors thought it was hilarious that the hypocrites up on the Hill were pointing the finger at one of their colleagues when so many of them had their own problems . . . The Teddy Kennedy [revelations] were picked up the next week by the *National Enquirer* and the *National Examiner*. I didn't know whether to take the supermarket tabloids' interest as a compliment or a [warning] that I needed to watch myself about being a little too explicit in some of my reporting.

The ethics frenzy gradually escalated to include long simmering charges against Speaker Jim Wright, as well as allegations of lesser offenses against several other legislators in both parties. The partisan-fed orgy reached its climax, at least for the year, after personal-life rumors about new Speaker Thomas Foley surfaced in June 1989.

The Wright frenzy also demonstrated how pyramiding can provide the means to include lightning-rod incidents only tangentially related to the frenzy's target. In the midst of Wright's financial troubles, the *Washington Post* published a lengthy story about a woman who had been the victim of a brutal, near-fatal 1973 assault by Wright's top aide and relative by marriage, John Mack, who was then nineteen years old. Reporters at the *Post*, the *New York Times*, and many other news organizations had been aware of the crime and Mack's light twenty-seven-month incarceration for at least two years, but all had agreed it was not newsworthy since much time had passed and Mack had paid his debt to society.[38] It suddenly became newsworthy in May 1989, and the powerfully emotional reaction to the gruesome details of Mack's attempted murder did immeasurable but undoubted damage to Wright just as the public was being presented with the Speaker's career-threatening financial imbroglio. The *Post*'s full-page ''Style'' interview about Mack's victim appeared May 4, 1989; Mack quit his job May 11; Wright resigned his Speakership by month's end.

Occasionally there can be a ''build-down'' as well as a ''buildup'' in successive frenzies. Many in the press were shell-shocked by the severe criticism the news media received after the Hart-Rice disclosures, and some were skittish about pursuing similar stories in the immediate aftermath. Reporters for the *Richmond Times-Dispatch* and the *Virginian-Pilot* cited this as an inhibiting factor in their treatment of Chuck Robb's private life, for example. Rose Ellen O'Connor of the *Pilot* remembers: ''The Hart story really threw a kink in the works, because we didn't want to do a *People* magazine piece. So I was a little conservative in what I pushed [the newspaper to publish], and we limited the womanizing [part of the Robb story].'' This same attitude caused many journalists to be cautious about the ''Bush mistress'' rumor as well. Ironically Gary Hart's fate made conceivable some reporting on Bush's private life, yet it also proved advantageous to Bush in the end, as *Newsweek*'s Howard Fineman suggests: ''Having already gone through the self-doubt and flogging about the Hart episode, the press was a little squeamish about pursuing Bush. In that sense Bush first suffered and ultimately benefited from the press's rather gun-shy attitude after Hart." These press inhibitions were a temporary phenomenon, as the Tower confirmation hearings and many other episodes since then have demonstrated. Competitive pressures, the search for a pattern, the persistence of the character issue, and other factors under discussion in this volume ensure that taboos, once broken, are rarely reinstated and that a frenzy in gestation inevitably displays behavior induced by genes inherited from its ancestors.

Social Conditions and Public Opinion

In a healthy democracy, public opinion affects all major developments in government and politics, frenzies included. And changes in public opinion—as well as evolving social conditions and popular culture—have helped to create circumstances favoring the development of virtually all the recent frenzies. In many ways the "new journalism" has merely reflected the modern desires of readers and viewers who financially sustain it.

Since the 1950s America has undergone a social glasnost that is sweeping and astounding. In 1962 David Brinkley, then of NBC News, was not permitted to use the words *venereal disease* on television; today, modest viewers are grateful when the formal term and not the slang is employed over the airwaves. Moreover, the range of subjects considered fit for public discussion is virtually unlimited in the 1990s, as just a glance at television or popular magazines will reveal. At the same time, attitudes on everything from acceptable language to divorce to homosexuality have liberalized, and the news media have both led and followed this cultural revolution.[39]

Large-circulation personality magazines and "trash TV" have conditioned their audiences to thinking about the private lives of public figures. This "Oprah Winfrey–*People* magazine" mentality meshes nicely with the personalizing effect of television itself so that a kind of celebrity politics is created: Public careers become soap operas, coverage of elective stars becomes indistinguishable from the focus on the Hollywood or sports[40] variety, and the appetite for tidbits about officials' private lives grows as a natural consequence. Inquiring minds want to know, so "there is virtually nothing we would not print in the newspaper now, if we had the goods," asserts *Washington Post* ombudsman Richard Harwood.

One event (Watergate) and two contradictory social movements (feminism and fundamentalist Christianity) have had special impacts on the public opinion that feeds frenzies. The post-Watergate generation of Americans is more cynical about politicians, less tolerant of corruption, and ever receptive to the explosion of public myths. Watergate's legacy was the passage of much tougher conflict-of-interest and ethics laws across the country, which have simultaneously raised the standards of good behavior and set new hair-trigger traps for public officials.[41] As "ABC World News Tonight" anchor Peter Jennings puts it: "We in the media are playing against the backdrop of a fairly righteous, I almost said self-righteous, public at the moment, which calls men and women to higher standards than we might have held them to ten or fifteen years ago." Also after Watergate, politicians were encouraged by character-sensitive journalists and mood-sensing consultants to share more of the personal details of their lives with a suspicious electorate. Feminism reinforced the trend toward this examination of private character. "The women's movement made what we used to call the 'male prerogative' unfashionable," acknowledges *The New Republic*'s Fred Barnes. "Before feminism we envied and admired Jack Kennedy for dipping his wick all over town, but no longer." There is a parallel here to the civil rights movement's effect on journalism, as native Southerner Bill Kovach, who began his newspaper career in 1959, explains:

The notion that a powerful political figure, normally white male, would have an affair with a woman was long considered part of life. It wasn't until the women's movement came along and women became more active in helping define what behavior was acceptable that the definition of news changed, and how men treated women became newsworthy. It was the same way in the Old South where the most well meaning people in the world didn't consider the notion of segregation and discrimination a news story—not until the civil rights movement forced Southerners to confront the notion that, "wait a minute, by God, that's a story!"

　　Oddly enough, the rise of Christian fundamentalism has complemented feminism's enhancement of the character issue despite the ideological polarity of the two movements. In the 1980s, out of a rediscovered belief that government has a moral dimension, Christian evangelical preachers led their flocks to new heights of political activism. In the Christian view, public officials, as role models for the young, should be exemplary individuals in all sectors of life, private conduct most definitely included. Even as individual evangelicals, such as Jim Bakker and Jimmy Swaggart, fell from grace because of their own personal peccadilloes, the fundamentalist perspective had some appeal to an America more attuned to conservatism in the 1980s and less enamored of the sexual revolution after the onset of the AIDS epidemic. In addition to promiscuity, alcohol abuse became much less acceptable over the last decade—and therefore, more reportable for a press reflecting changing mores.

Just as overarching social trends determine the universe of legitimate frenzy subjects, so too does public opinion about any specific frenzy affect that frenzy's course. Granted, the effect is often diffuse and ambiguous. First of all, most of the public simply is not much interested in political events. Gallup surveys for the Times-Mirror Center for the People and the Press conducted from 1986 to 1989 showed that 80 percent of Americans paid close attention to the *Challenger* space-shuttle disaster and 69 percent followed carefully the story of a young Texas girl's rescue from a backyard well, but only 37 percent closely followed the Quayle frenzy, 28 percent the Hart-Rice exposé, and 15 percent Speaker Jim Wright's scandal.[42] Second, most polls about matters not near and dear to the public's heart can be misleading, since the minority that cares passionately about a candidate's offense—and as a consequence is permanently alienated from him or her—may be obscured by the majority's apathy. Third, one suspects the public does not always give completely honest answers to pollsters' questions about frenzies. As we shall see, many people claim to be wholly uninterested in the racy side of political scandals and critical of the press for reporting it. But "that's part of the hypocrisy of the great American public," says columnist Jack Kilpatrick. "They damn the media for being prurient, but by God, they've got their noses in the paper hanging on every word we write." This hypocritical voyeurism, combined with intense concern by a minority of individuals, guarantees a substantial readership and viewership for the media's coverage of frenzies. As for the general public indifference, most reporters seem to adopt the viewpoint of the *Wall Street Journal*'s Al Hunt:

People tell me all the time "Oh, the public's bored with that." The public's bored with everything. The public's not nearly into politics the way we think it is. We love to believe that everyone's on the edge of their seat, waiting to learn the latest junk, but they're not.

At the same time there is evidence that public opinion, or at least the opinion of those paying attention, does make some difference in the frenzy's outcome. The *Washington Post*'s Paul Taylor sees the interested public as "very shrewd" in its judgments: "Despite the fact that nuance and subtlety gets lost in coverage, people monitor these things with incredibly fine antennae and they decide whether we've gone too far or whether we've hit the nail on the head, and almost always that determines whether the target survives or doesn't survive." The public certainly has to be tolerant of, or predisposed to hear, the charges made against a candidate, or the electorate will ignore them—a decision frequently sensed by the press, which will consequently deemphasize the frenzy or desist entirely. Referring to the revelation about Pat Robertson's "miracle baby," ABC's Jeff Greenfield notes, "The public decided, 'who cares?' and in seventy-two hours it was gone. Very few people are so lacking in a sense of charity or compassion that they don't understand why he fudged his wedding date." Even when most people consider the totality of the accusations to be somewhat serious, as they did in the 1972 election about Watergate and in 1988 concerning Quayle, they can choose to overlook the implications. Given that solid majorities had decided to reject George McGovern and Michael Dukakis, Watergate and Quayle became secondary considerations in these two campaigns despite the substantial press attention focused on them.

Subject to the cautions expressed earlier, there is a rough pecking order of public concern about candidate vices. On the whole, voters seem more interested in establishing whether they would buy a used car from a politician than whether he or she could be beatified by the pope. When forced to choose the sin raising "the most serious questions about the ethics of the candidates," Americans select "taking money in return for political favors" (54 percent) and lying (33 percent) by a mile over excessive drinking (7 percent) and extramarital sex (4 percent).[43] A CBS News/*New York Times* poll (see below) did not require respondents to make choices but rather asked whether it was "important for the press to tell the American people that a pres-

ACCUSATIONS ABOUT PRESIDENTIAL CANDIDATE	YES, PRESS SHOULD REPORT IT (%)	RESPONDENT WOULD VOTE AGAINST CANDIDATE (%)
Uses Cocaine	89	91
Was Guilty of Cheating on Income Tax	81	65
Lied About War Record	72	46
Had Been Hospitalized for Psychiatric Treatment	70	55
Was Guilty of Drunk Driving	66	39
Was Unfaithful to His Wife	40	36

idential candidate" committed certain errors and whether those mistakes would "be enough to make you vote against him, even if you agree with him on most of the issues."[44] Once again, extramarital exploits came dead last on the public's list of election crimes.[45]

Interestingly, cocaine use is at the very top of the scale, an exception to the public's emphasis on a candidate's trustworthiness rather than personal habits, and this is undoubtedly a reflection of the seriousness of the drug problem in contemporary America. Voters make a clear distinction between cocaine and marijuana, however. Only 29 percent believe someone who has ever smoked marijuana "should be disqualified from being president" and that proportion drops to 19 percent when respondents are assured the candidate "only smoked it in college."[46] This small minority compares with the 88 percent and 95 percent who would disqualify a presidential candidate for "drinking too much" or "improperly using government information to make money for himself," respectively.

On the other hand, even marginal changes in a candidate's support can mean the difference between victory and defeat. In a case where a major frenzy results in considerable hemorrhaging of support, the results can be deadly. Even though as many people as not thought Gary Hart was telling the truth about his weekend with Donna Rice in a May 1987 *Los Angeles Times* national poll,[47] and despite a two-to-one margin favoring his staying in the race,[48] Hart's actual voter support for the nomination fell disastrously from 41 percent to 27 percent at the same time.[49]

This sort of polling ambiguity is frequently observed during a frenzy. On the one hand, many people are sympathetic to the candidate being stripped naked in the public arena; on the other hand, they do not like the newly revealed side of the politician, and their attentions turn to his or her rivals. When Hart reentered the presidential race in December 1987, half of all Democratic voters agreed with his decision and six in ten claimed they would have no problem voting for a candidate who had committed adultery.[50] When the real votes were cast in Iowa and New Hampshire shortly thereafter, Hart received virtually none.

The public's immediate response to all three recent vice presidential frenzies was especially sympathetic, concealing the long-term political damage done to the presidential nominees in each case. Only 28 percent of a *Newsweek* sample thought Tom Eagleton's hospitalizations and electric-shock treatments made him "unfit to be vice-president" and just 31 percent wanted him to resign from the Democratic ticket.[51] Yet the unanimous judgment of political professionals was

that in the nuclear age most voters would never cast ballots for someone with a record of such severe mental illness. In Geraldine
Ferraro's case, only 25 percent of the public said her handling of the
family finances problem had made them less favorable to her, and 36
percent claimed the press coverage "would have been easier if she
had been a man" (compared to only 8 percent who felt a man would
have been treated more severely).[52] But the controversy essentially
neutralized Ferraro as a campaign asset, eliminating the one significant advantage Walter Mondale seemed to have at the starting gate
of his uphill challenge to President Reagan. The initial rush of support for Dan Quayle appeared the strongest of the three vice presidential nominees', perhaps owing to the unprecedented intensity of
negative coverage on a wide range of topics. Fully 69 percent thought
the Quayle coverage had been "excessive," and 55 percent believed
it to be "unfair" as well.[53] In spite of this first-blush reaction, however, Quayle remained the chief albatross around George Bush's
neck throughout the 1988 election and may well have cost Bush a
percentage point or two in the final reckoning.

While the public is usually kinder to the politicians than are the
press and political professionals—at least in survey responses—it can
occasionally be harsher. Most journalists and consultants privately
snickered more than scowled at the Dukakis campaign's "attack
video" exposure of Joseph Biden's plagiarism, but the voters viewed
the dirty trick without much charity. Nearly three-quarters (72 percent) of the respondents in a Harris survey believed the Dukakis
camp to have been "unethical" in its actions[54]—a far greater proportion than had been upset by Biden's original transgression.[55] Yet the
vagaries of politics dictated that Biden drop out of the contest while
Dukakis went on to win it.

Already acknowledged is the public's hypocrisy of maintaining
avid interest in private-life scandals while pretending indifference
and condemning the media for covering them. Nevertheless, there
appears to be some genuine concern about the growing invasion of
privacy occurring during some frenzies. During the 1988 election season 68 percent in a CBS News/New York Times poll agreed that "too
much attention is being paid to the private lives of people seeking
high public office," and by 51 to 38 percent, Americans believed that
"television and newspapers [were] probing too deeply into the private lives of candidates rather than "getting at what the public ought
to know.'"[56] In the wake of the Hart stakeout, Americans judged the
Miami Herald's methods to be "unfairly probing into a candidate's

private life" rather than "a good job of investigative reporting" by 56 to 29 percent.[57] And after the John Tower and Jim Wright episodes a random sample of adults even narrowly decided (by 42 to 40 percent) that "we are placing too high ethical demands on our government officials"—an unusual result given the public's enduring post-Watergate expectations of politicians.[58] According to a recent study of the public's view of Congress the citizenry placed the lowest priority on stories concerning "investigations of wrongdoing"; its top priority was coverage of congressional actions that affect everyday lives.[59] This may have been another hypocritical response, but it might also suggest that the voters' scandal saturation point is reached from time to time.

The emphasis in this section has been on the public opinion's effect on press coverage, but of course the reverse effect is at least as powerful: The news media's choice of subjects and slant directly influences public opinion. Often, when media organizations conduct polls, they are merely holding up a mirror to their own coverage. The impact of the press's intense focus during a frenzy is clearly seen by opinion trends registered after the Ford "free Poland" debate gaffe in October 1976, when President Ford's pollster conducted continuous surveying from the debate's end through the following day.[60] (See figure 4.1.) The public's "instant analysis" was quite different from that of the press. Immediately following the debate the sample picked Ford as "having done the better job" in the debate match-up by 44 to 33 percent. The news media judged Ford the loser, however, almost entirely on the strength—or weakness—of the "free Poland" remark. All three networks focused on the costly mistake in their postdebate commentary. NBC's John Chancellor remembers running from the debate hall to his network's headquarters as the candidates concluded: "I told the producer to queue up the Poland gaffe, and he said, 'I've already done it.' There was no question in anyone's mind that that was the [sound bite]." Most of the major newspapers reinforced this message the following morning; so did the next evening's television coverage by concentrating on anti-Ford fallout among Eastern European ethnic groups and a press conference with the Ford campaign's key strategists at which the first eleven questions had been about Poland.[61] The drumbeat of negative coverage took a heavy and steady toll on Ford's standing over the twenty-four-hour period. The president's original debate performance edge of 44 to 33 percent became a massive Jimmy Carter lead of 62 to 17 percent—an astounding net change of 56 percentage

PRO Gerald Ford
PRO Jimmy Carter
PRO Eugene McCarthy*

Both
Neither
Don't Know/Undecided

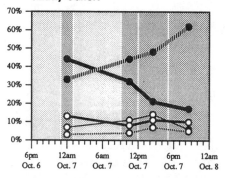

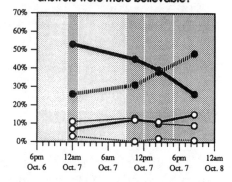

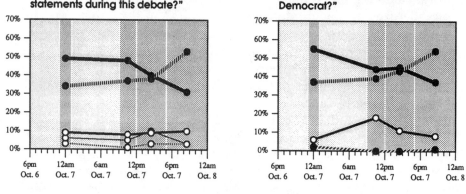

"Who do you think did the 'better job' in this debate — Gerald Ford or Jimmy Carter?"

"Generally, do you believe that (Jimmy Carter's or Gerald Ford's) answers were more believable?"

"Personally, did you most agree with (Gerald Ford's or Jimmy Carter's) statements during this debate?"

"If the presidential election were being held today, which candidate would you vote for: Gerald Ford, the Republican, or Jimmy Carter, the Democrat?"

* Eugene McCarthy was an independent candidate for president. Support for McCarthy was a volunteered response.

SOURCE AND NOTES: Compiled from data provided by President Ford's pollster, Robert Teeter of Market Opinion Research, Inc. The poll was a random-sample telephone survey from 11pm EST on October 6, 1976 to 12 midnight EST on October 7, 1976. The exact time periods of the survey on which the graph points are based are depicted by the darker shade of grey background. Between 103 and 148 interviews were conducted in each segmented time period.

FIGURE 4.1
Change in Public Reaction to the October 6, 1976, Ford-Carter Presidential Debate Through the Following Day

points. The horserace results ("If the election were held today . . . ")
showed a complete reversal. On debate evening Ford led by 55 to 37
percent; the next evening Carter romped out front by 54 to 37 percent. The decline for Ford and the rise for Carter was fairly constant
from time period to time period, as the impact of the news media's
analysis presumably penetrated an ever-increasing proportion of the
population. Over the final month of the campaign, Ford recovered
some of the lost ground and almost overtook Carter, but there is little
question that the events of October 6 and 7 were critical. The making
of the president in 1976 occurred at many points, but the news frenzy
over "free Poland" was surely one of them.

Humor

"Humor is the best medicine," goes the old aphorism, but for a
politician in trouble, humor can be a deadly brew, a compound of
sweet poison that finishes him or her off. For centuries editorial cartoonists have humbled the mighty, and occasionally helped to bring
them down; most recently, cartoonist Steve Benson of the *Arizona Republic* played a role in Governor Evan Mecham's downfall with a
daily dose of cutting satire.[62] But the most costly humor to a modern
campaign is that sponsored by the princes of television comedy:
Johnny Carson, Jay Leno, David Letterman, and Dana Carvey.[63]
Their one-liners and skits reinforce and extend the disasters that be-
fall candidates, transforming the pols from subjects of sympathy to
objects of ridicule, changing the way voters perceive the real events
on the campaign trail. Political reporters such as ABC's Ann Compton have sensed the relationship between late-night comedy and
real-life politics:

Much of the legend is set not on the evening news. . . . It's set by Carson,
and Letterman, and "Saturday Night Live." In a campaign, the gossip and
the fun bleeds into the coverage. It's not actually in the news, but it affects
the way people receive the news.

The comics have significantly shaped the images of many recent
officeholders and seekers. "Saturday Night Live" 's Chevy Chase
portrayed President Ford as an idiot and a stumblebum, preparing
the way for the interpretation of the "free Poland" gaffe as more
prima facie evidence of Ford's stupidity. President Carter's "killer
rabbit" provided fodder for endless gags about his political inepti-
tude and impotence.

Gary Hart, Dan Quayle, and John Tower may be entitled to royal-
ties for all the time they have filled as the subjects of monologues.

Letterman's "Top Ten Pickup Lines" for each beleaguered politician became instant classics, as this sampler suggests:

HART[64]	QUAYLE	TOWER
"Can a Kennedyesque guy buy you a drink?"	"Can my father buy you a drink?"	"I could have your picture on every bomber in the Air Force."
"Want to go to a nearby polling place?"	"Didn't we flunk out of school together?"	"Care to be part of a congressional probe?"
"Have you ever seen a front-runner naked?"		"Didn't we meet at Gary Hart's pool party?"

When Hart reentered the presidential contest in late 1987, he was nearly laughed back out of it. Said Letterman: "In, out, in, out—isn't that what got him in trouble in the first place? . . . The Hart campaign has had to operate on a shoestring; Gary has pretty much limited his activities to phone sex." Quayle also has proved to be a nearly irresistible butt of quips both as a nominee and as vice president. At times he has outranked all other national and world figures to become the top target of late-night television.[65]

Letterman and company are not the only sources of popular ridicule that spear candidates. The free-lance punch lines fanned by increasingly important "talk radio"[66] take a toll, too. Perhaps the most damaging joke about Quayle's National Guard Service was not ready for prime time: "What do you get when you cross a hawk with a chicken? A Quayle." Bumper stickers that catch the public's fancy make their contribution, as did this one aimed at Arizona's Evan Mecham: "Don't get mad! Get Evan."

Occasionally the most politically devastating laugh line is supplied by the candidate instead of a paid comedian. Near the end of the 1984 presidential primaries, a punchy Gary Hart expressed relief to be in California and out of New Jersey, where he had held "samples from a toxic waste dump" while his wife cuddled a koala bear in the Golden State.[67] Californians appreciated the New Jersey joke, but Garden State voters did not. Newspapers headlined the quip, and Hart lost the New Jersey primary in a landslide.

The Dynamics of the Feeding Frenzy: A Model Summary

Late-night humor is no laughing matter for many candidates, but it is merely the icing on a many-layered cake. Chapters 3 and 4 have presented and analyzed these layers—the conditions and stages of a

feeding frenzy (see figure 4.2). The prior conditions include those internal to the press's operation as well as the just-discussed external
factors that shape journalists' worldviews at any given time. All
these conditions taken together help to determine the intensity and
extent of the frenzy's fire once the spark of the candidate's mistake or
offense flashes.

That spark can be generated directly by the candidate (as Gerald
Ford did with his Poland gaffe on nationwide television) or indirectly
by the press (for example, the *Miami Herald*'s Hart stakeout) or a rival
camp (the Dukakis staff's "attack video"). Usually the press jumps
to cover the offense, though occasionally it needs a nudge, as in
Debategate. When *Time*'s Laurence I. Barrett revealed the Reagan
campaign's 1980 unauthorized acquisiton of the Carter briefing papers in his 1983 book, *Gambling with History*,[68] journalists seemed to
yawn collectively at this latest example of "politics as usual." But as
mentioned earlier, former Carter aides and a Democratic congressional investigation jump-started a scandal probe.[69]

The news media's interest in a candidate's mistake is always
piqued by the error's sexiness or universality as well as the
politician's hypocrisy, partial disclosure, attempts at lying and cover-
up, or "spins" (that is, attempts to downplay or deflect) by the staff
and political consultants. The Carter White House committed a classic goof in refusing to release the innocuous photograph capturing
the attack of the "killer rabbit," for instance.[70] Instead, "they left it to
the cartoonists to illustrate" and exaggerate the story, explains its author, Brooks Jackson.

Press reactions to any revelation include a ratcheting up of coverage, with more resources devoted to the issue and generous doses of
pack journalism and rampant speculation. "The conventional wisdom becomes set in concrete so quickly," observes *National Journal*'s
James Barnes. "You get a sense that everyone is on the phone on one
big party line, and everybody's so sure what's going to happen."
Columnist Robert Novak adds, "There's a hype, a hysteria in the air
where all disbelief is suspended, and the press is always going to the
next step: 'When's Quayle going to be dropped from the ticket?' 'Are
they going to have a miniconvention to replace Dukakis [because of
his alleged mental illness]?' "

The candidate under fire also usually reacts predictably, directing
his or her anger at the press, sometimes as an excuse to avoid full disclosure or to buy time before defusing the controversy or withdrawing altogether. There is probably less time to buy for a little-known
candidate, such as Joseph Biden, who was defined by the allegations

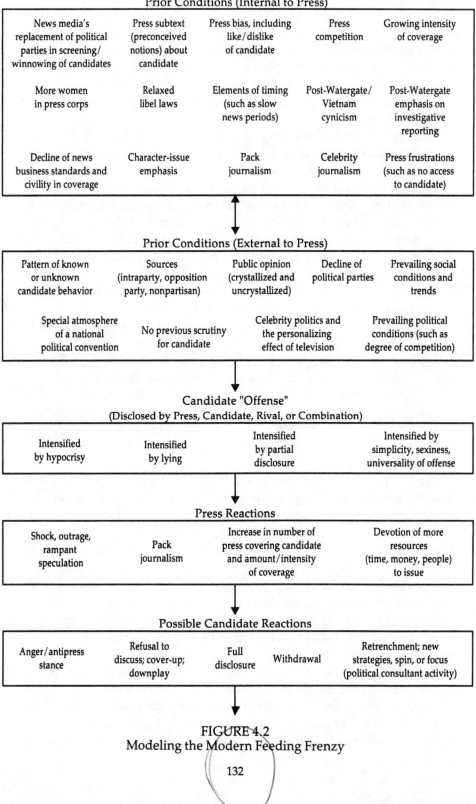

Prior Conditions (Internal to Press)

News media's replacement of political parties in screening/ winnowing of candidates	Press subtext (preconceived notions) about candidate	Press bias, including like/dislike of candidate	Press competition	Growing intensity of coverage
More women in press corps	Relaxed libel laws	Elements of timing (such as slow news periods)	Post-Watergate/ Vietnam cynicism	Post-Watergate emphasis on investigative reporting
Decline of news business standards and civility in coverage	Character-issue emphasis	Pack journalism	Celebrity journalism	Press frustrations (such as no access to candidate)

Prior Conditions (External to Press)

Pattern of known or unknown candidate behavior	Sources (intraparty, opposition party, nonpartisan)	Public opinion (crystallized and uncrystallized)	Decline of political parties	Prevailing social conditions and trends
Special atmosphere of a national political convention	No previous scrutiny for candidate	Celebrity politics and the personalizing effect of television		Prevailing political conditions (such as degree of competition)

Candidate "Offense"
(Disclosed by Press, Candidate, Rival, or Combination)

Intensified by hypocrisy	Intensified by lying	Intensified by partial disclosure	Intensified by simplicity, sexiness, universality of offense

Press Reactions

Shock, outrage, rampant speculation	Pack journalism	Increase in number of press covering candidate and amount/intensity of coverage	Devotion of more resources (time, money, people) to issue

Possible Candidate Reactions

Anger/antipress stance	Refusal to discuss; cover-up; downplay	Full disclosure	Withdrawal	Retrenchment; new strategies, spin, or focus (political consultant activity)

FIGURE 4.2
Modeling the Modern Feeding Frenzy

132

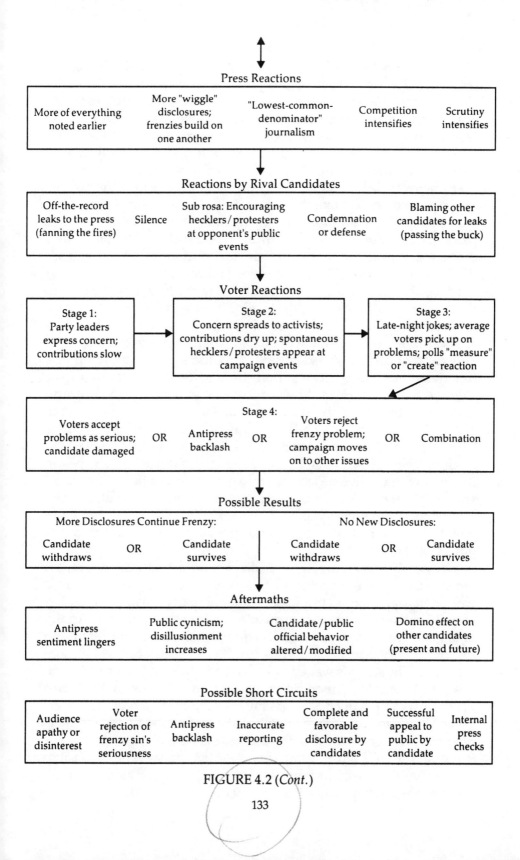

Press Reactions

| More of everything noted earlier | More "wiggle" disclosures; frenzies build on one another | "Lowest-common-denominator" journalism | Competition intensifies | Scrutiny intensifies |

Reactions by Rival Candidates

| Off-the-record leaks to the press (fanning the fires) | Silence | Sub rosa: Encouraging hecklers/protesters at opponent's public events | Condemnation or defense | Blaming other candidates for leaks (passing the buck) |

Voter Reactions

| Stage 1: Party leaders express concern; contributions slow | Stage 2: Concern spreads to activists; contributions dry up; spontaneous hecklers/protesters appear at campaign events | Stage 3: Late-night jokes; average voters pick up on problems; polls "measure" or "create" reaction |

Stage 4:

| Voters accept problems as serious; candidate damaged | OR | Antipress backlash | OR | Voters reject frenzy problem; campaign moves on to other issues | OR | Combination |

Possible Results

| More Disclosures Continue Frenzy: | | | No New Disclosures: | | |
| Candidate withdraws | OR | Candidate survives | Candidate withdraws | OR | Candidate survives |

Aftermaths

| Antipress sentiment lingers | Public cynicism; disillusionment increases | Candidate/public official behavior altered/modified | Domino effect on other candidates (present and future) |

Possible Short Circuits

| Audience apathy or disinterest | Voter rejection of frenzy sin's seriousness | Antipress backlash | Inaccurate reporting | Complete and favorable disclosure by candidates | Successful appeal to public by candidate | Internal press checks |

FIGURE 4.2 (*Cont.*)

133

of plagiarism before he had the opportunity to define himself for the larger public. Also critical at this juncture is whether television decides to make the story a major focus. If it does, the battle escalates dramatically since "television *is* the front page," as "CBS Evening News" executive producer Tom Bettag termed it. Of course, TV news coverage is not quite an independent variable in all this, as Bettag's on-air colleague Dan Rather explains: "If the *Washington Post*, the *New York Times*, or the *Los Angeles Times* runs a front-page story, particularly for more than one day, the heat's on to run it and we usually do. I don't enjoy saying that, but that's the way it works." This competitive pressure also contributes to the previously discussed lowest-common-denominator journalism and "wiggle" disclosures (also called "water-torture" journalism).[71]

Irresistibly, rival candidates are drawn to the fray, whether to fan the fires with off-the-record leaks to the press or to maneuver and attract the candidate's supporters if it looks as though the frenzy victim will not survive. Undercover, campaigns have frequently been known to encourage hecklers and demonstrators to show up at a frenzy target's public events, both to raise the temperature of the controversy and to give the news media colorful video backdrop and a hook to extend the life of the story. Dan Quayle was such a target in 1988 ("This Quayle is a chicken" was a common placard), just as Richard Nixon had been in 1952. It was in response to a protest sign reading "No Mink Coats for Nixon—Just Cold Cash" that Nixon came up with the line he later used to good effect in the "Checkers" speech: "My wife Pat wears a good Republican cloth coat."[72] (The "mink coat" reference was to a Truman administration scandal in which a secretary had accepted the gift of a nine-thousand-dollar mink coat.)

Many of the rival campaigns' challenges are actually on the record, with contenders attempting in full public view to capitalize on a wounded opponent's troubles. National party chairpersons frequently initiate attacks, too, as do interest groups offended by a gaffe or aligned with other campaigns. Thus, Polish Americans leapt into the fray to criticize Gerald Ford in 1976, *Playboy*-offended fundamentalist Christians savaged wayward son Jimmy Carter the same year, and Japanese Americans took on Spiro Agnew in 1968. Not every rival camp launches an assault on a tempting target, however. Some adhere to the old rule of politics that commands, "Never interfere with an enemy who is in the process of committing suicide." For instance, the 1972 Nixon campaign, so intent on surreptitious sabotage earlier that election year, stayed conspicuously away from all comment as the Eagleton crisis unfolded.[73]

At long last the public beyond the campaign circle is drawn into the controversy. Earlier, party leaders, activists, and contributors went on alert, but with an intensifying frenzy, campaign donations may dry up, unprompted protesters begin trailing a candidate, and average voters start to pay attention. Public opinion polls measure citizens' reactions (or create them, depending on the wording and interpretation of questions),[74] and the first late-night jokes creep into the monologues. At this juncture, the electorate—as (fallibly) measured by polls and pundits—may either judge the candidate's offense as serious, forcing him or her to withdraw or limp along in a damaged state, or deem it insufficiently weighty to merit severe punishment, in which case the candidate survives to fight another day. (The giveaway hint that it's all over is often when an official's staunchest allies defect; Arizona's Barry Goldwater served as such a messenger for both Richard Nixon in 1974 and Evan Mecham in 1988.[75]) New disclosures can revive the frenzy at any time, of course, though as the *Wall Street Journal*'s Al Hunt insists: ''Whether it should or it shouldn't, the news business has to move on. You can't freeze-frame a campaign and hold it there until every [leftover] question gets answered.'' This appeared to be the prevailing sentiment in the press corps both in 1984 after Ferraro's late-August press conference on her family finances and in 1988 once Quayle had endured close press scrutiny for about two weeks.

The aftermaths of feeding frenzies as well as possible short circuits in the frenzy process will be explored at length in chapters 7 and 8, but a few possibilities in both categories are suggested at the end of figure 4.2. The consequences range from lingering antipress sentiment among the public and politicians, to growing cynicism after another would-be emperor is unclothed, to increased scrutiny of the remaining candidates. Antidotes to the frenzy's power might include a direct and successful appeal to the public by the candidate (à la the ''Checkers'' speech) or a public backlash against press tactics (perhaps stakeouts) that rebounds to the candidate's favor.

This model of the modern feeding frenzy is merely a sketch of the dynamics that might apply in a given controversy. By no means does the frenzy always unfold in precisely this way, nor does the model convey the complexity of interactions among the various institutions and individuals constituting the political universe. Despite these obvious limitations, the model suggests a beginning of the next task at hand: a fuller description and analysis of the excesses that have characterized press coverage of some feeding frenzies.

5

Rumor and Excess

Junkyard Dog Journalism on the Prowl

Almost every big story is invariably carried to excess; the news media tend to run everything into the ground.
>   TOM BETTAG, executive producer, "CBS Evening News"

Maybe there's more of a relationship between news and pornography than we realize.
>   HOWARD FINEMAN, chief political correspondent, *Newsweek*

A critic in search of press excess need not exert him- or herself. As most journalists freely admit, it is everywhere, and nowhere in such abundance as during a feeding frenzy. This chapter will explore the extent and the circumstances of many frenzy excesses, concentrating especially on the nefarious and increasingly common practice of publishing or airing rumors for which a convincing body of evidence does not exist.

Journalists offer many reasons and excuses for the excesses documented here. Some are convincing and acceptable. Deadline pressures take an inexorable toll on quality and accuracy. ("In the middle of a massive campaign explosion we have to decide what to report by 7:00 P.M.; we don't have two weeks to debate the nuances," argues David Hoffman of the *Washington Post*.) Since the press prints only what it is told and can find out, it unavoidably publishes partial truths and distortions of reality. And every human frailty possessed by journalists is magnified because of the attention given their work by the millions who read and hear them daily.

Yet a critic's central concern about the abuses and excesses to be described shortly is that so many in the media appear to shrug their shoulders and dismiss the "inevitable" problems with one of three hackneyed formulations that might have been borrowed from *Bartlett's Familiar Quotations* or textbooks about the Fourth Estate:

"This is the price we pay for a free press."
"The public has the right to know."
"Life, and especially politics, isn't fair."

As this chapter's stories unfold, the reader may well want to ask a set of companion questions: Must the price of a free press be so high in some instances? Does the public have the right to know gossip, rumor, and innuendo? Should the news media add in such generous measure to the inherent unfairness of politics?

The Parade of Excess

The Reverend Pat Robertson once came up with a strange but appropriate (for him) theological explanation for the frenzies sweeping not only politics but religion: "Maybe God is cleaning house all around."[1] If political frenzies are divinely inspired, the press is serving as God's instrument with evangelical fervor. Many of the root problems generating journalistic abuses have already been identified in this volume: competitive pressures, pack journalism, biases of various sorts, the decline of news standards, and the corrosive post-Watergate cynicism, to mention a few. Moreover, many of the excesses that result—lowest-common-denominator journalism, "wiggle" disclosures, the overemphasis on the character issue, and so on—have also been discussed. Traces of these regrettable aspects of coverage can be found in virtually all the recent frenzies, even ones where the public official was unquestionably in the wrong. In the case of Mayor Marion Barry, for instance, every trivial tidbit and morsel about his 1990 drug arrest became a new story fed to viewers and readers, including completely false rumors broadcast during the competitive war that erupted among local television stations at the time.[2] The cameras and bright lights that were focussed on Mayor Barry intruded on the privacy of innocent and publicity-shy patients in a drug treatment center,[3] and even the movements of Barry's young son were recorded for the public to see.

Just the sight and sound of the frenzied press pack can be excessive. "Once we start, we're awful," observes CBS's Bruce Morton. "Pack journalism is ugly: four dozen reporters yelling questions, two dozen cameras in pursuit of the prey. It's not very thoughtful and it's certainly not journalism at its best." ABC's Brit Hume notes that the excessive nature of the pack is contained even in the terminology pack reporters use:

The famous phrase we employ is, ''the candidate was dogged today by controversy. . . . '' Now usually he wasn't dogged by anybody except us. We go pester somebody about something all day, and then write a lead based on it.

As the frenzy takes hold, the press becomes mesmerized by the subject and obsessed with the target. "The press absolutely blocks out every other topic and can't talk about anything else," says Ellen Hume, formerly of the *Wall Street Journal.* Journalists get carried away, caught up in an overreaction of their own making. With a loss of perspective, they cease making judgments about how much is too much and instead lock into the story line for the duration of the unfolding soap opera. In Joseph Biden's case, according to his former press secretary, Larry Rasky, "The end result was a perversion of the real Joe Biden. A hundred news organizations blurted out the same thirty seconds of information over a giant media megaphone, and Biden was damaged more because of the quantity of coverage and the absence of context than [by] any of the revelations."

The lack of balance in the coverage of most frenzies often encompasses trial by media, with an inherent presumption of guilt. "What concerns me as much as anything is the rush to judgment, with guilt assumed and extenuating circumstances rarely reported," admits "NBC Nightly News" anchor Tom Brokaw. The media also can lavish attention on a budding scandal out of all proportion to the offense.[4] This is true even when first reports are kept in perspective, as was the case with Robertson's "miracle baby." (As mentioned in an earlier chapter, the frenzy began as a brief reference buried in a lengthy *Wall Street Journal* profile.) Frequently the worst possible interpretation of a given set of circumstances becomes the press "spin," as Gerald Ford discovered after his Poland debate statement. While *Washington Monthly* editor Charles Peters "loved it because I'm a Democrat," he also calls the controversy "hideous and phony": "Any reasonable, well-informed person knew exactly what Ford meant, and the press certainly did. This was the most spectacular example of a story the press in their hearts knew was false, but willfully seized on anyway." Adds ABC News's Ann Compton:

I was at the presidential debate and in the travel pool the next day when we hounded Ford at every stop with, "What do you mean?" Now we all knew in our hearts exactly what he meant. We had been to Poland, we had seen the strength of the Catholic Church there. We knew that Poland felt this yearning for Western values and religious freedoms. What we got Ford on was a technicality, that the state of Poland was a Warsaw Pact nation. . . . The Poland frenzy lasted too long and was unforgiving.

Press mistreatment of candidates can take many other forms, including guilt by association and sensationalism. The strained efforts to link Geraldine Ferraro and her husband, John Zaccaro, to the Mafia in 1984 provided a sad example. In many instances using the most tenuous connections—such as a reputed mobster's renting of an apartment in a building Zaccaro inherited from his father in 1971 and immediately sold—some reporters seemed hell-bent on proving Ferraro's underworld ties. The *Wall Street Journal*'s Albert Hunt criticized one of his own newspaper's editorial writers, Jonathan Kwitney, as ''particularly unfair. He went back for generations trying to see if anybody's name ended in a vowel.''[5] CNN's Frank Sesno believes ''there were strong ethnic overtones in the commentary, basically saying 'they're Italian, so they must be connected with the Mafia.' '' In some stories, too, unnamed ''law enforcement officials'' were conveniently on hand to express a considered, nonspecific opinion that the allegations were true.[6] Sensationalism was present in the Ferraro case and is a part of most frenzies, but it moves front and center in any incident involving sex. From ''Geraldo'' to the print tabloids, Barney Frank and his male prostitute were assured top billing. Yet much of the establishment press was happy to ride the publicity wave as well. ''I doubt *Newsweek* put Frank on its cover because the magazine is profoundly interested in homosexuality,'' ABC's Peter Jennings wryly commented. The *Washington Times,* which first broke the scandal, showcased Frank in banner headlines for days.[7] A disapproving rival, the *Washington Post*'s Len Downie, charged that the *Times* was ''clearly crusading to drive Frank out of office; they wanted his scalp.'' And indeed, many of the front-page leads lend support to Downie's allegation: ''Tide is rolling against Frank,'' ''Democratic leaders desert Frank: 'Death drums are pounding,' lawmaker says,'' and so on. Congressman Frank's refusal to resign and his subsequent reelection in 1990 proves beyond doubt that politicians can sometimes survive the press's excesses—and their own.

More disturbing than sensationalism are the unethical practices, uncorrected errors, and invasion of innocent individuals' privacy that occur in some frenzies. Watergate's investigation established the modern standard for ends-justifies-means rule bending, with *Wash-*

ington Post sleuths Bob Woodward and Carl Bernstein underhand-
edly obtaining confidential telephone records and other information.[8]
An apparently more common unethical practice about which several
of our nonpress interviewees complained is the so-called "refused-
call barb," an unflattering reference to a public figure included in a
reporter's story to punish the official for not returning the reporter's
phone call. (It is impossible to know with any certainty whether this
complaint is justified, but it probably sometimes happens.) A far-
worse frenzy side effect is the uncorrected error, repeated daily and
compounded nightly as a controversy uncoils. Professor Hal Scott of
Harvard Law School, a close friend of his former law-school colleague Douglas Ginsburg, had the unpleasant experience of being
misidentified as the source of reports about Ginsburg's marijuana
use. (See chapter 4 for a discussion of one real source of the revelation.) Despite his denials and frantic efforts to correct the record,
Scott was unable to keep up with the incorporation taking place, as
first one media organization and then another picked up and amplified the original false report.[9] When adults such as Scott are penal-
ized it is regretable, but when the children of public officials bear any
unnecessary burden it is tragic. Unfortunately, from time to time a
child can be drawn into the frenzy net, either by proximity (Mayor
Barry's son) or because a prominent candidate or officeholder becomes a favorite target of the news media. Gary Hart's two college-
age children were harassed by reporters at their schools during
Hart's time of trial in 1987.[10] Spiro Agnew was another such politician, and his palpable hatred of the press was returned in kind. In
retrospect, says NBC's John Chancellor, "I think we were sometimes unfair to Spiro Agnew, and it's amazing that I'm saying
this—he was unfair to us!" Chancellor's competitor at ABC, Brit
Hume, supplied one such instance involving one of Agnew's
young-adult sons:[11]

When I was working for Jack Anderson in 1970 I was involved in something
I'll be sorry for all the rest of my days. The story centered on Vice President
Agnew's son Randy, who had broken up with his wife and moved in with a
male hairdresser in Baltimore. . . . We just shouldn't have done that story;
we had no reason to believe that [Randy's situation] was a result of anything
his father had done, and the vice president wasn't going around attacking
homosexuals either.

Hume's honest regret is a warning about press excess that ought to
be heeded. As Hume's ABC colleague Peter Jennings suggests,

"We're not always as conscious as we should be about the emotional and political litter we leave in our wake."

Rumors

People may expect too much of journalism. Not only do they expect it to be entertaining, they expect it to be true.

reporter and editor LEWIS LAPHAM[12]

Lapham is wrong. People have every right to expect the truth from the press, and most journalists fully accept their responsibility to report the news accurately. Despite deadline pressure, and even though the news is only the proverbial "rough first draft of history," newspeople by and large do a remarkably good job of delivering a reasonably reliable version of events. That is why the trend toward publishing and airing unverified rumors is so deeply disturbing, a throwback to the unbridled days of the early nineteenth century when journalists were little more than gossipmongers.

Granted, the reader's appetite for titillation has always motivated the press, and "half the people in the newsroom are here because they like to gossip and get paid for it," as the *Washington Post*'s Milton Coleman puts it. Then, too, rumors are part of the fabric of the political community, woven into the day-to-day contact reporters have with political consultants, activists, and officials. But the trafficking in innuendo has accelerated dramatically in recent years. A newsman for one of America's most prestigious publications recalled that in 1988 rumors were coming in so fast and furious "we had to separate them into categories of 'above the belt' and 'below the belt.' " When the telephone would ring at the desk of National Public Radio's Nina Totenberg, her colleague Cokie Roberts would tease, "Sex or drugs, Nina?" The sewer of hearsay has become the new mainstream of American politics for a long, sick season. Partly, the age of pervasive negative campaigning has created the conditions conducive to the spread of sleaze. Political consultants apply the knife of gossip with surgical skill, "getting a dozen people aggressively asking, 'have you heard the one about . . . ' until enough chatter develops so that the press starts to think it's true," as Democratic political operative Michael McCurry describes it. But mainly, tattle is taking center stage in politics because everyone knows the press will print it, even without proof, if not on the front page then in "style" sections or gossip columns where lower standards sometimes prevail.[13] And under the lowest-common-denominator rule, only one media outlet need give the story legitimacy before all can publish or broadcast it guilt-free.

The on-the-record rumor mill is being fed by a growing belief among some journalists that even *unproved* facts, if widely accepted as true, can have a substantial effect on a campaign or public official, and are therefore reportable. "If you haven't been able to confirm the rumors, but the rumors won't die, that is a legitimate news story," insists one senior television journalist. Also supposedly appropriate for public consumption are allegations made by only indirectly connected but "credible" sources, whether evidence is on hand or not. Both guideposts represent a substantial and unwise lowering of the threshold for publishing and broadcasting information, which results in unwarranted damage being done to public figures and inaccurate reports reaching the public. It may sometimes seem to journalists that "everyone knows" the scuttlebutt, but that is only because a newsperson's universe of contacts is public affairs oriented. In truth, the circulation of any unpublished political rumor is usually restricted to a small circle of political elites—until the press makes it a general topic of conversation via newsprint and the airwaves. Consider the unfairness and injustice in these five recent examples:

- When Michael Dukakis's campaign sent out the "attack video" that torpedoed Joseph Biden's candidacy, Richard Gephardt at first received the blame. Private speculation about the identity of the perpetrator was unavoidable, but when the conventional wisdom fingered Gephardt and this conclusion seeped into print—as it did almost everywhere—the Missouri congressman's campaign for the Democratic presidential nomination was dealt a body blow. Gephardt's 1988 press secretary, Don Foley, offered this assessment:

  It did us a lot of damage. Up until that time Dick Gephardt was viewed by most people as someone who would not engage in dirty campaigning, and he had a Boy Scout image. But this incident painted him as somebody who was a bit overanxious for the prize; in the eyes of a lot of people this took the shine off of the Gephardt aura.

  Even when Dukakis's staff was revealed to be behind Biden's troubles, the tarnish seemed to stick to Gephardt's image.
- Not long after Biden's plagiarism became the focus of the nascent 1988 campaign, the Champaign, Illinois *News-Gazette* published an article based purely on hearsay alleging that Jesse Jackson had left

the University of Illinois in 1960 after plagiarizing an English term paper. The sole sources for the story were two college acquaintances of Jackson who told the newspaper they had heard about the incident from others. The Associated Press sent out a dispatch based on the *News-Gazette* account that was used by many major newspapers throughout the country.[14] As it turned out, the professor who supposedly discovered Jackson's perfidy could not recall it, and the president of the University of Illinois certified that Jackson's academic record contained no notation of any disciplinary action for plagiarism.[15]

- Texas's 1990 Republican gubernatorial candidate Clayton Williams was victimized by published suggestions that "honey hunts," a special Western kind of sexual frolic, had taken place on his ranch. Not a shred of evidence that any such hunt occurred was ever produced by the press or his opponents, but state newspapers printed the rumor on the pretext of his denial when he was asked about it by a *Houston Post* reporter.[16] *Newsweek* followed up by headlining a "Periscope" item, "Rumors of a Honey Hunt," and helpfully recounted all variations of the canard:

In one version of the story, it's a form of entertainment favored by Williams and his chums, who strip to their underwear at his ranch and shoot water pistols at nymphs dancing in the nude. Another version has Williams inviting prostitutes to tag along at deer hunts and cattle roundups. A third sends Williams to Africa on safari with hookers in tow.[17]

- In a lengthy profile of Governor Gaston Caperton (D., W. Va.) and his marital and political troubles, the *Washington Post* strongly implied that Caperton might be a homosexual.[18] Noting that the governor's divorce raised "questions about [his] personal life," the article surmised that Caperton "was able to deal with new rumors about his sexuality by letting it be known that he was seeing" a prominent Wheeling woman. While such rumors were apparently circulating in West Virginia, stoked mainly by Caperton's Republican opponents, close family and political associates of Caperton have convincingly insisted the homosexual characterization is untrue, and thus the *Post* placed an unfair, additional burden on an unpopular, struggling governor. Incidentally Caperton has since wed the Wheeling woman, now West Virginia's first lady.
- *Westword*, a Denver weekly newspaper, published a cover story headlined "The Rumor About Romer" in June 1990. "Romer" was (and is) Colorado's Democratic Governor Roy Romer, and the

"rumor" was that he had maintained a longtime sexual relationship with his top female aide.[19] Both individuals strenuously denied it, their anger all the more intense because *Westword* offered no proof—just numerous unnamed sources who "think" the two are "much more than friends and co-workers." *Westword*'s limited circulation might have contained the damage, but the *Denver Post* picked up the story, quoting *Westword*, of course.[20]

These five incidents are not isolated examples, but part of a pattern every bit as convincing as the "character" continuums that capture the attention of the contemporary news media. Again and again, the same questionable practices noted in the above examples have arisen in national politics, affecting the careers of Jack Kemp, Gary Hart, Michael Dukakis, Dan Quayle, George Bush, John Tower, and Tom Foley. Each of these national cases will be examined in turn, in the rough chronological order of their development.

JACK KEMP[21]

Some candidates have provided the press with satisfactory answers to questions about rumors on numerous occasions, only to be asked the same questions over and over again. For two decades this has been the problem facing Jack Kemp, the former New York congressman and 1988 Republican presidential candidate who currently runs the Department of Housing and Urban Development for the Bush administration.

When Kemp was a star quarterback for the Buffalo Bills in the 1960s, he donated much of his free time to the campaigns of prominent Republicans. In 1967 Kemp was rewarded for his efforts with a three-month, off-season job as an assistant to one of California Governor Ronald Reagan's highest-ranking aides. Unfortunately for Kemp, this was precisely the time when a "homosexual clique" among Reagan's staff was exposed. An internal investigation mounted by Reagan's legal affairs adviser Edwin Meese and communications director Lyn Nofziger identified the members of the ring that included Kemp's boss, and those involved were asked to resign. The reason for the resignations was not reported at the time, but two months later, after Nofziger leaked word of the incident to six reporters, an October 31, 1967, syndicated column by Drew Pearson reported "that a homosexual ring [had] been operating in [Reagan's] office." Pearson also said that an "athlete" was involved.[22]

Pearson's column was the original published source of a false rumor that would grow and persist for decades: that Jack Kemp had been or was still a homosexual. Everywhere Kemp turned in the 1970s, the gossip seemed to follow him. It was the subject of private speculation in his congressional campaigns (Kemp was first elected to the U.S. House from a Buffalo district in 1970), it surfaced behind the scenes at the 1976 Republican National Convention, and it threatened his presidential ambitions as he geared up for a possible White House run in the late 1970s.

Some of Kemp's advisers decided on a bold move to spike the rumor: Absolutely confident the allegation was false, they would attempt to have the rumor fully investigated by a reputable journalist, with the results published independently of the campaign. One of Kemp's closest confidantes, writer Jude Wanniski, told all to the *New York Times*'s White House correspondent Martin Tolchin, who was preparing an October 1978 article about Kemp for *Esquire*.[23] When Tolchin questioned Kemp about the matter, the congressman stated flatly, "There is absolutely not a shred of evidence. There is nothing, and there was nothing." Kemp explained that he had simply invested in property with his Reagan administration boss. Unknown to Kemp, his boss had used the property (a Lake Tahoe ski lodge) for parties with other homosexual members and associates of the administration. Kemp said he had never seen the place, and that his investment was strictly a financial decision. Tolchin confirmed Kemp's account, published his findings, and concluded, "Everyone who has looked into the case has come to the same conclusion." It seemed like a vindication, but two months later columnists Rowland Evans and Robert Novak were moved to write a column about the "ugly and malicious calumny" being spread about Kemp by an unnamed, high-ranking Carter White House aide as well as John White, then chairman of the Democratic National Committee. Sure enough, the "garbage" and "gutter communications" riling Evans and Novak was once again the gossip about Kemp's sexual orientation. The columnists launched their own exhaustive inquiry, and summarized the results for their readers:

After considerable checking, we can now report that the rumor comes as close to being disprovable as any personal slander ever is. For example, contrary to one recurrent part of the rumor, there never was any police file on Kemp; he was not investigated.

One principal in the 1967 case whom we tracked down with some difficulty to his new job and life said he never had known or been told of any illicit association between Kemp and those who resigned under a cloud. Indeed, the sole source of the rumor that has haunted Kemp's career for eleven years is the fact that he traveled, on an official basis, several times with one of the Reagan aides who later resigned. That, and nothing more, is the "case" against Kemp.[24]

Yet, in a telling commentary on human nature, the charge continued to be remembered better than the emphatic exoneration. Despite these back-to-back 1978 debunkings, the squalid rumor continued its underground life. In the summer of 1985, as Kemp was gearing up for his 1988 presidential campaign, his aides again decided to confront the rumor in interviews with reporters for *Vanity Fair* and *Newsweek*.[25] Kemp's press secretary, John Buckley, had learned of the *Vanity Fair* reporter's interest in the "gay" rumor; one of Kemp's friends from the National Football League had tipped Buckley after an inquiry from the reporter. So Buckley called the newswoman (Marie Brenner), informed her that he had "heard the drums along the Mohawk," knew what she was up to, and proposed the following ground rules:

You can ask him any question you want. If you find anything based on your investigation, print it. If you find that the guy is gay, print that he's gay. But if you can't find anything, do one of two things. Either don't go into it, or print the fact that you've looked into it and there is nothing there.

And that, says Buckley, became the Kemp camp's formula for rumor control, at least in the beginning of the campaign. At about the same time, Howard Fineman of *Newsweek* approached Buckley, interested in the same subject. It was not a coincidence. According to Buckley, Brenner had told colleagues of her belief that *Newsweek* had had the goods on Kemp for years but had not published them; this got back to *Newsweek*, which decided it had better investigate what it didn't have.

Fineman's article ran before Brenner's, but both reached the same predictable conclusion: The rumors were untrue. Fineman retraced the history of the gossip, and quoted Lyn Nofziger: "They are vicious rumors [and] there is no evidence at all that anything happened." Kemp himself opened up to Fineman, expressing his hope "that any fair-minded person who reads about a rumor—many of which float in and out of Washington all the time—will dismiss something that has nothing to back it up." Instead Kemp's explanations only fueled more speculation and investigation. CBS's "West 57th" show explored the rumor but eventually decided not to air the matter. "I could have done what everyone else was doing at the time [which] was gathering all the rumors up and passing them off as a story," executive producer Andrew Lack says. "[But] four rumors don't make a story. I found no evidence that supported those rumors or . . . that would lead you to believe that [the rumors] were true, and so I dropped the story."

NBC's "Today" show, on the other hand, took a less admirable approach, and aired a story about Kemp on March 13, 1986, in which Kemp was asked point-blank whether he was gay or had ever been involved in a homosexual incident; he once again "categorically" and "absolutely" denied the rumors.[26] The segment's producers showed pictures of the *Newsweek* and *Vanity Fair* stories, not as Kemp's vindication or as proof that the rumors were false, but rather as a pretext justifying their decision to pop the question themselves. Kemp's answers to the "Today" questions were reported in an Associated Press story that was subsequently picked up by a number of daily newspapers.

"Today" show executive producer, Steve Friedman, defended the Kemp segment, claiming that "it would have been journalistically unsound not to raise [the rumor issue]. We gave Kemp an opportunity to put the rumor to rest, which he did"[27]—for the umpteenth time. John Buckley, on the other hand, called Friedman a "scumbag," decried NBC's "irresponsible journalism," and despaired that there would ever be an end to the scurrilous rumor. The Kemp campaign had incorrectly assumed that the questioning by reporters on this subject would stop once one prestigious news organization (such as *Newsweek*) showed that the rumor was false. "It's quicksand," Buckley says. "Because once you stick your toe in, you start getting sucked in." Moreover, by cooperating with the media and even encouraging "tell-all" stories, a candidate can aid and abet the spreading of the very rumor he hopes to squelch. For instance, reporters who call around attempting to verify or debunk gossip inevitably disseminate it. One can almost hear the calls made by political consultants to cronies around town the instant they finished talking to journalists seeking insight on Kemp's past: "Guess what NBC (or CBS or *Newsweek*) is looking into. . . ." This effect is heightened when reporters use tactics like those one television reporter employed, according to Buckley: "She led people to believe that she knew Kemp was gay, and she tried to browbeat people into confirming it. It was just outrageous."

Meanwhile, all the stories helped perpetuate the Kemp rumor, further damaging his campaign. Kemp's fundraisers encountered a number of major contributors who refused to give, citing their fear that "scandal" would engulf the candidate.[28] After the "Today" fiasco, the Kemp staff changed their rumor-control method, essentially refusing to cooperate when reporters sought to explore the topic further. But the campaign's leaders understood that if Kemp's presidential bid began to succeed, it would all be revisited with greater intensity. Kemp's failure to catch on in 1988, perhaps in some measure due to the rumor that would not die, had one small benefit for the exasperated candidate, his family, and staff: No additional confrontations with what *Washington Post* columnist Richard Cohen termed "sexual McCarthyism"[29] occurred. In the absence of damning evidence, without even an accuser, Jack Kemp had nonetheless been forced by various media organizations to deny repeatedly that he "is now or has ever been" a homosexual. As Cohen sadly observed, "Journalism has had prouder moments."

GARY HART

There are often disturbing excesses in the most justifiable of feeding frenzies. Gary Hart is a case in point. The Colorado candidate invited his troubles and brought controversy to himself. But at times even Hart critics sympathized with his plight. In 1984 legitimate concerns about his age, name change, and so on became "obsessive," as his then press secretary Kathy Bushkin noted: "How many times did he need to answer those questions? There were other important topics that also needed to be addressed." The scrutiny of Hart's résumé became ridiculously overwrought after the initial disclosures, too, with Hart criticized, among other things, for deemphasizing in his official biography his work as national campaign director of George McGovern's 1972 presidential campaign.[30] What ambitious politician would not have wanted to downplay a leadership position in a campaign that lost forty-nine states? (Already reviewed in chapter 3 was the role played by published, unproved rumors about Hart's womanizing proclivities in creating the subtextual aura of inevitability that preceded his 1987 private life revelations.[31])

The Donna Rice exposé itself is the focus of much concern about the press's investigative methods and procedures. First of all, the justification cited by the *Miami Herald* that made its news story on Hart "legitimate" was the candidate's "pattern of behavior," according to political editor Tom Fiedler. And what established this pattern? "The allegations had already been in place; the rumors had been there." In other words, gossip—allegations and rumors—constituted presumptive evidence of Hart's behavior, requiring a press trap to prove the candidate's guilt for the public to see. In Hart's case the presumption was almost certainly correct, but the standard of probable cause was a dubious one[32]—a disturbing precedent waiting to be applied to future candidates in less compelling circumstances.

The *Herald*'s stakeout also comes in for criticism, since it was less than airtight.[33] The rear entrance to Hart's town house was not watched continuously, nor was the surveillance maintained at all for two hours in the middle of the night. The poorly edited story was rushed into print as well (missing some of the *Herald*'s own Sunday editions) and for the wrong reason: The reporters did not want to give Hart any extra time to concoct an alibi or give a covering story to another newspaper. Jim Savage, a member of the stakeout team, explained why the paper would not "sit" on the story for another day to allow for more checking and precision: "We knew Hart had an aggressive group of operatives, and we would have given them twenty-four more hours to counterattack." This strategy might have been more appropriate for a competing presidential campaign than a newspaper. Overall, journalists inside and outside the *Herald* have ambivalent feelings about the Hart stakeout. A large majority believe it accomplished a good end (the exposure of Hart's character and judgment flaws), and some agree with the *Washington Post*'s Bob Woodward that the *Herald*'s stakeout was "unseemly but necessary and important—and it's not against the law to sit in a car." Many others, however, made statements like National Public Radio's Nina Totenberg's:

Most of us did not get into this profession to become private eyes. While completely legitimate, I find staking out houses to be extremely distasteful. If given the chance, I doubt very much I would have done it. That's just not the way I want to spend my time.

By no means is the *Herald* alone as a target of criticism for excessive behavior during the Hart affair. The *Washington Post*'s handling of the "other woman" story was also highly unpopular with many journalists. One of the *Post*'s own most-respected reporters, Bill Peterson, had refused to participate in the newspaper's New Hampshire request to question Hart because he was "queasy" about the

invasion of the candidate's privacy and also believed there were "un-
answered questions and holes" in the detective's report that revealed Hart's liaison.[34] Outside the newspaper, the *Post* was judged
severely because of the widespread belief that the editors in effect
"negotiated" Hart's withdrawal from the race in exchange for not
publishing the details of the candidate's long-term relationship with
a Washington woman.[35] Hart's precipitous withdrawal may well
have occurred on account of the *Post*'s inquiries; when informed of
the *Post*'s information, an exasperated Hart threw in the towel and
headed back to Colorado within hours.[36] And the *Post* did indeed decide not to publish the full story of the relationship once Hart had left
the race; at that point, according to the *Post*'s Ann Devroy, the story
became moot, irrelevant to a presidential contest that no longer included Gary Hart. But the decisions made by Hart and the newspaper were reached separately; inextricably bound together, they were
at the same time isolated and independent. Furthermore, as related
in an earlier chapter, the *Post* apparently had already given Hart's
D.C. mistress a promise of anonymity.

The second reason for the drubbing administered to the *Post* was
the question asked Hart by one of its reporters, Paul Taylor, at a news
conference a few days after the *Herald*'s exposé. Taylor posed an ex-
cruciatingly personal and unprecedented series of queries to a presidential candidate, twice requesting a reply to this interrogatory:
"Have you ever committed adultery?"[37] It was "overstepping the
bounds . . . a cheap shot, an unfair ambush question," said the *Los
Angeles Times*' media reporter, Tom Rosenstiel, reflecting the opinion
of many news colleagues. "The *Post* wanted Hart to deny guilt on
adultery, so they could print their [D.C. mistress] story to prove Hart
lied." Taylor, of course, saw it differently. Responding to a torrent of
criticism from the *New York Times*, he pointed out that Hart had insisted nothing "immoral" went on with Donna Rice. "What did Mr.
Hart mean by his denial of immoral behavior? . . . What I did was ask
Gary Hart the question he asked for."[38]

Legitimate or not, Taylor's prying was part and parcel of the
"mass pursuit of naked sensationalism"—as Hart's campaign manager called it[39]—that enveloped the Hart frenzy. Respectable newspapers were competing with the tabloids, playing one-upmanship in
titillation. No personal detail was too private for exploration. When
Mrs. Hart rejoined her husband on the campaign trail after the Rice
revelations, Hart press secretary Kevin Sweeney was accosted by
"frantic reporters" who wanted to know, "Did Gary and Lee kiss?

Did they kiss on the lips?" The news media swarmed over both the "damage central" and "damage control" locations with equal force: A hundred journalists and cameras were camped out on the *Post*'s doorstep (anticipating the D.C. mistress story), and about the same number were surrounding the Hart house in Colorado, many hanging from trees and others flying by in helicopters, with the television contingent shining huge, bright klieg lights on the home at night.

In the end Hart bitterly bowed out, but his unintentional legacy to politics was already clear. Rumors of illicit activity, if widespread enough, had become a sufficient news peg to entrap and publish. Moreover, "Gary Hart helped the press to cross a line," observed the *New York Times*'s Michael Oreskes. "We turned an effort to understand a candidate's character into a rationale for asking any question about anything—and Hart was so excessive he protected us from our own excesses." Ironically, Oreskes's own distinguished newspaper proved his point well in the wake of Hart's debacle. First the *Times* submitted to all the remaining candidates lawyerlike queries about adultery, including this fascinating "hypothetical" pair: "How should a hypothetical Presidential candidate who has *not* committed adultery answer the question, "Have you ever committed adultery'?" and "How should a hypothetical candidate who *has* committed adultery respond?"[40] (Only one candidate of fourteen surveyed seemed pleased by the *Times*'s effort: the Rev. Pat Robertson.) As if this fishing expedition was not enough, the *Times*'s Washington bureau sent requests to each candidate for essentially all the raw data of his entire life: complete medical records (with waivers on his physicians' need for confidentiality), academic transcripts from high school and college, employment files, state and federal income tax returns for the previous five years, birth certificate, marriage and driver's licenses, details of civil and criminal court cases involving the candidate, lists of "closest friends in high school and college [as well as] present friends, business associates, chief advisors and major fund-raisers." An additional request was the most callous: access to all FBI and other law-enforcement files available on the politician— files that are frequently filled with uncensored and unproved gossip and rumor. Many candidates objected to the *Times*'s intrusiveness, not to mention the burden of compiling the information. ("Why should we do their work for them?" one candidate's press secretary asked.) After substantial criticism from many quarters, the *Times* dropped the request.[41] But the precedents set during the Hart frenzy would not be so easily discarded.

MICHAEL DUKAKIS

While the judgmental evaluation of Hart's frenzy is necessarily equivocal, no such ambiguity is possible about Michael Dukakis's 1988 "mental health" controversy, one of the most despicable episodes in recent American politics. The corrosive rumor that the Democratic presidential nominee had undergone psychiatric treatment for severe depression began to be spread in earnest at the July 1988 national party convention. The agents of the rumormongering were "LaRouchies," adherents of the extremist cult headed by Lyndon LaRouche, who claims, among other loony absurdities, that Queen Elizabeth II is part of the international drug cartel.[42] The LaRouchies passed around leaflets headlined "Is Dukakis the new Senator Eagleton?" and after the convention they contacted numerous reporters and media organizations to follow up, stoking the competitive fires by telling each that rivals were already hot on the story's trail. (ABC's Sam Donaldson said he was personally approached by a LaRouchie who possessed press credentials, but all the others were telephoned.)

Shortly after the Democratic convention, the Bush campaign—with its candidate trailing substantially in most polls—began a covert operation to build on the foundation laid by the LaRouchies. As first reported by columnists Evans and Novak,[43] Bush manager Lee Atwater's lieutenants asked outside Republican operatives and political consultants to call their reporter contacts about the matter. These experienced strategists knew exactly the right approach so as not to leave fingerprints, explains Steve Roberts of *U.S. News & World Report*:

They asked us, "Gee, have you heard anything about Dukakis's treatment? Is it true?" They're spreading the rumor, but it sounds innocent enough: they're just suggesting you look into it, and maybe giving you a valuable tip as well.

At about the same time the *Detroit News* sent a questionnaire to Bush and Dukakis mildly reminiscent of the earlier *New York Times* grand inquisition, asking in part whether the candidates had ever been hospitalized or treated for depression or other mental illness. The Bush camp was delighted and began to alert key Republicans around the nation to the forthcoming Detroit story, which they hoped would include revelations about Dukakis's past. This fed the already developing frenzy and brought to a boil the speculation in political circles—all of it reaching the ears of reporters. Incredibly, the fever pitch of gossip even broached the subject of Dukakis's possible resignation from the ticket and the identities of his potential replacements.[44]

The Bush strategists actually received little satisfaction from the *Detroit News*'s August 2 story, which contained no discussion of Dukakis's mental history because Dukakis had refused to provide his medical records. But in anticipation of the story, the behind-the-scenes gossip had become so intense that a reporter from the *Boston Herald* asked Dukakis about the subject at a July 29 press conference. Dukakis merely shrugged and brushed the question aside, yet the *Boston Globe* (but not the *Herald*) printed an account of the encounter in the two bottom paragraphs of a page 6 article on July 30. Included was a brief explanation of the rumor and a notation that no evidence supporting it had been uncovered. Dukakis's press secretary, Dayton Duncan, also issued a blanket denial that the candidate had ever been treated for any form of mental illness.

At this juncture the conservative *Washington Times* swung into action. On August 2 (the same day as the *Detroit News*'s nonstory), the *Times* published a front-page article entitled "Dukakis Psychiatric Rumor Denied."[45] The story was officially pegged to Duncan's statement and the *Globe*'s report, but the paper also revealed that a Dukakis press aide had piqued its interest with a telephone call on July 28. As the *Times* editorially explained later, the aide wanted "to deny rumors that hadn't been placed in print—and which we had no intention of printing. . . . Such denials traditionally produce news reports, especially when they're unaccompanied by documentary proof."[46] With this highly questionable rationale for publishing a rumor without evidence, the *Times*'s August 2 story suggestively drew a strained parallel between Dukakis's situation and Thomas Eagleton's 1972 resignation from the Democratic ticket. This was child's play compared to the thoroughly deceptive, front-page banner headline the *Times* ran two days later: DUKAKIS KIN HINTS AT SESSIONS.[47] The lead paragraph began, "The sister-in-law of Massachusetts Gov. Michael Dukakis said yesterday 'it is possible' the Democratic presidential candidate consulted 'on a friendly basis' with psychiatrist Donald Lipsitt." (Lipsitt was a Dukakis family acquaintance who lived in their neighborhood.) Four paragraphs later the extent of the sister-in-law's actual knowledge, and her real opinion, became clear: "It's possible, but I doubt it. . . . I don't know." This manipulation of the facts was so egregious that both of the bylined reporters quit the *Times* in protest.[48] Incidentally, the psychiatrist in question, Dr. Lipsitt, was not even interviewed by the *Times*; when the *Baltimore Sun* contacted him, he emphatically denied treating Dukakis, discussing any personal problems with him, or referring him to any other doctor.[49]

Many newspapers, including the *Sun* and the *Washington Post*, had at first refused to run any mention at all of the Dukakis rumor since it could not be substantiated.[50] But on August 3, an incident occurred that made it impossible, in their view, not to cover the rumor. During a White House press conference, a correspondent for *Executive Intelligence Review*, a LaRouche organization magazine, asked Reagan if he thought Dukakis should make his medical records public. A jovial Reagan replied, "Look, I'm not going to pick on an invalid." Reagan half apologized a few hours later ("I was just trying to be funny and it didn't work"), but his weak attempt at humor propelled into the headlines a rumor that had been only simmering on the edge of public consciousness. Opinions differ as to whether the "gaffe" was intentional. The *Sun's* Jack Germond says no. "Reagan was always making mischievous cracks without thinking." Steve Roberts strongly disagrees: "I was sitting twenty feet from Reagan when he said it, and I'm convinced it was a shrewd and calculated way of planting that story. Reagan and his staff knew much of the press was trying to ignore the rumor, but when a president says something like that you can't ignore it."

Whether spontaneous or planned, there is little doubt that "Reagan and the Bush people weren't a bit sorry once it happened," as CNN's Frank Sesno asserts. The Bush camp immediately tried to capitalize on and prolong the controversy by releasing a report from the White House doctor describing the Republican nominee's health in glowing terms.[51] But this was a sideshow compared with the rumor itself. The mental health controversy yanked the Dukakis effort off track and forced the candidate and then his doctor to hold their own press conferences on the subject, attracting still more public attention to a completely phony allegation. False though it was, the charge nonetheless disturbed many Americans, raising serious doubts about a candidate who was still relatively unknown to many of them. "It burst our bubble at a critical time and cost us half our fourteen-point [poll] lead," claims the Dukakis staff's senior adviser, Kirk O'Donnell. "It was one of the election's turning points; the whole affair seemed to affect Dukakis profoundly, and he never again had the same buoyant, enthusiastic approach to the campaign." Dukakis lost the 1988 election for many reasons,[52] and it would be foolhardy to contend that his residence would now be 1600 Pennsylvania Avenue had this ugly rumor never been given so much publicity. However, the rumor added unfairly to his burdens, and Dukakis was treated shabbily.

As is usually the case, though, the candidate unnecessarily complicated his own situation. Until events forced his hand, Dukakis adamantly and stubbornly refused to release his medical records or an adequate summary of them, despite advance warning that the mental health issue might be raised. Gossip had circulated for years in Massachusetts[53] about Dukakis's "deep" depressions after the death of his brother Stelian in a 1973 automobile accident and again in 1978 when he was defeated for reelection as governor.[54] Dukakis's wife Kitty had called his reaction to the 1978 loss "like a public death," although it would be a strange individual who would not be considerably affected by such a voter rejection or by the death of a close relative. More to the point in 1988, a senior civil servant with direct access to Reagan and Bush White House aides delivered a very specific warning right after the convention to Dukakis adviser O'Donnell. The Bush side intended to undermine the Democrat's reputation by stoking the mental health rumor, the source said with assurance. Yet, even apprised of this fact, Dukakis still held firm for nondisclosure. Some of Dukakis's top staffers are convinced that the nominee mainly wanted to protect Kitty, fearing that a policy of complete openness on health records would eventually lead to requests for fuller information about his wife's past medical treatment and counseling for drug dependency. This protectiveness had been on public display before: In 1982 Dukakis lied about the purpose of Kitty's hospitalization, passing off her amphetamine dependency as hepatitis.[55] Finally, when Dukakis was confronted with the first queries about mental health in 1988, he reacted badly, giving curt replies and refusing all elaboration. Noted Ellen Hume, then of the *Wall Street Journal*, "Dukakis handled the matter so poorly that the press started to suspect he was covering something up. He fed our worst instincts, and he wasn't prepared to understand just how cynical and skeptical the corps has become."

Dukakis's failing in Hume's accounting was also the press's. Most of the aggressive reporting in this frenzy was directed at the victim of the rumormongering. Andrew Rosenthal of the *New York Times* recalls the "really awful" press conference with Dukakis's doctor:

First we questioned him extensively about whether Dukakis had ever gone to a psychiatrist, which would have supposedly proved [Dukakis] to be crazy in some way. Then once we established Dukakis had never gone to a shrink, we asked whether it was abnormal not to seek professional help when under as much stress as he apparently had been. The doctor was just dumbfounded; he said, "First you ask me if Dukakis is crazy because he went to a psychiatrist, now you ask me if he's crazy because he didn't go."

While focusing on the relatively innocent casualty, most journalists gave light treatment to the perpetrators. In retrospect, several newspeople said they regretted not giving more attention to the LaRouche role in spreading the rumor, given what Hume called the LaRouchies' well-deserved reputation as "dirty tricksters."[56] President Reagan also received no more than a light rap on the wrist in most newspapers and broadcasts for his successful move to highlight the rumor. "The incident was an outrage right from the get-go, but all the more so because of the president's misuse of his national platform," commented CBS's Dan Rather. And the press was far too reluctant to expose and alienate a source or two in order to piece together the clever rumor-marketing effort conducted by Republican party operatives. Kirk O'Donnell asked a question that begs attention from the press: "If they're pushing false rumors, why should they be protected?" Overall, one of the most important lessons of the Dukakis mental health frenzy is an enduring one, with applicability to many of the rumors discussed in this chapter. "The media are really liable for criticism when we get stampeded by competitive instincts into publishing or airing stories that shouldn't be on the record," says Nina Totenburg. "We were stampeded on the Dukakis story, and we should never have let it happen."

DAN QUAYLE

The megafrenzy of post-Watergate campaigns, the perils of Dan Quayle, became perhaps the most riveting and certainly the most excessive feature of 1988's general election. For nearly three weeks, coverage of the presidential campaign became mainly coverage of Quayle. Most major newspapers assigned an extraordinary number of reporters to the story (up to two dozen), and the national networks devoted from two-thirds to more than four-fifths of their total evening-news campaign minutes to Quayle.[57] Combined with the sexy material being investigated, this bumper crop of journalists and stories produced, in the words of a top Bush-Quayle campaign official, "the most blatant example of political vivisection that I've ever seen on any individual at any time; it really surpassed a feeding frenzy and became almost a religious experience for many reporters." Balance in coverage, always in short supply during a frenzy, was almost absent. First one controversy and then another about Quayle's early life mesmerized the press, while examination of the most relevant parts of his record, such as his congressional career, got short shrift.

"You saw lots of reporters camped out at the registrar's office at De-Pauw University [Quayle's alma mater] and at the National Guard headquarters in Indiana, but you didn't see many talking to people on the Hill about what sort of reputation he had," said David Beckwith, then of *Time* magazine and now Quayle's press secretary.[58]

It is not surprising to find Quayle's staff criticizing the press. What may startle observers who view the media as thin-skinned and defensive is their widely shared retrospective agreement with the charge that the Quayle frenzy was chock-full of excesses (see table 5.1). Even the minor but revealing digs at Quayle are well remembered by concerned journalists. *U.S. News & World Report's* Michael Barone recalled that CBS's estimate of Quayle's financial worth, broadcast at the GOP convention, was an astounding six hundred million dollars: "It was part of the press's irresponsible attempt to paint Quayle as a mindless rich kid, to put him into a slot that he didn't quite fit." (While Quayle will eventually inherit a large family trust fund, his total assets in 1988 totaled approximately one million dollars.[59]) Another previously mentioned aspect of the press's "slotting" of Quayle at the convention was an insistence by some broadcasters on calling him "J. Danforth Quayle III" rather than "Dan," by which he was usually known. This denial of a courtesy commonly extended to all politicians was decried by Roger Mudd: "The one thing you don't do is make fun of a person's name. With [the surname of] Mudd, I've been through it myself, and it's probably the cheapest shot you can take at anybody."

Of course, it was the big-ticket items about Quayle—his National Guard Service, the alleged affair with Paula Parkinson, and his academic record—that attracted the most attention. As discussed in an earlier chapter, the question of whether Quayle used special influence to gain admission to the National Guard and avoid the Vietnam War draft when he graduated from college in 1969 served as the original lightning rod for criticism of the young senator. At the convention, wild rumors flew, such as the false one that Quayle's family had paid fifty thousand dollars to gain him admission to the guard. The controversy was beginning to come to a boil when Bush and Quayle traveled to Indiana on August 19 at the conclusion of the Republicans' national conclave. At Huntington, Indiana, a hometown crowd of twelve thousand had gathered to root for Quayle, and in a classic setup that will be examined further in chapter 8, Quayle answered questions from a swarm of reporters as Hoosiers alternately cheered the candidate and booed the journalists. This threatening atmosphere may explain what NBC's John Chancellor called

TABLE 5.1
JOURNALISTS' SECOND THOUGHTS ON THE QUAYLE FRENZY

I had second thoughts from the first day. Our pursuit of Quayle was relentless, and our demeanor was terrible.

Peter Jennings, "ABC World News Tonight" anchor

In most of the interviews done with Quayle when he made his circuit of the convention anchor booths, he was never given the benefit of the doubt. There was a built-in antagonistic tone that communicated a clear message: here was a dummy, selected because Bush didn't want anybody to outshine him, and Quayle was a hollow-headed, Orphan Annie–eyed man who was just a cipher. The hunter instinct was on public display there in those two or three days in a way that I've never seen it before. . . . I don't think the viewer was allowed to make his own decision about Quayle because the questions and the treatment of Quayle so prejudged him that the newspeople got in the way of the story.

Roger Mudd, PBS and "MacNeil/Lehrer NewsHour"

Some of the coverage was hysterical, and some inaccurate information flying around the convention hall got on the air.

Tom Brokaw, "NBC Nightly News" anchor

The Quayle coverage was excessive and a feeding frenzy in the truest sense of the phrase; whenever the tiniest bit of red meat appeared, everybody dove for it.

Frank Sesno, CNN correspondent

The Quayle matters were pursued almost irrationally; the coverage was based on presumptions and perceptions more than a solid foundation of real information.

Richard Harwood, *Washington Post* ombudsman

There was a breathless quality that permeated the coverage that wasn't helpful; it made it feel like we were reporting a massive scandal instead of just describing a man. . . . Nor did we give the material to the readers in a way that allowed them to assess the guy; it was a hurl-it-all-into-their-face kind of coverage.

Michael Oreskes, *New York Times* correspondent

SOURCE: Interviews conducted for this volume.

some "astonishingly vicious questions" from the press, but the nationally televised encounter in Huntington lives on in popular memory as an example of frenzy journalism. Even before the jeering crowd appeared, many members of the press corps were spoiling for a fight, says Brit Hume:

Riding on the press bus into Huntington I heard remarks of a highly personal nature directed at Quayle. Once we got there, the press acted disgracefully. Some reporters were shouting and screaming at Quayle, arguing with him, saying things that were not questions at all, but comments. Ellen Hume of the *Wall Street Journal* told him that "while people were fighting and dying in Vietnam, you were writing press releases." And after it was all over, there was a lot of whining among reporters about the crowd yelling at us and the "inappropriate setting." Oh stop: if we can't take that, it's time for us to hang up our spurs.

Ellen Hume (no relation to Brit) defends her admittedly aggressive brand of questioning, noting that it is standard practice in the post-Watergate White House pressroom, where the daily exchanges are usually not fully televised, as was Huntington. Her "press release" comment was also a retort to Quayle, who suggested that journalists were calling National Guard service "dishonorable." Most of all, insists Hume, "We have an obligation to crack through the propaganda and the fake imagery that we are being handed by these guys, and if we have to look ugly in the process, so be it. I never became a reporter to be popular."

The National Guard issue was unquestionably a legitimate one for the press to raise, although once the picture was clear—Quayle's family did pull strings, but not to an unconscionable degree—[60] some journalists appeared to be unwilling to let it go. Far less legitimate was the press's resurrection of a counterfeit, dead-and-buried episode involving the party girl/lobbyist Paula Parkinson. No sooner had Quayle been selected for the vice presidential nomination than the anchors and correspondents were mentioning the 1980 sex-for-influence "scandal," about which Quayle had long ago been cleared of any wrongdoing and involvement with Parkinson. "When Quayle's name first came up as a vice presidential possibility, before his selection, the word passed among reporters that Bush couldn't choose Quayle because of his 'Paula problem,' " admitted one television newsman. "It was the loosest kind of sloppy association . . . as if nobody bothered to go back and refresh their memory about the facts of the case." Ellen Hume, at the request of her bureau chief, asked Quayle about the Parkinson incident at the first press conference after his nomination was announced; the candidate was "clearly rattled" by the inquiry, according to Hume—and likely a little irritated as well—raising the antennae and the interest of the hungry pack. Soon the issue was in full flight. The *Los Angeles Daily News* contacted the two attorneys who represented Parkinson during the 1981 FBI investigation, and they discovered (in their notes of the FBI's interview with their client) references to a pass Quayle supposedly made at her while they were dancing.[61] (Parkinson claims she turned him down flat.) The resulting article was tastefully headlined, in part, HE ASKED FOR SEX.

Almost simultaneously Paula Parkinson—living in Texas under an alias—resurfaced, though not to give free interviews.[62] After a swirl of rumors about Parkinson's publication plans, the chosen outlet, *Playboy* (for whom Parkinson had posed nude in 1980) graciously agreed to release key quotes from its forthcoming Parkinson spread "to prevent . . . further speculation." Parkinson's statement was of course spiced with hot-button words and phrases (*flirted, extremely close dancing, wanted to make love,* and the like) The sultry story was now irresistible to television, and all three networks devoted considerable attention to it. ABC and CBS led their nightly newscasts with it, while NBC included the Parkinson allegations as part of a multi-issue Quayle package.[63] As the lawyer explained Quayle's purported proposition, the NBC camera slowly panned up a provocative photograph of Parkinson, with special focus on her ample breasts. The NBC correspondent who did the piece, Pulitzer Prize–winning investigative reporter Jim Polk, confessed that he thought it was "a cheap shot":

It was an unfair accusation to begin with. I personally talked to Quayle back in 1980 when this first came up, and I thought he answered it squarely and honestly then. Besides being an old charge, even if the worst of Parkinson's allegations were true, nothing happened between them. . . . As it is, [the Parkinson segment] is buried way down in my story, and I didn't want it in at all, but the show's producer [put it in].

The CBS correspondent covering the controversy, Eric Engberg, disagreed with Polk, insisting, "The only fair alternative is to put it all out there, and let people decide which story they think is more believable." Yet given Parkinson's reputation,[64] the seriousness of the alleged offense even if true, and the press of far weightier concerns in the campaign, it is difficult to justify the media's hyped recycling of this trivial-if-racy bit of history.

Parkinson was not the only woman linked to Quayle, and journalists, convinced there might have been fire in the Parkinson smoke, went in search of a pattern. They thought they had found one in a woman named "Dawn" (not her real name). This untold tale of personal and partisan intrigue became a high priority for the Bush campaign as well as several media outlets (including CBS News and the *Wall Street Journal*). Some Democrats in South Carolina tipped national and state reporters to a wild liaison that had supposedly taken place in the late spring of 1977 between then U.S. Congressman Quayle and a young South Carolinean. Quayle (along with two other congressmen, one a Democrat and one a Republican) had been invited down to Myrtle Beach for a celebrity golf tournament by the local Democratic congressman, John Jenrette, a high-living politician later convicted of Abscam-related offenses and defeated for reelection in 1980. One of the 1988 Democratic tipsters had a personal as well as a political motive for torpedoing Quayle: Former State Senator Tom Turnipseed had been defeated in a 1980 congressional race after it was revealed that much earlier in life he had been treated for depression and had undergone electroshock therapy. Lee Atwater, the 1988 Bush-Quayle manager, had run the campaign of Turnipseed's successful Republican opponent, Floyd Spence, and in a preview of the Dukakis mental health incident, Atwater had clearly had a hand in advertising Turnipseed's problems. (At one point in the 1980 campaign, Atwater said he wouldn't respond to charges made by someone who had been "hooked up to jumper cables."[65]) In 1988 Turnipseed saw an opportunity for revenge, and he called the *Wall Street Journal*'s Jill Abramson, who had many years earlier worked in one of Turnipseed's campaigns for office. In addition to the Turnipseed situation, former congressman Jenrette was deeply involved in spreading the Quayle-"Dawn" rumor; claimed Atwater: "All that was Jenrette trying to get back in the limelight." Most of the press regarded Jenrette as a dubious character but in this case he had some credibility: Not only was he Quayle's host, but "Dawn" had apparently been a former girlfriend of his.

Other than Jenrette and Turnipseed, the root source of the rumor was a young man (now a South Carolina attorney) who had worked as a college aide to Jenrette and in that capacity served as the designated driver for the three visiting congressmen. The attorney had strongly suggested to a key South Carolina Democratic legislator that Quayle and one of the other congressmen had had a fun-filled night after spending hours drinking and dancing at a freewheeling Myrtle Beach bar called Cowboys—an establishment with its own mechanical-bull ride. When the attorney was contacted by the *Wall Street Journal*'s Abramson, however, he was far less forthcoming than Turnipseed had led Abramson to believe he would be: "He was nervous and he had conflicting loyalties. On the one hand, [Republican U.S. Senator] Strom Thurmond [also Atwater's mentor] had been good to him. But meanwhile, Turnipseed and all these Democrats were working on him incredibly hard, saying, 'It's your duty as a good Democrat to come clean about this.'" Once the attorney did open up a bit to Abramson, it was clear that his story was much less compelling than Turnipseed had hoped and implied. On the evening in question, the young college student had driven the somewhat older GOP congressman back to the hotel, alone, before midnight, leaving Quayle and the Democratic congressman at the bar. At the time most of the carousing was being done by the Democrat, who was aggressively pursuing women; Quayle had had a few beers and had danced from time to time, but according to the witness, the future vice president had been the quietest of the three legislators: "I can remember thinking that night, 'This guy [Quayle] is squeaky clean.' " The student returned home and went to bed, only to be awakened at 2 A.M. by a command from the Democratic congressman that a pizza be delivered to his hotel room. Specific instructions were given for the student to knock, put the food at the door, and leave without waiting for a response; the student received the distinct impression that the Democratic congressman was occupied with business other than paperwork. Quayle was staying in a separate room, and the student did not see him or hear from him. (One of many false rumors circulating among the 1988 press corps was that the student had delivered the pizza to Quayle's room and walked in on Quayle and "Dawn" having sex.)

Not long after Jill Abramson spoke to the attorney, the frenzy descended on him. His name was now being passed around freely by South Carolina Democrats, and reporters were being tipped by the dozen. Calls about Quayle and "Dawn" rained into his overwhelmed office. Concerned about the barrage of press inquiries and where they were leading, the attorney contacted his Washington benefactor, Senator Strom Thurmond, to warn him of the percolating problem involving Quayle. Thurmond was deeply concerned and called Atwater; the senator refused to discuss it over the phone and requested a personal meeting with Atwater and James Baker, the Bush-Quayle campaign chairman (now U.S. secretary of state). When Baker and Atwater arrived, Thurmond revealed the intelligence he had received, and all three placed a conference call to the attorney. Atwater got on the phone first because he wanted to deliver a private message. As it happened, Atwater remembered the man from 1978, when Atwater was working for Thurmond's reelection campaign and the attorney, then a student at Clemson University, had also been active in politics—chairing the university campaign unit of Thurmond's Democratic U.S. Senate challenger, Charles ("Pug") Ravenel. When Atwater told the attorney of his political recollection, the attorney paused and asked, "Does Thurmond know that?" Atwater assured him, "No, and he'll never know about it." (In a later interview, the RNC chairman deadpanned: "I did that intentionally, just to add a little something.")

Though Atwater could not have known it, the attorney needed no encouragement to tell what he knew; already worried about the gathering storm, he wanted to unburden himself and be done with it. Once Baker and Thurmond joined the call, the attorney reiterated what he had already told Abramson, CBS, and others—that at no time had he seen Quayle and any woman in the hotel together, nor had he had the slightest indication during all of his time with Quayle that the congressman was carrying on with anyone. According to the attorney, this declaration of Quayle's probable innocence provoked a candid exchange between Atwater (a Quayle booster) and Baker (who had not been enthusiastic about Quayle's nomination). As Atwater exclaimed, "You see, Jim, I told you, dammit. Danny's not a cockhound, he just runs around with that cockhound golf crowd."[66] Rather than Quayle, the Democratic congressman was the most likely source of the fuzzy memories about the trip's extracurricular sexual activities. Not only the pizza delivery was in evidence; the attorney reported to Atwater and company that the rather indiscreet Democratic legislator had regaled his colleagues with embarrassingly specific details of his evening's toothpaste-spiced sexual exploits. Furthermore, one of Congressman Jenrette's close friends had been designated to help provide female company to his guests if they so desired, and this friend's telephone number had apparently been given to the Democratic congressman (but not to Quayle).

Atwater had been quite worried that some media organization would break the potentially damaging story, but after his talk with the lawyer he was greatly relieved, and convinced that Quayle was not guilty of the main charge that might be hurled.[67] As for "Dawn," she was reportedly furious at Jenrette and his associates[68] for making her potentially the press's successor to Paula Parkinson; talk of legal action was briefly in the air, but dropped when no published mention of her occurred. Frustrated South Carolina Democrats, still convinced some hanky-panky took place, tried to hire a pilot to fly a "Dan and 'Dawn' " banner above the Darlington 500 stock-car race during a Quayle visit on September 4, 1988, as a way of getting the story into print. But the pilot would not do it, leading Turnipseed to suggest to the *Journal's* Abramson his suspicion that Atwater had paid the pilot off. Atwater laughingly dismissed the allegation, which is as unlikely and unproved as Quayle's nonexistent date with "Dawn."

Of course, the story (or nonstory) never broke during the campaign, but it almost did. One news organization had learned of the Thurmond-Atwater-Baker conference call and planned to use that unusual circumstance as the factual pretext for a published discussion of the "hidden crisis" about Quayle's past. A reporter for the organization interviewed Atwater about it, and the wily campaign manager flatly denied that the call had ever taken place. After the session Atwater telephoned the South Carolina attorney and let him know about the fib he had told. The attorney was not specifically asked to back up Atwater's untruth, but the implication was clear and the attorney quickly figured out what he was expected to do. The call from Atwater came just in time, as another reporter from the same news organization showed up at the attorney's office shortly thereafter. She grilled the attorney about the conference call; he claimed no knowledge of it. With two of the four telephone participants swearing the report was false (and the other two not commenting at all), the organization was forced to drop the story.

Some of the rumors engulfing the press corps about Quayle stretched even farther back into his past than did the womanizing gossip. Quayle's academic record was particularly fertile ground for rumormongers. By his own admission, the vice presidential nominee had been a mediocre student—and the evidence produced during the campaign suggests that *mediocre* was a charitable description. When the administration of Quayle's undergraduate college, DePauw University, proposed giving the new senator an honorary degree in 1982, many on the faculty heatedly protested and hundreds of students signed petitions objecting to the choice. In good part, the dissenters opposed Quayle's politics, but his exceedingly lackluster academic performance gave them powerful ammunition. (Quayle got his degree anyway.) At the time, though, a rumor swept DePauw, and especially its faculty, that Quayle had been caught plagiarizing during his senior year. This rumor, which had a specific teacher and class attached, was widely accepted as true and became part of the Quayle legend on campus.

Within a day of Quayle's selection as the vice presidential nominee, the rumor had reached the New Orleans convention hall. Apparently there were two primary sources. One was the core of Democratic operatives who had worked on U.S. Senator Birch Bayh's unsuccessful reelection campaign in 1980 (when Quayle defeated Bayh). Some staffers remembered the opposition research done on Quayle—research that included references to possible college plagiarism.[69] The other source was DePauw University faculty, who shared their recollections when reporters called them seeking "color" quotes for profile pieces on the country's newest political star.[70] Hours after the adjournment of the GOP convention, the *Wall*

Street Journal published a lengthy article on Quayle's problems that included unsubstantiated "rumors" of "a cheating incident."[71] The source cited was English Professor Robert Sedlack, who said, "There was an allegation that [Quayle] had plagiarized in a political science course." The reference to the plagiarism rumor was near the bottom of the article, noted the *Journal*'s Washington bureau chief, Al Hunt, who further justified its inclusion by pointing to the "credible, reputable faculty member who was willing to be quoted making the charge and who, in checking with other people, did not appear to be a guy who was on the payroll of the Indiana Democratic party." In fact, as noted in the *Journal* article, Professor Sedlack was an outspoken Democrat and president of the Greencastle, Indiana, city council, where DePauw is located.

The *Journal* mention helped to push the plagiarism rumor high up on the list of must-do Quayle rumors, and soon the press hunt was on—for every DePauw academic who had ever taught Quayle, for fellow students to whom he might have confided his sin, even for a supposedly mysterious, extant paper or bluebook in which Quayle's cheating was indelibly recorded for posterity. (A variation on the bluebook rumor was that it was up for sale to the highest media bidder.) Michael Lawrence, a former political science professor in whose class some said the incident had occurred, was tracked down to his new home in Albuquerque; he was hounded by reporters, some of whom accused him of keeping it under wraps. Several other present and former faculty members confessed that they did little but answer the telephone and the door for days. And reporters were often rewarded with tantalizing suggestions that the rainbow's pot of gold might be at the end of the next telephone connection. But it was fool's gold, recalled NBC's Jim Polk:

We chased professors all over the country. And each one kept saying, 'I think it's true and professor so-and-so knows all about it.' Then we'd call so-and-so and he'd say, 'no, not me, it's this other guy,' and by the time we finished running around in circles it was clear that there wasn't anybody who knew a real fact.

As it happens there appears to be a possible, logical explanation for the plagiarism allegation against Quayle, and it was apparently first uncovered by the meticulous and painstaking efforts of two *Journal* reporters, Jill Abramson and James B. Stewart (the latter a graduate of DePauw, a happy circumstance that gave him a leg up on the competition). Abramson and Stewart managed to locate almost

every DePauw student who had been a member of Quayle's fraternity, Delta Kappa Epsilon, during his undergraduate years. Approximately ten did indeed remember a plagiarism incident from 1969
(Quayle's graduating year), and the guilty student was in fact a golf-
playing senior who was a political science major and member of DKE
fraternity—but *not* Quayle. The similarities were striking and the
mix-up understandable after the passage of nearly twenty years.
What was remarkable, however, was that an undistinguished student such as Quayle would be so vividly remembered by faculty.
Abramson and Stewart also uncovered the reason for this, and even
two decades after the fact, their finding makes a political science professor blanch. Quayle, the future vice president of the United States,
was one of only two 1969 seniors to fail the political science comprehensive examination, a requirement for graduation. (He passed it on
a second try.) Abramson's conclusion was a reasonable one: "Jim
Stewart and I believed that people had confused Quayle's failure on
the comprehensive exam with his . . . fraternity brother's plagiarism,
especially since both events . . . occurred at about the same time."
Unfortunately for Quayle, and also the public, this reasonable but
not airtight supposition did not reach print, though it might have
provided a fair antidote to the earlier rumor-promoting article. Instead the firmly established fact of Quayle's comprehensive exam
failure was prominently displayed in the *Journal*, undoubtedly if un-
intentionally reinforcing suspicions that Quayle must have cheated
his way through college.[72]

Other academically oriented rumors congregated around Quayle's
admission first to Indiana University's law school and then to the
bar. Many wondered how a student with a poor undergraduate transcript could gain admission to a competitive law school. First reports
suggested that Quayle had once again been the beneficiary of a special favor, just as in his National Guard acceptance, by securing a
law-school berth under an equal-opportunity/affirmative-action
plan. In truth Quayle was admitted under a special program that allowed applicants to make a case for themselves based on factors
other than grades and LSAT scores, and they were required to take a
remedial summer course before enrolling in regular classes. Several
journalists who interviewed law-school officials reported that Quayle
personally convinced the admissions officers that he was a good
risk,[73] and this was no surprise to one of his undergraduate professors. While no Quayle fan, the faculty member commented: "Danny
could talk himself in or out of anything; he was a real charmer."
Then there was the rumor that Quayle had convinced or paid some-

one to take the bar exam for him. ABC's Ann Compton remembers a campaign morning when "that story went coast to coast among journalists in ten minutes" and "came close to being reported" by at least one media organization because it was presented as a proven fact, ready for the next edition of the Cleveland *Plain Dealer*. The version Jill Abramson heard included the fact that the *Plain Dealer* had actually found Quayle's substitute test taker. Calls to the *Plain Dealer* revealed no such story ready or contemplated for the presses,[74] and NBC News among others found an Indianapolis lawyer who remembered talking to Quayle at the examination's midpoint break.

An observer reviewing the academic stories about Quayle is struck mainly by two elements. First, despite the windstorm of rumor that repeatedly swept over the press corps, there was much fine, solid reporting with appropriate restraint shown about publication, with the exception of the original *Journal* article mentioning plagiarism as well as some pieces about Quayle's law-school admission. Of equal note, however, was the overweening emphasis placed on his undergraduate performance. As any longtime teacher knows, students frequently commit youthful errors and indiscretions that are not necessarily indicative of their potential or future development. Many students are also late bloomers, and maturity levels differ dramatically among college-age individuals. It is true, as the *Journal*'s Al Hunt contends, "Here was a guy who stood out for his lack of achievement"; from all indications there is little or nothing on his transcript about which Quayle can be proud. And Quayle made his own situation worse by steadfastly refusing to release his records, substantially increasing the damaging speculation that he has something to hide.[75] Yet, once again, a question of balance is raised: How much emphasis should have been placed on, and precious press resources devoted to, Quayle's life in his early twenties compared to his relatively ignored senatorial career in his thirties?

Another high-voltage rumor about Quayle concerned his alleged drug use in the early 1970s. This electrifying gossip galvanized the press from Washington to Los Angeles and became the hidden election-eve crisis of the 1988 presidential campaign. The rumor's real strength was its universally accepted premise: Any college student of Quayle's generation must have tried drugs. (Actually, many surveys at the time indicated that a substantial minority of college students had not experimented even with marijuana, much less harsher drugs.) This premise became the basis for the press's instantaneous fishing expedition at the Republican National Convention; ABC's Peter Jennings, in an anchor-booth interview with Quayle at mid-convention,[76] asked the nominee-designate directly, "Did you smoke marijuana?" and Quayle's response was unhesitating: "I did not."

Shortly thereafter, a telephone call was placed that would attempt to cast doubt upon the vice presidential candidate's veracity. Brett Kimberlin, a federal prisoner serving a fifty-year sentence for drug smuggling and a 1978 series of bombings in Speedway, Indiana, contacted *Los Angeles Times* reporter Douglas Frantz, who had written a story about Kimberlin in 1982 while the prisoner was serving time in Chicago and Frantz was on the staff of the *Chicago Tribune*.[77] With a conviction for perjury also on his record, the so-called Speedway Bomber was never considered a particularly credible accuser, but he told a detailed and circumstantially plausible story. He had met law student Quayle at a 1971 Indiana University fraternity party, claimed Kimberlin, who at the time was sixteen years old and a self-described "high-school pot dealer." According to Kimberlin:

Danny found out I had some pot for sale and he told me he wanted to buy some. At first I thought he might be a narc [narcotics policeman] because he looked square. But a friend of mine said he was all right, so I gave him my phone number in Indianapolis. A couple of weeks later he called and used the name DQ on the phone . . . and for the next sixteen to eighteen months I sold him an ounce of pot about once a month.

By Kimberlin's account, he and Quayle struck up such a good relationship that when Quayle got married, Kimberlin presented him with the gift of an ounce of hashish and "Acapulco Gold" marijuana. The relationship began to go sour, though, when Kimberlin watched the rising political star denounce drug use and insist he had never tried, much less regularly enjoyed, marijuana. As Kimberlin explains it, he had the purest of motives in "reluctantly" blowing the whistle on Quayle: "Everybody knows the way he smoked pot," and the American people needed to know what a "hypocrite" Quayle was.

"Everybody" may have known about Quayle's college affinity for pot, but Kimberlin had great difficulty pointing to any witnesses who could corroborate his story. Surely a socially popular, active student, such as Quayle, who smoked marijuana with regularity would be easy to finger, even after nearly twenty years. Kimberlin did indeed cite a few individuals to Frantz of the *Times*, who could support the fact that he had been telling this story for years: an impeccable group of fellow prisoners who had never personally laid eyes on Quayle. One of them, James Lewis, called Frantz from the penitentiary to vouch for Kimberlin's claim; Lewis is the alleged Tylenol killer and a convicted extortionist. In addition to these "reliable" sources, Kimberlin gave Frantz the names of an FBI agent and a former Indianapolis prosecutor who supposedly knew something about Quayle's crime or Kimberlin's charge; neither had ever heard anything about it. Later, Frantz—a DePauw graduate and golf team member whose career overlapped with Quayle's—utilized his college connections and spoke with a number of former DePauw students who had been involved with drugs, "and nobody had ever heard anything at all about Quayle smoking marijuana." A hard-driving investigative reporter, Frantz does "not like to lose a story," particularly one as significant as he believed this one could be. But his considered judgment about Kimberlin and his allegations were sound:

In this business you develop a strong instinct for what's bullshit and what's not. And this one looked like bullshit from the start. . . . Brett is an extremely intelligent, manipulative guy who really knows how to work the press. And this was simply some perverted desire of Brett's to get attention for himself.

Alas, the shrewd Mr. Kimberlin had no intention of letting the matter rest with Douglas Frantz. He had kept himself busy informing loads of other reporters about his charges, and playing one off against the other. As one journalist put it, "Kimberlin has an 'A' list of reporters and a 'B' list, and he ran down both before it was over, telling each one that everybody else was close to breaking the story." More importantly, he seemed to sense that "anything's possible in the waning days of a political campaign," as Bush/Quayle staffer Mark Goodin suggested. Goodin was assigned to monitor the situation in October, when rumors that Quayle would soon be linked to drugs were in every major newsroom in America. National Public Radio's Nina Totenberg was especially interested in Kimberlin's story. According to Kimberlin, his former girlfriend first contacted Totenberg in mid-October on his behalf, and after several conversations, Kimberlin signed an affidavit for Totenberg, which she then presented to the Bush campaign on October 28. Quayle's "categorical denial" followed, said Totenberg, who was unable to find "a reliable second source" so she could air it. Nonetheless, the Bush managers were apoplectic, and they quickly organized a contingency plan to manage the situation—and control the damage, should the story become public. Mark Goodin kept both James Baker and Lee Atwater fully apprised of all Kimberlin developments in the campaign's last week, including the deluge of interview requests pouring into his Oklahoma prison. NBC News sent a crew and conducted an on-camera, never aired interview with Kimberlin, and a full-scale press conference was scheduled for Friday, November 4, at 6 P.M. That afternoon's local newspaper, the *El Reno* (Okla.) *Daily Tribune*, carried a front-page article on the NBC interview and Kimberlin's story. At 5 P.M., as reporters and cameras were beginning to gather, the director of the federal Bureau of Prisons sent an unprecedented order to overrule the prison's warden; the press conference was cancelled and Kimberlin was placed in administrative detention.[78] Although the bureau had been in touch with a high official of the Reagan Justice Department prior to the issuance of the order, and Lee Atwater was quickly informed of the decision,[79] the director, J. Michael Quinlan, has denied that political considerations played any role in his actions, citing as his justification instead Kimberlin's concern about personal safety—a fear he supposedly expressed to Nina Totenberg.[80] (Both Kimberlin and Totenberg have denied that any such exchange took place.) Furthermore, after Kimberlin was released from detention on Saturday evening, he tried to call the Dukakis campaign using a friend as an intermediary; this third-party contact violated prison rules, and by 9:30 A.M. Monday (the day before the election) Kimberlin was back in solitary confinement until November 14. Kimberlin has since filed a suit against Quinlan for violation of his rights.[81]

The whole incident has convinced many reporters that a partisan effort was made to silence Kimberlin, and this has angered them and caused even more attention to be focused on Kimberlin's completely unsubstantiated charges. Before the election, only a few minor media organizations (the Oklahoma paper, WBAI radio in New York, and some left-wing fringe weeklies) had published or aired the story,[82] though if Kimberlin had actually held his press conference the already leaky dam might well have crumbled. (The press conference itself might have been seen by some as a newsworthy event, the hook allowing for publication.) After the election, the perceived cover-up and the lawsuit generated continuing coverage and repetition of Kimberlin's baseless allegations. In an April 1990 *Newsweek* highlight of the controversy, equal weight was seemingly given to Kimberlin's claims and Quayle's denial of the drug charge.[83] Certainly, the responsible federal officials, if not the Bush/Quayle campaign itself, have only themselves to blame for elevating Kimberlin to martyr status. But there is also a pitiful quality to the way in which the press let itself be manipulated by an apparently publicity-hungry federal prisoner guilty of heinous crimes. Journalists need to be more on their guard against individuals like Kimberlin who ''get enjoyment from seeing everybody spin their wheels,'' as ''60 Minutes'' producer Norman Gorin noted.

From drugs to women to plagiarism, rumors about Dan Quayle absorbed a disproportionate share of the press's time and resources in the 1988 general election campaign. Some of this focus was an inevitable and perhaps necessary byproduct of Quayle's national anonymity, not to mention the acknowledgment even among staunch Republicans that Quayle was nowhere near the most-qualified person Bush could have chosen to be next in line for the presidency. But once nominated, Quayle was entitled to have his abilities, public accomplishments, and ideas evaluated fairly—and at least as fully as the rumor of the week.

GEORGE BUSH

The rumor about George Bush's ''mistress'' had a run longer than all but a handful of Broadway productions—and for the political cognoscenti, it was every bit as entertaining. However, the relatively harmless behind-the-scenes fun turned into yet another public morality play as the 1988 campaign unfolded.

The story began almost two full presidential cycles earlier. In late February of 1981, about a month after Bush had taken the oath of office as vice president, a Washington, D.C., woman thought she heard a police officer say that Bush had been shot. Not finding any news about the incident on television, she began calling news organizations to get the details. This innocent effort begat a rumor that took Washington newsrooms by storm, and spurred every journalist's best sources to call in the same tip—with all the repetitions seeming to most newspeople like confirmation. After embellishments that naturally developed in the hundreds of retellings, the rumor boiled down to this: Vice President George Bush had been nicked by a bullet as he left a woman's town house late one evening. The woman was his mistress and—here is where two separate versions developed—she was either a longtime member of his staff or the widow of a former Midwestern Republican congressman. Journalists for all the great newspapers and networks swarmed over a Capitol Hill residential neighborhood where the incident was alleged to have happened. Ellen Hume, then of the *Los Angeles Times,* was going door to door, trying to find anyone who knew anything about the ''shooting,'' when she stumbled across Richard Roth of CBS doing the same thing. "We laughed and joined forces, but came up empty-handed," said Hume. The unfortunate woman who had first called the media was literally harassed by an invading army of journalists, none more obnoxious than a gumshoe from Jack Anderson's outfit who only left when the woman threatened to call the police. Both of the alleged mistresses were interviewed, too; both adamantly denied the specific incident and the general suggestion.

Gradually, it became apparent that the rumor was not true; an angry George Bush even had the FBI interview him about it so that he could get his denial on the official record. And the *Washington Post* decided to investigate and trace the development of this exceptionally powerful piece of gossip. The paper's findings were published in a March 22, 1981, front-page article[84] entitled "Anatomy of a Washington Rumor," by Benjamin Weiser and—appropriately enough—Janet Cooke, the reporter who three weeks later would resign after revealing she had fabricated a series about "Jimmy," a nonexistent eight-year-old D.C. heroin addict.[85] However, the *Post* piece made no mention at all of the story's "mistress" angle; Weiser remembers that, "Our reporters and editors basically concluded that the 'mistress' part, like the rest of the story, was untrue or at least not proved. We weren't going to publish something that we couldn't establish." Yet the mistress rumor was already too deeply rooted in the press corps' memory for the *Post*'s nonpublication of it to matter. Indeed, most reporters today seem to remember the article primarily as a discussion of the mistress allegation. (Of seventeen non-*Post* journalists with whom we discussed the *Post* article, fourteen misrecalled it as the first mention in print of the "Bush mistress" gossip.)

The staff aide romantically linked to Bush in this 1981 incident continued to be a press fascination as the months and years of Bush's vice presidency wore on. "She was a very divisive force in the Bush office, and people would quit because of her, but Bush would insist on keeping her," related *The New Republic*'s Fred Barnes. "People tried to figure out why he would keep [the woman] on his staff when she was driving good people away." The *Post*'s Walter Pincus noted that frequently "when a strong woman is in close proximity to a powerful man, and she appears to have great influence in his life, people start rumors about a personal relationship between them." This certainly occurred in Bush's case, and the rumor was believed even by some on Bush's staff. Ann Devroy (then of Gannett News Service and now with the *Washington Post*) spent several months in late 1981 and early 1982 examining Bush's vice presidential operation—and especially the role his alleged mistress played in it. The woman in question had worked for Bush for many years, and after Devroy interviewed three dozen close associates of Bush during various stages of his career, a less-than-flattering picture emerged of her. According to Devroy, "She was said to have fits of temper and screaming that totally disrupted the staff, to limit access to Bush unfairly, and to argue with everyone. And people kept hinting to me that there was a sexual relationship here." But when Devroy confronted the woman with her coworkers' suspicions, "She cried and screamed and expressed outrage." So Devroy looked elsewhere for proof, and after many weeks reached a conclusion: "I found absolutely no evidence of anything going on. After spending more time on this topic than any reporter I know of, I just came to disbelieve the rumor." Several other meticulous reporters like Devroy also investigated the situation, and reached the same conclusion. One journalist managed to find an airline pilot who had once been engaged to Bush's aide, but broke it off "because of his *suspicions* that she was having an affair with a married man whom he'd always *believed* to be George Bush." This was not exactly the kind of evidence that would stand up in divorce court.

Of course, the reporters who disproved the rumor to their satisfaction never published their findings, so all the others continued to believe the gossip, fueled from time to time by the reports of a Bush staff shake-up in which the alleged mistress was involved[86] or a series of mysterious Bush "disappearances" during 1978 and 1979 when Bush would tell his aides he was flying off to Washington for clandestine meetings with fellow former Central Intelligence Agency directors—meetings which all the other spymasters say were never held.[87] Again, the "mistress" rumor was never mentioned in these stories, but those in the know read between the lines for what they believed was the hidden subtext.

The rumor having been sustained in Bush lore for seven years, its surfacing in the 1988 campaign seemed preordained. And Bush's Republican primary opponents were not about to leave it for the Democrats to mine. As mentioned in chapter 4, both the Dole and Kemp campaigns were involved in spreading the gossip, and after Gary Hart's debacle, their efforts to get a major news organization to break the story went into high gear. Many broadcast network reporters and editors recalled a flurry of contacts in May and June of 1987 utilizing the familiar pressure tactic that "everybody else" was close to breaking the story. ABC News had assigned a half dozen personnel to try to divine the truth or falsity of the rumor, and they had come up with the same evidence as their predecessors at other media outlets: none. Yet the detailed calls from sources, some anonymous, kept coming. An exasperated Hal Bruno, fed up with the manipulation, undertook an unprecedented action:

I've never done it before, but I called my counterparts at other networks and news organizations and said, "Look, we don't have this, do you?" They said, "No, we don't have it. Are you getting the calls?" "Yeah, we're getting the calls." And we realized that there was an orchestrated effort to manipulate the news media. . . . We all agreed we would not be stampeded. What the callers wanted was to force us to ask this question in some sort of forum so it would legitimize a scandalous and unproven rumor. But we all dug in our heels and refused to be manipulated. The executives of ABC News then agreed that we shouldn't allow our network to be panicked into doing this story even at the risk of getting scooped.

Bruno's finger in the dike held, but meanwhile, Lee Atwater had picked up on his opponents' scheme and had decided on a bold move of his own: The campaign itself would break the story but on its own terms. As he described it:

The rumor had started filtering out to the states, and I had some worried state chairmen calling me. After Gary Hart, I knew this thing would inevitably break—probably first from some off-the-wall paper in an article written by a young gunslinging Billy-the-Kid reporter. And then I could just hear the major news organizations: "We don't want to go with this, but now that it's out, we've got to. . . ." So rather than let it come out in a way where I'm totally on the defensive, I made a decision to find one outlet where I could get it out specifically on my terms. And my terms were that I wanted the focus of the rumor to shift from the adultery question to my opponents' dirty tricks in putting out this unfounded rumor. Then all of a sudden, it would be over, because those putting the rumor out could no longer call around since they would be identifying themselves as the dirty tricksters.

The chance to carry out his plan came unexpectedly in the wake of a June 27, 1987, off-the-record luncheon between Atwater and two *Newsweek* staffers, D.C. bureau chief Evan Thomas and chief political correspondent Howard Fineman. Thomas and Fineman raised the subject of the rumor, and Atwater firmly denied it. On their return to the office, Thomas and Fineman decided to telephone Atwater and see if they could convince him to put the denial on the record so they could use it for a brief "Periscope" item in *Newsweek*'s June 29 edition. Atwater thought about their proposition, and finally said, "I might be willing to do some business with you." And he promised *Newsweek* a call from the Bushes' eldest son, George Junior. "Junior" was picked for a very simple reason, according to a senior Bush campaign official: "He couldn't be fired . . . and judging from the wrath of the candidate and his wife, they didn't exactly appreciate what was done, and still don't." Their chagrin was certainly understandable: In one of the largest-circulation news magazines, their son claims he asked his father whether he had ever committed adultery. "Junior" memorably summarized the vice president's response: "The answer to the Big A question is N.O."[88] The item was a hit for both sides. That issue of *Newsweek* received a great deal of publicity, and as for the Bush campaign, said Atwater, "After the 'Periscope' piece, we didn't receive another phone call about the rumor; it stopped it dead in its tracks." Fineman notes, "We were being used, but we were also using. . . . It's the standard Washington relationship."

One more campaign installment for the Bush mistress rumor remained in 1988. While this additional airing, like its predecessors, was not damaging to Bush, it demonstrated that even when the media's front door is shut, gossip can become legitimate news through the back door. In mid-October, when thousands of reporters crowded into Los Angeles for the final Bush-Dukakis debate, the *L.A. Weekly*, a local left-wing newspaper, published a front-page story discreetly entitled, "George Bush: Loverboy."[89] Its author Richard Ryan regurgitated all the old tales about Bush and his staff aide, adding generous scoops of speculation and prurient interpretation. Bush was "said" by anonymous sources to "have had a number of affairs over the years;" not a scintilla of proof was offered for what Ryan himself called "common gossip." Hal Bruno dismissed the piece by noting, "When we saw it, all of us laughed; this was less than what we had thrown away a year and a half earlier." CNN's Frank Sesno, who was accompanying Bush when the *L.A. Weekly* edition was distributed to the press, remembered, "Not a single member of the [press] pool questioned Bush about it because it was such total garbage." Unfortunately, two British tabloids, the *Evening Standard* and *Today*, as well as the New York *Daily News*, picked up the *L.A. Weekly*'s trash, though no responsible media outlet did so.[90] But on Wednesday, October 19, an event occurred that could not be ignored. A rumor that the *Washington Post* was going to publish an exposé on Bush's mistress ripped through Wall Street, triggering a forty-three-point drop in the Dow Jones average. To this day, no one knows exactly how the rumor was introduced to the financial district, though it was either a result of the *L.A. Weekly* story making the rounds, a plant by Democrats who wanted to get the word out, or a clever attempt by a market speculator to make money.[91] In any event, traders flooded the *Post* with calls asking about its publication plans. Normally the *Post* refuses all comment about what it may or may not print, but executive editor Benjamin C. Bradlee made an exception in this case in order to calm the market. On hearing the late-afternoon denial from a *Post* staffer, an excited broker told the staffer to "Hurry up! Call your broker and buy long!"[92]

Media organizations differed greatly in their approach to reporting the market drop. NBC News, the *New York Times*, and the *Boston Globe* mentioned only that an unspecified "damaging" story about Bush was incorrectly believed to be imminent; CBS News and the *Washington Post* included that the rumor was about Bush's personal life; the *Wall Street Journal* and *USA Today* were explicit, citing a "mistress" and an "extramarital affair," respectively, as the subject of the purported *Post* story. Wall Street's response had given the media a news peg for "legitimate" reporting of the Bush rumor, and some used the opportunity to broach the topic. Still more outlets discussed the gossip after the second newspeg was provided the very next day, Thursday, October 20. One of Dukakis's top aides, deputy national field director Donna Brazile, remarked on the record to reporters during a Northeastern campaign swing, "I think George Bush owes it to the American people to fess up. The American people have every right to know if Barbara Bush will share that bed with him in the White House."[93] Brazile quickly resigned in the brouhaha that followed, but her blunt assertions gave a green light to further coverage. The Associated Press, for example, prepared a detailed story for its subscribers about the rumor, and the article contained the initials of Bush's alleged mistress. Major newspapers all across the country ran the AP dispatch, complete with initials.[94]

After this two-day spate of stories based on Wall Street and Brazile, the rumor faded from print, though it was still very much alive in the newsrooms. The *Washington Post* was the focus of "a flood of irate calls," according to staff member Walter Pincus. "I've never been through anything quite like it. People, journalists among them, wanted to know why we were refusing to write about Bush's extramarital affairs. . . . It was toward the end of the campaign, it was clear that Dukakis was going to lose, and a lot of people were angry about that . . . including reporters."[95] Undeniably, there was a hesitancy to go further than reports had already gone—which, based on the nonevidence, was arguably much too far already. Even the tabloid press for once resisted the temptation to sensationalize when, a few days after the Wall Street plunge on October 22, protesters showed up at the annual Italian-American Foundation dinner in Washington with a banner a half block long emblazoned with the name of Bush's alleged mistress. (The demonstrators used a megaphone to chant, ''George loves [woman's name], the Vice President is an adulterer.'') Yet there were excellent reasons for the press's appropriate if tardy discretion. The first is the best: an utter absence of hard proof. Moreover, most editors and producers for major media organizations were well aware of this since their reporters had long ago investigated and discounted the rumor. For most journalists, the allegation simply lacked resonance, especially as contrasted with Gary Hart's or John Kennedy's compulsive womanizing; as one reporter expressed the sentiment, ''Suppose the worst were true and Bush had discreetly kept one mistress for twenty years: why kill the guy for that?'' And as mentioned in an earlier chapter, some journalists may have been reluctant to reopen the ''invasion of privacy'' controversy that had left its wounds in the wake of the Hart/Rice exposé. A good bit of the credit must also be assigned to Lee Atwater's strategy. ''The *L.A. Weekly* article [and subsequent events] never bothered me because I knew that the boil had already been pricked,'' the Bush manager commented. ''It was destined to be a one-day story, which is just a tree falling in the forest with nobody around.'' Furthermore, Brazile's resignation was ''proof positive'' of Atwater's theory that ''stories like that end up focussing on the dirty trickster putting the rumor out. Something like [the Bush rumor] can't come back to life without a new foundation.''

As for the rumor itself, Benjamin Weiser, coauthor of the *Post*'s original ''Anatomy of a Rumor'' piece, deserves the last word: ''I've not seen a single thing since my [1981] article that makes me think we missed it.'' Alas, Weiser has not had the final word; the gossip lives on and continues to find its way into print. In a postelection story about the appointment of Bush's alleged mistress to a State Department position, a senior editor at the *Washington Post* purposefully rewrote the initial reference to the woman to read: ''[Name], who has served President-elect George Bush in a variety of positions.''[96] *Washingtonian* magazine resurrected the *Post*'s old story about Bush's claimed attendance at nonexistent CIA directors' meetings and tied the incidents directly to ''alleged philandering.''[97] And Jack Anderson highlighted the staff aide's ''warm friendship'' with Bush in an April 1990 column.[98] It seems old rumors never die, and they do not fade from print either, even without proof.

JOHN TOWER[99]

Something truly extraordinary was at work in the U.S. Senate vote that sent John Tower down to defeat in March 1989—the first time ever that any new president had been denied one of his cabinet choices or that a former senator had been rejected for a cabinet post by his ex-colleagues. It may well have been that Tower was not a good choice for secretary of defense, that problems in his personal and professional life made him unfit to be near the top of the military chain of command. But one conclusion from an examination of the Tower affair is inescapable: The former Texas legislator was a victim of unfounded rumor and out-of-control press behavior that was at least as scandalous as his alleged offenses.

No one will be surprised that Tower himself, before his April 1991 death in a plane crash, called his confirmation defeat an ''exercise in character assassination.'' Nor will eyebrows be raised when Tower's one-time press spokesman, Dan Howard, criticizes the press for letting their ''standards slip in the pressure-cooker environment of a hot story.'' But one of Tower's chief accusers, conservative leader Paul Weyrich, whose testimony about Tower's alleged alcohol abuse and womanizing opened the floodgates to disparaging charges about the nominee, also is sharply critical of the media coverage:

Even though I wanted to see John Tower defeated, the press was very unfair to him. The man was not given a fair shake. While I approved of the outcome, I had the feeling you might get in watching your mother-in-law drive off the bridge in your new Cadillac.

Even more arresting is the self-criticism journalists direct at their own profession's handling of Tower. In retrospect, many newspeople believe the reporting became caught up in a frenzy fervor; competitive news organizations matched their rivals' unsubstantiated allegations tit for tat, whipping up public sentiment that played into the hands of the partisans conducting a rumor-fed lynching. ''Much of the reporting about Tower was unconscionable,'' declared NBC's Tom Brokaw. ''Everything became fair game, including the airing of very damaging allegations without documentation or confirmation.''

Tower was dismantled piece by piece beginning almost from the moment his confirmation hearings opened on January 25 and continuing over six agonizing weeks until the Senate vote rejecting him on March 9.[100] Many arguably legitimate questions were raised about

Tower's indiscreet private behavior and possible public conflicts of interest in his dealings with the defense industry, but it became extremely difficult for news consumers to separate fact from fiction in the barrage of anti-Tower allegations. As Tower's media aide Dan Howard noted,

Once this "feeding frenzy" started, it was almost impossible to cope with it. Basically, you had an open invitation by the media for anybody to make any kind of charge they wanted to against Senator Tower and be assured that it would find itself in some newspaper or on some television network. All that any enemy the guy ever had, or anybody with a political agenda had to do was pick up the telephone and call someone in the news media, and they were guaranteed of getting a hearing. At the peak of the frenzy, the media would print goddamn-near anything.

Some members of the news media were cleverly manipulated by Democratic U.S. senators, staff members, and consultants whose partisan agenda was to blunt the new president's popularity by means of a stinging, highly unusual cabinet defeat at the outset of his term. A prime instrument of sensational leaks about Tower to the press was a secret FBI investigative report to which only the senators (and the Bush administration) were directly privy. Such an FBI file is akin to a vacuum cleaner, with every allegation ever made against its target swept into its contents. "It was the same kind of raw material and unproven charges that [FBI director] J. Edgar Hoover tried to push on us about Martin Luther King, when most responsible journalists wouldn't touch it," commented veteran journalist Bill Kovach. The often inconclusive exposition in FBI reports can also be interpreted in divergent ways, depending on one's motives. "It was very difficult for us to judge [the charges'] validity since we couldn't see the report ourselves," remembers NBC's Andrea Mitchell. "We were forced to rely on the interpretations of partisan sources and senior senators whose tips were hard to ignore."[101]

Senate Armed Services Committee Chairman Sam Nunn (D., Ga.) postponed the committee confirmation vote on February 2 in order to permit the FBI to investigate additional charges against Tower, and during the nearly three weeks of FBI work, no hearings or formal debates were held. During that period, with no other activity to report, the news media focused on rumors. Day after day newspapers headlined unproven allegations and night after night the networks broadcast them.[102] Lesley Stahl on CBS, for example, cited "a drunken encounter between Tower and a Russian-born dancing school owner," despite the fact that the FBI was "unable to corroborate any of the story and we were unable to corroborate as well."[103] CBS's Rita Braver told viewers that Tower "may have been somehow swept up in the massive Justice Department investigation of defense contracting fraud known as Ill Wind" although there was "still no verification."[104] David Martin, CBS's Pentagon correspondent, focussed on a claim that Tower "maintained secretaries in Geneva as mistresses during the time he was chief negotiator for talks to reduce long-range nuclear weapons," commenting that "the allegation . . . could undermine his ability to lead the armed services" and moreover, uniformed personnel might be court-martialed for a similar offense.[105] (In all cases these were unconfirmed charges.)

The myriad reports of Tower's drinking were especially troublesome. Any consumer of the news, whether careful or casual, received the unmistakable impression that Tower had a serious drinking problem. Yet the press ignored the insistent testimonials to the contrary by many who knew the former senator well or worked closely and socialized regularly with him. More importantly, specific charges about his alcoholic overindulgences repeatedly did not check out.[106] An attendant claimed Tower drank too much vodka on a flight to Paris; other crew members disputed the story, and the attendant making the charge failed a lie-detector test. A waiter at the Monocle, a Capitol Hill restaurant, said he saw Tower drunk there, but a dozen other employees denied it. A businessman reported that Tower was tipsy at a reception in West Germany and cited five other witnesses; all five could not corroborate the incident. An Arizona public opinion pollster, described in one major newspaper story as a "solid, credible businessman with no ax to grind,"[107] insisted he saw Tower inebriated on three specific occasions at Washington's Jefferson Hotel, where Tower usually stayed when in town; the "unbiased" pollster had in fact worked for Arizona's Democratic U.S. Senator Dennis DeConcini, and Tower was not at the hotel on two of the three indicated dates. (On the third, two reliable witnesses swore that Tower was not at all incapacitated.)

Another damaging allegation that proved false arose at the height of the drama, on the first day of the full Senate's debate on the Tower nomination. A *Washington Post* article authored by Bob Woodward cited incidents of misconduct by Tower while he visited Bergstrom Air Force Base in Texas on two separate occasions during the 1970s.[108] A retired Air Force noncommissioned officer was the named source, and he vividly recalled Tower as being visibly drunk and having fondled two women, one of them in uniform. Tower heatedly denied the charges, and his aides went to work trying to clear him. "We traced down every commanding officer, every wing commander, every one of his supervisors," recalled Dan Howard, until they found the answer with the help of U.S. Senator John McCain (R., Ariz.). According to the Air Force, the individual had been relieved of duty in March 1977 and retired in April 1978 on grounds of "mixed-personality disorder with antisocial and hysterical features."[109] "He simply made the whole damn thing up," says Howard, though in the fevered atmosphere of the Tower frenzy, the validity of the charges was at first not seriously questioned. A CBS News interview with the retired Air Force man was scheduled for broadcast the evening of the *Post* story's publication, and it was narrowly averted when Senator McCain disclosed the newly obtained background revelations about the individual on the Senate floor at about 5:15 P.M. "It was a ballbuster right up to the wire," said Howard. Despite sidetracking the CBS segment and securing a front-page article in the next morning's *Post* about the Tower staff's findings, Dan Howard was disconsolate. "At the end of the day we were still stuck with the negative residue from that story [notwithstanding] the quick counterattack," noted Howard. As for Woodward, he admitted, "In a fast moving situation you report what you can get, and I wish I had [had] more time on that story to check."[110]

Despite the overall travesty of the episode, the *Post* deserves credit in one way: The paper published a corrective article quickly and with a front-page placement comparable to the original charge. One of the most frustrating problems faced by Tower and his staff was a traditional one about media coverage: the acquittal never catches up with the allegation. "We'd find ourselves chasing the same stories weeks after we'd clearly knocked them down," complains Howard. Tower adds: "When an allegation was disproven, the media often just went on to a new charge without bothering to note that the previous controversy had been resolved in my favor." NBC's Tom Brokaw says it happened because "the rumormongering was so out of control and repeated so often that it developed a framework of credibility." The sensational gossip that comprised this framework absorbed almost all the space and air time devoted to Tower's nomination. His undeniable qualifications and policy preparation for the post, as well as his generally acknowledged strong performance at the Senate confirmation hearings, received little mention.[111] Substance was boring; scandal was hot. Tower was far from blameless in bringing about his plight, and for many years he had lived the high life. "I freely admit my past excesses. . . . At the age of sixty-four I can look back with regret on a lot of things," Tower confessed to us.[112] But John Tower's sins cannot excuse the media's misdeeds. As ABC's Pentagon correspondent Bob Zelnick observes, "Most of the speculation done on his private life was uncalled for, and it never passed the threshold of relevancy that would have made it a fit subject to explore." The last point is debatable. Alcohol use and abuse is always a legitimate concern about someone in the military chain of command; indiscreet behavior can be dangerously compromising in any top official; and womanizing is highly inappropriate for a potential Defense Department chief who serves as a role model for the men and women of the armed forces. The real threshold that much of the printed and broadcast information about John Tower failed to pass was not relevancy but the most important standard of all: proof. This glaring inadequacy was the true source of the press's unfairness during the Tower affair.

TOM FOLEY

The smear is as old as politics, a time-dishonored technique designed to destroy an opponent by slander. Ironically, Congressman Thomas S. Foley of Washington was the victim of a smear at his moment of greatest political triumph, the ascension to the Speakership of the U.S. House of Representatives on June 6, 1989. An unholy alliance of Foley's own Democratic partisans and Republican party opponents orchestrated the conniving behind Foley's calumniation, with the press as an unwitting coconspirator.

As Speaker Jim Wright struggled under the weight of scandal in the spring of 1989, the eyes of Congress and the press increasingly turned to Wright's next in command and likely successor, Majority Leader Foley.[113] Some of Wright's closest allies sought a last-ditch rescue of their Speaker by use of the innuendo that Foley was homosexual. Like hundreds of other items of gossip, this completely unsubstantiated rumor had wafted through the halls of Congress for years, and a few journalists had picked up on it from time to time.[114] But now a few senior Democratic congressmen were spreading the rumor. As Steve Roberts explained it, "Wright's more devious supporters were creating a backfire of doubt about Foley as a way of slowing the momentum to get rid of Wright." The "documentation" used by the Wright backers was an FBI report on an apparently deranged individual who had made threats against Foley and claimed past homosexual contact with the Speaker-to-be. This report was filed in the office of the House sergeant at arms, where it was available to Wright's backers. Some concerned senior Democrats, including House Ways and Means Committee Chairman Dan Rostenkowski (D., Ill.), confronted Foley directly about the allegation, and Foley adamantly denied it.

Thus the Democratic rumor channel dried up, but the gossip continued to flow from two other sources. The Republican party was naturally delighted to see the Democrats in disarray, and wanted to be helpful in fostering additional chaos in the opposition party. Among the many Republicans passing along the rumor was an aide to House GOP Whip Newt Gingrich of Georgia. This staffer was particularly aggressive in her rumormongering, and she attempted to play one media outlet off against the other in the traditional game of "Beat Your Competitor" (that is, "The *Washington Post* has this already so you'd better hurry up and get it into print").[115] Less intentionally, some in the news media were also doing their part to keep the rumor alive. In mid-May Rowland Evans and Robert Novak quoted a Democratic party insider's small-circulation newsletter in their large-circulation column about the "alleged homosexuality of one Democrat who might move up the succession ladder."[116] Fred Barnes of *The New Republic* referred to a "rumor about sexual misconduct by Foley."[117] ("I wish now I hadn't put that sentence in," concedes Barnes.) CBS News was hot on the trail of the Foley rumor as well. Phil Jones, the network's widely respected Capitol Hill correspondent, worked for weeks to nail down a purported Foley homosexual liaison with a man who by May 1989 was a prisoner at Lorton reformatory (just outside the District of Columbia in suburban Virginia). Jones's ongoing work was well known to some of his colleagues inside CBS, and the suspicions raised by his research showed up on the air. In a late May "Face the Nation" program, Democratic Congressman William Gray of Pennsylvania was probed about his knowledge of any potential problem in Foley's background (he said there was none), and on the same broadcast Foley was shown being asked if "we'll be hearing, later on, that people . . . are looking into your background." (Foley's response: "No need to worry about that.")[118] On May 28 Dan Rather pursued the subject with an interviewee, House Majority Whip Tony Coelho of California. Rather was suggestive in this carefully phrased question: "Some of [the Republicans], with a wink I'm told, were passing the word that, 'listen, the worst of it is not even over yet,' that others in the Democratic leadership, Tom Foley . . . mentioned specifically [may be drawn in] . . . Do you know of anything of an ethical, character nature that would prevent Tom Foley from being the next Speaker . . . ?"[119] Rather later described the "anatomy of what happened":

That interview came at a time when I had been told by many people I trusted what was going on, and that operatives were trying hard and had a good chance to get the story placed. So at any moment, I'm possibly going to be reading in one of the better newspapers these allegations about Foley. Yet we didn't have the story where we were comfortable reporting it—and we never got to that point. So, I'm not proud of this, but I didn't want some-one to say, 'well, Rather gets an exclusive interview with Coelho and he doesn't ask him the tough question. . . . In hindsight, if I had it to do all over again, I probably wouldn't ask that.

The most explicit press airing of the Foley rumor came in a column by the *New York Daily News*'s Lars-Erik Nelson on June 5.[120] His inten-tions were good—an exposé of the Gingrich aide's rumormongering. But in so doing, Nelson revealed some of the heretofore unpublished details of the charges (such as the Lorton inmate's allegation). "In the process of making references to the rumor, some journalists spread gossip to millions that previously had the attention of about 2,000 people," observed the *Washington Post*'s media critic, Eleanor Randolph.

The press was primed, and the public stage set, for a grand de-nouement. The Republican National Committee's communications director, Mark Goodin, obliged by providing the plot's finale. Goodin circulated a four-page memo addressed to Republican lead-ers on Capitol Hill that was headlined: "Tom Foley: Out of the Lib-eral Closet." The homosexual allusion was further enhanced by a comparison of Foley's voting record with that of Massachusetts' avowedly gay Congressman Barney Frank. The memo was leaked from the Hill to several reporters, and its contents were publicly di-vulged on the very day Foley ascended to the Speakership. In most newspapers across America, the unproven rumor shared nearly equal billing with Foley's election,[121] and Foley felt compelled to de-clare on national television, "I am, of course, not a homosexual."[122] All this was too much for the fair-minded, and even for many fiercely Republican partisans. President Bush, House Minority Leader Rob-ert Michel (R., Ill.), and Senate Minority Leader Robert Dole (R., Kans.) denounced the memo. Its author, Mark Goodin, resigned his post, and Republican National Committee Chairman Lee Atwater—who denied advance knowledge of the memo—called Foley person-ally to apologize. Incidentally, Goodin maintains to this day that he did not "act intentionally to smear" Foley:

People just don't want to believe it, but I got in a rush and only glanced at the draft written by one of our researchers who was obviously trying to be very cute. I actually missed the [homosexual] double entendre . . . I look back occasionally and think 'how could you possibly have missed it?' And the simple answer is, I screwed up.

Interestingly, however, at the time he approved the memo, Goodin was well aware that at least one major media organization was already looking into Foley's life. CBS's Phil Jones, a personal and professional friend of Goodin's, had told the GOP staffer he was working on the story while Jones was pumping him for information about the subject.[123] Goodin also later cited Jones's potential Foley story to Lee Atwater in justifying his release of the memo. Goodin's apparent reasoning was that the memo might generate discussion of Foley's private life that could in turn provide a hook for Jones to break his story; Goodin was half right.

Clearly, then, journalists played a regretable if secondary role in spreading the allegation about Foley, just as they had for many of the other rumors discussed earlier in this chapter. But it ought also to be noted that some reporters, publications, and broadcasts refused to join the herd, and admirably refrained from abetting the gossip; a few even tried to contain it. Compared to many other newspapers the *Washington Post* downplayed the incident, burying it in a lengthy story on Foley's election as Speaker and refusing to include the detailed nature of the rumor. (The *Post* referred only to "a crude attempt to smear Foley on a personal basis."[124]) NBC's Andrea Mitchell was equally discreet in her initial report for the Nightly News,[125] mentioning a Republican "smear campaign" without particulars; then, over the next two evenings, she compiled two hard-hitting packages focussing the critical spotlight on those responsible for the innuendo.[126] "I was determined not to play into [the rumor-mongerers'] hands," says Mitchell. Cokie Roberts at National Public Radio took a similar approach, leading the fight to keep the rumor off the air. Her admiring colleague, Nina Totenberg, nonetheless notes that Roberts lost her battle due to the uncontrollable nature of a chaotic newsroom: "Here we had all these policy discussions about how far we should go, what was our obligation and to whom, and blah, blah, blah, and then the next morning at 3 A.M. some newscaster who was not part of the policy discussion reads the newswire copy over the air with some reference to homosexuality. And the cat's out of the bag." Earlier, Roberts had also done yeoman service in her other role as an ABC News Capitol Hill correspondent. In May when the Foley rumors first started swirling, she had received a call from the ABC "I-Team," an investigative unit of the network's news division. "These people are great believers in conspiracy theories," says Roberts, and they had a whopper for her to check out. A young man claiming to have had sex with an unspecified male "Democratic congressional leader"—the youthful homosexual did not know the congressman's name—said that the legislator could be identified by a distinctive one-and-one half inch scar on his penis.[127] "Can you find out if Foley has such a scar?" they asked Roberts. "I could not believe I was having this conversation," Roberts recalled, and she politely declined to carry the investigation forward. "I was not the person for this story; I was not going to conduct a stakeout in the men's room or do anything else necessary to get the information." Instead, Roberts called the press secretary to Democratic Whip Coelho, revealing that the same Democratic congressmen and staff members passing around other tales about Foley were responsible for this one.[128] This tipoff, combined with similar intelligence from elsewhere, spurred the Democratic leadership to confront the gossipers with a 'put up or shut up' command. Cokie Roberts's journalist-husband, Steven, was also able to do the right thing at his publication, U.S. News & World Report. Having already been told directly by a gay congressman with whom he went to high school that the Foley rumor was untrue—"he had never run across Foley's trail in the gay world"—Roberts and his editors at first decided to do nothing in print lest they perpetuate the false charges. But after the RNC memo and its attendant publicity had burst upon the scene, the U.S. News staff decided to publish a thorough exposé of the rumor-mongers. Tom Foley himself "had tears in his eyes and pleaded with the main reporter, Gloria Borger, and then our editor, Roger Rosenblatt, not to do this piece, but we believed we would be doing our readers an injustice by not explaining what had happened and why." The resulting story, entitled "Anatomy of a smear: Republicans and Democrats spread the Big Lie on Tom Foley," amply vindicates U.S. News's judgment by channeling the reader's attention to the injustice done Foley and more especially to the villainy of his accusers.[129] "We did a service by nailing the rumormongerers once we got the goods on them," Roberts justifiably boasts.

The frenzy abuses identified in parts of this chapter demonstrate the "coverage to excess" that has become so much a part of the news media's political focus. Occasionally, however, the abuse is in the opposite direction: the press's failure to discover or reveal official venality, or to apply a uniform standard of scrutiny to all candidates. This less prevalent but still noteworthy occurrence is the other side of the frenzy story.

CHAPTER

6

Frenzies That Weren't

The Other Side of the Story

"There are things we don't publish, lots of them, all the time," insists Len Downie, managing editor of the *Washington Post.* "There's far more restraint in this business than we're given credit for," asserts NBC News's Jim Polk. Despite all the excesses discussed in the previous chapter, considerable evidence exists to confirm Downie's and Polk's contentions. Many of the stories that reach print or broadcast are like icebergs: Only an eighth of the material gathered is ever made visible to readers and viewers, discretion keeping the other seven-eighths from view. Several of the cases already discussed (such as some of the Quayle and Bush gossip) demonstrate as much. Moreover, most of the rumors heard by members of the press are never published or aired at all, and not simply for lack of proof. Serious journalists are truly concerned about the appropriateness of publication in many instances, and together with their editors they try to exercise considered judgment. "At least once every other week we have really wrenching discussions about whether or not something should be published," reports *Time*'s Ted Gup. "I have files having to do with private indiscretions that would make wonderful chatter, but I'm not going to publish them." Of course, the problem is that not all journalists are as responsible as Gup, and in this age of lowest-common-denominator journalism, the rules of coverage are sometimes set by those on the ethical periphery. Moreover, the decisions about what is and is not revealed are often disturbingly arbitrary, with the informal rules being unfairly applied to different candidates in similar circumstances. In a couple of cases, as we shall see, one could even argue that *too* much discretion was employed by the press, and the public was denied legitimate information critical to evaluating a candidacy.

187

Frenzies Delayed and Denied

In chapter 2 we discussed the reasons for the lack of frenzies through the Kennedy and Johnson administrations. Once standards began to change, and the Rooseveltian rule was no longer universally honored, some potential frenzies were delayed or never happened at all simply by chance, circumstance, and missed opportunities. Ben Franklin of the *New York Times* spent months in Maryland during the 1968 presidential campaign "digging around, looking for the evidence of corruption on Governor Spiro Agnew's part. . . . We had strong intimations that Spiro had taken kickbacks [a form of illegal payoff by government contractors], which by then were a way of life in Maryland." Franklin at times came tantalizingly close to the story that would eventually cause Agnew to resign the vice presidency in disgrace, but alas he could not substantiate his suspicion by the end of the campaign. (Given the closeness of the final 1968 vote, it is entirely possible that corruption revelations about Agnew in mid-campaign would have been enough to elect Democrat Hubert Humphrey president.) The Watergate scandal, of which Agnew's resignation was a somewhat unrelated subset, was another frenzy delayed by early missed signals. CBS News's George Herman scooped everyone on the original GOP-sponsored burglary of the Democratic party's Watergate headquarters when a friend who worked part-time for the Democratic National Committee dropped by Herman's house for a neighborly visit in the summer of 1972:

He came to borrow the rose sprayer and said to my wife, "What has George heard about the break-in at the DNC?" So she called me, and the friend gave me the details he had heard on the job. Then I called the police department, making them believe I knew all about the story, and they told me everything. And I put it on the air immediately, an hour and a half before a wire service came out with it. . . . I knew that it was some kind of an espionage operation because the burglars had microfilm and cameras with them. But I really wasn't all that interested because I was working on some economic story that I thought was very important at the time.

Herman was certainly not alone in missing the significance of the break-in. Less than 3 percent of all the print stories and 17 percent of the broadcast pieces during the 1972 general election campaign even mentioned Watergate.[1] And the Watergate reporting team of the *New York Times* ignored an explosive tip from one of their newspaper's own photographers, who had been told by a Secret Service friend that President Nixon had an extensive Oval Office taping system.

The journalists dismissed the suggestion as too outrageous to be true—until Nixon aide Alexander Butterfield revealed just such a taping system to the Senate Watergate Committee fully eight months later.[2]

Some frenzies seem almost predestined to happen, so determined are a few politicians to advertise their odd proclivities. Tales of Jimmy Carter's homilies on sensitive subjects were legion in the 1976 campaign press corps even before his infamous "lust in the heart" *Playboy* interview. What has not been widely known is that Carter had given virtually the same talk with even juicier details in an on-the-record session to historian Doris Kearns Goodwin three months prior to *Playboy's* "scoop." While visiting Carter in Plains, Georgia, in July 1976, Goodwin asked Carter about a comment he had made to his campaign staff to avoid extramarital affairs. Carter responded by describing with graphic intimacy "about how every night when he prays to Jesus Christ he feels so guilty because he has to describe to Christ the dimensions of the women that he lusted after, and he felt that Christ didn't really want to hear this from him, but he has to go through it."[3] When Goodwin returned home and wrote a commissioned article for *Ladies Home Journal*, she decided to leave out what Carter had called his "battle of lust" because it was "too bizarre."[4] Additionally, at least one premier publication, the *New York Times*, refused the opportunity to print an exclusive advance article on the upcoming *Playboy* revelations. Jim Wooten, then covering the Carter campaign for the *Times*, relayed the *Playboy* offer to his editorial superiors, whose response was, according to Wooten: "We are not amused; thanks but no thanks." The editors believed the topic too racy, the source too seedy, and the opportunity to manufacture a phony issue too great[5]—all commendable sentiments in part that, by 1990s "anything goes" standards, appear hopelessly anachronistic. Incidentally, the *Times* only printed a "lust in the heart" story after other publications had done so and the furor was manifest. Furthermore, the *Times* cited Carter's use of the word *screw* only as "a vulgarism," and when Carter employed the obscenity "fuck" in a *Sunday Times Magazine* interview with Norman Mailer released the same week,[6] the *Times* substituted four dashes for the four-letter word.

The public release of the three frenzies discussed in this section—Watergate, Agnew's corruption, and Carter's *Playboy* spread—was merely delayed. Other recent potential frenzies never happened at all, though one wonders whether they could be contained as easily today. ABC's Sam Donaldson, covering the relatively unknown

Jimmy Carter in early 1976, was told by townspeople in Plains that Carter had "had a nervous breakdown" after losing the Georgia Democratic gubernatorial nomination in 1966. "Carter flatly denied it" when Donaldson questioned him about it, though he admitted "going on retreat and taking a few weeks off to try to keep his family together." Even though no medical records or other evidence was produced to disprove the allegation, Donaldson discounted the local gossip after discussing it with the presidential candidate's intimates. While circumstances differ—the incumbent president did not call Carter an "invalid," for instance—it is easy to imagine a story on "rumors concerning candidate Carter's past mental health problems" reaching print or air in the current climate. Similarly, the standard of proof necessary for private life exposés was higher only a few years ago. Knut Royce, now of *Newsday,* recalls his California investigation during the 1970s into a subgubernatorial male state officeholder's relationships with young men under age eighteen. "This was a felony, statutory rape, and we had affidavits from some of the [alleged victims], but we still found it next to impossible to meet the editor's standards," and so the charges were never published. In an election for governor during the 1980s in a southern state, a few reporters learned of an alleged extramarital relationship that had been carried on by the campaign's front-runner with one of the public employees under his command. (The candidate was already a statewide elective official.) Despite some intriguing evidence (hotel bills, love notes, and so on), no irrefutable confirmation of the affair was obtained and no public mention was ever made of the private tempest; the candidate won easily.

Of course, as in the case above, no irrefutable confirmation of Gary Hart's alleged affair with Donna Rice existed when the *Miami Herald* published its first story. Again and again, we have returned to Hart's 1988 frenzy as a watershed in the reporting about the private lives of politicians. While bad luck combined with recklessness (and perhaps predestination, as with Carter's *Playboy* interview) resulted in Hart's demise in 1987, it should be remembered that fortuitous timing prevented Hart's sexual exploits from receiving greater scrutiny in 1984, as explained in chapter 3. Good timing also may have stopped another potential Hart minifrenzy in its tracks. In 1984 James Perry of the *Wall Street Journal* wrote a long profile of Hart, published at the apogee of the candidate's meteoric rise.[7] In the story was the revelation that Hart and a friend had stolen a high-school chemistry test in advance of the examination, scoring near-perfect grades despite being very weak in the subject. The school principal almost refused to graduate the two seniors on account of the incident. Had Hart remained in the 1988 presidential contest, this might well have become a frenzy, or at least a flap, building on the Biden plagiarism controversy.

Timing is also evident in several other potential frenzies that never ripened. Pat Robertson's "miracle baby" revelation occurred when the character issue was in full bloom and thus received the maximum publicity; Ronald and Nancy Reagan's miracle baby (daughter Patti) was apparently never highlighted in Reagan's four presidential campaigns stretching from 1968 to 1984, even though some veteran Reagan watchers in the press corps were aware of the circumstances.[8] Some news outlets in 1987 were seriously discussing whether to disclose a U.S. senator's longtime relationship with a woman not his wife if the senator decided to run for president. Perhaps partly because word of the possible exposure had apparently reached the senator, he chose not to run. Nonetheless the story nearly came out publicly, and by accident, as ABC News's Jim Wooten forthrightly confessed:

I almost gave it away on the air in a live piece of schtick one night with Peter [Jennings]. . . . We were talking about a number of candidates who might have run for president, but didn't, and I was within a millisecond of discussing the senator's situation. The way I try to approach live television is to be conversational, you know, "Here's a story I want to tell you guys, sit down . . ." and so I almost did it. I broke out in a sweat because I came that close.

This senator was one of at least four current Senate members who purportedly keep mistresses, as cited by various interviewees. The reporters who claimed to have the goods on the solons all saw no reason to reveal the information since these legislators are relatively discreet; are not presidential candidates; are not guilty of the hypocrisy of parading their wives before the cameras at election time; seem at least in a couple of cases to have won the acquiescence of their spouses for the arrangement; and have chosen partners who are not on the congressional payroll, underage, or otherwise unsuitable. Of course, if any of these conditions were to change, so might the tentative decisions of the press not to report the affairs.

The Straight-Line Exception for Gays

These heterosexual relationships are off limits for the moment, but many journalists seem much more skittish about revealing homosexual entanglements, short of the truly outrageous cases such as that of

Barney Frank. Partly this may be because the public opprobrium attached to homosexuality is far greater, and therefore the potential
damage done by a story is more severe and long lasting. This seems
to be the principal rationale used by at least two news media organizations in deciding not to publish a story in 1988 about one of Michael
Dukakis's campaign aides. This individual was allegedly gay and
had also served as a foster parent to children, significant because
Dukakis as governor of Massachusetts had opposed allowing homosexuals to serve as foster parents. In this instance, though, the potential hurt that would have been inflicted on the staffer and his children
seemed to outweigh whatever element of hypocrisy existed in the situation. The *Washington Post* made a similar decision in 1980, when
the paper's top brass conferred and agreed to investigate a reliable
tip that several of Republican presidential candidate Ronald
Reagan's close advisers were gay. *Post* reporter Ted Gup was given
the assignment and, while the tip apparently proved to be accurate,
"There was no nexus between private sexual orientation and public
performance that we could see . . . except for a tortured argument
about the possibility of extortion, blackmail, and manipulation." The
Post chose not to make that argument, and while the subjects of the
investigation were made very uncomfortable in the process, nothing
was ever published about it.[9]

A particularly striking example of press discretion about homosexuality came in early June of 1990, when two gay activists held a Capitol Hill press conference to announce the names of three U.S.
senators and five U.S. House members they claimed were gay. It was
an example of "outing," a despicable new movement by gay extrem-
ists that calls for "uncloseting" politicians who are homosexuals
both to punish those who do not support the gay activists' agenda
and (somewhat contradictorily) to produce more "role models" for
the gay community. This practice is shunned even by many prominent avowed homosexuals as a violation of the privacy rights most
gays hold dear. After the press conference, not a single one of the
dozen correspondents covering it reported the names, nor was there
apparently the slightest interest in seeking proof of the allegations.[10]
(No evidence was provided by the event's organizers.) Since 1988
"outing" advocates have organized at least a half dozen demonstrations at the homes or offices of prominent officeholders (mainly congressmen but also a Midwestern governor), using signs, chants, and
speeches to label the targets as hidden homosexuals.[11] In only two
instances has the mainstream press identified the substance of the
"outing" allegations. One circumstance was partly unavoidable: In

1990 a gay activist announced on a live television news show panel his belief that a leading candidate for governor in his Northeastern state was homosexual. No proof was forthcoming, but nonetheless some other media outlets reported the scurrilous claim in full.[12] A second example of press complicity happened at about the same time on the other side of the continent. During a Western U.S. senator's 1990 reelection race, two of the incumbent Republican's most centrally located billboards were defaced with boldly visible statements such as "Closeted Gay. Living a Lie—Voting to Oppress." Several major West Coast newspapers, some Knight-Ridder newspapers (including the *Miami Herald* and the *Philadelphia Inquirer*), at least one local television station in the senator's home state, and National Public Radio named the senator in their accounts of the vandalism, thus acceding to the agenda of the vandals. This senator was one of those accused of "anti-gay" votes and thus hypocrisy, but in most cases the press appears to judge homosexual hypocrisy as more understandable than the heterosexual variety due to society's prejudices. As a consequence, journalists may see a less compelling need to publish or broadcast the inherent duplicity of gay public officials.[13]

Discretion or Timidity? The Cases of Chuck Robb and Jesse Jackson

Journalistic discretion, whatever the cause, may seem a welcome respite from the regular fare of scandal and tease. Yet too much discretion leads easily to abuses evident in John Kennedy's heyday. Such instances of excessive timidity are rare today, but they still can be found. One state example, Virginia's Charles Robb, and one national case, the Rev. Jesse Jackson, come to mind. When Robb was accused of attending drug parties, newspaper editorialists and political observers alike (including this author) rushed to his defense. Given Robb's straitlaced image, the charges seemed preposterous, and given his power and popularity, many were hesitant to question his behavior. After the initial, ground-breaking revelations by the *Richmond Times-Dispatch*, the newspaper that commendably devoted the most substantial time and resources to uncovering the facts was the Norfolk *Virginian-Pilot*. Yet pressure from Robb's staff and concern within the paper itself about the explosiveness of its findings resulted in a "heavily lawyered" article, according to *Pilot* editorial editor William Wood. The tone of the piece was also quite subdued, and a reader seeking to understand the scope and import of Robb's activities was forced to scan a full page and a quarter of newsprint, with the language couched so carefully that its meaning was obscured.[14] The withering hostility directed by Robb supporters to the newspaper—and particularly the story's investigative reporter, Rose Ellen O'Connor—took its toll. The pressure and inhibitions were all the greater on the newspaper and potential sources and witnesses as well, since Robb was virtually certain to win election to the U.S. Senate in a few months. "With a man as popular as Chuck Robb, you know it's damn hard," admitted the *Pilot*'s managing editor Jim Raper, who along with executive managing editor Sandra Rowe shepherded the story through to publication. The *Pilot*'s spread on Robb did in fact build a very strong case that, as governor, he had repeatedly and knowingly socialized with an exceedingly sleazy crowd that included drug dealers and that he had attended parties where cocaine was used. However, the newspaper also chose to leave out a great deal of information, particularly the explicit details about Robb's associations with "party girls" as well as women such as Tai Collins, a former Miss Virginia/USA, with whom Robb had a warm friendship for a time. "We bent over backwards to be conservative," remembered Rose Ellen O'Connor. "There had been a really bad backlash from the public after the Gary Hart [–Donna Rice] story, and so the climate was a problem. . . . If we erred, we wanted to err on the side of not printing enough, as opposed to printing too much." This approach, while admirable compared to press excesses in other frenzies, creates other problems—chiefly that, in an age of hype, a subdued story will be easily dismissed by the public, and information vital in evaluating a candidate will be disregarded. "There had been such great expectations built up about [the *Pilot*'s investigation] that many people—the political insiders at least—were let down by the story," says Bill Wood. "That dampened the response to [the revelations]." After the story appeared, according to Rose Ellen O'Connor, a "very credible" witness stepped forward, "a very respected, upstanding businessman in Virginia Beach who happened—through a series of coincidences—to be at a party" at which Governor Robb was present at Christmastime 1983. According to a sworn statement the businessman gave to the *Pilot*, he started to leave the party when a woman offered him a marijuana cigarette. "I was very concerned about being in the presence of illegal drugs because of my position in the community." His affidavit continued:

As I left I saw former Governor Charles Robb, who was then in office, sitting on a sofa with a young woman. . . . Another young woman was kneeling next to a coffee table directly in front of the sofa and was using what I presumed to be cocaine because she was inhaling it through her nose. Robb was less than two feet from the coffee table on top of which was a long row of lines of what I also presumed was cocaine. No attempt was made to hide the substance from the governor.

The *Pilot* chose not to publish a follow-up story because the new revelation "really didn't progress [the original story] that much further," said O'Connor. "We felt that any reasonable person could read our story and see that Robb had some knowledge" of the drugs available at parties he attended.[15] Robb has heatedly, "absolutely" denied being present when drugs were used; indeed, he has claimed, "I don't know if I would recognize cocaine if I saw it."[16] On the public record, Robb has also denied having any extramarital affairs, though privately some of his closest associates stress that Robb's declaration of sexual fidelity to his wife applies only to "full coital intercourse."

Better known and widely discussed has been the press's hesitancy to treat Jesse Jackson on the same terms as other presidential candidates. Not only did Jackson receive the most favorable coverage of any 1988 White House aspirant,[17] but with the exception of the alleged plagiarism incident described in the previous chapter, controversies that plagued his rivals' campaigns never had much of an impact on his, even when there was an obvious parallel. Jackson's wife Jacqueline was more than two months pregnant at the time of their 1962 marriage, but little was said about it in comparison to fellow preacher Pat Robertson's "miracle baby" frenzy.[18] A number of reporters had heard Jackson use the slurs "Hymie" and "Hymietown" over the years, but none until the *Washington Post*'s Milton Coleman thought this manifest example of prejudice sufficiently serious to report.[19] And Jackson's privacy was almost consistently respected despite strong circumstantial evidence linking him to women other than his wife. As early as 1975 Chicago journalist Barbara Reynolds, in her book on Jackson, reported on Jackson's "close personal relationship" with singer Roberta Flack, who crooned a passionate love song entitled "Jesse" on national television in 1974.[20] Other entertainers, including Nancy Wilson and Aretha Franklin, have also been tied to Jackson.[21] Still another celebrity, actress Margot Kidder ("Lois Lane" of *Superman* movie fame), nearly provided the hook for 1988 press scrutiny of Jackson's private life. Before the California primary, in the late spring of 1988, Kidder campaigned extensively with Jackson. As one reporter covering the campaign put it, "Jackie Jackson was conspicuously absent, and Kidder would almost take on the physical role of the campaign wife; she was there by his side campaigning with him everywhere." Late on the evening before the primary, Kidder came out of Jackson's hotel room apparently somewhat light-headed, and said on tape to CNN and ABC camera crews waiting for an expected Jackson-Dukakis conclave: "I'm Margot Kidder and I'm whacked." In the elevator after this encounter, Kidder remarked to a Jackson aide within earshot of a CNN crew that she hoped someone cleaned up Jackson's bedroom "since it's a mess."[22] The interest of the press was piqued by these events, and ABC's Brit Hume requested Marianne Keely, an off-the-air reporter for his network, to ask Jackson off-camera about Kidder's remarks. Jackson and later Kidder made it abundantly clear to Keely and others that the inquiry was not appreciated, and that all the circumstances, however suggestive, were in fact quite innocent. Jackson told Keely that his wife Jackie had been present that evening in his hotel room, and "the mess" to which Kidder referred was leftover food. A short time later ABC News received a letter from Kidder's lawyer threatening legal action and demanding that its personnel cease and desist from spreading rumors. The ABC reply insisted that its employees were innocent of rumormongering and noted that the network could not prevent other people from gossiping, but since it had no proof of a Jackson–Kidder relationship it would air no story. The only reference to the matter appeared in an AP dispatch filed by Rita Beamish on June 20, 1988, in which Kidder "angrily scoff[ed]" at "the inevitable campaign plane rumors that arise from her working relationship with Jackson." This single exception aside, the decision not to publish or air the unproved rumors was laudable, especially since the explanations offered by Jackson and Kidder were credible and plausible. On the other hand, the hesitation to pursue the more general topic of Jackson's alleged womanizing suggested a double standard in light of the press's aggressive pursuit of the character issue for other candidates. "I was convinced that a lot of people were afraid to touch that story for any number of reasons, first and foremost, a fear of being charged with being racist," commented CNN's respected anchor Bernard Shaw, who is black. Many interviewees also noted the paradox in Jackson's relationship with the press: Jackson insisted that he be treated as seriously as any other candidate—and when he was so treated, and was given the scrutiny that comes with the territory, Jackson often became incensed.

One newspaper that did devote substantial resources to investigating Jackson's private life was the *Atlanta Constitution*. But even the *Constitution* downplayed the matter, admitted the paper's respected former editor Bill Kovach (now curator of the Nieman Foundation) and staff writer Priscilla Painton.[23] Painton's extensive and aggressive research turned up substantial information about Jackson's links to several women, but the reporter and her editor chose to maintain a very high standard of proof not always present in the press's recent coverage of political figures. Painton makes an argument that Gary Hart would surely have welcomed in his time of trial:

Adultery is very hard to prove. Even if you have the woman involved claiming she's had a relationship, even if you have a time and a place, even if you have friends of the woman telling you this, even if you have the husband of the woman involved telling you this, it still boils down to their word against his. It's not like anything else in journalism where you can come up with documented proof.

Kovach pointed to his decision not to publish some of Painton's most suggestive material: "Priscilla got a lot of information about Jackson checking into motel rooms with a woman not his wife, and when the maid cleans up the room it's pretty obvious somebody was romping around in bed. I would not let those stories get into the paper because after all, he could have had a nightmare and she could have been sleeping on the floor. Jesse Jackson or anybody else could go into a lot of rooms with a lot of women and it does not necessarily prove anything." Jackson was undoubtedly delighted by Kovach's high standards, though the candidate took nothing for granted. Remembers Kovach: "For quite a long period Jesse became my morning alarm clock. I'd get a 5:30 A.M. call at least three or four times a week so he could complain about Priscilla's questions."

Many other reporters covering Jackson were well aware of at least some background on Jackson's private life but chose to tiptoe around it. Even the normally fearless Mike Wallace of "60 Minutes" nearly avoided the subject entirely in a featured interview with Jackson and his wife.[24] Journalists who did ask Jackson blunt questions seemed willing to accept answers that would not have been so easily swallowed coming from other candidates. For example, in the wake of Gary Hart's 1987 withdrawal, Jackson announced he had no "obligation to answer" queries about adultery because there was "not such activity" on his part, and regardless, it was only "a legitimate question . . . if national security is involved."[25] Later Jackson insisted "the second floor of the White House is off limits to the press."[26] Weighing the contrast between the treatment received by Jackson and that meted out to his competitors, Bill Kovach says bluntly, "Had he been a white candidate, there would have been considerably more effort devoted by more organizations to looking into [the allegations of womanizing]. There was a kind of self-censorship going on; it was fear of being attacked for piling on the black candidate."

Many of our interviewees made comments similar to that of ABC's Jim Wooten when he observed that "the media didn't do a very good job covering Jackson." Reporters cited many reasons for the "kid gloves" treatment Jackson usually received. As already mentioned, the press dreaded the charge of racism,[27] a common allegation leveled by black politicians who are under fire.[28] "The fear of being called racist led the press—and his Democratic opponents as well—to treat Jackson like he had fenders," columnist Jack Germond observes. Related to this is the ideological devotion of most journalists to the ideals of the civil rights movement and its practical application by means of affirmative action.[29] PBS's Paul Duke sees Jackson's status as the first major black candidate for president as the reason why "the press was sheepish about doing anything that would diminish him." Jackson's position as a role model for young inner-city blacks and the candidate's reverential reception at most African American gatherings probably reinforced the traveling media's instincts. Less praiseworthy was another assessment by many journalists: that Jackson was unelectable, and therefore close scrutiny of his character and positions was unnecessary.[30] On occasion, Jackson's inaccurate claims on the campaign trail went unexamined because of this sentiment,[31] but just as important, Jackson was not taken as seriously as his competitors merely on account of his color. The truly racist question of the 1984 and 1988 campaigns was, What does Jesse really want? when Jackson had made it abundantly clear that the presidency was his objective.

Other nonracial explanations for the special handling of Jackson are also apparent. Candidates who consistently provide good, colorful copy and who are by nature blunt and straightforward frequently receive favorable treatment from a grateful press. Jackson's clever tactics deserve credit as well. On his alleged extramarital sex life, Jackson and his wife launched a preemptive strike, aggressively staking out their privacy and warning reporters about invading it. Mrs. Jackson, for example, told Mike Wallace she would permit no "vulgar questions" in the "60 Minutes" interview, and on other occasions she admonished reporters not to "go digging" in an attempt to "destroy my family."[32] As for Jackson himself, "There's a disinclination to want to deal too harshly with Jesse," surmises columnist Robert Novak. "He's a tough fighter; you're not dealing with Michael

Dukakis there.'' Certainly Jackson's supporters' methods in dealing with Barbara Reynolds after publication of her (partly) unflattering biography of him might have warned off potential press challengers. After an enraged Jackson claimed the book had been ghostwritten by white editors, Reynolds was harassed by threatening telephone calls and pickets outside her apartment house.[33] Jackson has also been known to ask probing reporters an intimidating question or two, such as, How many blacks do you have on your staff? (Jackson's query may well have introduced some not entirely inappropriate white guilt from time to time; American newsroom personnel are 91 percent white, and just 6 percent of newspaper executives are members of minority groups.[34]) One rationale infrequently mentioned for Jackson's friendly relations with the news media does not stand up to inspection, however: a special regard for his position as a minister. Not only is the press corps irreverent by nature, but clearly no privileges on the order of Jackson's were extended to fellow preacher Pat Robertson. Indeed, many of Robertson's supporters believe his religious affiliation produced intensely critical, prejudicial coverage.[35]

Jesse Jackson notwithstanding, exercising too much discretion is usually the least of the press's worries. The excesses identified earlier in this volume are of far greater concern, foremost among them the publication or broadcast of rumor, gossip, and innuendo without reasonably strong evidence. The critical emphasis here is on the actual printing or airing of rumors, not the mere gathering of information about them. Any serious allegation is a fit subject for the press to explore and investigate in the newsroom, for one never knows in advance which alleyways are blind and which lead to significant relevations. But there ought to be a restoration of a high standard of proof before any charge is inked or aired: The facts that rumors are circulating widely and the political world is abuzz are most assuredly not a sufficient threshold. We will return to this vital argument in the concluding chapter, keeping in mind the wise words of the Nieman Foundation's Bill Kovach: ''The bell that's been rung can't be unrung . . . and that's reporting rumors. We didn't used to do that.''[36]

7

Consequences

Having examined some of the truths about feeding frenzies in previous chapters, we now turn to their consequences. Frenzies have major repercussions on the institution that spawns them—the press—including how it operates, what the public thinks of it, and whether it helps or hurts the development of productive public discourse. The candidates and their campaigns are obviously directly affected by the ways and means of frenzies; which politicians win and which lose, and the manner of their running, are affected by the rules of frenzy coverage. How the voters view politics at any given time—whether the electorate is optimistic or pessimistic, idealistic or cynical—is partly a by-product of what they learn about the subject from the news media. And above all, the dozens of feeding frenzies in recent times have had substantial and cumulative effects on the American political system, from determining the kinds of issues discussed in campaigns to influencing the sorts of people attracted to the electoral arena.

Consequences for the Press

We have already discussed some of the immediate consequences of the decline of press standards and the increase in competition: lowest-common-denominator journalism, the publication and broadcast of unproved rumor, the invasion of legitimate areas of privacy, and the strengthening of pack journalism. The focus in this section will be on two practical results of the press's own modern aggressiveness—its reduced access to elected officials and the growing hostility toward the press on the part of the general public.

One of the great ironies of contemporary journalism is that the effort to report more about candidates means that the news media often learn less than ever before about them. Wise politicians today consider everything they say to a reporter to be on the record, if not immediately, then eventually—perhaps of use the next time the newsperson writes a profile. Thus the pols are much more guarded around journalists than they used to be, much more careful to apply polish and project the proper image at all times. The dissolution of trust between the two groups has meant that "journalists are kept at arm's length by fearful politicians, and to some degree, the public's knowledge suffers because reporters have a less-well-rounded view of these guys," surmises veteran newsman Jerry terHorst. NBC News commentator John Chancellor agrees and believes his young colleagues have paid a steep price for "junkyard dog" journalism:

When the politicians realized they couldn't unbutton themselves in front of the press anymore they all got careful. And what we saw then was the closing of the candidate—his character, his inner thoughts, his feelings about a lot of things—he closed that off to us. And where it stands now, even with candidates you know pretty well, it's almost impossible to get beyond the facade. . . . Reporters work a hell of a lot harder these days to try to get some meaningful information about the candidates' characters and personalities. It's much harder now than it used to be.

The results are seen in the way in which presidential elections are conducted. Ever since Richard Nixon's 1968 presidential campaign,[1] the press's access to most candidates has been tightly controlled, with journalists kept at a distance on and off the trail. And as 1988 demonstrated, the less-accessible candidate (Bush) was better able to communicate his message than the more accessible one (Dukakis); the kinder and gentler rewards of victory went to the nominee who was able to keep the pesky media at bay. Harsh scrutiny—the current penalty for openness—reinforces the determination of campaign staffers to spin an impenetrable cocoon around their candidate. The positive aspect of this development is that the press is no longer co-opted by the pols the way it was in the all-too-chummy days of the Rooseveltian rule, when many of the insights gleaned by access-rich reporters were self-censored and withheld from readers. But the loss of all sense of camaraderie between journalists and politicians also means that reporters do not see the "real" candidate easily, that their dispatches accordingly will be impoverished and lack the perception afforded by proximity.[2]

However, it is by no means certain that the public *wants* the press to be proximate to candidates anymore. In recent years "there has been a significant erosion of public confidence in the press," concluded

the Times-Mirror Center for the People and the Press.[3] Consider
these findings from the Times-Mirror studies and other surveys:

- In 1985, 55 percent of Americans believed that news organizations
  generally "get the facts straight," while 34 percent thought reports were often "inaccurate." By 1988 the proportions had
  shifted decisively away from "get the facts straight" (40 percent)
  and toward inaccuracy (50 percent).
- By a two-to-one margin, Americans said that, "in covering stories
  about the personal and ethical behavior of politicians, news organizations are driving the controversy" rather than "only reporting
  the news."
- Asked to grade the candidates, the parties, the voters, the pollsters, the campaign consultants, and the press "for the way they
  conducted themselves in the 1988 campaign," respondents gave
  the press by far the lowest average score.[4]
- The proportion of voters who felt the press had "too much influence on which candidates became president" climbed over the
  course of the 1988 election season from 47 percent in May to 58
  percent by November.
- When asked to judge "who was most responsible for the negative
  aspects of the 1988 campaign," 17 percent blamed the candidates,
  32 percent the campaign managers, and 40 percent the news
  media.[5]
- When a random sample of Americans chose the professional
  group with "the lowest ethical standards," journalists placed second, just a percentage point below lawyers. Even congressmen
  were judged less harshly.[6]
- In addition to survey findings demonstrating public concern about
  press intrusiveness into politicians' private lives, the citizenry also
  overwhelmingly wants a public official to have the same right as a
  nonpublic person to sue the news media for libel. Fully three-
  quarters believe the libel laws ought to be the same for public officials and private citizens alike, and two-thirds think a news
  organization ought to have to pay damages to an official for a false
  report *even if* the organization thought the report was true at the
  time of publication.[7]

Unquestionably, the press spectacle during feeding frenzies has
contributed mightily to the decline in public support for the news
media. The polls almost always show a considerable uptick in public
criticism of journalistic practices during and after a frenzy. The cu-

mulative effect produced over time by many frenzies translates into lessened support for the press. Many journalists do not need surveys to tell them antipress sentiment is on the rise; they see it in their mail and telephone calls and they sense it on the road. The *Wall Street Journal*'s Jill Abramson fielded some angry calls from the public after her focus on Dan Quayle's college academic record: "One guy wanted to know if I was going to tackle his kindergarten performance next." The pro-Quayle, press-bashing mob at Huntington, Indiana, in late August 1988 gave many journalists a taste of ancient Rome's Colosseum. The crowd chanted, "Sam Donaldson, go home," with particular gusto, even though, says Donaldson, "I wasn't within a thousand miles of Indiana; thanks a lot, folks." Ellen Hume of the *Wall Street Journal* was in the thick of it, however, and CNN's live broadcast featured her grilling of Quayle in a tight close-up. "The *Journal* was flooded with angry phone calls demanding my firing, and my editors took enormous heat," recalls Hume.

Of course, journalists who thirst for popularity are in the wrong business. Frequently, voters are incorrectly blaming the messenger for delivering a disagreeable truth about a well-liked politician, and the press's special mission is to point out that a naked emperor is wearing no clothes even to a people determined to believe otherwise. Yet reporters would be foolhardy to ignore emphatic signs of the public's growing displeasure with them. In a recent *Los Angeles Times* poll, one-third of the Americans surveyed refused to back the First Amendment.[8] In another study, as many respondents said that "the government should *require* that news organizations give coverage to all sides of a controversial issue" as preferred that "the government should not be involved" in allocating coverage.[9] The press's First Amendment rights ought to be unassailable, whatever the media's shortcomings—but in a freewheeling democracy, privileges cannot always be guaranteed. Thoughtful journalists see their profession's own excesses as partly responsible for the citizenry's often lackluster support for press freedoms. "Our behavior definitely contributes to this," observes the *Washington Post*'s Richard Harwood. His *New York Times* colleague, executive editor A. M. Rosenthal, made a similar case in a passionate exposition after the stakeout of Gary Hart, and his argument applies more generally to his frenzy-addicted profession:

We are begging the nation to treat us as unworthy of respect. In time, without any question, we will lose the support of the American people in our constant struggles against those who would erode the First Amendment. We cannot claim it was designed for voyeurs.[10]

Consequences for the Candidates

One glance down the list of case studies used for this volume gives a reliable indication of a frenzy's consequences for a politician. All the candidate-victims were damaged by their controversies, most of them severely, and some were eliminated outright from competition for high office. The Romneys, Eagletons, Harts, and Bidens on the list comprehend fully that a frenzy's penalty can be the political equivalent of capital punishment. Even the less serious frenzies disrupt a campaign, take a candidate off his or her stride, and send the polls plummeting, as we saw with Gerald Ford's "free Poland" gaffe and Michael Dukakis's mental health crisis. Undoubtedly frenzies also cause the politicians, as well as their families and supporters, emotional pain and agony. In some cases the pols' constituencies are damaged, too; fairly or not, the images of Arizona and Washington, D.C., were badly tarnished by the scandals swirling around Governor Evan Mecham and Mayor Marion Barry. While it may be difficult to work up sympathy for electorates that chose the likes of Mecham and Barry, compassion is easily extended in cases of rumor-wronged innocents, such as "mentally ill" Michael Dukakis and "gay" Jack Kemp. In Kemp's case, for example, the consequences of calumny were as serious as they were unjust. John Buckley, Kemp's former campaign press secretary, explained:

I know for a fact that a number of influential people who wanted to endorse Kemp did not because they were worried a "scandal" was going to break. The rumor was one of the reasons the influential *Manchester Union Leader* in New Hampshire was hostile to Kemp. There were people that could have raised money for Kemp who didn't raise money for him because they were moral Christian people who were convinced that he was immoral. The Robertson campaign used it against Kemp in Iowa in the evangelical community.

For Kemp and many others, a frenzy problem becomes a hindrance but not necessarily a fatal handicap. Kemp did not capture the presidency for many reasons, but he was able to gain a spot in the Bush cabinet. Edward Kennedy recovered sufficiently from Chappaquiddick to win several reelections to the U.S. Senate and achieve exceptional prominence in that body, though a successful White House bid is now probably well out of his reach. Other politicians with a strong base like Kennedy's in Massachusetts can also survive a frenzy and regroup. Pat Robertson's fundamentalist Christians were little bothered by his pre-born-again miracle baby, and some of Marion Barry's African American constituency stuck by him to the bitter end and would have worked enthusiastically to reelect him had he chosen to run for mayor in 1990. As longtime Barry-watcher Tom Sherwood of WRC-TV comments, "People were always waiting for the other shoe to drop with Barry, and it always did; then people would say, 'now the mayor's finished'—but they ignored the fact that he was a centipede who had more shoes left to drop than Imelda Marcos."

Not just the candidates and officeholders caught up in a frenzy are affected by it, of course. The consequences of each case are felt beyond its borders, and the behavior of public officials is often modified. After Dukakis and Eagleton, not many pols were patronizing their friendly neighborhood psychiatrists. After Biden, they carefully checked the accuracy of their résumé and meticulously attributed borrowed passages in their speeches. After Tower, they cut back on liquor, and after Hart, they employed extra discretion in their illicit affairs.

Any megafrenzy such as the one that engulfed Dan Quayle is a somewhat different animal, with the complexity of the creature producing contradictory consequences. On the one hand, Quayle himself was badly battered and bruised. Of the four candidates on the two major-party tickets, he received by far the most negative coverage.[11] The residue of his campaign shellacking was visible after the election as well, with Americans consistently expressing doubts about his qualifications to assume the presidency should that become necessary.[12] Quayle's vice presidential spokesman, David Beckwith, sees little chance that his boss can overcome the frenzy-generated image burdens anytime soon: "For the indefinite future there will be lingering questions about Quayle based on what people saw or thought they saw in the campaign, and it's going to be with him for a number of years." It would be difficult for a vice president to get the public's attention long enough to change an impression formed by a large dose of unfavorable coverage in the campaign. And in his next campaign, Quayle can be certain that remnants of his past frenzy will resurface and redevelop. For example, "Quayle's still refusing to release his academic records, and that subject will be resurrected," predicts CNN's Ken Bode.[13]

Oddly enough, though, in some ways Quayle's campaign woes helped the man who chose him, George Bush. As mentioned in an earlier chapter, voter concern about Quayle probably cost Bush enough votes in November to deny the GOP ticket a popular-vote landslide. Yet Quayle served as a lightning rod for Democratic and press criticism, deflecting fire from Bush himself—and in the end, most people vote for president, not vice president. "If the media and the Dukakis campaign had spent nearly as much time trying to strike up a populist theme or trying to develop some real issues instead of going on a rabbit chase after Dan Quayle, they might have drawn blood," said Bush manager Lee Atwater. Moreover, Bush's "wimp" image was transformed into a "take-charge" one overnight as he forcefully defended his running mate and steadfastly refused to give in to pressure to dump him. The controversy also caused the Bush camp to focus its effort early, while an overconfident Dukakis retreated to Massachusetts apparently convinced that adverse reaction to Quayle would do the Democratic party's work for him. The news media also became spooked by the wave of public hostility generated by their Quayle coverage, and this aided the Republicans at a later stage of the autumn campaign. After Quayle's mechanical, remarkably poor performance in the October 5 vice presidential candidates' debate in Omaha—indelibly remembered on account of Democrat Lloyd Bentsen's "You're no Jack Kennedy" remark—television news commentators tumbled over one another to declare Quayle's showing a fine one.[14] And most attempts to probe Quayle's character and record fizzled after the initial period of overkill. "We became obsessively and excessively concerned with Quayle's military record, and after the understandable public backlash occurred, we backed off pursuing legitimate elements of his background," observes Los Angeles Times media reporter Tom Rosenstiel. Washington Monthly editor Charles Peters adds, "It's a crazy thing that happens with the press. It does an overkill on a story, then in reaction to the public reaction, it pulls back and the story disappears almost entirely." The search for the golden mean is not restricted to philosophers, and it proves as elusive in press coverage as in every other sector of life.

Consequences for the Voters

What seems to gall the voters most about frenzies is not the indignities and unfairnesses inflicted on candidates in the process, however bothersome they may be. Rather, people often appear to be irate that candidates are eliminated before the electorate speaks, that irreversible political verdicts are rendered by journalists instead of by the rightful jury of citizens at the polls. The press sometimes seems akin to the Queen of Hearts in *Alice's Adventures in Wonderland*, who declares, "Sentence first—verdict afterwards."

The denial of electoral choice is an obvious consequence of some frenzies, yet the news media's greatest impact upon voters is not in the winnowing of candidates but in the encouragement of cynicism. There is no doubt that the media, particularly television, have the power to influence people's political attitudes. With the decline of political parties, news publications and broadcasts have become the dominant means by which citizens learn about public officials, and while news slant and content cannot change most individuals' basic views and orientation, they can dramatically affect *what* people think about and *how* they approach a given subject.[15] The massive press focus during many frenzies guarantees that even casual news consumers will find out about the controversy; the media's agenda-setting function for society is never more in evidence. Since redundant media concentration is usually essential in order to capture the attention of a distracted public, this intensity is not necessarily bad, assuming the frenzy does not center on a trivial, irrelevant event. However, the approach taken by the media—the way in which a frenzy is framed and the context into which it is put—is critical to the public's view of politics. And the approach usually taken by journalists is clear: a repetitive, disproportionate stress on scandal, a "more of the same" theme, a "what can you expect from politicians" tone that deepens, extends, and reinforces the enduring public suspicion of all things political.[16] Post-Watergate reporting about government has been unrelentingly negative, scandal giving way to scandal, so that Americans not unreasonably conclude that all politicians must indeed be crooked even if only a few get caught. The substantial majority of public officials who do their jobs honestly and well are not nearly as newsworthy under the old maxim, "Bad news is news, good news is unreported."

The electorate's media-assisted cynicism has been on exhibit in a host of studies and surveys.[17] The late-summer Gallup poll rankings of the major-party presidential candidates are one crude but revealing measure of declining public confidence in political leaders, as reflected in the *combined* "very favorable" ratings that respondents gave the Democratic and Republican nominees:[18]

1952	– 84%	1972	– 63%
1956	– 94%	1976	– 69%
1960	– 77%	1980	– 51%
1964	– 76%	1984	– 68%
1968	– 63%	1988	– 42%

An irregular but marked drop is registered in the post-1964 favorability scores (average: 59 percent) compared with those recorded from 1952 to 1964 (average: 83 percent). By no means can this trend be ascribed solely to media coverage, however; disillusioning events (Vietnam, Watergate, the Iran hostage crisis, recessions, the Iran-Contra affair, and others) crowd the post-1964 calendar. But this period of growing cynicism also coincides almost precisely with the new era of freewheeling, "anything goes" journalism, and surely the kind of coverage these defining events received made a difference in the public's interpretation of them.

The voters' view of Congress, if anything, has deteriorated further than their judgment about presidential candidates. Just before Speaker Jim Wright's resignation in May 1989, a *Los Angeles Times* poll showed that 75 percent of Americans believed that the other members of Congress were guilty of "doing the same things" as Wright "very often" or "fairly often," while only 16 percent responded "fairly seldom" or "very seldom."[19] A *Newsweek* survey after Wright departed found that, by a margin of four to one among those who detected a change, people thought "the ethical conduct of members of Congress" had declined rather than improved in recent years.[20] The tragedy here is that virtually every professional observer of Congress has concluded precisely the opposite, that "the modern Congress is a far cleaner place than Congresses of old," as *Roll Call* editor James Glassman has written.[21] Corruption was commonplace in the nineteenth century and widespread through a good bit of the twentieth century as well, with an attitude toward ethical behavior that was far more cavalier than the current one. Unfortunately, many reporters apparently do not have any greater sense of history than does the general public, according to Steven Roberts:

A lot of the reporters who cover Congress think they're all scoundrels and they sensationalize the news that way. It's an easy, cheap stereotype that makes good copy—and it's wrong. There was more ink devoted to Wilbur Mills's exploits with Fanne Foxe than to Wilbur Mills's writing half the tax laws on the books. Does that serve the readers and make sense? Not to me.

Consequences for the Political System

The enhanced—some would say inordinate—influence possessed by the modern press is pushing the American political system in certain unmistakable directions. On the positive side are the increased openness and accountability visible in government and campaigns, which have been achieved during the past two decades. But this is balanced by two disturbing consequences of frenzied press coverage: the trivialization of political discourse and the dissuasion of promising political candidacies.

As to the former, the news media has had plenty of company in impoverishing the debate, most notably politicians and their television consultants. Nonetheless, journalists cannot escape some of the responsibility. First, the press itself has aided and abetted the lowering of the evidentiary standard held necessary to make a charge stick. In addition to the publication of rumor and the insinuation of guilt by means of innuendo, news outlets are willing to target indiscriminately not just real ethical problems, but possible problems and the perception of possible problems. (John Tower's frenzy demonstrated as much.[22]) Second, the media often treat venial sins and mortal sins as equals, rushing to make every garden-variety scandal another Watergate. Not only does such behavior engender cynicism in readers and viewers, but it cheapens and dulls the collective national sense of moral outrage that ought to be husbanded for the real thing. Third, the press often devotes far more resources to the insignificant gaffe than to issues of profound national and global impact; on many occasions, titillation has replaced transportation on the country's agenda, sex has substituted for serious debate, and peccadilloes have supplanted policy on the front pages. T. R. Reid of the *Washington Post* supplied a fitting anecdote about his attempt to get a substantive story into his newspaper ahead of a sensationalized one. Shortly after Gary Hart announced his candidacy for president in 1987, Reid and other reporters secured a comment from Hart on the subject of taxes that was remarkable in light of Walter Mondale's experience in 1984, to say nothing of the Republican party's strongly antitax rhetoric. Mondale had announced in his Democratic National Convention acceptance speech that, if elected, he would raise taxes—a declaration that most analysts came to deem politically foolish. While quibbling with Mondale's semantical approach, Hart told Reid that it would be "irresponsible" for any presidential candidate to rule out a tax increase, given the size of the federal budget deficit, and that he was leaning toward a combination of tax increases on imported oil, luxuries, and high-income Americans. "This was a fairly daring thing for any candidate to say, and I considered it big news," says Reid, and when he telephoned his editors, they agreed. But on the same day came the manufactured, inconsequential story of Hart's reaction to the possibility that rival candidates were spreading rumors about his womanizing (see chap. 3[23]). Back to the telephone went Reid, who argued that the gossip "was bullshit, not nearly as impor-

tant as the tax story, plus we'd pledged to stay away from those rumors unless they were proven.'' Excited editors huddled, then gave
Reid his writing orders: The gossip was the headline, and the break-
through tax statement would be buried deep in the article.[24] ''They
just couldn't resist,'' concluded Reid. Louis D. Brandeis, later a distinguished justice of the United States Supreme Court, well expressed the dangers inherent in such editorial decisions in a seminal
1890 law review article with his colleague Samuel D. Warren:

[Gossip] belittles by inverting the relative importance of things, thus dwarf-
ing the thoughts and aspirations of a people. When personal gossip attains
the dignity of print, and crowds the space available for matters of real interest to the community, what wonder that the ignorant and thoughtless mistake its relative importance. Easy of comprehension, appealing to that weak
side of human nature which is never wholly cast down by the misfortunes
and frailties of our neighbors, no one can be surprised that it usurps the
place of interest in brains capable of other things. Triviality destroys at once
robustness of thought and delicacy of feeling.[25]

Simultaneously, reporters have become inclined to ask narrowly
drawn, unrevealing questions rather than broad ones that assist voters in making their election-day choices. For example, newspeople
were more interested in telling their audiences whether Joe Biden
and Dan Quayle had plagiarized college term papers than whether
Biden and Quayle were intelligent and understood government. The
answer to the first query was not only basically unenlightening but
may very well have provided a misleading clue to the candidates'
overall capacities and aptitudes. Yet it is the realization that the press
will pursue the narrow rather than the broad aspects of their pasts
and characters that fills candidates' with fear and prevents them
from letting down their guard. Instead of giving extended insight
into their real thoughts and personalities, the ultracautious pols will
deliver only sanitized, programmed, prefabricated sound bites
spiced with pabulum. ''Did you ever wonder why we have these
highly structured debates with no spontaneous give-and-take between the nominees?'' asks ABC's Brit Hume. ''Because these candidates don't think they can afford to make any kind of honest
mistake, since we'll just go wild over it. If we ever want to get candidates to be more forthright, news organizations are going to have to
rethink their approach to gaffes and other such stories.''

The second troubling consequence of modern media coverage for
the political system has to do with the recruitment of candidates and

public servants.[26] Simply put, the price of power has been raised dramatically, far too high for many outstanding potential officeholders.[27] An individual contemplating a run for office must now accept the possibility of almost unlimited intrusion into his or her financial and personal life. Every investment made, every affair conducted, every private sin committed from college years to the present may one day wind up in a headline or on television. For a reasonably sane and moderately sensitive person, this is a daunting realization, with potentially hurtful results not just for the candidate but for his or her immediate family and friends. To have achieved a nongovernmental position of respect and honor in one's community is a source of pride and security, and the risk that it could all be destroyed by an unremitting and distorted assault on one's faults and foibles cannot be taken lightly. American society today is losing the services of many exceptionally talented individuals who could make outstanding contributions to the commonweal, but who understandably will not subject themselves and their loved ones to abusive, intrusive press coverage. Of course, this problem stems as much from the attitudes of the public as from those of the press; the strain of moral absolutism in portions of the American people merely finds expression in the relentless press frenzies and ethicsgate hunts. In addition, the absurdities of modern standards of public purity are everywhere. For instance, a candidate with marital difficulties would do well to get a divorce rather than reach an accommodation with his or her spouse because divorce is deemed acceptable while extramarital relationships, even past ones in a surviving marriage, are potential grist for the press mill (as Ohio's Governor Richard Celeste discovered[28]). All this leads not just to the discouragement of candidates who possess a mixture of great virtue and hidden vice but the encouragement of other kinds of politicians: those with a naïve, saintly image; ideologically driven crusaders; psychologically unbalanced individuals whose lust for power and craving for impersonal affection overcome fear of the risks of public unmasking; and comprehensively conventional, uncreative contenders whose lack of vision is matched only by their dullness. Qualities of shrewdness, worldliness, balance, and pragmatism—which are essential to success in governing—are sadly missing here.

Some journalists argue that concern about the deterrence of good candidates is overdrawn and outweighed by the advantages of close scrutiny. "A lot of the people that that is said about couldn't get elected in a hundred years [while press scrutiny] maybe keeps a lot of the fuckers out of government," as *Washington Post* executive editor

Ben Bradlee indelicately puts it. And, notes *Time*'s Ted Gup, "If people don't want to undergo profound scrutiny, then perhaps they have something to hide or have onion-thin skin and shouldn't be in public office." Adds *Post* ombudsman Richard Harwood, "Some people may be discouraged from running, but we've never had to call off an election for a lack of candidates." Other reporters see frenzies not as deterrents but as opportunities to test how a politician deals with stress and unexpected pressure. "Campaigns are supposed to confront candidates with tough choices, because once in office they will have to cope with crises that come from nowhere," asserts CBS's Eric Engberg. These arguments are indisputable in part: Frenzies have indeed eliminated some unworthy potential officeholders, and they certainly have measured crisis-managing skills. Yet a long campaign is fraught with enough revealing tests of a politician's mettle; it is wholly unnecessary to manufacture any on tangential matters. And while no ballot will ever be devoid of names, some may well be lacking good ones if the price of power continues inflating. It comes down again to the sorts of persons our society wishes to nudge toward and away from public service. *New York Times* columnist Anthony Lewis is surely correct when he suggests, "If we tell people there's to be absolutely nothing private left to them, then we will tend to attract to public office only those most brazen, least sensitive personalities. Is that what we want to do?"

If these are the unfortunate consequences, then what remedies can counteract them by preventing the excesses of frenzy coverage?

8

Remedies

I have lent myself willingly as the subject of a great experiment, . . . to demonstrate the falsehood of the pretext that freedom of the press is incompatible with orderly government.

THOMAS JEFFERSON[1]

Mr. Jefferson's experiment is still our own—a continuing challenge to citizens, politicians, and journalists alike. Unfettered freedom of the press is cherished by every American who values robust democracy, and few would seriously suggest tampering with the principle. Yet the extraordinary degree of constitutional protection afforded the news media (matched by no other national institution or private enterprise) carries with it corresponding and weighty obligations: to inform the citizenry as fully and accurately as possible, to check governmental power responsibly, and to report with fairness and balance. Feeding frenzies are not representative of day-to-day journalism in every respect; nonetheless the coverage of them is indicative of serious problems and excesses that cast into doubt the press's fulfillment of its side of the implied constitutional bargain. There is no question of what the press, under the First Amendment, has the right to do. Rather, the question is: What is the right thing for the press to do, what news is truly fit to print and how should it be presented?

The Dividing Line Between Public and Private

Whatever one's view of journalism in the 1950s and early 1960s, it *was* an easier, tidier enterprise. Public life was public life, and private life was private life, and never (or rarely) did the twain meet. Now the line between the two seems blurred and fuzzed and in constant motion. The disputed no-man's-land is a gray area that "has become a large red zone of press–politics combat," observes Marvin Kalb, former CBS newsman and director of the Joan Shorenstein Barone Center on the Press, Politics, and Public Policy at Harvard University.

On one side of the line are those who defend some or all aspects of the modern press's closer examination of public officials' private lives. They say that the voters need the information to judge character, and that the press has no business withholding it; if anything, assert a few, the press is still not being forthcoming enough. On the opposing side are mainly candidates but also some reporters who believe that the news media are too intrusive today, that not enough privacy is reserved for public servants. There is no direct relationship between private behavior and public performance, they insist, so why report it? (Comments from both contingents are featured in tables 8.1 and 8.2.)

In discussions with many dozen journalists on this subject, the only clear aspect of the debate is the division and uncertainty that surrounds it. But two boundaries are accepted by most reporters. First, a large majority reject the old Rooseveltian rule as too permissive. No longer does anyone want, as columnist Robert Novak put it, "to grow up believing that a crippled president like Roosevelt can walk or a terribly ill president like FDR in his last years is healthy." And newspeople certainly do not yearn for the good old days when a U.S. senator could stagger around drunk during floor debate and no one would report it. Virtually no one defends the press cover-up for John F. Kennedy, either. "The press helped to sell a lie, and we have the obligation to tell the truth," says *Washington Post* columnist Richard Cohen. "JFK's narrow margin of victory might well have been the number of people who were attracted to this handsome, loving couple enjoying the greatest marriage ever seen; if we had told the truth and people had known he was screwing everything that moved, would he have won the presidency?" The press's shame during Camelot has generated a silent but powerful mantra in the current generation of journalists: "No more JFKs." To their credit, newspeople today would never even consider overlooking a candidate's or president's personal recklessness and compulsive sexual behavior, much less willingly act as propagandists by projecting a false image of domestic harmony and perfection such as the one that benefited Kennedy. The second boundary on personal-life investigation embraced by most people in the contemporary news business is the belief that the "anything goes" rule that replaced the Rooseveltian one has taken coverage too far, exposing many private lives too fully and including wholly unacceptable aspects such as the airing of unproven rumors. Thus, the press—at least during thoughtful periods—rejects both extremes in private-life coverage, the "tell almost

TABLE 8.1
PUBLIC VERSUS PRIVATE LIFE: HOW MUCH SHOULD THE PRESS TELL?

COMMENTS SUPPORTING THE EXPANSIVE VIEW OF PRESS COVERAGE

There isn't a whole lot of privacy left, and I don't think there should be a whole lot left, for the obvious reason that it tells you something about people's character.
Bob Woodward, *Washington Post*

When we're dealing with the handful of public figures who would hold power over the 250 million rest of us, there's damn little that I would put off limits. If it's relevant, nothing, basically, is private.
Brooks Jackson, Cable News Network

The media shouldn't be a sort of priesthood, deciding what the public is justified in knowing; we're in the business of revealing information rather than husbanding it or containing it.
Kenneth Walsh, *U.S. News & World Report*

It's up to the voters, not journalists, to decide what's relevant. Denying voters this information, for fear they will give it more weight than it deserves, is patronizing.[2]
Michael Kinsley, *The New Republic*

I can't be in the business of saying, "Well, what should we say to the American people tonight? What is good for them to know? What is *nice* for them to know?"
Sam Donaldson, ABC News

If you work under the shield of the First Amendment, then you're obligated to print things, even if they cause unpleasantness or controversy—sometimes particularly if they do.
Robert Shogan, *Los Angeles Times*

An individual reporter may feel that something doesn't violate his moral code, but it might violate somebody else's moral code, and certainly when you vote for president one of the things you have a right to know is if a candidate's living by a moral code you approve of.
George Herman, CBS News (ret.)

RESERVATIONS ABOUT THE EXPANSIVE VIEW OF PRESS COVERAGE

Reporters are not qualified by training to be character cops . . . We don't know psychology and yet we are players in a mob psychology, all trying to analyze the candidate's private behavior without being close enough to him to understand it.
Tom Rosenstiel, *Los Angeles Times*

We have plunged into . . . private lives with a minimal awareness of why we are doing so, what we are looking for, and whether some of our techniques are proper. At most news organizations, guidelines are either nonexistent, inconvenient, retroactive or resemble Swiss cheese.[3]
Tom Oliphant, *Boston Globe*

I'm uncomfortable with the new emphasis on private lives, and I wish we could draw back a bit from it, though I don't think there's any possibility of that.
Dan Balz, *Washington Post*

Whether faithful or unfaithful as a husband—unless a candidate's character impacts . . . on important public policy, national interest or national security questions—private moral questions have no place in a presidential campaign. They are a matter between the candidate and his/ her family, their own conscience, and their God.[4]
1988 presidential candidate Jesse Jackson

SOURCE: Unless otherwise noted, interviews conducted for this volume.

TABLE 8.2
RANDOM THOUGHTS AND ANECDOTES ABOUT THE PRIVATE-LIFE DEBATE

ON DISTINGUISHING PRIVATE LIFE FROM PUBLIC LIFE

Every reporter in the long run has to define his own ethics about privacy. I've worried over this and discussed it with my colleagues and even with my wife and I don't think there is a simple answer.

Robert Pierpoint, CBS News

We have no clear, black and white guidelines; there's no bright shining line on privacy that we will not cross. You have to judge each case, agonizingly, as best you can.

Leonard Downie, *Washington Post*

A bunch of us were sitting around the Times as the Gary Hart story was unfolding and our bureau chief, Craig Whitney, said, "If anybody hears anything about any other candidates we certainly want to know about it." And I said, "Just a minute. Does that mean we are committed to writing about the sex lives of everybody in this race?" And Whitney said, "No, we are committed to *talking* about the sex lives." Which only summed up our dilemma.

Steven Roberts, *U.S. News & World Report*

The line between public and private life is a little bit like [former Supreme Court Justice] Potter Stewart's line about obscenity: I don't know if I can define it, but I know it when I see it.

Chris Wallace, ABC News

My opinion shifts with each story.

Bernard Shaw, CNN

ON THE STANDARDS FOR PRIVATE LIFE DISCLOSURE

A president who fucks around, a presidential candidate who fucks around, that now is considered by most journalists, and me, as relevant to the performance of his public job.

Benjamin Bradlee, *Washington Post*

Early in my career I went through a period when I was convinced a reporter should print just about anything he knew. But over the years my view has changed, and I am now working here at CBS to move the line of privacy to be more inclusive.

Dan Rather, CBS News

I've hardly ever seen any reporters come in with proof positive of a sexual affair. But you've got to have at least two sources who confirm it in order to publish. Usually for a big story I require three sources, but in cases of sex that's tough to get unless it's really kinky.

Albert Hunt, *Wall Street Journal*

I don't care if a public official goes home and sleeps with a sheep, unless he's on the agricultural committee dealing with sheep subsidies.

Andrew Lack, CBS News

Given our changing culture it is certainly conceivable to me that kinds of private sexual behavior now considered unacceptable in a president, a senator, or a governor, in twenty years may not have a stigma attached to them.

David Broder, *Washington Post*

(continued)

TABLE 8.2 (Cont.)

On Journalists' Views of Politicians' Private Lives

I don't cry too much for these guys because they take great advantage of their public positions all the time to help their private lives. They take trips at taxpayers' expense, they hire pretty women on their staffs and have nice affairs with them, and do lots of things like that that most other people can't and don't and wouldn't do. And so, if they're a little nervous about being held to higher standards about that kind of behavior, I think it's only right.

Leonard Downie, *Washington Post*

In order to convince voters that they are wholesome and trustworthy people, candidates have opened up for public inspection their own lives, their marriages, their children. They use their wives, use their homes, and willingly go public with all those private moments that they think will help them get elected. And it seems to me that once a public official does that, the line shifts rather rapidly to a point where virtually nothing remains private. It is only when those private moments damage the candidate that you hear the cry, "you are invading my privacy."

Roger Mudd, of PBS, "MacNeil/Lehrer NewsHour"

There is something unseemly about living too much in public.

E. J. Dionne, *Washington Post*

We had this case once involving the head of a relatively small governmental agency. The guy had been the CEO of a Fortune 500 company and was caught cheating at his club's golf championship. He was expelled from the club but told if he got treatment by a psychiatrist he could reapply. . . . We talked to the psychiatrist, we talked to the club rules committee, we talked to everybody, absolutely cold-cock had it, but we did not run it because the fellow was too unimportant and was not in a position to do much harm. But I told him I'd run the story if he ran for office.

Benjamin Bradlee, *Washington Post*

Source: Interviews conducted for this volume.

nothing" of the Rooseveltian rule and the "tell just about everything" of the anything-goes substitute, despite the rules' appealing purity and simplicity. However, in most news organizations no specific guidelines exist to enable journalists to navigate successfully between these extremes when a frenzy storm hits, thereby increasing the chances that the almost irresistable competitive dynamics of the frenzy will determine the rules of coverage. (In our interviews, many journalists complained about their organizations' tendency to make up the rules on a case-by-case basis with no attempt at standardization.) Every newspaper and broadcast outlet needs a relatively precise and clear set of guidelines to govern private-life frenzies. Based on the lessons learned from recent frenzies, as well as the opinions and preferences of our interviewees, we would suggest a kind of "fairness doctrine." It is designed to be fair to voters by giving them appropriate and sufficient information they can use in judging candidates and officeholders; fair to candidates by ceding them some reasonable reservoir of privacy while articulating the rules which the press appears to expect them to live under; and fair to journalists and editors by spelling out areas of legitimate and illegitimate investigation, freeing them from some uncertainty and confusion about their undertakings. A "fairness doctrine" that is sensible and can be widely accepted among the press, politicians, and public might include the following provisions:

PRIVATE LIFE SUBJECT TO PUBLICATION AND BROADCAST

1. All money matters (investments, transactions, earnings, taxes, and so on) of the candidate and, to the extent that they directly bear on the financial well-being of the candidate, the financial arrangements of his or her spouse and immediate family.

2. All health matters that may affect the candidate's performance in office.

3. Any incident or charge that reaches the police blotter or a civil or criminal court.

4. Sexual activity where there is a clear intersection between an official's public and private roles; for example, relationships with staff members or lobbyists, where elements of coercion or conflict of interest inherently exist.

5. Sexual activity that is compulsive and/or manifestly indiscreet, and therefore potentially dangerous; for example, the cases of John Kennedy and Gary Hart.

6. Any ongoing private behavior that is potentially or actually debilitating, such as alcohol or drug abuse.

7. Any illegal drug use (whether ongoing or not) that has occurred as an adult within perhaps the decade prior to candidacy, and any incident over the same period in which the candidate has condoned the use of illegal drugs in his or her presence, whether participating or not.

8. Any private behavior (whether or not included in the above categories) that involves the use of public funds or taxpayer-subsidized facilities in a substantial way.

PRIVATE LIFE SHIELDED FROM PUBLICATION AND BROADCAST

1. Nonlegal matters involving the candidate's underage children and also other family members, except to the extent that the relatives seek the limelight or influence the official.

2. Current extramarital sexual activity as long as it is discreet, non-compulsive, and the official's partner(s) are not connected to his or her public reponsibilities and are not minors; in addition, all past sexual activity and personal relationships that occurred many years earlier should *not* be examined. (Offenses older than a decade might be exempted from scrutiny as a reasonable statute of limitations.)

3. Sexual orientation per se, unless compulsive behavior or minors are involved.

4. Drug or alcohol abuse that was a youthful indulgence or experimentation; also adult abuse at least a decade old, when the individual has fully recovered and clearly abandoned the harmful practices.

5. Internal family matters, such as child rearing and nonfinancial relationships with relatives and nonpolitical friends.

ADDITIONAL PROVISIONS AND QUALIFIERS

1. Every charge printed or aired by the news media must either be proven or be accompanied by a substantial body of evidence. Excluded from publication and broadcast under this provision: rumors and sizable chunks of most FBI reports. Also discouraged: fishing expeditions, such as the 1988 *New York Times* questionnaire mentioned earlier in this volume.

2. Situational ethics inevitably apply to each case. Scrutiny ought to be greatest, with the fewest exceptions, concerning candidates for president and vice president, and correspondingly less intense for lower-level elective and nonelective offices. (As *U.S. News & World Report's* Michael Barone puts it, "There's no equal opportunity clause that applies to the presidency; it's not important that every person get an opportunity to be president, but it's important that we get a good president.") Similarly, job-specific exceptions can be made. For example, *any* past drug offense may be relevant to the appointment of the federal drug czar. Also, offenses committed after a politician's declaration of candidacy, when any prudent individual will be on his or her best behavior, are justifiably subject to added emphasis.

3. A candidate's degree of hypocrisy and lying can also rachet coverage up or down (as discussed in chapter 4). For instance, a bold philanderer who avidly uses family issues and his own loved ones to gain political advantage begs to have his lies and hypocrisy exposed.

4. Since no one is sure what, if any, implications much of a person's private life has on his or her public performance, private-life incidents that reach print ought to be interpreted cautiously by the media. After all, some faithful husbands (Calvin Coolidge, Richard Nixon) produced flawed presidencies and others (Harry Truman, Gerald Ford) did creditable jobs; some philandering presidents (such

as Warren Harding) were failures and others (Franklin Roosevelt) historically towering.

A strong case can be made that under these standards, voters are given all the information about a candidate's private character they need to make a responsible choice, while facts that invade an official's legitimate privacy and add little but prurient, gossipy titillation are withheld. Granted, these guidelines are not airtight, will not end the debate about privacy, and do not pretend to be a rote substitution for considered editorial judgment when a new frenzy arises. But they are an improvement over the inconsistent, ad hoc seat-of-the-pants decision making existing in many news organizations today. The current lack of clearly articulated standards leads inexorably to increasing intrusiveness, more lowest-common-denominator journalism, and additional instances of unproven rumors reaching print. The standards suggested here are the result of a mental exercise that ought to take place in media outlets across America before the frenzy-spawning pressures build in the next presidential election cycle. Of course, the precise standards separately agreed upon by the various print and broadcast outlets will differ from organization to organization; it could not be otherwise in such a diverse, competitive industry. But the opinion leaders in journalism—the networks, the prestigious newspapers, the major weekly newsmagazines—can individually and collectively set the standards that matter for their profession. If they publicize those standards and hold to them, whatever the provocation from sources or left-wing weeklies or rebel competitors, they can effectively reduce the impact of frenzies, rumormongering, and junkyard-dog journalism.

Whether or not the "fairness doctrine" becomes widely adopted in whole or in part, there is another way for the media to provide voters with invaluable glimpses into the souls of candidates and public officials while reducing the spotlight's intensity on purely private lives. Journalists ought to put more emphasis on *public* character than *private* character, for the former is at least as revealing of an individual's make-up as bedroom behavior. Part of the public side of character is on the record and easily accessible, such as courage demonstrated by taking issue stands that may be unpopular with the public at-large or special interest groups. Other aspects, less frequently commented on, include a finely developed sense of humor or irony, the ability to rebound from setbacks and frustrations, the degree to which a person tends to shade the truth or deny reality, and an individual's general openness or secretiveness.[5] The two most telltale indicators of public character are surprisingly little explored: how the candidate relates to his or her working associates and peers, and how he or she deals with staff. Concerning the former, columnist David Broder points out that Gary Hart's determination to go it alone and play by his own set of rules was shown just as convincingly by his public life as his private one:

What frustrates me about the Gary Hart thing was we should not have had to wait for a Donna Rice incident to raise large questions in people's minds about the character of Gary Hart. Here was a man who had served in the United States Senate for twelve years, and yet it was hard to find another senator who said, "I know Gary very well, know him inside out, feel very comfortable with the idea of his being president." This was a job where if you're going to be a success at all, you have to be able to build relationships with other political players. This guy had never demonstrated the slightest inclination or capacity to build any kind of relationship with any other politician. Now that was something that we should have been able to write about.

If anything, the exploration of a candidate's relationships with his or her staff is even more eye opening—and it is a completely aboveboard, legitimate topic for press commentary and analysis. Already, journalists extensively cover *who* a politician's key subordinates are, but rarely do they write about *how* staff are treated. Personality traits that include bad temper, pettiness, laziness, and stupidity as well as hints of underlying racist or sexist attitudes can all be on display here. Several 1988 presidential candidates had reputations for browbeating staff members, and none more so than Jesse Jackson.[6] Yet a search through all the major 1988 profiles and feature articles on Jackson turned up only one in which the subject was given any serious attention.[7] If the press is willing, the staff room can substitute for the bedroom in investigating the nature of candidates' characters, and it can add a political dimension not found in the boudoir. As the *Wall Street Journal*'s Al Hunt asserts, "Political character ought to be much more important to us than the personal character revealed by who's screwing whom."

If reporters need some additional incentive to set aside a reservoir of privacy for public officials, the privacy-threatening celebrity trend in journalism itself might provide it. A number of our well-known interviewees complained about recent encroachments on their own personal lives, and this is certain to continue. Angry politicians and consultants, such as strategist Stuart Spencer, are demanding the same privacy standards be applied to "the powerful public figures in the

media'': ''Let's have a level playing field and see how they like it.''
And interestingly, some in journalism are not ruling out such fair
play.[8] *Washington Post* managing editor Len Downie was asked
whether his stated goal of increasing the scrutiny of the behavior of
influential leaders in government, business, and religion[9] applied to
prominent reporters, even his own: ''I include the news media in that,
sure.'' It may be time to modify the ''anything goes'' rule before the
press is hoist by its own petard.

On Reporting Rumors

> *Rumor thrives on motion,*
> *stronger for the running.*[10]
>
> *Aeneid, 4*

The single most disturbing development in modern journalism is
the loosening of standards that permits the publication or broadcast
of unproven rumor. Responsible news veterans are deeply concerned about this trend. ''It's just the shabbiest journalism to go with
rumors. If you can't pin it down, you shouldn't put it in the paper or
on the air,'' declares NBC News commentator John Chancellor. Columnist David Broder emphatically agrees: ''It's not a close question
for me. If you can't make the distinction between rumors and journalism, between gossip and journalism, then you're in the wrong
business.'' Adds his *Washington Post* colleague, media-beat reporter
Eleanor Randolph, ''We print enough things as it is that turn out not
to be true, without adding rumors to the mix.''

Several excuses are offered to explain the regretable deterioration
in standards. Skillful political consultants who plant and carefully
nurture rumors receive some blame, though it is difficult to believe
the current crop are any more adept at manipulating the press than
their predecessors. The consultants may be no different today, but
the rules of journalism have indeed changed. Earlier generations of
political operatives were frequently unable to convince reporters to
print the goods on candidates even when proof was available, thanks
to the prevailing Rooseveltian rule. Some current reporters suggest
that they have an obligation to the public to discuss all the factors
affecting a political campaign, including the rumors that regularly
sweep the electoral caravan. ''That's too easy an out, just a way of
breaking into some juicy gossip,'' says Broder. Moreover, any news

attention to unproved rumor multiplies whatever effect the rumor may be having on a candidate, so media intervention is not simply a matter of passive, neutral reporting. "There is a false sense among reporters that, 'Oh, everybody's already talking about it anyway so it doesn't hurt to print it.' But they don't realize that everyone *isn't* talking about it—at least not until they publish it," notes former *Wall Street Journal* staffer Ellen Hume. The political rumor mill churns in a tiny, enclosed echo chamber, but when its mutterings are broadcast, they can become a deafening roar, reverberating around the networks' Grand Canyon and drowning out all other campaign dialogue.

Rationalizations aside, the real reason for the new attractiveness of rumor is the spread of lowest-common-denominator journalism. "The range of standards acceptable to individual reporters and their outlets has become enormous, and stories produced under the lowest standards are now sometimes getting the widest circulation," says Dan Howard, who experienced the phenomenon as John Tower's spokesman. Responsible media organizations must fight back by adopting strict rules about the use of "rumor news" broken by other outfits. First, a story from another organization ought to be independently verified by a media outlet's own reporters before the subject is given prominence on its pages or airwaves.[11] Publication or broadcast by a single organization should not automatically open the floodgates to publication and broadcast everywhere. "Something shouldn't become part of the public debate simply because one newspaper has printed something," argues the *New York Times*'s Andrew Rosenthal. "You always have to ask whether the story meets the standards set by *your* newspaper." Adds *Time*'s Ted Gup, "There's no shame in being scooped on a story that shouldn't be published."

The best antidote the press can administer to rumormongering, then, is simply not to give any publicity to gossip, thereby refusing to play into the hands of the schemers. This prohibition should include back-door mentions as well, such as the qualifying phrases "plagued by" or "dogged by rumors of . . ." ABC's Sam Donaldson believes the news media should occasionally go even further, self-censoring stories like the one that dwelt upon links between Dan Quayle and Paula Parkinson:

It was wrong to say Quayle was involved in the Paula Parkinson affair. Clearly he wasn't. "Involved" is a word that sends a certain signal and has a certain meaning, a code that we all understand. So if you're not going to take the time to carefully explain it all—''He went down there, he stayed in a separate room, he wasn't a part of the hanky-panky''—then you just don't mention it at all. You can't have it both ways in something like that.

In addition, the media would do well to follow the admirable if extraordinary steps taken by ABC's Hal Bruno to foil the efforts of the ''Bush mistress'' rumor pushers. As we have seen, Bruno initiated talks with his rivals at other networks to put a stop to the media manipulation being undertaken by Bush's Republican opponents. Fears of a news cartel or conspiracy are unfounded in these situations, says Bruno:

> This is unheard of in the news business, but there are times when we've got to talk to each other. We simply can't let people stampede us into asking a question at a press conference or some public forum that will legitimize a scandalous, unproven rumor. This doesn't mean the media are conspiring together; you'll never undermine the fierce competition that exists among us.

Last, under certain conditions, journalists might want to debunk a persistent and debilitating rumor that may be unfairly inflicting great damage on a political figure. This suggestion is a ''back to the future'' idea, since Ben Bradlee (then of *Newsweek*) did precisely this in demolishing the 1962 rumor about John F. Kennedy's ''prior marriage'' to a twice-divorced socialite (see chap. 2). To a lesser degree, the *Post* accomplished the same thing for George Bush in 1981, though as related in chapter 5 the newspaper did not explicitly raise the ''mistress'' part of the rumor. However, there are distinct dangers in such media rebuttals. ''The trouble with setting up a straw man and knocking him down is that sometimes people only see the straw man and fail to notice you've dispatched him, and this is especially true on television,'' warns ABC News's Peter Jennings. This in extremis remedy should be reserved for the truly insidious rumors that will not subside on their own.

Of course, from time to time rumors do break into print through no fault of the media, as with President Reagan's ''invalid'' pronouncement concerning Michael Dukakis's mental health or Jack Kemp's own strategic choice to kick his ''gay'' rumor out of the campaign closet. But the news media still have clear obligations in these instances. The most obvious is to downplay the rumors and not to sensationalize. ''Run stories like that deep inside the paper or way down inside another story,'' advises the *Detroit News*'s Jim Gannon. ''In effect, you signal the readers not to take it too seriously.'' Second, once the amassed evidence is enough to convince even Perry Mason that a rumor is false, news organizations have the duty not to keep raising dead-and-buried tales from the crypt. Some outlets were nothing short of irresponsible in their unrelenting rehashing of the Kemp "gay" gossip, for instance. Third, when a perfidious rumor comes out in the open thanks to the efforts of rumormongerers, the press ought to go after the evildoers. "We ought to devote just as much energy to trying to trace down who's responsible as we do in investigating the original tip," declares Hal Bruno. *U.S. News & World Report* did just such a good deed in the case of the calumny about Tom Foley, for example[12] (see chap. 5).

Unfortunately, the same favor was not extended to Michael Dukakis after the classic dirty trick played on his campaign in the form of the mental health controversy. Not only should the press have criticized President Reagan more severely for his churlish effort to undermine Dukakis, but the rumor should have been forthrightly labeled as the lie and the smear it was, rather than timidly described in many places as merely "unproved," suggesting to between-the-lines readers that there might be a kernel of truth to a malicious falsehood.[13] Moreover, greater investigative resources should have been devoted to uncovering the LaRouche and Republican origins of the gossip and those groups' efforts to spread it. "We should have tried much harder to nail the sources of that rumor because it did Dukakis a lot of damage," asserts Jeff Greenfield of ABC News.

None of this is to suggest that journalists should be at all limited in the subjects they can explore and check out, so long as a high standard for publication or broadcast is maintained. As ABC's Chris Wallace notes: "I feel comfortable asking all kinds of impertinent, personal, or sensitive questions while not on live [television], but what I decide to put on the air has to pass a much higher and more serious threshold." CBS's Bob Schieffer agrees: "We're obligated to check out all kinds of distasteful things, but unless we're absolutely certain something personally damaging is true, we have the obligation to put it away and say nothing about it." Alas, there are perils even in checking out rumors. As mentioned in other chapters, gossip can be spread more widely in the political community, and on good authority, when reporters call well-connected sources to verify such tips. And one suspects that media organizations have occasionally worked oblique rumor references into stories as a way to justify the substantial resources invested in chasing rumors down. But these are relatively minor concerns compared with the brazen practices criticized earlier, which lead inescapably to one conclusion: Professional journalists must report facts, not rumors, and responsible editors must only publish the news that is fit to print—gossip and rumors being most definitely excluded from the mix.

Internal Checks and Balances

No one and no institution outside the press can or should limit what the press does, but those in the profession who care about its standards and want to fend off threats to its liberty ought to try to temper the excesses associated with feeding frenzies. The best solution is old-fashioned leadership and determination to cure the ills within each media organization. For instance, at CBS News, Dan Rather says he has learned from the problems exhibited in past frenzies and that now his "goal for this outfit is to be less a part of the frenzy, less a part of the herd, more difficult to stampede, more willing to set higher standards and go our own way on these stories." Ideally, every editor would insist on the same, killing investigative stories that fail to make a real case, refusing to give in to lowest-common-denominator journalism, resisting competitive pressures, and providing voluntary accountability when mistakes are made. A frenzy of good editing alone could counteract many bad effects of feeding frenzies. But, in truth, not enough editors are able to do this because, as David Broder notes, "It's very hard to be both the person who is goading your staff to 'go get the story' and the one who is saying in a very detached and skeptical way, 'Is this story really there?' " "In my experience many editors don't really perform the editing function; instead of canning bad stories, they make excuses for getting them into print," suggests the *Baltimore Sun*'s veteran columnist Jack Germond. "We don't have nearly enough accountability in this profession. Reporters who go too far on a story or screw up are rarely disciplined in a significant way by their editors," says CNN's Frank Sesno.

Besides editors, prominent journalists also have a responsibility to provide leadership for their profession and to call a halt to the excesses seen in many frenzies. Occasionally, senior reporters and columnists have indeed helped to restore civility and balance to coverage. For instance, James J. Kilpatrick's well-reasoned criticism of the press's Billygate antics is credited with ending the out-of-control spiral of competitive "wiggle" stories.[14] "He basically said, 'What is all this shit? I've been reading it and reading it, and I can't see that you've got anything that matters.' And he clearly had the effect of toning down the coverage," remembers an approving David Broder. Broder himself has often served as an ethicist in the press corps, never hesitating to criticize press practices or inadequacies. Several syndicated columnists, including Ellen Goodman of the *Boston Globe* and Mike Royko of the *Chicago Tribune* lambasted the *New*

York Times for its intrusive 1988 candidate questionnaire, encouraging the newspaper to take a second look and eventually withdraw it. But these internal circuit breakers occur all too seldom during political seasons, partly because of the intensity of the competition but also because journalism is a special animal. In just about all professions the individuals generally acknowledged to be the leading lights are E. F. Huttons—when they speak, others listen and usually follow their precepts and heed their warnings. But in journalism, most scribes and correspondents pride themselves on their independence and contrariness. "No one is the keeper of the conscience of journalism," insists the *Post*'s Bob Woodward, and, adds PBS's Paul Duke, "Reporters tend to say 'screw you' to anyone who tries to set standards for the whole business." Appearance also matters: "It can look like sour grapes, that because you got beaten you're whining about 'excesses' and trying to knock down the other guy's story," explains CNN's Brooks Jackson.

Whatever the combination of reasons, neither opinion leaders in the press nor the traditional editorial arrangements are likely to produce self-policing sufficient to right many of the wrongs of frenzies. Nevertheless, news organizations can be structured to encourage self-criticism in several useful ways. While no panacea, the institution of the ombudsman is advantageous—and can be made more so.[15] The ombudsman is a newspaper's public editor or reader's representative who acts as an internal critic, receiving and evaluating complaints against the paper's reporters and coverage. Ideally, the ombudsman is hired on contract for a fixed term with a set salary and working conditions, impervious to tinkering by management, so that he or she is truly independent; moreover, the ombudsman's column should have guaranteed, unedited access to prime space in the newspaper on a regular basis. Alas, the reality falls far short of the ideal. Since the Kentucky newspapers *Courier Journal* and the *Louisville Times* established the first U.S. ombudsman in 1967, only a few dozen newspapers have followed suit.[16] Despite the conflict of interest inherent in the concept of their critiquing their own work, many editors fiercely oppose the ombudsman concept, believing it to be a usurpation of their proper function. And needless to say, editors and reporters do not relish the potential second-guessing of their work by an ombudsman in the cold print of their own newspaper. Legendary CBS newsman Edward R. Murrow once remarked that journalists are not thin-skinned, they are no-skinned (a condition, the author concedes, from which academics suffer equally). Also, the relative handful of newspapers that have overcome their doubts and appointed an ombudsman have not always made the position truly independent, leaving some skeptics to suggest that ombudsmen often do more to justify the paper's actions to readers than truly to check a paper's excesses. (One critic termed the ombudsman "a chicken in charge of the foxes' den."[17]) Yet anyone who regularly reads the *Washington Post* is struck by the good that a thoughtful and autonomous ombudsman can accomplish. The *Post*'s current (and years ago, its first) ombudsman, Richard Harwood, and some of his predecessors[18] have slain sacred cows by the dozen, tilted at windmills in the off-season, and cantankerously raised hell with predictability. The measure of Harwood's success is not only the frequently favorable comments from readers who were previously convinced that the "arrogant" *Post* would never listen to an average person's complaint, but also the off-the-record grumbling we encountered from *Post* reporters and editors deeply resentful of Harwood's often on-target criticisms.

As the *Post* has proved, the potential of the ombudsman position in its ideal construction is still great, and every major newspaper and newsmagazine ought to have one. And why should the idea be restricted to the print media? Each network news show should also have its own independent internal critic, with a mandate to critique its coverage and guaranteed access to a few minutes of airtime every week. Throughout this volume, newspeople have candidly expressed retrospective regret about the media's frenzy excesses. If all the network shows and every sizable publication employed a truly independent ombudsman, then a powerful circuit-breaker mechanism would be in place to slow press excesses *during* a frenzy, heading off mere regrets after the fact.

Perhaps surprisingly, the initial network reception to this ombudsman proposal has been generally favorable, at least from the anchors. CBS's Dan Rather calls it "a pretty good suggestion." NBC's Tom Brokaw thinks, "there ought to be room somewhere in the news cycle for each network to do it." ABC's Ted Koppel notes that "from a sales point of view, I would find that to be a particularly fascinating segment to put on 'World News Tonight' or 'Nightline.' " And given the unsurpassed importance of television coverage during an election campaign, the print media ought regularly to review what the networks focus on as well. Each major newspaper should summarize and comment on the campaign stories run on all three networks the previous evening. This would institutionalize the excellent-but-more-intermittent attention devoted to television by newspaper reporters assigned to the media beat. The *New York Times*, the *Los Angeles Times*, the *Washington Post*, and other large papers have maintained top-notch reporters on this beat; their coverage of newspaper and television reportage has already provided a welcome and more widely circulated supplement to the work published in the specialized journalism reviews.

Thus, there is no shortage of helpful innovations that are completely harmonious with the First Amendment, if the press is only willing. But one old idea that probably does not deserve to be reinvented is the National News Council.[19] The council existed for almost eleven years (1973-84), having been formed under the auspices of a prominent, private research organization, the Twentieth Century Fund.[20] In its short lifetime, the nonpartisan council's eighteen members (eight from the press, ten from the public) investigated 242 complaints about the accuracy and fairness of various national media organizations, with findings circulated in reports and press releases.[21] This publicity was the council's only sanction, since it lacked the power to enforce its recommendations. Many of the larger newspapers and broadcast outlets were hostile to it or largely ignored its work, and for this and other reasons the council was dissolved in 1984.[22] While some opposition to the council was no doubt generated because of jealous turf-guarding, other concerns were well grounded. No matter how well intentioned at inception, an organization like the council can easily be captured by factions of ideology or financial interest at some point in its existence. As is often the case with so-called "fair campaign practices commissions," no one watches or regulates the regulators closely, and yet the sweet-sounding name and idealistic founding motivations can carry significant weight with the public. Better to encourage the media to appoint ombudsmen and adopt the other decentralized reforms suggested in this volume; an added incentive for news organizations to be responsive to these tamer proposals is the real possibility that demands for a revival of the news council will be heard otherwise.[23]

Raising Standards

Much of this study has focused on the need to raise standards in many specific respects: resisting the reporting of rumors; preserving areas of legitimate privacy for public officials; treating all candidates alike; decreasing sensationalism, wiggle disclosures, and lowest-common-denominator journalism; and so on. But the job of elevating press standards is a broader mission than these items suggest, encompassing journalists' attitudes, their methods of operation, and the substance of their coverage.

Newspeople could probably induce officials to give better answers to legitimate questions, and preserve more public tolerance in the process, if their cynicism could be dampened and their civility augmented. First of all, as ABC's Brit Hume observes, "We need to be unyieldingly skeptical but ought to draw back from the relentless cynicism we've engaged in recently." Mark Twain may have been correct when he opined, "The only way for a newspaperman to look at a politician is down," but a journalist also needs to acknowledge that not everything a politician does is completely self-interested and manipulative; politicians, like the rest of us, are mainly destined for purgatory, not heaven or hell. David Broder has even proposed that the press balance its attacks on officeholders by regularly saluting those who serve well.[24] Few reporters will probably ever share National Public Radio reporter Cokie Roberts's generosity of spirit toward politicians ("I see most of them as hardworking, underpaid public servants"), but then both Roberts's father and mother have served in Congress.[25] And not many in the new school of journalism seem to share the sentiments of the gregarious Jack Germond, who admits that he enjoys the social company of carousing pols and who declares: "I like most politicians and I'm willing to forgive them the things they do, just as they forgive us." But all journalists might want to take to heart the delightful slogan of one of their most marvelous institutions, the Gridiron Club: "Singe but never burn." Since 1885 the annual Gridiron dinner has good-naturedly roasted presidents and press alike, relaxing the tensions that inevitably exist between reporters and politicians.[26] A little of the Gridiron spirit of tolerance, and its underlying premise that government and press are wary adversaries but not bitter enemies, could be usefully applied to coverage the year round. So could an effort to restore more of a "sense of decorum and propriety in reporting—not stuffiness but civility," as Howell Raines of the *New York Times* described the goal. Civility means not asking whether Gary and Lee Hart kissed on the lips, not calling individuals involved in a frenzy at 2 A.M. (as one DePauw University professor experienced in the midst of Dan Quayle's plagiarism controversy), and not screaming impertinent questions at a beleaguered official. Granted, many reporters shout because they are frustrated and lack access, but the *Los Angeles Times*'s Jack Nelson still sees this kind of behavior as counterproductive: "I've always felt that members of the press who shout and make asses of themselves . . . don't do themselves any good, don't elicit information, and make the public weary and leery of the press." And one other old-fashioned but preferable standard to which modern journalists might return is a more rigid separation and labelling of commentary and straight, factual reporting. "There's too much spinning of stories to one side or the other, too great a selectivity in the presentation of the facts in this post-Watergate group," insists veteran Jerry terHorst. "Many of these young journalists want to change the world by starting on page one, which is supposed to be straight news." NBC News's John Chancellor agreed and recalled a recent conversation with former NBC News executive Tom Pettit "about why our correspondents following the presidential campaign always had to end their pieces with some snippy little piece of criticism":

I said, "Pettit, why the hell can't they just come on and say, 'Tomorrow the candidate goes to Cleveland,' " and Pettit replied, "Because with this generation, it would come out, 'Tomorrow the candidate goes to Cleveland—and no one knows why.' "

Not just form but also substance is in need of improvement. During campaigns the press's fixation on polls, gaffes, and frenzies drains reporters' energy and often detracts from coverage that might be truly useful to an undecided voter. The polling obsession is particularly galling.[27] Not only is much of the polling hyped and misleading, but knowledge about which candidate is alleged to be ahead is the most worthless piece of information voters can have, unless they are on the way to a betting parlor. There is absolutely no doubt that polling interferes mightily with the campaign dialogue—the ongoing discussion among the candidates and the electorate on policy issues. Consider this frank admission from Bush's 1988 manager, Lee Atwater:

The only time I ever felt sorry for Dukakis was right before the second presidential debate in October when ABC News released their fifty states poll, which basically said Dukakis was cooked and done. Now imagine a guy getting ready to go to something as important as a debate and seeing that right beforehand. . . . That's like somebody coming up to you right before you go on stage to play Hamlet and saying, "Hey, by the way, your mother just died."

There will be no shortage of good material to fill the holes left by fewer polling reports. A weekly newspaper and television box score on the issues would be a welcome addition, including past positions taken, an update on that week's issues, and a list of topics still being ducked by one or more candidates. Repetition is not a bad thing, particularly because voters tune into an election at different times. For the same reason, the often-superb lengthy profiles and biographical pieces run by papers and network news programs early in the campaign season ought to be repeated just before election day. More analysis and criticism of the paid television advertisements and the political consultants who make them ought to be institutionalized as a regular part of the coverage. Partly as a response to the press's tardy review of the manipulative 1988 Bush spots, national and state journalists did a much-more-thorough job of ad review in the 1990 midterm elections, and even greater emphasis is likely in 1992.[28] The broadcast media can inform the electorate in other ways, too, by reversing recent trends and giving viewers more, not less, information about politics. In figures compiled by Harvard researcher Kiku Adatto, the three networks (combined) devoted 26 percent fewer minutes to the 1988 presidential campaign on their evening news broadcasts than they did to the 1968 campaign, and the average length of the uninterrupted sound bite fell from 42.3 seconds to 9.8 seconds over the same two decades.[29] Regretably, the networks have also been cutting back their national party convention coverage in recent years,[30] and their local affiliate stations—urged on by management consultants who tell them how "bored" the public is with politics—are far worse, substituting extra crime reports, health tips, help-line call-ins, and just about anything else for political news.[31] "Soft" news is also a growing component of the network evening broadcasts. While the shows have usually always included a closing human interest feature, these "jumping porpoise" segments eat up more than twice as many precious news minutes today as in the early 1970s.[32] Along with the decline in hard news has come the near-disappearance of news commentary on the prime network broadcasts. Only NBC's John Chancellor remains in place as a regularly appearing commentator. No one has appeared on ABC's "World News Tonight" or the "CBS Evening News" for a number of years.[33] Perhaps feeling lonely, Chancellor wondered aloud: "Why in the world can't each evening news program have some old geezer who's been around . . . go on the air and reflect on things?" Better yet, each network should have several commentators from various perspectives to offer their views in round-robin fashion.[34]

Whether or not the networks attempt to expand their commentary and political coverage, they ought at least to upgrade the quality of what actually appears on the air. This means resisting, much better than in 1988, the wily efforts of the political consultants to turn the evening news shows into conveyor belts for contrived images and soundbites.[35] Press frustration with this kind of manipulation is one root cause of feeding frenzies, as chapter 3 discussed, and therefore a lessening of journalists' discontent might help to reduce the incidence or intensity of frenzies. One way to accomplish this good end would be for the media to refuse to give more than perfunctory coverage to "stealth" candidates who insulate themselves from the press; in other words, the networks could trade a degree of news visibility for reasonable direct access to candidates.[36] Alternately, the networks could scrub the usual repetitive video packages of campaign hoopla and look-alike rallies held in picturesque locales, and turn the time over to the candidates. As CBS's Bob Schieffer explained the idea:

Let's offer each [major-party presidential] candidate four minutes as a block of time on the evening news broadcast to discuss defense issues. One candidate comes on the air on Wednesday night, his opponent on Thursday night, and answers questions from the anchor on the chosen topic. This could be repeated every other week or so for the duration of the general election campaign, with a different subject each time. If one candidate refused to come on, we'd just announce he'd refused, and his opponent still gets the scheduled four-minute appearance.

Four minutes does not sound generous, but in fact it is a sizable block of time in a broadcast that (minus commercials) only lasts about twenty-two minutes. And if all three networks made similar arrangements, the evening airwaves would fairly hum with policy discussion and substance, compared to the near silence at present.

This intriguing idea and others, if well implemented, could raise the level of televised campaign discourse considerably. As for the level of journalistic standards and integrity, other changes are in order. The age of celebrity journalism is in full blossom, and many of its manifestations are deeply disturbing. David Broder has correctly warned about "co-optation, subversion by seduction, [and] the insidious inhibition of intimacy [inherent in] a new hybrid creature, an androgynous blending of politician and journalist called the Washington Insider."[37] It is not simply the "revolving door" through which some individuals have passed repeatedly, one year a government official, the next a journalist, then back to government, and so on—moves that obviously bring into question their objectivity, independence, and true loyalties.[38] Of greater concern is the developing ethos of stardom.[39] Many reporters, especially the television ones, are better known than most of the officials they cover. The name recognition is unavoidable, but the reveling in their own celebrity and their acquiescence in the tawdry and professionally compromising aspects of stardom is eminently eludible. One cannot really begrudge them their enormous salaries, since (from baseball players to game-show letter turners) income is frequently mismatched with true value. As CBS's Bruce Morton puts it, "You could argue that a first-rate sixth-grade teacher is worth more than a television anchor in terms of the good they do for society." The anchors seem to recognize as much; reacting to Barbara Walters's 1976 $1-million-a-year contract with ABC News, then foot soldier Dan Rather commented, "Is any TV journalist worth a million dollars a year? No, unless they find a cure for cancer on the side."[40] (Rather's CBS earnings approximated $4 million in 1990.[41]) Less excusable is some television journalists' pursuit of fame and participation in events that eviscerate their claims to professionalism. Repeatedly, anchors and reporters—especially Tom Brokaw, Connie Chung, and Barbara Walters, as well as Sam Donaldson, Diane Sawyer, even John Chancellor[42]—have showed up on entertainment shows such as "Late Night With David Letterman" and Johnny Carson's "Tonight Show," and have submitted to self-indulgent and occasionally embarrassing lines of questioning. (For example, Letterman once engaged CBS's Lesley Stahl, an able and aggressive reporter, in a degrading, sexist discussion of her "good teeth."[43]) Other television reporters have crossed the line of good taste and good ethics as well. Tom Brokaw hosted a "Christmas in Washington" special in which he sang carols on stage with President and Mrs. Reagan.[44] Barbara Walters helped to conduct a farewell awards dinner for Nancy Reagan at which she commented, "Didn't she always look and behave just right? Weren't we always so proud?"[45] Deborah Norville played host (for a substantial fee) at a Phillip Morris sales conference, reading "news" about tobacco and interviewing company guests.[46] Unprofessional hucksterism and boosterism of the sort exhibited in these examples partly accounts for the low regard in which some high-profile television journalists are held. TV news celebrities often complain about not being taken as seriously as their print brethren, but their own actions sometimes give ample cause for derision.

This is but the tip of a polluted iceberg, trivial bits of a larger problem in television journalism: the movement away from news values and toward entertainment values. "TV has always been part show business," contends CBS's Bill Plante, and of course he is correct. Even his news division's patron saint, Edward R. Murrow, was not above hosting a personality interview show, "Person to Person." And television news, like every media outlet, needs to be appealing enough to attract a sustaining audience. As Sam Donaldson characterized it, "We're a moneymaking organization and I'm damn proud of it; someone's got to pay this inflated salary of mine!" But many serious broadcast journalists, even those who benefit from the star system, are deeply concerned about the trend in their medium's news. Dan Rather states flatly: "The entertainment values [are] overwhelming the journalistic values, and the values of the star system [are] overwhelming the meritocracy in journalism." Many reporters and anchors, especially on the morning and weekend news shows but increasingly on the critical evening broadcasts as well, are being selected not for their reportorial experience and skills but for their looks and likability. "It's gotten progressively much worse over the years," laments Judy Woodruff, who left CBS to become a key player on PBS's enlightening MacNeil/Lehrer NewsHour. "Especially with women, the people selected for high-profile posts tend to be young and good looking." The prototype was the late Jessica Savitch of NBC News.[47] As Sam Donaldson described her (in a view corroborated by some at her own network), "She was always near the top in the polls showing the public's 'most trusted' newspersons, but Jessica Savitch knew nothing about news. The camera loved her, and she had a special quality reading that teleprompter script that had been written by someone knowledgeable. But she had no idea what she was saying." Tragically, Savitch is replicated in local television stations all across America. CBS newsman Wyatt Andrews, who served apprenticeships in a number of large stations, commented, "At every station I worked at . . . there was an airhead anchorman or anchorwoman—I mean absolutely brainless people who didn't utter a word that wasn't written for them, who didn't have a thought that wasn't put in their head by a producer." Veteran Douglas Kiker of NBC News is equally appalled by "this new generation of 'news readers' and 'personalities' who wouldn't recognize a good story if it stood there and said, 'I am a big news story'." One of his wizened colleagues, talking off the record, sadly recounted the recent arrival of "news actors and actresses—the Barbie and Ken dolls"—at his beloved network: "They look very experienced on paper, and they're dynamite-smooth delivering the news on the air—glib, authoritative. But their years of experience consist of having read the teleprompter, not gathering the news."

The results of this deterioration are plain to see. When standards fall, viewers are treated to a larger dose of soft news and even "recreations" of real-life events.[48] The titillating topics that form the core of many feeding frenzies also move to center stage. Unlike the complex issues that require sophistication and study to report, most frenzies are a news entertainer's delight, featuring the sensationalistic simplicity on which trash TV thrives. When likability matters more than sound journalism, young television reporters are given the wrong message and encouraged to embrace the wrong values. "The danger is in the signals sent to journalism school graduates, that what matters is not an agile brain but a pretty face, not straight-ahead, hardnosed reporting, but getting onscreen and making people sweat like Diane Sawyer or Connie Chung," says Wyatt Andrews. When form matters more than substance, big-salary personalities substitute for street-wise reporters and foreign bureaus. One "deeply worried" longtime CBS correspondent rightly bemoans the loss of fourteen of twenty-eight CBS Washington bureau positions over the decades of his employment, while the news division's money was drained to "support multimillion dollar salaries and find vehicles [that is, shows] for the news 'stars' we hired." When the Q-rating—the networks' polling measurement of the popularity of on-air personalities[49]—is king and news personnel become the focus of public relations management, the First Amendment becomes a shell, its raison d'être destroyed since reporters fear to raise unpleasant hard news subjects. "The main problem with star journalism is that it leads to timidity in reporters," admits CBS News executive producer Tom Bettag. "The stars have to avoid controversy, which is usually bad for ratings."

There may be no quick fix to "star journalism" in the age of tight corporate control and fierce competition for a dwindling audience market share. But there are some acceptable stopgap solutions, the most effective of which is self-denial and a simple stiffening of spines among concerned anchors and reporters. CNN's Bernard Shaw has shown the way, actively rejecting "the cult of personality," as he describes it, that surrounds many of his competitors. Shaw politely refuses autograph requests and late-night show invitations alike because, "I'm not an entertainer, I'm not a star, and I greatly resent what's happening to this profession." Roger Mudd, formerly of CBS and now of PBS, is even more emphatic about "the responsibility of well placed journalists to say no":

I'm bewildered, disheartened and crushed that men and women with great talent and integrity would find it necessary to demean the profession to the extent of participating in a comedy show. The idea that being on the air several nights a week in this marvelous six-thirty P.M. position is not enough, that you must match wits with David Letterman and Johnny Carson, that you must reveal a warm side of yourself, a nonprofessional side—it's everything I believe in upside down.

Another positive step to raise standards and counteract celebrity journalism would be to curtail some journalists' propensity to cash in on their stardom. News organizations ought to forbid their employees from receiving honoraria (speaking fees) over a set amount. The U.S. Senate limits its members to two thousand dollars per appearance, for instance, and that would appear to be a reasonable cap. Currently, some of the networks' and newspapers' hottest properties are receiving ten to twenty-five thousand dollars, and occasionally up to an incredible fifty thousand dollars per appearance.[50] Given the enormous potential for conflict of interest here—reporters may cover many of the interests represented by the sponsoring groups—and in order to build public confidence in their public-service profession, superstar journalists ought to be willing to make this sacrifice; with their regular take-home pay, few will need to apply for public assistance. And there is also the question of hypocrisy, the human foible that newspeople use to justify so many feeding frenzies. Like most media outlets, the *Washington Post* has strongly attacked public officials' acceptance of honoraria. Comments *Post* ombudsman Richard Harwood:

We run a chart . . . once a week in the paper about the honoraria that congressmen get. If you ever ran a chart about the honoraria that is being collected in this newsroom, it would knock your eyes out. And there are a lot of people in Washington who make so much money talking to these lobbies and special interest groups that they would quit their jobs before they would give up their speaking fees.

At the very least, and whether or not large fees are banned, every news organization should regularly require its reporters to disclose fully their speaking fees and sources of income, and the disclosures should be available for public inspection.

Remedies from the Candidate's Perspective

While the remedies suggested here for press excesses would no doubt delight most politicians, candidates and officeholders can make their own contributions toward ending the worst aspects of feeding frenzies. Naturally, realistic remedies on the candidate's side of the equation must make political sense. In nature some animals avoid becoming frenzy victims by fleeing or freezing, options not practical for pols fixed clearly in the sights of deadly aimed television cameras. Equally impractical today is an attempt to ignore whatever charges have been made. This used to be the standard political advice doled out by grizzled veterans: For example, in 1962 Richard Nixon wrote, ''The man in political life must come to expect the smear and to know that, generally, the best thing to do about it is ignore it—and

hope that it will fade away.''[51] But in the modern age of negative attack politics, to make no defense when charges fly is a ticket to political oblivion. As Gary Hart discovered in 1984 about his name
change, age, and so on, the questions cannot be brushed off and will
be raised continuously until credible answers are given. Of course,
Hart suffered from a poor relationship with many in the traveling
press corps, but even when most journalists personally like a candidate (Gerald Ford and Geraldine Ferraro are examples), good press
relations no longer carry a candidate very far when a frenzy hits. The
press is determined not to be co-opted, as in the days of FDR and
JFK, and appeals for mercy generally (and often appropriately) fall
on deaf ears. Pat Robertson learned as much in 1988 when he
pleaded with the *Wall Street Journal* not to print the ''miracle baby''
reference. ''He said it would embarrass his son, and when he first
called, I thought he was talking about a twelve-year-old boy, and I
worried, 'My God, we're going to scar a kid for life,' '' remembers
the *Journal*'s Albert Hunt. ''Robertson's son turned out to be thirty-
five years old''—and the ''miracle baby'' passage went into the story.
Building up chits with the press through favors and good relations
used to provide some insulation when disaster struck. ''You built
up deposits in a press bank account so you could draw down in
times of trouble; now you can never make enough deposits because
at any time a mega-withdrawal, a frenzy, can take place,'' said Lee
Atwater.

The most rational, logical solution for candidates is to avoid the
sins and circumstances that spawn frenzies. ''When one of my congressional candidates asks me about the rules today, I tell him that if
he's married and is going to have his wife and six-year-old daughter
sitting on his knee in the brochure, he'd better not be fucking his
secretary,'' explains Republican operative John Buckley. *U.S. News &
World Report*'s Michael Barone goes beyond advising the avoidance of
hypocrisy: ''If you want sex, get married and stick to your wife. If
you're unmarried, don't have sex.'' These are excellent suggestions,
as are the Ten Commandments, but history suggests that such perfection is also a bit contrary to human nature. Given the nearly certain assumption that flesh-and-blood candidates will falter on the
way to the Promised Land, the next-best option is to be prepared for
the inevitable stumbles. Democrat Bruce Babbitt's 1988 campaign
was certainly ready for the drug frenzy that briefly enveloped the
presidential field after Douglas Ginsburg's confession of drug usage.
More than a year earlier, during a long bicycle trip with the candidate
and his wife across Iowa, Babbitt's press secretary, Michael Mc-

Curry, sounded out his boss on all potential past foibles. Says Mc-Curry: "In this new age the first thing the press secretary to a presidential candidate should do is to have a long, exhaustive, up-close and personal interview with the candidate." Babbitt frankly confessed his 1960s marijuana experimentation, saving time and preventing mixed signals when the real onslaught began many months later. As it happened, after discussions with his campaign advisers, Babbitt took a direct but offhand approach. While on an airplane shortly after the Ginsburg revelations, Babbitt approached a *Washington Post* reporter, Maralee Schwartz, and teased, "I hear the subject of the day is marijuana. What about it, Maralee, have you ever used it?" Schwartz said yes, then logically turned the question on Babbitt, who casually admitted his past. This matter-of-fact method of revelation helped to reinforce the press corps' belief that it was "no big deal," as McCurry suggested.

Most candidates and their staffs try to prepare for conceivable eventualities, especially when they have some hint of a future crisis. As reviewed in chapter 5, the Bush-Quayle camp went into high gear when the first rumblings of prisoner Brett Kimberlin's allegations reached them. Former Reagan White House counsel Fred Fielding interviewed Quayle extensively about the matter, and staff aide Mark Goodin compiled a thick file on Kimberlin's sordid criminal record to share with inquiring reporters. "I wanted to appeal to reporters' better instincts, to make sure they understood what kind of source they actually had here," explained Goodin. When a campaign team has more leisure—between election cycles—it often tries to short-circuit the bad aspects of the candidate's subtext or to clean up worrisome remnants of past frenzies, although such efforts can backfire. Senator Joe Biden, running for reelection in 1990, insisted during a C-SPAN interview that he had "never plagiarized in law school," a conclusion seemingly supported by the *Wilmington* (Delaware) *News Journal*'s widely circulated account of a probe into the Biden matter by the Delaware Supreme Court's Board of Professional Responsibility. As it turned out, however, the board had not judged the act of plagiarism at all; rather, it had merely exonerated Biden's decision not to disclose the incident on his application to practice law, an important distinction the *News Journal* had failed to make clear. To Biden's renewed embarrassment, the plagiarism controversy again found its way into the headlines.[52]

What is often surprising is how frequently candidates do not learn the plainest lessons taught by past frenzies. After Spiro Agnew, Thomas Eagleton, and Geraldine Ferraro, one might have thought a presidential nominee would not have selected a little-known, nationally untested running mate, but George Bush picked Dan Quayle anyway. At least Bush avoided McGovern's compounding error; when Quayle looked his shakiest in the hours after his nomination, Bush specifically refused to back him "1,000 percent," as McGovern had done for Eagleton. Instead, Bush said only that he was "comfortable" with Quayle "at this point," but if "evidence of wrongdoing" were presented, "I'd be happy to consider it."[53] By contrast, Gary Hart apparently drew no lessons at all from his own 1984 frenzy. A wise politician is always acutely aware of the press's subtext about him and wary of taking actions that confirm the undesirable elements of it; Hart ignored many warnings and recklessly validated his own womanizing subtext by means of Donna Rice in 1987. Moreover, to this day he denies that the subtext even existed. In a letter to this author, Hart wrote: "Clearly I disagree with your . . . suggestion that in my case there was something 'strange' about me, or that I was 'a playboy.' If these were such well known facts in the minds of the press, they seem[ed] to neglect them over the better part of fifteen years of public life."[54]

Whatever the degree of preparation, when a frenzy commences, disclosure—complete and quick—is usually the best policy. Any delay in a campaign should be only for purposes of gathering the facts and double-checking to ensure accuracy, since wiggle disclosures are sometimes generated by later corrections of the record; here again, adequate preparation can be critical. The most difficult aspect of this rational remedy, at least for the campaign staff, is getting the candidate to embrace it. For instance, Michael Dukakis abruptly refused to discuss his medical records at first, despite his advisers' recommendation to the contrary, a costly error that fueled press speculation about his mental history. Often hurt and angry, a politician is more inclined to lash out or hunker down, or when actually guilty, to cover up. Yet after Watergate and Chappaquiddick, the best assumption for a campaign is the worst-case scenario: that all the relevant information will eventually come to light, that obstinacy and subterfuge can convert a two-day story into a weeks-long water-torture frenzy, and that any attempt at cover-up will be potentially disastrous. The Bush–Quayle camp learned this anew when Brett Kimberlin's press conference was cancelled and he was incarcerated shortly before the 1988 election. While the campaign dodged the bullet, press interest in the prisoner and his charges intensified after Kimberlin's apparent silencing and has continued long after the election.

By contrast, full and even excessive disclosures helped to end frenzies as diverse as Billygate, Ferraro's finances, and Nixon's secret fund. Granted, disclosure does not always work, especially if the root problems are too serious (as with Eagleton) or too juicy (Jack Kemp's "gay" rumor). And disclosure can come too late to be of much assistance. After many damaging weeks of allegations and well publicized gossip, John Tower went on ABC's "This Week with David Brinkley" to rebut in forceful terms the suggestion that he was an alcoholic and to take an extraordinary pledge: "I hereby swear and undertake that if confirmed, during my tenure as Secretary of Defense, I will not consume beverage alcohol of any type or form, including wine, beer, or spirits of any kind."[55] Dramatic though the appearance was, opinions in the Senate and the country had already hardened. "We should have done it much earlier. We could have rallied some undecided voters and brought some borderline senators our way," Tower spokesman Dan Howard believes in retrospect.

Sometimes an apology is attached to full disclosure, and contrition—as an act of uncharacteristic humility—usually assists a pol in the effort to move beyond a problem. It is a more effective tactic when coupled with plausible efforts to duck full responsibility for the controversy. Thus Michael Dukakis expressed sorrow for the "attack video" but shifted blame to his staff; many candidates have ascribed drug use to the foolhardiness of youth; and after his cocaine bust Mayor Marion Barry portrayed himself the victim of entrapment and disease, attributing his many mistakes to an uncontrollable passion that deprived him of free will. Throughout his frenzy-dotted career, Barry perfected a new type of apology: He insisted on his innocence after each new incident but simultaneously promised never to do it again, in the process turning over enough new leaves to defoliate a forest. At least Barry recognized that some sort of contrived repentance was necessary. Gerald Ford let his pride and stubbornness prevent him from acknowledging any error after his "free Poland" gaffe in 1976.

Most politicians are "take charge" individuals by nature, so they tend to judge the remedies suggested so far as too defensive. Candidates prefer to seize the offensive, as Richard Nixon did in the famed "Checkers" televised address on September 23, 1952. Ted Kennedy employed a similar appeal to Massachusetts voters a week after Chappaquiddick, on July 25, 1969, and a study by Professors Michael J. Robinson and Philip M. Burgess demonstrated that it was indeed effective in regaining support lost on account of the accident.[56] Other recent candidates, including Thomas Eagleton, Gary Hart, and Dan

Quayle, considered but rejected such an approach, in part because of the press's increased (and warranted) propensity to analyze such dramatic appeals instantly and critically. Imagine, for instance, what journalists would do today with Nixon's "Checkers" fib that his wife Pat "was born on St. Patrick's Day"—part of a passage in which Nixon argued that he and his wife were not quitters because "the Irish never quit."[57]

Politicians can take the offensive in other ways today. Their consultants and advisers go on "spin patrol," trying to focus the press and public opinion on aspects of a frenzy that are most favorable to their candidate. Thus, instead of asking why Dan Quayle avoided Vietnam combat, his camp framed the debate as one where Quayle's critics were questioning the patriotism of those who honorably served in the National Guard instead of fleeing to Canada or burning their draft cards. Surrogates can add spark to a candidate's counteroffensive, particularly spouses (such as Lee Hart or Dagmar Celeste) when a husband's fidelity is under attack. Marilyn Quayle not only stood by her man during the Paula Parkinson onslaught, she partly quelled the controversy with a well-timed humorous remark: "Anyone who knows Dan Quayle . . . knows that if there's a golf course around, that's all he's going to look at."[58]

The most satisfying form of counteroffensive for a politician caught in a frenzy is a direct assault on the news media even though any attempt to make the press the issue is fraught with peril. It does not work if, like Evan Mecham, you have already alienated the voters. More importantly, earning the enmity of people who buy ink by the barrel and normally have the last word is rash. "The only time it is truly safe to bash the media is if you are visibly wronged," said Lee Atwater, "And even then you ought to shoot back in as general a way as possible, never going after journalists by name." The Bush campaign, including Atwater of course, found such a general and ingenious way to "shoot back" when they were reeling from the reaction to Quayle's nomination. As described in chapter 5, the vehicle was the post-convention, allegedly impromptu press conference held by Quayle in the midst of an aggressively antipress hometown crowd in Huntington, Indiana. While Bush campaign chairman Jim Baker strenuously denied to an angry press corps that Huntington was a "set-up" immediately after its conclusion, and though Atwater swore that "no conspiracy" existed, most journalists remain convinced that the concept, if not its precise execution, was intentional. Howard Fineman of *Newsweek* was one of the many who refuse to see Huntington as a mere happenstance:

The Bush people wanted images of Dan Quayle—the hotdog who had been chewed up in the shark tank—being literally embraced by average, heartland Americans. Did they want the press to be on the defensive? Yes, no doubt. That's why they went there. They wanted to get the press out of its cocoon and surrounded by "real Americans." Did they deliberately turn on the microphone so that the whole town could hear the nasty press questions? No, I don't think so. They would love to claim credit for it, but they are afraid to because that would reveal just a little too much manipulation on their part. But they did everything else to set up that situation.[59]

The fabled "Huntington massacre" included a potpourri of assaults on the press. The master of ceremonies whipped up the crowd by sarcastically 'welcoming' the corps as it disembarked from the buses and "ran the gauntlet through a large booing mob screaming ugly things," recalls a participant, *Dallas Times Herald* reporter Bob Drummond. In addition to a sea of "single finger salutes," Drummond was greeted by a placard-wielding Republican "who whacked me in the face with his sign." The press conference and the press's egress after the show were marked by near-constant catcalls and heckling, and the press buses finally made their way out of the area with "the good people of Huntington again offering us middle fingers in their universal gesture of farewell," says Drummond. The actual question-and-answer session with Quayle, broadcast over a live microphone to the rally participants and on CNN to tens of thousands, was a cramped, acoustically primitive affair that forced journalists to shout their questions and claw their way to the front. In the sweltering August heat, with the crowd's provocations, and given an opportunity to talk directly with Quayle at last, some reporters let their adrenalin pump excessively. "We went for the jugular, and we looked vicious," admits *U.S. News & World Report*'s Kenneth T. Walsh. "It ended up being the kind of day I relish," Atwater declared. "I'm flattered that reporters give us credit for planning it. We didn't, but here's the real point: If the press hadn't . . . asked asshole questions, it never would have happened. We didn't tell them, 'Please go out there and be an asshole.' " In the end, the media frenzy about Quayle was checkmated by a real or pseudo *vox populi* frenzy at Huntington. Most of our interviewees saw Huntington as a turning point, after which the press began to pull back from intensive scrutiny of Quayle. "The Bush people were very smart to take advantage of the public's unhappiness with the press," observes the *Washington Post*'s E. J. Dionne. "In a contest pitting Dan Quayle against Lloyd Bentsen, Bentsen wins, but if it's Quayle vs. the press, they knew Quayle could run a pretty good race."

The Voter's Contribution

It is entirely appropriate that we conclude our discussion of feeding frenzies by turning to the foundation of any representative democracy, the electorate. For in any system such as ours, the standards under which the political players and reporters operate are ultimately set by the voters collectively. Just as citizens are legitimately entitled to claim credit for the accomplishments of the society they sustain, they also must bear responsibility for the problems that exist in it. Concerning feeding frenzies, the predispositions and preferences of voters directly and indirectly influence frenzy development and denouement in three ways:

1. *Public interest or disinterest*[60]: As chapter 4 examined, public opinion plays a role in regulating the fate of frenzies. If the public chooses to tune out the controversy, or expresses anger about the press's conduct (à la the Huntington massacre), then the story will gradually be buried deeper in the back pages and new revelations will have less impact. After all, news delivery is a business that depends on public subscription, and however much they take to heart their First Amendment obligations, media organizations will generally not seek to alienate their viewers and readers for a lengthy period.

2. *Choice of outlets and information*: In any given frenzy, and in many respects overall, some media outlets will be more responsible and less excessive than others. To the extent that people choose to watch broadcasts and read publications with higher standards, the best in journalism is encouraged—and the reverse is also true. CBS's Dan Rather, in a radio tribute to his late, respected colleague Robert Schakne, noted that, "The feel-good alleged news correspondents, the good-news pretenders, are a dime a dozen and on every station. They're everywhere now. . . . One of the reasons, dear listener, is that not enough of you care."[61] This is not unrelated to the crisis of citizen education in the United States. One of the century's most outstanding political scientists, V.O. Key, was surely correct when he wrote, "voters are not fools"[62]; they understand their basic interests and generally vote accordingly, and therefore rationally, at the polls. But if not foolish, the electorate is ill informed. The knowledge by which voters determine their interests is paltry,[63] their attention to political subjects is generally scant, and their devotion to quality newspapers—especially among the young—has declined sharply.[64]

3. *Public attitudes about politics*: The voters' cynicism about politics

is at least equal to, and reinforces, journalists' similar malady. All too ready to believe any charge of corruption or moral turpitude against a politician, the public is often as unwilling as the press to view candidates and officeholders in a balanced way, with vices weighed against virtues. Perhaps it is also a matter of hypocrisy, that maligned transgression that both press and public seem so unwilling to overlook in politicians. The public refuses to take Jesus's advice— "judge not that ye be not judged"—because they apparently do not fear judgment, and believe themselves to be far superior to the equally human class of politicians. One of the most humorous bits of public opinion data ever gathered was the response to the following question: "Is there anything in your past that you think might prevent you from holding a high government office?" Even after preceding queries had made clear that disqualifying offenses included drug use, alcohol abuse, extramarital affairs, cheating on taxes, and so on, 80 percent answered "no."[65] Heaven must be a far larger place than anyone has imagined.

It follows, then, that the remedies from the voters' perspective for the excesses of frenzies must emphasize a dramatic improvement in the quantity and quality of civic knowledge. While individuals can accomplish this on their own, the schools must take the lead, stressing from kindergarten through college the study of current events, American government, and political history. A better informed citizenry will more wisely evaluate and select media outlets, and care more about issue substance and less about frenzy sensationalism. A little more trust and tolerance and a bit less cynicism and hypocrisy about politics and politicians is also warranted. The public would also do well to support strengthening the political party system in the United States[66] since one root cause of frenzies has been the decline of the parties. The press has attempted to substitute its "character issue" screening for the peer review once provided by party leaders, but it is poorly suited for the task. Journalist Walter Lippmann understood as few seem to do today that the press is *not* the equivalent of parties—the former being a disjointed mass of separately run businesses collectively charged with checking power, the latter being the fundamental building blocks of democracy with the responsibility for organizing power and mobilizing public opinion. As Lippmann explained it in 1922:

The press is no substitute for institutions. It is like the beam of a searchlight that moves restlessly about, bringing one episode and then another out of darkness into vision. Men cannot do the work of the world by this light alone. They cannot govern society by episodes, incidents, and interruptions.[67]

When all is said and done on this subject, it is a good bet that more will be said than done. "The press is a business, and it is almost never going to do things purely out of altruism," noted Bill Plante of CBS News. Nor can the news-gathering process, chaotic by nature, become fully orderly, nor should any measure of press freedom be sacrificed to tame or prevent the excesses that have concerned us in this volume. "As long as America continues to be a free country, you will have a lot of bad journalists writing a lot of garbage," declares Ted Koppel. But it would be tragic to see the prediction of Koppel's ABC colleague, Brit Hume, come true: "My guess is that it will take some monstrous episode which is so bad and so obviously excessive that the press is forced to step back."

As I have learned in the course of interviewing, good journalists do not shrink from examining their profession's weaknesses; to the contrary, they welcome it as an opportunity to improve the quality of reporting as well as to bolster public confidence in their craft. It is toward the fulfillment of these vital twin goals that the suggestions offered in this study have been made. "The duty of the press is to print the news and to raise hell," says Tom Brokaw, and that will never change. But Roger Mudd added an essential qualifier: "We are not in the business to protect public officials, but we are in the business to be fair to them." Feeding frenzies have included substantial elements of unfairness not just to candidates but to the general public and to the high standards good journalists hold dear. Alexis deTocqueville celebrated news organizations because "they maintain civilization."[68] As press conduct during feeding frenzies has proved repeatedly, they can also decivilize politics. The legions of responsible and dedicated newsmen and -women must work to moderate the excesses that destroy confidence in their profession and threaten support for press freedoms. Journalists and journalism must feed less at frenzies and more at the table of fairness and civility.

Afterword

The Frenzies of '92

The year 1992 was the best of times and the worst of times for press coverage of politics. On the one hand, many news organizations made a determined effort to focus on issues in the presidential campaign, and thus inform their readers and viewers more fully than ever before. Yet, on the other, such well-intended plans still could not stop journalistic standards from sinking to new lows along the way.

How could this have happened, especially after the press had fervently promised not to repeat—much less augment—the mistakes of the 1988 campaign? The same factors that produced so many earlier feeding frenzies (as outlined in chapters 3–5) once again took control. Lowest-common-denominator journalism accelerated, the obsessive character issue was still front-and-center, and unproven rumors were even more carelessly splashed across many front pages than four years before. From time to time the campaign was hijacked by the tabloids, and the establishment press meekly followed the lead of their low-life brethren as the focus shifted from substance to sleaze. This appalling phenomenon was memorialized by the press itself at its 1992 Gridiron Club dinner,[1] with a ditty sung to the old melody of "Kids":

TABLOIDS

Sleaze, we provide just what readers want today.
Sleaze, whether in the Senate or in the hay.
Print any kind of rumor, legend, lie or myth.
We hit stuffed shirts, bigwigs, perverts, preachers,
Any kind of target.

Sleaze, sodomy, and rape are our stock-in-trade.
Sleaze, it's the steamy stuff of which profit's made.
Keeping our circulation healthy in ev'ry way.
What's the matter with sleaze today?

ESTABLISHMENT PRESS

Please, we're too pure to cover such sordid stuff.
Please, in the high-class press there's not space enough.
Sleaze makes our readers queasy when they get the point.
Goodness gracious, no salacious copy
Ever mars our columns.

But—there is one exception to standard bland,
Sleaze can be quite all right if it's second-hand.
Bless the *Star* and *Inquirer,* though we pretend they're worst,
Just as long as they print sleaze first.

What's Hot and What's Not About Campaign '92 Coverage

In addition to the "Geraldo Syndrome" lyrically described above, Campaign '92 was replete with regrettable press practices and stumbles, many of them just more of the same from past years. In 1988 the press dutifully swallowed Republican media events whole (such as Bush's visit to a flag factory); the next cycle's uncritical reviews went to Democratic media events, such as the packaged Clinton–Gore bus trips. Despite a brief summer effort by CBS to expand the length of presidential candidates' sound bites,[2] the average sound bite on the networks' evening news continued to shrink—to 8.4 seconds in 1992.[3]

Short sound bites were but a tiny part of the overall problem. The three oldest networks cut back their national party convention coverage substantially in 1992, devoting only a miserly two or three hours per night.[4] CNN and C-SPAN's gavel-to-gavel efforts admirably filled the void for citizens fortunate enough to have cable TV, but nothing can excuse the networks' diminishing devotion to these vital quadrennial conclaves of American democracy.[5] What airtime the networks offer is also increasingly filled with the chattering of their celebrity anchors and correspondents, rather than the actual words and deeds of the candidates, parties, and campaigns.[6] From Labor Day to Election Day the TV reporters and anchors consumed 71 percent of the evening newscast time devoted to the 1992 campaign, while the presidential candidates were given a mere 12 percent of the time.[7] It is not just that the voters often benefit from seeing and hearing from the candidates directly; it is also that the network correspondents and pundits, predictable dispensers of inside-the-Beltway conventional wisdom, are so frequently off-base. During Bill Clinton's difficult spring of Gennifer Flowers, marijuana usage, and draft evasion, for example, virtually every major television newsperson and commentator wrote Clinton off, as the following sampling suggests:[8]

Clinton . . . will either not be the nominee or not be the president.

Margaret Warner, *Newsweek*

In November's general election Clinton will be clobbered by Bush.[9]

John McLaughlin, "The McLaughlin Group"

I think he's got to get out of the race in the next two or three days; otherwise he's going to get badly damaged.

Ed Rollins, Republican (and, briefly, Perot) political consultant

I think he is dead . . . Clinton is unelectable.

Robert Novak, CNN commentator

With commentary of this ilk, one can easily understand why Bill Clinton and his fellow candidates sought refuge on the talk shows (Larry King Live, Donahue, etc.), and other nontraditional television forums (MTV, Arsenio Hall, and so on). This approach is obviously good for candidates who want to escape the usual news-media filter and speak to voters at length and without instant analysis. Ross Perot, who launched his protocandidacy on Larry King's CNN show, was the first to demonstrate talk TV's power, but Bill Clinton quickly set the record for quantity and variety of appearances on "alternative" television. Come the fall, George Bush joined in, albeit somewhat reluctantly, as he made the rounds of Larry King and the network morning shows. Overall, Clinton appeared on talk shows forty-seven times, Perot thirty-four times, and Bush only sixteen times.[10]

Talk-show democracy added a surprise element to Campaign '92, and it proved its worth not just to candidates but also to voters, the political system and even the press. Thanks to talk shows, voters probably glimpsed more facets of the presidential candidates than ever before, and they also were often able to make a direct connection with the contenders, due to the call-in component that was usually present. The political system was strengthened by this new diversity of approach, because the talk shows broadened the audience for politics, educating some citizens not regularly reached by news programming. The competition provided by nontraditional venues also proved healthy for the traditional news organizations. Voters' issue-oriented questions were a welcome change from the horserace-obsessed fare of many reporters, for instance, and kept the press focused on people's real concerns.[11] Also helpful was the reminder—a revelation to some of the news media's oversized egos—that many citizens believed they could happily do without much of the press. Of course, what voters frequently missed on the talk shows was the hard questioning and tough follow-ups that expose politicians' inconsistencies, the type of interrogation that only trained journalists can usually provide. So talk-show democracy has its limits, and it ought to be seen as either a complement or a supplement to mainstream news coverage. Nonetheless, the talk-show phenomenon, likely now a permanent part of the campaign landscape, is a useful revolt against the press insiders, and potentially a powerful tool to produce wider participation and interest in politics.

Throughout the year, some journalists derided candidate appearances on talk shows as undignified, characterizing the shows as more entertaining than informational. Whatever the truth of those criticisms, journalists ought to be at least as concerned with the Hollywoodized behavior of some of their colleagues. In 1992, as before,[12] an apparently insatiable thirst for celebrity led many prominent television newspersons to blur the line between journalism and entertainment by appearing on such comedy/variety shows as Jay Leno, David Letterman, and Arsenio Hall. As usual, these infotainment artists (led by all-time-appearance record-holder Tom Brokaw of NBC) filled guest slot after guest slot without a peep of criticism from anyone in their star-struck profession.[13]

Talk-show democracy also had its effects on the network evening newscasts. CBS, ABC, and NBC all employed panels of "average voters" for intermittent discussions throughout the fall with Dan Rather, Peter Jennings, and Tom Brokaw. Like all other unscientifically selected, nonrandom samples, these so-called "focus groups" were unbalanced in some way. For example, ABC's and CBS's participants seemed disproportionately hostile to Bush, while not a single undecided voter in NBC's small sampling eventually went to Clinton's column.[14]

Other network innovations included regular "truth checks" on claims made in candidate advertising and speeches. In this area, the work of ABC's Jeff Greenfield, CBS's Eric Engberg, CNN's Brooks Jackson, and NBC's Lisa Myers, among others, was one of the highlights of 1992's television press coverage. However, there was at times an unfortunate tendency to present only one possible, narrow interpretation of a TV spot's assertions or a candidate's statements, when alternate explanations were equally credible, if less critical. The newspaper "ad watches" that rapidly and blessedly became a standard feature of campaign coverage around the country usually avoided this pitfall, allowing space for the criticized campaigns to respond. Television should do the same.

The network news divisions also made an effort to match the serious mood of 1992 voters by focusing on the key issues—especially the economy. All of the evening newscasts beefed up their issue-oriented segments, and the regular viewer probably did receive adequate tutelage in the major areas of campaign debate. Surprisingly, as a proportion of total election news, issue coverage declined from 40 percent in 1988 to 32 percent in 1992, while horserace coverage galloped ahead (35 percent in 1992, compared to 25 percent in 1988).[15] Yet the absolute numbers of issue segments in 1992 almost precisely matched those of 1988,[16] and many of the 1992 issue pieces were, by network TV standards, lengthy and in-depth. Additionally, the issue pieces were competing with an unprecedented orgy of horserace polls, including at least four sets of daily "tracking polls" in the final weeks of the campaign. Senior broadcast and print journalists are among the first to admit that polling—and reporting about it—got completely out of hand in the latter stages of 1992.[17] The survey results determined the headlines and drove the context of the coverage to an appalling degree, while the faults and inherent inadequacies of polls (high refusal rates, difficulties in screening out nonvoters, and so on) rarely received appropriate attention. Compounding these difficulties was the pronounced tendency of each news organization to hype its survey, to the minimization or exclusion of surveys with different results. And almost all the preelection polls missed the size of the Perot vote—a final caution that ought to give all journalists pause before the next poll-a-rama begins.

Because of time constraints, the three oldest networks are unable to match the news efforts of CNN and C-SPAN. CNN's "Inside Politics" and its six-part series "Democracy in America" were major contributions to voter education, and C-SPAN's complete coverage of almost all major campaign events (gloriously without commentary) allowed viewers to evaluate the candidates for themselves.

Many print-news organizations also deserve credit for thorough, issue-oriented coverage. Indeed, at virtually every major newspaper and newsmagazine, the sheer volume of 1992 campaign-related stories and analyses was impressive, and maybe overwhelming. Few print outlets made enough effort to produce reader-friendly and reader-responsive coverage. A clear exception, and a model for the future, was the *Charlotte Observer* in North Carolina.[18] After polling to determine voters' concerns, the newspaper asked candidates to address the "citizens' agenda" rather than the one designed by the politicians' political consultants. Reporters wrote fewer campaign strategy stories and far more issue pieces, with reader reactions high-lighted rather than the responses of spin doctors and political pros. The paper opened up a telephone line and invited readers to propose questions for the candidates, which *Observer* reporters then asked the national and state contenders when the opportunity came. Every Sunday morning the paper focused on a particular issue and chal-lenged readers to propose solutions; Sunday evening the local ABC affiliate (WSOC–TV) aired a program featuring the candidates' stands on the issue, and voters' reactions. Thousands of citizens participated in the *Observer* undertaking and, incredibly, WSOC's programs twice matched or exceeded the ratings of NFL football games on another channel. Voter turnout in this media market also increased substan-tially over 1988, at a pace greater than in North Carolina or in fact the nation as a whole.[19]

The *Charlotte Observer* clearly welcomed the constructive criticism of its readers, and all news outlets with truly independent ombuds-men can make the same claim (see chapter 8). Regrettably, the televi-sion networks continue to resist the on-air ombudsman concept, to the detriment of their viewers. An internal critic with access to the airwaves could serve as a lightning rod for the complaints and anger of a skeptical public that is increasingly shutting out the mainstream press. The average citizen believes, with some justification, that Big Media is as unresponsive and inaccessible as Big Government and Big Business, and that precious little opportunity exists for personal, two-way communication between the networks and their news con-sumers. (Arbitron ratings do not suffice.) "Nightline's" occasional town meetings on ABC, and CNN's weekly "Reliable Sources," the only current television program that scrutinizes press behavior, are steps in the right direction, but only the institution of the ombudsman could act as an internal and external circuit-breaker on feeding fren-zies and questionable press practices. When I debated NBC News president Michael Gartner on this subject in the summer of 1992, he dismissed the idea out-of-hand, insisting, "That's *my* role."[20] Could a vigorous NBC ombudsman have prevented the "Dateline NBC" fiasco of November 1992, involving a rigged crash test of a General Motors pickup truck, either by flagging the practice before airtime or by handling GM's post-air complaint in a fair-minded fashion? Gart-ner initially stonewalled GM and publicly defended his network's shoddy performance, but then, under threat of legal action, he agreed to a lengthy, humiliating on-air apology by the "Dateline NBC" anchors. In March 1993 Gartner resigned as a consequence of this enormously damaging incident—which itself was a consequence of declining standards, infotainment's forward march, and the lack of internal checks in a major network. As a direct result of its investigation of the "Dateline NBC" disaster, NBC News in March 1993 did in fact appoint an ombudsman, David McCormick (who would also serve as the senior producer for broadcast standards). While McCormick was to receive complaints and investigate them internally, there were no initial plans to give him access to airtime—and thus no opportunity for him to act as a fully empowered, independent viewer advocate. Nonetheless, his designation gives at least some cause for hope.

Media Bias, Front and Off-Center

Indeed, coverage of the campaign vindicated exactly what conservatives have been saying for years about liberal bias in the media.

Jacob Weisberg, *The New Republic*[21]

I sensed and observed a bias toward Clinton and more liberal policies and positions.

Richard Benedetto, *USA Today*[22]

There seems little doubt—at least in this corner—that press coverage was tilted against Bush during much of the campaign.

David Gergen, *U.S. News & World Report*[23]

[The pro-Clinton] bias of reporters, editors, the whole crew . . . brought about a tilt that was more pervasive and obvious than I've ever seen.

Hugh Sidey, *Time*[24]

The coverage has not been equal, not been fair.

Reid Collins, CNN[25]

A surprising number of prominent journalists and commentators, not all from the conservative wing of their profession, insist that in the 1992 general election the press leaned heavily in Bill Clinton's direction. Republicans are overwhelmingly of this opinion, having long ago consigned journalists to the rung of hell reserved for covert Democrats. The Perotistas would concur: George Bush and Ross Perot may not agree on much, but dislike for those Bush called the "nutty talking heads" and Perot termed "jerks" and "teenage boys" is one unifying element. (The first half of Bush's favorite slogan, "Annoy the Media—Reelect Bush" could easily have been adopted by Perot.)

Naturally enough, much of the media establishment disagrees with Bush, Perot, *and* the bold journalists whose critiques are cited above. NBC's political director, Bill Wheatley, declared, "I don't believe there was an active bias at work,"[26] while his network colleague, anchor Tom Brokaw, offered his own sound bite to dampen the controversy: "Bias, like beauty, is most often in the eye of the beholder."[27] Thus, fairness prevailed, say most of the news business's high priests, and the press did not defeat Bush: Bush beat Bush.

The more one studies the remarkable case of 1992, the greater the likelihood of judging both sides of this debate partly in the right. For 1992, the conclusions about press tilt are essentially the same as those reached when this controversial subject was initially taken up in chapter 3: "of course" the news media are biased, but "press tilt has a marginal-to-moderate effect, no more and no less. . . ."[28]

First, the bias itself. Television viewers could be forgiven for sometimes believing that the acronyms ABC, NBC, and CBS stood for the American Broadcasters for Clinton, the National Broadcasters for Clinton, and the Clinton Broadcasting System. From Labor Day to Election Day, the Center for Media and Public Affairs found that 71 percent of the substantive comments made about George Bush on ABC, NBC, and CBS by reporters and other "nonpartisan" sources were negative. Bill Clinton's evaluations among the same group were 52 percent *positive.* These totals excluded horserace remarks about who was likely to win the election—portrayals that favored Clinton by an even greater margin.[29]

Another study, by PR Data Systems and Mead Data Central, suggests that print-news organizations exhibited a similar bias. A painstaking content analysis of AP, UPI, and eleven major U.S. daily newspapers over the general election period showed that nearly three-quarters (72 percent) of all negative characterizations made in presidential debate stories and accompanying headlines were about Bush. Clinton garnered just 15 percent of these unfavorable mentions, and Perot only 13 percent.[30] By contrast, Clinton was the beneficiary of almost half (48 percent) of the glowing characterizations and headlines, while Perot garnered 30 percent of the positive mentions and Bush a paltry 22 percent. Most observers rated Perot the best performer in the first debate, Clinton in the second, and Bush in the third, so even a healthy front-runner's bonus could scarcely entitle Clinton to such a lion's share of kudos if fairness prevailed. The tilt to Clinton in the news pages was matched on the editorial pages, too, as Clinton became the first Democrat since Lyndon Johnson in 1964 to win more newspaper editorial endorsements than the Republican nominee.[31]

Seemingly, everywhere one looked in the summer and autumn of 1992, Bush and Quayle were being bashed and Clinton and Gore were being hailed in the media. The *Washington Post* certainly fit the pattern, and when its ombudsman, Joann Byrd, scrutinized the newspaper's contents (including headlines and photographs) covering the campaign's last two and a half months, she reached the conclusion that her paper had a "very lopsided" tilt in Clinton's direction.[32] For instance, the *Post*'s Style section featured a glowing account of a Clinton–Gore bus trip, headlined "New Heartthrobs of the Heartland." And, in one of the most embarrassing juxtapositions of the campaign, the *Post* hyped its mid-September public opinion poll showing a 21 percentage-point lead for Clinton with a front page, top-left headline, "Clinton's Lead Appears Solid, May Be Growing." Just a week later, when its next poll revealed a much narrower 9-point lead for Clinton, the *Post* buried the story inside on page A6 with the amusingly protective headline, "Clinton Slide in Survey Shows Perils of Polling."[33] The news media tilt was supplemented by late-night comics, and even some prime-time entertainment shows, such as "Murphy Brown," which piled on the Republicans and promoted the Democrats (see table A1).[34]

There were notable exceptions, of course. Broadcast personality Rush Limbaugh, with a weekly radio audience of over 12 million and growing rapidly, aimed daily broadsides at the Clinton bandwagon.[35] The *Washington Times* was slanted against Clinton from its masthead to its classified ads, with headlines and news stories so enthusiastically pro-Bush that at times it appeared to be a throwback to the nineteenth century's cheerleading party press.[36] And many of the news approaches to Hillary Rodham Clinton suffered from a subtle—or (sometimes) blatant—sexism.[37] But even added together, these anti-Clinton transgressions were no match for the collective pro-Clinton fare of the leading networks and newspapers.

There is general agreement that the economy torpedoed Bush and elected Clinton. But was it the economy itself, or the media depictions of it, that turned voters against Bush? No one can say with any certainty, but the networks' descriptions of economic conditions sounded more like the Great Depression than the moderate recession and prolonged period of sluggish growth that characterized 1990–92. Fully 96 percent of the economic evaluations on the evening newscasts during much of the general election were negative, as were 83 percent of the predictions about the economy's future performance.[38] The latter undoubtedly helped to drive down consumer confidence still further, and make Bush's predictions of recovery seem fanciful and "out of touch" to voters.

TABLE A.1
Late-Night Political Humor in the 1992 Campaign.

Candidate	Total Number of David Letterman, Jay Leno, and Arsenio Hall Jokes	Examples
George Bush	608	*On Bush's alleged affair: "Wouldn't it be ironic if Barbara got a chance to throw him out of the White House before we got a chance to?" (Jay Leno, June 25, 1992)
		*"Bush is now being accused of manufacturing the current crisis with Iraq. If it's true, it'll be the first manufacturing job he's brought to the U.S. in years." (Jay Leno, September 2, 1992)
		*On Bush meeting with the Postmaster General: "It wasn't an emergency or anything. Bush just needed one of those change-of-address kits." (Jay Leno, October 27, 1992)
Bill Clinton	423	*"Top Ten Surprises in the United Nation's Sex Study: No. 10—Of the 100 million acts of love daily, most occur in Bill Clinton's campaign van." (David Letterman, June 25, 1992)
		*"Bill Clinton said yesterday, 'It's not appropriate to go after someone's wife in the media.' He said, 'Going after someone's wife is better done discreetly, like at a cocktail party.'" (Jay Leno, August 25, 1992)
		*On Clinton saying he's capable of commanding the U.S. military because he's headed the Arkansas National Guard: "Isn't that like saying you can fly the Space Shuttle because you've seen every episode of Star Trek?" (Jay Leno, August 31, 1992)
Dan Quayle	357	*On Quayle being like Hamburger Helper: "You know he's in the Cabinet. You just hope you never have to use him." (Jay Leno, June 19, 1992)
		*On Quayle's trip to Los Angeles: "Just what L.A. needs—another dumb blond." (Arsenio Hall, June 24, 1992)
		*On Quayle meeting with Ronald Reagan: "That must have been interest-

TABLE A. 1 (Cont.)
LATE-NIGHT POLITICAL HUMOR IN THE 1992 CAMPAIGN.

CANDIDATE	TOTAL NUMBER OF DAVID LETTERMAN, JAY LENO, AND ARSENIO HALL JOKES	EXAMPLES
Dan Quayle (Cont.)		ing—someone who doesn't know what he's doing meeting with someone who can't remember what he did." (Jay Leno, September 9, 1992)
		*"Top Ten Ways Quayle Prepared for the Vice Presidential debate: No. 7—Read book of inspirational stories about dumb guys who went up against smart guys—and won. No. 2—Reread his 'how a bill becomes a law' comic book."(David Letterman, October 13, 1992)
Ross Perot	334	*"I haven't seen a guy so mixed up about being in a race since Michael Jackson." (Arsenio Hall, September 25, 1992)
		*"If he is not elected president he should go out to the airport. He'd make a great Hare Krishna." (Jay Leno, October 8, 1992)
		*"Top Ten Reasons Clinton Is Losing His Lead: No. 2—More and more people like the idea of a tiny, insane millionaire running things." (David Letterman, October 29, 1992)
Jerry Brown	106	*On Brown's showing in the New York primary: "He finished fifth, behind Clinton, Tsongas, uncommitted, and the older, fatter Elvis." (Johnny Carson, April 8, 1992)
		*On Brown's 800 Number: "They put you on hold and play a recording of his concession speech." (David Letterman, April 26, 1992)
		*On a break-in at Brown's campaign headquarters: "Not too serious, I understand. The thieves got away with three mood rings, two lava lamps, some magic crystals, [and] a couple of the beaded curtains." (Jay Leno, June 22, 1992)
Al Gore	49	*On Al Gore, Sr.'s comment that his son was raised for the job of vice president: "How do you raise someone [for that]?

TABLE A.1 *(Cont.)*
LATE-NIGHT POLITICAL HUMOR IN THE 1992 CAMPAIGN.

CANDIDATE	TOTAL NUMBER OF DAVID LETTERMAN, JAY LENO, AND ARSENIO HALL JOKES	EXAMPLES
Al Gore *(Cont.)*		Do you put them in their room with nothing to do? Take them to a funeral and let them hang around?" (Jay Leno, July 10, 1992)
		*On Gore's speaking style: "I never thought I'd miss the charisma of Paul Tsongas." (Jay Leno, October 13, 1992)

NOTE: Other politicians who were frequent targets (and their total numbers of 1992 late-night jokes) include: Edward Kennedy (59), Patrick Buchanan (56), Ronald Reagan (53), and Paul Tsongas (51).

SOURCES: Numbers of jokes on "The Tonight Show with Jay Leno," "Late Night with David Letterman, and "The Arsenio Hall Show" were compiled by the Center for Media and Public Affairs. All of calendar year 1992 was surveyed. The joke examples were selected from campaign issues of *Hotline* from January 1, 1992 to November 3, 1992.

These media characterizations of the economy were no minor matter. The state of the economy was unquestionably the central issue of the campaign, and the chief source of President Bush's woes. A positive press spin suggested that economic recovery could have helped Bush regenerate lost momentum, and would have undercut Clinton's major campaign thrust. But not only did Bush not receive an assist; the news media repeatedly ignored or downplayed nearly every encouraging sign of an ongoing recovery that was slowly picking up steam. Near the end of the campaign, when the U.S. gross domestic product was announced to have grown by a strong 2.7 percent in the third quarter, most major media outlets pooh-poohed the news,[39] some even implying that the government's books had been cooked to make Bush look good at a critical moment. After the election, when the government released the final revised GDP growth rate for the third quarter, the statistic turned out to be 3.4 percent—an even better showing than Bush had been able to trumpet.

Was this just an isolated incident, one wherein skeptical reportorial juices were flowing freely as Election Day approached? Not according to a number of experienced financial reporters who attended the Commerce and Labor Departments' briefings throughout the campaign.[40] Some colleagues, they noted, openly cheered bad economic statistics and booed good ones, hoping for the best spin from Clinton's perspective. These personal reactions would be revealing but harmless enough, as long as the resulting stories were not affected by the bias. Yet many news reports of economic statistics seemed to share the same slant. When the civilian unemployment rate rose, the headlines logically reflected that bad news.[41] But when it fell in the summer and autumn, that fact was sometimes deemphasized (or even buried) in print stories, with more obscure, unfavorable jobless statistics—such as private, nonfarm payroll employment—highlighted in the headlines. For example, in early September, when overall unemployment edged down a tenth of a point, to 7.6 percent, the front pages of both the *Washington Post* and the *New York Times* headlined instead the loss of 67,000 private nonfarm jobs.[42] Said one financial reporter for a major news service, "Financial markets paid attention to the [private nonfarm] number, but even professional economists weren't uniformly focussed on that drop, and I have never [before] seen a paper lead with it in a general news report."[43]

The media's Democratic tilt is not new to many voters. A postelection survey by the Times–Mirror Center for the People and the Press found that 35 percent of the voters believed the press had been unfair to George Bush, while just 19 percent termed the press unfair to Bill Clinton.[44] Even many reporters acknowledged as much. An October 1992 study by the Times–Mirror Center revealed that 55 percent of the journalists surveyed believed Bush's candidacy was damaged by press coverage, while only 11 percent thought Clinton was similarly harmed.[45]

True, the press targeted Clinton early on, thanks to Gennifer Flowers, the draft charges, and marijuana noninhaling—but this was the time when key reporters had tagged Clinton "easy meat" for the Republicans in the fall, and many newspersons were privately hoping a "stronger" Democrat would enter the fray. Once Clinton was the nominee and the alternative to four more years of Bush, the tone of his coverage changed markedly. Adding to Clinton's advantage was the shame and regret many reporters felt about their handling of the Flowers affair, not to mention embarrassment about their mispredictions of Clinton's "inevitable" demise.

What motivated the tilt? The obvious but incomplete explanation is party preference and ideology. A Freedom Forum survey of journalists revealed that newspersons are predominantly and increasingly Democratic: 44 percent of reporters in 1992 called themselves Democrats, up from 38 percent in 1982; while only 16 percent identified with the Republican party, down from 19 percent ten years earlier.[46] Whether Democratic, Republican, or independent, most reporters are ideologically liberal, especially on social issues. Thus, the Democratic National Convention platform was almost universally labeled "moderate" despite containing an absolutist prochoice position on abortion and, for the first time ever, controversial pledges to end the ban on gays in the military, and seek civil rights legislation for homosexuals. (President Clinton and the news media were to discover, shortly after the new president's inauguration, just how explosive the proposal on gays in the military was.) By contrast, the Republican National Convention platform was repeatedly characterized as right-wing and extreme, even though it was little changed from the ones with which Ronald Reagan and George Bush won landslide Electoral College victories in 1980, 1984, and 1988.

The abortion issue in particular generated an extra shove in the Democratic direction in 1992, since another GOP presidential victory could have eventually provided the fifth Supreme Court vote to overturn *Roe* v. *Wade*, the decision guaranteeing abortion rights. Many reporters claim that their personal views on abortion and other issues do not influence coverage, but this assertion rings more true for some than for others. Journalists are not automatons, and at the very least their personal preferences influence the kinds of subjects they choose to cover, and the approach they take to that coverage. A few newspersons are quite blunt about the influence their views have on coverage. Margaret Carlson, *Time*'s deputy bureau chief in Washington who once worked in the Carter administration, explained: "You couldn't have fought the battles you have fought to get where you are and not find what the Republicans say about women offensive—it's not possible, you cannot be that objective."[47] Of course, most Republicans find Carlson's statement not only offensive but proof positive of press bias. Another example often cited by the GOP is the statement by ABC News's Carole Simpson that she "believed Anita Hill" in her 1991 charges of sexual harassment against Supreme Court Justice-to-be Clarence Thomas. This declaration came less than a week before Simpson was to moderate the second presidential debate in Richmond, Virginia on October 16.[48]

Other factors besides ideology were also at work in 1992. The press is traditionally tougher on an incumbent administration, whatever its party affiliation, especially in hard times. The White House occupant's flaws are always well known, and the press's battles with him have usually left tender bruises that are easily inflamed or require the revenge of the per.. By contrast, the challenger is relatively unsullied, his transgressions less known or threatening. George Bush was an irresistibly inviting target because he had blown a massive lead and become unpopular with most viewers and readers—a development that actually predated the nasty turn in his press coverage. Bush took on the unmistakable look of a potential loser, and the possible fall of a once-invincible leader became a compelling story that shaped the context in which all other reporting was done. The scent of losing also emboldened enemies from the president's own party and ideology to carp and lash out, without fear of retribution, which made it all the more difficult for Bush to communicate a persuasive message. After all, the news media often only echo and amplify the biting criticism they readily find in the pundit class or on the campaign trail, and the source can as easily be on the right (Bush critics Patrick Buchanan, William Safire, and George Will, for instance) as on the left. In fact, the most dismissive, vicious remarks about Bush came from conservative, not liberal, commentators; the president's right flank was breathtakingly exposed, and relatively few ardent defenders of the Bush faith could be found to counteract the torrent of abuse heaped upon him.[49]

Surprisingly, given Bush's apparent congeniality, many senior reporters also disliked him personally—and this group extended well beyond Dan Rather. Various explanations were offered privately, including Bush's inaccessibility, perceived favoritism, and even reverse class snobbery (the old "preppie factor" that long dogged the upper-crust Bush). Some journalists also harbored resentment about the way in which Bush won the presidency in 1988, especially his team's shrewd manipulation of the media and the use of Willie Horton, the pledge-of-allegiance issue, and the like; 1992 became the payback, the just dessert, for 1988. But whatever the cause, the press usually gives more favorable treatment to politicians they personally like (Bill Clinton, Ronald Reagan) than ones they do not like (Gary Hart, George Bush), regardless of ideology.

In addition, the newsrooms across America are now dominated by the baby-boomers, and in the main they identified with the Democrats' young and hip boomer ticket. The 46-year-old Clinton's Fleetwood Mac, saxophone, and experiences in the 1960s counterculture era had more resonance and relevance to youthful journalists than the 68-year-old Bush's country music, horseshoes, and World War II.

Perhaps most fundamentally, journalists' careers and personal satisfaction depend in good part on the importance of the news they cover. The defeat of an incumbent president, the end of the Reagan–Bush era, and the election of a Kennedyesque successor with the accompanying massive changes in policy and personnel all was simply better news, with the promise of years of drama and upheaval to come. More than a few newspersons who did the reporting on candidate Clinton knew they would likely win the assignment to cover President Clinton, sharing the White House limelight and—with visions of Ben Bradlee advising JFK dancing in their dreams—maybe even the Oval Office. Most of us just *hope* for change that will benefit our professions or businesses; journalists are in a position to nourish their kind of change to fruition.

So, on the whole, the press was certainly a Clinton ally in 1992.[50] But George Bush probably could still have won the election had he held fast to his "no new taxes" pledge, capitalized early on his Persian Gulf victory, focused purposefully on domestic ills, and spent the campaign convincing Americans of the worth of his recovery plan, instead of mainly attacking Clinton's character and record. Bush and his managers ignored a fundamental lesson of American presidential elections: voters cast ballots retrospectively, and any contest for the White House inevitably becomes a referendum on the performance of the incumbent administration, not the challenger. So the fault, dear George, lay less in your press clippings than in yourself and your truly awful campaign—one of the most inept in modern history.

This is not to exonerate the press. Consumers have a right to expect more balance and fairness than they get in campaign coverage. Once again, vigorous ombudsmen who relentlessly challenge their news organizations can play a vital role, and the need for *video* ombudsmen is especially apparent in this area. The television networks need internal critics even more than do most newspapers, wherein a variety of opinions is regularly available. It would also help if more conservative-minded young people could be attracted to news reporting; if news accounts and agendas are inevitably biased, perhaps readers and viewers would benefit from an ideological mix. "Diversity," after all, is the holy buzzword of the 1990s. Why not in the newsroom, too?

The Frenzies of '92: Déjà Vu All Over Again

There was a frenzy or two in store for most candidates in 1992, and voters could be forgiven for thinking they had seen it all before. The circumstances were familiar: mistresses, imagined or real; drug use; the Vietnam draft; deeply rooted subtexts; unsubstantiated rumors in print and on air. Moreover, several frenzies were not just *similar* to past ones, but precisely the *same* controversies resurrected whole from past election cycles. A comprehensive accounting is beyond the scope of this Afterword, but herewith a sampling of the Frenzies of '92.

BILL CLINTON

Damaged but unbowed, Bill Clinton survived more feeding frenzies than anyone else in modern history save Dan Quayle. Unlike Quayle, he emerged from the media's trial-by-fire holding the keys to the White House. Few in Clinton's camp, and hardly anyone outside of it, imagined this happy ending in the snows of New Hampshire when Flowers bloomed early in 1992.

Ever since Clinton had begun to consider a 1992 White House bid seriously, profiles of the prospective candidate had often included vague and completely unsubstantiated references to Clinton's "womanizing" and "marital difficulties."[51] Clinton himself was concerned enough about the early press coverage, as well as the specter of what lay ahead (given the Gary Hart precedent), that he brought his wife to a Washington press breakfast in September 1991. The couple attempted to head off further inquiries by admitting they had not had "a perfect marriage" free of difficulties, yet insisting that the details were no one's business, especially since the marriage had overcome those past problems. All the Clinton's close friends and associates privately confirmed to reporters that the pair had indeed worked through their difficulties and were happily married.

The Clinton's thoroughly reasonable claim to privacy was not to prevail, of course. When Clinton announced his presidential candidacy on October 3, 1991, most stories in the mainstream press contained the obligatory unsourced paragraph noting that Clinton was "dogged by rumors of marital infidelity," and the subsequent candidate profiles over the succeeding weeks retained this questionable dimension.[52] Some broadcast journalists also helped to create the climate conducive to Clinton's adultery frenzy. On January 19, 1992, ABC's Cokie Roberts served as a moderator for a WMUR-TV (Manchester, N.H.) debate among the Democratic presidential hopefuls that was seen nationally on C-SPAN. Roberts turned to Clinton and launched this broadside of innuendo:

There is concern among members of your party that [with] these allegations of womanizing . . . the Republicans will find somebody, and that she will come forward late, and that you would lose the all important—to Democrats—women's vote. What do you say?[53]

Despite all the well-intentioned seminars and the promises to conduct business differently than in 1988, the press had splashed enough rumor-combustible gasoline about Clinton in the early months of Campaign '92 so that only a spark was needed to start an enormous fire. Arkansas state employee and cabaret singer Gennifer Flowers decided to be the spark, for a hefty and still undetermined amount of money. On January 23, 1992 the *Star*, a gossipy, trashy supermarket tabloid, released a squalid cover story on Flowers's supposed "12-year affair with Bill Clinton."[54] Subsidiary headlines included "Mistress Tells All," "Dems' front-runner lied to America, says his former lover," and "The secret love tapes that prove it." Over the next week this incident would not only nearly torpedo the Clinton campaign but prove anew the dominance of lowest-common-denominator journalism.

Gennifer Flowers was a name unfamiliar to the public but well known to many in the political press. For many months she and several other women had been romantically linked to Governor Clinton by his opponents, and even by some neutral observers in Arkansas. Given the centrality of the post–Gary Hart character issue, most major broadcast and print-news organizations had sent reporters—some had dispatched teams of them—to Arkansas, to investigate. *Not one news outlet uncovered enough evidence to warrant a single published or broadcast story.* The claims simply did not check out, were unprovable, or suffered from other fatal flaws. Therefore, one might presume that well-prepared news organizations, having already thoroughly investigated these allegations, would discard them as without merit once they reached print in a sleazy, suspect publication. After all, such was the case with the Bush mistress rumor in October 1988 (see pp. 175–177).

Certainly, some news outlets attempted to do just that.[55] On the first evening, only NBC among the networks even mentioned the subject, but some large local television stations, such as WNBC in New York City, covered it extensively. More importantly, ABC's "Nightline" devoted its program to the "media's handling of the Clinton allegations," a backdoor way of discussing the infidelity claim.[56] The ABC, CBS, and CNN networks waded in with stories on the second day (Friday, January 24), as did most major newspapers, with the exception of the *New York Times,* which appropriately downplayed the frenzy from beginning to end.[57] But the floodgates opened after Clinton made the decision to appear on "60 Minutes" with his wife right after the Super Bowl on Sunday, January 26. Up to 50 million Americans watched the affectionate Clintons try to shake off the charges without discussing their marital history in detail. Whatever their success, the broadcast fully legitimized public discussion of the tabloid story, and all networks led with the subject on their Monday broadcasts, aided by a *Star*-sponsored Monday afternoon press conference attended by over 200 journalists. At this session, edited tapes, surreptitiously recorded by Flowers, were played disclosing ambiguous telephone conversations between Clinton and Flowers—he called her "baby" once in closing, and a sexual allusion was made.[58] Flowers also fielded questions ranging from Clinton's preferences in sex acts to his wearing or nonwearing of condoms. In one of the worst news decisions of the election year, CNN chose to carry this tawdry press conference live, a decision which in retrospect CNN political director Tom Hannon regretted.[59]

There can be little doubt that in another election year the Flowers incident would have proved fatal to Clinton's candidacy. As it was, Clinton fell from near-certain winner of the New Hampshire primary to a poor second-place finish (well behind the victor, former U.S. Senator Paul Tsongas). Clinton survived and eventually triumphed because, first, the importance of the economy and the voters' determined focus on it overrode all other issues in 1992; second, Clinton was the beneficiary of a weak Democratic candidate field, and most party leaders recognized that probably he alone of the announced contenders would have a reasonable chance of victory in November;[60] and third, the establishment news media were genuinely embarrassed about their latest detour into the gutter, and happy to move on to other matters at the earliest opportunity. *Newsweek*, the Arkansas *Democrat–Gazette*, and other publications quickly seized upon discrepancies in Flowers's story and résumé, while few major news organizations ever put much stress on the seemingly incriminating elements of the tapes.[61]

The Flowers frenzy yet again made obvious the inability (or unwillingness) of the mainstream media to resist a juicy story from the seamier side of their business. Instead of news standards trickling down from best to worst, they were now bubbling up from worst to best—truly a Mad Hatter's affair. And, without either group of media overtly acknowledging the favor done the other, it was beginning to resemble a cooperative arrangement, as former *New York Times* reporter Christopher Lydon suggested:

The upscale media baited the trap with hints about womanizing; their down-market cousins bagged the trophy; and the quality commentators returned, bright clothespins on their noses, to dissect the evidence and tell us what it meant. To audiences it did not look like real warfare in the media but rather like a face-saving division of labor.[62]

One salutary effect of the Clinton–Flowers story was to turn the public even more strongly against this type or reporting. A CNN/*Time* poll at the height of the Flowers incident found that 82 percent of the respondents believed the press paid too much attention to candidates' personal lives, and only 25 percent wanted to "be informed about the private lives of presidential candidates, including any extramarital affairs"—down dramatically from the 41 percent who wanted to be told such things in 1987.[63] Furthermore, the public gave a forceful thumbs down on lowest-common-denominator journalism. "If a competing medium reveals charges about a candidate's personal life," only 4 percent thought" an editor should consider the charge to be news in itself and report it on that basis." Rather, 42 percent preferred that the editor "check out the stories and do a story only if it can be independently verified," while another 50 percent wanted the editor to "ignore the charges unless they seem clearly connected to the candidate's public duties."[64] While the press was less critical of itself, it was not particularly proud of its performance. In a June 1992 *Times–Mirror* survey of journalists, more than a third (36 percent) admitted that news organizations had handled the Clinton controversy "not too responsibly" or "not at all responsibly."[65]

The press fiasco that was Gennifer Flowers may have helped insulate Clinton from additional intrusive coverage of his private life, despite many opportunities and provocations. As is standard practice (see chapter 4), journalists were inundated with "helpful" calls from agents of Clinton's Democratic rivals, as well as the Republican party and long-time Clinton foes in Arkansas. The Clinton campaign undertook a "bimbo eruption watch" that was kept busy throughout the primaries and general election.[66] Clinton aide Betsy Wright oversaw the effort, which included monitoring seven such allegations in the preconvention period and nineteen similar charges in the days following the Democratic National Convention. Some of the "bimbo fever" was traced to the large, six-figure sums of money being offered to women by tabloid publications. By-and-large, the Clinton effort at containment was successful, both because the accusing women had credibility problems and the post-Flowers press had little stomach for the chase. Even when one outlet published or aired a story, few if any others were willing to follow up. An April *Washington Times* top-of-the-front-page piece on Roger Clinton's use of his brother's Little Rock gubernatorial mansion for sexual liaisons went nowhere; even the *Times* noted that no evidence existed that Bill Clinton even knew about Roger's romantic activities.[67] In its lead story on July 13, the "CBS Evening News" examined an apparently baseless claim by a conservative independent political committee that a young woman committed suicide after being made pregnant by Bill Clinton in the

1970s. (As the report noted, the woman's family denied the allegations, which correspondent Eric Engberg termed a "nasty hoax.")[68] Shortly after the Democratic convention, syndicated television talk-show host Sally Jessy Raphael irresponsibly featured the completely unsubstantiated claims of former Miss Arkansas Sally Miller Perdue, who said she had a brief affair with Clinton in the fall of 1983. No major news organization picked up the story, which was also being pushed by the far-left New Alliance Party headed by presidential candidate Lenora Fulani.[69]

The real tests for the press came as the campaign moved into its tense final days in October. Often, in this pressure-cooker atmosphere, it becomes easier for questionable stories to reach print or air, and to ricochet across the media landscape before good judgment can intervene. In mid-October, *Penthouse* magazine chose to release its upcoming December issue interview with Gennifer Flowers, and in thirteen raunchy pages she leveled explosive charges (such as her claim to have aborted Clinton's child) and described in excruciating detail the couple's purported sex acts and pet names for various body parts. If ever the press might yield to the temptation to sell papers, this opportunity would be choice. Yet the matter was downplayed and sanitized almost everywhere (except in the *Washington Times*), perhaps prodded by *Penthouse* publisher Bob Guccione's statement that he had sought to verify Flowers's charges, "often without success."[70] The Republicans took up where *Penthouse* left off, as they desperately sought to turn the tide in the campaign's waning hours.[71] During the final week, a number of major news organizations received telephone calls from GOP officials demanding that a story be written about Clinton's "current extramarital affair" with a reporter covering the Clinton campaign that the Secret Service "knew all about." On election eve (November 2), U.S. Representative Guy Vander Jagt (R., Mich.), the chairman of the National Republican Congressional Committee, publicly made this charge at an Omaha news conference. When only a local television affiliate aired the allegation, Vander Jagt sent a transcript of his comments to national news organizations. No one aired or published the story, and the Secret Service denied that any of their employees had knowledge of a Clinton affair.

Gennifer Flowers was Clinton's defining feeding frenzy, but hardly the only one to which he was subjected. The frenzy over Clinton's draft record was almost as disruptive for the candidate as the Flowers episode, and it lasted longer. Like Dan Quayle, Bill Clinton was forced to relive the painful Vietnam era through the ambiguities in his own past. Quayle had served in the National Guard while Clinton avoided service entirely, but both had clearly benefited from special connections and privileged treatment not available to most young men, and both suffered most from their own lack of candor and mishandling of the issue. Both the 1988 Bush/Quayle ticket and the 1992 Clinton organization were inexplicably unprepared for press inquiries on a legitimate subject—a national candidate's military record—and they let information about their pasts dribble out, in a confusing and contradictory way. Clinton had even less excuse than Quayle, who was unexpectedly chosen for the 1988 GOP ticket and had not faced prior intense press scrutiny on his Vietnam record. By contrast, Clinton had been extensively questioned on the matter during earlier campaigns in Arkansas, and he also had ample opportunities during the presidential primaries to lay out the particulars of his draft status. Instead, as the *Washington Post*'s Dan Balz concluded, Clinton wounded himself "largely because it took him months to reveal" the details, "and sometimes only after repeated questioning from news organizations."[72] The more evasive Clinton sounded and the hazier his usually sharp memory, the more the media's interest was piqued. At the height of the frenzy, for instance, the *Los Angeles Times* had eight staff members working on the story. "We've had a bigger bureau in Little Rock than we've had in New York," boasted the *Times*'s Jack Nelson,[73] and as a result the newspaper broke new ground repeatedly.

As is often the case with similar controversies, the issue became not just draft evasion but also the candidate's trust and credibility: Was Clinton telling the truth? Every new "wiggle disclosure" was hyped because it suggested that the candidate had lied, or hidden something from public view; and every news organization tried to get a piece of the big story, and thus was likely to uncover an unrevealed fact. So Clinton could correctly insist, as he did about one such minor disclosure, that "You've got a feeding frenzy on about something that even if it's true, it doesn't amount to a hill of beans,"[74] and yet it did matter, in another sense. The draft story became one more vehicle for the omnipresent character issue, another chance for the press to test a presidential contender, and another opportunity for the opposition to seed land mines.[75]

Building on the doubts about Clinton created or reinforced by the draft debate, the Bush campaign tried to generate a potentially more destructive frenzy that went to the heart of Clinton's patriotism. Had Clinton been disloyal in participating in a 1969 anti–Vietnam War demonstration on foreign soil (in London) and by visiting the Soviet Union while that nation was supplying arms to America's Southeast Asia adversary? Perhaps this controversy really began in the pages of

Feeding Frenzy's first edition, when CBS News's Eric Engberg—two years before Bill Clinton even decided to run for the White House—projected the scenario of the Oxford Rhodes Scholar president who had been a KGB trainee in Moscow (see page 82).[76] More likely it started in September 1992 on the floor of the U.S. House of Representatives, where a group of Republican congressmen led by California's conservative fire-breather Robert K. Dornan had been asking the Moscow question and darkly suggesting an answer: that young Clinton was somehow a Communist dupe. But since the insinuations were based on mere speculation, most news organizations ignored the matter. The rumor continued to fly, however, in part because C-SPAN necessarily broadcast these House floor discussions as part of its comprehensive coverage of Congress. The *Washington Times* went far beyond C-SPAN's dutiful reporting, of course, touting the Democrat's 1969–70 Moscow trip in a banner headline ("Clinton toured Moscow at war's peak"),[77] and quoting a retired British intelligence officer as asserting that Clinton "fit the profile perfectly" of a candidate ripe for recruitment as a Soviet "agent of influence."

With the gas on the stove turned to high, President Bush decided to throw the lighted match himself. On October 7, 1992, in an appearance on CNN's "Larry King Live," Bush gave a seemingly well-rehearsed answer when King asked him about the Moscow trip:

Larry, I don't want to tell you what I really think 'cause I don't have the facts. I don't have the facts. But to go to Moscow, one year after Russia crushed Czechoslovakia, not remember who you saw—I think, I really think the answer is level with the American people. . . .[78]

Bush's remarks intensified a wave of electrifying rumors in press ranks. The Bush forces, it was said, knew Clinton had had KGB contacts; was part of a Soviet-sponsored and -financed antiwar network; had once prepared to renounce his American citizenship as part of his effort to evade the draft; and had possessed more than one passport under different names. Within a few days, though, it became clear that Bush had no facts at all to sustain his innuendo, despite an ill-fated, improper search of Clinton's and his mother's passport files by members of the Bush team;[79] and that not a single stitch of evidence existed to verify any of the rumors floating about. Press commentary and punditry turned harshly critical of Bush, and he paid a political price for his venture into McCarthyism.

This pseudo-issue never fully died, though many members of the press did their best to inter it. Variations on the theme continued to circulate right up to election day, and even Rhodes House at Oxford University was besieged by reporters "in pursuit of imaginary material to support various calumnies about Clinton's Oxford days."[80] In the final week of the campaign one Oxford-related rumor briefly took on a printed life and nearly became a last-minute controversy. On October 29, 1992, a widely circulated Boston bond wire[81] reported a rumor that CNN and ABC News's "20/20" show would soon be airing photographs or videotape of Clinton burning the American flag at an antiwar rally in England. ABC was flooded with calls from domestic and foreign news organizations, propelling a frazzled network news publicist, Arnot Walker, to secure a retraction (of sorts) by the bond wire about a day later.[82]

Gennifer Flowers, the draft controversy, and Clinton's antiwar activities all were part of the character issue for the Democratic nominee. A great deal of the press's energy, not to mention newsprint and airtime, were wasted in pursuit of unrevealing aspects of these and other campaign matters. At the same time the news media once again failed to focus on some truly consequential facets of character. For example, in the case of Bill Clinton, a much ignored but significant and easily documentable character trait is his often uncontrolled temper—surely a legitimate worry for voters about any potential occupant of the Oval Office.[83]

There were many open public examples of Clinton's blowing up during the campaign, but oddly the press never pointed to the obvious pattern of behavior (contrary to their usual mode of operation, as discussed in chapter 3).[84] When Clinton was incorrectly told in late February that Jesse Jackson was supporting one of his rivals, Iowa U.S. Senator Tom Harkin, his angry outburst—"It's an outrage; it's a dirty, double-crossing, back-stabbing thing to do"—was picked up by an open satellite microphone and then aired by a Phoenix television station and, later, by some of the networks.[85] About a month later, Clinton exploded on stage in response to a heckling AIDS activist who was in attendance at a fund-raiser; Clinton's videotaped retort was widely aired.[86] In an April "Nightline" production that followed Clinton around during one day's campaigning for the New York primary, Clinton was shown sharply berating an aide because of some loud heckling at a Wall Street rally.[87] Reporters also personally watched other blowups at staff members, Secret Service agents, and fellow newspersons, and they were privy to his advisers' estimates that Clinton lost his temper at staff from five to ten times a day.[88] Yet the first major publication to devote serious attention to the subject was the British newsmagazine, *The Economist*, in an article published four days *after* the election.[89] Concluded *The Economist,* in an observation that American journalists should have offered the American electorate for its consideration before they cast their ballots: "None of this proves that Mr. Clinton is an ogre. But it does show that . . . the "real" Mr. Clinton is rather more complex than the folksy, schmoozy man that America thinks it has just elected as its next president." The U.S. media finally awoke from its slumber about Clinton's temperament after the president-elect cursed and dressed down his personal aide, David Friendly, on November 7 for permitting photographers near him on the golf course.[90] Interestingly, while the press widely reported this incident (and a later one shortly after Clinton was inaugurated[91]), almost no mention was made when Clinton had angrily rebuked the same Mr. Friendly *prior* to election day for allowing cameras to record his morning jog from the driveway of the Arkansas governor's mansion.[92]

GEORGE BUSH

The presidency is a special kind of frenzy hell. Chief executives generally lurch from controversy to controversy, and troubled, unpopular incumbents running for reelection are especially vulnerable since they have an arguable record to defend, and must also contend with the constant, intense press attention that comes with the office. George Bush, every bit as much as Queen Elizabeth II did, could claim 1992 as an *annus horribilis,* and it showed in his press coverage. Whether it was the misrepresentation of Bush's supposed amazement at an advanced model of the supermarket scanner or wildly inaccurate rumor-mongering about the state of his health, Bush's press could hardly have been worse during much of the campaign season. In the former case a *New York Times* reporter who was not even in attendance when the president watched a demonstration of the new scanner in February 1992 wrote a front-page story citing the incident as proof that Bush was out of touch with recession-ravaged average Americans—an image which stuck easily to the upper-class candidate for the duration of the campaign.[93] In the latter case, baseless speculation by two commentators on CNBC cable network in July 1992 created an avalanche of gossip and coverage about whether poor health would force Bush from the presidential race.[94] This phony but damaging charge of physical infirmity[95] reinforced the appearance of lame-duck status, making the president's impending political demise seem all the more inevitable.

But the most memorable 1992 Bush frenzy was a pitiful reprise and extension of the "Bush mistress" rumor that had dogged the president for many years and was discussed in detail in this volume's first edition (see chapter 5). As noted earlier, "The gossip lives on," and its return was depressingly predictable, because "Old rumors never die, and they do not fade from print either, even without proof."[96]

The rumor's 1992 encore had roots in Clinton's suffering over Gennifer Flowers. The press corps, reflecting some combination of its own shame over the Flowers incident, a pro-Democratic bias, and a misplaced desire for "fairness," decided that there ought to be—or inevitably, there would be—a focus on Bush's private life. The long-time unsubstantiated rumor of romance between Bush and his own Jennifer, a reference to his former staff aide, Jennifer Fitzgerald,[97] provided the opportunity for journalism's avenging angels. (Perhaps the symmetry in the women's names alone proved irresistible). Of course, real angels would certainly have known that two wrongs don't make a right, in journalism as in the rest of life.

This golden-oldie frenzy had been building behind the scenes for months before it burst into full public view in August 1992. The Clinton camp had been arguing to the press corps since late winter that balance and simple fairness required an examination of Bush's private life. Hillary Rodham Clinton carried this contention into print in an April interview with *Vanity Fair:* "Bush and his carrying on . . . [are] apparently well known in Washington."[98] Both Clintons quickly apologized, but other Democratic campaign operatives continued this line of attack with the press. By mid-April the *New York Times* was suggesting in a front-page headline that "Bush May Get a Closer Look After What Clinton Endured," noting "long-denied rumors that Mr. Bush had an extramarital affair are already back in play. . . ."[99] A May *Times–Mirror* poll of the press found nearly three-quarters saying "If the Clinton character stories continue, news organizations will be obligated to follow up rumors concerning President Bush's personal life."[100] Garry Trudeau threw his comic strip "Doonesbury" into the fray, with fictional *Washington Post* reporter Rick Redfern directly asking President Bush, "Have you ever had an extramarital affair?"[101] Finally, in June and July, *Newsweek* and *Time* made their dubious contributions to the developing frenzy. In another regrettable example of lowest-common-denominator journalism, *Newsweek* chose to reproduce the cover of a forthcoming *Spy* magazine with this blazing headline: "1,000 Reasons Not to Vote for George Bush: No. 1—HE CHEATS ON HIS WIFE."[102] *Spy,* a fringe publication (circulation

150,000) known for its outrageousness, claimed that Bush had had three extramarital affairs, but presented no proof or convincing substantiation. Alas, the lack of evidence was no bar to *Newsweek,* which spread the gossip to a far wider audience (circulation 3,240,000). Describing his newsmagazine as just part of the "food chain" of journalism, *Newsweek's* Jonathan Alter justified the item by explaining that it was simply a "heads up" to readers about a big story to come.[103] Of course *Newsweek* simultaneously promoted an unsubstantiated rumor, making a frenzy based on it all the more likely. *Time* weighed in with its Democratic Convention issue, when the following question to Bill Clinton was reprinted in full: "When you hear talk about Gennifer Flowers, do you want to talk about Jennifer Fitzgerald?"[104] At the time, Fitzgerald's name had generally not been used in print by mainstream news organizations since, unlike Flowers, she was making no public statements or allegations, and no proof (such as tapes) had been produced that might justify an invasion of her privacy. That did not stop *Time,* which assigned a rough moral equivalency to the Flowers and Fitzgerald cases.

The stage was then set for the main act of this dreadful rerun. Naturally, a tabloid newspaper, the *New York Post,* once again filled the title role in the year of lowest-common-denominator journalism. Having produced a "WILD BILL" cover page during the Flowers episode, the *Post* topped itself in August with a screaming "exclusive" cover entitled "THE BUSH AFFAIR."[105] The entire production was based on a single footnote in a new book about a Washington lobbyist.[106] The book's author, Susan Trento, quoted former U.S. ambassador Louis Fields as saying he arranged in 1984 for then–Vice President George Bush and his high-ranking aide Fitzgerald to share a guest cottage in Geneva, Switzerland, while Bush was participating in arms disarmament talks. Fields claimed Bush and Fitzgerald "stayed in adjoining bedrooms" and that the arrangement made the ambassador "uncomfortable." (Barbara Bush was traveling in the United States at the time.) What is most important is what Fields did not say: He had no proof, no first-hand knowledge of an affair, and no corroborating witnesses; and he admitted he was not sure about his suspicion. In other words, this was nothing more than garden-variety, across-the-back-fence gossip and speculation, which the *New York Post* managed to spin into 64 column inches of lurid prose. Nor could other reporters confirm the non–tape-recorded comments, given to Susan Trento's husband a half-dozen years earlier. Conveniently for this pseudo-story, Ambassador Fields had died in 1988.

Some news organizations did not bother to dwell on the story's shortcomings. The very morning the *Post* appeared, "CBS This Morning" anchor Harry Smith held up the *Post*, called it "a conservative newspaper," and asked Bush campaign official Mary Matalin, "If your campaign ends up plagued by the same sort of rumors that have plagued Bill Clinton, will this even the playing field?"[107] Later that day, CNN reporter Mary Tillotson decided to ask Bush to comment on the *Post*'s scandal sheet—during live CNN coverage of a Kennebunkport news conference held by the president with visiting Israeli Prime Minister Yitzhak Rabin. Citing the Republican emphasis on "family values and character" as her rationale, Tillotson elicited an angry response from Bush: "I'm not going to take any sleazy questions like that from CNN. . . . I'm outraged. . . . I'm not going to respond other than to say it's a lie."[108] Tillotson's question and Bush's answer made the subject nearly impossible to ignore, so the media floodgates opened wide, with extensive coverage given on all national networks. Actually, one lone voice tried to stem the tide at a network. ABC's Hal Bruno, who had been instrumental in dampening down similar media rumors in 1988 (see chapter 5), argued against any reporting of the recycled Bush mistress story "so ABC could be the only network not to air it."[110] But he lost the internal battle, mainly because Bush responded to Tillotson's provocation. Bruno, and many others, are critical of Tillotson's judgment, but also of editors and news executives who permit their reporters to exhibit such behavior. "The inmates are running the asylum," says Bruno. "The people at the top need to tell the reporters NO."

The worst indignity, and the frenzy's low point, occurred on television the evening of August 11 (the same date of the *New York Post* story and Tillotson's query). Well before the incident involving a faked fire in a GM truck crash test, "Dateline NBC" managed to disgrace itself. Doing his most convincing Geraldo impersonation, co-anchor Stone Phillips marched into the Oval Office and asked the President of the United States, "Have you ever had an affair?"[111] This was the question Gary Hart was asked in 1987, of course,[112] but only after substantial evidence had been amassed by the inquiring reporter's newspaper, suggesting that Hart had lied about his private-life activities. No such proof existed in Bush's case, but mere technicality could not deter an ambitious broadcaster who, like so many in his profession hoping to make a name for themselves, longed to go where no journalist had ever gone before. Even some of Phillips's NBC colleagues were appalled. "If you can't prove it, you can't print it or broadcast it," remarked John Chancellor. "I don't think that question should have been asked. . . ."[113] President Bush, often painfully inarticulate, was roused to eloquent anger by Phillips's impertinence, and his first-blush judgment was sound: "You're perpetuating the sleaze by even asking the question, to say nothing of asking it in the Oval Office, and I don't think you ought to do that, and I'm not going to answer the question. . . . And I should think you'd be a little ashamed of yourself."

Asked by co-anchor Jane Pauley what effect his exchange with Bush might have, Phillips noted that it would help to "level the playing field" on the character issue between Bush and Clinton—and a viewer could be forgiven for believing he had detected a tinge of pride and satisfaction in Phillips's voice as the newsman announced the product of his labors. But whatever the combination of factors and motives in the 1992 Bush "mistress" exposé (fairness, bias, family values boomerang, and the like), the methods of rumor-mongering and lowest-common-denominator journalism were unacceptable. And the result was still less appealing, best summarized in a syndicated editorial cartoon by Jeff MacNelly. Entitled "The 1992 Presidential Debate," it featured Gennifer debating Jennifer, with the sad spectacle moderated by talk-show "journalist" Geraldo Rivera.[114]

ROSS PEROT

No other presidential candidate in American history has been treated to a wilder media rollercoaster ride than Ross Perot, and Perot's extraordinary evolving relationship with the news business helped to define a jarringly strange political year. An early love affair between Perot and journalism eventually turned into mutual contempt, as the press sought to unmask a super salesman while the sometime candidate found solace away from the press, on the talk-show circuit. Ironically, despite numerous press efforts and a series of mini-scandals, the only real frenzy that engulfed Perot (a bizarre charge that Republicans had plans to disrupt his daughter's wedding) was essentially self-generated.

Nothing was conventional about the "Perot for President" campaign—least of all its inception. Appearing on CNN's "Larry King Live" in February 1992,[115] Perot indicated his willingness to run for president if voters put him on all fifty state ballots. While Perot's personal money began to flow freely to fund the effort, there was also a great deal of genuine, enthusiastic grassroots support for the Texas billionaire-turned-politician. The "mom-and-pop" nature of the ballot drive in many locales was a made-to-order attraction for television, as was the Texan's homespun, simplistic, straight-talking style. Perot rapidly became *the* story, portrayed as a breath of fresh air—a welcome alternative to a failed Republican president and a slick, sleazy Democratic pol. Even more than Clinton, Perot invented the talk-show approach to politics, and as he went merrily from TV studio to TV studio his poll numbers kept climbing. The mainstream press could not get much access to Perot, in part because he did little stumping, had no traditional campaign schedule or entourage, and at first was immune from criticism by Bush and Clinton, both of whom were afraid to alienate his millions of followers. Oddly, given that Perot had shut them out, many normally skeptical big-name journalists signed on as boosters in the early months of Perot's protocandidacy, serving up powder puff, gee-whiz coverage, such as the March 29 Perot segment on "60 Minutes" in which an enthralled Morley Safer gushed, "And what Americans love most is a maverick, an untamed cowpoke willing to ride in and clean up the town, especially one who's willing to blow $100 million to get hired for a job he doesn't really want." Of course, journalism was welcoming a good story, and one supposedly untainted by the cynical machinations of partisan politics. But just as reporters take on an unseemly guise in pursuing a frenzy, so too are they unattractive and out of place in the role of cheerleader.

The press's natural instincts finally brought the extended honeymoon with Perot to an end. As Perot shot up in the opinion polls, the scrutiny of his candidacy increased. The defining moment of the new press–Perot relationship occurred on Sunday, May 3, when Tim Russert of NBC's "Meet the Press" pushed Perot hard for details of his deficit-reduction plan. When a flustered Perot couldn't deliver the goods, the candidate groused about "the interesting game we're playing today. It would've been nice if you'd told me you wanted to talk about this and I'd had all my facts with me. . . ." The Wizard of Texarkana had lost a bit of his magic, and the press began to pay attention to the man behind the curtain.

Fascination intermittently gave way to investigation, as tough pieces on Perot appeared in many publications and on broadcasts. The *Wall Street Journal* focused on Perot's alleged videotaping of employees, sometimes to obtain evidence of marital infidelity.[116] The *Washington Post* revealed Perot's attempts to smear a senior Pentagon official, Richard Armitage, with whom Perot disagreed on the Vietnam MIA issue.[117] The *Post* also exposed Perot's work as a source for reporter Bob Woodward in 1988, when Perot sought to uncover damaging information about then–Vice President Bush and his family.[118] This story proved controversial for the *Post* as well, mainly because of Woodward's decision to break a confidentiality agreement with Perot, formerly his off-the-record informant.[119] The *New York Times* focused on unflattering aspects of Perot's professional dealings,[120] and columnist William Safire hit Perot hard again and again about a host of alleged transgressions.[121] All three networks also broadcast skeptical pieces investigating Perot's activities and contradicting some of his assertions; many zeroed in on the rapidly emerging "Inspector Perot" image.

Singly, none of these charges reached the boiling point of a feeding frenzy; cumulatively, while they began to soften some of Perot's support, many voters were not yet paying close attention, so the effect was still limited. But there were more potentially explosive controversies on the way.[122] *Newsweek* and ABC News were exploring whether Perot had had his daughter Nancy's Vanderbilt University boyfriend (who was a professor) investigated while she was at the college. ABC, which had seven reporters assigned to Perot, had also discovered a Perot employee named Bobby Joe King, who had been fired in March 1986 after disclosing he was HIV-positive.[123] Other Perot employees may also have been dismissed because of their, or their dependents', illnesses.

Ross Perot short-circuited these and other stories with his abrupt and somewhat mysterious withdrawal from the presidential race on July 16, 1992, the last day of the Democratic National Convention. The press quickly turned the spotlight on an energized Democratic campaign, and Perot receded to the background. Hints of the independent's potential reentry continued to trickle out from his core supporters,[124] but reporters had shelved, stored, or discarded their Perot investigations to deal with more pressing election matters. By the time Perot actually reentered the race on October 1, there was only about a month to go, and little time, talent, or energy to spare for more background research on Perot. Much of the coverage was also on prearranged autopilot because of four debates, scheduled issue pieces and candidate profiles, and the usual avalanche of horserace speculation and opinion. In other words, intentionally or not, Perot chose to exit and reenter at precisely the optimal moments to minimize the amount and the effects of tough investigative reporting.

Moreover, the press was less interested in doing investigative research on Perot because most reporters viewed Perot II as a minor candidate. He was relegated to single-digit support in the polls, and his coverage was dismissive (as suggested by the October 12 cover of

Newsweek, labeling Perot's reentry an "EGO TRIP"). As it turned out, this electoral reading of Perot was badly off the mark, but it nevertheless served to protect him from the scrutiny he might otherwise have faced had he been seen as a stronger force. There were in fact a few exceptions to the once-over-lightly coverage of Perot. For instance, CBS News revealed that Perot's petition committee paid $56,000 to private investigators to check out certain campaign volunteers,[125] and *U.S. News & World Report* and *The New Republic* published stories about Perot's keeping tabs on his daughter's Vanderbilt University professor–boyfriend.[126]

Perot might have escaped a full-blown frenzy, save for himself. As was so often the case with other frenzies discussed in this volume, Perot brought the press club down on his own head, and proved to be his own worst enemy. The media instrument of Perot's self-mugging was CBS's "60 Minutes." In a segment aired on Sunday, October 25,[127] Perot made sensational charges: The Republicans had planned to disrupt his daughter Carolyn's church wedding in August 1992; conspired to circulate to the tabloids a phony, computer-generated photograph of Carolyn in a lesbian pose,[128] in order to smear her; and intended to wiretap his office and break into his computerized stock-trading program, and ruin him financially. "This is Watergate II," declared Perot, who also announced that the potential attacks on his daughter were the real reason for his July withdrawal from the presidential race. Perot offered loads of specifics about the alleged dastardly deeds, but not a shred of proof to support any of them.[129] Nor was this the first unsubstantiated plot Perot had "uncovered." In earlier times he had insisted he had been targeted by drug lords as well as five armed terrorists hired by the North Vietnamese to assassinate him.[130]

Even for conspiracy-addicted reporters who might have been inclined to believe the worst about a desperate Republican campaign, Perot's charges were over the top and simply incredible. Widely derided for his Perot-noia, the independent presidential candidate's allegations were believed by only a quarter of the voters (though half of his own supporters).[131] Perot struck back hard at the press, telling reporters to "run your bizarre stories and your twisted, slanted stories," continuing an all-out war with the establishment media waged in the spring and intensified after Perot's reentry. (Minutes after rejoining the race, Perot said to the assembled newspersons, "I don't care what you do. Just have fun, get raises and bonuses, play gotcha. . . ."[132])

Perot also used press-bashing to counteract the predictable media chorus that suggested Americans were "throwing their vote away" by casting a ballot for an Independent candidate unlikely to win. Almost one in five voters apparently agreed with Perot, deciding they would be squandering their vote more recklessly by supporting Bush or Clinton. Meanwhile, Perot brought the oddest presidential campaign in American history to a close as it had begun, by talking to Larry King to thank him for "a hell of a ride."[133] Perot's love–hate relationship with the media had been easily divisible: The talk shows were lovable, the working press detestable. And all future candidates took note of the media lessons Perot taught.

DAN QUAYLE

It was business as usual—same old, same old—in the press's treatment of Dan Quayle in 1992. Four years of incumbency in the vice presidency, general acknowledgment behind the scenes that Quayle had been an effective second-in-command, and substantive accomplishments during his term mattered not a whit. Much of the press continued to hold Quayle in contempt as a dim-witted, lightweight, rich, and pampered pretender to the throne. Many journalists extended the scorn they felt for Quayle to any colleagues who dared suggest that Quayle might not be as bad as his press clippings suggested. The *Washington Post*'s David Broder and Bob Woodward wrote an extensive seven-part series on Quayle for their newspaper in January 1992 that credited the vice president with *some* political talent and administrative savvy.[134] While Broder and Woodward's overall judgment of Quayle was actually quite mixed, it was entirely too positive for the media's conventional wisdom mainstream, and the two respected and experienced *Post* reporters were widely ridiculed in the journalistic community.[135]

Oddly, Quayle shared a problem in press coverage with Bill Clinton. In the first half of 1992, the press painted a portrait of Clinton that few trained observers of his record could recognize; instead of an accomplished, creative governor with an impressive tenure, Clinton was portrayed as a scandal-ridden pol from a backwater state. Unlike Quayle's, however, Clinton's image—less set in concrete—was more fairly drawn in the second half of the election year. But the principle was the same: When the news image of a public figure is so dramatically at odds with the official record and his reputation among associates, then something is wrong with the press coverage.

What was unquestionably wrong with Quayle's press coverage in

1992 was the revival of an old, unsubstantiated rumor previously dissected and debunked in this volume: the allegations by federal prisoner Brett Kimberlin that he was young Dan Quayle's marijuana supplier (see chapter 5).[136] As reviewed earlier, there is a perfectly legitimate side to the Kimberlin case—whether he was silenced and unduly punished for his allegations by a Republican-controlled administration. Although the Department of Justice's inspector general concluded in July 1993 that politics played no role in the matter, one Democratic U.S. senator and other observers who have investigated the matter insist that Kimberlin was unfairly treated.[137] But a press that ought to know better repeatedly used Kimberlin's possibly excessive punishment to air without qualification the convict's completely unsubstantiated charges about Quayle's supposed drug purchases. Kimberlin—a convicted perjurer, bomber, and drug dealer—has a well-deserved reputation as a smooth-talking press manipulator who has supplied reporters with phony leads and outrageous "corroboration" of his allegations. Yet despite journalists' direct and indirect access to this information, and their respected colleagues' conclusions that his drug allegations are baseless, some have eagerly portrayed Kimberlin in the most sympathetic light possible, bolstering his feeble credibility on the pot-buying tales.[138] Additionally, many accounts of Kimberlin's woes failed to make even the most rudimentary notations about the prisoner's lack of substantiation for the Quayle allegations.[139] The press offenders have included not just tabloids for which such violations of high standards of fairness are routine, but also pillars of mainstream journalism, including the *Washington Post*, the *New Yorker*, and the Associated Press.

While hardly in the same class, Garry Trudeau, creator of "Doonesbury," was equally and persistently guilty of failing to distinguish between the legitimate and illegitimate aspects of Kimberlin's case as he repeatedly returned to the subject in 1991 and 1992.[140] More than two dozen newspapers refused to run some of the offending Trudeau comic strips, and *Newsday* ran them with a proper disclaimer—but over 1,300 newspapers published them with no clarification at all.[141] Kimberlin, not cartoonist Trudeau, had the last laugh in October 1992 as he paraded his drug accusations against Quayle on national television, courtesy of the "Today" show.[142] But his most revealing comment came when he was asked about his allegations. Said Kimberlin: "I stand by my *story*"[143] (emphasis added). Unfortunately, so did much of the news media.

Garry Trudeau's championing of Brett Kimberlin was not the only time Quayle was caricatured in 1992. The "Murphy Brown" speech and the "potatoe" incident made Quayle the butt of an even larger proportion of late-night television jokes than usual. Quayle's unhappy season began on May 19, 1992 in a speech he delivered in San Francisco on "restoring basic values [and] strengthening the family."[144] Toward the conclusion of a serious address with some thoughtful passages about the decline of families as a root cause of the recent Los Angeles riots, Quayle condemned "bearing babies irresponsibly" and added:

It doesn't help matters when prime-time TV has Murphy Brown—a character who supposedly epitomizes today's intelligent, highly paid, professional woman—mocking the importance of fathers, by bearing a child alone, and calling it just another "lifestyle choice."

In many respects there was nothing exceptional about this passage. Quayle and the Republicans had already been developing their "family values" issue, and virtually every major Democrat, including Bill Clinton, Jesse Jackson, and Mario Cuomo, had preached similar sermons against unwed motherhood.[145] Nor was rhetorical reference to a television show, or criticism of television's standards and morals by politicians, very unusual.[146] Yet Quayle's poke at Murphy Brown set off a firestorm that consumed for many weeks the vice president's usefulness on the campaign trail.

Partly, this was the result of Quayle's choice of an exceptionally popular CBS television show and character, a news anchorwoman played by Candice Bergen. As a subsequent poll showed, she was considerably better liked than the vice president, even as a potential president,[147] and Quayle simply could not compete with her legions of fans who resented Quayle's passing harsh judgment on her. (They saw Quayle's message much as the New York Daily News did, in its headline QUAYLE TO MURPHY BROWN: YOU TRAMP!) Partly, too, Quayle's tar-and-feathering was because of a seemingly unresolved, illogical, and hypocritical aspect of his criticism and its root Republican philosophy. Once impregnated, Brown chose not to have an abortion—the GOP preference—but, instead of being celebrated for her pro-life stance, she was condemned. Most of all, Quayle was pummeled in this circumstance because he could not escape his press subtext,[148] the dismal caricature of him that had been created and validated and reinforced over four years of virtually nonstop derision. The Quayle subtext instantly established an unshakable premise for the Murphy Brown episode: This cartoon stick-figure, this callow gaffe-prone youth, this nincompoop of a vice president, had attacked a nonexistent television sitcom character! David Letterman captured

Quayle's quandary better than any columnist or commentator when he deadpanned, "Mr. Vice President, I don't know how to tell you this, but Murphy Brown is a fictional character."[149] Other less humorous pundits used the opportunity to relive past Quayle controversies, including the usual parade of unsubstantiated rumors. This sound bite from Jesse Jackson was widely used, for example: "No exam-cheating, pot-smoking, draft-dodging, privileged youth vice president . . . can speak with moral authority about abandoned moral values and assuming personal responsibility."[150]

The Murphy Brown controversy intermittently stretched almost to October, thanks to a "family values" Republican National Convention as well as a revenge-minded Hollywood. Emmys were awarded to Candice Bergen and her series in a late August production filled with anti-Quayle invective.[151] And in late September the "Murphy Brown" season opener was a virtual nonstop rebuke to Quayle.[152] But by April 1993, when Quayle had left office and the issue he raised could be considered outside of his subtext, *The Atlantic* magazine ran a much-discussed cover story by a liberal academic, with the headline "DAN QUAYLE WAS RIGHT" followed by "The dissolution of two-parent families, though it may benefit the adults involved, is harmful to many children, and dramatically undermines our society."[153]

Quayle's image as a lightweight, already secure as a result of Murphy Brown and a dozen earlier frenzies, was irreversibly elevated to dogma on June 15, 1992 with the so-called [or so-spelled] "potatoe" incident. Quayle was visiting an elementary school in Trenton, N.J. when, as planned, he conducted a spelling bee for sixth-grade students. Working off an inaccurate flash card prepared by a teacher,[154] he corrected twelve-year-old William Figueroa when the child spelled "potato" on the blackboard—prompting the nervous boy to add an unnecessary "e" at the end of the word.

It proved to be a costly letter for Quayle. Reporters ran for their dictionaries, and CNN aired the clip over and over, all day long. "Quayle Opens Mouth, Inserts Toe," read a typical newspaper headline.[155] MTV broadcast a spoof (Pink Floyd singing "We don't need no education"), David Letterman invited Figueroa on his show, and Jay Leno joked that Quayle "should stop watching 'Murphy Brown' and start watching 'Sesame Street.'"[156] The elementary-school principal was inundated with press calls from England to Colombia, and journalists camped outside the Figueroa home.[157]

As all fair observers will attest, the average day of almost any national candidate contains at least a gaffe or two—a mispronounced word, a garbled sentence, confusion about one's current location (the towns all blur together). Only rarely does the press focus on any single one, much less blow a minor slip-up into a monumental goof. But Quayle's subtext guaranteed inordinate attention. Young Figueroa himself saw the point, and was quoted as saying the misspelling "showed the rumors about the vice president are true—that he's an idiot." As for the news media, they were unwilling to let Quayle remove his dunce cap easily. When the vice president tried to laugh off the incident by noting that "Mark Twain once said, 'You should never trust a man who has only one way to spell a word,'" the Associated Press surveyed Twain experts and quickly put a report on its wire that "Twain may never have said that."[158] Whether Twain did or did not, the piling-on was clearly excessive, the whole episode one of the silliest frenziettes ever. The "potatoe" incident, once pursued, became an embarrassment for Dan Quayle, but it ought to have embarrassed the press even more.

The unfairness in Quayle's coverage is all the more apparent when compared with that of his opponent. If Dan Quayle was the ultimate media goat, then Albert Gore was the classic media darling. Nary a discouraging word was said about Gore, a former journalist,[159] in most media quarters; to the contrary, he was hailed upon his selection by Clinton, and given one of the softest rides for a national party nominee in recent times.[160] The double standard that existed through the campaign continued even after election day. Shortly after becoming vice president–elect, Gore and his wife, Tipper, went hiking in some woods near Washington. They got lost and had to depend on the Secret Service for rescue. Modest-to-nonexistent accounts of the event were carried by most news organizations, despite Gore's reputation (subtext?) as a bright and resourceful environmentalist. As Thomas Palmer of the Boston Globe observed, "Who doubts that, had Dan and Marilyn Quayle lost their way, they would have been featured on Page 1?"[161]

JERRY BROWN

The unconventional presidential campaign of former California governor Jerry Brown experienced one of 1992's most perplexing, murky, and unresolved frenzies. It involved charges that, while governor in the 1970s, Brown tolerated the use of marijuana and cocaine in his presence at one of his residences (a house in the Laurel Canyon section of Los Angeles). If true, these offenses were serious ones, not only because Brown was his state's chief law-enforcement officer but also

because California law defined such acts as misdemeanors (for marijuana) and felonies (for cocaine).[162] ABC News was the sole original
conduit for the allegations, which were made by former state police
officers reportedly assigned to guard the governor and his residence.

ABC's "World News Tonight" first broadcast this bombshell on
April 9, 1992, at the top of the newscast. Correspondent John
McWethy, normally assigned to the State Department, focused the
piece on two unnamed accusers who were presented anonymously,
in shadows, one of them with his voice electronically altered.
McWethy claimed that two other officers—who also were not pictured—had corroborated the charges. (The next night, ABC
announced that a fifth policeman and a sixth source, a Brown "political aide," had substantiated the claims; not one was identified by the
network.) In the "World News Tonight" feature, Brown was given
only a brief sound bite, videotaped that day while campaigning, in
which he vigorously denied all the allegations.

That evening's "Nightline" provided a much better forum to
explore the charges and permit Brown an extended response. Host
Ted Koppel acknowledged from the outset that "This kind of story
can be devastating to a man who is running for president of the
United States." Correspondent McWethy then reported that he had
come across the story "quite by accident,"[163] but after securing four
sources, "The decision was made to go with the story." After noting
that the sources agreed that "Brown held numerous parties [in the
house] where both marijuana and cocaine were used in large quanti-
ties," two officers anonymously recounted tales of "ashtrays with
seeds or leftovers of marijuana . . . in every room, except the bath-
room," the "very strong odor" of marijuana that "would permeate
the house," and "traces of white powdery substances" later confirmed on "five or six" occasions to be cocaine by "little test kits that
are used to identify various controlled substances."[164] Why didn't the
officers report the offenses? Said one, "Our primary concern was the
protection of the governor, and not to arrest him." Added McWethy:
"They also feared they would be fired because they had raised the
issue with their superiors, and nothing was ever done about it." After
noting that nearly 50,000 Californians a year were cited for marijuana
possession, one of the anonymous former policemen made this
arresting—or nonarresting—remark:

As a police officer, you made arrests on a lot flimsier . . . evidence than that
[found in Brown's house]. I felt very uncomfortable going in there. I tried to

avoid going into the house after a while, because of the frequency of it. After that, I never made an arrest again for marijuana possession.

McWethy closed by referring to one of his sources who had refused to appear on camera, a "rookie cop" whose experiences at the Brown house "burst his bubble," "may have driven him out of law enforcement into another field altogether," and "still bothered" him eighteen years later.

Correspondent Ken Kashiwahara then presented Brown's side of the story, mainly by concentrating on Brown associates for whom "the charges just don't ring true." The governor's former chief of staff, B. T. Collins, who had since turned publicly critical of Brown, claimed that Brown assiduously avoided people who used alcohol or other drugs. A former police officer who knew the accusing officers' superiors insisted that *no* reports of drug activity at Brown's house were *ever* made. Brown's police driver for four years called the allegations nonsense, saying he had been in Brown's home "probably a thousand times" and had never even "observed a party going on." The caterer for many of Brown's gatherings at his home also denied seeing any drug use. While noting that other friends of Brown remembered that he never had alcohol in his home, and hated the smell of cigarette smoke, Kashiwahara also included the comments of Don Walters, a local newspaper reporter who covered Governor Brown. Walters claimed he had attended Brown fund-raisers where marijuana was smoked, and that the governor's security people had told him of wild parties held in the Laurel Canyon house. (One naturally wonders why Walters had not reported these stories earlier, in his own newspaper.)

Koppel then turned to a live, shadowed interview with one of the police officers making the allegations. After reiterating that he repeatedly smelled marijuana outside the house and while waiting in side rooms on the inside, and that he observed drug residue in the house at times when Brown was visiting, the officer was asked, "On a scale of one to ten . . . [what is] your conviction that Governor Brown knew that drugs were being used in his house . . . ?" The officer replied: "Between a six and an eight." Koppel then noted that before the show the officer had answered the same question with "a four or a five"— with either rating, well short of a certainty.

Finally it was Brown's turn, and in a live interview Brown castigated the story, the witnesses, and ABC News: "There's no truth to this. . . . This is a bizarre story. . . . The whole story is ridiculous. . . .

There's not a shred of substantiation other than this anonymous guy.
. . . These so-called parties, they don't exist. I don't host parties,
period!" After announcing that his campaign was "very seriously
contemplating a legal action" (that never came), Brown—like any
other resourceful politician—tried to turn the situation to his advantage, twice repeating his toll-free telephone number and requesting
contributions from those who did not believe that this was "the way
the media ought to treat a candidate for president."

Partly because of ABC's use of completely anonymous sources,
which generated caution and skepticism, and perhaps partly because
Brown's long-shot presidential campaign was already on the skids,
most other news organizations—including rival networks—downplayed or ignored the ABC charges. The *New York Times* barely mentioned them,[165] and the *Los Angeles Times* and *Washington Post* concentrated on the multitude of public and police figures, some of them
conservative Republicans not usually friendly to Brown, who found
the allegations unlikely or incredible.[166] At least one network executive from NBC, CBS, Fox, and CNN publicly criticized the ABC story,
and a CBS vice president claimed that CBS had been offered the same
allegations but chose not to air them.[167] Lowest-common-denominator
journalism clearly did not prevail in this frenzy, though an observer
wonders what might have happened had Brown been a frontrunner
instead of an also-ran at the time the disclosures hit the press.

About a week after the initial ABC broadcast, the story briefly came
to life again, as two of ABC's original police sources decided to publicly identify themselves. On the April 15 "World News Tonight,"
Robert E. Ford, a California state policeman in the 1970s who had
later moved to Colorado, insisted that Brown *had* to have known
about the drug use occurring in his home, and further alleged that his
supervisors told him to ignore such or face transfer.[168] The supervisors denied it. Shortly thereafter another ex-policeman, James C.
Pashley, who had been John McWethy's first source, went public in an
interview with the *Los Angeles Times*.[169] Pashley added another charge:
that Brown and his girlfriend, singer Linda Ronstadt, had left marijuana butts in soft-drink cans on one occasion. Pashley said he discovered them after the couple, who had been alone, left the house. Brown
responded by claiming he had not begun dating Ronstadt until after
Pashley had left the state police. The period of alleged drug activity at
Brown's house also differs somewhat in the separate accounts given
by Pashley and Ford, his former immediate supervisor.[170]

The regenerated frenzy fizzled almost at once. The moribund
Brown candidacy had become nearly irrelevant, though indeed there

were practical consequences for the still-campaigning Californian. At the least, Brown found it difficult to continue criticizing opponent Bill Clinton for generating "a scandal a week."[171]

All that remained were contradictions and questions. Were any or all of ABC's sources lying—and, if so, what were their motivations? Did Brown hold parties in the house, or (as he insists) not? Who were the alleged drug-using guests at these gatherings, if in fact they occurred? (The police say they were given the guest list, but would any of those people corroborate the allegations, even off the record?) Was any report, formal or informal, ever made to the officers' superiors?[172] It is abundantly apparent that ABC jumped the gun on an unripe and unready story, then dropped it before all the major questions could be answered. Many obvious, credible individuals with near-constant contact with Governor Brown were neither called nor featured, initially. Also, it is doubtful that ABC's four original sources were pushed as hard as possible to go public; had they done so, it would have greatly strengthened the first report. After all, within just a week, two of the four revealed their identities, suggesting that they were hardly unalterably opposed to unmasking. Some of this sloppiness would be at least defensible if there had been vital time pressures involved (the need to broadcast before an important election day, for example), but no such deadline existed in this case. And, after making sensational charges, ABC apparently ceased to pursue the story. Thus, Brown was suspended in the nether world between conviction and vindication, and the public was left to wonder about the truth or falsity of the allegations. This was a serious matter that deserved careful and thorough investigation, but ABC's handling of it ignored a time-honored principle of responsible journalism: *Important stories, like fine wine, should not be served before their time.* And not served at all if they are vinegar.

CONGRESSIONAL AND STATE FRENZIES

The House "Bank" Scandal

The institution of Congress and some of its members suffered through frenzies in 1992, not the least of which was the overheated brouhaha surrounding the U.S. House of Representatives' "bank." Since 1830, House members had been able to keep their paychecks and other funds in non–interest-bearing accounts maintained by the office of the sergeant-at-arms. Members were also granted "overdraft protection"—that is, they were allowed to write checks well beyond the level of their accounts, up to an amount equal to the next month's salary (and sometimes more). This was certainly a generous arrangement; few commercial banks permit such interest-free loans, even for their best customers. But then, the House "bank" was not a bank at all, just an internal perk of office. And the permissible overdrafts were not "bad checks," either. However, these distinctions were rarely made by a press and public eager to skewer their least-loved branch of government.

A General Accounting Office report in September 1991 revealed over 8,000 overdrafts in a recent twelve-month period, triggering a frenzy that rapidly reached every congressperson. Within a month the House had voted to close its "bank," and the House Ethics Committee was investigating. After a futile attempt to keep the overdrafters unknown, the House disclosed the names of 267 current full members and 58 former and nonvoting members who had written overdrafts. Only a handful were guilty of flagrant abuses (such as using massive overdrafts for personal investments), while the large majority had kited a few checks for small amounts. Nonetheless, virtually all offenders were pilloried in their local media, and the national press had a field day of Congress-bashing. Public approval ratings of Congress, never stellar, fell into the cellar, and some primary defeats and retirements of incumbents were directly tied to the overdrafts.[173]

Granted, the "bank" was poorly run, Congress had been intermittently warned through the decades about the slipshod operation, and congressional perks were overly generous in many ways. But, compared to the wholesale waste involved in pork-barrel spending, congressional mass-mailing to constituents, or the savings-and-loan debacle that was partly a product of congressional action (and inaction), the House "bank" was incredibly small potatoes. Further, most of the news media, perhaps egged on by the radio and television talk-show hosts, greatly overemphasized this tiny aspect of congressional operations, and made only a feeble attempt to explain the differences between a real bank and the House version, or to separate the truly guilty from those committing venial sins or less. Despite the impression left by the press, the House did *not* run a bank, most of the overdrafts could *not* fairly be classified as bad checks, and—with a small number of individual exceptions—this was *not* much of a scandal.

Congressman Jim McCrery

One particular House member was engulfed in a frenzy far more hurtful than the check-kiting affair. U.S. Representative Jim McCrery of Louisiana was the latest target of gay activists who take it upon themselves to declare public figures to be homosexual (whether they are or not). As earlier discussed (see chapter 6),[174] this revolting practice is termed "outing," and such blatant, press-abetted invasions of privacy have become all too common in recent years, extending recently to a high official of the Department of Defense and one of President Clinton's Cabinet nominees.[175] Unfortunately, the mainstream press has not yet learned to ignore this unsavory and intrusive sideshow. In the case of McCrery, a national gay magazine, *The Advocate*, published a full cover story on the congressman's alleged "double life."[176] The justification for the outing was McCrery's conservative voting record on "family values" issues, though the congressman is not particularly outspoken on them, certainly not a leading advocate of antigay measures, and by no stretch of the imagination a "gay-basher." More importantly, the only on-the-record evidence offered by named individuals to support the charges about the married congressman's sexual orientation consisted of the recollections of one college friend (now a gay activist) who alleged a long-past relationship with McCrery, as well as another individual who claimed to have driven with McCrery to gay bars years ago. Despite the lack of clear substantiation—and the relevance and privacy considerations, even if the allegations were true—news media throughout McCrery's district gave the article wide publicity, helpfully assisted by a press conference called by the extreme gay activist group ACT-UP.[177] The congressman was surely correct when he responded by noting "the sleazy attacks which I have had to endure . . . and now my wife is having to live through . . . should not have to be endured by anyone, in or out of public office."[178] Meanwhile, sensible voices within the gay community itself are speaking out against outing. Author and AIDS activist Randy Shilts, writing in the *Los Angeles Times,* insisted: "It's bizarre . . . for a minority fighting the moral judgments of fundamentalist preachers to set itself up in the business of compelling others to submit to their moral judgments."[179] Unfortunately, the publication practices of many news organizations encourage and promote Queer Nation and ACT-UP's privacy invasions instead of reasoned concern for the preservation of the legitimate privacy rights of public people.

Governor David Walters

Another public official whose family has recently suffered from press excess is Oklahoma Governor David Walters.[180] In early November 1991 his 19-year-old son, Shaun, was charged with misdemeanor

pect smoking pipes in his apartment. News coverage of the incident involving the governor's son became intense, especially among
television stations, and in a single week the Walters' family counted
forty-seven TV and newspaper stories about the young man. The
state police were attempting to germinate seeds they found in
Shaun's apartment (they proved *not* to be pot), and these efforts produced regular television updates on the case. According to his
mother, the press staked out Shaun, and in order to avoid them he
was forced to crawl in and out of a hole in the back fence, and
through a window, to gain access to his apartment. On December 11
he pled "no contest" to the drug paraphernalia charge, though he
claimed he was merely holding the pipes for a friend. On December
15 he was discovered unconscious from an overdose of antidepres-
sant drugs.[181] On December 26 Shaun Walters died, in what the
authorities ruled was a suicide. "We watched helplessly as the media
dogged him," said his father in a eulogy at his son's funeral. No one
would contend that the press was wrong to mention the arrest, but
the son was not the father, and such frenzied coverage was both
unwarranted and, from the Walters family's perspective, unforgiv-
able. Most children of public officials have not willingly chosen the
spotlight, and the news media have an obligation to treat them with
sensitivity and care. The case of Shaun Walters shows the tragic consequences of doing otherwise.

Senator Charles Robb

The amazing saga of the incredible shrinking senator continued
from 1991 to 1993, as Virginia U.S. Senator Charles Robb became
embroiled in controversy after controversy, eliminating the once-
prominent national politician from presidential and vice presidential
consideration alike, and weakening his previously unassailable position in his home state. What was once a "frenzy that wasn't" (see
chapter 6)[182] became a series of frenzies whose ill effects were compounded by Robb's prevarications, deceptions, intimidations, and
general mishandling.

At the core of Robb's problems remained his shocking indiscretions
while serving as Virginia's governor from 1982 to 1986, including his
association with a sleazy Virginia Beach social set, and his attendance
at dozens of parties where cocaine was not only plentiful but also
openly displayed and used. Some of these parties were large affairs,
some very intimate gatherings of four, but all were inappropriate sites
for a state's chief law-enforcement officer. Prostitutes (some of them

so-called "coke whores" who perform their services for drugs instead of money) and cocaine dealers were among the regular participants.[183] Robb and his defenders often point to the "unreliable reputations" of some of these individuals, who have spoken out about his sordid activities. A fair retort would be a simple question: What in the world was a governor of Virginia doing partying with people of this sort, week after week after week, despite explicit warnings from his friends and allies about the company he was keeping?[184]

Since sex sells in the media, it may not be surprising that the first truly intense public scrutiny of Robb occurred not because of drugs but because of allegations of illicit sex. In April 1991 the *Washington Post* and NBC News (in its "Exposé" program) focused on Tai Collins, the strikingly beautiful 1983 Miss Virginia-U.S.A., who claimed to have had a sexual relationship with Robb during his governorship.[185] Robb denied a relationship, proclaiming on many occasions, "The only person I have ever loved, emotionally or physically, is my bride. . . ." Robb quickly added a useful subordinate clause, however: "Like any other red-blooded American, I have some fun from time to time, but I don't think that's either disqualifying or inappropriate." Perhaps with this in mind, and only after disputing Collins' claim that she and he had ever had anything more than a private drink, he admitted to the *Post* that he had invited the 21-year-old Collins to his suite in New York's Pierre Hotel in February 1984, where he recalled they shared a bottle of wine followed by Robb's disrobing and Collins's treat of a nude massage. Collins reported that sex followed; Robb, somewhat incredibly, said his willpower was such that he called a halt to the encounter before its consummation. Collins went on to do a *Playboy* cover story on her relationship with Robb, including a well-attended autograph tour.[186] Also because of the "Exposé" broadcast (which featured chapter 6's Virginia Beach businessman who had observed a woman snorting cocaine at Governor Robb's feet),[187] new attention was drawn to Robb's knowledge of drug use.

In yet another of many serious errors in his handling of the controversies swirling around him, Robb inexplicably released the 78-page transcript of the entire two-and-one-half-hour interview with NBC "Exposé" producer Marion Goldin. (NBC did not make it, and would not have made it, available, save for the bits used in its 12-minute segment on Robb.) The press zeroed in on salacious material NBC opted not to use, as well as Robb's rambling, evasive, and morally obtuse answers that included some stunning admissions.[188] At one point Robb, despite his legal responsibilities as governor, indicated he would not have turned in an individual, or individuals, involved in "limited" drug use at a party; only "wide-scale" activity would have drawn his interest. Robb was also asked whether he had been in a hot tub with two Virginia Beach prostitutes named "Frankie" and "Jamie." Here was his not-so-ringing denial: "No. I, I don't want to go into any, uh, uh, specifics about anything that I, uh, I might have done, but I can assure you that I don't, don't ever reca[ll]. . . . I, I was never knowingly in the company of anyone who had the occupation that you suggested."

Ever since the *Richmond Times–Dispatch* published the first report of Robb's party activities in May 1987, the Robb staff had engaged in often frantic efforts to learn the extent of Robb's sins and to try to cover them up. It is important to note that Robb's closest advisers and paid staffers simply did not know the parameters of their boss's transgressions, and as one of them later put it privately, "We could not defend him unless we knew what to defend him against." In October 1990, Robb's Senate chief-of-staff, David McCloud, authorized an in-house investigation that involved a senior aide, Bobby Watson, and a political associate of his, retracing Robb's steps through the Virginia Beach sands. The report of their findings was full of sex and drug discoveries, and the next month Watson traveled to Boston to interview a young college woman concerning a particularly troubling relationship she had allegedly had with Robb. (The voyage was paid for with Robb campaign funds, but was intentionally misreported to the Federal Election Commission to hide the trip's purpose.[189]) Unfortunately, the staff efforts at damage control also contained intimidation of those investigating Robb's activities, including a threat to use the Internal Revenue Service against Billy Franklin, a private investigator with links to the Republican party who published a book brimming with sex and drug allegations against Robb.[190]

The cover-up began unraveling in June 1991 when Robb's longtime bitter rival, Virginia Democratic Governor L. Douglas Wilder, alleged to a *Washington Post* reporter that Robb possessed one or more illegally wiretapped conversations recorded from his (Wilder's) cellular telephone.[191] Sure enough, for nearly two-and-one-half years, Robb's office had been in possession of an October 1988 tape recording of then–Lt. Gov. Wilder discussing Robb's Virginia Beach problems with a Tidewater supporter. On the tape, Wilder pronounced Robb "finished" politically because of the drug charges, and oddly, this was apparently enough to convince Robb and his staff that the tape (referred to as "Beach Music" by them) was proof positive of

Wilder's perfidy. To the contrary, it was mainly idle chit-chat and gossip between two friends engaging in a supposedly private conversation, and in another part of the tape Wilder actually defended Robb against suggestions of racism. Within a day of Wilder's disclosure to the *Post* that the tape existed, both the *Post* and the *Roanoke Times* published excerpts of it.

Robb wasted no time in lying about his handling of the tape. He insisted, "I had no idea of the origin of it," and through his press secretary Robb announced that the tape had arrived in his office anonymously in a plain brown envelope. In fact, he knew a great deal about the tape's origins. Robert Dunnington, a Virginia Beach party associate of Robb's who was an electronics buff, had by chance recorded the conversation and then passed it along to Bruce Thompson, Robb's close friend at the Beach who had sponsored many of the parties Robb attended. Appointed by Robb to two state boards, Thompson had been reportedly called "a leader of the Virginia Beach underworld"[192] by police, and had successfully bargained for immunity from prosecution in exchange for his cooperation in a federal drug probe in 1987. Thompson personally gave the tape to McCloud in Virginia Beach in February 1989, and McCloud almost immediately informed Robb of the details of the acquisition, as well as the contents of the tape.[193]

Robb also claimed his staff were "specifically forbidden" to leak the tape to the press, but Robb's top three aides all have denied this. The tape was in fact played for *Post* reporter Kent Jenkins, Jr., by two Robb aides, and a transcript was leaked to the *Roanoke Times'* Rob Eure. Within two days of the transcript's publication, Robb placed his chief of staff (McCloud), political director (Watson), and press secretary (Steven Johnson) on leave; a little over a month later, on July 19, 1991, Robb announced the requested resignations of the three. All later pled guilty to wiretapping violations, with Johnson and Watson's penalties considered very minor; McCloud also was convicted for filing a false campaign report to the FEC. In addition, Robert Dunnington entered a guilty plea on a wiretapping violation, and the Norfolk grand jury returned an indictment against Bruce Thompson, who pled guilty to charges of wiretapping and witness tampering. Interestingly, an FBI-wiretapped conversation of Thompson talking with Robert Dunnington and his brother revealed Thompson reminiscing that "We were all tryin' to cover [Robb's] ass at the time."

After a lengthy investigation during which he became a target of the probe, Robb narrowly averted indictment from the same grand jury. The jury's surprising decision in January, 1993 not to indict was no accident. Robb's prominent defense attorney, Charles R. C. Ruff, had enjoyed extraordinary access to the Justice Department, and Ruff's long-time friend and former employee George Terwilliger,[194] the senior Justice official supervising the Robb case, reportedly undercut the local prosecutor by sending a high-ranking deputy to the jury to read a highly unusual personal statement reminding the jurors that they alone, and not the prosecutor, had the power to indict Robb.[195]

Meanwhile, the loss of all the senator's men barely seemed to slow the Robb office's cover-up efforts. Members of his new staff continued to spread personal smears about those on the senator's enemies list, and a particularly vicious memorandum from one of the Robb staff holdovers, Christine Bridge, had an unrecognized ironic twist. In the March 1991 memo, which came to light in May 1992, Bridge proposed a Machiavellian scheme to undermine Douglas Wilder—the governor from Robb's own party—and, in the process, shift the spotlight of controversy from Robb to Wilder.[196] "We know," she warned, "that Wilder [and his aides] are vindictive, petty, untrustworthy, devious and that they will lie to your face, spread scurrilous rumors, and use any tactics of intimidation and threat that they feel are necessary for their purposes." Most fair observers would say her characterizations fit the Robb staff equally well or better. Bridge's conclusion is also apt: "They represent the kind of politics that are alien to Virginia government as we have known it."[197] Another irony is that much of the press bought into the Robb staff's portrayal of the senator's problems as part and parcel of the Robb–Wilder feud. The focus on the feud, like the concentration on the sexual dimension, deflected some attention from the more serious aspects of the story (drugs, intimidation, and so on).

As for Senator Robb, the grand jury's decision has left him free to run for reelection in 1994, yet his status as a kind of unindicted co-conspirator has also cost him dearly. He cannot escape the harsh judgment earned by his actions during and since Virginia Beach. His hubris and arrogance in believing that the rules of political life did not apply to him have badly damaged the phony Boy Scout image he so carefully cultivated for years. And the refusal to own up to his failings, to apologize for conduct unbecoming a governor, has compounded his difficulties. Few who have closely monitored the senator's prevarications can have any respect for sanctimonious and utterly preposterous statements such as this one: "I have told the truth and I stand by *every word* I have ever uttered on the subject" (emphasis added).[198] As Robb's stonewalling has continued, in fact, his own words have served as the most appropriate commentary on his troubles. In perhaps Robb's only recent statement on which all persons—friends *and* foes—are agreed, the senator declared, "I have never claimed to be a rocket scientist. . . ."[199] And at the same June 1991 news conference, Robb offered the press, and history, a telling epitaph for his scandal-drenched career: "If any of the allegations which I have categorically denied were in fact true, I would clearly be unfit for the office I hold or the office that I held previously."

Senator Robert Packwood

As noted in the Robb case, in chapter 6 we discussed "frenzies that weren't," and 1992 had its share of those. Republican presidential candidate Patrick J. Buchanan received remarkably gentle coverage from his media chums and former colleagues for many weeks after his announcement of candidacy. This was despite having views antithetical to those of most journalists, and a long list of highly controversial public actions and positions during the Nixon administration (in which he served as an influential aide), and by way of his newspaper columns and television appearances.[200] Also, as already discussed, the press eagerly focused on rumors of President Bush's nonexistent health problems, but journalists could have more profitably looked closely at Democratic candidate Paul Tsongas's health. By-and-large, the news media bought without thorough investigation Tsongas's claims of robustness and complete remission of his cancer, yet shortly after the presidential election Tsongas was hospitalized with a recurrence of the dread disease.[201]

Without minimizing these examples, there was no more prominent instance of a "frenzy that wasn't" than the one involving U.S. Senator Robert Packwood of Oregon. In November 1992, Packwood was narrowly reelected to a fifth term after barely avoiding a preelection character frenzy that probably would have resulted in his defeat. The character bullet was his sexual harassment of many women, including some of his employees, over many years. Holding the gun but not firing until the election was past was the *Washington Post*.

On Sunday, November 22, the *Post* published a lengthy front-page story outlining the senator's unwanted sexual advances as reported by ten women, mainly his former staff members and lobbyists.[202] The extremely detailed accounts of Packwood's gross misbehavior were convincing and appalling—so much so that the frenzy that followed was a completely justifiable one. Outrage toward Packwood in Oregon and indeed across the nation also spawned questions about the media: What did they know about Packwood's foul deeds, and when did they know it? The *Post* naturally bore the brunt of the first wave of indignation. As it happened, a freelance writer, Florence Graves,

first contacted the *Post* in September 1992 with information she had
gathered on the subject, and by early October she had been hired to
work on the story with the paper's own reporters and editors. A serious effort was made to nail down the details by Election Day, but the
difficulty of doing so with many reluctant women, as well as Packwood's own clever delaying tactics,[203] made early publication impossible. As *Post* executive editor Leonard Downie explained: "On Election Day we still needed to do much more reporting, writing, and
editing before we had a story sufficiently full, accurate, and fair to
publish. We wanted to publish as quickly as possible but not before
the story was truly ready."[204] In other words, the *Post* acted responsibly, and did what ABC News should have done before it broadcast
the drug-party allegations about Jerry Brown.

Rather than looking in the *Post*'s direction, critics could profitably
aim their fire at Oregon's media organizations, and especially the
state's largest newspaper, *The Oregonian*. Almost unbelievably, Packwood had forcibly kissed one of the newspaper's own Washington
correspondents in March 1992. The reporter told her two supervising
editors about the incident shortly thereafter, but nothing was done—
even though the paper had also independently received allegations
about Packwood from one of the women featured in the *Post*'s eventual exposé.[205] The red-faced *Oregonian* editors admitted their embarrassment,[206] but since the paper was editorially a strong backer of
Packwood, some onlookers understandably wondered whether the
newspaper really wanted to tell the big story that had literally bussed
it full on the mouth.

FINAL THOUGHTS ON THE FRENZIES OF '92

Having attended more than a fair share of postelection conferences
on "the press and politics" over the years, this author is tempted to
compare journalists' responses to criticism to Marion Barry's apoc-
ryphal rejoinder to his accusers (cited in chapter 8): "I didn't do it,
and I'll never do it again." Of course, the problem in 1992 was that
the press *did* do it again—some of the same recycled frenzies, more
lowest-common-denominator journalism, and many of the same
rumors reported without sufficient substantiation.

As I have argued throughout this volume, these practices should
stop—but there is little reason to believe they will. First, the press is
not highly motivated to change, especially after 1992. Overall, it
gives itself high grades for its work in the 1992 campaign, with eight
of ten journalists rating the coverage as excellent or good.[207] Second,

the fact that the public in the end seemed to ignore or downgrade most of the character charges against Clinton has led many in the news media to conclude that their excesses do not matter much; the electorate will sort it all out, and therefore the press is free to continue its mischief-making. But 1992 was a special year, as are all years with an electorally powerful, overarching issue such as a bad economy. Another more "normal," less-engaging campaign like 1988's will see the character issue and its associated press foibles become far more influential.

The news business's somewhat self-satisfied, *laissez faire* attitude about its seamier side is blissful ignorance. While the media generally may be pleased with their performance in 1992, the candidates and the voters are not. George ("Annoy the media") Bush and Ross ("The press is a bunch of jerks") Perot made media-bashing an integral part of their stump speeches, and they gave the distinct impression that the attacks are not simply a campaign tactic, but deeply felt. Bill Clinton may have been the press's chosen one in the warm autumn of 1992, but he and his staff have never forgotten or forgiven the media's deep freeze the winter before. A well-rooted distrust of, and a thinly veiled contempt for, the press was obvious in the way the President and his close advisers dealt with the media, at least until David Gergen's appointment to the White House staff in the late spring of 1993.[208]

The voters were not much happier about the press coverage than the candidates. Six out of ten surveyed Americans gave the news media a grade of C (29 percent), D (16 percent), or F (15 percent) for their efforts in 1992—not very different from the public's evaluation of media performance in 1988, the year most reporters believe to be their profession's nadir.[209] Substantial majorities throughout the campaign also believed news organizations had "too much influence" on the election's outcome.[210] This may be one reason why Americans were so willing to turn to talk shows as an alternative, less-filtered source of information about the candidates.[211] Many voters now believe that they do not need or want journalists as their intermediaries, and the "insider" press has become just as repulsive to them as "insider" politicians, PACs, and political consultants. As a consequence, when the candidates started avoiding the mainstream press and taking the talk-show route, most voters applauded—or at least were indifferent to the complaints of unhappy, ignored journalists. The press's accumulated arrogance, biases, and excesses may have cost it the public support necessary to fulfill its vital, premier role in holding candidates and public officials accountable. This ought to be of concern not only to journalists but to the rest of us who depend on the news media to have the access to pose tough questions on our behalf.

The year 1992 was a singularly damaging one for public confidence in the news media. Large groups of Americans, especially Republicans and Independents, became measurably and intensely more dissatisfied with the media because of what they considered to be biased coverage and unfair frenzies. Such grassroots sentiment has real consequences for the media, from lack of support for their work (as suggested above), to smaller audiences, to reduced morale in the news corps. Could growing public resentment of the press's ways and means be one reason why the ranks of disgruntled journalists have swollen? Two decades ago just 7 percent of working reporters expected to leave their profession within five years, but by 1992 that proportion had grown to 21 percent.[212] And those newspersons who said they were "very satisfied" with their jobs declined by almost half, from 49 percent to 27 percent of the sampled individuals.[213] Could public anger at the media be fueling an unorganized revolt at the polling places when news organizations attempt to conduct exit surveys on Election Day? On November 3, 1992, both national exit polls (one taken by the broadcast networks in consortium, and the other by the Los Angeles Times) erred in early projections. Clinton's margin was placed at more than double the 5 percentage points it turned out to be, while both Bush and (especially) Perot were said to have done considerably worse than final results showed.[214] Many analysts believe that resentful Bush and Perot voters disproportionately refused to participate in the surveys because they were sponsored by the disliked news media.[215]

Obviously, news organizations cannot and should not determine their campaign coverage with an eye to their own popularity. But even if journalism does not need the public's adulation to play its essential role, it does require the voters' respect, and their basic belief in the high quality of both its information and its underlying fairness. These indispensable elements are on the wane, drained over the years by frenzy after frenzy, controversy upon controversy, perceived inequity on top of inequity. In a major recent study by the Los Angeles Times,[216] far more Americans said their confidence in the news media had lessened rather than increased over the years; two-thirds believed the media "give more coverage to stories that support their own point of view than to those that don't"; by 56 percent to 36 percent, people "think incidents such as the one in which NBC News doctored the truck explosion without informing its audience" are "common"; and 58 percent feel "Most news reporters are just concerned about getting a good story, and they don't worry very much about hurting people." More disturbingly, in a clear reversal from public opinion in the mid-1980s, a majority of Americans now judge the news media to be "abus[ing the] privilege of freedom of the press" rather than being "careful to use this power reasonably."

What effect does this stern judgment have on popular support for the First Amendment? Only a slim majority (53 percent) say "It's important to have a free press even when the press acts irresponsibly," while 45 percent choose this worrisome statement instead: "Sometimes there is too much freedom of the press." As one might expect, the foundations of public backing for an unfettered press are weakest (and probably growing more feeble over time) among conservatives, and those over age 45 who have had the opportunity to observe the media's performance over a longer period. At least among certain influential groups, the public's contempt for journalism is on a par with that for politicians, and this means that, increasingly, those in or seeking office will stoke antipress fervor in order to avoid the accountability that only vigorous, respected mainstream journalism can provide.

How can this disagreeable trend be reversed? I return again to the many remedies discussed in chapter 8, and particularly to the beneficial role of the ombudsman.[217] Many large newspapers and networks have hired reporters to serve on the "media beat," and their job is to explain and criticize the methods and stories of print and broadcast journalists around the country. This is a useful and necessary service; by general consensus, news organizations have failed miserably in helping their readers and viewers to understand what they do, and how (and why) they do it. But an essential complement to the "media beat" reporter is the fully independent ombudsman, an internal critic with license to serve not just an explanatory function but as a reader's or viewer's advocate. The public has warmly welcomed such press officers where they exist and, as the Los Angeles Times found, Americans favor the idea of "the media regulating themselves" rather than regulation by the government or the courts.[218] Sadly, though, only a few dozen newspapers have appointed ombudsmen. And, as earlier argued, the on-air video ombudsman is desperately needed at the networks and individual station affiliates as a critical check on broadcast behavior, and also as a receptive outlet for the legions of frustrated and angry media targets and viewers who currently have no easy "talk-back" recourse.[219] The obdurate unresponsiveness of many broadcast and print outlets to innovative proposals such as the ombudsman is both revealing and deeply discouraging to those who want good journalism to triumph. Without ombudsmen, the arguments against a revival of the National News Council (see chapter 8, page 229) are much weaker. Despite opposition from senior news organizations, perhaps it is time for the Council concept to be reconsidered.

One of television's best journalists, ABC's Ted Koppel, once confessed to a nationwide audience an astoundingly frank view of those who go into his profession:

It's long been a suspicion of mine that many of us who choose journalism as a career do so because it allows us to remain adolescents past the age of forty. . . . We are rarely held to account for the consequences of our reporting, we are free to hold others to much higher standards than we are inclined or able to meet ourselves and, in exchange for all of this, especially [for] those of us in television journalism, our egos are regularly massaged while we are paid more than we're worth.[220]

Exaggeration aside, a close observer of journalism will recognize truths in Koppel's offering. Yet the public of late has been sending journalism a blunt message: Grow up—the party's over. No longer are thoughtful news consumers so willing to accept uncritically the biases and arrogant dictates of mainstream media's elites, such as the CBS News president who reportedly said "Our job is to give people not what they want, but what we decide they ought to have."[221] Of course the *public* has its *own* need for maturation, as demonstrated by "what people [apparently] want." The public's obsession with gossip and celebrity, taste for tabloids and trash TV, and preference for "A Current Affair" and "Entertainment Tonight" over "Face the Nation" and "The MacNeil/Lehrer NewsHour" feed the worst aspects of our media culture.[222] Seventy years ago Walter Lippmann identified this root cause of the press's ills, what he called "the failure of self-governing people to transcend their casual experience and their prejudice," including their "hunger for sideshows and three-legged calves."[223]

The challenge of creating an informed society that, in Lippmann's phrase, will seek "the full important" instead of "the curious trivial" is one that must be embraced by *both* the public *and* the news media, if only because reform of one and not the other will surely produce failure. Broadening civic education for the citizenry, and elevating print and broadcast standards among the press, must be simultaneously pursued by our institutions of learning and the leading lights of journalism. For in the broadest sense of constitutional practice, the First Amendment's right to a free press belongs *jointly* to the people *and* the press, and both have obligations to the other if the right is to be fully secured. And fully secure the right is *not:* While much of the news media denies it, the foundations of public support for their work have badly eroded in recent years. Will the band just play on, or will journalists respond in good faith to constructive criticism and meet a concerned citizenry halfway?

Interviews Conducted for This Study

In all, 208 individuals were interviewed during the course of research for this volume. Following is a list of the 182 on-the-record interviews. Of the 182, 84 were conducted in person and 98 by telephone. (An asterisk denotes telephone interview.) The length of the interviews varied greatly, with in-person sessions generally lasting one to three hours and telephone interviews fifteen minutes to one and one-half hours; 25 of the interviewees were interviewed more than once. Unless otherwise noted, only each individual's affiliation at the time of the interview is listed. Please see the preface for additional comments and details about the interviews. The names of off-the-record interviewees (about two dozen overall) do not appear in this listing. They provided background information only, and no direct quotations from these interviews are used in the text of this volume.

JILL ABRAMSON, *Wall Street Journal*, Washington, D.C., August 4, 1989.
*WYATT ANDREWS, CBS News, January 11, 1990.
*GEORGE ARCHIBALD, *Washington Times*, May 23, 1989.
LEE ATWATER, chairman, Republican National Committee, Front Royal, Va., January 6, 1990.
DAN BALZ, *Washington Post*, Washington, D.C., November 21, 1989.
JAN W. BARAN, general counsel, George Bush for President (1988 campaign), Washington, D.C., February 22, 1990.
FRED BARNES, *The New Republic*, Washington, D.C., August 4, 1989.
JAMES A. BARNES, *National Journal*, Washington, D.C., August 18, 1989.
MICHAEL BARONE, senior writer, *U.S. News & World Report*, Washington, D.C., September 7, 1989.
LAURENCE I. BARRETT, formerly national political correspondent and currently deputy bureau chief, *Time*, Washington, D.C., August 11, 1989, and *July 6, 1990.
*ROBERT BECKEL, Democratic political consultant, December 28, 1989.
*DAVID BECKWITH, press secretary to Vice President Dan Quayle, December 27, 1989.
TOM BETTAG, "CBS Evening News" executive producer, New York, N.Y., January 19, 1990.

CHARLES BIERBAUER, CNN, Charlottesville, Va., September 27, 1989.

*PAUL BLUSTEIN, *Washington Post,* June 5, 1989.

*KEN BODE, formerly of NBC News and currently director of the Center for Contemporary Media, DePauw University, January 12, 1990.

BENJAMIN BRADLEE, executive editor, *Washington Post,* Washington, D.C., September 15, 1989.

*MAX BRANTLEY, managing editor, *Arkansas Gazette,* September 25, 1989.

DAVID S. BRODER, *Washington Post,* Washington, D.C., August 25, 1989.

*TOM BROKAW, anchor, "NBC Nightly News," January 22, 1990.

HAL BRUNO, ABC News, Charlottesville, Va., September 28, 1989; *January 31, 1990; and *June 27, 1990.

JOHN BUCKLEY, National Republican Congressional Committee, Washington, D.C., July 7, 1989.

*KATHRYN A. BUSHKIN, 1984 press secretary to Gary Hart and currently with *U. S. News & World Report,* March 20, 1989.

*ROBERT E. CALVERT, DePauw University political science professor, August 9, 1989, and July 2, 1990.

*JOHN CHANCELLOR, NBC News, January 29, 1990.

*GARRY CLIFFORD, *People* magazine, December 29, 1989.

JOHN COCHRAN, NBC News, Charlottesville, Va., September 28, 1989.

*RICHARD COHEN, columnist, *Washington Post,* December 5, 1989, and January 2, 1990.

MILTON COLEMAN, *Washington Post,* Washington, D.C., September 22, 1989.

ANN COMPTON, ABC News, Charlottesville, Va., September 28, 1989.

*JIM CONNOR, formerly of NBC News, January 9, 1990.

*ALFREDO CORCHADO, *Wall Street Journal,* February 7, 1990.

*CONGRESSMAN PHIL CRANE (R., Ill.), 1980 Republican presidential candidate, October 25, 1989.

*BILL DEDMAN, *Washington Post,* January 16, 1990.

ANN DEVROY, *Washington Post,* Washington, D.C., October 5, 1989, and *June 15, 1990.

E. J. DIONNE, formerly *New York Times* and currently *Washington Post,* Charlottesville, Va., November 1, 1989.

SAM DONALDSON, ABC News, Washington, D.C., October 5, 1989.

LEONARD DOWNIE, managing editor, *Washington Post,* Washington, D.C., September 15, 1989.

*BOB DRUMMOND, *Dallas Times Herald,* October 31, 1989.

PAUL DUKE, host of "Washington Week in Review," Washington, D.C., August 17, 1989.

*THOMAS B. EDSALL, author and political reporter, *Washington Post,* July 16, 1990.

ALAN EHRENHALT, *Congressional Quarterly,* Washington, D.C., August 24, 1989.

ERIC ENGBERG, CBS News, Washington, D.C., January 5, 1990.

*TOM FIEDLER, political editor, *Miami Herald,* April 10, 1989; January 3, 1990; and January 29, 1990.

HOWARD FINEMAN, *Newsweek* chief political correspondent, *March 29, 1989, and Washington, D.C., August 24, 1989.

*WARREN FISKE, *Virginian-Pilot,* August 7, 1990.

*DON FOLEY, 1988 press secretary to the Richard Gephardt presidential campaign, January 8, 1990.

*BEN FRANKLIN, formerly of the *New York Times,* January 22, 1990.

*DOUGLAS FRANTZ, *Los Angeles Times,* September 1, 1989.

*AARON FREIWALD, *Legal Times,* October 6, 1989.

*BARBARA GAMAREKIAN, *New York Times,* February 24, 1989.

JAMES GANNON, bureau chief, *Detroit News,* Charlottesville, Va., September 28, 1989.

David Gergen, *U.S. News & World Report*, Washington, D.C., January 5, 1990.

Jack Germond, columnist, *Baltimore Sun*, Washington, D.C., August 18, 1989.

*Steve Goldberg, Media General, November 20, 1989.

*Mark Goodin, former Republican National Committee official, January 10, 1990.

*Norman Gorin, producer, "60 Minutes," March 16, 1990.

*Jeff Greenfield, ABC News, October 13, 1989.

Ted Gup, *Time*, Washington bureau, Washington, D.C., July 10, 1989.

*John Hall, visiting professor of journalism, University of Michigan, and freelance investigative journalist, March 8, 1990, and March 13, 1990.

Steven Haner, executive director, Virginia Republican Joint Legislative Caucus, Williamsburg, Va., September 28, 1990.

Michael Hardy, *Richmond Times-Dispatch*, Richmond, Va., August 10, 1989.

Richard Harwood, *Washington Post* ombudsman, Washington, D.C., July 10, 1989.

*Brian Healy, CBS News, September 8, 1989.

*George Herman, CBS News (retired), October 30, 1989.

Ken Highberger, CONUS Communications, Charlottesville, Va., September 25, 1989.

*David Hoffman, *Washington Post*, Washington, D.C., October 5, 1989.

*John Holland, "NBC Nightly News," March 8, 1990.

Jerald terHorst, President Ford's first press secretary and formerly *Detroit News* reporter, Washington, D.C., August 4, 1990.

*Dan Howard, former spokesman for Senator John Tower, January 11, 1990, and February 15, 1990.

Brit Hume, ABC News, Charlottesville, Va., September 28, 1989, and *June 27, 1990.

Ellen Hume, executive director, Joan Shorenstein Barone Center, Kennedy School of Government, Harvard University, Boston, Mass., December 18, 1989.

Albert Hunt, D.C. bureau chief, *Wall Street Journal*, Washington, D.C., August 11, 1989.

Terry Hunt, Associated Press, Charlottesville, Va., September 28, 1989.

*Michael Isikoff, *Washington Post*, July 5, 1990.

Brooks Jackson, *Wall Street Journal*, *May 23, 1989; Milwaukee, Wis., February 24, 1989; and Washington, D.C., August 4, 1989.

*Kent Jenkins, Jr., *Washington Post*, August 8, 1990.

Peter Jennings, ABC News, September 28, 1989.

*Mark Johnson, former press secretary to 1988 Democratic presidential candidate Richard Gephardt and press secretary to U.S. House Speaker Jim Wright, July 23, 1990.

*David Johnston, *New York Times*, January 31, 1990.

*Phil Jones, CBS News, September 8, 1989.

Marvin Kalb, director, Joan Shorenstein Barone Center, Kennedy School of Government, Harvard University, Boston, Mass., December 18, 1989.

*Marianne Keely, reportorial producer, ABC News, January 30 and June 27, 1990.

Douglas Kiker, NBC News, Washington, D.C., October 5, 1989.

James J. Kilpatrick, syndicated columnist, Washington, D.C., September 7, 1989.

*Brett Kimberlin, federal prisoner, October 12, 1989.

Susan King, WJLA-TV (Washington, D.C.), Charlottesville, Va., September 27, 1989.

*Wayne King, *New York Times*, January 2, 1990.

Ted Koppel, ABC News, and host of "Nightline," Washington, D.C., January 5, 1990.

*Bill Kovach, curator, the Nieman Foundation, March 6, 1990, and July 25, 1990.

*Andrew Lack, CBS News, January 9, 1990.

GEORGE LARDNER, *Washington Post*, Washington, D.C., August 25, 1989.

*JAMES LATIMER, *Richmond Times-Dispatch* (retired), September 26, 1989.

*MICHAEL LAWRENCE, former DePauw University professor, August 10, 1989.

*ANTHONY LEWIS, columnist, *New York Times*, November 20, 1989.

*BILL LIVINGOOD, executive assistant to the director, U.S. Secret Service, February 2, 1990.

MRS. NACKEY LOEB, publisher and president, *Manchester Union-Leader*, Goffstown, N.H., June 23, 1989.

*MARY LUKENS, aide to pollster Robert Teeter, March 17 and 21, 1989.

JOHN MASHEK, *Boston Globe*, Charlottesville, Va., September 28, 1989.

BARBARA MATUSOW, *Washingtonian* magazine, Washington, D.C., September 22, 1989.

*BILL MCALLISTER, *Washington Post*, March 27, 1990.

*SARAH MCCLENDON, independent Washington, D.C. news correspondent, March 5, 1990.

DAVID MCCLOUD, administrative assistant to U.S. Senator Charles Robb, Washington, D.C., July 3, 1990.

MICHAEL MCCURRY, Democratic Congressional Campaign Committee, Washington, D.C., August 28, 1989.

CHARLES MCDOWELL, *Richmond Times-Dispatch*, Washington, D.C., August 22, 1989.

MARY MCGRORY, *Washington Post*, Washington, D.C., November 21, 1989.

*DICK MEYER, CBS News producer, July 9, 1990.

ANDREA MITCHELL, NBC News, Washington, D.C., December 21, 1989.

*DAN MORANO, Brett Kimberlin's lawyer, October 4, 1989.

*G. C. MORSE, press secretary to Governor Gaston Caperton, March 26, 1990.

BRUCE MORTON, CBS News, Washington, D.C., October 16, 1989.

ROGER MUDD, PBS and "MacNeil/Lehrer NewsHour," Arlington, Va., January 5, 1990.

JACK NELSON, D.C. bureau chief, *Los Angeles Times*, Washington, D.C., August 24, 1989.

ROBERT NOVAK, syndicated columnist, Washington, D.C., August 25, 1989.

*ROSE ELLEN O'CONNOR, *Virginian-Pilot* and *Los Angeles Times*, November 14, 1989; November 20, 1989; December 28, 1989; and March 6, 1990.

*KIRK O'DONNELL, senior adviser to 1988 Dukakis presidential campaign, June 29, 1990.

MICHAEL ORESKES, Washington, D.C., *New York Times*, November 21, 1989.

*PRISCILLA PAINTON, *Time*, January 29, 1990.

*JAMES PERRY, *Wall Street Journal*, September 8, 1989.

CHARLES PETERS, editor, *Washington Monthly*, Washington, D.C., September 22, 1989.

*BILL PETERSON, *Washington Post*, April 5, 1989 and July 13, 1990.

*ROBERT PIERPOINT, CBS News, October 26, 1989.

*WALTER PINCUS, *Washington Post*, May 26, 1989.

BILL PLANTE, CBS News, Washington, D.C., November 21, 1989.

MARTIN PLISSNER, CBS News, Washington, D.C., September 7, 1989.

JIM POLK, NBC News, Washington, D.C., October 5, 1989.

HOWELL RAINES, D.C. bureau chief, *New York Times*, Washington, D.C., November 21, 1989.

*ELEANOR RANDOLPH, *Washington Post*, Washington, D.C., July 10, 1989.

JIM RAPER, managing editor, *Virginian-Pilot and Ledger Star*, Norfolk, Virginia, December 26, 1989, and *July 5, 1990.

*LARRY RASKY, former press secretary, Joseph Biden presidential campaign, January 2, 1990.

DAN RATHER, CBS News, New York, N.Y., January 19, 1990.
*T. R. REID, *Washington Post*, March 5, 1990.
CHARLES S. ROBB, U.S. senator (D., Va.), Washington, D.C., July 3, 1990.
COKIE ROBERTS, National Public Radio and ABC News, Washington, D.C., October 5, 1989.
STEVEN V. ROBERTS, *U.S. News & World Report*, Washington, D.C., August 18, 1989.
*CARL ROCHELLE, CNN, January 9, 1990.
*GLEN ROCHKIND, producer, NBC News, January 11, 1990.
*LOIS ROMANO, *Washington Post*, Washington, D.C., July 31, 1989.
*ANDREW ROSENTHAL, *New York Times*, January 11, 1990.
*TOM ROSENSTIEL, media reporter, *Los Angeles Times*, October 30, 1989.
*KNUTE ROYCE, *Newsday*, April 16, 1990.
TIM RUSSERT, D.C. bureau chief, NBC News, Washington, D.C., January 4, 1990.
JIM SAVAGE, *Miami Herald*, Washington, D.C., November 11, 1989, and December 28, 1989.
JEFF SCHAPIRO, *Richmond Times-Dispatch*, Richmond, Va., August 10, 1989.
*CODY SCHEARER, freelance reporter, March 8, 1990, and March 14, 1990.
*BOB SCHIEFFER, CBS News, November 22, 1989.
*MARALEE SCHWARTZ, *Washington Post*, July 20, 1990.
FRANK SESNO, CNN, Charlottesville, Va., September 27, 1989.
*MICHAEL SHANAHAN, McClatchy Newspapers, July 23, 1990.
WALTER SHAPIRO, *Time*, New York, N.Y., December 19, 1990.
*TOM SHERWOOD, WRC-TV (Washington, D.C.), and formerly of the *Washington Post*, November 24, 1989, and January 18, 1990.
MARK SHIELDS, columnist and television commentator, Washington, D.C., September 22, 1989.
ROBERT SHOGAN, *Los Angeles Times*, Washington, D.C., September 22, 1989.
*ROBERT SHRUM, Democratic political consultant, July 3, 1990.
*WILLIAM SLOAT, Cleveland *Plain Dealer*, September 8, 1989.
LARRY SPEAKES, spokesman for President Reagan, Washington, D.C., August 24, 1989.
*STUART SPENCER, Republican political consultant, November 21, 1989.
*JOHN ROBERT STARR, *Arkansas Democrat*, March 15, 1990.
*STEVEN STOCKMEYER, Washington, D.C. consultant, August 10, 1990.
*KEVIN SWEENEY, 1987 press secretary to Gary Hart, March 22, 1989.
*PAUL TAYLOR, *Washington Post*, April 5, 1989, and March 14, 1990.
STEPHEN TAYLOR, Unistar Radio Network, Charlottesville, Va., September 28, 1989.
*PETER TEELEY, formerly Vice President George Bush's communications director, May 30, 1989.
BILL THOMAS, *Roll Call*, Washington, D.C., August 24, 1989.
*CHARLIE THOMPSON, ABC News "20/20" and CBS News "60 Minutes," December 27, 1989, and March 14, 1990.
*NINA TOTENBERG, National Public Radio, October 4, 1989.
*JOHN G. TOWER, former U.S. senator (R., Tex.), January 12, 1990.
*KAREN TUMULTY, *Los Angeles Times*, March 13, 1989 and January 3, 1990.
*TOM TURNIPSEED, South Carolina Democratic politician, August 21, 1989.
*CHRIS WALLACE, ABC News, November 22, 1989.
*EDWARD WALSH, *Washington Post*, March 13, 1989.
KENNETH T. WALSH, *U.S. News & World Report*, Washington, D.C., August 11, 1989.
O. T. WATKINS, Director of Advertising, *Washington Times*, May 30, 1989.
*BERNIE WEINRAUB, *New York Times*, January 9, 1990.
*BENJAMIN WEISER, *Washington Post*, June 14, 1989.
*TOM WESTBROOK, president, Tell-Back Inc., Spokane, Wash., March 21, 1989.

*PAUL WEYRICH, president, Free Congress Foundation, January 5, 1990.

*HAL WINGO, *People* magazine, December 29, 1989.

BILL WOOD, editorial editor, *Virginian-Pilot and Ledger Star*, Charlottesville, Va., September 28, 1989, and Norfolk, Virginia, December 26, 1989.

JUDY WOODRUFF, PBS and "MacNeil/Lehrer NewsHour," Washington, D.C., October 17, 1989.

BOB WOODWARD, *Washington Post*, Washington, D.C., December 21, 1989.

JAMES WOOTEN, ABC News, Washington, D.C., September 15, 1989.

*BOB ZELNICK, ABC News, January 9, 1990.

Notes

Preface to the Paperback Edition

1. Comment made to the author at the second presidential debate, Richmond, Va., October 16, 1992. As quoted in Carol Horner, "A mouth with the media's ear," *Philadelphia Inquirer*, October 29, 1992, D4.

2. Comment made to the author at the Republican National Convention, Houston, Tex., August 20, 1992.

Chapter 1. Inquisition, American Style

1. Quoted by Richard E. Cohen, "Fall from Power," *National Journal* 21 (August 19, 1989): 2086.

2. Quoted by Eleanor Randolph, " 'Quayle Hunt' Turns News Media Into Target for Angry Public," *Washington Post*, August 25, 1988, A10.

3. From a random-sample telephone survey of 1,000 adults nationwide conducted by Yankelovich Clancy Shulman for *Time* and CNN, October 15–17, 1990. The exact wording of the question was, "Do you think that the media focus on the most important issues or do they spend too much time focusing on things that are irrelevant, like candidates' personal lives?" About 17 percent responded "the most important issues" while 5 percent were undecided.

4. William Safire, "Stop Keyhole Journalism," *New York Times*, May 11, 1987, A17.

5. Russell Baker, "All Shall Be Disclosed," *New York Times*, May 12, 1987, A31.

6. The "Saturday Night Live" television show concocted just such a skit at the height of the 1988 presidential campaign's preseason preliminaries, with Democratic candidate Bruce Babbitt playing the role.

7. Quoted in Michael Wines, "In Bed With the Press," *Washington Journalism Review* 9 (September 1987): 17.

8. From a speech delivered at Yale University on November 11, 1987.

9. Quoted by Carol Matlack, "Crossing the Line?" *National Journal* 21 (March 25, 1989): 724–29.

10. The word *frenzy* is derived from the Greek *phrenitis*, meaning a temporary madness or delirium.

11. Arthur A. Myrberg, Jr., "Shark Behaviour," in John D. Stevens, ed., *Sharks* (New York: Facts on File Publications, 1987): 84. See also Jose I. Castro, *Sharks of North America Waters* (College Station: Texas A & M University Press, 1983): 29; and William Safire, "Fish Story," *New York Times*, September 4, 1988, A22.

12. Michael J. Robinson, "The Media in 1980: Was the Message the Message?", in Austin Ranney, ed., *The American Elections of 1980* (Washington, D.C.: American Enterprise Institute, 1981), p. 191.

Chapter 2. The Press of Yesteryear

1. From *Democracy in America*, vol. 1 (New York: Vintage, 1945), p. 194.

2. Many persons in and out of journalism insist it is not strictly a profession since there are no formal educational requirements, examinations, peer reviews, or

uniform codes of ethical standards. But journalism is a rigorous calling that attracts, in the main, individuals of considerable skill and erudition—more so than some other occupations indisputably labelled professions.

3. See Mitchell Stephens, *A History of News: From the Drum to the Satellite* (New York: Viking, 1989).

4. Ibid., p. 2.

5. Charles Press and Kenneth VerBurg, *American Politicians and Journalists* (Glenview, Ill.: Scott, Foresman, 1988), pp. 8–10.

6. A claim for Jefferson's purity may be suspect coming from a professor at Jefferson's University, but this biased assertion has the added virtue of truth. See Merrill D. Peterson, *Thomas Jefferson and the New Nation* (New York: Oxford University Press, 1970), pp. 185–87.

7. Press and VerBurg, *American Politicians*, pp. 36–39.

8. For a delightful rendition of this episode, see Shelley Ross, *Fall from Grace* (New York: Ballantine, 1988), chap. 12.

9. The name strictly derived from printing the comic strip "The Yellow Kid" in color.

10. Doris A. Graber, *Mass Media and American Politics*, 3rd ed. (Washington, D.C.: Congressional Quarterly Press, 1989), p. 12.

11. See Thomas C. Leonard, *The Power of the Press: The Birth of American Political Reporting* (New York: Oxford University Press, 1986), chap. 7.

12. Louis D. Brandeis and Samuel D. Warren, "The Right to Privacy," *Harvard Law Review* 4 (December 15, 1890): 196.

13. Richard L. Rubin, *Press, Party, and Presidency* (New York: Norton, 1981), pp. 38–39.

14. Stephen Bates, *If No News, Send Rumors* (New York: St. Martin's, 1989), p. 185.

15. See Richard Harwood, "The New Untruths," *Washington Post*, July 23, 1989, D6.

16. However, there is the matter of journalists' acceptance of honoraria—large speaking fees from special interests. This topic will be taken up in chapter 8.

17. Nan Britton, *The President's Daughter* (New York: Elizabeth Ann Guild, Inc., 1927).

18. Press and VerBurg, *American Politicians*, p. 24.

19. Bates, *If No News*, p. 98.

20. Steve Neal, *Dark Horse* (Garden City, NY: Doubleday, 1984), pp. 38–44, 143, 145, 186, 192–93.

21. See Ronald Steel, *Walter Lippmann and the American Century* (New York: Vintage, 1981).

22. Edward Polliard, "Ike Wants to Know His Running Mate Is Morally Clear," *Washington Post*, September 21, 1952, A1.

23. John Wilds, *Afternoon Story* (Baton Rouge: Louisiana State University Press, 1976), p. 236.

24. Rudy Maxa, "Gossip Is to News What Yeast Is to Bread," *Washington Journalism Review* (April–May 1979): 24–25.

25. Marjorie Williams, "The Bottle and the Genie: Drinking in Washington," *Washington Post*, March 12, 1989, F1, 4–5. See also Steven Waldman, "Tippling in Washington," *Newsweek* 113 (March 6, 1989): 23.

26. Ibid. Former Senator John Tower (R–Texas) also included some frank reminiscences of senatorial drinking in his book, *Consequences: A Personal and Political Memoir* (Boston: Little, Brown, 1991).

27. See John Ed Bradley, "Blaze's Glory," *Washington Post Magazine*, December 10, 1989, pp. 24–30, 70–72; and Thomas C. Reeves, *A Question of Character: John F. Kennedy in Image and Reality* (New York: Free Press, 1991).

28. Both Adams and Baker published accounts of their travails. See Sherman Adams, *First-hand Report* (Westport, Conn.: Greenwood, 1961); and Bobby Baker with Larry L. King, *Wheeling and Dealing* (New York: W. W. Norton, 1978).

29. (Boston: Atlantic Monthly, Little Brown, 1981), p. 54. See also Thomas Brown, *JFK: History of an Image* (Bloomington: Indiana University Press, 1988), especially pp. 70–79.

30. See, as a sampler, "Jack Kennedy's Other Women," *Time* 106 (December 29, 1975): 11–12; Peter Collier and David Horowitz, *The Kennedys* (New York: Summit Books, 1984); and John H. Davis, *The Kennedys: Dynasty and Disaster* (New York: Mc-Graw-Hill, 1984), pp. 613–19; and Ross, *Fall From Grace,* chap. 18.

31. Stern is now deceased; this is based on the reminiscence of Lardner alone. The original article by Stern was subtly entitled "Probers Doubt Kennedy Knew of Poison Plot Against Castro," *Washington Post,* November 16, 1975, A6.

32. However, the investigative reporting of Dan Thomasson and Tim Wyngaard of the Scripps-Howard Washington bureau should also be credited.

33. William Safire, "The President's Friend," *New York Times,* December 15, 1975, A31.

34. "Jack Kennedy's Other Women."

35. The letters to the editor in *Time* 107 (January 12, 1976): 4, and *Newsweek* 87 (January 26, 1976): 4, give a flavor of the outrage some readers felt after the assault on the memory of their hero.

36. See Judith Campbell Exner, *My Story* (as told to Ovid Demaris) (New York: Grove, 1977); Kitty Kelley, "The Dark Side of Camelot," *People* 29 (February 29, 1988): 106–14; and Gerri Hirshey, "The Last Act of Judith Exner," *Vanity Fair* 53 (April 1990): 162–67, 221–26.

37. C. David Heymann, *A Woman Named Jackie* (New York: Lyle Stuart, 1989), pp. 278–89. See also pp. 231–35.

38. Ibid., pp. 290–92.

39. Bates, *If No News,* p. 146.

40. Heymann, *A Woman Named Jackie,* pp. 226–27. NBC News correspondent Douglas Kiker, who had seen a transcript of the tape, remarked: "The dialogue was such that it had to be authentic. In between the passion portions Kennedy was asking, for example, why a famous *Washington Post* columnist at the time had so much power—things that you just had to be an insider to know."

41. R. W. Apple, "Changing Morality: Press and Politics," *New York Times,* May 6, 1987, B8.

42. Robert Pierpoint, *At the White House: Assignment to Six Presidents* (New York: G. P. Putnam's Sons, 1981), pp. 192–94.

43. See, for example, Maxine Cheshire with John Greenya, *Maxine Cheshire, Reporter* (Boston: Houghton Mifflin, 1978), pp. 45–48. There has even been a report of a television news correspondent acting as an intermediary in arranging meetings between Kennedy and Blaze Starr. See John Ed Bradley, "Blaze's Glory," pp. 24–30, 70–72. Another of my own journalist-interviewees in a not-for-attribution comment told of a JFK liaison with a female White House reporter.

44. See *Time* and *Newsweek* letters cited in note 35 above.

45. East Orange, N.J.: Association of Blauvelt Descendants, 1957.

46. See Benjamin C. Bradlee, *Conversations with Kennedy* (New York: W. W. Norton, 1975), pp. 45–46, 115–17; see also Tom Goldstein, *The News at Any Cost* (New York: Simon & Schuster, 1985), pp. 76–77.

47. "The Blauvelt Campaign," *Newsweek* 60 (September 24, 1962): 86–87.

48. Bradlee, *Conversations with Kennedy,* p. 153.

49. Both of these incidents were related by John Mashek of the *Boston Globe.*

50. J. F. terHorst et al., *The Flying White House: The Story of Air Force One* (New York: Bantam, 1979), pp. 206–8.

51. A high-ranking political associate of former president Nixon told us that "He uses the term 'media asshole' so frequently it sounds like one word."

52. Nixon and the psychiatrist claimed the visits were about physical, not mental, ailments, but others were unconvinced of this. See William M. Blair, "Psychiatric

Aid to Nixon Denied," *New York Times*, November 14, 1968, p. 34; "Doctor Discusses Treatment of Nixon," *New York Times*, July 1, 1969, p. 25; and Jack Anderson, "Nixon's Visits to Doctor Recalled," *Washington Post*, July 29, 1972, D31.

53. Bates, *If No News*, pp. 101–2.

54. See Ross, *Fall from Grace*, pp. 191–93.

55. More than twenty years later, the press exposés on Chappaquiddick continue. See, for example, one of a dozen lengthy articles published near the twentieth anniversary of the accident: Tom Matthews, "Chappaquiddick," *Newsweek* 114 (July 3, 1989): 52–53.

56. Richard L. Lyons, "Rhodes Seems Certain to Take Ford's Place," *Washington Post*, October 17, 1973, A2; Spencer Rich, "Senate Panel Clears Ford Unanimously," *Washington Post*, November 21, 1973, A1. The charge about Ford and the psychiatrist had been made in a book by Robert N. Winter-Berger, *The Washington Pay-Off* (Secaucus, N.J.: Lyle Stuart, 1972), pp. 255–62.

57. Seth Kantor, "Riegle Tapes Reveal Talks with Girlfriend," *Detroit News*, October 17, 1976, A1–4.

58. For instance, see Jonathan Walters, "A Night on the Town Just Isn't What It Used to Be in Jefferson City," *Governing* 2 (July 1989): 26–31: and Rob Gurwitt, "In the Capitol Pressroom, the Old Boys Call It a Day," *Governing* 3 (July 1990): 27–30.

59. Anthony King, "Transatlantic Transgressions: A Comparison of British and American Scandals," *Public Opinion* 7 (December/January 1985): 20–22, 64; and Richard Harwood, "From Rags to Tabloids," *Washington Post*, February 5, 1989, D6.

60. The references here are to Australian Prime Minister Bob Hawke's adultery (confessed tearfully on national television in March 1989), the womanizing of Argentina's President Carlos Menem, and exposure of the mistresses of Greek Prime Minister Andreas Papandreou and his rival and eventual successor, Constantine Mitsotakis.

61. Barbara Matusow, "Washington's Journalism Establishment," *The Washingtonian* 23 (February 1989): 94–101, 265–70.

62. See Eleanor Randolph, "Extra! Extra! Who Cares?" *Washington Post*, April 1, 1990, C1, 4.

63. Sunday papers are exceptions to the trend. More than one hundred new Sunday papers were created in the 1980s, and Sunday circulation as a whole has increased 25 percent since 1970.

64. Harold W. Stanley and Richard G. Niemi, eds., *Vital Statistics on American Politics* (Washington, D.C.: Congressional Quarterly Press, 1988), Table 2-8, p. 58.

65. Ibid.

66. See Evans Witt, "Here, There, and Everywhere: Where Americans Get Their News," *Public Opinion* 6 (August/September 1983): 45–48; June O. Yum and Kathleen E. Kendall, "Sources of Political Information in a Presidential Primary Campaign," *Journalism Quarterly* 65 (Spring 1988): 148–51, 177.

67. This was the fundamental conclusion of Shanto Iyengar and Donald R. Kinder, *News That Matters* (Chicago: University of Chicago Press, 1987).

68. According to a study by Frank N. Magid Associates cited in the *Washington Post Magazine*, May 13, 1990, p. 17; published in *The Rundown* 9 (September 4, 1989): 264.

69. Matusow, "Washington's Journalism Establishment," 268.

Chapter 3.   The Boys in the Bush

1. The press population explosion is observed in government as well as campaigns. President Reagan's press spokesman Larry Speakes compares the dozen reporters on hand at the White House for Harry Truman's 1945 announcement of the

atomic bombing of Hiroshima with the three thousand reporters on a "South Lawn platform half as long as a football field" for the 1981 return of the American hostages from Iran.

2. Reporters T. R. Reid and Lloyd Groves of the *Washington Post* have defined the ratio of media members to the general public as the "hype index." The higher the index number, the greater the hype.

3. Only George Bush had received more coverage. Center for Media and Public Affairs, "Quayle Hunt: TV News Coverage of the Quayle Nomination," *Media Monitor* 2 (September 1988): 1–4.

4. Quayle's ninety-three stories compared to the fifty-three registered by the Reagan-Gorbachev summit over ten days in December 1987 (all networks combined).

5. John and Mary R. Markle Foundation, *Report of the Commission on the Media and the Electorate: Key Findings* (New York: Markle Foundation, May 1990), pp. 16–18. See also Thomas E. Patterson, "The Press and Its Missed Assignment," in Michael Nelson, ed., *The Elections of 1988* (Washington, D.C.: Congressional Quarterly Press, 1989), p. 98; Marjorie R. Hershey, "The Campaign and the Media," in Gerald M. Pomper et al., eds., *The Election of 1988: Reports and Interpretations* (Chatham, N.J.: Chatham House, 1989), pp. 96–98; James Glen Stovall, "Coverage of the 1984 Presidential Campaign," *Journalism Quarterly* 65 (Summer 1968): 444–45; Thomas E. Patterson, *The Mass Media Election* (New York: Praeger, 1980); and Michael J. Robinson, Nancy Conover, and Margaret Sheehan, "The Media at Mid-Year: A Bad Year for McLuhanites," *Public Opinion* 3 (June/July 1980): 41–45.

6. Robert S. Lichter, Stanley Rothman, and Linda S. Lichter, *The Media Elite* (Bethesda, Md.: Adler and Adler, 1986).

7. William L. Riordan, *Plunkitt of Tammany Hall* (New York: Dutton, 1963), pp. 82–83.

8. Quoted in "Dagmar Celeste Calls Governor Good Mate," Cleveland *Plain Dealer* (AP dispatch), June 10, 1987, B10.

9. David L. Altheide, *Creating Reality: How TV News Distorts Events* (Beverly Hills: Sage, 1976), pp. 144–45.

10. See the excellent study by Robert M. Entman, *Democracy Without Citizens: Media and the Decay of American Politics* (New York: Oxford University Press, 1989), pp. 49–50.

11. See David S. Broder, *Behind the Front Page* (New York: Simon & Schuster, 1987), pp. 98–114.

12. David Shribman, "Robertson's Conversion From Rakishness to Faith Culminates in His Crusade for the White House," *Wall Street Journal*, October 6, 1987, 70.

13. T. R. Reid, "Painfully, Robertson Corrects Record," *Washington Post*, October 8, 1987, A1, 6.

14. Quoted in John Stacks and David Beckwith, "More Hurt Than Angry," *Time* 124 (September 3, 1984): 21.

15. For an overview, see James M. Perry, "Washington's Times and Post Do Battle in Scandal Involving 'Call Boys,' Fraud and Social Climbing," *Wall Street Journal*, July 28, 1989, A12.

16. Quoted in James M. Naughton, "Data on Eagleton Reported Lacking," *New York Times*, July 29, 1972, A10.

17. Quoted in Daniel Pederson, " 'I Am Not Perfect'," *Newsweek* (October 24, 1988): 25.

18. Timothy Crouse, *The Boys on the Bus* (New York: Ballantine Books, 1972), p. 7.

19. See William Boot, "Campaign '88: TV Overdoses on the Inside Dope," *Columbia Journalism Review* 27 (January/February 1989): 24.

20. Michael Barone, "A New Breed of Baby Boomer?" *Washington Post*, August 18, 1988, A23.

21. Broder, *Behind the Front Page*, pp. 238–39.

22. American Society of Newspaper Editors, *The Changing Face of the Newsroom* (Washington, D.C.: ASNE, May 1989), p. 29.

23. For example, see E. J. Dionne, Jr., "Bridge Led to Detour Over 20 Years," *New York Times*, July 18, 1989, A12. Twenty years after Chappaquiddick, a new book on the accident by a reporter who covered it reached the top of the *New York Times* best-seller list: Leo Damore, *Senatorial Privilege: The Chappaquiddick Cover-Up* (New York: Dell/Bantam, 1989). Damore built on the solid investigative work done in the 1970s by such journalists as Robert Sherrill.

24. Michael Cornfield and David Yalof, "Innocent by Reason of Analogy: How the Watergate Analogy Served Both Reagan and the Press During the Iran-Contra Affair," *Corruption and Reform* 3 (1988): 185–206.

25. See Nicholas von Hoffman, "Mediagate: When the Press Gets Goody-Goody," *Washington Post*, August 25, 1980, B9; and Eleanor Randolph, "Watergate Leaves Lasting Mark on Media," *Washington Post*, August 8, 1984, A12.

26. See Tom Wolfe, *The New Journalism* (New York: Harper & Row, 1973), especially pp. 9–32.

27. The first and best in White's series was *The Making of the President 1960* (New York: Atheneum, 1961). See also Joe McGinniss, *The Selling of the President 1968* (New York: Trident, 1969).

28. See James David Barber, *The Presidential Character* (Englewood Cliffs, N.J.: Prentice-Hall, 1972), p. 445.

29. I have attempted to make the case for doing precisely this in Larry J. Sabato, *The Party's Just Begun: Shaping Political Parties for America's Future* (Glenview, Ill.: Scott, Foresman, 1988).

30. See the journalists quoted by John B. Judis, "The Hart Affair," *Columbia Journalism Review* 25 (July/August 1987): 21–25.

31. Gary Hart, "Why Our Media Miss the Message," *Washington Post*, December 20, 1987, C4.

32. See Alessandra Stanley and Maureen Dowd, "The Dweebs on the Bus," *Gentleman's Quarterly* 57 (September 1988): 430–33, 482–87; and Molly Ivins, "The Reporters Under the Bed," *Mirabella* 1 (June 1989): 120–21.

33. American Society of Newspaper Editors, *The Changing Face of the Newsroom*, pp. 27–28; and figures supplied by the Gannett Foundation drawn from ongoing research conducted by Jean Gaddy Wilson of the University of Missouri.

34. Suzannah Lessard, "Kennedy's Woman Problem, Women's Kennedy Problem," *Washington Monthly*, December 1979, pp. 10–14.

35. Suzannah Lessard, "The Issue Was Women," *Newsweek* 109 (May 18, 1987): 32, 34.

36. See Judis, "The Hart Affair."

37. The author wishes to acknowledge the invaluable counsel and editorial assistance provided by Professor Scott Matheson of the University of Utah School of Law in preparing this section.

38. 376 U.S. 254 (1964). See also Steven Pressman, "Libel Law: Finding the Right Balance," *Editorial Research Reports* 2 (August 18, 1989): 462–71; and David Elder, "Defamation, Public Officialdom and the *Rosenblatt* v. *Baer* Criteria—A Proposal for Revivification: Two Decades After *New York Times Co.* v. *Sullivan*," *Buffalo Law Review* 33 (1984): 579–680.

39. *Curtis Publishing Co.* v. *Butts*, 388 U.S. 130 (1967); *Associated Press* v. *Walker*, 388 U.S. 130 (1967).

40. *New York Times Co.* v. *Sullivan*, 376 U.S. 254, 279–80 (1964). *St. Amant* v. *Thompson*, 390 U.S. 727, 731 (1968).

41. Randall Bezanson, Gilbert Cranberg, and John Soloski, *Libel Law and the Press* (New York: Free Press, 1987), p. 122.

42. Ibid., p. 201.

43. David Anderson, "Libel and Press Self-Censorship," *Texas Law Review* 53 (1975): 422; Scott M. Matheson, Jr., "Procedure in Public Person Defamation Cases: The Impact of the First Amendment," *Texas Law Review* 66 (1987): 215.

44. The average costs of defending a libel case are estimated to be between $95,000 and $150,000. See the Gannett Center for Media Studies, "The Cost of Libel: Economic and Policy Implications" (New York: Gannett Center, 1986), p. 3.

45. Anthony Lewis, *"New York Times* v. *Sullivan* Reconsidered: Time to Return to 'The Central Meaning of the First Amendment,' " *Columbia Law Review* 83 (1983): 603.

46. In a case involving the *Alton* (Illinois) *Telegraph* (circulation 38,000), the paper faced a $9.2 million jury judgment based on a never-published memorandum prepared by two of its reporters that was sent to a federal investigator. The newspaper was forced to file for bankruptcy to avoid having to sell all its assets. It finally reached a settlement that allowed the paper to stay in business, but its near demise sent an unmistakable signal to media outlets everywhere. See John Curley, " 'Chilling Effect,' How Libel Suit Sapped the Crusading Spirit of a Small Newspaper," *Wall Street Journal*, September 29, 1983, 1. See also Howard Kurtz, "Spate of Libel Judgments May Alter News Practices," *Washington Post*, November 24, 1990, A4, 5, and W. John Moore, "Press Clipping," *National Journal* 22 (December 22, 1990): 3086–3090.

47. Rodney Smolla, *Suing the Press* (New York: Oxford University Press, 1986), p. 16.

48. Bezanson, Cranberg, and Soloski, *Libel Law and the Press*, p. 8.

49. Dom Bonafede, "Go Away," *National Journal* 21 (February 11, 1989): 378.

50. Laurence I. Barrett, "Orator for the Next Generation: Does Joe Biden Talk Too Much?" *Time* 129 (June 22, 1987): 24–25.

51. Douglas A. Harbrecht, "Is Joe Biden More Than 'Just A Speech'?" *Business Week* 2991 (March 30, 1987): 59–60.

52. "More Urge Than Surge," *The Economist* 303 (June 13, 1987): 41–42.

53. See, for example, Michael Barone and Grant Ujifusa, *The Almanac of American Politics 1990* (Washington, D.C.: National Journal, 1989), pp. 229–30.

54. See Brooks Jackson, "Rabbit Redux: Carter and the Press," *Wall Street Journal*, April 30, 1989, A16. Radio newsman Paul Harvey was the first to use the AP story, according to Jackson, and this helped to trigger the pressure from newspapers to allow earlier-than-scheduled publication.

55. See Broder, *Behind the Front Page*, pp. 30–31.

56. "Jackson and the Jews," *The New Republic* editorial, March 19, 1984, pp. 9–10; Victor Gold, "Letter to Jesse, From Hymie's Son," *National Review* 36 (May 18, 1984): 28–29.

57. See William Boot, "Iranscam: When the Cheering Stopped," *Columbia Journalism Review* 25 (March/April 1987): 25–30.

58. See "A Voice for the Yuppie Generation," "Election Extra," *Newsweek* 104 (November/December 1984): 45–46.

59. See Eleanor Randolph, "The Press and the Candidate: Hart Sex Life Was Longtime Focus of Rumors," *Washington Post*, May 9, 1989, A1.

60. This anecdote was related by CBS News's Eric Engberg.

61. Howard Fineman, "Gary Hart: A Candidate In Search of Himself," *Newsweek* 109 (April 13, 1987): 25–27. McEvoy later claimed the quote was "hypothetical" and off the record; Fineman insists it was an on-the-record remark.

62. Paul Taylor, "Hart to Withdraw From Presidential Campaign," *Washington Post*, May 8, 1987, A1. For another tale of Hart's romances, see the interview with

314

one of his mistresses in Roger Simon, *Road Show* (New York: Farrar, Straus, & Giroux, 1990), pp. 83–93.

63. Devroy commented: "We had all decided in our minds that we would have published [the Hart affair details]. . . . This is a character portrait the voters ought to have had" as long as he was a serious candidate.

64. Broder, *Behind the Front Page,* p. 264.

65. See Charles Kaiser, "Reporting the Scandal," *Newsweek* 103 (July 18, 1983): 20.

66. Mondale and Bentsen had briefly run for the 1976 Democratic presidential nomination, while Bush challenged Reagan on the GOP side in 1980.

67. Along with several of my students, I personally witnessed this incredible case of mistaken identity.

68. Quoted in David R. Runkel, *Campaign for President: The Managers Look at '88* (Dover, Mass.: Auburn House, 1988), p. 207.

69. Jim Wooten of ABC News cited a fascinating circumstance that can serve as a miniequivalent of a political convention's feeding frenzy: the campaign train. In 1976 Carter had a whistle-stop tour across Pennsylvania when the news broke of his *Playboy* "lust in the heart" interview. Says Wooten: "Everybody was captive on the train, and the news just swept it. The Carter people were besieged with questions. It was just a sensation, a real feeding frenzy!" There was apparently a similar chain reaction on Eisenhower's campaign train when the Nixon "secret fund" scandal broke. See Richard Nixon, *Six Crises* (Garden City, N.Y.: Doubleday, 1962), chap. 2; and "The Remarkable Tornado," *Time* 60 (September 29, 1952): 11–12.

70. Press and VerBurg, *American Politicians,* pp. 293–301, esp. pp. 296–98.

71. Colleen O'Connor, "Again, Sex and Politics," *Newsweek,* June 15, 1987: 33.

72. See Eleanor Randolph, "Frustrated Reporters Add Megaphones, Binoculars to Notepads," *Washington Post,* November 2, 1988, A25.

73. The brief treatment here of press "bias" only touches on the major elements of the dispute. Readers seeking more information should consult the references in succeeding footnotes, as well as these general overviews of the topic: Lance Bennett, *News: The Politics of Illusion,* 2nd ed. (New York: Longman, 1988), pp. 117–39; Ronald Berkman and Laura W. Kitch, *Politics in the Media Age* (New York: McGraw-Hill, 1986), pp. 77–104; Entman, *Democracy Without Citizens,* pp. 30–40; Doris A. Graber, *Mass Media and American Politics,* 3rd ed. (Washington, D.C.: Congressional Quarterly Press, 1989), pp. 7–8, 76–77, 103, 209–12; Press and VerBurg, *American Politicians,* pp. 92–98; Austin Ranney, *Channels of Power: The Impact of Television on American Politics* (New York: Basic Books, 1983), chap. 2; Mitchell Stephens, *A History of News: From the Drum to the Satellite* (New York: Viking, 1989), pp. 264–67; Martin A. Lee and Norman Solomon, *Unreliable Sources: A Guide to Detecting Bias in the News Media* (New York: Lyle Stuart, 1990).

74. See, for example, William A. Rusher, *The Coming Battle for the Media: Curbing the Power of the Media Elite* (New York: William Morrow, 1988).

75. Ted J. Smith III, "The Watchdog's Bite," *American Enterprise* 1 (January/February 1990): 65.

76. American Society of Newspaper Editors, *The Changing Face of the Newsroom,* p. 33; William Schneider and I. A. Lewis, "Views on the News," *Public Opinion* 8 (August/September 1985): 6–11, 58–59; and Lichter, Rothman, and Lichter, *The Media Elite.* Note, however, that the Lichter sample was probably weighted disproportionately to the most liberal segment of journalism. See Entman, *Democracy Without Citizens,* p. 32.

77. See Dom Bonafede, "Crossing Over," *National Journal* 21 (January 14, 1989): 102; Richard Harwood, "Tainted Journalists," *Washington Post,* December 4, 1988, L6; Charles Trueheart, "Trading Places: The Insiders Debate," *Washington Post,* January 4, 1989, D1, 19; and Kirk Victor, "Slanted Views," *National Journal* 20 (June 4, 1988): 1512. For example, among the journalist-interviewees in this volume who

once worked for Democratic candidates or administrations are Ken Bode, Kathy Bushkin, John Chancellor, Jeff Greenfield, Mark Shields, and Tim Russert. The only easily identifiable journalist-interviewee who formerly served Republican candidates and officeholders is David Gergen. (See the Appendix for their current affiliations.)

78. "*Roe* v. *Webster*," *Media Monitor* 3 (October 1989): 1–6.

79. Richard Harwood, "A Weekend in April," *Washington Post*, May 6, 1990, B6. See also David Shaw, "Abortion and the Media," (four-part series), *Los Angeles Times*, July 1, 1990, A1, 50–51; July 2, 1990, A1, 20; July 3, 1990, A1, 22–23; July 4, 1990, A1, 28–29.

80. "Post Haste," *The New Republic* 201 (December 4, 1989): 9–10. *Post* editors forbade employees from engaging in the practice after the first reported occurrence of it, but to no avail.

81. The importance of the agenda-setting function is discussed throughout Shanto Iyengar and Donald R. Kinder, *News That Matters: Television and American Opinion* (Chicago: University of Chicago Press, 1988). See especially the conclusions reached on pp. 4, 33.

82. David Whitman, "Who's Who Among the Homeless," *The New Republic* 199 (June 6, 1988): 18–20. See also *Washington Post*, April 19, 1989, D10.

83. Times-Mirror Center for the People and the Press, "The People and the Press, Part 5: Public Attitudes Toward News Organizations," based on an in-person random-sample survey of 1,507 adult Americans, conducted by the Gallup organization between August 9–28, 1989 (margin of error: plus or minus 3 percent).

84. David Gergen, "The Message to the Media," *Public Opinion* 7 (April/May 1984): 5–6.

85. See Sig Mickelson, *The Electric Mirror: Politics in an Age of Network Television* (New York: Dodd, Mead, 1972), pp. 4–5, 164–67.

86. Patrick J. Buchanan, "Pundit vs. 'Re-Pundit' on Writers' Rights and Reasons," *Richmond Times-Dispatch*, December 29, 1988, A14.

87. Quoted in an AP dispatch from Richmond, Va., dated October 10, 1989.

88. Edith Efron, *The News Twisters* (Los Angeles: Nash Publishing Co., 1971). See the criticisms of Efron's study in Paul Weaver, "Is Television News Biased?" *Public Interest* (Winter 1972): 57–74; and also in Robert L. Stevenson, Richard A. Eisinger, Barry M. Feinberg, and Alan B. Kotok, "Untwisting The News Twisters: a Replication of Efron's Study," *Journalism Quarterly* 50 (Summer 1973): 211–19.

89. Michael J. Robinson and Maura Clancey, "General Election Coverage: Part 1," *Public Opinion* 7 (December/January 1985): 49–54, 59.

90. See Robert S. Lichter, Daniel Amundson, and Richard E. Noyes, "Election '88 Media Coverage," *Public Opinion* 11 (January/February 1989): 18–19, 52; and Eleanor Randolph, "CBS Hanging Tough on Vice President," *Washington Post*, February 13, 1988, A15.

91. See Robert S. Lichter, Daniel Amundson, and Richard E. Noyes, *The Video Campaign: Network Coverage of the 1988 Primaries* (Washington, D.C.: American Enterprise Institute, 1988).

92. See Mark Hertsgaard, *On Bended Knee: The Press and the Reagan Presidency* (New York: Farrar, Straus, & Giroux, 1988).

93. For example, see Robert Cirino, *Don't Blame the People* (New York: Random House/Vintage, 1972).

94. Fairness and Accuracy in Reporting (FAIR), "All the Usual Suspects: MacNeil-Lehrer and Nightline" (New York: FAIR, May 1990). Two Boston College sociologists, William Hoynes and David Croteau, conducted the study for FAIR, a liberal group critical of the news media.

95. See Nick Thimmesch, "The Editorial Endorsement Game," *Public Opinion* 7 (October/November 1984): 10–13. However, there has been an accelerating trend toward neutrality on the editorial pages. In 1964, 1968, and 1972 only 23 percent of

the pages made no endorsement in the presidential contest; in 1984 the figure was 33 percent and in 1988, 55 percent. See Martin P. Wattenberg, *The Decline of American Political Parties* (Cambridge, Mass.: Harvard University Press, 1990), chap. 9.

96. See Sarah Lyall, "Family Paper First to Report Quayle's War Role," *New York Times*, August 19, 1988, A17.

97. Quoted in *Hotline* 2 (January 16, 1989): 1.

98. This is sometimes termed "structural bias."

99. See, for example, William C. Adams, " '84 Convention Coverage," *Public Opinion* 7 (December/January 1985): 43–48.

100. Jody Powell, *The Other Side of the Story* (New York: William Morrow, 1984), p. 108.

101. Michael J. Robinson and Margaret Sheehan, "Brief Encounters With the Fourth Kind: Reagan's Press Honeymoon," *Public Opinion* 3 (December/January 1981): 56–57.

102. Bates, *If No News*, pp. 53–55.

103. See "The Remarkable Tornado," *Time* 60 (September 29, 1952): 11. The anti-Dukakis *Boston Herald* gave the *Post*'s unfair treatment of Nixon a run for the roses in 1988 when it published eighteen articles on the Dukakis-Biden "attack video" incident in a single day's newspaper (October 1, 1987). The articles absorbed all the news space in the first eleven pages.

104. See Jules Witcover, "William Loeb and the New Hampshire Primary: A Question of Ethics," *Columbia Journalism Review* 10 (May/June 1972): 14–25.

105. Richard Harwood, "Everybody's Sin But Our Own," *Washington Post*, April 16, 1989, B6.

106. Broder, *Behind the Front Page*, pp. 351–57; Tom Goldstein, *The News at Any Cost* (New York: Simon & Schuster, 1985), pp. 79–81.

Chapter 4. A Thousand Points of Gossip

1. The consultant-reporter "sweetheart" arrangement is discussed throughout Larry J. Sabato, *The Rise of Political Consultants* (New York: Basic Books, 1981).

2. Shrum's consulting partner, David Doak, was also accused of the anti-Biden attack by conservative talk-show host John McLaughlin during a televised program. A week later McLaughlin retracted the allegation.

3. See Jill Abramson and James Lyons, "Behind the Biden Plagiarism Flap," *Legal Times* 10 (September 21, 1987): 1, 3.

4. As reported on "20/20," December 18, 1987, in a piece produced by Charlie Thompson.

5. Ibid. According to Thompson, Armandt's husband was missing and presumed dead, apparently murdered in California in connection with a drug-running operation. Rice's former boyfriend was serving a ten-year sentence for drug-related offenses.

6. Fiedler is entirely believable on this score, not only because he knows the voices of both Armandt and his tipster but also because his source did not know that Bimini was Hart and Rice's destination on the *Monkey Business* trip. Armandt, of course, was herself on the cruise and could easily have supplied that bit of information to enhance her credibility during the call to Fiedler.

7. Bill Dedman, "Rice Points to a Friend as Tipster," *Atlanta Journal and Constitution*, May 17, 1987, A1.

8. In off-the-record conversations with me, high-ranking Virginia Republican officeholders and party officials have confirmed the party's role in the recruitment of, and fundraising to pay, the private detective.

9. The aide was N. Jeffrey Lord, associate director of the White House Office of

Political Affairs. See Maureen Dowd, "Biden Is Facing Growing Debate on His Speeches," *New York Times*, September 16, 1987, A1, D30.

10. See also Martin Schram, *The Great American Video Game: Presidential Politics in the Television Age* (New York: William Morrow, 1987), p. 197.

11. Tower went into some detail on his ex-wife's maneuverings against him in his book, *Consequences: A Personal and Political Memoir* (Boston: Little, Brown, 1991).

12. See, for example, Brooks Jackson, "Hart's Newest Issue Is His Age," *Wall Street Journal*, March 9, 1984, 52. Jackson has developed his own plausible theory on Hart's age-cheating, as he explains in an interview:

Hart said that his staff changed it on his bio and he didn't catch it. Well, it was in his license and his application to the bar. The age change, if you look closely, happened about the time he was 29 years old. He was 29 two years in a row. My conclusion was that the much-heralded child genius of the McGovern campaign just didn't want to turn 30.

13. In our conversation with him, Edsall was careful not to violate the confidentiality of his source. Information on that score and most of the details appearing here were obtained from others.

14. Hart's Washington paramour had not been overly discreet. According to one senior D.C. bureau chief, who (along with his wife and other reporters) had socialized at the woman's apartment, "On this particular person's bedside table was a picture of her and Gary." In addition, more than two dozen of our interviewees mentioned the woman by name, though most had heard it from other reporters. Many versions of the *Post*'s scoop are repeated among journalists, but some are highly inaccurate. Contrary to the belief of some, for example, the *Post* had not been sitting on the story for weeks or months. Incidentally, while the *Post* received the materials on May 5, 1987, Hart's recorded night with the woman had taken place almost five months earlier. The timing of the delivery obviously was designed to capitalize on the Rice revelation, and the fact that the detective was staking out Hart rather than the jealous husband's wife suggests that, even in the absence of evidence that Hart was seeing his wife, the prominent husband had the personal or political motivation to do Hart in. See also Paul Taylor, *See How They Run: Electing the President in an Age of Mediaocracy* (New York: Alfred A. Knopf, 1990), chap. 2.

15. Gerald R. Ford, "Poland: I Told You So," *Washington Post*, October 11, 1989, A29; Leo P. Ribuffo, "Is Poland a Soviet Satellite? Gerald Ford, the Sonnenfeldt Doctrine, and the Election of 1976," *Diplomatic History* 14 (Summer 1990): 385–403.

16. Jack W. Germond and Jules Witcover, *Whose Broad Stripes and Bright Stars? The Trivial Pursuit of the Presidency 1988* (New York: Warner Books, 1989), pp. 176–78. Hart's then press secretary, Kevin Sweeney, told us that he was among those giving specific warnings to the candidate.

17. E. J. Dionne, "Gary Hart: The Elusive Front Runner," *New York Times Magazine*, May 3, 1987, p. 28.

18. Riordan, *Plunkitt of Tammany Hall*, p. 77.

19. Robb himself applied this adjective to the party group with which he traveled. See *Newsweek* 112 (November 14, 1988): 19.

20. See Walt Harrington, "Lynda (Johnson Robb)," *Washington Post Magazine*, July 9, 1989, p. 19.

21. See Rose Ellen O'Connor, "Robb Enjoyed Glitzy Va. Beach Social Scene," *Virginian-Pilot and Ledger-Star*, August 28, 1988, A1, 6. The lengthy story was based on more than two hundred interviews and months of research.

22. See Larry Sabato, *Virginia Votes 1987–1990* (Charlottesville, Va.: University of Virginia Center for Public Service, 1991), chap. 2.

23. See Ronald J. Watkins, *High Crimes and Misdemeanors: The Term and Trials of Former Governor Evan Mecham* (New York: William Morrow, 1990); also Peter

Goudinoff and Sheila Tobias, "Arizona Airhead," *The New Republic* 199 (October 26, 1987): 15–16.

24. A Barry sampler, all from the *Washington Post*, would include: Eric Pianin, "Barry Defends His Integrity, Denies Drug Use," March 17, 1983, A1, 32; Eric Pianin and Joe Pichirallo, "Barry-Johnson Relationship Described," August 11, 1984, A1, 11; Victoria Churchville and Arthur S. Brisbane, "D.C. Officials Confirm Barry's Visit to Model," May 3, 1987, D1, 9; Tom Sherwood, "Barry's Tie to Johnson Won't Go Away," June 21, 1987, A1; Tom Sherwood and Sharon LaFraniere, "Tests Show Cocaine in Hotel Room," December 25, 1988, A1, 20; Sharon LaFraniere, "Lewis Says He Smoked Crack With Barry," August 31, 1989, A1; Sharon LaFraniere, "Barry Arrested on Cocaine Charges In Undercover FBI, Police Operation," January 19, 1990, A1.

25. See Daniel Pederson, " 'I Am Not Perfect'," *Newsweek* 112 (October 24, 1988): 25; Alfredo Corchado, "San Antonio's Mayor, a Hero of Hispanics, Falls From Grace Amid Moral Lapse, Media Scrutiny," *Wall Street Journal*, October 17, 1988, A24.

26. See the many examples cited in Bates, *If No News*, pp. 10–11.

27. Eleanor Randolph, "Post's Woodward Cites Rumors of Drug Use at Paper," *Washington Post*, June 8, 1984, B2. *Washington Monthly* editor Charles Peters, a long-time *Post* watcher, claims some *Post* staff "were taking everything in sight in the seventies, and a lot of coke in the eighties."

28. LBJ biographer Doris Kearns Goodwin discovered the discrepancy and discusses it in the American Press Institute, *Covering the Candidates: Roles and Responsibilities of the Press* (Reston, Va.: American Press Institute, 1987), pp. 47–48. Amazingly, when Goodwin confronted Johnson with the truth, he explained that his ancestor had actually died in the more important battle of San Jacinto—also utterly false.

29. Brent Larkin and Mary Anne Sharkey, "Celeste womanizing worries aides," Cleveland *Plain Dealer*, June 3, 1987, A1. Celeste's denial was detailed in the third paragraph of the story.

30. Andrew Rosenthal, "Dukakis Releases Medical Details to Stop Rumors on Mental Health," *New York Times*, August 4, 1988, A1, D20.

31. The frank details of Eagleton's radical shock treatments might have removed whatever figleaf of privacy the senator retained. Quayle's academic record is, by all accounts, unusually dismal.

32. In the short term, Dukakis was set back badly in Iowa, the first caucus state. For the long term, the incident deprived Dukakis of the services of his political alter ego, campaign manager John Sasso (who was forced to shoulder the responsibility and resign.) Many observers believe that Sasso could have prevented the disastrous drift in Dukakis's postconvention campaign. Sasso returned to Dukakis in September, but by then the die was cast.

33. The reporter, Linda Ashton, refused all comment to us. See the testimony of Congressman Bob Livingston (R., La.) during the Hearing on Congressional Ethics and the Role of the Media, U.S. House of Representatives Bipartisan Task Force on Ethics, September 20, 1989, *Committee Report*, pp. 259–60.

34. The newspapers were the *Dallas Morning News* and the *Houston Chronicle*. See *Hotline* 3 (April 6, 1990): 8–9. This was not the last episode in Texas's 1990 gubernatorial drug wars. In late October a former Mattox press secretary, by then a resident of New Mexico, gave a sworn statement to the *Albuquerque Journal* that he saw Richards use cocaine at a Dallas bar in 1977.

35. See Beth Barrett and Mark Barnhill, "New Accusation Against Quayle," *Los Angeles Daily News*, August 23, 1989, A1.

36. "The Nunn Standard," *Wall Street Journal* editorial, February 28, 1989, A22.

37. George Archibald, "Sex and Booze Turn Hill Into a School for Scandal," *Washington Times*, March 2, 1989, A1.

38. See Richard Harwood, "The Mack-Small Story," *Washington Post*, May 14, 1989, C6; Bill Thomas, "Why Small Told All," *Roll Call*, May 29–June 4, 1989, p. 16. Anonymous letters in January 1987 had tipped off many in the press to Mack's troubles. Only the *Fort Worth* (Texas) *Star Telegram* published a story as a result, and it was somewhat sympathetic to Mack, who was the brother of Wright's son-in-law. Wright had also helped to secure Mack's parole by means of letters and a job offer. See also Janet Hook, "Passion, Defiance, Tears: Jim Wright Bows Out," *Congressional Quarterly Weekly* 47 (June 3, 1989): 1289–94. The original *Post* article on Mack's victim was by Ken Ringle, "Memory and Anger: A Victim's Story," *Washington Post*, May 4, 1989, B1.

39. See, for example, Ted Gup, "Identifying Homosexuals: What Are the Rules?" *Washington Journalism Review* 10 (October 1988): 30–33.

40. Coverage of sports figures has changed radically, too. Babe Ruth's absence from baseball on account of venereal disease was once attributed by a knowing press to a bellyache, while contemporary athletic heroes have all their private warts examined in public.

41. See Elder Witt, "Is Government Full of Crooks, or Are We Just Better at Finding Them?" *Governing* 2 (September 1989): 33–38; Suzanne Garment, "Political Imperfections: Scandal Time in Washington," *Public Opinion* 10 (May/June 1987): 10–12, 60.

42. Times-Mirror Center for the People and the Press, "The People and the Press, Parts 1 through 5" Washington, D.C.: Times–Mirror Corporation, 1986–89).

43. From the Harris poll, a telephone random-sample survey of 1,253 adults conducted nationwide from April 19–23, 1989, with a margin of error of plus or minus 3 percent.

44. Telephone random-sample survey of 749 adults taken nationwide May 5–6, 1987, with a margin of error of plus or minus 4 percent.

45. Adultery was the only offense a majority (52 percent) said wasn't "any of the press's business."

46. CBS News/ *New York Times* telephone random-sample survey of 589 adults nationwide conducted on November 8, 1987, in the wake of Judge Douglas Ginsburg's withdrawal from consideration for a Supreme Court seat (margin of error: plus or minus 4 percent).

47. Telephone random-sample survey of 1,118 adults conducted from May 7 to 8, 1987, with a margin of error of plus or minus 4 percent.

48. Ibid.

49. NBC News/ *Wall Street Journal* telephone random-sample poll of 1,026 adults conducted May 6, 1987, with a margin of error of plus or minus 4 percent.

50. CBS News/ *New York Times* national telephone random-sample survey of 613 adults conducted December 15, 1987. The margin of error for the Democratic voter group taken alone was plus or minus 6 percent.

51. National telephone random-sample survey of 513 adults conducted July 27–29, 1972 (margin of error: plus or minus 4 percent). See "A Crisis Named Eagleton," *Newsweek* 80 (August 7, 1972): 12–19.

52. CBS News/ *New York Times* telephone random-sample survey of 1,135 registered voters nationwide, conducted September 12–16, 1984 (margin of error: plus or minus 3 percent).

53. Conducted for the Times-Mirror Company on August 24–25, 1988; a telephone random-sample survey of 1,000 registered voters, with a margin of error of plus or minus 3 percent.

54. A random-sample telephone survey of 1,000 voters conducted October 2–7, 1987, with a margin of error of plus or minus 3 percent.

55. The *Washington Post*–ABC News random-sample telephone poll of 2,015 adults conducted September 17–22, 1987, had shown that just 28 percent of those

who had heard about Biden's problems were "bothered a lot" by them, and 55 percent said he should continue his presidential campaign (margin of error: plus or minus 3 percent).

56. Random-sample telephone survey of 589 adults conducted November 8, 1987, with a margin of error of plus or minus 4 percent.

57. CBS News/ *New York Times* random-sample telephone survey of 749 adults conducted May 5–6, 1987, with a margin of error of plus or minus 4 percent.

58. A Yankelovich Clancy Shulman random-sample telephone survey for *Time* and CNN of 506 adults nationwide conducted June 1, 1989, with a margin of error of plus or minus 4 percent.

59. Center for Responsive Politics, *Dateline: Capitol Hill* (Washington, D.C.: Center for Responsive Politics, 1990): 1. Findings are drawn from a random-sample telephone survey of 1,270 adults conducted in January and February 1989, with a margin of error of plus or minus 3 percent.

60. The total sample was 498. See Figure 4.1 for further details of the survey. Tell-Back, Inc. of Spokane, Washington, also conducted a nonscientific "instant pulse-reading" for the Ford campaign, in which fifty registered voters (all weak partisans or independents) used devices to record their immediate reactions to each statement made in the debate. The plotted graph of those reactions shows little response (positive or negative) to Ford's "free Poland" remark, while other points of contention, such as Ford's military action to free the ship *Mayaguez* and Carter's criticism of the Arab oil embargo, generated strong voter emotions. See also the Notre Dame student sample results compiled by social psychologist Lloyd Sloan described in the *Detroit Free Press*, November 27, 1976, A14. Students who saw only the debate and no television analysis scored Ford the winner by 47 to 27 percent, while students who watched television after the debate awarded the victory to Carter by a large margin.

61. Boxes 27 and 28, October 6–7, 1976, DuVal papers, Gerald R. Ford Library.

62. See Lindsay Gruson, "Split Over Mecham Goes Deeper Than Politics," *New York Times*, March 19, 1988, A6.

63. See Richard Zoglin, "Politics, Late-Night Style," *Time* 97 (September 12, 1989): 66.

64. Letterman also introduced a list of the "Top Ten Things Gary Hart and Donna Rice Could Have Done While They Were Together," of which the most ironically telling was "Discussed having sex. Decided against it."

65. See the compilation from the Center for Media and Public Affairs published in the *Washington Post*, August 12, 1989, C3.

66. See Michael Barone and Joannie M. Schrof, "The Changing Voice of Talk Radio," *U.S. News & World Report* 108 (January 15, 1990): 51–53.

67. Bill Peterson, "Hart Falls Into a Cross-Country Campaign Trap," *Washington Post*, May 27, 1984, A5.

68. Laurence I. Barrett, *Gambling with History* (New York: Doubleday, 1983). Barrett himself devoted just two paragraphs and a footnote to Debategate, and *Time* magazine had bumped a piece containing Barrett's scoop for "lack of space" in February 1981.

69. See Charles Kaiser, "Reporting the Scandal," *Newsweek* 91 (July 18, 1983): 20.

70. The photograph, eventually released by the Reagan White House, deflates the story both by proving Carter's assertion and by the ordinariness of the pictured encounter.

71. See chapter 3. The term *water-torture journalism* is attributed to *New York Times* executive editor A. M. Rosenthal. See Thomas Griffith, "Water-Torture Journalism," *Time* 121 (May 23, 1983): 52.

72. See *New York Times*, September 11, 1952, p. 77.

73. Lou Cannon, "Nixon Asks for Silence on Eagleton," *Washington Post*, July 27, 1972, A16.

74. See Sabato, *The Rise of Political Consultants*, chap. 2.

75. Goldwater was a GOP U.S. senator in 1974 when he urged Nixon to resign as president, and he was the retired "grand old man" of the Arizona Republican party when Mecham heard from him in 1987 and 1988.

Chapter 5. Rumor and Excess

1. From the "700 Club" of June 27, 1989, Christian Broadcasting Network, as quoted in *Hotline* 2 (June 28, 1989): 1.

2. See Tom Shales, "Hot on the Mayor's Trail," *Washington Post*, January 24, 1990, C1; and "Breeding the Barry Story," *Washington Post*, February 6, 1990, C1, 8.

3. Karlyn Barker, "Barry Asks Media to Give Florida Patients Solitude," *Washington Post*, February 20, 1990, B7.

4. See the comparison of Billygate to Reagan administration scandals in Entman, *Democracy Without Citizens*, pp. 42–55.

5. See Jonathan Kwitney and Anthony M. DeStefano, "Rep. Ferraro and a Painful Legacy," *Wall Street Journal*, September 13, 1984, 28.

6. Eleanor Randolph, "Ferraro Emerges From 'Full-Court Press' in Media's Good Graces," *Washington Post*, August 23, 1984, A4.

7. Paul M. Rodriguez and George Archibald, "Sex Sold from Congressman's Apartment," *Washington Times*, August 25, 1989, A1, 7; Michael Hedges, "Deserted by Press, Frank Stands Firm Against Resigning," *Washington Times*, September 18, 1989, A1, 10; Ralph Z. Hallow and Paul M. Rodriguez, "Tide Is Rolling Against Frank," *Washington Times*, September 19, 1989, A1, 5; Paul M. Rodriguez and Ralph Z. Hallow, "Democratic Leaders Desert Frank," *Washington Times*, September 20, 1989, A1, 8.

8. See Bates, *If No News*, pp. 169–70. See also Carl Bernstein and Bob Woodward, *All the President's Men* (New York: Warner, 1975).

9. Hal S. Scott, "Betrayal," *The New Republic* 199 (December 14, 1987): 12–13.

10. This was the claim of Kevin Sweeney, Gary Hart's press secretary in 1987.

11. See also Brit Hume, *Inside Story* (Garden City, N.Y.: Doubleday, 1974), pp. 49–60.

12. As quoted in W. Lance Bennett, *News: The Politics of Illusion* (New York: Longman, 1983), p. 64. Lapham has been a reporter for several newspapers and more recently the editor of *Harper's*.

13. See David Broder's discussion of a "sorry episode" at the *Washington Post*, when a false rumor about the Jimmy Carters wiretapping the Ronald Reagans during the 1980–81 postelection transition reached print via a *Post* gossip column: Broder, *Behind the Front Page*, pp. 314–16. Broder also unwittingly provided another example in our interview with him. He claimed that reporters still allow public officials some measure of personal privacy, pointing proudly to the fact that no journalist had printed any mention of Senate Democratic Majority Leader George Mitchell's well-known relationship with Republican Janet Mullins, the Bush State Department's assistant secretary for public affairs. Yet when Broder's newspaper next ran a "style" section profile on the divorced Mitchell, notice of the romance was included. See Lois Romano, "George Mitchell, the Civil Senator," *Washington Post*, June 27, 1990, B2.

14. See, for example, "Jackson Linked to Plagiarism in College," *Boston Globe* (AP dispatch), December 25, 1987, p. 24.

15. See Mitchell Locin, "Jackson: Plagiarism Story Is a 'New Low,' " *Chicago*

Tribune, December 26, 1987, p. 5; and Constanza Montana, "Jackson's File Clean, U. of I. Chief Reports," *Chicago Tribune*, December 31, 1987, p. 10. Neither the university president nor the college professor cleared Jackson completely; too much time had passed for records and memories to be complete. But the *News-Gazette's* hearsay sources certainly did not present an airtight case meriting publication of damaging information about a presidential candidate.

16. See *Hotline* 3 (April 23, 1990): 10–11.

17. See *Newsweek* 115 (May 7, 1990): 6.

18. Bill McAllister, "W. Virginia Politics Gets 'Soap Opera' Spin," *Washington Post*, March 25, 1990, A1, 6–7.

19. See *Hotline* 3 (June 7, 1990): 6–7. The rumor had apparently circulated behind-the-scenes for years.

20. Jeffrey A. Roberts, "No Comment on Romer Rumor," *Denver Post*, June 6, 1990, B1, 3.

21. My research assistant Mark Stencel wrote a first draft of parts of this section on Kemp.

22. Lou Cannon, *Reagan* (New York: G. P. Putnam's Sons, 1982), pp. 132–38.

23. Martin Tolchin, "Jack Kemp's Bootleg Run to the Right," *Esquire* (October 24, 1978), pp. 58–69 at p. 67.

24. Rowland Evans and Robert Novak, "Ugly Political Rumors," *Washington Post*, December 29, 1978, A15.

25. See Marie Brenner, "Jack the Jock," *Vanity Fair* 49 (January 1986): 50–56, 102–4; and Howard Fineman, "Kemp: New Ideas, Old Questions," *Newsweek* 106 (December 2, 1985): 54.

26. Myron S. Waldman, "Kemp, Asked Again, Says No Again," New York *Newsday*, March 14, 1986, 31.

27. Paul Taylor, "Rep. Kemp Angry Over NBC Question on Homosexuality," *Washington Post*, March 14, 1986, A4.

28. I can confirm the fundraisers' claims with one bit of anecdotal evidence. After speaking to a national American Medical Association meeting in 1987 and offering an assessment of the upcoming presidential contest, I was pulled aside by a board member of the AMA's political action committee who was a major Republican party donor and activist. He advised me not to bother including Kemp in my analysis at future gatherings since "he has no chance to win because he's as queer as a three-dollar bill."

29. Richard Cohen, "Sexual McCarthyism," *Washington Post*, March 18, 1986, A19.

30. See David Scribman, "Persistent Questions About Discrepancies on Hart Background," *New York Times*, March 24, 1984, A28.

31. On this point, see also Judis, "The Hart Affair."

32. As explained in the previous chapter, some reporters had had more direct confirmation of Hart's womanizing, and for them the charges had a firmer foundation.

33. See Martha Brannigan and Michael Allen, "Anatomy of Story on Presidential Candidate's Weekend," *Wall Street Journal*, May 6, 1987, 6.

34. Peterson, an outstanding reporter known for his devotion to high journalistic standards, said he did not think the story was "solid enough" to warrant interrupting Hart and his wife late at night, especially because it was their first chance to meet privately since the Rice story broke. "I'm a Midwesterner. . . . I've got a very strong sense of right and wrong, and that was beyond the line," commented Peterson. In addition, Peterson claimed the detective had not surveilled the woman's apartment for the entire night on the evening when Hart was alleged to be inside. "Shades of the *Miami Herald!* Did we want to repeat the same mistake again?" won-

dered Peterson. Incidentally, Peterson had feared that his refusal to cooperate with the *Post*'s Paul Taylor in New Hampshire would cost him his job, but in fact, his colleagues were understanding and supportive, not only at the time but through a long and painful bout with lung cancer. Five days after my second interview with Peterson in July 1990, he succumbed to the disease at the age of forty-seven.

35. This theory was set forth, for example, in Hendrik Hertzberg, "Sporting News," *The New Republic* 199 (June 15, 1987): 42.

36. See Germond and Witcover, *Whose Broad Stripes and Bright Stars?* pp. 203–9.

37. Hart refused to answer Taylor's questions, as well as this one from Tom Oliphant of the *Boston Globe*: "Except for the times you and your wife were separated, has your marriage been monogamous?"

38. Paul Taylor, "Asking Gary Hart the Question He Asked For," *New York Times* (letter to the editor), May 22, 1987, A30.

39. William Dixon, as quoted in an AP dispatch from Boston on July 14, 1987.

40. Phil Gailey, "Presidential Hopefuls Uneasy About Questions on Adultery," *New York Times*, May 14, 1987, A1.

41. See Michael Wines, "In Bed with the Press," *Washington Journalism Review* 9 (September 1987): 17. In 1990 the *Arkansas Gazette* followed the *New York Times*'s precedent by asking each candidate for governor whether he had ever used illegal drugs or engaged in extramarital sex (in addition to requests for tax returns, medical records, and financial data). The sex question was dropped before all candidates were polled. See *Hotline* 3 (March 15, 1990): 5–6.

42. Dennis King, *Lyndon LaRouche and the New American Fascism* (Garden City, N.Y.: Doubleday, 1989). See especially pp. 121–22.

43. Rowland Evans and Robert Novak, "Behind Those Dukakis Rumors," *Washington Post*, August 8, 1988, A13. Reporters from six major news organizations (all three networks, the *Washington Post*, *U.S. News & World Report*, and the *Los Angeles Times*) told us they had been contacted by Bush operatives about the rumor—and in addition, they knew of colleagues at other outlets who had also been called. See also Thomas B. Rosenstiel and Paul Houston, "Rumor Mill: The Media Try to Cope," *Los Angeles Times*, August 5, 1988, 1, 18.

44. Several reporters mentioned this rife speculation during interviews. Evans and Novak, "Behind Those Dukakis Rumors," also included a reference to it in their column.

45. By Ralph Z. Hallow and Amy Bayer, A1, 6.

46. "Invalid?!" *Washington Times* editorial, August 5, 1988, F2. This editorial was more explicit; the August 2 story made a brief reference to the aide's unsolicited call, however.

47. By Amy Bayer and Gene Grabowski, August 4, 1988, A1, 8.

48. *Columbia Journalism Review* 27 (January/ February 1989): 21.

49. Rosenstiel and Houston, "Rumor Mill," p. 18.

50. See Edward Walsh, "Dukakis Acts to Kill Rumor," *Washington Post*, August 4, 1988, A1, 6.

51. Gerald M. Boyd, "Doctor Describes Bush As 'Active and Healthy,'" *New York Times*, August 6, 1988, A7.

52. Larry J. Sabato, *The 1988 Election in America: The Change That Masks Continuity* (Glenview, Ill.: Scott Foresman, 1989), pp. 24–27, 43–46.

53. Another Massachusetts-based incident also fed the Dukakis rumor. A past president of the state psychiatric society, who had owned an upscale mental health clinic, possessed land that was chosen by the Dukakis administration as the site for a new prison building—guaranteeing the landowner a handsome profit. The FBI had been investigating whether special favors were involved, and this apparently encouraged groundless speculation that the owner was being paid off for covering up

Dukakis's medical history. (The FBI dropped the investigation, incidentally.) See Jonathan Alter, "The High Velocity Rumor Mill," *Newsweek* 112 (August 15, 1988): 22.

54. Conservative Ed King ousted the one-term governor in a Democratic primary; Dukakis had his revenge four years later when he staged a successful comeback and defeated King to regain the statehouse.

55. Andrew Rosenthal, "Dukakis Releases Medical Details to Stop Rumors on Mental Health," *New York Times*, August 4, 1988, A1, D20.

56. Dennis King, in *Lyndon LaRouche*, p. 122, commented upon "the usual [media] reluctance to cover anything relating to LaRouche."

57. The network Quayle coverage on evening news shows, August 18–27, 1988, compiled by my research assistant Leslie Greenwald from Vanderbilt University's *Television News Index and Abstracts* (Nashville, Tenn.: Vanderbilt Television News Archive, August 1988), was as follows:

NETWORK	TOTAL NUMBER OF QUAYLE STORIES	TOTAL QUAYLE MINUTES	TOTAL LEAD* MINUTES FOR QUAYLE	PERCENTAGE OF TOTAL CAMPAIGN COVERAGE DEVOTED TO QUAYLE
ABC	22	49:50	35:00	85.5
CBS	20	42:50	32:40	67.5
NBC	18	38:20	30:20	68.2

*"Lead" means the first item on the evening news.

58. See also Richard E. Cohen, "Prime Time," *National Journal* (September 3, 1988): 2221. For an assessment of Quayle's U.S. House and Senate careers, see Richard F. Fenno, Jr., *The Making of a Senator: Dan Quayle* (Washington, D.C.: Congressional Quarterly Press, 1988). Fenno also offers a revealing commentary on the press's portrayal of Quayle's career in his book, *Watching Politicians: Essays on Participant Observation* (Berkeley: Institute of Governmental Studies, University of California at Berkeley, 1990), pp. 27–54.

59. Quayle's official 1988 financial statements showed his assets amounted to between $859,700 and $1.2 million.

60. Retired Major General Wendell C. Phillippi, a former senior official of the Indiana National Guard, admitted that he was contacted by Quayle in 1969 and called Alfred F. Ahner, a ranking officer in the guard. Phillippi was then managing editor of the *Indianapolis News*, a paper owned by Quayle's grandfather. Ahner denied giving Quayle any preferential treatment, and guard vacancies apparently existed at the time of Quayle's application. Ahner and many others noted that calls from former guard officials such as Phillippi seeking help for guard applicants were quite common in the Vietnam era. Undoubtedly Quayle received extra attention because of Phillippi's rank, and his swearing-in may have been expedited as well. But, as CNN's Frank Sesno notes, "The family connections Quayle used were probably little different than those employed by other relatively well-connected, upper-middle class families at the time." See Michael Isikoff and Joe Pichirallo, "The Quayle Furor: Questions Linger," *Washington Post*, August 26, 1988, A1, 6.

61. Beth Barrett and Mark Barnhill, "Former Lobbyist's Lawyers Say She Told FBI He Asked for Sex," *Los Angeles Daily News*, August 23, 1988, 1.

62. Lois Romano, "Parkinson Silent on Quayle Trip," *Washington Post*, August 18, 1988, C2; Michael Isikoff and Joe Pichirallo, "Allegations Called 'Lies' by Quayle," *Washington Post*, August 24, 1988, A1.

63. The network reports aired on August 23, 1988.

64. Engberg makes a valid point when he notes, "In investigative reporting

we're rarely involved with witnesses who are the kind of people you'd want to invite to your sister's wedding. Individuals with checkered pasts are frequently the only ones in the room." But caution is in order when dealing with such people; they are sometimes schemers and manipulators well trained in the media arts.

65. See David Rogers, "Bush Campaign Manager Atwater, Often Viewed as Rough Tactician, Now Can Take Lower Profile," *Wall Street Journal*, August 11, 1988, 54. While mortally ill with an inoperable brain tumor in 1990, Atwater wrote Turnipseed a letter of apology and asked for forgiveness.

66. Atwater gave us a similar and even more colorful exclamation during an interview.

67. Interviewed journalists who were assigned to the chase were not willing to say flatly that Quayle was innocent, of course, since few rumors of this sort can ever be completely disproved. Nevertheless, most would agree with Phil Jones of CBS, who went to South Carolina in search of the rumor and "looked into it in depth; no other reporter got as far as I did. And if we had had a story, we would have put it on the air. We didn't have a story."

68. The attorney is not included in this number; he had never heard of "Dawn" until one of Jenrette's closest aides called him and mentioned the name in the middle of this flap.

69. The best recollection of Indiana political observers and Bayh campaign veterans is that the rumor never surfaced on the air or in print in 1980. Indeed, the Bayh campaign appears to have had no hard evidence that the plagiarism had occurred.

70. See Kirk Johnson, "Some Say Politics Tints How Quayle Is Recalled," *New York Times*, August 23, 1988, A16.

71. David Rogers and Jeffrey H. Birnbaum, "Quayle Family Contacts Helped Him Avoid Draft," *Wall Street Journal*, August 19, 1988, 38.

72. Jill Abramson and James B. Stewart, "Quayle Initially Failed a Major Exam at DePauw, Former School Official Says," *Wall Street Journal*, August 23, 1988, 54.

73. See Lisa Belkin, "Quayle Fields Another Question About Admission to Law School," *New York Times*, September 10, 1988, A8. The Cleveland *Plain Dealer* had broken the story the previous day. See Keith C. Epstein and Bill Sloat, "Special Deal for Quayle," *Plain Dealer*, September 9, 1988, A1.

74. In fact, Bill Sloat of the *Plain Dealer* had done a great deal of investigative work on the subject. He notes that the National Guard attendance records showed Quayle on duty the day of the bar exam, but after further research he concluded that Quayle was most likely at the exam, whatever the guard records showed.

75. Most rumors on the DePauw campus persisting to the current day stem partly from Quayle's refusal to release his transcript, which would contain not just grades but also notations about disciplinary actions taken against him or courses he was forced to drop by the instructor—the latter a penalty used in Quayle's day for plagiarizers. (Any such "DR"—that is, "drop"—designation on his transcript would undoubtedly trigger an immediate frenzy.)

76. The interview was conducted on Wednesday evening, August 17, 1989.

77. Douglas Frantz, "Hypnosis: 'Parlor trick' Entrances the Courts," *Chicago Tribune*, February 7, 1982, A6.

78. See Aaron Friewald, "Isolation for Inmate with Quayle Claims," *Legal Times*, December 19, 1988, 1. See also Norman Solomon, "Quayle Bait," *San Francisco Bay Guardian*, May 30, 1990, A21.

79. However, Atwater told us that he was not pleased with the confinement decision: "I remember thinking, 'Oh shit, that's the worst fucking thing that can happen.' "

80. Aaron Friewald, "Prisons Director Defends Quayle Accuser's Isolation," *Legal Times*, January 30, 1989, 1.

81. Michael Isikoff, "Official Had Quayle Accuser Detained," *Washington Post*,

July 4, 1990, A9. See also Norman Solomon, "Court Battle Over Quayle Pot Connection Gets Underway," *San Francisco Bay Guardian,* July 11, 1990, A9.

82. Mark Hosenball and Michael Isikoff, "Pssst: Inside Washington's Rumor Mill," *The New Republic* 200 (January 2, 1989): 16–19. Associated Press editors in Oklahoma City and New York wisely decided to keep the story off the wire, although their decision has been criticized; see Martin A. Lee and Norman Solomon, *Unreliable Sources* (New York: Lyle Stuart, 1990), pp. 162–167.

83. "Quayle Watch: Jailhouse Politics?" *Newsweek* 115 (April 2, 1990): 5.

84. Benjamin Weiser and Janet Cooke, "Anatomy of a Washington Rumor," *Washington Post,* March 22, 1981, A1, 14.

85. Cooke actually received the Pulitzer Prize for the series, which she returned after the truth emerged. See Tom Goldstein, *The News at Any Cost* (New York: Simon & Schuster, 1985), pp. 215–17. Incidentally, after Cooke's fraud was exposed, Benjamin Weiser said he and "every other reporter who ever did a story with her" went back and "double-checked the facts." Notes Weiser: "I cannot speak for other reporters, but in my case, looking back at the Bush story, I can tell you that everything in there I can vouch for."

86. See David Hoffman, "George Bush—Man and Politician" (multipart series), *Washington Post,* August 12, 1988, A1, 10–11.

87. See Bob Woodward and Walter Pincus, "George Bush—Man and Politician" (multipart series), *Washington Post,* August 10, 1988, A1, 8.

88. "Bush and the 'Big A' Question," *Newsweek* 111 (June 29, 1987): 6.

89. Richard Ryan, "The Covert George Bush: The Mistress Question," *L.A. Weekly,* October 14–20, 1988, pp. 1, 21, 39, 48.

90. Hosenball and Isikoff, "Pssst."

91. Many political reporters seem to lean to the Democratic scenario, while business reporters suspect that the alternate explanations are more likely. But no one we interviewed has any real evidence that would support one theory over another. *Washington Post* executive editor Benjamin Bradlee offered to buy dinner for any reporter who could find an investor who made a substantial amount of money off the rumor, but no one was able to collect.

92. Paul Blustein, "False Rumor of Post Story Batters Stocks," *Washington Post,* October 20, 1988, E1.

93. Michael K. Frisby, "Dukakis Aide Quits for Remarks on Bush," *Boston Globe,* October 21, 1988, 1.

94. See Eleanor Randolph, "Bush Rumor Created Dilemma for Media," *Washington Post,* October 22, 1988, A9.

95. See also Walter Pincus, "The Story That Wasn't There," *Washington Post,* December 8, 1988, A26.

96. Maralee Schwartz, Ann Devroy, and Gwen Ifill, "Bush Office Aide Expected to Get a Protocol Post," *Washington Post,* January 10, 1989, A21.

97. Jayne O'Donnell, "So Where the Heck Was George? Not Meeting With Ex-CIA Chiefs," *The Washingtonian* 24 (November 1988): 21.

98. Jack Anderson and Dale Van Atta, "Bush Friend Gingerly Investigated," *Washington Post,* April 17, 1990, D14.

99. My research assistant Miguel Monteverde conducted many of the interviews for this section and prepared a briefing paper that served as a first draft for parts of this discussion.

100. A thorough review of the Tower nomination fight is beyond our scope here. See instead Tom Morgenthau, "Tower's Troubles," *Newsweek* 113 (March 6, 1989): 16–22; Committee on Armed Services, U.S. Senate (101st Congress, 1st session), *Hearings on Nomination of John G. Tower to Be Secretary of Defense* (January 25, 26, 31, February 1, 23, 1989) (Washington, D.C.: U.S. Government Printing Office, 1989); Helen Dewar, "Senate Kills Tower's Nomination as Defense Chief, 53–

47," *Washington Post*, March 19, 1989, A1, 16. Tower's own reflections are contained in his book, *Consequences: A Personal and Political Memoir* (Boston: Little, Brown, 1991).

101. Andrea Mitchell was one of several reporters—another was Andrew Rosenthal of the *New York Times*—who distinguished themselves by deciding against the broadcast or publication of sensational rumors that could not be adequately substantiated, even when rival news organizations used them. For example, Mitchell was approached by a source who spoke of Tower's alleged personal misconduct while representing the United States at arms negotiations in Geneva in the 1980s. After thorough investigation, Mitchell and NBC chose not to use the story because:

It came down to the issue of whether this was at all relevant to his public performance of duty. . . . I talked to other members of the U.S. delegation . . . many of whom did not like him and felt that he was immoral, but all of them said it wasn't applicable to his performance of duty.

102. Transcripts of all ABC, CBS, and NBC evening news broadcasts on the Tower nomination between January 25, 1989, and March 10, 1989, were reviewed for this study.

103. "CBS Evening News," February 7, 1989.

104. "CBS Evening News," February 8, 1989.

105. "CBS Evening News," February 17, 1989.

106. See Ann Devroy, "The Tower 'Sightings,' " *Washington Post*, February 24, 1989, A1, 9.

107. Ibid.

108. Bob Woodward, "Incidents at Defense Base Cited: Drunkenness, Harassment of Women Alleged," *Washington Post*, March 2, 1989, A1, 27.

109. Dan Balz and Bob Woodward, "Allegations About Visit to Base Challenged," *Washington Post*, March 3, 1989, A1, 16.

110. However, Woodward is still not ready to issue a complete mea culpa: "It's still not clear to me whether this guy [the Air Force officer] has a mental problem or not, and in fact the records don't say it." Dan Howard responds by explaining that the records are deceptive because the officer was "allowed to retire, supposedly with problems in his knees," as a face-saving measure.

111. Howard cites an excellent example in the speech outlining views on defense matters that Tower gave to the National Press Club on March 1, 1989:

I had spent enough time with [Tower] to know that he was a very intelligent man, that he knew NATO and European politics extraordinarily well and he knew a lot about the military, and I wanted to get some of that aired. So he gave a speech for the National Press Club that had a great deal of content about his thinking on defense. And we knew going in that almost all the news stories would center on the Q and A afterward and would probably be on matters other than the speech, but we had to make a try. He gave a hell of a speech, but none of the news stories referred to any of the content. None of the questions following the speech referred to the content. The press didn't give a damn what his qualifications were or what his views were on the future of the alliance, or whatever. It was all back on the scandals.

112. A high Bush administration official who has known Tower for years and who worked diligently for Tower's confirmation also acknowledged to us the basic truth of Tower's womanizing: "Every time I saw the guy, he was trying to get laid."

113. For background, see Janet Hook, "Passion, Defiance, Tears: Jim Wright Bows Out," *Congressional Quarterly Weekly* 47 (June 3, 1989): 1289–95; and Chuck Alston, "Smear Tactics Overshadow Election of New Speaker," *Congressional Quarterly Weekly* 47 (June 10, 1989): 1373–75.

114. *Time*'s Ted Gup, who has written about the subject of homosexuality and

politics, had "heard rumors about Foley being gay for years" but, like other journalists, had never taken the gossip seriously.

115. After the aide's shenanigans were exposed, Gingrich applied a rather light penalty: suspension without pay if she did it again.

116. Rowland Evans and Robert Novak, "Democrats and the Perils of Regicide," *Washington Post*, May 15, 1989, A17. The newsletter, called "Memorandum," was published on April 26 by Horace Busby, a former top aide to President Lyndon B. Johnson.

117. Fred Barnes, "Musical Chairs," *The New Republic* 202 (June 12, 1989): 14–15. Despite its listed publication date, the magazine was actually on the newsstands several weeks earlier.

118. The program aired May 29, 1989. See *Hotline* 2 (May 30, 1989): 14–15.

119. Ibid. Coelho, of course, answered no.

120. Lars-Erik Nelson, "Newt Tastes Blood and Has Feeding Frenzy," *New York Daily News*, June 5, 1989, p. 27.

121. Typical was the front-page headline in the *Boston Globe* on June 6, 1989: FOLEY BECOMES HOUSE SPEAKER; GOP IS RAPPED FOR RUMORS.

122. The declaration came during a CNN interview on June 7, 1989. Foley cited his twenty-one-year marriage.

123. This is another example of the way reporters facilitate the spread of rumor and political intelligence. In many cases, of course, this is an unavoidable by-product of a journalist's necessary attempt to determine the truth of information he or she has received.

124. Tom Kenworthy and Don Phillips, "Foley Elected Speaker of House," *Washington Post*, June 7, 1989, A4.

125. "NBC Nightly News," June 6, 1989.

126. "NBC Nightly News," June 7 and 8, 1989.

127. According to Cokie Roberts, the young homosexual had been interviewed by the FBI in connection with an earlier investigation of Maryland Democratic Congressman Roy Dyson's staff-hiring practices. Dyson's administrative assistant had advertised for male staff aides and made unusual after-hours demands on them; he committed suicide the morning the *Washington Post* published an article about it all. See Eric Pianin and Robert Barnes, "Ex-Dyson Aides Recall Unorthodox Demands," *Washington Post*, May 1, 1988, A1, 33.

128. The FBI report, mentioned ibid., was apparently also in the hands of the U.S. House sergeant at arms. See the earlier discussion in this section.

129. Gloria Borger, "Anatomy of a Smear," *U.S. News & World Report* 106 (June 19, 1989): 40–41. See also Dan Balz and Ann Devroy, "Fallout from Foley Memo Puts Atwater on Defensive," *Washington Post*, July 3, 1989, A1, 4.

Chapter 6. Frenzies That Weren't

1. Doris A. Graber, "Press and TV as Opinion Resources in Presidential Campaigns," *Public Opinion Quarterly* 40 (Fall 1976): 285–303, especially table 6, p. 298. For discussions of the reasons behind the press's laggard performance on Watergate, see Ben H. Bagdikian, "The Fruits of Agnewism," *Columbia Journalism Review* 11 (January/February 1973): 9–21; and Jules Witcover, "The Trials of a One-Candidate Campaign," *Columbia Journalism Review* 11 (January/February 1973): 24–28. The role played by competition in Watergate coverage was discussed in chap. 3.

2. See Harrison Salisbury, *Without Fear or Favor* (New York: New York Times Books, 1980), p. 433.

3. Quoted in American Press Institute, *Covering the Candidates: Role and Responsibilities of the Press* (Reston, Va.: American Press Institute, 1987), pp. 50–51.

4. Goodwin admitted, "Any [editor] would have fired me . . . If you put histo-

rians in reporters' shoes, I'm not sure how long we'd last there." Goodwin's humble observation certainly applies to political scientists as well.

5. See David Gelman, "The Great Playboy Furor," *Newsweek* 88 (October 4, 1976): 70.

6. Norman Mailer, "The Search for Carter," *Sunday Times Magazine*, September 26, 1976, 19.

7. James M. Perry, "Senator's Start," *Wall Street Journal*, March 13, 1984, A1, 20.

8. Patti Reagan was born seven months after her parents' marriage. Nancy Reagan admitted the birth was "precipitous" in her memoirs published after President Reagan's retirement in 1989. See Nancy Reagan, *My Turn: The Memoirs of Nancy Reagan* (with William Novak) (New York: Random House, 1989). It is true that the subject seems more relevant for a born-again preacher like Robertson than for an ex-denizen of hedonistic Hollywood like Reagan. But Reagan campaigned in 1980 as a "family values" candidate who was the darling of many Christian evangelicals.

9. See Ted Gup, "Identifying Homosexuals: What Are the Rules?" *Washington Journalism Review* 10 (October 1988): 30.

10. See the excellent account of the press conference and its aftermath in Glenn R. Simpson and Craig Winneker, "What to Do When Members Are Cited As Homosexuals," *Roll Call*, June 4, 1990, pp. 14, 16. Simpson and Winneker also suggest a thoughtful framework for reporting about politicians' private lives that is similar to some of the recommendations made later in chap. 8.

11. See Benjamin Weiser, "Gay Activists Divided on Whether to 'Bring Out' Politicians," *Washington Post*, September 19, 1989, A4; Valerie Richardson, "Gay Activists Drag 'Hypocrites' Out of Closet," *Washington Times*, September 20, 1989, A5. See also Eleanor Randolph, "The Media, at Odds Over 'Outing' of Gays," *Washington Post*, July 13, 1990, C1, 4.

12. See *Hotline* 3 (June 6, 1990): 6–7 and (June 7, 1990): 7. The candidate chose not to comment, citing privacy rights.

13. For an example of discreet and responsible handling of "outing," see the policy set forth in Alan K. Ota, "Outing: Practice puts press on spot," *The Sunday Oregonian*, June 24, 1990, M1. A different but exceptionally instructive case of press discretion in a situation involving homosexuality occurred in Mississippi in 1983. The leading candidate for governor, Democrat Bill Allain, was accused of buying sex from male prostitutes just two weeks before the election. Despite the prostitutes' sworn affidavits and passed lie-detector tests, most media outlets were exceptionally cautious in their handling of the material, and they refused numerous opportunities to sensationalize a blockbuster story. Allain denied all charges and won the election handily. See Curtis Wilkie, "Too Hot to Handle," *Washington Journalism Review* 6 (March 1984): 38–39, 58.

14. See Rose Ellen O'Connor, "Robb Enjoyed Glitzy Va. Beach Social Scene," *Virginian-Pilot* and *Ledger-Star*, August 28, 1988. A1, 6.

15. The businessman resisted going on the record at the time because of fears of potential financial ruin from retribution by Robb supporters or a politically inspired tax investigation. He was motivated to approach the newspaper because he was incensed that "the number one law enforcer in the state of Virginia [was] watching this go on," and then denied knowledge of it later. The author personally examined the affidavit and interviewed the businessman as background for the discussion in this section. He claims to be a Democrat who voted for Robb in his successful gubernatorial bid in 1981 (while supporting Republican presidential candidates since 1980). He also insists that when he saw Robb at the Christmas party, Robb "had to know what was going on; either that, or he was blind." The businessman finally allowed his name to be used in an NBC News "Exposé" segment on Robb aired April 28, 1991. Incidentally, the *Virginian-Pilot* interviewed many other individuals who offered testimony about the prominent presence of drugs at the beach parties as well as Robb's

association with women other than his wife. But many of these people, unlike the businessman, were of dubious reputation. While one should not discount their claims on this basis alone—see CBS News's Eric Engberg's comments in note 64 of chapter 5 above—a newspaper's readership is unlikely to be convinced by such testimony, and may well be offended by it.

16. I questioned Robb closely on this point, especially since he suffered from cataracts in both eyes. When I suggested that he might have been unable to see any cocaine near him, he responded emphatically that his vision "wasn't *that* impaired." Robb later added that, while he was "not even quite sure" how people went about ingesting cocaine, if he had seen someone line up white powder and put it in his or her nose, "I would know that that was very funny behavior because . . . that's not the way most people either eat or . . . smoke a cigarette. Yes, I would know that was very strange behavior." Robb also insisted, "In my now-fifty-one years I have never seen drugs, except what I see in television and news pictures."

17. Robert S. Lichter, Daniel Amundson, and Richard Noyes, *The Video Campaign: Network Coverage of the 1988 Primaries* (Washington: American Enterprise Institute, 1988).

18. Jackson pointed out that he had never fibbed about his wedding date, as had Robertson, though Robertson's frenzy was at least as much about "preacher hypocrisy" as his attempted cover-up.

19. See David S. Broder, *Behind the Front Page*, pp. 247–50.

20. Barbara A. Reynolds, *Jesse Jackson: The Man, the Movement, the Myth* (Chicago: Nelson-Hall, 1975) pp. 418–19.

21. See Elizabeth O. Colton, *The Jackson Phenomenon* (Garden City, N.Y.: Doubleday, 1989), pp. 82, 125–26.

22. Kidder turned from the Jackson aide to the CNN crew and reportedly said, "Oh shit—the press is here. I'm not supposed to say things like that."

23. See Painton's three-page profile of Jackson, in which all the intimations about his private life are relegated to the tail end of the massive article. Priscilla Painton, "Jackson's Charisma, Principles Winning Converts, But Contradictions Linger," *Atlanta Constitution*, October 19, 1987, A1, 6. While de-emphasized by its placement, this section of Painton's article includes the following passage:

Reports that Jackson has had affairs have dogged him all of his married life. . . . In the last four years, he's been tied to two prominent women in Washington-based black organizations, as well as a woman now involved in his campaign.

Several people who have been close to Jackson over the years—including a former top aide—say privately that they know many of the stories to be true.

24. The program aired Sunday, October 11, 1987. At the outset, Mrs. Jackie Jackson told Wallace she would "not discuss certain vulgar questions," and Wallace desisted after ascertaining that she never "worried" when Reverend Jackson was "on the road." Later Wallace asked the candidate about his "personal morality" in light of Gary Hart's withdrawal; Jackson sidestepped the question and Wallace did not follow up.

25. As quoted in Julia Malone, "Jackson Queried on 'Gary Hart Problem,' " *Atlanta Constitution*, June 6, 1987, A16.

26. As quoted in Colton, *The Jackson Phenomenon*, p. 126.

27. This press fear extends to other situations and minority groups. Alfredo Corchado of the *Wall Street Journal* said some journalists for national and local publications who contacted him about San Antonio Mayor Henry Cisneros's extramarital affair were reluctant to publish anything about America's leading Hispanic politician lest they "be perceived as ethnic bashing." And when the *Washington Post* was accused of antiblack bias in its coverage of the African-American community in the mid-1980s, the executive editor publicly apologized for the offense given, and the publisher pledged that the paper would show more "sensitivity" to black concerns. In the wake of these *mea culpas*, more than a dozen articles critical of black Mayor

Marion Barry were de-emphasized, delayed, or killed entirely. See Crocker Coulson, "Pulling Punches," *The New Republic* 196 (May 25, 1987): 10–12.

28. Chicago Mayor Harold Washington, Washington Mayor Marion Barry, and U.S. Representative Gus Savage (D., Ill.), among many others, have attacked the press for racism when their conduct was questioned. See Douglas Frantz and Mitchell Locin, "Irate Washington retaliates," *Chicago Tribune*, April 8, 1983, 2; Eric Pianin, "Barry Defends Integrity, Denies Drug Use," *Washington Post*, March 17, 1983, A32; Jim McGee, "Peace Corps Worker Alleges Rep. Savage Assaulted Her," *Washington Post*, July 19, 1989, A8.

29. See the discussion of press bias in chapter 3. Also see Robert S. Lichter, Stanley Rothman, and Linda S. Lichter, *The Media Elite* (Bethesda, Md.: Adler and Adler, 1986), pp. 64–65.

30. See Dom Bonafede, "Blame the Scribes," *National Journal* 20 (July 9, 1988): 1803–6.

31. For instance, Jack Germond cited some "wild defense-spending figures" used by Jackson in a 1984 New Hampshire Democratic debate at Dartmouth University, where neither the candidates during the debate nor the press afterwards bothered to correct Jackson.

32. Quoted in Monica Langley, "Hart Campaign Debacle Prompts Media Debate About Whether a Politician's Sex Life Is News," *Wall Street Journal*, July 27, 1987, 44.

33. David Maraniss, "Jackson: Playing to the Camera," *Washington Post*, December 27, 1987, A8–9.

34. The American Society of Newspaper Editors compiled these figures on minority employment in 1990.

35. Kirk Victor, "Slanted Views," *National Journal* 20 (June 4, 1988): 1512.

36. Quoted in American Press Institute, *Covering the Candidates*, p. 37.

Chapter 7. Consequences

1. See Joe McGinniss, *The Selling of the President 1968* (New York: Trident, 1969).

2. See Alessandra Stanley and Maureen Dowd, "The Dweebs on the Bus," *Gentleman's Quarterly* 57 (September 1988): 486.

3. Times-Mirror Center for the People and the Press, "The People and the Press, Part 5: Attitudes Toward News Organizations," conducted by the Gallup Organization in August to October, 1989. Unless otherwise noted, the survey findings cited below are from the Times-Mirror study.

4. The panelback Gallup telephone survey of 2,022 registered voters was taken November 9–10, 1988 (margin of error: plus or minus 2.5 percent). The question and results were:

"Students are often given the grades A, B, C, D, or Fail to describe the quality of their work. Looking back over the campaign, what grade would you give to each of the following groups for the way they conducted themselves in the campaign?"

| | A | B | C | D | FAIL |
	%	%	%	%	%
The voters	19	30	28	10	7
George Bush	15	34	26	13	11
Republican Party	11	34	31	12	10
Pollsters	13	29	29	12	11
Michael Dukakis	9	29	40	13	7
Democratic Party	7	26	45	13	7
Campaign consultants	5	20	37	14	8
The press	8	22	33	19	16

5. Eleven percent gave another answer; Gallup random-sample telephone poll for *Newsweek* taken October 20–21, 1988, with 1,013 registered voters in the sample (margin of error: plus or minus 3 percent).

6. Random-sample telephone survey of 506 adults conducted June 1, 1989 by Yankelovich Clancy Shulman for *Time* and CNN (margin of error: plus or minus 4.5 percent).

7. Times-Mirror Center for the People and the Press, "The People and the Press," part I: "Attitudes Toward the News Media," conducted by the Gallup Organization in January 1986. See especially pp. 35–36.

8. Only 66 percent agreed with the First Amendment when it was read to them blind, without identification as part of the Constitution; 15 percent flatly disagreed, 14 percent "haven't heard enough to say," and 5 percent were not sure. This was a random-sample telephone survey of 2,217 adults conducted nationwide from September 14–19, 1989 (margin of error: 2.5 percent).

9. Times-Mirror Center, "The People and the Press," part 5. About 48 percent chose each contrasting statement, with 4 percent expressing no opinion.

10. A. M. Rosenthal, "Special to the Miami Herald," *New York Times*, May 7, 1987, A35.

11. Thomas E. Patterson, "The Press and Its Missed Assignment," in Michael Nelson, ed., *The Elections of 1988* (Washington, D.C.: Congressional Quarterly Press, 1989), p. 103.

12. See, for example, the *Washington Post*–ABC News poll in Ann Devroy, "Quayle Still Seen Unqualified to Assume Presidency," *Washington Post*, August 16, 1989, A4.

13. Several of our interviewees suggested that Quayle's academic controversies will be revived, if not in 1992 when he will presumably seek reelection as vice president, then in 1996 during a run for the presidency.

14. William Boot, "Campaign '88: TV Overdoses on the Inside Dope," *Columbia Journalism Review* 27 (January/February 1989): 23.

15. See Shanto Iyengar and Donald R. Kinder, *News That Matters* (Chicago: University of Chicago Press, 1987); Thomas E. Patterson, *The Mass Media Election* (New York: Praeger, 1980); Press and VerBurg, *American Politicians*, pp. 62–66; Shanto Iyengar, Mark D. Peters, and Donald Kinder, "Experimental Demonstrations of the 'Not So Minimal' Consequences of Television News Programs," *American Political Science Review* 76 (December 1982): 848–58; and Roy L. Behr and Shanto Iyengar, "Television News and Real-World Cues and Changes in the Public Agenda," *Public Opinion Quarterly* 49 (Spring 1985): 38–57.

16. Alas, the deepening American cynicism is not restricted to politics. See Donald Kanter and Phillip Mirvis, *The Cynical Americans* (San Francisco: Jossey-Bass, 1989).

17. In addition to those mentioned below, see Austin Ranney, *Channels of Power: The Impact of Television on American Politics* (New York: Basic Books, 1983), pp. 75–79.

18. The exact wording of Gallup's question, and the percentages recorded by each major-party nominee, are as follows:

All persons in the survey were handed a card and asked: "You will note that the ten boxes on this scale go from the highest position of +5 for someone you have a very favorable opinion of all the way down to the lowest position of −5 for someone you have a very unfavorable opinion of. How far up or down the scale would you rate [nominee] and [nominee]?"

HIGHLY FAVORABLE RATINGS
(+5, +4)

AUGUST 1952		AUGUST 1972	
Eisenhower	47%	Nixon	40%
Stevenson	37	McGovern	23
	84		63

AUGUST 1956		SEPTEMBER 1976	
Eisenhower	66%	Carter	41%
Stevenson	28	Ford	28
	94		69
AUGUST 1960		AUGUST 1980	
Nixon	38%	Reagan	31%
Kennedy	39	Carter	20
	77		51
AUGUST 1964		JULY 27–30, 1984	
Johnson	55%	Reagan	42%
Goldwater	21	Mondale	26
	76		68
SEPTEMBER 1968		AUGUST 24–25, 1988	
Nixon	38%	Bush	25%
Humphrey	25	Dukakis	17
	63		42

SOURCE: George Gallup, *The Gallup Poll* (Wilmington, Del.: Scholarly Resources, Inc., 1985), p. 150. The August 1988 figures were obtained directly from the Gallup Organization.

Note that for 1988, Gallup used telephone rather than in-person surveying, and consequently changed its scale to four verbal response choices (very favorable, mostly favorable, mostly unfavorable, and very unfavorable). Under this new system the "very favorable" response is the rough (but not exact) equivalent of the previous +4, +5 scores.

19. Random-sample telephone survey of 2,160 adults nationwide conducted from April 22–25, 1989 (margin of error: plus or minus 3 percent).

20. Random-sample telephone survey of 750 adults nationwide conducted June 1–2, 1989 by the Gallup Organization. (Margin of error: plus or minus 4 percent). 39 percent said ethical conduct had declined, 8 percent said it had improved, and 50 percent said it had stayed about the same.

21. James K. Glassman, "The 'Ethics' Frenzy," *Washington Post*, May 28, 1989, B1, 2.

22. See R. Jeffrey Smith, "How Valid Is Nunn's Ethical Line in Dust?," *Washington Post*, March 3, 1989, A17; and George F. Will, "... With Empty Cartridges," *Washington Post*, March 1, 1989, A23.

23. A brief discussion of this incident appears on p. 42.

24. T. R. Reid, "Hart Creates Mini-Flap on Campaign Day 2: Reporters Seize on Rumor-Monger Comment," *Washington Post*, April 15, 1987, A11.

25. Louis D. Brandeis and Samuel D. Warren, "The Right to Privacy," *Harvard Law Review* 4 (December 15, 1890): 196.

26. On this general subject, see also Laurence I. Barrett, "Rethinking the Fair Game Rules," *Time* 130 (November 30, 1987): 76, 78; Richard Cohen, "The Vice of Virtue," *Washington Post*, March 10, 1989, A25; Charles Krauthammer, "Political Potshots," *Washington Post*, March 1, 1989, A23; Norman Ornstein, "The Post's Campaign to Wreck Congress," May 29, 1989, A25; and "Ethicsgate," *Wall Street Journal* editorial, July 15, 1983, 26.

27. Increasing intrusiveness and scrutiny is also one factor in the lessened attractiveness of nonelective governmental service. See Lloyd M. Cutler, "Balancing the Ethics Code," *Washington Post*, March 13, 1989, A15; Ann Devroy, "Current Climate of Caution: Expanded FBI Checks Slow Confirmations," *Washington Post*, March 13, 1989, A1, 4–5.

28. See Richard E. Celeste and Dagmar I. Celeste, "The Celestes on Loving, Living," Cleveland *Plain Dealer*, July 7, 1987, A7.

Chapter 8. Remedies

1. In a letter to Thomas Seymour dated February 11, 1807.

2. Michael Kinsley, "No Sex Please, We're Journalists," *Washington Post*, November 17, 1988, A25.

3. Testimony at the Hearing on Congressional Ethics and the Role of the Media, U.S. House Bipartisan Task Force on Ethics, September 20, 1989, p. 244.

4. As quoted in Wayne King, "Hatcher to Head Effort Toward a Jackson Race," *New York Times*, June 6, 1987, A33.

5. See the comments of LBJ biographer Doris Kearns Goodwin in American Press Institute, *Covering the Candidates: Role and Responsibilities of the Press* (Reston, Va.: American Press Institute, 1987), pp. 44–47.

6. Incidents of Jackson's public rudeness to, and berating of, his staff are legion and well known to political journalists. For examples cited by former staff members themselves, see Elizabeth O. Colton, *The Jackson Phenomenon* (Garden City, N.Y.: Doubleday, 1989), pp. 23, 95, 98, 108, 143–45, 166, 173–77; and Donna Britt, "The Organizer, Up From the Chaos," *Washington Post*, October 7, 1989, C4. The latter case concerns ex-Jackson aide Donna Brazile.

7. See Priscilla Painton, "Jackson's Charisma, Principles Winning Converts, but Contradictions Linger," *Atlanta Constitution*, October 19, 1987, A1, 6.

8. This has already happened in Great Britain, where the private lives of some reporters and editors are considered fair game for exposure and comment. See, for example, Glenn Frankel, "In London, A Lust for Libel," *Washington Post*, January 31, 1990, C1, 9.

9. Downie's statement was printed in the following *Post* article: Laura Sessions Stepp and Bill Dedman, "Priest Urges Boycott of Post Advertisers," *Washington Post*, September 11, 1989, E3.

10. Virgil, *Aeneid* 4.175 (New York: St. Martin's Press, 1967), p. 72.

11. This was one of the *Washington Post*'s rules during Watergate.

12. As reviewed in chapter 5, columnists Evans and Novak, *Newsweek*'s Howard Fineman, and others performed the same service for Jack Kemp at various stages of his elongated ordeal.

13. See the similar but more general argument made by Walter Shapiro, "Is It Right to Publish Rumors?" *Time* 132 (July 10, 1989): 53.

14. See Broder, *Behind the Front Page*, pp. 106–7.

15. See Norman E. Isaacs, *Untended Gates: The Mismanaged Press* (New York: Columbia University Press, 1986), pp. 132–46.

16. M. L. Stein, "How Editors View Ombudsmen," *Editor and Publisher* 122 (May 13, 1989): 15–16.

17. Eugene J. McCarthy, "Press Undergoing Self-Examination: A Ridiculous Sight," *Roll Call* 35 (June 26–July 2, 1989): 20. I am also grateful to Professor Timothy E. Cook of Williams College and Warren Cikins of the Brookings Institution for their thoughts on the ombudsman concept.

18. The other *Post* ombudsmen were Ben Bagdikian, Robert Maynard, Charles Seib, Bill Green, Robert McCloskey, and Sam Zagoria.

19. See Isaacs, *Untended Gates*, chaps. 6 and 7; Doris A. Graber, *Mass Media and American Politics*, 3rd ed. (Washington, D.C.: Congressional Quarterly Press, 1989), pp. 369–70; and William A. Rusher, *The Coming Battle for the Media* (New York: William Morrow, 1988), pp. 115–18, 173–74.

20. Funding was also provided by the Markle Foundation.

21. Sandra Bramen, "Public Expectations of Media Versus Standards in Codes of Ethics," *Journalism Quarterly* 65 (Spring 1988): 71–77, 240 at pp. 72–73. See also Patricia I. Dooley, David Klaassen, and Richard Chapman, *A Guide to the Archives of the National News Council* (Minneapolis: Silha Center for the Study of Media Ethics and Law, 1986).

22. See Patrick Brogan, *Spiked: The Short Life and Death of the National News Council* (New York: Twentieth Century Fund, 1985).

23. There have already been calls for a renewed National News Council. See Norman Isaacs, *Untended Gates*, pp. 130–31; and Robert S. McCord, "Press and Ethics: Who's Looking at the Problem?" *Wall Street Journal*, July 3, 1987, 12. One state, Minnesota, hosts a news council that has operated since 1971. See Robert Schafer, "The Minnesota News Council: Developing Standards for Press Ethics," *Journalism Quarterly* 58 (Autumn 1981): 355–62.

24. David Broder, "Democracy and the Press," *Washington Post*, January 3, 1990, A15.

25. Roberts's father was the late Hale Boggs, Democratic Majority Leader of the U.S. House, and her mother is former Congresswoman Lindy Boggs (D., La.), who succeeded her husband in 1973 and served until her retirement in 1991.

26. See Marianne Means, "Why We Invited Richard Nixon to Dinner," *Washington Post*, January 14, 1989, A21.

27. See my *The Rise of Political Consultants* (New York: Basic Books, 1981), chap. 2. Among the media-related polling problems discussed is the tendency of news outlets to overstate the significance of each new poll, especially if their group has produced it.

28. See *Hotline* 3 (May 14, 1990): 22; David S. Broder, "Should News Media Police the Accuracy of Ads," *Washington Post*, January 19, 1989, A22. See also Randall Rothenberg, "Politics on TV: Too Fast, Too Loose?" *New York Times*, July 15, 1990, E1, 4; and Thomas B. Rosenstiel, "Policing Political TV Ads," *Los Angeles Times*, October 4, 1990, A1, 20, 21.

29. Kiku Adatto, "Sound Bite Democracy: Network Evening News Presidential Campaign Coverage, 1968 and 1988" (Cambridge, Mass.: Joan Shorenstein Barone Center, John F. Kennedy School, Harvard University, June 1990), tables 3 and 5, pp. 23, 25. The total three-network general election coverage of the 1968 presidential campaign was twenty-one hours, forty-six minutes. In 1988 the total was sixteen hours exactly.

30. Dom Bonafede, "Blinking Eyes," *National Journal* 20 (August 6, 1988): 2061.

31. Television critic Ron Powers once skewered many local news broadcasts by applying to them the well-earned label, "Eyewitless—a Twinkie of the Airwaves." As quoted in W. Lance Bennett, *News: The Politics of Illusion* (New York: Longman, 1983), p. 1.

32. The "jumping porpoise" genre includes such earth-shattering stories as the ones about the anniversary of the chocolate chip cookie and a Christmas lawsuit against Santa Claus. Using the Vanderbilt University Television News Indexes from 1972 to 1988, my research assistant Leslie Greenwald timed the human interest features for the months of October and March in each presidential or congressional election year. In October 1972 and 1974 these features accounted for just 1.7 percent of the evening news shows (all networks combined). By March 1988 the proportion was 4.9 percent; in October of that year it was 4.1 percent. One of the best "jumping porpoise" stories is actually about whales—the October 1988 rescue of three gray whales trapped in ice off Barrow, Alaska. See Tom Rose, *Freeing the Whales: How the Media Created the World's Greatest Non-Event* (New York: Birch Lane, 1989).

33. Earlier in the 1980s CBS had featured Bill Moyers (since departed for PBS) and before him, veteran Eric Sevareid, whose distinguished CBS career stretched from 1939 to 1977. ABC had used George Will for a time in the early 1980s as an evening commentator.

34. It is certainly true that, with the coming-of-age of CNN, C-SPAN, and PBS, the main commercial networks may feel less pressure to feature politics and news commentary. But the success of these alternative channels does not relieve the networks of their responsibilities, especially since they still control about a two-thirds share of the overall viewing audience. Nonetheless, CNN, C-SPAN, and PBS have made outstanding contributions in broadening the scope of political coverage for

highly educated and motivated viewers, and they look to do still more in the future. See, for example, the tentative-but-promising proposals for PBS's coverage of the 1992 presidential election in Alvin H. Perlmutter, Inc., *The Voter's Channel: A Feasibility Study* (New York: Alvin H. Perlmutter, Inc. for the John and Mary Markle Foundation, June 1990).

35. See the perceptive article by William Boot, "Campaign '88: TV Overdoses on the Inside Dope," *Columbia Journalism Review* 27 (January/February 1989): 23–29.

36. Boot, ibid., describes how this could be accomplished in practice.

37. David S. Broder, "Beware the 'Insider' Syndrome: Why News Makers and News Reporters Shouldn't Get Too Cozy," *Washington Post,* December 4, 1988, L2. Also see Broder, *Behind the Front Page,* pp. 359–64.

38. The problem is less serious for commentators and columnists than for working journalists; furthermore, a simple trip through the door, if the beginning of a person's semipermanent transition from politics to journalism, is not particularly worrisome. See Richard Harwood, "Tainted Journalists," *Washington Post,* December 4, 1988, L6; and Charles Trueheart, "Trading Places: The Insiders Debate," *Washington Post,* January 4, 1989, D1, 19.

39. On the subject, see especially Matusow's revealing book, *Anchor.* See also Fred Graham, *Happy Talk: Confessions of a TV Newsman* (New York: W. W. Norton, 1990); and Richard Zoglin, "Star Power," *Time* 134 (August 7, 1989): 46–51.

40. Quoted in Peter Boyer, "Broadcast Blues," *Vanity Fair* 51 (January 1988): 64.

41. Eleanor Randolph, "The Real Dan Rathers," *Washington Post Magazine,* July 8, 1990, pp. 12–17, 27–31 at p. 14.

42. Barbara Walters and Connie Chung are the champion publicity seekers of television news, followed closely by Tom Brokaw, as measured by their appearances on Johnny Carson's "Tonight Show" and "Late Night with David Letterman." The combined number of guest slots logged by each major news personality on Carson (for 1966–90) and Letterman (1982–90) is as follows:

Barbara Walters	21	Deborah Norville	2
Connie Chung	18	Mike Wallace	2
Tom Brokaw	15	Jessica Savitch	2
Jane Pauley	12	Jeff Greenfield	2
Sam Donaldson	7	Lesley Stahl	2
John Chancellor	6	Dan Rather	1
Diane Sawyer	5*	Peter Jennings	1
David Brinkley	3	Ted Koppel	1
Morley Safer	3	Maria Shriver	1
Hugh Downs	3	Charles Kuralt	1
George Will	2	Mary Alice Williams	1
Walter Cronkite	2	Paula Zahn	1

*This total includes Sawyer's cohosting with Letterman of a prime-time special broadcast in November 1986.

43. The show was aired on January 31, 1989.

44. The show was aired on December 15, 1985.

45. Quoted in Paula Span, "Salute to Fashion's First Lady," *Washington Post,* January 11, 1989, C3.

46. Cited in Jonathan Alter, " 'Looksism' in TV News," *Newsweek* 114 (November 6, 1989): 72–73.

47. See Gwenda Blair, *Almost Golden* (New York: Simon & Schuster, 1988); and Alanna Nash, *Golden Girl* (New York: Dutton, 1988).

48. See Richard Zoglin, "TV News Goes Hollywood," *Time* 134 (October 9,

1989): 98, 103; and Tom Shales, "Beyond Reality: Simulating the News," *Washington Post*, July 27, 1989, C1.

49. See Richard Cohen, "Get Liked or Get Lost," *Washington Post*, October 13, 1989, A26.

50. See Carol Matlack, "Crossing the Line?" *National Journal* 21 (March 24, 1989): 724–29; Richard Harwood, "Honoraria for Journalists," *Washington Post*, January 29, 1989, D6; Eleanor Randolph, "Should Journalists Report Their Own Honoraria?" *Washington Post*, April 14, 1989, A1, 8; Burling Lowrey, "The Media's Honoraria," *Washington Post*, April 26, 1989, A27.

51. Richard M. Nixon, *Six Crises* (Garden City, N.Y.: Doubleday, 1962), p. 129.

52. The C-SPAN interview with Biden aired on August 19, 1990. The Wilmington newspaper article that boosted Biden was by Robin Brown, "Biden Cleared, Sets Sights on White House," *Wilmington Sunday News Journal*, May 28, 1989, A1, 8. The story was picked up by the *Washington Post* and UPI, among others, giving Biden a favorable burst of publicity as he made early preparations for his 1990 reelection campaign. The plagiarism issue first reemerged in a front-page article by George Archibald, "Biden Changes His Story, Insists 'I Never Plagiarized in Law,' " *Washington Times*, August 23, 1990, A1, 9.

53. Interview with Bush by correspondent David Beckwith in *Time* 132 (August 29, 1988): 20. Beckwith is now Quayle's press secretary.

54. Letter to me dated May 1, 1989. Ironically, the letter was written on the second anniversary of his rendezvous with Donna Rice.

55. The show aired on Sunday, February 26, 1989.

56. Michael J. Robinson and Philip M. Burgess, "The Edward M. Kennedy Speech: The Impact of a Prime-Time Television Appeal," *Television Quarterly* 9 (Winter 1970): 29–39.

57. Mrs. Nixon was born on March 16, 1912, not March 17 (St. Patrick's Day). This may not seem much of a discrepancy, but it is probably enough for some to do "character" analysis on Nixon today. Incidentally, no one in the press or in Nixon's political opposition pointed out the slight overstatement, if it was even noticed at that time.

58. Donnie Radcliffe, "The Candidate's Wife, Diving into the Maelstrom," *Washington Post*, August 18, 1988, C9.

59. In fact, a senior member of the Bush staff has since admitted that the microphone *was* deliberately turned on so that the whole town could hear. See Bush vice presidential chief-of-staff Craig Fuller's statement in Taylor, *See How They Run*, p. 176.

60. I am grateful to my colleague Steven E. Finkel for his thoughts on this subject, which have influenced my own as expressed here.

61. Quoted in "Dan Rather's Lament," *Washington Journalism Review* 11 (November 1989): 52.

62. V. O. Key, Jr., *The Responsible Electorate* (Cambridge, Mass.: Harvard University Press, 1966), p. 7.

63. See, for example, Scott Keeter and Cliff Zukin, *Uninformed Choice* (New York: Praeger, 1983). This is a study of voter knowledge in the 1976 and 1980 presidential elections.

64. See the concluding section of chapter 2.

65. Random-sample telephone survey by Yankelovich Clancy Shulman for *Time* and CNN; the sample was 504 adults nationwide, taken March 2, 1989, with a margin of error of plus or minus 5 percent.

66. I have attempted to make this case at length in my *The Party's Just Begun: Shaping Political Parties for America's Future* (Glenview, Ill.: Scott, Foresman, 1988).

67. Walter Lippmann, *Public Opinion* (New York: Free Press, 1965), p. 19. Thomas E. Patterson has developed this argument at length in his article, "The Press and Its Missed Assignment," in Michael Nelson, ed., *The Elections of 1988* (Washing-

ton: Congressional Quarterly Press, 1989), pp. 95–98. For a fascinating discussion of how Great Britain's strong party system helps counterbalance press power in that country, see Anthony King, ''Transatlantic Transgressions: A Comparison of British and American Scandals,'' *Public Opinion* 7 (December/January 1985): 20–22, 64.

68. Alexis de Tocqueville, *Democracy in America*, vol. 2 (New York: Vintage, 1945), p. 119. Tocqueville was referring to newspapers, of course, but his declaration can be applied equally to the broadcast media of our time.

Afterword

1. Held in Washington, D.C. on March 28, 1992.

2. In July, "CBS Evening News" announced that whenever Bush, Clinton, or Perot appeared on the broadcast, the candidate's sound bite would be at least 30 seconds in length. Then the length was shortened to 20 seconds. Finally, the rule was abandoned altogether.

3. Center for Media and Public Affairs, "Clinton's the One," *Media Monitor* 6 (November 1992): 2. The average sound bite was 9.8 seconds in 1988, and 42.3 seconds in 1968.

4. NBC News and the Public Broadcasting System arranged some joint efforts that expanded NBC's coverage—though not on the NBC network's airwaves.

5. There are many who do not believe that political parties matter these days, but I beg to differ. See the author's *The Party's Just Begun: Shaping Political Parties for America's Future* (Glenview, Ill.: Scott, Foresman, 1988), chap. 1.

6. Note, for example, the fate of one of George Bush's key campaign speeches in September 1992, which was consigned to network oblivion. See Mickey Kaus, "Sound-Bitten," *The New Republic* 204 (October 26, 1992): 16–18.

7. Voters and pundits accounted for the remaining 17 percent of the time. Center for Media and Public Affairs, "Clinton's the One," p. 2.

8. These examples are taken from the three dozen contained in the postelection videotape, "They All Laughed," produced by Dara Monahan and Adrienne Rich. It was shown on election night in Little Rock and again to an obviously pleased Bill Clinton during his inaugural week ceremonies. The source of each quotation is as follows: Margaret Warner (CNN's "The Capital Gang," February 29, 1992), John McLaughlin ("The McLaughlin Group," April 12, 1992), Ed Rollins ("Nightline," January 27, 1992), and Robert Novak ("The Capital Gang," February 15, 1992 and March 3, 1992).

9. McLaughlin's miss was par for the course in his "Group." One analyst checked the accuracy of his inside-the-Beltway Group's predictions for one year (August 1990 to August 1991) and found the overall correct batting average to be 43.2 percent, well below the 50 percent level of a coin toss. See Scott Shuger, "The McLaughlin Grope: If These Washington Pundits Are So Smart, How Come They're So Often Wrong," *Los Angeles Times Magazine*, April 26, 1992, pp. 20–22, 50, 53.

10. Compilation extends from January 1, 1992 to November 3, 1992. See The Freedom Forum, Media Studies Center, *The Finish Line: Covering the Campaign's Final Days* (New York: The Freedom Forum, January 1993), pp. 16, 124–25.

11. See, for example, Howard Kurtz, "The Talk Show Campaign," *Washington Post*, October 28, 1992, A1, 14.

12. See pp. 234–36, 282.

13. Among those joining Brokaw on the role of dishonor were Ted Koppel, Andrea Mitchell, Cokie Roberts, and Tim Russert.

14. I recorded and watched all three networks' evening newscasts from January 1, 1992 to November 3, 1992, and these comments reflect my own impressions of the overall coverage.

15. Center for Media and Public Affairs, "Clinton's the One," pp. 2–3.

16. *Ibid.* In the 1992 general election there were 258 horserace stories and 233 issue segments; in 1988, 145 horserace stories and 232 issue segments.

17. The Freedom Forum, *The Finish Line*, pp. 13–16, 55–59, 129–30, 147–48.

18. I am grateful to the *Observer's* political reporter Tim Funk for providing background material used in this section. Another newspaper with a similar consumer-oriented approach in 1992 was the *Wichita Eagle* in Kansas. See also David Shaw, "Some Papers Seek Readers' Guidance in Shaping Coverage," *Los Angeles Times,* April 1, 1993, A18.

19. Mecklenburg County, North Carolina's turnout was 51.2 percent in 1988 and 60.2 percent in 1992. North Carolina's turnout in 1988 was 44.7 percent and in 1992 50.8 percent. The nation's turnout in 1988 was 50.0 percent and in 1992 55.2 percent. No claim of a direct causal relationship between the newspaper and higher turnout can be made, of course, but it is certainly a reasonable hypothesis.

20. The debate was sponsored by the Freedom Forum just prior to the opening session of the Democratic National Convention, New York City, July 13, 1992.

21. "Hot Springs Eternal," *The New Republic* 204 (November 23, 1992): 46.

22. The Freedom Forum, *The Finish Line*, p. 129.

23. "Was the Press Unfair to Bush?" *U.S. News & World Report* 109 (November 9, 1992): 100.

24. The Freedom Forum, *The Finish Line*, p. 128.

25. Comment made on CNN's "Reliable Sources," aired September 5, 1992.

26. As quoted in Howard Kurtz, "Networks Stressed the Negative in Comments About Bush, Study Finds," *Washington Post,* November 15, 1992, A7.

27. As quoted in *National Journal* 24 (October 3, 1992): 2247. A recent study lends new credence to Brokaw's slant on bias. See Albert C. Gunther, "Biased Press or Biased Public? Attitudes Toward Media Coverage of Social Groups," *Public Opinion Quarterly* 56 (Summer 1992): 147–67.

28. See pp. 86–93. For other views on bias in the 1992 campaign, see Jeffrey L. Katz, "Tilt?" *Washington Journalism Review* 15 (January/February 1993): 23–27; Graeme Browning, "Too Close for Comfort?" *National Journal* 24 (October 3, 1992): 2243–2247; and Thomas C. Palmer, Jr., "Reputation for bias seems well earned," *Boston Globe,* January 3, 1993, 65, 68.

29. Perot also received a much better press than Bush; 45 percent of his evaluations from nonpartisan sources were positive. But Clinton's press, as noted, was more favorable still. Moreover, Bush received the most negative press coverage of any candidate in either party when the whole of election year 1992 is considered. (This finding takes into account Clinton's rough passage through the crises of the primaries.) In the general election, the horserace evaluations were 82 percent positive for Clinton; 49 percent positive for Perot; and just 24 percent positive for Bush. These findings come from the Center for Media and Public Affairs, "Clinton's the One," pp. 3–5. My own monitoring of all network evening news broadcasts from January to November 1992 confirms these general conclusions.

30. The data base of articles, retrieved by NEXIS using key words as the basis for the search, covers all of September and October of 1992. Editorial and op-ed pages were excluded. Percentages cited here have been rounded.

31. Clinton won editorial endorsements from 183 newspapers, compared to Bush's 138. Perot won only four endorsements. See "Clinton's the Choice," *Editor & Publisher* 125 (October 24, 1992): 9–10, 44–45; also *Editor & Publisher* 125 (November 7, 1992): 15. In 1988, Bush won 195 endorsements to Michael Dukakis's 51.

32. Joann Byrd, "73 Days of Tilt," *Washington Post,* November 8, 1992, C6.

33. The details are contained in Joann Byrd, "Poll Play," *Washington Post,* October 4, 1992, C6.

34. One of the most frightening poll statistics of 1992 was the CBS News finding that 18 percent of adult Americans—and 30 percent of the 18-to-29 age group—reported that they received some presidential campaign news first from late-night

comics. The telephone survey of 1,355 adults was taken October 16–17, 1992. Its margin of error was plus or minus 3 percent.

35. See Jerry Hagstrom, "Campaign Sideshow?" *National Journal* 24 (September 5, 1992): 2037.

36. See Howard Kurtz, "Who What When Where Why Be Objective? Politics, and the Times," *Washington Post,* November 15, 1992, F1, 5.

37. See Katherine Corcoran, "Pilloried Clinton," *Washington Journalism Review* 15 (January/February 1993): 27–29.

38. Center for Media and Public Affairs, "The Boom in Gloom," *Media Monitor* 6 (October 1992): 1–3. The time period covered by the study was July through September 1992.

39. The CBS Evening News "Reality Check" segment aired in the top block of the October 28, 1992 broadcast was typical, with the good-news number buried in an avalanche of older bad-news numbers.

40. Interestingly, three reporters—interviewed separately—all requested anonymity, lest their revelations result in ostracization by colleagues.

41. For example, on June 6, 1992 the top, right headline on the front page of the *Washington Post* read "Jobless Rate Rose to 7.5 Pct. in May," and on July 3, 1992, the *Post's* headline with the same placement read "Jobless Rate Hit 7.8 Pct. in June."

42. The *Washington Post* headline on September 5, 1992 read "167,000 Jobs Lost in U.S. Last Month," while the *New York Times* headline on the same date read "167,000 Jobs Lost by U.S. Businesses." Both headlines appeared in the top, right position.

43. This reporter continued:

These reports are only part of the story. There is also a story in what we reporters did not pay much attention to. For one, consumer spending was starting to revive in the summer, and was driving up economic growth. [Some newspeople] were disgusted when the Commerce Department reported in October that gross domestic product rose [by 2.7 percent]. They charged that "George cooked the books." The fact is the government had been reporting a pickup in spending for several months. So had private retailers. But everybody played it down.

Perhaps more importantly, everybody ignored the rise in U.S. productivity, even though Bill Clinton labeled productivity one of his chief concerns about the U.S. economy. U.S. productivity was surging through the summer, as businesses around the country found ways to get more out of their workers. The rise meant all those wrenching layoffs might actually be helping strengthen American businesses. But who wanted to hear that in the middle of an historic election?

44. A telephone reinterview survey of 1,012 voters conducted November 5–8, 1992, based on an original random-sample survey of adults conducted May 28–June 10, 1992. Margin of error: plus or minus 3 percent. Approximately 27 percent also thought the press had been unfair to Ross Perot. Another survey by Gannett News Service and Louis Harris found that among the 36 percent of the public that perceived a news bias in favor of either Bush or Clinton, 77 percent said journalists were biased in Clinton's favor. This random-sample telephone poll of 1,021 adults was taken September 21–23, 1992, and had a margin of error of plus or minus 3 percent.

45. A telephone survey of 290 journalists selected to be roughly representative of the profession, conducted October 7–29, 1992.

46. David Weaver and G. Cleveland Wilhoit, *The American Journalist in the 1990s* (New York: The Freedom Forum, 1992), pp. 6–7. The study was based on telephone interviews with 1,410 representative American print and broadcast journalists conducted from June 12 to September 12, 1992.

47. As quoted in The Freedom Forum Media Studies Center, *The Homestretch: New Politics, New Media. New Voters?* (New York: The Freedom Forum, Columbia University, October 1992): 49–50. Note also Carlson's mischaracterization of Marilyn Quayle's statements about women at the Republican National Convention. During the Carter administration, Carlson was special assistant to the chairman of the Consumer Product Safety Commission.

48. See Mike Allen, "ABC reporter to be moderator here," *Richmond Times–Dispatch*, October 10, 1992, B1, 6. Simpson later was criticized for comments she made during the debate, which some observers interpreted as unfavorable to both Bush and Perot.

49. Howard Kurtz, "Cannon on His Right . . .," *Washington Post*, September 7, 1992, A10.

50. Not surprisingly, the Clinton–press axis quickly deteriorated once the new President was sworn in. The same old imperative (getting a good story) produced a new dynamic that overrode ideology and other sources of tilt. See Howard Kurtz, "Media Pendulum Swings Again for the President," *Washington Post*, January 31, 1993, A1, 18.

51. The outlets publishing rumors extended well beyond the *Washington Times*. See, for example, Ronald Brownstein, "Clinton's New Ideas Now Hold Audiences' Attention," *Los Angeles Times*, August 11, 1991, A1, 15. Brownstein attributes the charges to Clinton's political opponents in Arkansas, but of course just the reporting of the unproven charges accomplished the goals of Clinton's detractors.

52. See, for example, David Shribman, "Clinton, Arkansas's Best-Known Over-achiever, Widens His Horizons to Include the White House," *Wall Street Journal*, October 8, 1991, A24.

53. Tape provided by WMUR-TV. Clinton replied in part: "I've been on the ballot seventeen times in seventeen years [in Arkansas]. . . . I think it is highly unlikely, given the competitive environment in which I've been in, that you have anything to worry about on that score. . . . I have proved . . . that I can deal with the kind of sleaze the Republicans put out. . . ."

54. The issue hit the newsstands on Monday, January 27, 1992, but was faxed to major news organizations early, to generate advance publicity.

55. See Thomas B. Rosenstiel, "Clinton Allegation Raises Questions on Media's Role," *Los Angeles Times*, January 29, 1992, A1, 20; Howard Kurtz, "Five Days From Tabloid Tattle to Front-Page Fare," *Washington Post*, January 28, 1992, A8; and William A. Henry III, "Handling the Clinton Affair," *Time* 139 (February 10, 1992): 28–29.

56. In "Nightline"'s defense: Clinton had tentatively agreed to appear on the program, but canceled in late afternoon, possibly because of bad weather or perhaps because he thought better of fully opening up the subject for public discussion. Had Clinton refused from the outset, "Nightline" might have scheduled another subject for the evening.

In the interest of full disclosure, the author was one of the guests on this show, and used the occasion to denounce lowest-common-denominator journalism. Mandy Grunwald, one of Clinton's media advisers, did the same.

57. The *Times* relegated the Flowers story to short pieces at the bottom of its political page, or a few paragraphs in stories on other topics.

58. Reportedly, Flowers taped fifteen such conversations without Clinton's knowledge from 1990 until early 1992. Clinton tacitly acknowledged that he was the male voice on the tapes when he apologized to New York Gov. Mario Cuomo for unflattering references to Cuomo's Italian heritage contained on one tape excerpt. The sexual allusion is a lighthearted reference by Flowers to Clinton's prowess at oral sex, but Clinton's response is noncommittal or garbled. All in all, it is difficult to reach any firm conclusion from the tapes about the extent of the Clinton–Flowers relationship, although clearly she is more than a passing acquaintance. The edited nature of the released tape excerpts should also induce caution.

59. Rosensteil, "Clinton Allegation," A20.

60. It was already too late in the nominating process for other candidates to enter the race and qualify for many states' primary and caucus contests.

61. See *Newsweek* 116 (February 3, 1992): 19–20; and Don Johnson and Terry Lemons, "Ex-agent contradicts LR Singer," *Arkansas Democrat–Gazette*, January 26,

1992, A19. Another aspect of the Flowers controversy discussed on the tapes but not much followed up concerned Clinton's hiring of Flowers for a state job, which she had repeatedly requested of him. See Timothy Clifford and Shirley E. Perlman, "The Flowers Job: Officials' Changes Gave Her an Advantage," *Newsday*, February 6, 1992, 5.

62. Christopher Lydon, "Sex, War, and Death," *Columbia Journalism Review* 29 (May/June 1992): 58.

63. See data and discussion in Martha FitzSimon, "What the Polls Say About Campaign Coverage," *Covering the Presidential Primaries* (New York: The Freedom Forum Media Studies Center, June 1992), pp. 51–61, especially pp. 53–55, 58.

64. See data in "Politicians and Privacy," *The CQ Researcher* 2 (April 17, 1992): 341.

65. A telephone survey of 400 print and broadcast journalists selected to be roughly representative of the profession, conducted in May 1992.

66. See Micheal Isikoff, "Clinton Team Works to Deflect Allegations on Nominee's Private Life," *Washington Post*, July 26, 1992, A18.

67. See Jerry Seper, "Brother bragged of liaisons in Clinton's mansion," *Washington Times*, April 14, 1992, A1.

68. See the *Hotline* 5 (July 14, 1992): 19.

69. Isikoff, "Clinton Team Works. . . ." Also see the *Hotline* 5 (July 20, 1992): 15.

70. Carried in an Associated Press dispatch and printed widely on October 17, 1992.

71. See Ann Devroy, ". . . And the Losers: Bush Defeat Blamed on Bad Campaign and Bad Economy," *Washington Post*, November 5, 1992, A31.

72. Dan Balz, "Miscalculations Mark Clinton's Attempt to Settle Draft Record Issue," *Washington Post*, September 8, 1992, A12.

73. Comment by Nelson on CNN's "Reliable Sources," September 19, 1992.

74. Quoted in Balz, "Miscalculations."

75. Once again, news organizations were called—anonymously and otherwise—and informed that rival publications and networks were about to break new stories on Clinton's draft record.

76. Many readers of this volume have commented on the eerie similarity between Engberg's speculation and the actual course of the 1992 campaign. When I reported this to Engberg, he responded by wondering, "You don't suppose that [Bush campaign staffers] stole my scenario, do you?" Letter to the author dated February 18, 1993.

77. Published Monday, October 5, 1992 on A1.

78. *Hotline* 6 (October 8, 1992): 5.

79. The following article summarizes what was known about the Clinton passport search *prior* to the election: Bill Turque, "The Clinton File Mystery Grows," *Newsweek* 119 (November 2, 1992): 49. After the election the improper nature of the search became fully apparent, and two high-ranking Bush administration staffers in the State Department were dismissed or demoted. See Eric Schmitt, "Passport Search Brings Dismissal," *New York Times*, November 11, 1992, A1, D19; and David Johnston, "Prosecutor Named to Review Search of Files on Clinton," *New York Times*, December 18, 1992, A1, 34.

80. From the 1992 Christmas letter of Anthony Kenny, the Warden of Rhodes House.

81. Technical Data, Thomson Financial Systems. This bond service leases time on the Dow Jones wire service. The author of the item was David Ader, who noted in his story that "If it hurts Clinton, it helps bonds." Apparently, the rumor first took on life in the Tokyo market and quickly spread around the world.

82. The semi-retraction noted that "The official denials are coming in. Adamantly. A spokesman for ABC news called the rumor 'vicious' and said no such tapes exist. Period. CNN denied the rumor earlier." Materials for this paragraph were provided by Arnot Walker, who was also interviewed by telephone on February 5, 1993.

83. See again the discussion about Senator Edmund Muskie's temper, and its influence on reporting of his "cry" in the snow of New Hampshire (p. 75).

84. See pp. 71–79.

85. See "Jackson Takes High Road in Open-Mike Flap," *Washington Post*, February 29, 1992, A20. CNN, NBC, and Fox networks used the videotape in news broadcasts.

86. Activist Robert Rafsky said, "I'm dying of AIDS while you're dying of ambition," to which Clinton replied, "If I was dying of ambition I wouldn't stand up here and put up with all this crap. . . ." See *Washington Post*, February 23, 1993, B7 (Mr. Rafsky's obituary).

87. The show, entitled, "One Day in New York," aired on April 2, 1992. Clinton barked at the aide: "I don't know what you people are thinking about, subjecting me to this. Can you hear that? There are more jeers than cheers."

88. See "The Bill Clinton nobody knows," *The Economist*, November 7, 1992, 38. See also Jeffrey H. Birnbaum, "President's Temper Unsettles Staffers Unused to His Ways," *Wall Street Journal*, February 17, 1993, A16.

89. Ibid.

90. *Hotline* 6 (November 9, 1992): 10.

91. On February 16, 1993, President Clinton swore at a junior aide when the latter attempted to block two local D.C. dignitaries from accompanying Clinton to a photo opportunity with blue-collar workers. See *Hotline* 6 (February 17, 1993): 9.

92. Birnbaum, "President's Temper."

93. The press "pool report" by the two reporters directly observing Bush's reactions to the scanner technology in Orlando, Florida noted nothing unusual about Bush's reactions. But other news organizations (also not present) quickly reiterated the *New York Times's* version of events. See Andrew Rosenthal, "Bush Encounters the Supermarket, Amazed," *New York Times*, February 5, 1992, A1.

94. The commentators were left-wing pundit Christopher Hitchens and (several days afterward) Wall Street analyst John Westergaard. See Mark Jurkowitz, "Ins and Outs," *Boston Phoenix*, October 16, 1992, 6–7.

95. If nothing else, Bush's endurance during the long campaign of 1992 disproved the speculation.

96. See pp. 171–77 at 177.

97. I refrained from using Ms. Fitzgerald's name in the first edition since, by-and-large, only reporters and political elites knew her, and the rumors about her were completely unproven. The latter is still true, but alas, Ms. Fitzgerald's anonymity did not survive the campaign, and she was the focus of hundreds of mentions in high-profile articles and broadcasts. In my view, this is unfair to her and deeply regrettable, yet she is also part of the official on-the-record history of the 1992 presidential campaign.

98. Gail Sheehy, "What Hillary Wants," *Vanity Fair* 55 (May 1992): 140–217 at 147.

99. By Andrew Rosenthal, April 13, 1992, A1, 17.

100. A *Times–Mirror* survey of more than 400 print and broadcast journalists conducted in May 1992. The survey was not purely random but was broadly representative of the journalistic community.

101. This Sunday strip ran on May 24, 1992. Bush (or his invisible representation) answered "No."

102. "Taking Aim at the Bush Rumors," *Newsweek* 119 (June 15, 1992): 6.

103. Comments made on CNN's "Reliable Sources," aired June 13, 1992. Alter himself asked and then answered the key question: "Did [*Spy*] come up with the goods? No, not really."

104. See *Time* 140 (July 20, 1992): 26.

105. The issue appeared August 11, 1992, and included three lengthy (for the *Post*) related stories on the "affair."

106. Susan B. Trento, *The Power House: Robert Keith Gray and the Selling of Access*

and Influence in Washington (New York: St. Martin's Press, 1992). The footnote appears on page 413 in chapter 14. CNN actually beat the *Post* in the race to get this footnote on the record. On August 3, more than a week before the *Post* published, CNN's Bob Franken mentioned on-air that Democrats were sending around the excerpt of Trento's book to members of the press. See *Hotline* 5 (August 4, 1992): 6–7.

107. *Hotline* 5 (August 11, 1992): 11–12.

108. *Hotline* 5 (August 12, 1992): 8–9. This was not the first time Tillotson had raised the subject of the Bush rumors; she had mentioned them on-air during an August 3, 1992 broadcast. See *Hotline* 5 (August 4, 1992): 6. Interestingly, one report has it that if Tillotson had not asked Bush about the *Post* story, two other women reporters were prepared to do so, while some male reporters opposed raising the subject. See *National Journal* 24 (October 10, 1992): 2327. See also the discussion in this volume about the role of women journalists in the new emphasis on the character issue, pp. 68–69.

109. See pp. 173–74.

110. Discussion with the author at the Republican National Convention, Houston, Tex., August 17, 1992.

111. Show aired August 11, 1992. For a transcript of the relevant section, see *Hotline* 5 (August 12, 1992): 6–7.

112. See pp. 148–51.

113. Comment made on CNN's "Reliable Sources," aired August 15, 1992.

114. MacNelly's work is syndicated by his home newspaper, the *Chicago Tribune*.

115. The exact air date was February 20, 1992.

116. David Rogers and Jill Abramson, "Under Cover: Ross Perot Takes Surveillance Tactics to Unusual Lengths," *Wall Street Journal,* June 12, 1992, A1, 6.

117. David Remnick, "H. Ross Perot—the Strengths and the Strangeness," *Washington Post,* March 29, 1992, C7. See also Karen DeWitt with Michael Kelly, "Perot Pursued Charges Against Official for Years," *New York Times,* June 28, 1992, A18.

118. Bob Woodward and John Mintz, "Perot Launched Investigations of Bush," *Washington Post,* June 21, 1992, A1, 18.

119. See William Safire, "Deep Ross," *New York Times,* June 29, 1992, A15.

120. See Steven A. Holmes, "Federal Contracts Gave Perot His Big Break," *New York Times,* May 5, 1992, A1, 28; and Michael Kelly, "Perot Under Fire: Sifting Facts and Motives," *New York Times,* June 25, 1992, A1, 27.

121. William Safire, "Old Pro Perot," *New York Times,* May 7, 1992, A27; "Perot's Plea of Hardship," May 28, 1992, A23; "Perot 'Hardship' Mystery Deepens," June 1, 1992, A17; "Perot Versus Social Security," June 15, 1992, A19; "Deep Ross," June 29, 1992, A15. See also Howard Kurtz, "Perot's Late Entry Into Race Greatly Compresses Media Scrutiny," *Washington Post,* June 25, 1992, A18.

122. See Marie Brenner, "Perot's Final Days," *Vanity Fair* 55 (October 1992): 74–104 at 82.

123. King was employed by EDS Federal Systems, and at the time Perot was the head of the company. According to Brenner, ibid., ABC had planned to air this exposé on Thursday, July 16, 1992—the very day that Perot withdrew. It was not broadcast.

124. I received a call from a strong Perot supporter about the time of the Republican National Convention in August. This Perotista claimed that Perot had personally assured him he planned to reenter the race "in early October." Perot jumped back in the contest on October 1.

125. The segment was broadcast on September 29, 1992. See also the follow-up on September 30.

126. Thomas Toch, "All in the Perot Family," *U.S. News & World Report* 113 (October 5, 1992): 22–23; and Sidney Blumenthal, "He's Ba-a-ck!" *The New Republic* 207 (October 19, 1992): 12–15.

127. Perot made similar charges in a *Boston Herald* interview and at campaign rallies in Pennsylvania and New Jersey on the same day as the "60 Minutes" segment

was broadcast. See Paul Richter and Sara Fritz, "Perot Charges Plot Forced Him Out," *Los Angeles Times*, October 26, 1992, A1, 18; and Howard Kurtz, "Aides Struggle to Push Perot Charges of GOP Tricks Off Center Stage," *Washington Post*, October 28, 1992, A11.

128. Perot did not specifically mention the lesbian pose, but another of his daughters gave the gory details to the press. See Richard L. Berke, "Perot Says He Quit in July to Thwart G.O.P. 'Dirty Tricks,'" *New York Times*, October 26, 1992, A1, 12.

129. The FBI had earlier investigated the bugging allegations (at Perot's instigation) and found no evidence of wrongdoing.

130. Laurence I. Barrett, "Perot-noia," *Time* 140 (November 9, 1992): 28–29. For more background see Sidney Blumenthal, "Brother Ray," *The New Republic* 207 (November 16, 1992): 18–22.

131. See survey results in *Newsweek* 119 (November 9, 1992): 23.

132. *Hotline* 6 (October 2, 1992): 5. In the previous week, Perot had rebuked NBC's Katie Couric and Lisa Myers for trying to "prove their manhood" by their tough questioning of him.

133. Perot telephoned King at the latter's home on the day after the election, November 4.

134. The series ran on the front page of the *Post* on January 5–10 and 12, 1992. It has been reprinted in book form: David S. Broder and Bob Woodward, *The Man Who Would Be President* (New York: Simon & Shuster, 1992).

135. Marshall Ingwerson, "Vice President Struggles to Overcome Poor Image," *Christian Science Monitor*, August 20, 1992, 1, 4. See also William Boot, "The Woodbro Rehab Project," *Columbia Journalism Review* 31 (September/October 1992): 57–60.

136. See especially pp. 168–71.

137. The U.S. senator was Carl Levin of Michigan. See *Hotline* 6 (October 5, 1992): 16–17; and (July 22, 1993): 10.

138. Perhaps the worst offender was Mark Singer, "The Prisoner and the Politician," *The New Yorker* 68 (October 5, 1992): 108–33. This lengthy, fawning profile of Kimberlin, published less than a month before the election, includes a description of the prisoner (derived from comments by his mother) as "a loving, gentle-spirited pacifist who, before and during his imprisonment, has never flagged in his devotion to his family" (p. 109). Singer reports almost without question or challenge every aspect of Kimberlin's dubious drug allegations against Quayle.

139. For example, see the Associated Press dispatches on Kimberlin dated October 3, 1992 and October 10, 1992; and the *Washington Post*, October 9, 1992, B6, and October 10, 1992, A14.

140. One particularly extended Trudeau series on Kimberlin ran daily from November 11 to November 30, 1991. In the strip published on November 19, 1991, for instance, "*Washington Post* reporter" Rick Redfern tells his wife that Kimberlin "claims he sold marijuana to Quayle on 15 or more occasions." His wife replies, "I can't believe we're talking about a vice president." Says Redfern: "Well, they're the ones with too much time on their hands." On May 10, 1992, Trudeau returned to Kimberlin, hailing him in one unfunny panel as "a model prisoner with an extraordinary number of official commendations and degrees earned in prison."

141. See Howard Kurtz, "Garry Trudeau's Cartoon Beat," *Washington Post*, May 30, 1992, B1, 5. Earlier, after the first Kimberlin–Quayle series had been published and criticized, Trudeau defended himself in an article, "Investigative Cartooning: Why Does the White House Quail at My 'Doonesbury' Strip?" *Washington Post*, January 15, 1992, C1, 4. In it Trudeau called his work "a kind of reality cocktail—part fact, part fiction, part serious and part frivolous. . . ." But if he chooses to focus on real-life allegations that affect a public person's reputation, he ought to be held to the same standards of fairness and accuracy as any other editorialist.

142. Kimberlin appeared on the show that aired October 8, 1992.

143. *Hotline* 6 (October 8, 1992): 32–33.

144. See *Vital Speeches of the Day* 58 (June 15, 1992): 517–20.

145. See quotations cited in David Whitman, "The war over 'family values,'" U.S. News & World Report 109 (June 8, 1992): 35–36.

146. Attacks on television's and Hollywood's excessive sex and violence is a modern staple of political campaigning. Also, other politicians have referred to specific TV shows to underline their points. See E. J. Dionne, Jr., "Quayle v. Brown: Unplanned Furor Eclipses Message," Washington Post, May 21, 1992, A24.

147. An ABC/Washington Post telephone survey of 1,512 adults taken June 3–7, 1992 put Quayle's favorable rating at 26 percent and his unfavorable rating at 54 percent. "Murphy Brown" registered a 50 percent favorable rating and a 21 percent unfavorable rating. The margin of error was plus or minus 3 percent. The controversy cost Quayle support. In February 1992 his favorability rating had been 39 percent, unfavorable 46 percent.

148. See pp. 71–79.

149. The gag was part of "Late Night with David Letterman" on May 20, 1992.

150. Carried in an Associated Press dispatch and published in many newspapers on May 22, 1992. For instance, see Christopher Connell, "Quayle declares he'd attack Murphy Brown again," Baltimore Sun, May 22, 1992, A14. No explanation was given in the dispatch for the "exam-cheating" or "pot-smoking" references. For background, see pp. 167–71 of this volume.

151. See Rick Du Brow, "Bergen, 'Brown' Win Big at Emmy Awards," Los Angeles Times, August 31, 1992, A1, 9.

152. The episode was panned for its harshness. See Tom Shales, "Murphy Brown's Quayle Shoot," Washington Post, September 22, 1992, B1, 8.

153. Barbara Dafoe Whitehead, "Dan Quayle Was Right," The Atlantic 271 (April 1993): 47–84. See also David Broder, "On Crisis of Family Values, Dan Quayle Was Right," Washington Post, March 24, 1993, A21.

154. The school principal later insisted that the flash card had been prepared not by one of his teachers but by another Trentonite who participated in an after-school program.

155. This one ran in the Atlanta Constitution on June 16, 1992, p. A7, with "news services" listed as the author.

156. These examples are cited in Howard Kurtz, "Why Quayle's 'Potatoe' Gaffe Won't Fade," Washington Post, June 21, 1992, A16.

157. Evelyn Nieves, "Spelling by Quayle (That's With an E)," New York Times, June 17, 1992, A23.

158. Kurtz, "Why Quayle's 'Potatoe' Gaffe Won't Fade." After Quayle's office cited a published source, AP later moved a second story that noted several books mentioned Twain as the quotation's author.

159. Gore was a reporter for the Nashville Tennessean from 1971 to 1976, before his entry into electoral politics.

160. The gap in favorable references on the network evening news broadcasts was far greater between Gore and Quayle than between Clinton and Bush. A September 1992 study by the Center for Media and Public Affairs found that, throughout August, three out of every four quoted sources on the air praised Gore, while two out of every three sources criticized Quayle. See Media Monitor 6 (August/September 1992): 3. Not much changed through election day, despite an occasional media elbow in Gore's side. See, for example, the NBC News segment on Gore's campaign contributions for the junk bond industry aired October 9, 1992, and quoted in Hotline 6 (October 13, 1992): 10–11.

161. Thomas C. Palmer, Jr., "Reputation for bias seems well earned," p. 68.

162. Under California law, knowledge of ongoing drug use inside one's home, even if one does not personally partake, is classified as the legal equivalent of possession of the drug. However, the statute of limitations on any such crime that might have occurred during Brown's gubernatorial tenure (1975–83) had already expired by 1992.

163. About a week later, the full story came to light. McWethy had been interviewing in late March a former California state policeman, James C. Pashley, about a case involving alleged improper construction of the C-17 cargo jet produced by the McDonnell Douglas Corporation. McWethy and his ABC News team were hosting Pashley at a dinner, when the conversation turned to Pashley's other career experiences, including his service guarding Brown. Pashley casually mentioned the drug matter, and McWethy pressed it, insisting it was of public interest given Brown's then-current presidential candidacy. Pashley suggested other sources to McWethy, and the ABC investigation began. See Kenneth Reich, "Source of Brown Story Unmasks Himself," *Los Angeles Times*, April 18, 1992, A2.

164. The Brown campaign pointed out that cocaine test kits were not standard-issue equipment for the state police security detail, but the officers said they secured them from friends in the Los Angeles Police Department. John McWethy explained this apparent discrepancy during the April 9, 1992 "Nightline" broadcast.

165. See "ABC Reports Drugs Used at Brown Home," *New York Times*, April 10, 1992, A26. Barely five column inches long, the story appeared at the bottom-left of the page.

166. See, for example, Thomas B. Rosensteil and Melissa Healy, "Brown Denies TV Report of Drug Parties," *Los Angeles Times*, April 10, 1992, A4; Kenneth Reich and John Hurst, "State Police Deny Brown Drug-Party Reports," *Los Angeles Times*, April 11, 1992, A16; Donald P. Baker and Lou Cannon, "Brown Denies Report of Marijuana, Cocaine Parties at His House," *Washington Post*, April 10, 1992, A12; and Lou Cannon and John F. Harris, "California Police Officials Skeptical of Allegation Against Brown," *Washington Post*, April 11, 1992, A10. Conservative Republicans backing Brown included state Senator Ed Davis, who was Los Angeles police chief during Brown's first term as governor; Howard Newsham, a retired California state police commander; and political consultant Ed Rollins, who had been GOP chief of staff in the state legislature during part of Brown's governorship.

167. See Sharon Bernstein, "ABC Still Defending Its Brown Story," *Los Angeles Times*, April 16, 1992, F11; and Howard Kurtz, "ABC Criticized for Broadcast of Report," *Washington Post*, April 11, 1992, A10. See also Lawrence N. Hansen, *Reflections: The Press Looks at Itself, Politicians, and the Public* (Washington: Centel Public Accountability Project and the Joyce Foundation, 1992), p. 15.

168. Mark Gladstone and Kenneth Reich, "Source of Brown Drug Charges Emerges," *Los Angeles Times*, April 16, 1992, A17.

169. Kenneth Reich, "Source of Brown Story Unmasks Himself."

170. Ibid.

171. See Burt Solomon, "For Attack-Dog Campaigner Brown . . . Barking Back at Press Is a Snap," *National Journal* 24 (April 18, 1992): 952–53.

172. Not surprisingly, the current California state police officials say no. But given this organization's potential involvement and self-interest, only an independent investigation would be credible.

173. See Marjorie Randon Hershey, "The Congressional Elections," in *The Elections of 1992: Reports and Interpretations* (Chatham, N.J.: Chatham House, 1993), pp. 162–65.

174. See pp. 192–93.

175. In August 1991 *The Advocate*, a gay magazine produced in Los Angeles, published a cover story "outing" the well-known Defense Department official, justifying its action by pointing to the ban on gays in the military. (The individual in question had no power to change the policy, and may not have personally supported the policy.) The official was then fully identified in reports carried by the *Detroit News*, the *New York Daily News*, and the *Village Voice*, as well as in a Jack Anderson column published by many newspapers.

Shortly after her nomination as Clinton's secretary of Health and Human Services, Donna Shalala was forced to deny untrue reports that she was a lesbian. The radical gay group "Queer Nation" had been calling news organizations with the claim, with no substantiation whatsoever. *The Capital Times* in Madison, Wisconsin, published a story that included the allegation and the denial, followed by a similar nationwide Associated Press story on New Year's Eve 1992 that was widely carried with no-win headlines such as "Not homosexual, appointee says." See also Jeffrey Toobin, "The Shalala Strategy," *The New Yorker* 69 (April 26, 1993): 53–62 at 59, 62.

176. Chris Bull, "The Outing of a Family Values Congressman: U.S. Representative Jim McCrery's Double Life," *The Advocate* (September 22, 1992): 38–45. McCrery is a Republican. By no means is this the most extreme example of "outing." (See ibid. for much worse examples.) In a telephone conversation on April 29, 1993, Bull well defended his piece and offered justifications for this outing from an activist's perspective. But in my view, none of those rationales legitimizes the invasion of privacy inherent in this cruel practice.

177. See Tim Curran, "Big Events Oct. 3 in Louisiana," *Roll Call*, September 24, 1992, pp. 14, 22; and *Hotline* 6 (September 2, 1992): 16.

178. Press release, "Statement by Congressman Jim McCrery," August 30, 1992, p. 1.

179. Shilts wrote this comment in the August 7, 1991 edition of the *Los Angeles Times*. It is quoted in "'Outing' of Gay Politicians Divides the Press," *CQ Researcher* 2 (April 17, 1992): 351.

180. See Roberto Suro, "Bitter Oklahoma Leader Strikes Back at the Press," *New York Times*, February 25, 1992, A12. Walters is a Democrat.

181. Shaun Walters had received medical treatment and stress counseling over the previous three years.

182. See pp. 193–95.

183. About a dozen of Robb's Virginia Beach social companions have been convicted on drug violations or received immunity from prosecutors in exchange for testimony or information. See again the citations to chapter 6, and for a general review of the background to the Robb story, see John F. Harris, "Charles S. Robb: The Unmaking of a Politician," *Washington Post*, June 7, 1992, A1, 18.

184. Political and personal friends of Governor Robb in Richmond and Tidewater cautioned him about his party associates.

185. Donald P. Baker, "Robb Acts To Head Off TV 'Exposé,'" *Washington Post*, April 26, 1991, A1, 14. The "Exposé" show was aired on April 28, 1991. All major Virginia newspapers carried extensive stories on Collins between the publication of the *Post* piece and the airing of the NBC broadcast.

186. The October 1991 issue of *Playboy* featured a scantily clad Collins on the cover with the title, "The Woman Senator Charles Robb Couldn't Resist." See pp. 91–97, 164. See also Bob Gibson, "Collins reveals own tale," *Daily Progress*, August 21, 1991, A1, 9.

187. See pp. 194–95 and 275 *n*. 15, 276 *n*. 16.

188. See the excellent column by Robert G. Holland, "The Robb Tapes: Sex, Drugs, Intimidation, and Gross Stupidity," *Richmond Times–Dispatch*, May 8, 1991, A16. See also Holland's "The Unmaking of a President, 1991," *Richmond Times–Dispatch*, June 19, 1991, A12.

189. In May 1992, David McCloud pled guilty to a misdemeanor charge for falsely reporting to the FEC. On a 1988 report he had listed Watson's travel expenses as a "fund raising" cost.

190. The "Exposé" show included a surreptitiously made tape recording of David McCloud threatening to bring down the wrath of the IRS upon Franklin. Franklin's book was entitled *Tough Enough: The Cocaine Investigation of United States Senator Chuck Robb* (Virginia Beach: Broad Bay Publishing Co., Inc., 1990). Franklin alleges that Robb repeatedly used cocaine.

191. Donald P. Baker, "Wilder Says He's Bugged," *Washington Post*, June 8, 1991, A1, 9. Wilder had known of the wiretapping for some months prior to this, but had not made the information public.

192. John Harris, "Charles S. Robb: The Unmaking of a Politician," A18.

193. Robb apparently did not personally listen to the tape, so he would have "plausible deniability," but the tape was kept approximately twenty feet from his desk, and the senator also requested a transcript from his staff.

194. Ruff, as U.S. attorney for the District of Columbia from 1979 to 1982, had promoted Terwilliger in his office and later recommended him for a U.S. attorney's post in Vermont.

195. See Alicia Mundy, "Ruff Justice," *Legal Times* 15 (February 8, 1993): 2, 13; and "Spare the Robb: Did Friendly Insiders Spoil the Senator?" *Washington Post,* February 21, 1993, C1. Mundy also reports that a high official in the Bush White House expressed interest in the case to Justice. Robb was a Bush favorite, having voted for the Persian Gulf War authorization and to confirm Clarence Thomas to the U.S. Supreme Court.

196. Rob Eure, "Memo outlined ways to save Robb," *Virginian–Pilot,* May 20, 1992, A1, 6.

197. The memo was dated March 28, 1991 and was addressed to David McCloud.

198. Statement of Senator Robb contained in a press release dated May 20, 1992. See also Dale Eisman, "Taking the Chuck Robb Challenge," *Virginian–Pilot,* June 30, 1991, C1; and Margaret Edds and Warren Fiske, "You can't take their words for it," *Virginian–Pilot,* July 20, 1991, C1.

199. Robb made the comment at a press conference held June 12, 1991 at the U.S. Senate Radio/TV Gallery.

200. It may also be true that some journalists were grateful to Buchanan for taking on Bush, enlivening an otherwise unopposed contest and giving an unliked president fits.

201. Granted, no medical authority can predict the future course of a disease with certainty, but Tsongas's battle with cancer had been life-threatening and reporters often did not challenge enough the rosy health picture presented by Tsongas and his campaign. Fortunately, Tsongas was released from the hospital in late December 1992 and appeared to be on his way to another recovery, despite a brief rehospitalization in early 1993.

202. Florence Graves and Charles E. Shepard, "Packwood Accused of Sexual Advances," *Washington Post,* November 22, 1992, A1, 26–27. Packwood is a Republican.

203. The Post requested an interview with Packwood on October 23, but Packwood agreed to meet only on October 29. At that session the senator denied the charges and asked for time to respond. Days later he passed along derogatory information about the accusers that had to be checked out, as well as a request to prepare a statement for any story before publication.

204. Quoted from Leonard Downie, Jr., "Getting the Packwood Story," *Washington Post,* November 29, 1992, C7. See also Joann Byrd, "All the News That's Ready to Print," *Washington Post,* November 29, 1992, C8; and Richard Cohen, "It's Not Just Packwood's Dirty Linen," *National Journal* 24 (December 5, 1992): 2797.

205. Howard Kurtz, "Oregon Paper Says It Failed to Confirm Charges Against Packwood," *Washington Post,* December 2, 1992, A17.

206. Ibid. and *Hotline* 6 (December 1, 1992): 22.

207. Times–Mirror Center for the People and the Press, "The Press and Campaign '92: A Self Assessment" (Washington: Times–Mirror Center, December 1992), pp. 1, 15.

208. As Clinton's close friend and top White House adviser, Bruce Lindsey, told some journalists, "You all have been asses ever since we started." Quoted in Richard E. Cohen, "Vox Sop," *Washington Post,* January 3, 1993, C5. See also Burt Solomon, "How a Leak-Loathing White House Is Putting the Press in Its Place," *National Journal* 25 (February 13, 1993): 416–17; and Jeffrey H. Birnbaum, "Resentful of Negative Coverage, Clinton Spurns the Media, but He May Need to Woo Them Back," *Wall Street Journal,* April 15, 1993, A16.

209. The exact comparison between the 1992 and 1988 ratings is as follows:

	November 1992					November 1988				
Public's grade of press performance	A	B	C	D	F	A	B	C	D	F
	11%	25%	29%	16%	15%	8%	22%	33%	19%	16%

Source: Times–Mirror Center for the People and the Press, Washington, D.C. Based on random-sample telephone reinterviews of approximately 1,000 voters each in November 1988 and November 1992, shortly after each year's presidential election. The margin of error is plus or minus 3 percent.

210. Ibid. Polls taken in January, February, and September 1992 showed that 53 to 58 percent said the press had "too much influence," only 4 to 5 percent said the press had "too little influence," while 33 to 40 percent said press influence was "about right."

211. See Richard Harwood, "The Growing Irrelevance of Journalists," *Washington Post*, October 23, 1992, A21.

212. Weaver and Wilhoit, *The American Journalist in the 1990s*, pp. 10–11.

213. Ibid.

214. See "Problems in Exit Polling," *The Public Perspective* 4 (January/February 1993): 19–23. The network consortium is called Voter Research and Surveys (VRS).

215. Ibid. Somewhat the same phenomenon was detected in the 1988 presidential election.

216. The *Los Angeles Times* used a telephone survey of 1,703 adult Americans taken March 6–9, 1993, with a margin of error of plus or minus 3 percent. See the excellent, accompanying two-part series on the media by David Shaw, "Trust in Media Is on Decline," *Los Angeles Times*, March 31, 1993, A1, 16–18; and "Distrustful Public Views Media as 'Them'—Not 'Us,'" *Los Angeles Times*, April 1, 1993, A1, 18–19.

217. See pp. 226–29 and the discussion in the Afterword.

218. In response to the question "What, if anything, should be done about abuses of freedom of the press?" 51 percent said "The news media should regulate themselves," 27 percent wanted the courts to "Make it easier for the news media to be sued for libel," and 12 percent thought "The news media should be regulated by the government."

219. As noted earlier, NBC has appointed an ombudsman, but the post is strictly a behind-the-scenes position, at least so far. Also, the Canadian Broadcasting Corporation has had a particularly active ombudsman since the position was established in July 1989. The current CBC ombudsman, William Morgan, indicated in a telephone interview that he takes up a complaint only after the show in question has had an opportunity to respond *and* if the complainant remains dissatisfied. Currently, the CBC ombudsman is off-air, but this may change once an ongoing task force reports on possible improvements to the position.

220. Opening of "Nightline" show on "Politics and the Media: Reporting or Distorting," aired September 16, 1992.

221. Quotation often attributed to Richard S. Salant, who served as CBS News president from 1961 to 1964 and again from 1966 to 1979. Salant, who died in 1993, was an enormously influential figure in television journalism during its developmental decades.

222. See Donald Kellermann, "The People and the Press" (Washington: Times–Mirror Center for the People and the Press, December 1992), p. 3.

223. Walter Lippmann, *Public Opinion* (New York: Harcourt, Brace and Co., 1922), p. 365.

Selected Bibliography

Books

ABRAMSON, JEFFREY B., F. CHRISTOPHER ARTERTON, and GARY R. ORREN. *The Electronic Commonwealth*. New York: Basic Books, 1988.

ALTHEIDE, DAVID L. *Creating Reality: How TV News Distorts Events*. Beverly Hills: Sage, 1976.

American Press Institute. *Covering the Candidates: Role and Responsibilities of the Press*. Reston, Va.: American Press Institute, 1987.

ARTERTON, F. CHRISTOPHER. *Media Politics: The News Strategies of Presidential Campaigns*. Lexington, Mass.: Lexington Books, 1984.

BATES, STEPHEN. *If No News, Send Rumors*. New York: St. Martin's, 1989.

BENNETT, LANCE. *News: The Politics of Illusion*. 2nd ed. New York: Longman, 1988.

BERKMAN, RONALD, and LAURA W. KITCH. *Politics in the Media Age*. New York: McGraw-Hill, 1986.

BLACK, CHRISTINE M., and THOMAS OLIPHANT. *All By Myself: The Unmaking of a Presidential Campaign*. Boston: Globe Pequot, 1989.

BRODER, DAVID S. *Behind the Front Page*. New York: Simon & Schuster, 1987.

COOK, TIMOTHY E. *Making Laws and Making News: Media Strategies in the U.S. House of Representatives*. Washington, D.C.: Brookings, 1989.

COSE, ELLIS. *The Press*. New York: William Morrow and Co., Inc., 1989.

CROUSE, TIMOTHY. *The Boys on the Bus*. New York: Ballantine, 1973.

DIAMOND, EDWIN. *The Tin Kazoo: Television, Politics, and the News*. Cambridge, Mass.: MIT Press, 1975.

ENTMAN, ROBERT M. *Democracy Without Citizens: Media and the Decay of American Politics*. New York: Oxford University Press, 1989.

EPSTEIN, EDWARD JAY. *Between Fact and Fiction*. New York: Random House, 1975.

———. *News from Nowhere: Television and the News*. New York: Random House, 1973.

GINSBERG, BENJAMIN, and MARTIN SHEFTER. *Politics by Other Means: The Declining Importance of Elections in America*. New York: Basic Books, 1990.

GOLDBERG, ROBERT, and GERALD JAY GOLDBERG. *Anchors: Brokaw, Jennings, Rather and the Evening News*. New York: Birch Lane, 1990.

GOLDSTEIN, TOM. *The News at Any Cost*. New York: Simon & Schuster, 1985.

GRABER, DORIS A. *Mass Media and American Politics*. 3rd ed. Washington, D.C.: Congressional Quarterly Press, 1989.

———. *Media Power in Politics*. 2nd ed. Washington, D.C.: Congressional Quarterly Press, 1989.

GREENFIELD, JEFF. *The Real Campaign: How the Media Missed the Story of the 1980 Campaign*. New York: Summit, 1982.

HESS, STEPHEN. *The Ultimate Insiders: U.S. Senators in the National Media*. Washington, D.C.: The Brookings Institution, 1986.

HIRSCH, ALAN. *Talking Heads: Television's Political Talk Shows and Pundits*. New York: St. Martin's, 1991.

ISAACS, NORMAN E. *Untended Gates: The Mismanaged Press*. New York: Columbia University Press, 1986.

IYENGAR, SHANTO, and DONALD R. KINDER. *News That Matters*. Chicago: University of Chicago Press, 1987.

KURTZ, HOWARD. *Media Circus: The Trouble With America's Newspapers*. New York: Times Books/Random House, 1993.

LEE, MARTIN A., and NORMAN SOLOMON. *Unreliable Sources: A Guide to Detecting Bias in the News Media*. New York: Lyle Stuart, 1990.

LEONARD, THOMAS C., *The Power of the Press: The Birth of American Political Reporting*. New York: Oxford University Press, 1986.

LICHTER, S. ROBERT, STANLEY ROTHMAN, and LINDA S. LICHTER. *The Media Elite*. Bethesda, Md.: Adler and Adler, 1986.

LICHTER, S. ROBERT, DANIEL AMUNDSON, and RICHARD NOYES. *The Video Campaign: Network Coverage of the 1988 Primaries*. Washington, D.C.: American Enterprise Institute, 1988.

MATUSOW, BARBARA. *The Evening Stars: The Making of the Network News Anchor*. Boston: Houghton Mifflin, 1983.

MITROFF, IAN, and WARREN BENNIS. *The Unreality Industry*. New York: Birch Lane Press, 1989.

MICKELSON, SIG. *The Electric Mirror: Politics in an Age of Network Television*. New York: Dodd, Mead, 1972.

NIMMO, DAN, and JAMES E. COMBS. *Mediated Political Realities*. 2nd ed. New York: Longman, 1988.

ORREN, GARY R., and NELSON W. POLSBY, eds. *Media and Momentum: The New Hampshire Primary and Nomination Politics*. Chatham, N.J.: Chatham House, 1987.

PALETZ, DAVID L., and ROBERT M. ENTMAN. *Media Power Politics*. New York: Free Press, 1981.

PATTERSON, THOMAS E. *The Mass Media Election*. New York: Praeger, 1980.

PATTERSON, THOMAS E., and ROBERT D. McCLURE. *The Unseeing Eye: The Myth of Television Power in National Elections*. New York: G. P. Putnam's Sons, 1976.

PERRY, JAMES A. *Us and Them: How the Press Covered the 1972 Election*. New York: Clarkson Potter, 1973.

PRESS, CHARLES, and KENNETH VERBURG. *American Politicians and Journalists*. Glenview, Ill.: Scott, Foresman, 1988.

RANNEY, AUSTIN. *Channels of Power: The Impact of Television on American Politics*. New York: Basic Books, 1983.

ROSENSTIEL, TOM. *Strange Bedfellows: How Television and the Presidential Candidates Changed American Politics, 1992*. New York: Hyperion Press, 1993.

ROSS, SHELLEY. *Fall from Grace: Sex, Scandal, and Corruption in American Politics from 1702 to the Present*. New York: Ballantine, 1988.

RUSHER, WILLIAM A. *The Coming Battle for the Media: Curbing the Power of the Media Elite*. New York: William Morrow, 1988.

SCHRAM, MARTIN. *The Great American Video Game: Presidential Politics in the Television Age*. New York: William Morrow, 1987.

SIMON, ROGER. *Road Show*. New York: Farrar, Straus & Giroux, 1990.

STEPHENS, MITCHELL. *A History of News: From the Drum to the Satellite*. New York: Viking, 1989.

TAYLOR, PAUL. *See How They Run: Electing the President in an Age of Mediaocracy*. New York: Alfred A. Knopf, 1990.

WATTENBERG, BEN J. *The Good News Is the Bad News Is Wrong*. New York: Simon & Schuster, 1985.

Articles

ADAMS, WILLIAM C. "'84 Convention Coverage." *Public Opinion* 7 (December/January 1985): 43–48.

————. "Media Coverage of Campaign '84: A Preliminary Report." *Public Opinion* 7 (April/May 1984): 9–13.

ADATTO, KIKU. "The Shrinking Sound Bite." *The New Republic* 202 (May 28, 1990): 20–23.

ALTER, JONATHAN. "How the Media Blew It." *Newsweek* 112 (November 21, 1988): 24–26.

AMUNDSON, DANIEL, and ROBERT S. LICHTER. "Heeere's Politics." *Public Opinion* 11 (July/August 1988): 46–47.

BAGDIKIAN, BEN H. "The Fruits of Agnewism." *Columbia Journalism Review* 11 (January/February 1973): 9–21.

BALZ, DAN. "Capitol Hill Stuck in Ethics Quagmire." *Washington Post*, May 28, 1989, A1, A20.

————. "The Public Politics of Rumors." *Washington Post*, June 8, 1989, A1, A10.

BARBER, JAMES DAVID. "Candidate Reagan and the Sucker Generation." *Columbia Journalism Review* 25 (November/December 1987): 33–36.

BARNES, JAMES A. "Changing Company Town." *National Journal* 21 (February 4, 1989): 278–80.

BARRETT, LAURENCE I. "The Dark Side of Competition . . . Woodward, Bernstein." *Columbia Journalism Review* 12 (July/August 1974): 14–15.

————. "Rethinking the Fair Games Rules." *Time* 130 (November 30, 1987): 76, 78.

BONAFEDE, DOM. "Blame the Scribes." *National Journal* 20 (July 9, 1988): 1803–6.

————. "Crossing Over." *National Journal* 21 (January 14, 1989): 102.

————. "Go Away." *National Journal* 21 (February 11, 1989): 378.

————. "Scoop or Snoop?" *National Journal* 20 (November 5, 1988): 2791–94.

————. "Taking On the Press." *National Journal* 21 (April 8, 1989): 856–60.

BOOT, WILLIAM. "Campaign '88: TV Overdoses on the Inside Dope." *Columbia Journalism Review* 27 (January/February 1989): 23–29.

————. "Iranscam: When the Cheering Stopped." *Columbia Journalism Review* 25 (March/April 1987): 25–30.

BOYD, JAMES. "The Ritual of Wiggle: From Ruin to Reelection." *Washington Monthly* 2 (September 1970): 28–43.

BRAMEN, SANDRA. "Public Expectations of Media Versus Standards in Codes of Ethics." *Journalism Quarterly* 65 (Spring 1988): 71–77, 240.

BRANDEIS, LOUIS D., and SAMUEL D. WARREN. "The Right to Privacy." *Harvard Law Review* 4 (December 15, 1890): 193–220.

BRODER, DAVID S. "Beware the 'Insider' Syndrome: Why News Makers and News Reporters Shouldn't Get Too Cozy." *Washington Post*, December 4, 1988, L2.

Center for Media and Public Affairs. "Quayle Hunt: TV News Coverage of the Quayle Nomination." *Media Monitor* 2 (September 1988): 1–4.

CLANCEY, MAURA, and MICHAEL J. ROBINSON. "General Election Coverage in Campaign '84: Part 1." *Public Opinion* 7 (December/January 1985): 49–54, 59.

COOPER, THOMAS W. "Ethics, Journalism and Television: Bibliographic Constellations, Black Holes." *Journalism Quarterly* 65 (Spring 1988): 450–55, 496.

DEWAR, HELEN. "Defeat of Tower Reflects Dramatic Changes in Senate." *Washington Post*, March 13, 1989, A1, A6–7.

DIAMOND, EDWIN. "Fairness and Balance in the Evening News." *Columbia Journalism Review* 11 (January/February, 1973): 22–23.

————. "Gotcha: The Media's Frenzied Patrol of the Candidates." *New York*, October 26, 1987, pp. 50–53.

————. "New Wrinkles on the Permanent Press." *Public Opinion* 7 (April/May 1984): 2–4, 58.

EASTLAND, TERRY. "Ethicshock." *The Washingtonian* 23 (August 1989): 77–80.

FUNKHOUSER, G. RAY. "The Issues of the Sixties: An Exploratory Study in the Dynamics of Public Opinion." *Public Opinion Quarterly* 37 (Spring 1973): 62–75.

GARMENT, SUZANNE. "Political Imperfections: Scandal Time in Washington." *Public Opinion* 10 (May/June 1987): 10–12, 60.

———. "Sleaze, Scandal, and Successful Elections." *Public Opinion* 11 (September/October 1988): 15–17.

GERGEN, DAVID. "The Message to the Media." *Public Opinion* 7 (April/ May 1984): 5–8.

GLASSMAN, JAMES K. "The 'Ethics' Frenzy." *Washington Post*, May 28, 1989, B1–2.

GUP, TED. "Identifying Homosexuals: What Are the Rules?" *Washington Journalism Review* 10 (October 1988): 30–33.

GUZZARDI, WALTER. "The Secret Love Affair Between the Press and Government." *Public Opinion* 8 (August/September 1985): 2–5.

HENRY, WILLIAM A., III. "Cover Story: Journalism Under Fire." *Time* 122 (December 12, 1983): 76–93.

HENTOFF, NAT. "Woodward, Bernstein and 'All the President's Men'." *Columbia Journalism Review* 12 (July/August 1974): 10–13.

HERSHEY, MARJORIE RANDON. "The Campaign and the Media." In *The Election of 1988: Reports and Interpretations*, edited by Gerald M. Pomper et al. chap. 3, pp. 73–102. Chatham, N.J.: Chatham House, 1989.

HERTZBERG, HENDRICK. "Sluicegate." *The New Republic* 196 (June 1, 1987): 11–12.

HOLLSTEIN, MILTON. "Congressman Howe in the Salt Lake Media: A Case Study of the Press as Pillory." *Journalism Quarterly* 54 (Autumn 1977): 454–58, 465.

HOSENBALL, MARK, and MICHAEL ISIKOFF. "Pssst: Inside Washington's Rumor Mill." *The New Republic* 200 (January 2, 1989): 16–19.

IVINS, MOLLY. "The Reporters Under the Bed." *Mirabella* 1 (June 1989): 120–21.

JOHNSTON, DAVID. "The Anonymous-Source Syndrome." *Columbia Journalism Review* 25 (November/December 1987): 54–58.

JUDIS, JOHN B. "The Hart Affair." *Columbia Journalism Review* 25 (July/August 1987): 21–25.

KING, ANTHONY. "Transatlantic Transgressions: A Comparison of British and American Scandals." *Public Opinion* 7 (December/January 1985): 20–22, 64.

LEEDEN, MICHAEL. "Public Opinion, Press Opinion, and Foreign Policy." *Public Opinion* 7 (August/September 1984): 5–7, 60.

LESSARD, SUZANNAH. "The Issue Was Women." *Newsweek* 109 (May 18, 1987): 32, 34.

LICHTER, ROBERT S. "How the Press Covered the Primaries." *Public Opinion* 11 (July/August 1988): 45–49.

———. "Misreading Momentum." *Public Opinion* 11 (May/ June 1988): 15–17, 57.

LICHTER, ROBERT S., DANIEL AMUNDSON, and RICHARD E. NOYES. "Election '88 Media Coverage." *Public Opinion* 11 (January/February 1989): 18–19, 52.

LICHTER, ROBERT S., and LINDA S. LICHTER. "Covering the Convention Coverage." *Public Opinion* 11 (September/October 1988): 41–44.

LICHTER, ROBERT S., and STANLEY ROTHMAN. "Media and Business Elites." *Public Opinion* 4 (October/November 1981): 42–46, 59–60.

MCCARTNEY, JAMES. "What Really Happened in Manchester?" *Columbia Journalism Review* 10 (May/June 1972): 26–27.

MATLACK, CAROL. "Crossing the Line?" *National Journal* 21 (March 25, 1989): 724–29.

———. "Rules of the Game." *National Journal* 21 (June 3, 1989): 1386.

MATUSOW, BARBARA. "Washington's Journalism Establishment." *The Washingtonian* 23 (February 1989): 94–101, 265–70.

MOORE, DAVID. "The Legacy of William Loeb." *Public Opinion* 5 (December/January 1983): 43–44.

ORNSTEIN, NORMAN. "The Post's Campaign to Wreck Congress." *Washington Post*, May 29, 1989, A25.

PATTERSON, THOMAS E. "The Miscast Institution: The Press in Presidential Politics." *Public Opinion* 3 (June/July 1980): 46–51.

———. "The Press and Its Missed Assignment," pp. 93–110. In *The Elections of 1988*, edited by Michael Nelson. Washington, D.C.: Congressional Quarterly Press, 1989.

PLISSNER, MARTIN. "Inkbites." *Washington Post*, March 20, 1989, A11.

RANDOLPH, ELEANOR. "Candidates Limit Media Access." *Washington Post*, September 21, 1988, A1, A14.

———. "Frustrated Reporters Add Megaphones, Binoculars to Notepads." *Washington Post*, November 2, 1988, A25.

———. "'Quayle Hunt' Turns News Media into Target for Angry Public." *Washington Post*, August 25, 1988, A10.

ROBINSON, MICHAEL J. "Just How Liberal Is the News? 1980 Revisited." *Public Opinion* 6 (February/March 1983): 55–60.

———. "Pressing Opinion." *Public Opinion* 9 (September/ October 1986): 56–59.

ROBINSON, MICHAEL J., and MARGARET SHEEHAN. "Brief Encounters With the Fourth Kind: Reagan's Press Honeymoon." *Public Opinion* 3 (December/January 1981): 56–61.

ROBINSON, MICHAEL J., NANCY CONOVER, and MARGARET SHEEHAN. "The Media at Mid-Year: A Bad Year for McLuhanites." *Public Opinion* 3 (June/July 1980): 41–45.

ROSENSTIEL, THOMAS B., and PAUL HOUSTON. "Rumor Mill: The Media 'Try to Cope.'" *Los Angeles Times*, August 5, 1988, 1, 18.

SCHNEIDER, WILLIAM, and I. A. LEWIS. "Views on the News." *Public Opinion* 8 (August/September 1985): 6–11, 58–59.

SHAPIRO, WALTER. "Is It Right to Publish Rumors?" *Time* 132 (July 10, 1989): 53.

SMITH, TED J., III. "The Watchdog's Bite." *American Enterprise* 1 (January/February 1990): 62–70.

STANLEY, ALESSANDRA, and MAUREEN DOWD. "The Dweebs on the Bus." *Gentleman's Quarterly* 57 (September 1988): 430–33, 482–87.

STEIN, M. L. "How Editors View Ombudsmen." *Editor and Publisher* 122 (May 13, 1989): 15–16.

STEVENSON, ROBERT L., et al. "Untwisting *The News Twisters*: A Replication of Efron's Study." *Journalism Quarterly* 50 (Summer 1973): 211–19.

STOVALL, JAMES GLEN. "Coverage of the 1984 Presidential Campaign." *Journalism Quarterly* 65 (Summer 1968): 443–49, 484.

SWERDLOW, JOEL. "The Decline of the Boys on the Bus." *Washington Journalism Review* 3 (January/February 1981): 15–19.

THIMMESCH, NICK. "The Editorial Endorsement Game." *Public Opinion* 7 (October/November 1984): 10–13.

WHEELER, MICHAEL. "Reining in Horserace Journalism." *Public Opinion* 3 (February/March 1980): 41–45.

WILDAVSKY, AARON. "The Media's 'American Egalitarians.'" *Public Interest* 88 (Summer 1987): 94–104.

WILKIE, CURTIS, "Too Hot to Handle." *Washington Journalism Review* 6 (March 1984): 38–39, 58.

WINES, MICHAEL. "In Bed with the Press." *Washington Journalism Review* 9 (September 1987): 16–19.

WINSHIP, TOM. "Answering Hart and Kennedy." *Columbia Journalism Review* 25 (May 1988): 39–41.

WITCOVER, JULES. "The Trials of a One-Candidate Campaign." *Columbia Journalism Review* 11 (January/February 1973): 24–28.

———. "William Loeb and the New Hampshire Primary: A Question of Ethics." *Columbia Journalism Review* 10 (May/June 1972): 14–25.

WITT, EVANS. "Here, There, and Everywhere: Where Americans Get Their News." *Public Opinion* 6 (August/September 1983): 45–48.

YUM, JUNE O., and KATHLEEN E. KENDALL. "Sources of Political Information in a Presidential Primary Campaign." *Journalism Quarterly* 65 (Spring 1988): 148–51, 177.

Name Index

Abramson, Jeffrey B., 351
Abramson, Jill, xi, 161–163, 165–167, 203, 301, 316, 325, 344
Adams, Sherman, 33, 308
Adams, William C., 316, 352, 353
Adatto, Kiku, 232, 335, 353
Ader, David, 342
Agnew, Randy, 140
Agnew, Spiro, 7, 8, 19, 48, 63, 64, 72, 80, 84, 88, 108, 134, 140, 188, 189, 239
Ahner, Alfred F., 324
Ailes, Roger, 1, 83
Albosta, Donald J., 81
Allain, Bill, 329
Allen, Michael, 322, 341
Alston, Chuck, 327
Alter, Jonathan, 273, 324, 336, 343, 353
Altheide, David L., 311, 351
Amundson, Daniel, 315, 330, 352, 353, 354
Anderson, David, 313
Anderson, Jack, 10, 57, 95, 140, 172, 177, 310, 326, 347
Andrews, Bert, 31
Andrews, Wyatt, 51, 235, 236, 301
Apple, R. W., 309
Archibald, George, 119, 301, 318, 321, 337
Ard, Michael J., viii
Armandt, Lynn, 98, 316
Armitage, Richard, 276
Arterton, F. Christopher, 351
Atwater, Lee, 22, 83, 97, 98, 108, 152, 161–164, 169, 170, 174, 175, 177, 184, 185, 206, 231, 238, 242, 243, 301, 325

Babbitt, Bruce, 20, 81, 92, 117, 238, 239, 307
Bagdikian, Ben H., 328, 334, 353
Baker, Bobby, 33, 308
Baker, Donald P., 347, 348
Baker, James, 162, 163, 169, 242
Baker, Russell, 4, 307
Bakker, Jim, 55, 122
Bakker, Tammy Faye, 55
Balz, Dan, 215, 268, 301, 327, 328, 342, 353
Baran, Jan W., 301
Barber, James David, 65, 312, 353
Barker, Karlyn, 321
Barnes, Fred, 68, 76, 114, 122, 172, 183, 301, 328
Barnes, James A., 131, 301, 353

Barnes, Robert, 328
Barnhill, Mark, 318, 324
Barone, Michael, 60, 86, 88, 157, 219, 238, 301, 312, 313, 320
Barrett, Beth, 318, 324
Barrett, Laurence I., 11, 78, 131, 301, 313, 320, 333, 345, 353
Barry, Marion, 7, 17, 103, 104, 111, 112, 137, 140, 204, 205, 241, 296, 318, 321, 331
Bates, Stephen, 308–310, 316, 318, 321, 351
Bayer, Amy, 323
Bayh, Birch, 164, 325
Beamish, Rita, 196
Beckel, Robert, 301
Beckwith, David, 104, 157, 205, 301, 311, 337
Behr, Roy L., 332
Belkin, Lisa, 325
Benedetto, Richard, 253
Bennett, Lance, 314, 321, 335, 351
Bennis, Warren, 352
Benson, Steve, 129
Bentsen, Lloyd, 82, 206, 243, 314
Bergen, Candice, 281, 282
Berke, Richard L., 345
Berkman, Ronald, 314, 351
Bernstein, Carl, 19, 61, 63, 140, 321
Bernstein, Sharon, 347
Bettag, Tom, 134, 136, 236, 301
Bezanson, Randall, 313
Biden, Joseph, 7, 14, 53, 57, 71, 73, 74, 84, 91, 96–97, 99, 112, 116, 118, 119, 126, 131, 138, 142, 191, 204, 205, 210, 239, 313, 316, 317, 320, 337
Bierbauer, Charles, 302
Birnbaum, Jeffrey H., 325, 343, 349
Black, Christine M., 351
Blaine, James G., 28
Blair, Gwenda, 336
Blair, William M., 309
Blumenthal, Sidney, 344, 345
Blustein, Paul 248, 326
Bode, Ken, 67, 77, 96, 100, 109, 205, 302, 315
Boggs, Hale, 33, 335
Boggs, Linda, 335
Bolling, Richard, 33
Bonafede, Dom, 313, 314, 331, 335, 353
Boot, William, 311, 313, 332, 336, 345, 353
Borger, Gloria, 186, 328
Bork, Robert, 20, 101

Boyd, Gerald M., 323
Boyd, James, 353
Boyer, Peter, 336
Bradlee, Benjamin, 32, 41, 42, 103, 115, 176,
    212, 216, 217, 224, 262, 302, 309, 326
Bradley, Ed, 89
Bradley, John Ed, 308, 309
Bramen, Sandra, 334, 353
Brandeis, Louis D., 28, 210, 308, 333, 353
Brannigan, Martha, 322
Brantley, Max 302
Braver, Rita, 180
Brazile, Donna, 16, 176, 177, 334
Brenner, Marie, 146, 322, 344
Bridge, Christine, 294
Brinkley, David, 60, 121, 241, 336
Brisbane, Arthur S., 318
Britt, Donna, 334
Britton, Nan, 29, 308
Broder, David S., 9, 30, 39, 42, 64, 216, 221,
    222, 226, 230, 233, 279, 302, 311, 312, 314,
    316, 321, 330, 334–336, 345, 346, 351, 353
Brogan, Patrick, 335
Brokaw, Tom, 138, 158, 178, 181, 228, 234, 246,
    250, 254, 302, 336, 338
Brooks, Jack, 6
Brown, Jerry, 257, 283–287, 296, 346–347
Brown, Robin, 337
Brown, Thomas, 308
Browning, Graeme, 339
Brownstein, Ronald, 341
Bruno, Hal, 37, 58, 82, 84, 112, 174, 175, 224,
    225, 274, 302
Buchanan, James, 27
Buchanan, Patrick J., 89, 91, 258, 261, 295, 315,
    349
Buckley, John, 146, 147, 204, 238, 301
Buckley, William F., 91
Bull, Chris, 348
Burgess, Philip M., 241, 337
Busby, Horace, 328
Bush, Barbara, 176, 273
Bush, George, vii, 1, 7, 15, 16, 20, 22, 57, 73, 75,
    82, 83, 86, 89, 90, 91, 95, 96, 97, 104, 107,
    108, 110, 117, 120, 126, 144, 152–160, 162,
    169, 170–173, 175, 176, 177, 179, 184, 187,
    201, 204–206, 224, 231, 232, 239, 240, 242,
    243, 248, 249, 250, 253–258, 259, 260, 261,
    262, 269, 271–275, 276, 279, 295, 297, 298,
    311, 314, 323, 325–327, 331, 333, 337, 338,
    339, 340, 342, 343, 344, 346, 349
Bush, George, Jr., 175
Bush, Marvin, vii
Bushkin, Kathryn A., 76, 77, 110, 148, 302, 315
Butterfield, Alexander, 189
Byrd, Joann, 255, 339, 349

Caddell, Patrick, 96, 97
Calvert, Robert E., 302
Cannon, Lou, 321, 322, 347
Caperton, Dee, 18

Caperton, Gaston, 7, 18, 143
Capone, Al, 34
Carlson, Margaret, 260, 340
Carson, Johnny, 129, 234, 236, 257, 336
Carter, Billy, 7, 11, 55, 72
Carter, Jimmy, 7, 10, 11, 48, 60, 64, 72, 74, 75,
    81, 90, 92, 105, 106, 108, 127–129, 131,
    134, 145, 189, 190, 314, 320, 321, 333
Carvey, Dana, 129
Castro, Fidel, 34, 309
Castro, Jose I., 307
Celeste, Dagmar, 55, 242, 311, 333
Celeste, Richard, 7, 17, 55, 84, 101, 116, 117,
    211, 318, 333
Chancellor, John, 63, 64, 104, 127, 140, 157,
    201, 222, 231, 234, 274–275, 302, 315,
    336
Chapman, Richard, 334
Chase, Chevy, 129
Cheshire, Maxine, 309
Chiles, Lawton, 117
Chung, Connie, 234, 236, 336
Church, Frank, 34, 35
Churchville, Victoria, 318
Cikins, Warren, 334
Cirino, Robert, 315
Cisneros, Henry, 7, 17, 18, 57, 102, 112, 117,
    330
Clancey, Maura, 89, 315, 353
Cleveland, Grover, 28
Clifford, Garry, 302
Clifford, Timothy, 342
Clinton, Bill, vii, 248–249, 250, 253, 254, 255,
    256, 257, 259, 260, 261–262, 263–271, 272,
    273, 274, 275, 276, 279, 281, 286, 296, 297,
    298, 338, 339, 340, 341, 342, 343, 346, 347,
    349
Clinton, Hillary Rodham, 255, 263, 264, 272
Clinton, Roger, 266
Cochran, John, 302
Coelho, Tony, 21, 183, 184, 186, 328
Cohen, Richard E., 77, 115, 148, 214, 302, 307,
    322, 324, 333, 337, 349
Coleman, Milton, 12, 115, 141, 195, 302
Collier, Peter, 309
Collins, B.T., 285
Collins, Reid, 253
Collins, Tai, 194, 291, 348
Colton, Elizabeth O., 330, 334
Combs, James E., 352
Compton, Ann, 108, 113, 129, 138, 167, 302
Connell, Christopher, 346
Connor, Jim, 302
Conover, Nancy, 311, 355
Cook, Timothy E., xi, 334, 351
Cooke, Janet, 172, 326
Coolidge, Calvin, 219
Cooper, Thomas W., 353
Corchado, Alfredo, 102, 302, 318, 330
Corcoran, Katherine, 340
Cornell, Douglas, 38

Cornfield, Michael, 312
Cose, Ellis, 351
Coulson, Crocker, 331
Couric, Katie, 345
Cranberg, Gilbert, 313
Crane, Phil, 302
Cronkite, Walter, 87, 336
Croteau, David, 315
Crouse, Timothy, 59, 60, 311, 351
Cuomo, Mario, 281, 341
Curley, James, 17
Curley, John, 313
Curran, Tim, 348
Cutler, Lloyd M., 333

Damore, Leo, 312
Davis, Ed, 347
Davis, John H., 309
Davis, William True, 95
Day, Benjamin, 27
Deaver, Michael, 41
DeConcini, Dennis, 180
Dedman, Bill, 302, 316, 334
Demaris, Ovid, 309
DeStefano, Anthony M., 321
Devroy, Ann, 80, 104, 150, 172, 173, 302, 304,
    326–328, 332, 333, 342
Dewar, Helen, 326, 353
Dewey, Thomas E., 8
DeWitt, Karen, 344
Diamond, Edwin, 351, 353
Dickerson, Nancy, 43
Dickinson, Angie, 34
Dionne, E. J., 71, 81, 109, 110, 217, 243, 302,
    312, 317, 346
Dixon, William, 323
Doak, David, 316
Dole, Robert, 95, 96, 108, 173, 184
Donahue, Phil, 55, 98
Donaldson, Sam, 55, 60, 89, 109, 152, 189, 190,
    203, 215, 223, 234, 235, 240, 336
Dooley, Patricia I., 334
Dornan, Robert K., 269
Dougherty, Peter, viii
Dowd, Maureen, 312, 317, 331, 355
Downie, Leonard, 56, 88, 139, 187, 216, 217,
    222, 296, 302, 334, 349
Downs, Hugh, 336
Drummond, Bob, 243, 302
Du Brow, Rick, 346
Dukakis, Kitty, 155
Dukakis, Michael, 7, 14–16, 73, 86, 90, 96, 112,
    116, 124, 126, 131, 142, 144, 152–156, 161,
    170, 175, 176, 192, 196, 199, 201, 204–206,
    224, 225, 231, 240, 241, 316, 318, 323, 324,
    326, 331, 333
Dukakis, Stelian, 155
Duke, Paul, 31, 52, 114, 198, 227, 302
Duncan, Dayton, 153
Dunnington, Robert, 293
Dyson, Roy, 328

Eagleton, Thomas, 7, 9, 10, 46, 54–57, 64, 84,
    91, 95, 106, 115, 116, 119, 125, 134, 152,
    153, 204, 205, 239–241, 318, 319, 321
Eastland, Terry, 87
Edds, Margaret, 349
Edsall, Thomas B., 103, 302, 317
Efron, Edith, 89, 315
Ehrenhalt, Alan, 302
Eisenger, Richard A., 315
Eisenhower, Dwight, 8, 31, 33, 44, 45, 88, 105,
    314, 332, 333
Eisman, Dale, 349
Elder, David, 312
Elizabeth II, Queen, 152, 271
Engberg, Eric, 82, 160, 212, 250, 267, 269, 302,
    313, 324, 330, 342
Entman, Robert M., xi, 311, 314, 321, 351, 352
Epstein, Edward Jay, 351
Epstein, Keith C., 325
Eure, Rob, 293, 349
Evans, Rowland, 14, 91, 145, 152, 183, 322, 323,
    328, 334
Exner, Judith Campbell, 34–36, 309

Farrakhan, Louis, 12
Feinberg, Barry M., 315
Fenno, Richard F., 324
Ferraro, Geraldine, 6, 7, 12, 13, 53, 54, 57, 72,
    74, 80–82, 84, 89–91, 103, 105, 108, 119,
    126, 135, 139, 238, 239, 241, 321
Fiedler, Tom, 55, 98, 109, 110, 148, 302, 316
Fielding, Fred, 239
Fields, Louis, 273
Figueroa, William, 282–283
Fineman, Howard, 77, 78, 120, 136, 146, 174,
    175, 242, 302, 313, 322, 334
Finkel, Steven E., 337
Fiske, Warren, 302, 349
Fitzgerald, Jennifer, 272, 273, 343
FitzSimon, Martha, 342
Flack, Roberta, 195
Flowers, Gennifer, vii, 248, 259, 263, 264–266,
    267, 270, 272, 273, 341, 342
Foley, Don, 142, 302
Foley, Thomas, 7, 21, 22, 75, 88, 102, 120, 144,
    182–186, 225, 328
Ford, Gerald, 7, 10, 11, 40, 47, 60, 72, 74, 106,
    108, 109, 127–129, 131, 134, 138, 139, 204,
    219, 238, 241, 317, 320, 333
Ford, Robert E., 286
Foxe, Fanne, 7, 19, 47, 208
Frank, Barney, 7, 21, 22, 55, 56, 88, 100, 110,
    139, 184, 192, 321
Frankel, Glenn, 334
Frankel, Max, 10
Franken, Bob, 344
Franklin, Aretha, 195
Franklin, Ben, 188, 302
Franklin, Billy, 292, 348
Frantz, Douglas, 168, 169, 302, 325, 331
Freiwald, Aaron, 302, 325

Freud, Sigmund, 64
Friedman, Steve, 147
Friendly, David, 271
Frisby, Michael K., 326
Fritz, Sara, 345
Fulani, Lenora, 267
Fuller, Craig, 337
Funk, Tim, 339
Funkhouser, G. Ray, 353

Gailey, Phil, 323
Gallup, George, 333
Gamarekian, Barbara, 37, 302
Gannon, James, 59, 82, 224, 302
Garment, Suzanne, 319, 354
Gartner, Michael, 252–253
Gault, Charlayne Hunter, 89
Gelman, David, 329
Gephardt, Richard, 96, 97, 142
Gergen, David, 109, 253, 297, 303, 315, 354
Germond, Jack, 31, 32, 37, 71, 75, 109, 115, 154, 198, 226, 230, 303, 317, 323, 331
Giancana, Sam, 34
Gibson, Bob, 348
Gingrich, Newt, 20, 117, 183, 184, 328
Ginsburg, Benjamin, 351
Ginsburg, Douglas, 7, 20, 81, 100, 101, 113, 114, 117, 119, 140, 238, 239, 319
Gladstone, Mark, 347
Glassman, James K., 208, 333, 354
Gold, Victor, 313
Goldberg, Gerald Jay, 351
Goldberg, Robert, 303
Goldberg, Steve, 303
Goldin, Marion, 291
Goldstein, Tom, 309, 316, 326, 351
Goldwater, Barry, 44, 88, 89, 135, 321, 333
Goodin, Mark, 22, 169, 184, 185, 239, 303
Goodman, Ellen, 226
Goodwin, Doris Kearns, 189, 318, 328, 329, 334
Gorbachev, Mikhail, vii, 54, 311
Gordon, Lou, 8
Gore, Al, Jr., 20, 81, 117, 255, 257–258, 283, 346
Gore, Al, Sr., 257
Gore, Tipper, 283
Gorin, Norman, 171, 303
Goudinoff, Peter, 318
Graber, Doris A., 308, 314, 328, 334, 351
Grabowski, Gene, 323
Graham, Fred, 336
Graves, Florence, 295–296, 349
Gray, William, 183
Green, Bill, 334
Greenfield, Jeff, 118, 124, 225, 250, 303, 315, 336, 351
Greenya, John, 309
Griffith, Thomas, 320
Groves, Lloyd, 311
Grunwald, Mandy, 341
Gruson, Lindsay, 320
Guccione, Bob, 267

Gunther, Albert C., 339
Gup, Ted, 65, 187, 192, 212, 223, 303, 319, 327, 329, 354
Gurwitt, Rob, 310
Guzzardi, Walter, 354

Hagstrom, Jerry, 340
Haig, Alexander, 4, 80
Hall, Arsenio, 250, 256
Hallow, Ralph Z., 321, 323
Hamilton, Alexander, 27
Haner, Steven, 303
Hannon, Tom, 265
Hansen, Lawrence N., 347
Harbrecht, Douglas A., 313
Harding, Warren, 29, 34, 220
Hardy, Michael, 101, 303
Harkin, Tom, 270
Harrington, Walt, 317
Harris, John F., 347, 348, 349
Harris, Louis, 340
Hart, Gary, 3, 5–7, 12–14, 17, 25, 47, 48, 53, 55, 56, 60, 64, 66–69, 72, 73, 76–81, 84, 89, 91, 92, 97, 98, 100–103, 106, 109, 110, 112, 114–121, 123, 125, 126, 129–131, 140, 144, 148–152, 173, 174, 177, 190, 191, 194, 197, 203–205, 209, 216, 217, 221, 230, 238, 240, 241, 261, 263, 274, 312, 313, 316, 317, 320–323, 330, 331, 333, 354
Hart, Lee, 77, 130, 150, 230, 242
Hartpence, George, 102
Harvey, Paul, 91, 313
Harwood, Richard, 87, 121, 158, 203, 212, 228, 237, 303, 308, 310, 314–316, 319, 336, 337, 350
Hawkes, Bob, 310
Hays, Wayne, 47, 100
Healy, Brian, 303
Healy, Melissa, 347
Hearst, William Randolph, 28
Hedges, Michael, 321
Henry, William A., III, 341, 354
Hentoff, Nat, 354
Herman, George, 32, 40, 43–45, 188, 215, 303
Hershey, Marjorie Randon, 311, 347, 354
Hertsgaard, Mark, 91, 315
Hertzberg, Hendrik, 323, 354
Herz, Suzanne, viii
Hess, Stephen, 351
Heymann, C. David, 309
Highberger, Ken, 303
Hill, Anita, 260
Hirsch, Alan, 352
Hirshey, Gerri, 309
Hitchens, Christopher, 343
Hoffman, David, 80, 136, 303, 326
Hoffman, Dustin, 61, 62
von Hoffman, Nicholas, 312
Holland, John, 79, 303
Holland, Robert G., 348
Hollstein, Milton, 354

Holmes, Steven A., 344
Hook, Janet, 319, 327
Hoover, J. Edgar, 36, 179
Horowitz, David, 309
terHorst, Jerald, 40, 43, 48, 69, 201, 231, 303, 309
Horton, Willie, 261
Hosenball, Mark, 326, 354
Houston, Paul, 323, 355
Howard, Dan, 178, 179, 181, 223, 241, 303, 327
Hoynes, William, 315
Hume, Brit, 4, 63, 71, 90, 137, 140, 158, 159, 196, 210, 230, 246, 303, 321
Hume, Ellen, 69, 114, 138, 155, 156, 158, 159, 171, 172, 203, 223, 303
Humphrey, Hubert, 188, 333
Hunt, Albert, 31, 47, 123, 135, 139, 165, 167, 216, 221, 238, 303
Hunt, Terry, 303
Hurst, John, 347

Ifill, Gwen, 326
Ingwerson, Marshall, 345
Isaacs, Norman E., 334, 335, 352
Isikoff, Michael, 303, 324–326, 342, 354
Ivins, Molly, 312, 354
Iyengar, Shanto, 310, 315, 332, 352

Jackson, Andrew, 27, 29
Jackson, Brooks, 11, 39, 66, 75, 103, 104, 115, 131, 215, 227, 250, 303, 313, 317
Jackson, Jackie, 195, 198, 330
Jackson, Jesse, 7, 12, 48, 72, 75, 90, 100, 101, 115, 116, 142, 143, 193, 195–199, 215, 221, 270, 281, 282, 313, 321, 322, 330, 331, 334
Jackson, Michael, 257
Jefferson, Thomas, 27, 213, 308
Jenkins, Kent, xi, 293, 303
Jenkins, Walter, 44
Jennings, Peter, 55, 122, 139, 140, 158, 167, 191, 224, 250, 336
Jenrette, John, 161, 163, 325
Johnson, Don, 341
Johnson, Kirk, 325
Johnson, Lady Bird, 44
Johnson, Lyndon, 17, 26, 33, 41, 45, 62, 64, 74, 113, 188, 254, 318, 328, 333, 334
Johnson, Steven, 293
Johnston, David, 303, 342, 354
Jones, Charles O., xi
Jones, Phil, 183, 185, 303, 325
Judis, John B., 312, 322, 354
Jurkowitz, Mark, 343

Kaffu, Toshiki, 48
Kaiser, Charles, 314, 320
Kalb, Marvin, 213, 303
Kamen, Al, 20
Kanter, Donald, 332
Kantor, Seth, 310
Kashiwahara, Ken, 285

Katz, Jeffrey L., 339
Kaus, Mickey, 338
Keely, Marianne, 196, 303
Keeter, Scott, 337
Kellermann, Donald, 350
Kelly, Michael, 344
Kemp, Jack, 7, 13, 95, 96, 144–148, 173, 204, 224, 225, 240, 322, 334
Kendall, Kathleen E., 310, 355
Kennedy, Edward, 7, 9, 11, 22, 45, 46, 62, 64, 67, 69, 72, 106, 113, 116, 119, 204, 241, 258
Kennedy, Jackie, 37, 38, 40–42, 309
Kennedy, Joe, 41
Kennedy, John F., 9, 26, 33–43, 46, 48, 62, 64, 67, 76, 110, 122, 177, 188, 193, 206, 214–218, 224, 238, 308, 309, 333
Kennedy, Joseph, 117
Kennedy, Robert, 99
Kenny, Anthony, 342
Kenworthy, Tom, 328
Kerry, John, 117
Key, V. O., Jr., 244, 337
Kidder, Margot, 195, 196, 330
Kiker, Douglas, 43, 235, 303, 309
Kilpatrick, James J., 11, 87, 91, 123, 226, 303
Kimberlin, Brett, 168–171, 239, 240, 280, 303, 345
Kinder, Donald R., 310, 315, 332, 352
King, Anthony, 310, 338, 354
King, Bobby Joe, 277, 344
King, Dennis, 323, 324
King, Ed, 324
King, Larry L., 249, 279, 308, 345
King, Martin Luther, 16, 100, 179
King, Susan, 303
King, Wayne, 97, 303, 334
Kinnock, Neil, 14, 96
Kinsley, Michael, 215, 334
Kitch, Laura W., 314, 351
Klassen, David, 334
Kopechne, Mary Jo, 9
Koppel, Ted, 60, 71, 228, 246, 284, 285, 299–300, 303, 336, 338
Kotok, Alan B., 315
Kovach, Bill, 100, 122, 179, 197, 199, 303
Kraft, Joseph, 62
Krauthammer, Charles, 333
Kuralt, Charles, 336
Kurtz, Howard, 313, 338, 339, 340, 341, 344, 345, 346, 347, 349, 351
Kwitney, Jonathan, 139, 321

Lack, Andrew, 42, 147, 216, 303
LaFraniere, Sharon, 318
Langley, Monica, 331
Lapham, Lewis, 141, 321
Lardner, George, 35, 76, 102, 103, 115, 304
Larkin, Brent, 318
LaRouche, Lyndon, 15, 152, 154, 156, 225, 323, 324
Latimer, James, 304

Lawrence, Bill, 30
Lawrence, Michael, 165, 304
Lee, Martin A., 314, 326, 352
Leeden, Michael, 354
Lemons, Terry, 341
Leno, Jay, 129, 250, 256–258, 282
Leonard, Thomas C., 308, 352
Lessard, Suzannah, 69, 312, 354
Letterman, David, 129, 130, 234, 236, 250, 256, 257, 281–282, 320, 336
Levin, Carl, 345
Lewis, Anthony, 212, 304, 313
Lewis, I. A., 314, 355
Lewis, James, 168, 169
Lichter, Linda S., 311, 314, 331, 352, 354
Lichter, Robert S., 311, 314, 315, 330, 331, 352–354
Limbaugh, Rush, 255
Lincoln, Abraham, 27
Lindsey, Bruce, 349
Lippmann, Walter, 31, 62, 93, 245, 300, 337, 350
Lipsitt, Donald, 153
Livingood, Bill, 304
Livingston, Bob, 318
Locin, Mitchell, 321, 331
Loeb, Nackey, 92, 304
Loeb, William, 9, 92, 316
Long, Earl, 33
Long, Huey, 17, 31
Long, Russell, 32
Lord, Jeffrey, 316
Lowrey, Burling, 337
Luce, Henry, 30
Lukens, Mary, 304
Lyall, Sarah, 316
Lydon, Christopher, 265, 342
Lyons, James, 316
Lyons, Richard L., 310

Mack, Connie, 117
Mack, John, 120, 319
Macmillan, Harold, 36
MacNelly, Jeff, 275, 344
Magid, Frank N., 310
Mailer, Norman, 10, 189, 329
Malone, Julia, 330
Mansfield, Jayne, 34
Maraniss, David, 331
Marcos, Imelda, 205
Martin, David, 180
Mashek, John, 304, 309
Mason, Perry, 224
Matalin, Mary, 274
Matheson, Scott M., Jr., xi, 312, 313
Matlack, Carol, 307, 337, 354
Matthews, Tom, 310
Mattox, James, 18, 117, 118, 318
Matusow, Barbara, 304, 310, 336, 352, 354
Maxa, Rudy, 308
Maynard, Robert, 334
McCain, John, 181

McCarthy, Eugene, 59, 128, 334
McCarthy, Joseph, 33
McCartney, James, 354
McClendon, Sarah, ix, 100, 304
McCloskey, Robert, 334
McCloud, David, 292, 293, 304, 348, 349
McClure, Robert D., 352
McCord, Robert S., 335
McCormick, David, 253
McCrery, Jim, 288–289, 348
McCurry, Michael, 141, 239, 304
McDowell, Charles, 304
McEvoy, John, 78, 313
McGee, Jim, 331
McGinniss, Joe, 65, 312, 331
McGovern, George, 9, 10, 68, 76, 77, 106, 108, 115, 124, 148, 240, 317, 332
McGrory, Mary, 36, 304
McLaughlin, John, 55, 91, 249, 316, 338
McWethy, John, 284–285, 286, 347
Means, Marianne, 335
Mecham, Evan, 7, 16, 111, 112, 129, 130, 135, 204, 242, 317, 320, 321
Meese, Edwin, 144
Menem, Carlos, 310
Mercer, Lucy, 30
Meyer, Dick, 304
Michel, Robert, 184
Mickelson, Sig, 315, 352
Mills, Wilbur, 7, 19, 47, 110, 208
Mintz, John, 344
Mirvis, Philip, 332
Mitchell, Andrea, 179, 185, 304, 327, 338
Mitchell, George, 321
Mitroff, Ian, 352
Mitsotakis, Constantine, 310
Monahan, Dara, 338
Mondale, Walter F., 12, 64, 82, 89, 103, 105, 108, 126, 209, 314, 333
Monroe, Marilyn, 34
Montana, Constanza, 322
Moore, David, 354
Moore, W. John, 313
Morano, Dan, 304
Morgan, William, 350
Morgenthau, Tom, 326
Morse, G. C., 304
Morton, Bruce, 137, 234, 304
Morton, Thurston, 32
Moyers, Bill, 335
Mudd, Roger, 157, 158, 217, 236, 246, 304
Mullins, Janet, 321
Mundy, Alicia, 349
Murdoch, Rupert, 55
Murrow, Edward R., 227, 234
Muskie, Edmund, 7, 9, 48, 72, 75, 343
Myers, Lisa, 250, 345
Myrberg, Arthur A., 307

Nash, Alanna, 336
Naughton, James M., 311

Neal, Steve, 308
Nelson, Jack, 5, 63, 83, 230, 268, 304, 342
Nelson, Lars-Erik, 184, 328
Nelson, Michael, 311, 332, 337
Newsham, Howard, 347
Nichols, Bruce, viii
Niemi, Richard, 310
Nieves, Evelyn, 346
Nimmo, Dan, 352
Nixon, Patricia, 134, 242, 337
Nixon, Richard M., 7, 8, 18, 19, 26, 31, 33,
    41–43, 45–47, 62–64, 89, 92, 105, 108, 134,
    135, 188, 189, 201, 219, 237, 241, 242, 309,
    310, 314, 316, 321, 332, 333, 335, 337
Noah, Timothy, 4
Nofziger, Lyn, 144, 146
North, Oliver, 20, 86
Norville, Deborah, 234, 336
Novak, Robert, 14, 37, 43, 56, 62, 63, 78, 83, 91,
    95, 115, 131, 145, 152, 183, 198, 214, 249,
    304, 322, 323, 328, 334, 338
Novak, William, 329
Noyes, Richard E., 315, 330, 352, 354
Nunn, Sam, 119, 179, 318, 333

O'Connor, Colleen, 314
O'Connor, Rose Ellen, 111, 114, 120, 194, 195,
    304, 317, 329
O'Donnell, Jayne, 326
O'Donnell, Kirk, 154–156, 304
Oishi, Gene, 9
Oliphant, Tom, 215, 323, 351
Oreskes, Michael, 5, 58, 151, 158, 304
Ornstein, Norman, 333, 354
Orren, Gary R., 351, 352
Ota, Alan K., 329

Packwood, Robert, 295–296, 349
Painton, Priscilla, 197, 304, 330, 334
Paletz, David L., 352
Palmer, Thomas C., Jr., 283, 339, 346
Papandreou, Andreas, 310
Parkinson, Paula, 7, 15, 83, 90, 118, 119, 157,
    159, 160, 163, 223, 242, 324
Pashley, James C., 286, 347
Patterson, Thomas E., 311, 332, 337, 352, 354
Pauley, Jane, 275, 336
Pearson, Drew, 45, 144, 145
Pederson, Daniel, 311, 318
Pell, Claiborne, 20, 117
Perdue, Sally Miller, 267
Perlman, Shirley E., 342
Perot, Carolyn, 278
Perot, H. Ross, 249, 251, 253–254, 257,
    275–279, 297, 298, 338, 339, 340, 344–345
Perot, Nancy, 277
Perry, James M., 190, 304, 311, 329, 352
Peters, Charles, 67, 69, 87, 138, 206, 304, 318
Peters, Mark, 332
Peterson, Bill, 149, 304, 320, 322, 323
Peterson, Merrill D., 308

Pettit, Tom, 231
Phillippi, Wendell C., 324
Phillips, David Graham, 28
Phillips, Don, 328
Phillips, Stone, 274–275
Pianin, Eric, 318, 328, 331
Pichirallo, Joe, 318, 324
Pierpoint, Robert, 37–39, 216, 304, 309
Pincus, Walter, 172, 176, 304, 326
Plante, Bill, 234, 246, 304
Plissner, Martin, 304, 355
Plunkitt, George Washington, 54, 55, 110
Poindexter, John, 20
Polk, Jim, 160, 165, 187, 304
Polliard, Edward, 308
Polsby, Nelson W., 352
Pomper, Gerald M., 311
Powell, Jody, 11, 81, 92, 316
Powers, Ron, 335
Presley, Elvis, 257
Press, Charles, 308, 314, 332, 352
Pressman, Steven, 312
Pulitzer, Joseph, 28

Qaddafi, Muammar, 11
Quayle, Dan, 1, 6, 7, 15, 53, 54, 60, 73, 74,
    81–84, 86, 90, 91, 95, 99, 102, 104, 107,
    108, 113–116, 118, 119, 123, 124, 126,
    129–131, 134, 135, 144, 156–171, 187, 203,
    205, 206, 210, 223, 230, 239, 240, 242, 243,
    255, 256–257, 263, 267–268, 279–283, 307,
    311, 316, 318, 324–326, 332, 337, 345, 346,
    353, 355
Quayle, Marilyn, 242, 283, 340
Quinlan, J. Michael, 170

Rabin, Yitzhak, 274
Radcliffe, Donnie, 337
Rafsky, Robert, 343
Raines, Howell, 39, 55, 230, 304
Randolph, Eleanor, 95, 184, 222, 304, 307, 310,
    313, 314, 315, 318, 321, 326, 329, 336, 337,
    355
Ranney, Austin, 307, 314, 332, 352
Raper, Jim, 194, 304
Raphael, Sally Jessy, 267
Rasky, Larry, 138, 304
Rather, Dan, 59, 134, 156, 183, 184, 216, 226,
    228, 234, 235, 244, 250, 261, 305, 336, 337
Ravenel, Charles, 162
Ray, Elizabeth, 47
Reagan, Nancy, 191, 234, 329
Reagan, Patti, 191, 329
Reagan, Ronald, 7, 11–13, 15, 19, 20, 41, 54, 57,
    62, 63, 76, 81, 86, 89–93, 99, 100, 101, 114,
    126, 131, 144–146, 154–156, 170, 191, 192,
    224, 225, 234, 239, 256–257, 258, 260, 261,
    310, 314, 316, 320–322, 329, 333
Rebozo, Charles ("Bebe"), 45
Redford, Robert, 61, 62
Reeves, Thomas C., 308

Reich, Kenneth, 347
Reid, T. R., 209, 210, 305, 311, 333
Remnick, David, 344
Reynolds, Barbara A., 195, 199, 330
Ribuffo, Leo P., 317
Rice, Donna, 7, 13, 48, 55, 56, 60, 73, 78, 97, 98,
    103, 106, 109, 110, 114, 117, 118, 120, 123,
    125, 148, 150, 177, 190, 194, 221, 240, 316,
    320, 322, 337
Rich, Adrienne, 338
Rich, Spencer, 310
Richards, Ann, 18, 117, 118, 318
Richardson, Valerie, 329
Richter, Paul, 345
Riegle, Donald, 47
Ringle, Ken, 319
Riordan, William L., 311, 317
Rivera, Geraldo, 55, 139, 275
Rivers, Mendel, 33
Robb, Charles S., 7, 16, 99, 101, 110, 111, 113,
    114, 120, 193–195, 290–295, 305, 317, 329,
    330, 348–349
Robb, Lynda Johnson, 17, 317
Roberts, Charles, 41, 99
Roberts, Cokie, 68, 141, 185, 186, 230, 263, 305,
    328, 335, 338
Roberts, Jeffrey A., 322
Roberts, Steven V., 61, 67, 68, 79, 84, 110, 152,
    154, 182, 186, 208, 216, 305
Robertson, Pat, 7, 14, 28, 56, 57, 73, 112, 113,
    115, 116, 119, 124, 137, 138, 151, 191, 195,
    199, 204, 205, 238, 311, 329, 330
Robinson, Michael J., 22, 89, 241, 307, 311, 315,
    316, 337, 353, 355
Rochelle, Carl, 305
Rochkind, Glen, 78, 79, 305
Rodriguez, Paul M., 321
Rogers, David, 325, 344
Rollins, Ed, 249, 338, 347
Romano, Lois, 305, 321, 324
Romer, Roy, 143, 322
Romney, George, 7, 8, 48, 72, 74, 108, 204
Ronstadt, Linda, 286
Roosevelt, Eleanor, 30
Roosevelt, Franklin D., 26, 29–31, 33, 34, 49,
    214, 220, 238
Roosevelt, Theodore, 28, 74
Rose, Tom, 335
Rosenblatt, Roger, 186
Rosenstiel, Tom, 54, 150, 206, 215, 305, 323,
    335, 341, 347, 351, 355
Rosenthal, Andrew, 155, 203, 223, 305, 318,
    320, 324, 327, 332, 343
Ross, Shelley, 308–310, 352
Rostenkowski, Dan, 183
Roth, Richard, 172
Rothenberg, Randall, 335
Rothman, Stanley, 311, 314, 331, 352, 354
Rowe, Sandra, 194
Royce, Knut, 190, 305
Royko, Mike, 226

Rubin, Richard L., 308
Ruff, Charles R.C., 293, 349
Runkel, David R., 314
Rusher, William A., 314, 334, 352
Russell, Mark, 83
Russert, Tim, 276, 305, 316, 338
Ruth, Babe, 319
Ryan, Richard, 175, 326

Safer, Morley, 276, 336
Safire, William, 3, 35, 91, 261, 277, 307, 309,
    344
Salant, Richard S., 350
Salinger, Pierre, 41
Salisbury, Harrison, 328
Sasso, John, 14, 318
Savage, Gus, 331
Savage, John, 97, 110, 118, 149, 305
Savitch, Jessica, 235, 336
Sawyer, Diane, 234, 236, 336
Schafer, Robert, 335
Schakne, Robert, 244
Schapiro, Jeff, 99, 101, 110, 305
Schieffer, Bob, 66, 68, 69, 225, 233, 305
Schmitt, Eric, 342
Schneider, William, 314, 355
Schram, Martin, 317, 352
Schrof, Joannie M., 320
Schwartz, Maralee, 239, 305, 326
Scott, Hal S., 140, 321
Scribman, David, 311, 322
Sedlack, Robert, 165
Seib, Charles, 334
Seper, Jerry, 342
Sesno, Frank, 61, 88, 112, 139, 154, 158, 175,
    226, 305, 324
Sevareid, Eric, 335
Seymour, Thomas, 334
Shalala, Donna, 347–348
Shales, Tom, 321, 337, 346
Shanahan, Eileen, 32
Shanahan, Michael, 305
Shapiro, Walter, 74, 305, 334, 355
Sharkey, Mary Anne, 318
Shaw, Bernard, 196, 216, 236
Shaw, David, 315, 339, 350
Sheehan, Margaret, 311, 316, 355
Sheehy, Gail, 343
Shefter, Martin, 351
Shepard, Charles E., 349
Sherrill, Robert, 312
Sherwood, Tom, 103, 111, 205, 305, 318
Shields, Mark, 62, 305, 315
Shilts, Randy, 289, 348
Shogan, Robert, 76, 215, 305
Shribman, David, 341
Shriver, Maria, 336
Shrum, Robert, 96, 97, 305, 316
Shuger, Scott, 338
Sidey, Hugh, 253
Simon, Roger, 314, 352

Simpson, Carole, 260
Simpson, Glenn R., 329
Sinatra, Frank, 34, 82
Sinclair, Upton, 28
Singer, Mark, 345
Sloan, Lloyd, 320
Sloat, William, 305, 325
Smith, Harry, 274
Smith, R. Jeffrey, 333
Smith, Ted J., III, 314, 355
Smolla, Rodney, 70, 313
Solomon, Burt, 347, 349
Solomon, Norman, 314, 325, 326, 352
Soloski, John, 313
Span, Paula, 336
Speakes, Larry, 305, 310
Spence, Floyd, 161
Spencer, Stuart, ix, 221, 305
Stacks, John, 311
Stahl, Leslie, 179, 234, 336
Stanley, Alessandra, 312, 331, 355
Stanley, Harold W., 310
Starr, Blaze, 33, 34, 309
Starr, John Robert, 305
Steel, Ronald, 308
Stein, M. L., 334, 355
Stencel, Mark, viii
Stencel, Sandra, xi
Stephanopoulos, George, viii
Stephens, Mitchell, 307, 314, 352
Stepp, Laura Sessions, 334
Stern, Lawrence, 35, 309
Stevens, John D., 307
Stevenson, Adlai, 37, 332, 333
Stevenson, Robert L., 315, 355
Stewart, James B., 165, 166, 325
Stewart, Potter, 216
Stockmeyer, Steven, 305
Stovall, James Glen, 311, 355
Sullivan, Brendan, 86
Suro, Roberto, 348
Swaggart, Jimmy, 122
Sweeney, Kevin, 78, 97, 150, 305, 317, 321
Swerdlow, Joel, 355

Taylor, Paul, 123, 150, 305, 313, 317, 322, 323, 337, 352
Taylor, Stephen, 305
Teeley, Peter, 305
Teeter, Robert, 128
Terwilliger, George, 293–294, 349
Thimmesch, Nick, 315, 355
Thomas, Bill, 99, 102, 305, 319
Thomas, Clarence, 260, 349
Thomas, Evan, 174
Thomasson, Dan, 309
Thompson, Bruce, 293
Thompson, Charlie, 305, 316
Thompson, Frank, 33
Thompson, Paul, 57, 58
Thurmond, Strom, 161–163

Tillotson, Mary, 274, 344
Tobias, Sheila, 318
Toch, Thomas, 344
Tocqueville, Alexis de, 25, 246, 338
Tolchin, Martin, 145, 322
Toobin, Jeffrey, 348
Totenberg, Nina, 20, 114, 141, 149, 156, 169, 170, 185, 305
Tower, John G., 5, 7, 20, 21, 25, 56, 69, 85, 100, 110, 113, 117, 119, 121, 127, 129, 130, 144, 178–182, 205, 209, 223, 241, 305, 308, 317, 326, 327
Tower, Lilla, 100
Trento, Susan B., 273, 343–344
Trudeau, Garry, 272, 280, 345
Trueheart, Charles, 314, 336
Truman, Harry, 82, 134, 219, 310
Tsongas, Paul, 257, 258, 265, 295, 349
Tully, Paul, 14
Tumulty, Karen, 114, 305
Turnipseed, Tom, 161, 163, 305, 325
Turque, Bill, 342
Twain, Mark, 230, 283

Udall, Morris K., 92
Ujifusa, Grant, 313
Uno, Sosuke, 48

Van Atta, Dale, 326
Vander Jagt, Guy, 267
Vanocur, Sander, 4
VerBurg, Kenneth, 308, 314, 332, 352
Victor, Kirk, 314, 331

Waldman, Myron S., 322
Waldman, Steven, 308
Walker, Arnot, 270, 342
Wallace, Chris, 216, 225, 305
Wallace, George, 74
Wallace, Mike, 197, 198, 330, 336
Walsh, Edward, 78, 305, 323
Walsh, Kenneth T., 84, 215, 243, 305
Walters, Barbara, 234, 336
Walters, David, 289–290
Walters, Don, 285
Walters, Jonathan, 310
Walters, Shaun, 289–290, 348
Wanniski, Jude, 145
Warner, Margaret, 249, 338
Warren, Samuel D., 28, 210, 308, 333, 353
Washington, George, 27, 64, 113
Washington, Harold, 331
Watkins, O. T., 305
Watkins, Ronald J., 317
Watson, Bobby, 292, 293
Wattenberg, Ben J., 352
Wattenberg, Martin P., 316
Weaver, David, 340, 350
Weaver, Paul, 315
Weems, Dana, 98
Weinraub, Bernie, 305

Weisberg, Jacob, 253
Weiser, Benjamin, 58, 172, 177, 305, 326, 329
Welker, Herman, 32
Westbrook, Tom, 305
Westergaard, John, 343
Weyrich, Paul, 85, 178, 306
Wheatley, Bill, 254
Wheeler, Michael, 355
White, John, 145
White, Theodore H., 65, 312
Whitehead, Barbara Dafoe, 346
Whitman, David, 315, 346
Whitney, Craig, 216
Wildavsky, Aaron, 355
Wilder, L. Douglas, 89, 292–293, 294
Wilds, John, 308
Wilhoit, G. Cleveland, 340, 350
Wilkie, Curtis, 329, 355
Will, George F., 91, 93, 261, 333, 335, 336
Williams, Clayton, 18, 108, 143
Williams, Marjorie, 308
Williams, Mary Alice, 336
Williams, Pete, 32
Willke, Wendell, 30
Wills, Garry, 33
Wilson, Jean Gaddy, 312
Wilson, Nancy, 195
Wines, Michael, 307, 323, 355
Winfrey, Oprah, 121

Wingo, Hal, 306
Winneker, Craig, 329
Winship, Tom, 355
Winter-Berger, Robert N., 310
Witcover, Jules, 316, 317, 323, 328, 355
Witt, Elder, 319
Witt, Evans, 310, 355
Wolfe, Tom, 64, 312
Wood, William, 193, 194, 306
Woodruff, Judy, 235, 306
Woodward, Robert, 19, 61, 63, 76, 89, 113, 140,
    149, 180, 181, 215, 227, 276–277, 279, 306,
    318, 321, 326, 327, 344, 345
Wooten, James, 189, 191, 198, 306, 314
Wright, Betsy, 266
Wright, Jim, 1, 7, 21, 48, 120, 123, 127, 182, 183,
    208, 319, 327
Wyngaard, Tim, 309

Yalof, David, 312
Yum, June O., 310, 355

Zaccaro, John, 12, 13, 139
Zagoria, Sam, 334
Zahn, Paula, 336
Zelnick, Bob, 182, 306
Zoglin, Richard, 320, 336
Zukin, Cliff, 337

Subject Index

ABC News, 250, 277, 284–287
Abortion issue, 87, 260
Access, to candidates, 85–86, 132, 201, 233
Accountability, 208, 226
"Actual malice" rule, 69–70
ACT-UP, 289
"Ad watches," 250-251
Adversarial relationship, 63
Advocate, The, 289
Agnew's "Fat Jap" flap, 7, 8–9, 48, 72, 80
Alcohol abuse, 32-33, 47, 218, 219. *See also* Drinking
   rumor of Tower's, 178, 180, 182
Anchors, 235
Angles, 53, 61
"Anything goes" rule, 46, 48, 208, 214, 217, 222
Apathy, 123
Apology, 241
Associated Press, 280
Atlantic, The, 282
Attack journalism, 26

Baby-boomers, 261
Barry case, 7, 17, 103–104, 111–112, 137, 205, 241
Bias, 86, 92–93, 132, 137
   liberal, 86–90
   in 1992 presidential campaign, 253–262
   nonideological factors in, 91–92
   pro-Clinton, 340
Biden's plagiarism, 7, 14, 73, 96–97, 99, 112, 116, 118, 126, 239
Billygate, 7, 11, 55, 56, 63, 72, 226, 241
"Blackmail" standard, 85
"Blauvelt campaign," 41
Bush's "mistress," 7, 13–16, 73, 75, 95, 110, 117, 120, 224
   rumors about, vii, 171–177, 264
   and stock market drop, 175–176

"Call boy" scandal, 56, 57
Candidates, 1, 2, 3, 4, 65–68, 80
   media tune for, 233
   mistreatment of, 139
   presidential, 82, 84
   rating of, 207–208
   recruitment of, 210–212

relationships of with associates and staff, 221
   remedies from, 237–243
   vice presidential, 53–54, 82–83
Caperton case, 7, 18, 143
Carter's "killer rabbit," 7, 11, 72, 75, 79, 129
Carter's "lust in the heart," 7, 10, 48, 72, 74, 105, 189
"CBS Evening News," 266-267
CBS News, 250, 278
Celeste case, 7, 17, 84, 101, 116, 117
Chappaquiddick, 7, 9, 22, 45–46, 62, 64, 67, 72, 204, 241
"Character cop," 68
"Character frenzies," 117
Character issue, 27, 45, 64–68, 71, 122, 132, 137, 191, 245, 247
   and Clinton, 268, 270–271
   and women journalists, 68–69
Charlotte Observer, 251–252
"Checkers speech," 8, 134, 135, 241, 242
Check-kiting, congressional, 287–288
Cisneros case, 7, 17–18, 57, 102, 112, 117
Civic knowledge, 245
Civil rights movement, 61
   effect on journalism, 112
Civility, 230, 246
   decline in, 55, 132
Clinton-Gore bus trips, 248
CNN (Cable News Network), 50, 53, 248, 251, 264, 265, 274
Commentary, 232
   labeling of, 231
Competitive pressures, 56–58, 137, 226
Congress, voters' view of, 208
Congressional frenzies, 287–296
Conservatives
   and media, 88–90
   in media, 91
Constitutional values, 2
Consultants, 5, 141, 222, 232
Context, 81
Continuous public-affairs programming, 53
Contrition, 241
Corruption, financial, 33
Counteroffensives, 241–243
Coverups, 112, 116, 131, 240
   Eagleton and, 116
   Quayle and, 116

Critical mass, definition of, 6
Critics
    charges of, 1–2
    colleagues as, 2–3
    conservative, 1
    of left, 2
C-SPAN, 50, 53, 248, 251, 269
Cynicism, 63, 66, 132, 137, 230, 244, 245
    of public, 133, 207, 208, 209

"Dateline NBC," 252-253, 274
Deadline pressures, 136, 141
Debategate, 7, 11, 63, 76, 79, 81
Defamation suits, 70
Democrat-Gazette (Arkansas), 265
Democratic National Convention, 260
Dirty tricks, 116
    Dukakis and, 116
Disclosure, 132, 240–241
"Double whammy," 96
Drinking, 124. *See also* Alcohol abuse
    Johnson and, 43–44
    Mills and, 110
    Tower and, 110
Drug (ab)use, 125, 218, 219
    by Babbitt, 20, 81, 117, 238–239
    by Chiles, 117
    by Gingrich, 20, 117
    by Ginsburg, 7, 20, 81, 113, 114, 117, 140
    by Gore, 20, 81, 117
    by Kennedy, Joseph, 117
    by Kerry, 117
    by Mack, 117
    by Pell, 20, 117
    by press, 113
Drug frenzy, 238
Drug use, purported, 241
    by Barry, 17, 103–104, 137
    by Kennedy, John, 36
    by Mattox, 18, 117, 118
    by Richards, 18, 117
    by Robb, 7, 16, 110–111, 193–195
Drug-use frenzies, 117
Dukakis's "attack video," 7, 14, 96, 112, 116,
    126, 142, 241
Dukakis's mental health, 7, 15, 73, 224, 225,
    240
    rumors about, 152–156
Duplicity, 94, 112

Eagleton's mental health, 7, 9–10, 46, 56, 84,
    106, 126
Economist, The, 270–271
Economy, 251
    media characterizations of, 255–259
"Editorial crusade," 28
Editors, 226, 227
Elections, as a game, 54
End-justifies-means rule, 139
Entertainment values, 234–236

Ethics frenzies, 120
"Exposé," 291, 348

"Fairness doctrine," 218, 220
"Family values" theme, 281–282
Fear, 62
Feeding frenzies
    over Brown's house parties, 284–286
    over "Bush's mistress" rumors, 272–275
    causes of, 52
    circumstances that govern, 80–81
    over Clinton's military record, 267–269
    over Clinton's visit to Soviet Union,
      268–270
    congressional, 287–296
    definition of, 6
    delayed, 188–189
    denied, 189–191
    differences in, 22
    examples of, 7, 22
    first modern, 33
    over Flowers allegations, 264–267
    in foreign countries, 48
    as global, 49
    guidelines for, 217, 220
    insights about, 22
    model summary of, 130–131, 132–133,
      134–135
    of 1992 presidential campaign, 262
    outside components of, 94
    over Perot, 278
    over Quayle's "Murphy Brown" speech,
      280–282
    state, 289–290
Feeding frenzies, capsule summaries of, 8–22
    noncampaign, 18–22
    from presidential politics, 8–16
    from state and local levels, 16–18
Feeding frenzies, consequences of, 23, 200
    for Barry, 205
    for Bush, 205–206
    for candidates, 204–206
    for Kemp, 204
    for Kennedy, Edward, 204
    for political system, 208–212
    for press, 200–204
    for Quayle, 205–206
    for Robertson, 205
    for voters, 206–208
Feminism, 69, 121
    and character issue, 122
Ferraro's finances, 7, 12–13, 57, 72, 89, 103,
    105, 126, 139, 241
First Amendment, 3, 70, 203, 204, 213, 215,
    229, 236, 244
    popular support for, 298–299
Fish schooling, 59
Fishing expeditions, 219
"Focus groups," 250
Foley case, 7, 21–22, 75, 120, 225
    rumors in, 182–186

Ford's "free Poland" gaffe, 7, 10, 60, 72, 106, 108–109, 127, 129, 241
Frank case, 7, 22, 56, 110, 139
Freedom of the press, 3, 213
"Frenziettes," 22
   over Quayle's "potatoe" gaffe, 282–283
Front-runners, 80
Fundamentalism, 121
   and character issue, 122

Gamesmanship coverage, 54
"-Gate," 63, 64
"Gatekeeper," 4
Gatekeeping, 58
Gays in the military, 260
"Geraldo Syndrome," 248
Ginsburg case, 7, 20, 100–101, 113, 114, 117, 140
Gossip, 5, 6, 10, 15, 26, 28–29, 53, 55, 75, 141, 209–210, 222, 223, 225
Gridiron Club dinner, 247–248
Guilt, 62
   by association, 139
   presumption of, 138

Hart, questions concerning, 7, 12, 48, 72, 76–77, 100, 102–103, 238
Hart/Rice case, 7, 13–14, 48, 58, 60, 73, 78, 80, 97–98, 103, 106, 109–110, 114, 118, 120, 125, 190, 240
   rumors in, 148–151
Hays/Ray case, 47
"Hidden crisis," 164, 167
Homelessness issue, 87
Homosexuality, 88, 193
   discretion about, 191–192
   of Frank, 139, 192
Homosexuality, purported
   of Caperton, 18, 143
   of Foley, 21, 75, 182–186
   of Kemp, 7, 13, 144–148
Honoraria, 237
"Horserace" reporting, 54
House "bank" scandal, 287–288
Humor, 94
   and Carter, 129
   and Ford, 129
   and Hart, 129, 130
   and Mecham, 130
   and Quayle, 129, 130
   and Tower, 129, 130
"Hype index," 311
Hypocrisy, 31, 94, 98, 104, 113, 131, 132, 219, 237, 238
   Biden and, 112
   Cisneros and, 112
   Dukakis and, 112
   Ginsburg and, 114
   Hart and, 112, 114
   homosexual, 193
   "institutionalized," 39

   of press, 113
   of public, 123, 126
   Quayle and, 113, 114–115
   Robb and, 114
   Robertson and, 112
   varieties of, 112

Ideology, press bias and, 260
Incumbent administrations, press toughness on, 260–261
"Instant analysis," 127
Invasion of privacy, 4, 126, 139, 150, 177, 200
Investigative reporting, 2, 19, 132
Iran-Contra affair, 7, 19–20, 62, 76
"Irangate," 63

Jackson's "Hymietown" remark, 7, 12, 48, 72, 75, 115, 195
Journalism, 2-5. *See also* Media (press)
   corruption of, 29
   definition of, 26
   from description to prescription, 61
   early American, 26–29
   frenzy's causes within, 52
   "junkyard-dog," 26, 46, 49, 201, 220
   lowest-common-denominator, 58, 133, 134, 137, 142, 187, 200, 220, 223, 226, 229, 247, 264, 266
   modifiers of the word, 2
   new rules for, 29
   phases in, 25–26
   public attitudes toward, 88, 299, 349–350
   quality of, 51
Journalists, 1, 2, 4, 6
   background of, 87
   as generalists, 54
   "Hollywoodized," 250
   Watergate-era, 61–62
"Junkyard-dog" journalism, 26, 46, 49, 201, 220

Kemp case, 7, 13, 204, 241
   rumors in, 144–148, 224–225
Kennedy/Campbell affair, 34–35
   elements of, 36
Kennedy-Hart comparison, 67

"Lapdog" journalism, 25–26, 42, 43, 49
Libel laws, 202
   relaxation (loosening) of, 45, 69–70, 132
Liberals, and media, 90–91
Local media, 50, 53, 84
Los Angeles Times, 268, 286
"Lowest-common-denominator" journalism, 58, 133, 134, 137, 142, 187, 200, 220, 223, 226, 229, 247, 264, 266
Lying, 112, 124, 131, 132, 219
   Celeste and, 116
   Dukakis and, 116
   Eagleton and, 115, 116
   Hart and, 115, 116

Lying *cont.*
Jackson and, 115, 116
Johnson and, 113
Kennedy, Edward, and, 116
Quayle and, 115, 116
Robertson and, 115, 116

"Manchurian Candidate" defense, 82
Mass-circulation dailies, 27
Mecham case, 7, 16, 111, 112, 242
Media (press). *See also* Journalism
assumptions of, 65–66
attack on, 242–243
campaign coverage by, 52–54
checks and balances in, 226–229
condemnation by politicians of, 2
confidence in, 298–299
constitutional protections of, 213
contemporary, 49
critics of, 1–3
distortion of political process by, 3
duty of, 246
feelings about, 2
frustration of, 85–86, 132, 232
as "gatekeeper," 4
and gossip and rumor, 5–6
influential role of, 1
and Jackson, 195–199
and Johnson, 42, 43–45
and Kennedy, Edward, 46
and Kennedy, John, 33–42
manipulation of, 232
and Nixon, 42, 45
obligations of, 23
omissions by, 29–33, 36–45
political coverage by, 6
and politicians, 29–31
power of, 4–5, 207, 208
and private life, 3–4
privileges of, 23
public confidence in, 3, 201–204
quality of coverage by, 54
and Roosevelt, 29–30
as screening committee, 1, 4, 65, 132
scrutiny of, 222
standards of, 6, 21, 23, 24
voter reactions to, 297–298, 349–350
Media excesses, 11, 23, 28, 137–140
defenses of, 5
"Medialities," 22
Megafrenzies, 22, 156, 205
Military, gays in the, 260
Mills/Foxe case, 7, 19, 47
"Miracle baby," 28, 56, 124, 138, 191, 205, 238
Moral absolutism, 211
Morality tale, 28
MTV, 282
"Muckraking," 28
"Murphy Brown," 255, 346
"Murphy Brown" speech (Quayle), 280–281
Muskie's New Hampshire "cry," 7, 9, 48, 72, 75

National News Council, 299
National political conventions, 83
coverage of, 232
NBC, 250, 264, 350
Negative campaigning, 141
Networks, TV, 50, 228, 232
campaign coverage by, 248
cutbacks at, 51
innovations in coverage, 250–251
New Alliance Party, 267
"New journalism," 64, 121
New Republic, The, 278
New York Post, 273–274
New York Times, 259, 264, 272, 277, 286, 340
New York Times Co. v. *Sullivan,* 69
New Yorker, 280
News council, 229
"News cycle without end," 53
Newsday, 280
Newspapers, 53, 54–55, 227–229
circulation of, 49–50
Newsweek, 265, 272–273, 277
"Nightline," 252, 264, 284–285, 341
Nixon's "secret fund," 7, 8, 33, 92, 105, 241
Nonpolarized races, 80

"Objective" reporting, 29
Ombudsmen, 227–228, 229, 252–253, 350
need for, 262, 299
video, 299
Oneupmanship, 11, 57, 150
Openness, 208
Opinion leaders, 220, 227
Oregonian, The, 296
"Outing," 192, 288–289, 348
Overdrafts, congressional, 287–288

Pack journalism, 59–60, 71, 91, 132, 137–138, 200
effects of, 60–61
Partisan press, 27
Party newspapers, 27
Peer pressure, 59
"Penny press," 27
Penthouse magazine, 267
Personality politics, 65
Political advertisements, 232
Political character, 221
Political contributions, 89
Political parties, 1, 65, 132, 207, 245
Politicians, 1, 2, 3, 28, 230
relationships with press, 29
self-inflicted wounds of, 94
and sex, 27, 28, 29, 31, 33–42, 47, 48
undesirable kinds of, 211
Politicians, procedural errors of, 104, 105, 106, 107, 108
Bush, 107
Carter, 105
Eisenhower, 105
Ferraro, 108
Ford, 106
Hart, 106

McGovern, 106
Nixon, 105
Quayle, 104, 107, 108
Politicians, substantive offensives of, 104–107
Bush, 107
Carter, 105
Eagleton, 106
Eisenhower, 105
Ferraro, 105
Ford, 106
Hart, 106
McGovern, 106
Mondale, 105
Nixon, 105
Polling
horserace, 251
obsession with, 231
on public reaction to Clinton-Flowers coverage, 265–266
"Potatoe" incident, 282
Presidency, 81–82
"Presidential bubble," 109
Presidential campaign (1992), 247–253
cable coverage of, 248, 252
issue-oriented coverage of, 251–252
late-night political humor in, 256–258
media bias in, 253–262
network coverage of, 250–251, 252
polling during, 251
print media coverage of, 251–252
talk TV and, 249–250
Press corps
growth of, 49
size of, 53, 310–311
women in, 68–69, 132
Price of power, 211–212
Print media, 251–252
Privacy, 215, 216, 220, 221, 229
Privacy rights, 29, 192
violation of, 28
Private life
contrasted with public life, 66, 213–217
coverage of, 214
of public people, 25, 26, 27, 30, 35, 42, 46, 48, 65, 121
shielded from publication, 218–219
subject to publication, 218
Productivity, economic, 340
Professionalism, 234
Public character vs. private character, 220
Public life, price of, 4
Public opinion, 3, 94, 121, 132, 135, 244, 245
effect on media, 123–127
media effect on, 127, 129
Pyramidal frenzies, 118–119, 120
Quayle and, 118–119

Quayle's past, 7, 15, 60, 73, 114, 115, 116, 118–119, 124, 126, 130, 205, 223, 239, 240, 242
Quayle's past, rumors about, 156, 171
academic record, 164, 167

drug use, 167–171, 280
law school and bar exam, 166, 167
National Guard service, 157–159
Parkinson, relationship with, 159–160
plagiarism, 164–166
womanizing, 160–164
Queer Nation, 289, 348

Recklessness, 214
of Hart, 79, 190
of Kennedy, Edward, 67, 69
of Kennedy, John, 33, 36
"Refused-call barb," 140
"Reliable Sources," 252
Republican National Convention, 260
Republican party, Flowers-Clinton issue and, 267
Revisionism, 62–63
Roanoke Times, 293
Robb case, 7, 16, 99, 101, 110–111, 120, 193–195
Robertson's past, 7, 14, 28, 56–57, 73, 112, 115, 124, 138, 191, 205, 238
Roe v. *Wade*, 260
Romney's "brainwashing," 7, 8, 48, 72
Rooseveltian rule, 30, 31, 33, 35, 39, 42–43, 45, 46, 65, 69, 84, 113, 188, 201, 214, 217, 222
Rumors, 5, 7, 13, 15, 18, 55, 58, 75, 83, 90, 136, 137, 187, 199, 200, 209, 214, 219, 220, 229, 247
categories of, 141
checking out, 225
debunking of, 224
downplaying of, 224
excuses for airing, 222–223
rules about using, 223
Rumors, examples of, 142–143
Bush and, 171–177
Dukakis and, 152–156.
Foley and, 182–186
Hart and, 148–151
Kemp and, 144–148
Quayle and, 156–171
Tower and, 178, 180–182
Runaway elections, 92

Scandal coverage, kinds and manner of, 3
Scandals, 55, 56, 59, 62–63, 207
financial, 33
government, 5, 8
new type of, 22
real, 5, 29
Self-censorship, 30, 70, 198
Sensationalism, 1, 139, 229
Sex(ual) activity, 55, 56, 124, 216, 218, 219
and Frank, 110
and Hays, 47
and Johnson, 43
and Kennedy, John, 33–42
and Mills, 47
and Riegle, 47
as taboo topic, 33
"Sexual McCarthyism," 148

Situational ethics, 219
"60 Minutes," 264, 276
Skepticism, 63
Soft news, 232, 235
Sound bites, 248, 338
Sources, 94, 132
    accidental, 102–103
    and Celeste, 101
    and Cisneros, 102
    coworkers as, 100
    exes as, 100–101
    and Foley, 102
    and Ginsburg, 100–101
    and Hart, 101, 102–103
    intrapartisan, 95–98
    and Jackson, 100, 101
    lawyers as, 101
    nonpartisan, 100–103
    partisan, 99–100
    police guards as, 101
    prisoners as, 102
    and Quayle, 102
    reporters as, 102
    and Robb, 101
    Secret Service agents as, 101
    and Tower, 100
    varieties of, 95
"Spin patrol," 242
"Spins," 131, 138
Spy magazine, 272–273
Stakeouts, 47, 135, 149
Standards
    for candidates, 84–85
    decline in, 132, 137, 200
    evidentiary, 209
    lack of, 220, 222
    of probity, 55, 57, 84
    of proof, 55, 57, 190, 197
    of public purity, 211
    raising of, 229
"Star journalism," 2, 56, 132, 233–234, 236
Star tabloid, 264–265
State frenzies, 289–290
"Stealth" candidates, 233
Stupidity, 94, 109
Subtext, 71, 104, 132, 240
    and Biden, 71, 72, 73–74
    and Carter, 74–75
    and Ford, 74
    and Hart, 76–79
    and Jackson, 75
    and Muskie, 75
Sullivan standard, 70
Supreme Court, 69
"Sweetheart" arrangements, 94

Tabloids, hijacking of '92 presidential campaign by, 247
Talk-show approach to politics, 249–250, 276
"Teapot Dome," 22, 29
Technology, 50–51

    advances in, 52–53
Television, 50–51, 53, 54, 65, 134, 207
    cable, 50
    networks, 50–51, 228, 232
    personalizing effect of, 121
Texas governor's election, 7, 18, 143
Time magazine, 272, 273
Times-Mirror, 272
Timidity, 193
Timing, 79–80, 190, 191
Tips, 94–95
"Tit-for-tat" frenzies, 119
Tolerance, 230, 245
Tower case, 7, 20–21, 56, 100, 110, 117, 127, 129, 130, 241
    rumors in, 178, 180–182
"Trash TV," 55, 121, 235
Trial by media, 138
Trickle-down effect, 117
Trivialization, 6, 209–210

Uncorrected errors, 140, 141
Unethical practices, 139–140
U.S. News & World Report, 278

Vice presidency, 81, 82–83
Vice presidential frenzies, 125–126
Vices, hierarchy of, 124–125
Vietnam War, 26, 41, 42, 43, 81
Voters
    reaction to press coverage, 297–298
    remedies from, 244–245
Voyeurism, 123

Wall Street Journal, 276
Washington Post, 255, 259, 276–277, 280, 286, 291, 292–293, 295–296, 340
Washington Times, 255, 266, 267, 269
"Watchdog" journalism, 26, 42, 49
Watergate scandal, 7, 18–19, 22, 26, 41, 42, 46, 121, 124, 188
    legacy of, 122
    and media, 61–64
    and transformation of journalism, 19
Water-torture frenzy, 240
"Water-torture" journalism, 134
"West of the Potomac" rule, 30
Wiggle disclosures, 57, 61, 133, 134, 137, 226, 229, 240
WNBC, 264
Womanizing, purported, 13
    of Celeste, 7, 17
    of Clinton, 264–267
    of Hart, 77–79, 240
    of Jackson, 196–198
    of Tower, 21, 178
Women journalists, 68–69
"World News Tonight," 284, 286
Wright case, 7, 21, 120, 127, 182

Yellow journalism, 28

"Zero-sum" principle, 80